This

Book

Is Presented

To *Guy Lee Dozier*

By *Guy Lee Dozier*

Date *5-31-1971*

IN BLACK AMERICA

Harlem Congressman Adam Clayton Powell, Jr., and Brooklyn Congresswoman Shirley Chisholm displaying Black Power salutes, lead the first black parade in New York City's history.

IN BLACK AMERICA

PRESIDENTIAL PUBLISHERS

Los Angeles, California

To

J. RUPERT PICOTT

Editorial Staff

Editors and Writers:

Alice Bonner
Barbara Dwyer
Kenneth Edison
Virginia Hamill
Alicia Jones
Julie Maxie
Dave Sendler
Anne Sheldon

Copy Editors:

Portia Franklin
Jeanne Paul
Frederick Reinstein

Editorial Assistants:

Janice Booker
Denise Doolan
Marian Ecker
Martha Jackson
Zabe Rothchild
Jonas Santos
Alfred Smith
Merle Understein

Researchers:

Clifton Brown
Betty Dorfman
Gretchen Fox
Toni Garrett

Production Staff:

Kristi Brown
Anne Dixon
Renata Knutson
Allan S. Kullen
Archie Middleton
Margie Moeller
Rosemary Mornin
John J. O'Malley
Richard Parks
Sally Roof
Elizabeth Wilson

Foreword

IN BLACK AMERICA is the work of a dedicated team of people who have tried to present the inside story as they see it. Their goal, beyond simple factual presentation, was not to overwhelm the reader with a mass of data and events, but to penetrate to the core of what these occurrences meant; they did not seek merely to record information, but to improve understanding. In order to further this goal, the research data was supplemented by a pictorial tour; beginning in the past, when the stage was set for the 1960 decade of gigantic development, the illustrations culminate with the reality of the black movement of 1969.

It is a difficult task for any publisher—in this period of continuous flux—to produce a volume which not only chronicles facts, but expresses a mood, which through its words and pictures captures the thoughts and feelings of a people. The authors undertook this task. The story they tell evokes a whole gamut of emotions; it is exciting, upsetting, frustrating, inspiring, and, to every American—black or white—intensely real.

It is, then, with pleasure that I bring you this volume of *In Black America,* which I believe will occupy a lasting place in your memory and in your home.

Jules Pollack

President

Table of Contents

Introduction

AS THE DECADE of the 1970s unfolds we find ourselves looking back to the recent past in search of a perspective for the future. The state of affairs, politically and socially, regarding black Americans is at present nearly indefinable. After sixteen years of agitation and legislation to accomplish full integration of minority groups into the mainstream of American life, many people have come to abandon this course of action and are retreating to the old philosophy of separatism.

The near demise of the civil rights movement of the 1960s was clearly recognizable when the federal government downgraded racial imbalance as a top priority. No longer did people—black and white—demonstrate, or even really communicate, but instead each side seemed to have marked time while the problems continued to exist. Politically, blacks enjoyed the largest representation in the House of Representatives since Reconstruction, a Negro was sitting on the Supreme Court, and another was in the Senate. But the election of Richard M. Nixon to the presidency and the success of his white, middle-America approach opened to question the overall power that was generally conceded to the black electorate in those years.

The rise of a violence-prone rhetoric, as expressed by the Black Panthers and others, has taken the place of singing, praying, non-violent integrated protest groups. Because the Black Panthers have received much attention, the editors have included a separate article dealing with recent conflicts between the Panthers and the police. Andrew B. Haynes, Jr., conducted an investigation of police relations with the Black Panthers and with the black community as a whole and his report also reveals his views and experiences in the black movement. While this article may be considered controversial, it is at the same time thought-provoking and should serve as a point of departure for further research into the police situation versus the white community, as well as the intra-black struggles within the various militant factions.

Turning to the recent past, it is evident that much change has occurred since the loss of Martin Luther King, Jr. His death represented more than the loss of one man. It also symbolized a change in the philosophical approach of many blacks who no longer believe that prayer to a God in a far-off heaven is as effective as direct confrontation with people on earth. Basically, the shift in leadership among blacks has revealed a new type of power politics. Instead of the long-time policy of upper-class black leadership speaking to white America without benefit of advice from the masses, the trend has shifted to small power groups effectively articulating the frustrations of the grass roots population.

This means, of course, that the number of leaders within the black community has increased, and that they represent fewer people within their own particular sphere of influence. This development offers the potential for a more effective influence on the public, for several reasons. If, for instance in the case of the Black Panthers, there are several leaders within one large urban area who are successful in gaining the attention of local politicians, more points of view and more voices are heard than in the case of the former single leader who was regarded by the larger group as only a token representative. While it seems to many that efforts are being made to eliminate systematically the Panthers, there are other power blocks still in operation and anxious to prove the theory that many voices are better than one.

Perhaps the greatest threat to black America in the new decade lies in the area of political change. On other fronts many of the steps toward integration have already been accomplished in such a manner that there is little danger of backsliding. Blacks are moving rapidly in every branch of communication media. From television newscasting to Shakespearean drama, casting is now conducted on a nearly color-blind basis. This is not to suggest that prejudices and stereotypes do not still exist, but more positive change has occurred during the 1960s than in any previous period in our history. This is obvious, too, in athletics. Although a change in attitude by players and spectators preceded the civil rights era, the great change in the sports arena took place simultaneously with other developments.

Within the pages of this volume there are positive illustrations of integration in the theater, art, music, television, motion picture and sports worlds. Much of the entertainment available to the American public today features blacks in starring roles, especially in the field of music. Single stars such as Stevie Wonder and groups like the Temptations are also bringing profits into black America through the recording companies which they represent, in these two cases, Mo-Town Records.

Thus black-owned enterprises are thriving to an extent never known before in America. Money flows in from black and white purchasers who are interested in the product. The new emphasis on black power has motivated the "products" (recording stars, etc.) to align themselves with black capital, illustrating what could be done by "big" black business as the new decade opened.

Accepting the thesis, then, that black enterprise and business can and will be a positive growth factor in the 1970s, it is necessary to look at some of the problems which must be faced and eventually settled. Although black-owned cooperatives are fast becoming a reality in large urban centers, slum housing, poverty, and welfare continue to be the greater reality. For every ten investors who support black-owned cooperatives there remain a hundred who cannot afford to make the smallest purchase. This is a crucial American problem.

In 1954, when the United States Supreme Court reversed the doctrine of separate but equal education, the whole nation reacted. Some people, especially in the South where the policy of separatism was openly pursued, deeply resented the concept of integration. For the most part, blacks reacted with joy and had high hopes of achieving the American dream through an opportunity for better education, but in the closing years of the past decade this quest for integration was finding fewer and fewer supporters. So long as integration was sought for Southern schools only, the North was content to let the federal government administer whatever force was necessary. When, at last, it became apparent that segregation existed widely in Northern areas, where whites maintained a separate circle around black city dwellers, many Northern whites withdrew their support of integration.

More important were the new attitudes being formed in black America regarding integrated education. As more Negro children began to be integrated into predominantly white schools they found they were indeed part of an alien culture. The cry for black studies was just one illustration of the bewildered feeling within these black children as they began to doubt the worth of integration in terms of themselves.

Thus, as the 1960s ended, the nation once again was facing the question of the value of integration in its schools. The black separatists were arguing that the quality of education should be improved within the inner city and in the rural South, and that children should be free to attend their local schools, thus reestablishing the separate but equal philosophy so odious just sixteen years earlier. White separatists concurred in the decision of blacks who spoke against busing black children out of the ghetto areas. And integrationists, black and white, were still searching their hearts and minds before choosing to align themselves with one philosophy or another.

This, too, is an American problem and one that will have far-reaching effects long past the decade of the 1970s.

Two parallel movements have developed. There is the growth factor in business, media, housing, education, and other related areas for many blacks who climbed over the walls of segregation in the reform period of the 1960s. Yet there remain the millions who have not felt the effects of legislation, integration, and education. One cannot help but suggest, as we enter the new decade, that the voices of the Black Panthers and other related groups will be more acceptable to those favoring separation, a movement which has developed in large measure out of false hopes, unalleviated frustrations, and uncontained anger.

The Editors

SECTION I

A Pictorial Tour of Black America: Past and Present

The following pages give a brief but comprehensive picture of Black American life from its beginnings to the present day. Our story starts with the Black African background and then shifts rapidly to this continent. The reader is first guided through the period of early exploration, then through the rise of the slave trade and through a developing American economic system—much of it built on the backs of slaves. At the same time we see a thriving free Black population growing and developing parallel to the slave population.

All too often in the past the tendency has been to present the Negro in the role of a subjugated slave, with little or no recognition accorded the achievements and accomplishments of the free Black population. In order to present a more accurate picture, we are devoting many pages in this section to Negro leaders: churchmen, abolitionists, businessmen, etc., —as well as to the ordinary people who lived and worked in circumstances that were similar to those of their white counterparts. Also seen here are writers and poets, physicians and inventors, as well as entertainers, who broke down the barriers of race and achieved the acclaim of both Black and white Americans.

There are the unsung heroes, too, who fought and died on the battlefields of all of America's wars, yet were unable to leave a legacy of freedom for their own people. On many of the pages that follow we see the grim reality, over the years, of equality deferred, for many Black Americans, until death.

Today we are in a period of conflicting interpretations regarding the Black experience in America. The study which follows reflects these ambiguities. Some Negroes have found it impossible to escape the chains which earlier bound them in slavery. One sees pictures of slaves in 1850 and of poor people in 1968 which reflect little change in status in over one hundred years. From accounts of the early nineteenth-century leaders of slave revolts—the Nat Turners, the Denmark Veseys and the Gabriel Prossers of old—we can turn to the contemporary period and the new revolutionaries who are still seeking—with different weapons—to lead their people out of bondage.

Another similarity can be found between the Black abolitionists of antebellum days and the moderate civil rights leaders of the 1950's and early 1960's. The rhetoric has changed but the goal has remained the same. We see in these pages many of the Black Reconstruction legislators who played such a significant role for a few years after the Civil War. Then, shifting to the contemporary period, we see the current Black elected officials and wonder what their fate ultimately will be—wonder whether the present trend will last.

Will the picture of the past in Black America enlighten the future? To see an overall view—even a bird's-eye view made up, of necessity, of a mere sampling from the distant past—should serve to illuminate the future, for to know yesterday is to build a better tomorrow.

Window from Timbuktu.

While Europe was emerging from the Middle Ages and entering the Renaissance, civilizations of highly organized nation-states had been thriving in West Africa. The map below gives the location of the major West African civilizations that existed prior to the advent of the slave trade. Ghana, the first of the great empires, reached her peak in cultural and political achievement in about 1067. As she began to decline because of outside invasions, the empire of Mali rose to dominate the West African scene in the 1200's. Later, in the 1400's, Songhay, also in West Africa, became one of the most advanced cultures in existence in the world at the time.

The handsome carving shown here is a window from the city of Timbuktu, which was a part of both the Mali and the Songhay empires.

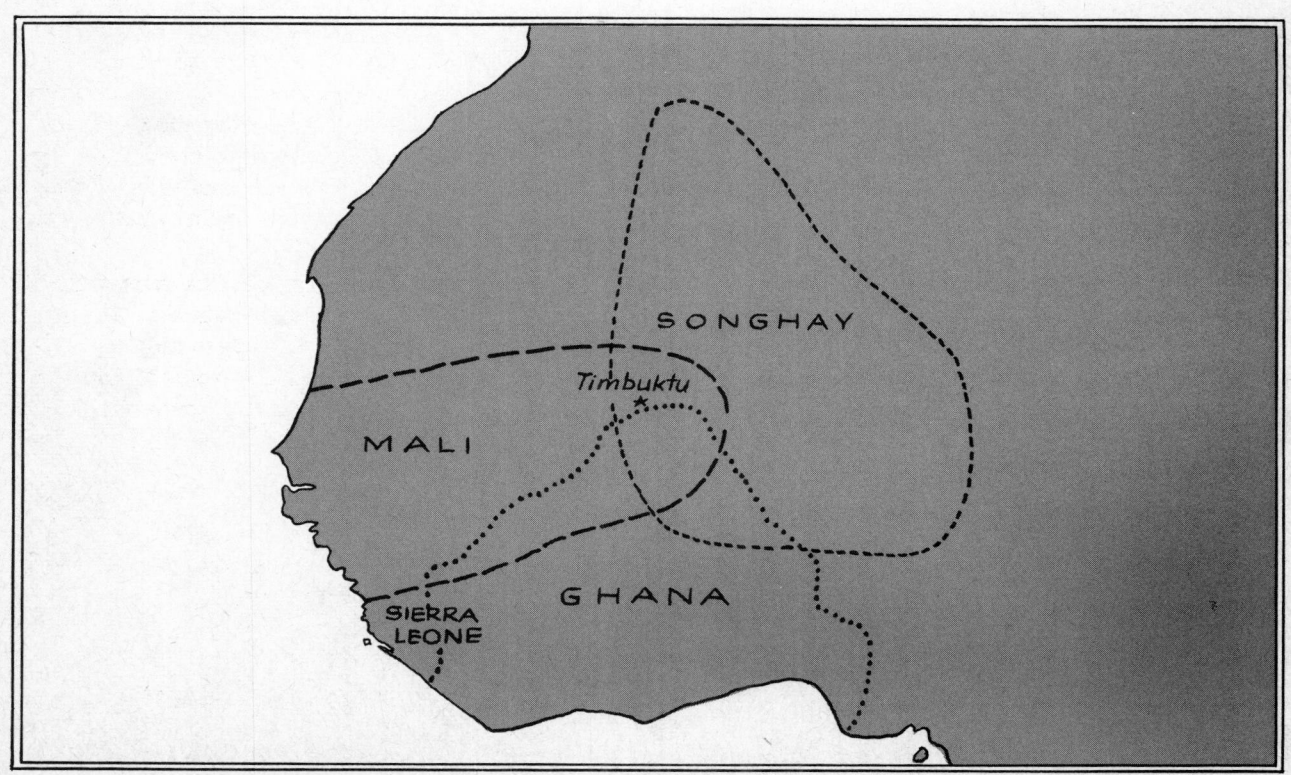

Early West African kingdoms.

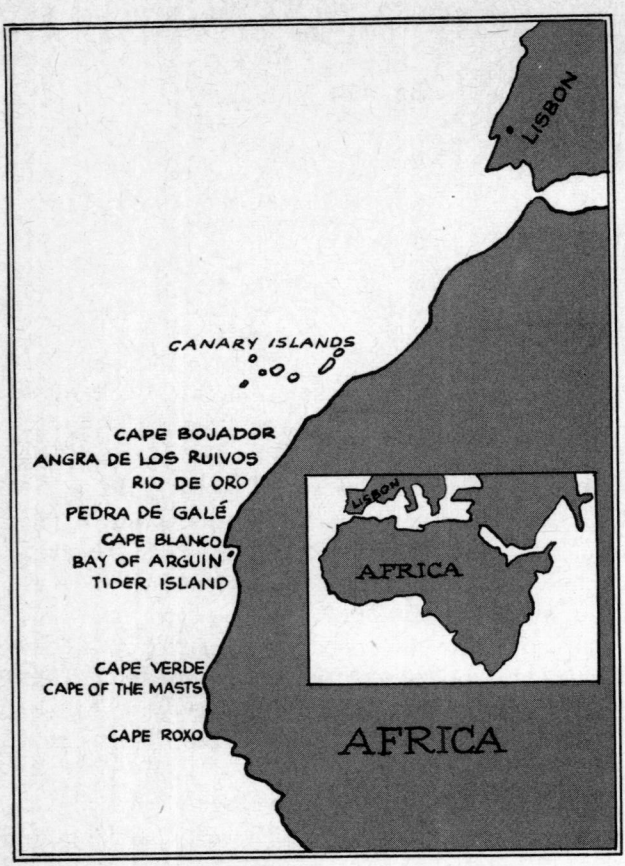

Portuguese exploration in Africa under the sponsorship of Prince Henry the Navigator, between 1420 and 1460.

The map shows the area of Africa explored by the Portuguese under the sponsorship of Prince Henry the Navigator.

The peak period of West African cultural achievement also saw the rise of the slave trade. This trade took many of the youngest and ablest warriors from their homeland and thus caused a dearth of leadership. Beginning in 1483, when six or eight Africans were taken back to Portugal, about five hundred to six hundred Africans per year were enslaved and taken to Spain and Portugal.

Some of these captives, and their descendants, played a vital part in the exploration and discovery of the New World along with the Spanish conquistadors. One of these Black explorers was Estevanico, who in 1539 was said to have discovered the Seven Cities of Cibola, located in present-day Arizona and New Mexico.

Estevanico sighting the Seven Cities of Cibola.

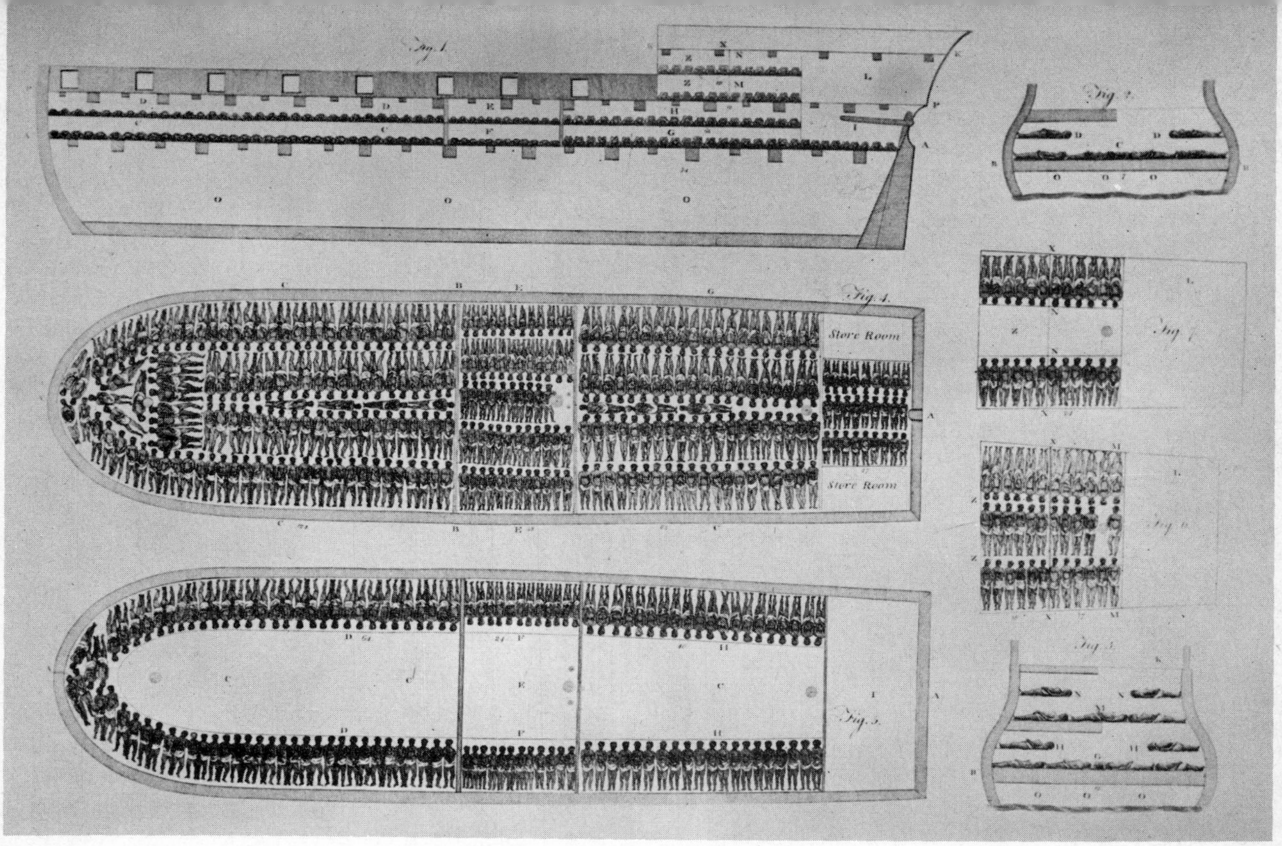

Plan of the slave ship Brookes, *1790.*

		Feet	Inches			Feet	Inches
AA	Overall length of Lower Deck	100	0	HH	Length of Platforms in Women's Room .	28	6
BB	Breadth of beam inside Lower Deck	25	4		Breadth of Platforms in Women's Room .	6	0
OOO	Depth of Hold	10	0	II	Length of Gun Room on Lower Deck ..	10	6
	Height between each deck	5	8		Breadth of Gun Room on Lower Deck ..	12	0
CC	Length of Men's Room on Lower Deck ..	46	0	KK	Length of Quarter Deck	33	6
	Breadth of Men's Room on Lower Deck .	25	4		Breadth of Quarter Deck	19	6
DD	Length of Platforms in Men's Room	46	0	LL	Length of Cabin	14	0
	Breadth of Platforms in Men's Room ...	6	0		Height of Cabin	6	2
EE	Length of Boys' Room	13	9	MM	Length of Half Deck	16	6
	Breadth of Boys' Room	25	0		Height of Half Deck	6	2
FF	Breadth of Platforms in Boys' Room	6	0	NN	Length of Platforms on Half Deck	16	6
GG	Length of Women's Room	28	6		Breadth of Platforms on Half Deck	6	0
	Breadth of Women's Room	23	6	PP	Upper Deck		

Stowing the cargo at night on a slaver.

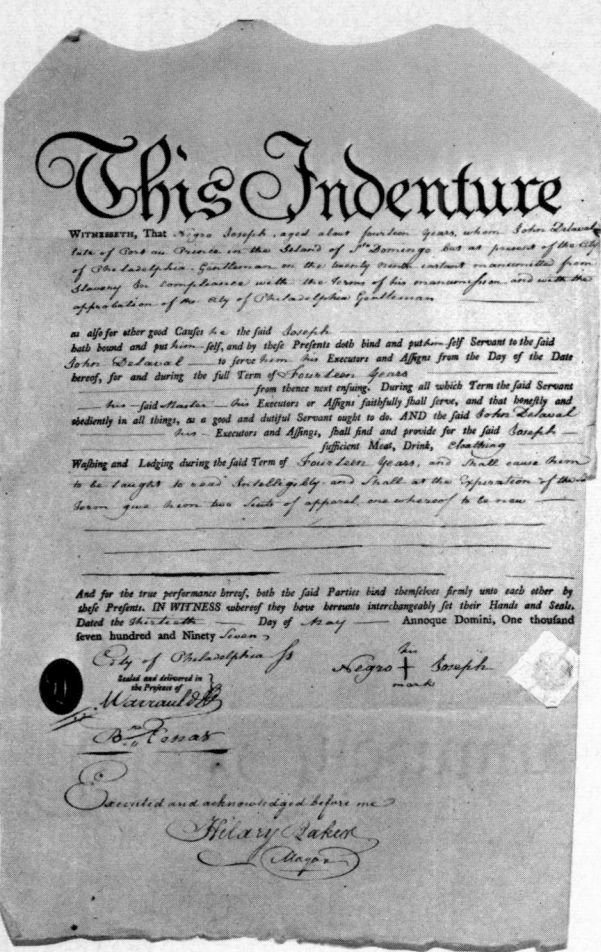

A certificate of indenture.

When in 1619 Blacks were first brought to the English colonies, they were placed in indentured servitude for a period of years and were later released as free people, as was the case with indentured Europeans. Before long, however, most Blacks were placed in a position of perpetual servitude or slavery by their white owners.

In Europe and Latin America, Blacks were given the opportunity to distinguish themselves. Henrique Diaz (d. 1661), a Brazilian Black soldier dedicated to the preservation of a Portuguese Brazil, fought the Dutch in their attempt to seize control of his country in the mid-seventeenth century. Diaz rose through the ranks to eventually become a general.

Gustavus Vassa (1745–1801) was an African from Guinea who was captured in boyhood and enslaved in Virginia; he later purchased his freedom. He became a seaman and a world traveler. After numerous voyages and adventures he settled in Great Britain, where he wrote his autobiography.

Toussaint L'Ouverture (1743–1803), a slave in French St. Domingue (now Haiti), liberated that colony, conquered Spanish Santo Domingo and was governor general of both. His country was recaptured by the French, and Toussaint was taken prisoner by treachery, but his successors ousted the French and proclaimed Haitian independence in 1804. The elder Alexandre Dumas (1802–1870), a Frenchman of African and French descent, was one of the leading novelists of his time. His *Three Musketeers* and *Count of Monte Cristo* survive as literary classics.

Receipt for payment of duty on a slave.

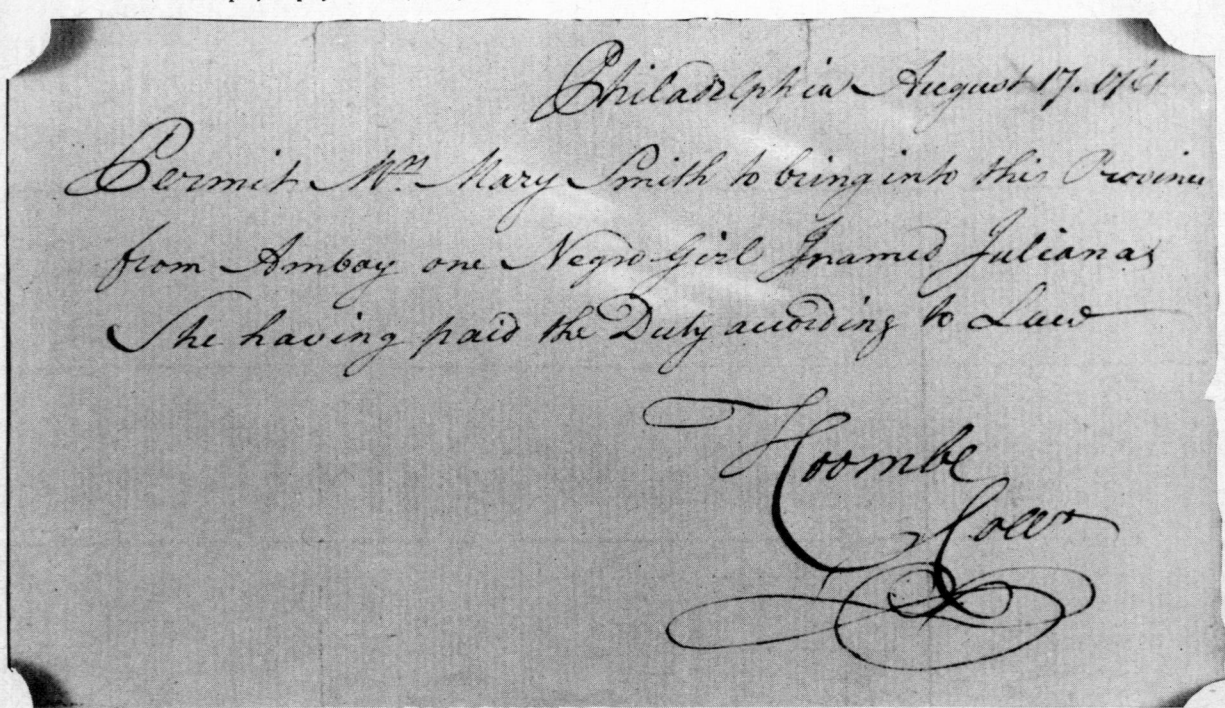

Henrique Diaz

Gustavus Vassa

François Dominique Toussaint L'Ouverture

Alexandre Dumas (père)

7

Richard Allen

The original pulpit from which Richard Allen preached.

An early view of the Mother Bethel A.M.E. Church.

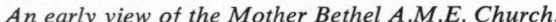

In 1787 Richard Allen and Absalom Jones, two free Black men of Philadelphia, established the Free African Society. This was the first known organization to be founded by Blacks for the improvement of the economic and social conditions of Negroes in the United States. Later, in 1794, while Jones and Allen were worshipping at St. George's Methodist Church in Philadelphia one Sunday, they were forcibly removed from the church by white members for refusing to sit in the "colored section." Following this ouster from the white church, Jones left the Methodist denomination and became the first Black Protestant Episcopal clergyman in the nation. Allen, realizing that worship could not be confined to benches reserved for "Black and White," organized the African Methodist Episcopal Church and became its first bishop. Shown here is the "second version" of his own church, the Mother Bethel A.M.E. Church. It is on the site of the original Mother Bethel Church.

Benjamin Banneker (1731–1806), noted astronomer and inventor, was among the planners of the Federal City, now Washington, D.C., in the 1790's.

Absalom Jones

Benjamin Banneker working on the laying out of the nation's capital.

Phillis Wheatley

Crispus Attucks

Peter Salem at the Battle of Bunker Hill.

Phillis Wheatley (c. 1753–1784), an African slave belonging to the Wheatley family in Boston, wrote and published widely acclaimed poetry. During the American Revolution she wrote a poem dedicated to General George Washington; for this, the general sent her a note expressing his appreciation of her considerable talents.

Crispus Attucks, a seaman in Boston, was the first of five men shot and killed by the British during the "Boston Massacre" in March 1770. During the Revolutionary War Blacks served in integrated units. Many of these Black soldiers, among them Peter Salem, a hero of Bunker Hill, were noted for their valor in battle.

Prince Hall, a free Black of Boston, founded the first Negro Masonic lodge in 1787. Obtaining the charter for his lodge from the grand lodge in England because of discrimination by the white American Masonic orders, Hall organized the group which is now called the Prince Hall Grand Lodge. Today this lodge has a membership of over 100,000.

The Prince Hall Monument in Boston.

To all and every our Right Worshipful & loving Brethren, we, Thomas Howard, Earl of Effingham, Lord Howard, &c., &c., &c., Acting Grand Master under the authority of His Royal Highness, Henry Frederick Duke of Cumberland &c., &c., &c., Grand Master of the Most Ancient and Honorable Society of Free and Accepted Masons, sends greeting:

Know Ye, that we, at the humble petition of our right trusty and well-beloved Brethren, Prince Hall, Boston Smith, Thomas Sanderson and several other Brethren residing in Boston, New England in North America do hereby constitute the said Brethren into a regular Lodge of Free and Accepted Masons, under the title or denomination of the African Lodge, to be opened in Boston aforesaid, and do further at their said petition, hereby appoint the said Prince Hall to be Master Boston Smith, Senior Warden, and Thomas Sanderson, Junior Warden, for opening the said Lodge, and for such further time only as shall be thought proper by the Brethren thereof, it being our will that this our appointment of the above officers shall in no wise affect any future election of officers of the Lodge, but that such election shall be regulated agreeable to such by-laws of said Lodge as shall be consistent with the general laws of the society, contained in the Book of Constitution; and we hereby will and require you, the said Prince Hall, to take special care that all and every the said Brethren are or have been regularly made Masons, and that they do observe, perform, and keep all the rules and orders contained in the Book of Constitutions; and further, that you do, from time to time, cause to be entered in a book kept for that purpose, an account of your proceedings in the Lodge, together with all such rules, orders and regulations, as shall be made for the good government of the same; that in no wise you omit once in every year to send to us, or our successors, Grand Masters, or to Rowland Holt, Esq., our Deputy Grand Master, for the time being an account in writing of your said proceedings, and copies of all such rules, orders, and regulations as shall be made as aforesaid, together with a list of the members of the Lodge, and such a sum of money as may suit the circumstances of the Lodge and reasonably be expected, toward the Grand Charity. Moreover, we hereby will and require you, the said Prince Hall, as soon as conveniently may be, to send an account in writing of what may be done by virtue of these presents.

The charter of the first Black Masonic lodge.

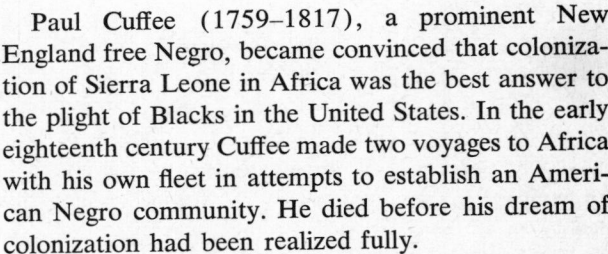

Paul Cuffee

Paul Cuffee (1759–1817), a prominent New England free Negro, became convinced that colonization of Sierra Leone in Africa was the best answer to the plight of Blacks in the United States. In the early eighteenth century Cuffee made two voyages to Africa with his own fleet in attempts to establish an American Negro community. He died before his dream of colonization had been realized fully.

James Varick (1750–1828) was a founder and the first bishop of the African Methodist Episcopal Church Zion, organized in Philadelphia in 1796 in response to white hostility.

Lemuel Haynes (1753–1833), married to a white woman, was the first Black minister to an all-white congregation. He served as pastor to the Congregational Church of Torrington, Connecticut, following the Revolutionary War. During that war Haynes had served as a minuteman and had seen action in the Battle of Lexington.

James Varick

Lemuel Haynes

The first newspaper wholly owned and operated by Blacks was *Freedom's Journal,* begun by John B. Russwurm and Samuel Cornish in 1827. Russwurm, the first Negro graduate of a college in the United States (Bowdoin College, in 1826), later abandoned journalism to become a colonizationist.

Peter Williams, pastor of St. Philip's Episcopal Church in Harlem, was chastized by his bishop for his militant stance against and outspoken opposition to the American Colonization Society in 1830.

Many Black leaders felt that the plan of the primarily white American Colonization Society of sending free Blacks to Africa was in reality a way to eliminate the voice of Black opposition to slavery.

Joining with Peter Williams and others in their opposition to the American Colonization Society was Charles L. Reason of New York. Reason favored the establishment of a colony for free Blacks in upper Canada, where he believed they would still be able to make their voices heard in the fight against slavery.

John B. Russwurm

Peter Williams

Charles L. Reason

James McCune Smith

James McCune Smith, a graduate of the University of Glasgow, in Scotland, was one of the earliest Negro physicians in the United States. Although his sizable practice kept him extremely busy, Smith engaged in historical writing. He was the author of several books, the best known of which was *Toussaint L'Ouverture,* published in 1841.

Martin R. Delany, a man of many talents and vocations, attended the Harvard Medical School; although he did not graduate, he soon became a successful physician. He was also an author, an editor, and, for a brief period, a colonizationist. Delany edited a weekly newspaper, and later, in 1852, published a chronicle of Black America entitled *The Condition, Elevation, Emigration and Destiny of the Colored People of the United States, Politically Considered.* This work is still considered historically valuable. During the Civil War, Delany was made a major; he was the highest-ranking Black field officer of that time.

The Reverend Morris Brown was the second bishop of the A.M.E. Church. In the early 1820's Brown had been a minister in Charleston, South Carolina. After the discovery of the Denmark Vesey conspiracy of 1822, Brown was forced to flee to Philadelphia.

Martin R. Delany

Morris Brown

Slave quarters.

Slave family.

A slave and his cabin.

15

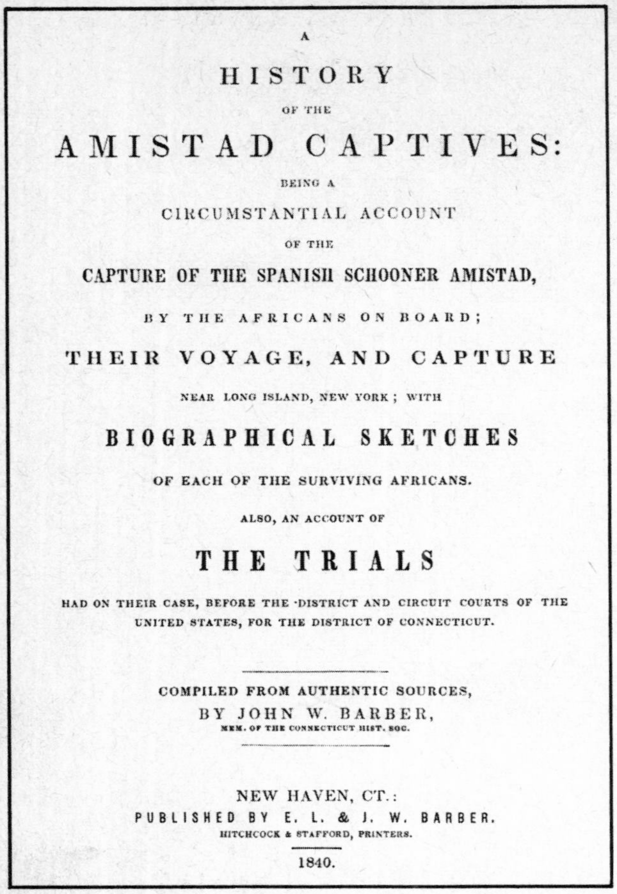

A
HISTORY
OF THE
AMISTAD CAPTIVES:
BEING A
CIRCUMSTANTIAL ACCOUNT
OF THE
CAPTURE OF THE SPANISH SCHOONER AMISTAD,
BY THE AFRICANS ON BOARD;
THEIR VOYAGE, AND CAPTURE
NEAR LONG ISLAND, NEW YORK; WITH
BIOGRAPHICAL SKETCHES
OF EACH OF THE SURVIVING AFRICANS.
ALSO, AN ACCOUNT OF
THE TRIALS
HAD ON THEIR CASE, BEFORE THE ·DISTRICT AND CIRCUIT COURTS OF THE
UNITED STATES, FOR THE DISTRICT OF CONNECTICUT.

COMPILED FROM AUTHENTIC SOURCES,
BY JOHN W. BARBER,
MEM. OF THE CONNECTICUT HIST. SOC.

NEW HAVEN, CT.:
PUBLISHED BY E. L. & J. W. BARBER.
HITCHCOCK & STAFFORD, PRINTERS.
1840.

Joseph Cinque

Slave revolts and rebellions were common throughout the history of Negro slavery in the United States. The best-known revolt today is Nat Turner's insurrection, which occurred in Southampton County, Virginia, in August 1831, and resulted in the death of fifty-five whites. After several weeks in hiding, Nat Turner was captured in the dismal swamp. He was hanged, together with some of his followers. Many other Blacks had been killed indiscriminately during the revolt.

Joseph Cinque, an African, together with other slaves, captured the ship *Amistad* off the coast of Cuba and, after killing the captain, forced two pas-

The discovery of Nat Turner.

sengers to sail the ship toward Africa. The two passengers in fact piloted toward the Americas, and eventually a patrol boat off the coast of New England sighted the *Amistad* and boarded her. They captured Cinque and his men and attempted to return them to slavery. In one of the most celebrated cases of the mid-1800's, John Quincy Adams, former President of the United States, defended the *Amistad* captives and eventually obtained their freedom.

The thread of militant Black protest against discrimination and inequality runs through the history of race relations in America. From time to time a particular person appeared who was especially outspoken. One such individual was David Walker, a Negro from North Carolina who moved to Boston. In 1829 he published his *Appeal . . . to the Colored Citizens of the World*. A long discourse on the evils of slavery, the *Appeal* urged Blacks to throw off the yoke which bound them by whatever means they could. So incendiary was this publication considered that a price was put on Walker's life, and in 1830 he died under mysterious circumstances.

In 1843, in addressing a convention of Blacks in Rochester, New York, Negro abolitionist Henry Highland Garnet admonished his listeners to take to the streets and fight, to use violence against violence, to obtain the equality that was rightfully theirs.

Charles Lenox Remond was one of the first men to become affiliated with the abolitionists after they organized and was probably the most prominent Black abolitionist prior to Frederick Douglass' entrance into the American Anti-Slavery Society.

WALKER'S

APPEAL,

IN FOUR ARTICLES;

TOGETHER WITH

A PREAMBLE,

TO THE

COLOURED CITIZENS OF THE WORLD,

BUT IN PARTICULAR, AND VERY EXPRESSLY, TO THOSE OF

THE UNITED STATES OF AMERICA,

WRITTEN IN BOSTON, STATE OF MASSACHUSETTS,
SEPTEMBER 28, 1829.

THIRD AND LAST EDITION,
WITH ADDITIONAL NOTES, CORRECTIONS, &c.

Boston:
REVISED AND PUBLISHED BY DAVID WALKER.
. . . .
1830.

Henry Highland Garnet

Charles Lenox Remond

Frederick Douglass

Frances Ellen Watkins Harper

Frederick Douglass — former slave, abolitionist, lecturer, writer, politician and perhaps the greatest nineteenth-century Black leader—is almost a legend, so outstanding were his accomplishments. Frances Ellen Watkins Harper was one of the foremost woman abolitionists of her time, as well as a creative poet and fiction writer. Robert Purvis, another leading Black abolitionist, was so fair in color that on one occasion he was invited to dance with the daughter of a Southern slaveowner.

William Wells Brown, an escaped slave, was the first Black novelist. His first novel, *Clotel,* the story

Robert Purvis (front row, third from right) and the executive committee of the Pennsylvania Anti-Slavery Society, 1851.

18

William Wells Brown

William Still

of a slave, was published in 1853. He also wrote of his escape from slavery, in *The Narrative of William Wells Brown*. William Still, agent of the Underground Railroad, in his book *The Underground Railroad* (1872), recorded his own experiences and those of others who so valiantly served the cause of freedom.

Perhaps the most fantastic escape ever devised and executed by an American slave was that of Henry Box Brown, who had himself shipped through the United States mails from slavery in the South to freedom in Philadelphia. He, too, described his adventures in a book.

The arrival of Henry Box Brown at Philadelphia.

19

Marie Weems

Harriet Tubman

Fugitive slaves with members of the Underground Railroad.

Looking for fugitive slaves.

Another slave who escaped through an ingenious method was Marie Weems, who at the age of fifteen donned man's clothing and fled to New York. Harriet Tubman, after her own escape to freedom, returned South nineteen times to bring more than three hundred slaves Northward to freedom. The passage of the Fugitive Slave Law of 1850 increased the dangers for those slaves who sought freedom through escape. The difficulties of the Underground Railroad multiplied as bounty hunters took to the pursuit of escaped slaves.

Five Black men were with John Brown when he led his raid on Harpers Ferry in 1859. They were Lewis S. Leary, Shields Green, Dangerfield Newby (first man in the Brown party to be shot), John Anthony Copeland and Osborne Perry Anderson.

Lewis S. Leary

Shields Green

Sojourner Truth with Abraham Lincoln.

An outstanding Black woman of this period was Sojourner Truth, an ex-slave. During the Civil War she served as a nurse and also as a spy for the Union. In 1864 she met with President Lincoln. She was an advocate of land ownership for freedmen.

In July 1863 New York City—especially the Negro areas—was torn by violence as poor whites rioted against the newly enacted draft laws (for which they blamed the Black population of the city). Many Negroes lost their businesses, homes and belongings.

The first Black man to lose his life in the Civil War was Nicholas Biddle, who was shot down in April 1861 as his Pennsylvania company was on its way to defend the nation's capital.

Biddle was a free man, but his example and that of other free Blacks was quickly followed by ex-slaves, who often risked their lives to escape in order to enlist in the Union Army.

New York during the draft riots of 1863.

22

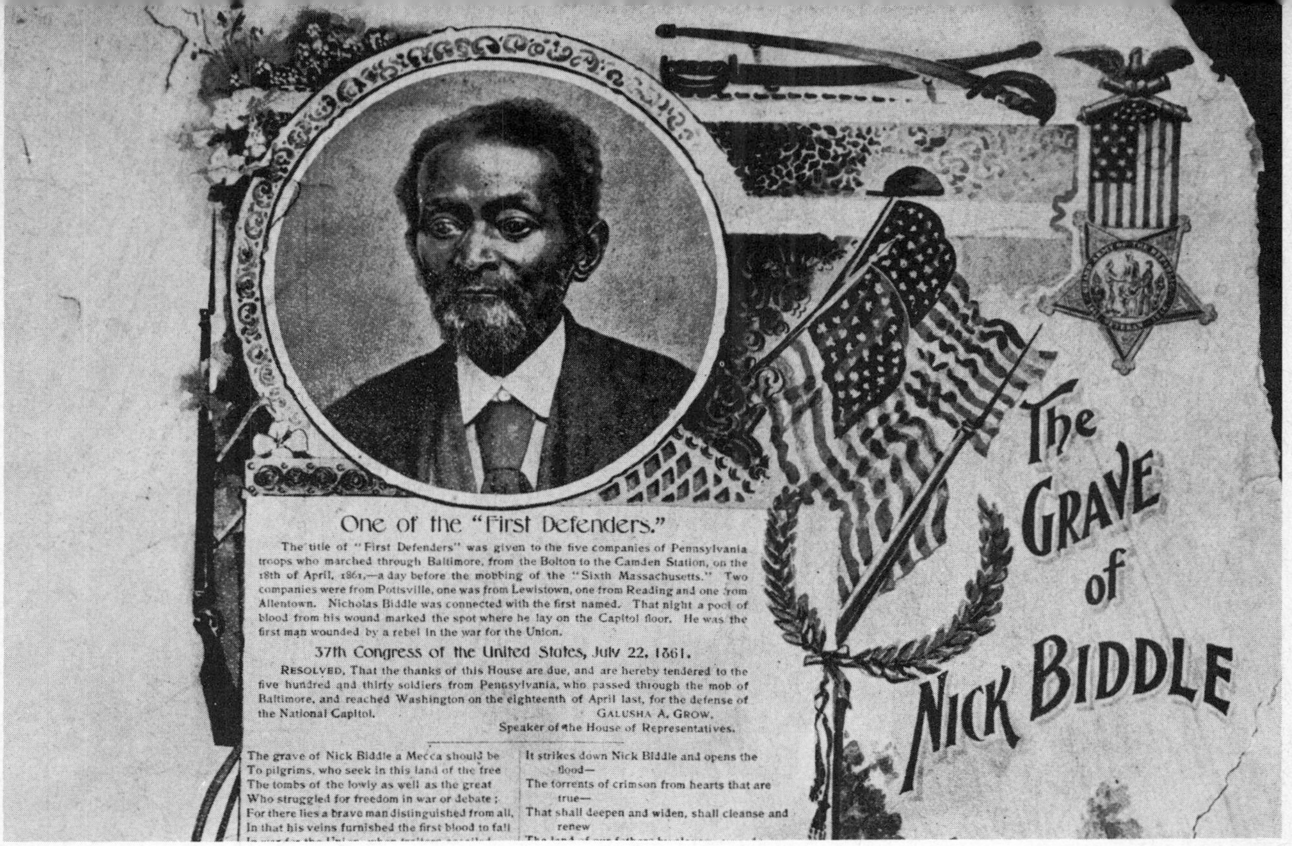
The Grave of Nick Biddle

One of the "First Defenders."

The title of "First Defenders" was given to the five companies of Pennsylvania troops who marched through Baltimore, from the Bolton to the Camden Station, on the 18th of April, 1861,—a day before the mobbing of the "Sixth Massachusetts." Two companies were from Pottsville, one was from Lewistown, one from Reading and one from Allentown. Nicholas Biddle was connected with the first named. That night a pool of blood from his wound marked the spot where he lay on the Capitol floor. He was the first man wounded by a rebel in the war for the Union.

37th Congress of the United States, July 22, 1861.

RESOLVED, That the thanks of this House are due, and are hereby tendered to the five hundred and thirty soldiers from Pennsylvania, who passed through the mob of Baltimore, and reached Washington on the eighteenth of April last, for the defense of the National Capitol.

GALUSHA A. GROW,
Speaker of the House of Representatives.

The grave of Nick Biddle a Mecca should be
To pilgrims, who seek in this land of the free
The tombs of the lowly as well as the great
Who struggled for freedom in war or debate;
For there lies a brave man distinguished from all,
In that his veins furnished the first blood to fall

It strikes down Nick Biddle and opens the flood—
The torrents of crimson from hearts that are true—
That shall deepen and widen, shall cleanse and renew

Testimonial to Nicholas Biddle.

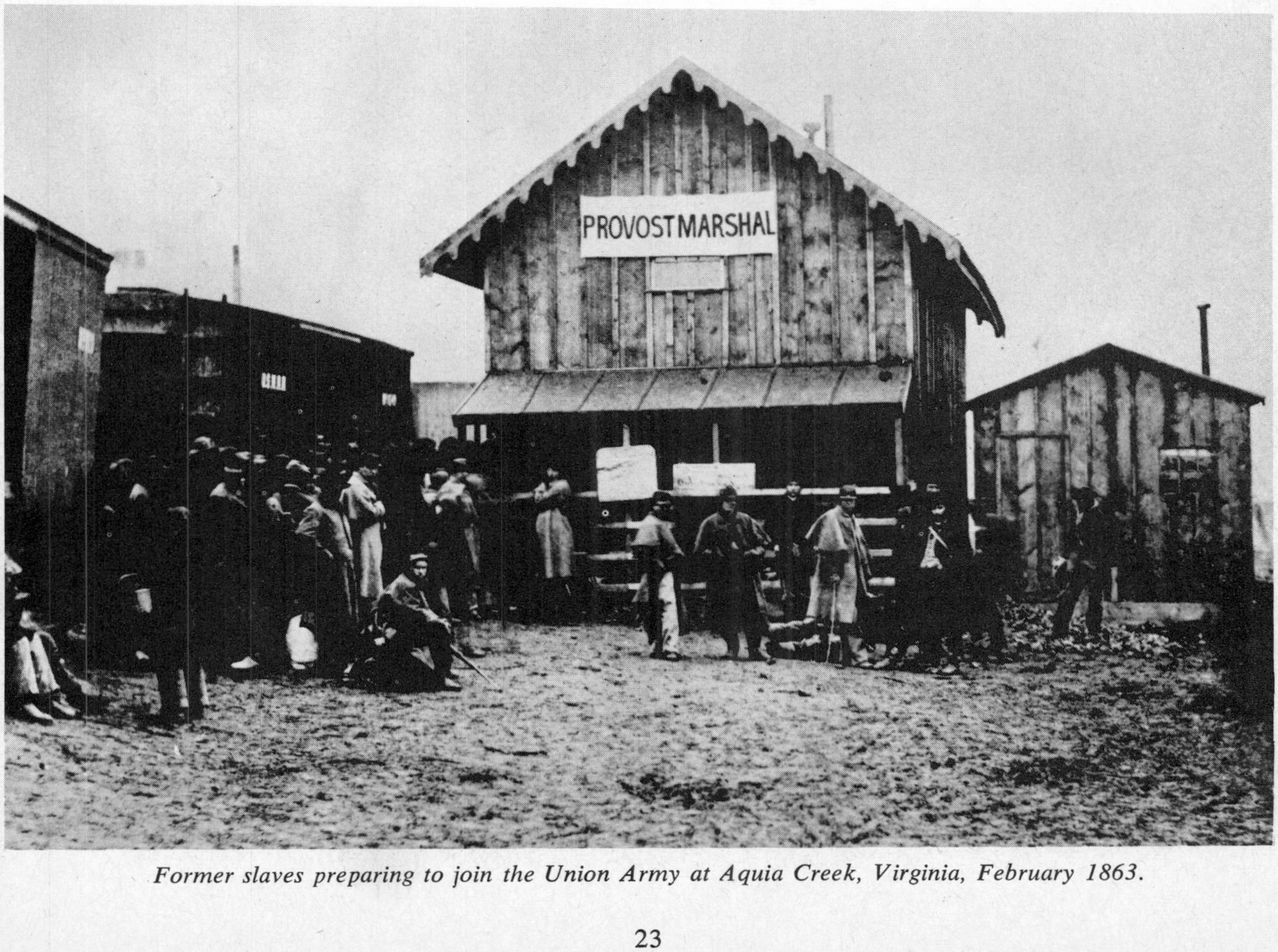

Former slaves preparing to join the Union Army at Aquia Creek, Virginia, February 1863.

COME AND JOIN US BROTHERS.

PUBLISHED BY THE SUPERVISORY COMMITTEE FOR RECRUITING COLORED REGIMENTS
1210 CHESTNUT ST. PHILADELPHIA.

Negro Union troops seizing a Confederate cannon.

The Battle of Fort Pillow.

Although many Blacks, both slaves and free men, hastened to volunteer for duty in the Union Army, their nation was not quick to receive them. Finally, in the summer of 1863, an official order for the recruitment and training of Black soldiers was issued. In the remaining two years of war Blacks fought in many major battles and endured more than the usual hardships of war because of their color.

In the Battle of Fort Pillow (Tennessee), in 1864, Confederate General Nathan Bedford Forrest (later an important figure in the Ku Klux Klan) employed tactics calling for the annihilation of all Black troops. So many were killed that the battle became known as the Fort Pillow Massacre. At Fort Wagner (on Morris Island near Charleston) in 1863, one of the earliest encounters in which Black soldiers were engaged, the Fifty-fourth Massachusetts regiment distinguished itself.

The Battle of Fort Wagner.

William H. Carney

William H. Carney, a sergeant with the Fifty-fourth Massachusetts Colored Infantry, although wounded himself, picked up the American flag when its bearer was shot down and led the charge at Fort Wagner, planting the flag at the top. Carney was twice wounded in battle.

John V. De Grasse, a distinguished Black Boston physician, served as assistant surgeon with the Thirty-fifth United States Colored Troops.

Major Alexander T. Augusta was surgeon with the Seventh United States Colored Troops. Although a major, Augusta was allotted the pay of an ordinary enlisted man. After repeated protests, Augusta eventually was given compensation. Augusta was later promoted to the rank of lieutenant colonel.

John V. De Grasse

Alexander T. Augusta

Susie King Taylor, wife of a noncommissioned officer in the First South Carolina Volunteers, spent some time in camp with her husband's company as a laundress, teacher and nurse. She later served as a hospital nurse.

Robert Smalls was a seaman on board the Confederate ship *Planter*. In the spring of 1862 Smalls took the wheel of the *Planter* and sailed it out of Charleston toward the Union Navy, which was offshore. He then surrendered the *Planter*. For this daring deed Smalls received monetary compensation and was made a pilot and later a captain in the Union Navy. He later served as a congressman from South Carolina.

Early in 1863 Secretary of War Stanton called for volunteer artillery companies from Massachusetts. Among those called on to recruit Negro troops was John Mercer Langston, of Ohio, who some years later was a United States congressman.

Susie King Taylor

Robert Smalls (top) with three of his crew.

John M. Langston presenting colors to Fifth U.S. Colored Troops at Camp Delaware, Ohio, 1863.

27

Charlotte L. Forten

Daniel Alexander Payne

Office of the Freedmen's Bureau, Memphis.

28

Workers on a Sea Islands plantation.

Charlotte Forten, daughter of a wealthy Philadelphia Negro, chose to abandon the life of a cultured New England "schoolmarm" and go South in 1862 to the South Carolina Sea Islands to teach ex-slave children.

Daniel A. Payne, a bishop in the A.M.E. Church, was instrumental in carrying out the purchase of Wilberforce University from white Methodists in 1863. He served as its first president, and was one of the few Negroes of his time to hold the office of college president.

In 1865 the Freedmen's Bureau was created to aid newly freed Negroes, to help them settle and find work and to protect them from injustices. The bureau later concerned itself with the education of Blacks.

Toward the close of the war General William T. Sherman had settled some forty thousand Blacks who had served with the Union on land confiscated from rebel plantation owners on the Sea Islands. A year later, however, this land was given back to its original owners and the Negroes were forced to accept free labor contracts at low wages or to leave.

Emancipated plantation workers listening to the terms of a free labor contract.

Robert B. Elliott

Peter H. Clark

Francis L. Cardozo

John R. Lynch

Reconstruction brought Black legislators to many areas for the first time. Peter H. Clark was the first Black man to sit in the Ohio legislature after the repeal of the Black Laws. Robert Brown Elliott, of South Carolina, was one of the most gifted and able of the Black Reconstruction legislators, serving South Carolina as both a state legislator and a United States congressman. Francis L. Cardozo, who had been educated in Scotland, held various state offices in Reconstruction South Carolina. He later served the United States government in various capacities.

John R. Lynch and John M. Langston were both elected United States Congressmen, from Mississippi and Virginia, respectively. Lynch later served as paymaster to the Army and Langston as minister to Haiti.

John Rock had the distinction of being, in 1865, the first Black lawyer admitted to practice before the Supreme Court.

John M. Langston

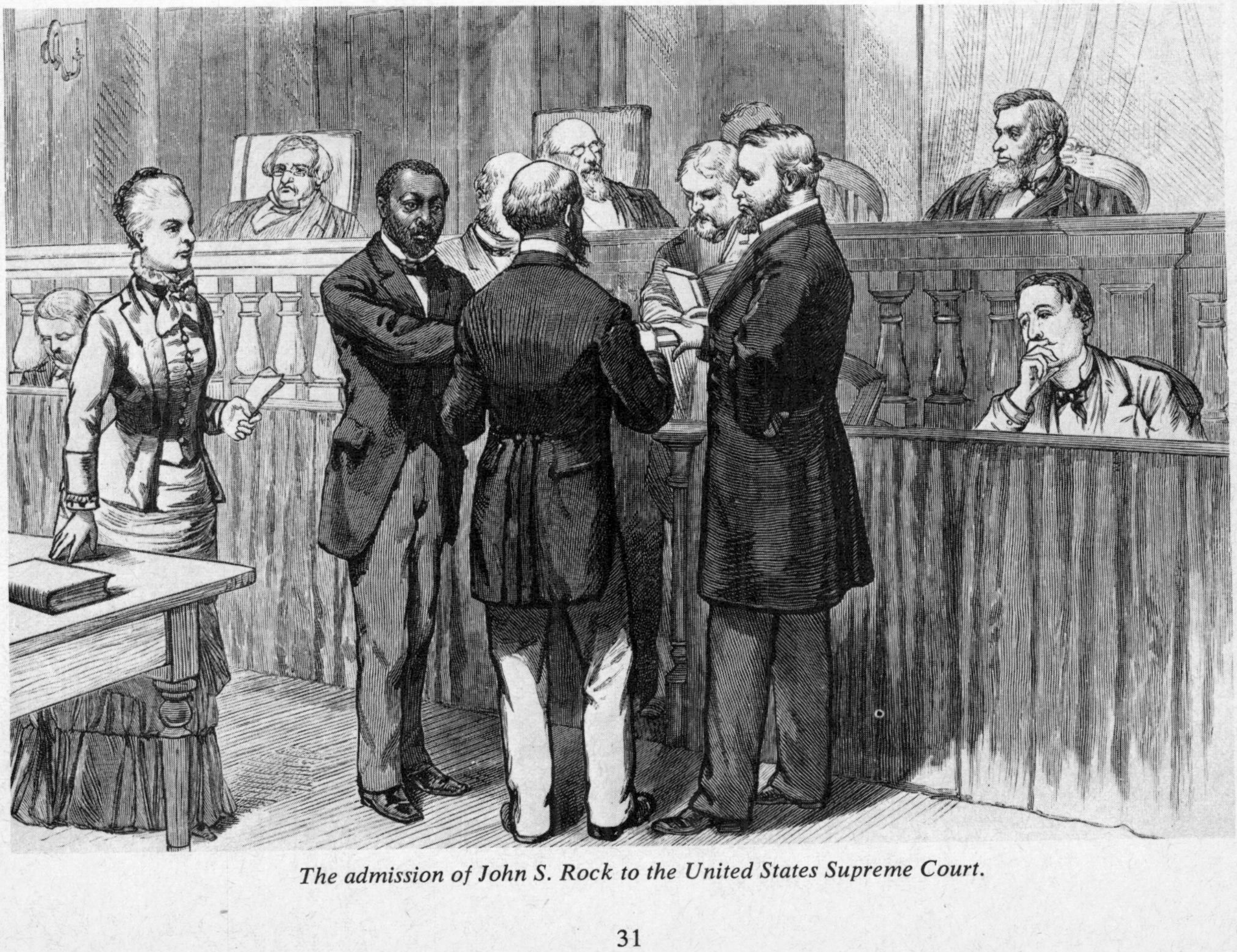

The admission of John S. Rock to the United States Supreme Court.

James T. Rapier

James T. Rapier, outstanding Alabama Reconstructionist, served in his state's constitutional convention in 1867. In 1872 he was elected to the United States Congress, where he served one term. Henry M. Turner, a Georgia post-war public servant, was a member of the state constitutional convention and a state legislator; later he was made a bishop in the A.M.E. Church. He also served as postmaster of Macon, Georgia, as a customs inspector and as a government detective.

John P. Green was elected to the Ohio legislature in 1881; he was one of the few Blacks to hold office after the collapse of Reconstruction in 1877.

Hiram Revels was the first Negro to serve in the United States Senate. Revels was appointed by the Mississippi legislature to fill the unexpired term of former President of the Confederacy Jefferson Davis. Blanche K. Bruce served one complete term in the United States Senate, representing the state of Mississippi.

Jefferson P. Long, of Georgia, was the first legally recognized Black member of the United States House of Representatives. J. Willis Menard was the first Negro listed as a United States congressman, but the contest was disputed and Menard was never seated.

Henry M. Turner

John P. Green

Blanche K. Bruce

Hiram R. Revels

Jefferson P. Long

J. Willis Menard

Richard H. Cain, from Ohio, went to South Carolina as a missionary to the freedmen. He served in the South Carolina state legislature, and later was elected to two terms in the United States House of Representatives.

Joseph H. Rainey, also from South Carolina, was a self-educated man and a barber by trade. When forced to serve as a laborer in the Confederate Army, Rainey escaped and took refuge in the West Indies. After the war Rainey served his state in several offices and then was elected to four terms in the United States Congress.

Pinckney Benton Stewart Pinchback was the only Black Reconstructionist to serve as a state governor. When the Louisiana governor was forced to resign, Pinchback was appointed acting governor for twenty-three days. In 1873 Pinchback was elected to the United States Senate but was never allowed to take his seat.

Richard H. Cain

Joseph H. Rainey

P. B. S. Pinchback

George H. White

Thomas E. Miller

Henry P. Cheatham

Henry P. Cheatham, born a slave, was educated at Shaw University, graduating in 1883. Between 1889 and 1893, Cheatham served as a United States Congressman from North Carolina.

Thomas E. Miller, born in South Carolina to free parents, was educated at Lincoln University. In 1875 he was admitted to the South Carolina bar; later he was elected to a term in the United States Congress. Afterward Miller became president of the State Colored College in Orangeburg, South Carolina.

George White, last of the Black congressmen in the nineteenth century, was elected from North Carolina to the United States House of Representatives in 1897 and served until 1901.

The leading Black musician of the turn of the century was Samuel Coleridge-Taylor (1875–1912), an Englishman. The son of a distinguished West African physician and an Englishwoman, Coleridge-Taylor was well known in both Britain and the United States (which he visited) as a composer and conductor. Among his best-known works are the *Hiawatha* trilogy, *A Tale of Old Japan*, *African Suite* and *African Romances*—this last a setting of six poems by Paul Laurence Dunbar.

Samuel Coleridge-Taylor

Justin Holland

Frederick Elliot Lewis

James Bland

Thomas Greene Bethune

Alexander C. Luca, Sr.

Cleveland O. Luca

Alexander C. Luca, Jr.

Bert Williams and George Walker.

John W. Luca

Two important Black composers and musicians of the second half of the nineteenth century were Justin Holland and Frederick Elliot Lewis. Holland, a guitarist, did considerable research on guitar technique. In addition to his compositions for guitar, he wrote his widely used *Holland's Modern Method for the Guitar.*

Frederick Elliot Lewis, a gifted violinist, pianist and organist, was well known in Boston musical circles. Between 1861 and 1878 he composed works for piano, orchestra and band.

An exceptional musical genius of this period was Thomas Greene Bethune (1844–1905), known as "Blind Tom." Born blind and in slavery, Bethune showed an aptitude for the piano at the age of four. He soon mastered the instrument and eventually won acclaim as a musician in both Europe and America. His master, who later became his guardian, took most of the profits of Bethune's talent.

An interesting group of singers and instrumentalists of the mid-nineteenth century was the Luca family. One of its members, Cleveland Luca, later lived in Liberia and composed that country's national anthem.

Ira Aldridge

Singers of the later nineteenth century included Flora Batson, Mme. Marie Selika (Mrs. Sampson Williams), Hamilton Hodges and Sidney Woodward.

Spirituals became popular with the advent of the Fisk Jubilee Singers in 1871. The original group, consisting of nine students, earned enough money in seven years of concerts in Europe and America to build Fisk University's Jubilee Hall.

One of the leading composers of popular songs of this period was James Bland (1854–1911), also a singer and entertainer, who wrote "Carry Me Back to Old Virginny," and "In the Evening by the Moonlight."

An outstanding turn-of-the-century musical comedy team was that of Bert Williams and George Walker, popular singers, dancers and comedians, who starred in such shows as *In Dahomey* and *Bandana Land*. Williams later was a star of the *Ziegfeld Follies*.

The greatest nineteenth-century American Negro actor, Ira Aldridge (1807–1867), found little opportunity for a career in the United States and settled in Britain. He played Othello with Edmund Kean as Iago, and was famous throughout Europe for his Macbeth, Shylock and King Lear. He died in Poland. The Shakespeare Memorial Theatre at Stratford-on-Avon has a chair in his honor.

The Fisk Jubilee Singers

Edward M. Bannister. Driving Home the Cows. *Oil. 1881.*

The best-known American Negro painters of the nineteenth century were Robert Duncanson (*c.* 1817–1872) and Edward M. Bannister (1828–1901). Duncanson, a painter of Romantic landscapes, was born in New York State of Scotch Canadian ancestry; he began his career in Cincinnati and Detroit and later went to Scotland. He later lived mostly abroad.

Bannister, a Canadian, came to Boston early in his career and by the 1870's had settled in Providence, Rhode Island. A fine landscape painter and an accomplished scholar, Bannister was a founder of the Providence Art Club.

Robert S. Duncanson. The Surprise. *Oil. 1868.*

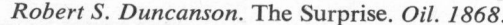

Jan Ernst Matzeliger

Elijah J. McCoy

The leading Black nineteenth-century inventor was Jan Matzeliger, who revolutionized the shoe industry with his shoe-lasting machine.

Elijah McCoy invented an automatic lubricating cup for machines in 1872. He later took out a total of fifty-seven patents for various inventions.

Granville T. Woods is credited with the invention of the automatic air brake. He also devised a system of transmitting telegrams between moving trains.

Lewis Latimer worked with Thomas A. Edison and Alexander Graham Bell. Latimer is said to have made the drawings for Bell's first telephone.

Granville T. Woods

Lewis H. Latimer

In 1893 Dr. Daniel Hale Williams performed the first successful open-heart operations in medical history. The surgical techniques used in this remarkable operation were studied by physicians across the country. Dr. Williams opened Provident Hospital, with a biracial staff, in Chicago and also organized the first training course for Black nurses, at Provident Hospital. He later organized a school of nursing at Freedmen's Hospital in Washington, D.C. He was the first Negro elected to the American College of Surgeons.

Freedmen's Hospital grew out of a small clinic established for Blacks during the Civil War. Today it has the second largest predominantly Negro medical school in the country.

Daniel Hale Williams

Freedmen's Hospital, Washington, D.C., in 1870.

Paul Laurence Dunbar

The best-known nineteenth-century Black writer was the poet, novelist and short-story writer Paul Laurence Dunbar (1872–1906). Dunbar's literary talents were already in evidence when he was a high school student in Dayton, Ohio. In 1893 his first volume of poems, *Oak and Ivy*, was published. His second volume of poems, *Majors and Minors* (1895), won him the friendship and encouragement of William Dean Howells. By 1896 Dunbar was famous as a poet. He wrote dialect verse, such as "When Malindy Sings," and poems in standard English, such as "We Wear the Mask." His poetry is widely read and loved today, although his fiction is largely forgotten.

Henry O. Flipper was the first Black man to graduate from the United States Military Academy. Flipper was assigned as a second lieutenant to the Cavalry, where he encountered hostility from his white colleagues. Flipper's career in the military came to a somewhat questionable end in 1881, when he was relieved of his commission for conduct unbecoming an officer. Although Flipper was later exonerated of the charges, he never returned to the Army.

John H. Alexander, the second Black West Point graduate, served with distinction as a Cavalry commander in the American West. He and his men policed the open plains in order to ensure peace between the Indians and the newly arrived settlers. So highly regarded was Alexander that shortly after his death the Army named a camp in Virginia for him.

Charles Young was the third Negro to graduate from West Point. Prior to his death in 1922, Colonel Young was the highest-ranking Negro in the Armed Forces. He served in Cuba during the Spanish-American War. He had also served in the American West. Young was sent to Liberia as military envoy. He died in Nigeria of a tropical illness.

Henry O. Flipper

Charles Young

John H. Alexander

A company of Negro soldiers, 1883.

A squadron of the Ninth Cavalry on maneuvers during the Indian wars.

Black soldiers who fought in the Spanish-American War.

The Ninth Cavalry, a Black unit, fought sixty battles with the Indians between 1868 and 1890. They also served in Cuba during the Spanish-American War.

Blacks of the Ninth and Tenth Cavalries saw action in Cuba with Theodore Roosevelt and his Rough Riders. An Associated Press eyewitness credited them with saving Lieutenant Colonel Roosevelt and his men from extermination by the Spanish forces at San Juan Hill.

George Washington Williams

Alexander Crummell

Booker T. Washington

George Washington Williams, a graduate of Newton Theological Seminary, was the author of the definitive nineteenth-century Black history, *The History of the Negro Race in America from 1619 to 1880* (1883). He served as minister resident to Haiti in 1885.

Alexander Crummell was the founder and first president of the American Negro Academy in Washington, D.C., which opened in 1897.

Booker T. Washington, leader and educator, was the founder of Tuskegee Institute, at which he sought to combine practical and academic education. Washington rose to nationwide prominence in 1895, the year of Frederick Douglass' death.

John Hope, distinguished educator, was president and founder of the Atlanta University system. He opposed the separatist philosophy of Booker T. Washington by seeking social as well as political equality for Blacks.

T. Thomas Fortune, publisher of the *New York Age*, was a militant spokesman for the Negro during the latter part of the nineteenth century.

F. L. McGhee was associated with the Niagara Movement. He was a Chicago attorney who headed the legal department of that organization during its brief existence.

John Hope

T. Thomas Fortune

Fredrick L. McGhee

W. E. B. Du Bois

Founders of the Niagara Movement in 1906. W. E. B. Du Bois is second from the right, second row; Carter Woodson is second from the right, back row.

In 1905 W. E. B. Du Bois called a conference in Niagara Falls of prominent Negroes for the purpose of organizing a Black pressure group. The result was the Niagara Movement. Although this movement did not grow in strength or membership during its four-year existence, it set the stage for the organization, in 1909, of a stronger and more permanent body, the National Association for the Advancement of Colored People. Du Bois became editor of its official publication, *The Crisis*, in 1910,

The Fourth Annual Conference of the NAACP.

and was regarded as one of the major spokesmen for Black people through much of the first half of the twentieth century.

Eugene Kinckle Jones was active with the National Urban League from the year of its founding, 1911. He was executive secretary until 1941. In 1948 he was appointed a member of the Fair Employment Board of the United States Civil Service Commission.

Carter G. Woodson, educator, historian, author and founder of the Association for the Study of Negro Life and History, was the second Black to receive a Ph.D. from Harvard (in the field of history). W. E. B. Du Bois, who had been the first, had obtained his degree in 1895; Woodson received his in 1912. As of spring 1969, the total number of Blacks to receive advanced degrees in history from Harvard was only six. In 1916 Woodson issued the first number of the *Journal of Negro History*, which was, and has remained, the main vehicle in which young and talented Blacks could publish their historical findings on the Negro.

Eugene Kinckle Jones

Carter G. Woodson

THE JOURNAL

OF

NEGRO HISTORY

CARTER G. WOODSON
EDITOR

VOLUME I

1916

THE ASSOCIATION FOR THE STUDY OF NEGRO LIFE
AND HISTORY, Inc.
LANCASTER, PA., AND WASHINGTON, D. C.
1916

Marcus Garvey

James Weldon Johnson

Marcus Garvey was known as a latter-day colonizationist and a Black nationalist. Garvey was born in Jamaica and came to the United States after having made a series of attempts to organize Blacks in his country. He founded the Black Star Line, with three ships, for the purpose of carrying disaffected Blacks back to Africa. His steamship company folded and Garvey was convicted of fraud, but he remained a hero to the Negro masses.

James Weldon Johnson, poet, author and militant, was executive secretary of the NAACP during the long and arduous years in which the organization was pressing for federal anti-lynching legislation. He wrote "Lift Every Voice and Sing," commonly known as the Negro National Anthem, and was the author of several books. *God's Trombones* is perhaps the best-known collection of his verse.

The Amenia Conference, held in 1916, was a

Meeting of the Amenia Conference in 1916.

Negro recruits, World War I.

biracial meeting of interested and prominent citizens who wished to lay a foundation for a more just and democratic society.

Despite such activities on the part of those who wished to end discrimination, Negroes still served in segregated Armed Forces in World War I.

Black soldiers and officer, World War I.

Walter White

Walter White followed James Weldon Johnson as executive secretary of the NAACP. White, also a novelist, dedicated his life to the eradication of racial discrimination, particularly racial hostilities in the South.

Robert H. Terrell, prominent Washington attorney, was named a judge of the municipal bench in the District of Columbia by President Taft. His wife, Mary Church Terrell, who died in 1954, was the most militant of women. Her career spanned nearly half a century. She was active as a newspaper writer and as a civil rights and women's rights worker.

Charles S. Johnson, sociologist and educator, established and collected materials for one of the most comprehensive collections on race relations in existence. It is at Fisk University. He worked out of Fisk and later became its president.

Oscar DePriest, congressman from Chicago, was in 1928 the first Negro to enter the United States Congress since the exit of George White in 1901.

George Washington Carver, famous scientist and humanitarian, was given the Roosevelt Medal for distinguished service to science in 1939. Carver was on the faculty of Tuskegee Institute.

Robert H. Terrell

Mary Church Terrell

Charles S. Johnson

Oscar DePriest

George Washington Carver (front row, center) with members of the Tuskegee faculty.

55

Richard B. Harrison

The first half of the twentieth century, particularly the period from the end of World War I to the Depression, witnessed a "Negro Renaissance" in the arts—especially in literature. The roots of this awakening lay in part in a growing awareness among writers and other creative people of their Black heritage and pride in that heritage—ideas which were furthered by new leaders such as Du Bois, and which could find expression in Du Bois' magazine *The Crisis.*

In the early twentieth century, however, serious Negro actors still found it almost impossible to establish a career. Richard B. Harrison (1864–1935), a distinguished Shakespearean actor, made his living giving programs of readings and found fame only in 1930 when he played the role of De Lawd in *The Green Pastures.*

The leading American Black composers of the early twentieth century were Harry T. Burleigh (1866–1949) and Will Marion Cook (1865–1944). Burleigh, who had studied with Dvořák, wrote many art songs. A singer of note, he was soloist to such New York churches and synagogues as St. George's Episcopal Church (J. P. Morgan's church) and Temple Emanu-El. Cook, who had also studied with

Harry T. Burleigh

Will Marion Cook

Countee Cullen

Claude McKay

Dvořák, wrote musical dramas, musical comedies and operettas, among them *Clorindy* and *St. Louis Woman*.

Scholar and philosopher Alain Locke (1889–1954) documented the Negro Renaissance in his anthology *The New Negro: An Interpretation* (1925). Outstanding writers of this period were the novelist and poet Jean Toomer (1894–1967), author of the novel *Cane*, and the poets Claude McKay (1890–1948) and Countee Cullen (1903–1946).

Alain Locke

Arna Bontemps

Jessie Fauset

The keynote of this awakening was set by McKay's protest poem "If We Must Die," written after the race riots of 1919. McKay's greatest poetry appears in his book *Harlem Shadows* (1922). He also wrote novels and sociological studies.

Countee Cullen's beautiful lyric poetry was published in several volumes, among them *Color* (1925) and *Copper Sun* (1927).

Later writers whose poems were published during the Negro Renaissance were Sterling A. Brown, poet, critic and scholar, Arna Bontemps, poet, novelist and scholar, and Langston Hughes.

Among fiction writers of this period were Rudolph Fisher, Eric Walrond and Jessie Fauset.

The outstanding Negro writer of the 1930's and 1940's was Richard Wright (1908–1960), author of *Uncle Tom's Children* (1938), a collection of stories, and the novel *Native Son* (1940).

Leading musicians of this period included the singers Marian Anderson and Roland Hayes and conductor Hall Johnson, whose choir was well known to movie audiences and radio listeners.

Richard Wright

Roland Hayes

Richmond Barthé

Richmond Barthé. The Birth of the Spirituals. *Bronze*.

In the early twentieth century the best known Negro artist was probably the painter Henry O. Tanner. Well-known artists of the 1920's and 1930's included sculptors Richmond Barthé and Augusta Savage and painters Archibald Motley, Malvin Gray Johnson and William E. Scott.

The Hall Johnson Choir

59

Paul Robeson

The serious Negro actor entered the American theatre scene with the production in 1917 of three Negro plays by white writer Ridgely Torrence. The next such important milestone was in 1920, with Eugene O'Neill's *Emperor Jones,* starring Black actor Charles Gilpin. This was followed, in 1924, by O'Neill's *All God's Chillun Got Wings,* starring Paul Robeson, and such plays as Dorothy and DuBose Heyward's *Porgy* and Paul Green's *In Abraham's Bosom.*

Paul Robeson, noted for his Othello in the 1940's, is equally well known as a singer. He had been a leading athlete in his college days, as well as an outstanding scholar.

Leading actresses of the 1920's and 1930's included Rose McClendon, Abbie Mitchell and blues singer Ethel Waters. Actresses who were well known to film audiences were Hattie McDaniel and Butterfly McQueen.

The blues had become a widespread idiom in the

Hattie McDaniel

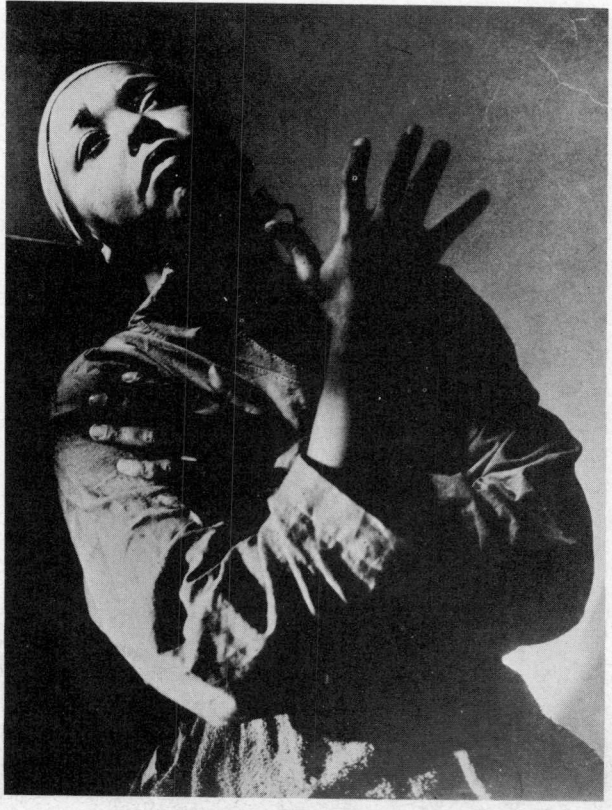

Ethel Waters in Mamba's Daughters.

South well before World War I. They achieved greater popularity just before the war through such blues compositions as W. C. Handy's "Memphis Blues" and "St. Louis Blues." Among other notable early jazz and blues composers and performers were Jelly Roll Morton, King Oliver, Kid Ory, Bunk Johnson and Sidney Bechet. A leading blues singer of the period before the 1920's was Ma Rainey. During the 1920's and 1930's, leading blues singers included Sara Martin, Bertha "Chippie" Hill, Mamie Smith and, of course, Bessie Smith.

Popular songwriters of the 1920's and 1930's included Noble Sissle, Eubie Blake, Shelton Brooks, jazz musician Duke Ellington, Andy Razaf and jazz pianist and singer Thomas "Fats" Waller.

Musicals starring Negroes were extremely popular in the 1920's and 1930's, and a number of stars gained worldwide fame through this medium. Among these performers were Florence Mills, Josephine Baker and dancer Bill Robinson.

W. C. Handy

Jelly Roll Morton

Thomas "Fats" Waller

Florence Mills

Bessie Smith

Josephine Baker

Josh Gibson

Joe Louis

Josh Gibson, the power-hitting, sure-handed all-star catcher of the Homestead Grays from the 1920's through the 1940's, was known as the "Babe Ruth of Negro baseball."

Joe Louis, the "Brown Bomber," held the heavyweight title for over eleven years, longer than any other man. A dedicated American, Louis aided Army morale during World War II with both boxing exhibitions and speaking engagements.

Jesse Owens, the Ohio State track immortal, won four gold medals during the 1936 Olympic Games in Berlin. Adolph Hitler was so upset by Owens' achievements that he left the stadium rather than present the medals to the victorious Owens.

Jesse Owens

Satchel Paige

Ageless Leroy "Satchel" Paige, with his wide assortment of pitches, was one of the greatest control pitchers in baseball history. Although almost seventy, he is now with the Atlanta Braves, gathering enough time to get his well-earned pension.

The New York Renaissance, called simply the "Rens," was one of the greatest basketball teams of its day. From 1923 through 1941 they won 1,588 games and ten world championships. Their finest season was 1938–39, when they won 112 games.

The New York Rens

The American labor movement had long been active on the behalf of white workers when, in 1925, A. Philip Randolph organized the Brotherhood of Sleeping Car Porters, which became the strongest Black union. In 1929 this union received a charter from the AFL. Randolph, who has been a vice-president of the AFL-CIO, is a leading civil rights activist. He planned a march on Washington in 1941 to protest discrimination in defense industries. The march was called off when President Roosevelt took steps to do away with certain discriminatory practices.

George L. P. Weaver rose in the ranks of the labor movement from Red Cap to an executive position with the CIO, to the post of assistant secretary of labor during the Kennedy and Johnson administrations.

Robert Weaver, a member of Franklin D. Roosevelt's "Black Cabinet" in the 1930's, became the first Negro Cabinet member when President Lyndon Johnson made him Secretary of Housing and Urban Development. Following the election of President Richard Nixon in 1968, Weaver was named president of City University, New York's, new Bernard M. Baruch College.

A. Philip Randolph

George L. P. Weaver

Robert Weaver

Adam Clayton Powell, Jr.

Adam Clayton Powell, United States congressman from Harlem since 1945, gained his considerable following in the 1930's. As assistant pastor (and later as pastor) of the Abyssinian Baptist Church in Harlem, Powell was an active civil rights worker. In the 1930's he organized a series of boycotts against businesses located in Harlem which refused to hire Negro workers. So successful were these boycotts that Powell was propelled into first local and later national politics, where he has had an active career.

One of the greatest travesties of justice in this country occurred in the early 1930's when nine Black youths were arrested and convicted in Alabama on what was obviously a false charge of raping two white women. The plight of the "Scottsboro Boys" attracted world-wide concern. Twice the Supreme Court reversed the youths' convictions, but Alabama justice failed to operate on their behalf, and although one of the women testified that the rape charge was false, some of the Scottsboro Boys served lengthy prison terms.

The nine Scottsboro boys

Mary McLeod Bethune

Mordecai W. Johnson

Mary McLeod Bethune embarked on her long and active career when in 1904 she founded a girls school in Florida on money earned from baking and selling pies. This school eventually became Bethune-Cookman College. Mrs. Bethune rose through the ranks of Negro leadership, eventually becoming a member of President Franklin D. Roosevelt's "Black Cabinet." During Roosevelt's administration Mrs. Bethune served on the advisory committee of the National Youth Administration. She was a director with the American Red Cross and founder of the National Council of Negro Women.

Mordecai Johnson, a Baptist minister, became, in 1926, the first Negro to assume the presidency of Howard University.

Negroes felt the hardships of the Depression years especially keenly. Many Negroes had to make a living as migrant workers. These conditions were ameliorated to some extent with the advent of World War II.

A migrant worker's tailoring and cleaning shop.

Dorie Miller

The John Hope, *one of fourteen Liberty Ships named for Negro leaders.*

Dorie Miller was the first Black hero of World War II. Miller was a messman on a ship at Pearl Harbor at the time of the Japanese attack. Though untrained as a gunner, Miller manned an antiaircraft gun after its operator had been shot down. He was credited with having destroyed four enemy planes and was awarded the Navy Cross. In 1943 he was killed in action.

Fourteen World War II Liberty Ships were named for Black leaders.

When the Liberty Ship *Booker T. Washington* was launched in 1942, Hugh Mulzac, a Negro with twenty-two years' experience and training, was made her captain. Mulzac refused the Navy's choice of an all-Negro crew, and he was allowed to choose his men not on the basis of race but on performance.

Benjamin O. Davis, Sr., was the first Negro to hold the rank of brigadier general in the United States Army. He received the single star in 1940 and served in that capacity throughout World War II.

Captain Hugh Mulzac (third from right) with some of his crew after the Liberty Ship Booker T. Washington *had completed its maiden voyage.*

Benjamin O. Davis, Sr.

Lieutenant General George S. Patton, Jr., pinning a Silver Star on Private Ernest A. Jenkins. Private Jenkins was cited for his part in the destruction of an enemy gun and the capture of fifteen German soldiers.

Members of an Army medical unit.

Ann Petry

Langston Hughes

The theme of social consciousness—of awareness of the Black working-class man—which had occupied Negro writers in the 1930's continued through the 1940's. At the same time, a more aggressive tendency was seen in the work of such novelists as Chester Himes. The 1940's also saw a greater emphasis in Negro fiction on the Black protagonist as an individual rather than a social symbol.

Among the leading novelists who began publishing at this time were Chester Himes (*If He Hollers Let Him Go,* 1945) and Ann Petry (*The Street,* 1946; *Country Place,* 1947).

The variety of trends in Black fiction continued to increase in the 1950's and 1960's, until today we find such divergent approaches as those of John Oliver Killens and Henry Van Dyke.

Langston Hughes was still considered the leading Black poet. Among his later volumes of poetry are *One-Way Ticket* (1949) and *Ask Your Mama* (1961). A versatile writer, Hughes also published plays (*Tambourines to Glory,* 1959), short stories (*The Best of Simple,* 1961), autobiographies (*The Big Sea,* 1963), biographical works (*Famous American Negroes,* 1954) and anthologies.

John Oliver Killens

Henry Van Dyke

Dean Dixon

Josh White

One of the most distinguished American Negro musicians to come into the limelight in this period was Dean Dixon. Dixon, a New Yorker, graduated from the Juilliard School in 1936 and got his Master's degree from Columbia three years later.

Dixon's experience as a conductor dates back to the early 1930's, when he organized his own symphony orchestra at the YMCA in Harlem. While still a student at Columbia he was invited to conduct an orchestra at New York's Town Hall. He has conducted the NBC Symphony, and at twenty-six he was the youngest conductor ever to lead the New York Philharmonic. Dixon later left the United States and went to Europe. He has conducted most of the leading symphony orchestras in Europe and in Israel.

Two of the leading singers today are Leontyne Price and William Warfield, both of whom first became known in the 1950's. Miss Price, who made her Metropolitan Opera debut during the 1960–61 season, is considered one of the greatest dramatic sopranos in opera today. William Warfield is well known not only on the concert and opera stages, but to movie and television audiences as well.

The popularity of folk song has continued to increase since the Second World War. Josh White's singing and guitar playing have earned him a devoted following since the 1930's. A unique folk and calypso singer who first became popular in the 1950's was Harry Belafonte, also known as an actor and producer.

Leontyne Price and William Warfield in Porgy and Bess.

Harry Belafonte

E. Franklin Frazier

John Hope Franklin

E. Franklin Frazier, noted scholar and sociologist, who was head of the sociology department at Howard University, published, during the 1940's and 1950's, a number of studies on Black America. Among these were *Black Bourgeoisie* (1957), *The Negro Church* and *The Negro in the United States*.

John Hope Franklin, historian and author, is considered one of the foremost scholars of Negro history today. He has taught at many universities, both in the United States and abroad, including Cambridge. He is now head of the history department at the University of Chicago.

James M. Nabrit, Jr., former president of Howard University, was appointed a delegate to the United Nations by President Johnson.

Stephen Wright, former president of Fisk University, is currently director of the United Negro College Fund.

James M. Nabrit, Jr.

Stephen J. Wright

Bayard Rustin

Civil rights leaders of the pre-"Black power" period are today considered passé by many young militants. Men who have previously sought alliance with and help from the white community are now "on the fence" as to where their own power base lies.

Bayard Rustin, executive director of the A. Philip Randolph Institute, directed and supervised the successful 1963 March on Washington. This was the first massive integrated protest to be carried out in the nation's capital.

Whitney M. Young, Jr., dynamic head of the Urban League, has sought to foster cooperation between white business and the Black community. Although he has been successful to a marked degree, Young has encountered much criticism from Blacks who disapprove of his close ties with the white establishment.

Roy Wilkins, executive secretary of the NAACP, has also been forced, of late, to cope with angry militants who object to the older, more traditional, approaches followed by the NAACP. Wilkins still maintains his leadership of the largest civil rights group in the country, but he is operating under stress both within his organization and without.

Whitney M. Young, Jr.

Roy Wilkins

James Farmer, founder and former director of the Congress of Racial Equality, was ousted from this position with the takeover of CORE by a more militant group. Farmer ran for Congress on the Republican ticket in the 1968 elections, losing to Mrs. Shirley Chisholm. (He was one of the few Negroes to take a job in the Nixon administration and is assistant secretary of administration with the Department of Health, Education and Welfare.

Floyd McKissick, for a time considered a member of the angry, militant sector of the Black leadership, headed CORE after Farmer's resignation. In 1968 it appeared that McKissick, too, was following too "soft" a line for the Black membership. McKissick took a year's leave of absence and left the management of CORE to acting director Roy Innis.

Stokely Carmichael, who claims to have coined the term "Black power" while a worker with the Student Nonviolent Coordinating Committee, became chairman of SNCC in 1966. Fire and violence often followed in the wake of Carmichael's appearances across the nation, as he preached the new doctrine of Black violence in return for white violence. For a brief span, Carmichael seemed to be the new Messiah to his followers, but internal discord coupled with financial losses crippled SNCC; Carmichael left the organization in 1968 for a brief tenure with the Black Panther Party.

James Farmer

Floyd McKissick

Stokely Carmichael

Medgar Evers

Daisy Bates

Medgar Evers was a field secretary for the NAACP in Mississippi before his tragic assassination in 1963. Charles Evers came to Mississippi later that year and took over his brother's leadership of the Black rural population of the state. In 1969 Charles Evers became mayor of Fayette, Mississippi. The election of a Black mayor in the state that is the most belligerent member of the former Confederacy is a tribute to the abilities of both of the Evers brothers.

Daisy Bates, leader of the 1957 school integration movement in Little Rock, Arkansas, was president of the Arkansas NAACP. Mrs. Bates saw the nine children successfully enrolled in Central High School and aided them through their trying early days in the school.

James Meredith, the first Negro to be enrolled in the University of Mississippi, stayed to take his degree despite threats, violence and heckling from both students and faculty members.

James Meredith receiving his degree from the University of Mississippi.

The late Malcolm X, leader of the Black masses, was a former disciple of Elijah Mohammad and the Black Muslims. After coming to believe that Black separatism would ultimately destroy the goal of equality, Malcolm left the Muslims and formed his own organization, with an emphasis on Black unity within the system. His death by assassination did not still Malcolm's message, but elevated the dead man to martyrdom and his words to scripture.

H. Rap Brown, a member of SNCC, became the most militant of the Black spokesmen. Brown toured the country preaching Black violence, and coined the phrase "Violence is as American as cherry pie." He has been charged with inciting a riot in Cambridge, Maryland, in 1967, and has been convicted of carrying a gun across a state line. His book *Die, Nigger, Die!* published in 1969, has sold extremely well.

Eldridge Cleaver, former convict in the California penal system, wrote a penetrating analysis of Black racial attitudes in his *Soul on Ice*. Cleaver has been minister of information for the Black Panther Party. In 1968 he was the Presidential candidate of the Peace and Freedom Party. Cleaver is at present living abroad.

H. Rap Brown

Malcolm X

Eldridge Cleaver

Martin Luther King, Jr., Baptist minister in Montgomery, Alabama, organized the Montgomery Improvement Association in 1955, after Mrs. Rosa Parks' famous refusal to move to the back of a bus. The MIA led a successful boycott by the Negro community of the Montgomery public transit system. This boycott and its resultant publicity brought Dr. King to a position of leadership which he used to further the civil rights cause until he was struck down by an assassin's bullet in April, 1968. He became one of the outstanding leaders of his time. Dr. King received the Nobel Peace Prize in 1964; he was the youngest man ever to have won this distinction.

During the last few years of his life, Dr. King was frequently at odds with many of the younger, more militant, Blacks, especially those of the urban community. Dr. King's assassination temporarily welded Blacks together, but it also signified the end of the nonviolent phase of civil rights protest.

Martin Luther King, Jr.

Dr. King during the Selma to Montgomery march, 1965.

Livingston L. Wingate

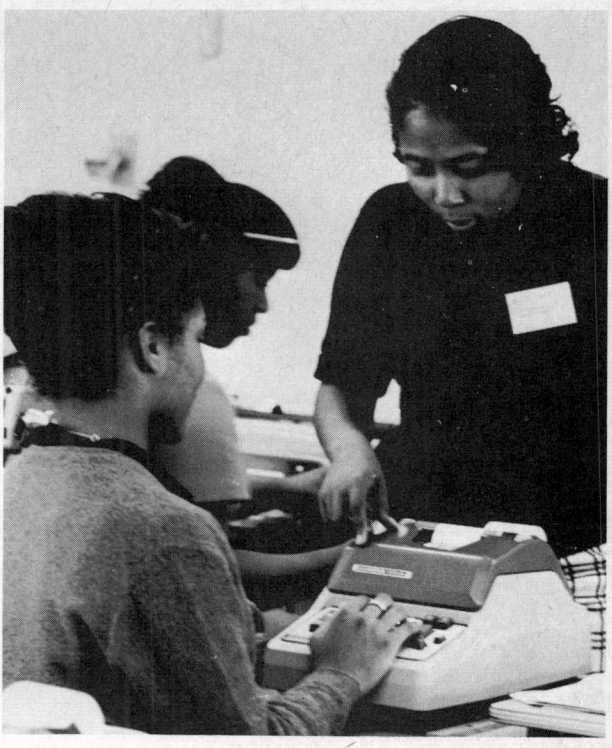

Detroit's New Careers Program in action. The program trains young people in job skills.

Livingston Wingate was formerly director of the Harlem Youth Program (HARYOU Act), which is a successful example of the self-help programs now in operation in many cities. Wingate, a long-time associate of Adam Clayton Powell, is now director of the New York City branch of the Urban League and is still based in Harlem.

The programs begun by people like Wingate and

Cyril Tyson of Newark led to a variety of projects aimed at creating self-help opportunities for Negroes. The development of Black businesses, from small shops to large capital investments, became an important concern of urban Black leaders. The Small Business Administration in Washington began to assist potential Black entrepreneurs—although not to the extent of the need.

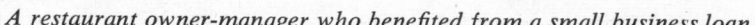

A restaurant owner-manager who benefited from a small business loan.

Augustus Hawkins

Augustus Hawkins has been United States congressman from the 21st district of California since 1963. His majorities in the elections of 1962 and 1964 were among the largest ever won by a Congressional candidate. Hawkins had been a California assemblyman since 1934 and had authored or co-authored more than three hundred laws for his state.

Charles C. Diggs, Jr., has been a United States congressman from Detroit since 1954. As civil rights "whip" of the Democratic study group, Diggs was a prime mover in securing passage of the important open housing section of a 1966 omnibus civil rights bill. Congressman Diggs has recently become chairman of the House Foreign Affairs Subcommittee on Africa.

Robert N. C. Nix has been a United States congressman from Pennsylvania's 2nd district since 1958. Nix serves as chairman of the House Subcommittee on Postal Operations.

Charles C. Diggs, Jr.

Robert N. C. Nix

In 1966 Edward W. Brooke became the first Negro to be elected to the United States Senate since Reconstruction. Senator Brooke, a Republican, first gained prominence in Massachusetts while serving as chairman of the Boston Finance Committee in 1961–62. His successful campaign against graft and corruption led to his being elected attorney general of Massachusetts in 1962. In 1966 a predominantly white electorate sent Brooke to the Senate.

Representative William L. Dawson has been representing Chicago Negroes in Congress since 1943. Dawson has held several important posts in Congress. He is chairman of the House Committee on Government Operations.

When Representative John Conyers, Jr., was elected in 1964, Michigan became the first state to send two Negroes to Congress at the same time. (The other is Congressman Diggs.) Congressman Conyers has championed the "one man, one vote" principle. Conyers was among the Black leaders who organized a national committee of inquiry, to evaluate presidential candidates during the election campaign in 1968.

William L. Dawson

Edward W. Brooke

John Conyers, Jr.

Julian Bond

Julian Bond is one of a number of Negroes who have gained national prominence through their work in state governments. Bond, who is still in his twenties, is a member of the Georgia state legislature. A founder of the Atlanta University student organization which was a forerunner of SNCC, Bond later served as information director of SNCC. Because of Bond's opposition to the Vietnam war, the Georgia legislature denied him his seat; Bond was later seated by order of the United States Supreme Court. Bond was nominated for the Vice-Presidency at the Democratic national convention in 1968, but he withdrew his name, as he was too young to qualify for the office.

In 1967 Carl B. Stokes became the first Negro to be elected mayor of a major American city. Law practice and service in the Ohio legislature helped prepare Stokes for this crucial position. Mayor Stokes, who has had serious urban problems to cope with, has worked hard to improve police-community relations and to bring increased government aid into the ghetto.

Walter Washington of Washington, D.C., was in 1967 the first Negro to be appointed mayor of a

Carl B. Stokes

Walter Washington

Lucius Amerson

Carl T. Rowan

major American city and the first mayor of the District of Columbia. Mayor Washington has done much to bring city government closer to the people and has won the respect of both Black and white Washingtonians. President Nixon found it politically wise to reappoint him in 1969, despite the fact that Washington is a Democrat.

Lucius Amerson is the sheriff of Macon County, Alabama. His recent election points to the gains Black candidates are making in elections in predominantly Black areas in the South now that bloc voting and general election reforms have gone into effect.

Carl Rowan, noted journalist and former diplomat, holds degrees from Oberlin College and the University of Minnesota. Rowan was on the staff of the *Minneapolis Tribune* when President Kennedy appointed him deputy assistant secretary of state for public affairs in 1961. In 1964 President Johnson appointed Carl Rowan director of the United States Information Agency. Rowan had previously been ambassador to Finland.

Representing the 30 per cent white and 70 per cent Black and Puerto Rican Bedford-Stuyvesant district of Brooklyn, "Fighting Shirley Chisholm" defeated Republican James Farmer, former head of CORE, to become the first Negro congresswoman in the United States. Her activism in Congress has already received much publicity.

Shirley Chisholm

Thurgood Marshall

Many Black American jurists have made lasting contributions to the civil rights cause. Perhaps the most important of these contributors is Justice Thurgood Marshall, who has dedicated his entire professional life to the courtroom battle for civil rights. An outstanding constitutional lawyer, Marshall became director of the NAACP's Legal Defense and Educational Fund in 1939. He and his team of lawyers won civil rights decision after civil rights decision before the Supreme Court during the Warren era. Perhaps the most famous of these cases was the landmark school desegregation victory of *Brown* v. *The Topeka Board of Education* in 1954. In 1962 President Kennedy appointed Justice Marshall to the bench of the United States Court of Appeals for the second circuit. Subsequently, President Johnson appointed Justice Marshall United States Solicitor General, and in 1967 Marshall became the first Negro Supreme Court justice.

Constance Baker Motley, who was associate counsel to the NAACP Legal Defense Fund from 1948 to 1965, won the court battle which opened the doors of "Ole Miss" to James Meredith. In 1966 Mrs. Motley, who two years previously had won a seat in the New York State senate, was appointed judge of the Federal Circuit Court for the southern district of New York.

Constance Baker Motley

A. Leon Higginbotham

A graduate of the Yale Law School, A. Leon Higginbotham, Jr., assumed his present position of judge of the United States District Court for the eastern district of Pennsylvania in 1964. Earlier he had been a commissioner to the Federal Trade Commission. He has also been a member of President Johnson's National Commission on the Causes and Prevention of Violence.

The past six years have seen eruptions of urban violence of a severity not seen since the 1940's. Cambridge, Maryland, in 1963, had one of the first of these recent civil disorders. In 1964 there were severe riots in the ghettoes of such major cities as New York, Jersey City, Chicago, Philadelphia and Rochester. The Watts area of Los Angeles saw rioting in 1965, and Washington, D.C., was one of the cities to have riots in April 1968, following the assassination of Dr. Martin Luther King.

The cry "Black power" was first heard in June 1966 during a march through Mississippi which James Meredith had organized to spur voter registration among Negroes. "Black power" is an ambiguous term; there are many different interpretations of its meaning. Whatever it may stand for, the slogan has served as a symbol around which Negroes of various philosophies could unite and show common cause in areas in which they share similar goals.

Scene in North Philadelphia during the August 1964 riots.

Black power conference in Newark, July 1967. Seated, left to right, are Ron Karenga, H. Rap Brown, Ralph Featherstone and Jesse Jackson.

Scene during street fighting in Memphis on March 28, 1968.

Solidarity Day during the Poor People's Campaign, June 19, 1968.

In March 1968 the Memphis garbage collectors were striking for the right to form a union and for wage contracts. Dr. Martin Luther King, Jr., came to Memphis to aid the strikers and to try to prevent violence. A march was scheduled for March 28, but was interrupted by street fighting and disorders. A youth was killed and more than four hundred people were arrested. Dr. King left Memphis but returned a few days later. It was on his return trip that he was assassinated.

A march on Washington planned by Dr. King to unite the poor—Black, brown and white—and known as the Poor People's Campaign was carried out in May and June of 1968, despite the leader's death. Although the results of this campaign cannot yet be determined, the loss of Dr. King's dynamic leadership and spiritual guidance was reflected in the chaotic conditions that prevailed throughout much of the campaign's stay at Resurrection City, on the Lincoln Memorial grounds.

Resurrection City during the Poor People's Campaign, May–June, 1968.

With increasing integration in the 1960's, many Black actors and playwrights were seen by Broadway (and Off-Broadway) audiences. Among the actors who were now seen in leading roles were Ossie Davis, Ruby Dee, Claudia McNeil, Diana Sands, James Earl Jones, Roscoe Lee Browne, Robert Dean Hooks, Lou Gossett, Barbara Ann Teer, Clarence Williams, III, Gloria Foster and Ethel Ayler. Actor Frederick O'Neal became president of Actors Equity. One of the great successes of the 1968–69 Broadway season was James Earl Jones' performance in *The Great White Hope*.

Outstanding recent plays by Negroes have included Lorraine Hansberry's *A Raisin in the Sun*, LeRoi Jones' *Dutchman*, Ossie Davis' *Purlie Victorious*, Adrienne Kennedy's *Funnyhouse of a Negro*, James Baldwin's *Blues for Mister Charlie*, Douglas Turner Ward's *Day of Absence* and Ronald Milner's *Who's Got His Own*. One of the outstanding plays of 1968 was Lonne Elder, III's, *Ceremonies in Dark Old Men*.

The 1960's also saw a demand by leading "white" nightclubs for entertainers who previously had been known for years to Negro clubs. One such performer was comedienne Jackie "Moms" Mabley.

Jackie "Moms" Mabley

Marian Anderson

Shirley Verrett

Louis Armstrong

In the 1960's opera and concert stages saw far more Black performers than ever before. Since the Metropolitan Opera dropped its color bar in 1955 with the debut of Marian Anderson (as Ulrica in Verdi's *Masked Ball*), many Black singers have performed on its stage. These have included Leontyne Price, Robert McFerrin, George Shirley, Mattiwilda Dobbs, Martina Arroyo, Grace Bumbry, Gloria Davy, Reri Grist, Felicia Weathers and noted concert star Shirley Verrett.

Major concert managements now began to represent such musicians as pianists Natalie Hinderas, Andre Watts and Eugene Haynes, violinist Sanford Allen and cellist Kermit Moore. Leading Black conductors of the 1960's include Henry Lewis, who became one of the conductors of the Los Angeles Symphony, Paul Freeman, one of the conductors of the Dallas Symphony, and Everett Lee, conductor of an orchestra in Sweden.

Among composers are William Grant Still, Ulysses Kay, William Dawson, Coleridge-Taylor Perkinson and Howard Swanson.

Many jazz musicians who had gained a wide following during the 1920's, 1930's and 1940's were just as popular in the 1950's and 1960's. Among these were Louis Armstrong, Duke Ellington, Count Basie, Lionel Hampton, Earl "Fatha" Hines and

Count Basie

Dizzy Gillespie

Earl "Fatha" Hines   *Julian "Cannonball" Adderley*

singers Ella Fitzgerald and Lena Horne. One of the greatest jazz singers of the 1930's and 1940's, Billie Holiday, died in the late 1950's. Pearl Bailey, whose enormous popularity dates from the 1950's, has scored a tremendous success on Broadway recently in the leading role in *Hello Dolly!*

A jazz bandleader, singer, comedian and enter-

tainer who first achieved great popularity around 1930 is Cab Calloway. He has recently starred with Pearl Bailey in *Hello Dolly!*

One of the most important influences on "cool" jazz was the playing of bebop artist Charlie Parker. Among the best-known cool jazz musicians are Thelonius Monk, Dizzy Gillespie, Julian "Cannonball"

Duke Ellington, with Diahann Carroll and Paula Kelly.

Cab Calloway

Phil Moore with Patrice Munsel.

The Fisk Jubilee Singers

Adderley, Miles Davis and Cecil Taylor. Leading musicians of "avant-garde" jazz, which grew out of cool jazz, have been John Coltrane and Ornette Coleman.

One of the first Negroes to play an important role behind the scenes in Hollywood is songwriter Phil Moore, who has also conducted the first interracial studio orchestra.

The Fisk Jubilee Singers are still well known to audiences throughout the country.

The first Negro to become an established movie hero (and who is still a top Black film star) is Academy Award winner Sidney Poitier. His films have included *Cry the Beloved Country, The Blackboard Jungle, The Defiant Ones, Porgy and Bess, A Raisin in the Sun, Lilies of the Field, In the Heat of the Night, Guess Who's Coming to Dinner* and *For Love of Ivy.*

Among actors and entertainers who have had leading screen roles in recent times are Harry Belafonte, Eartha Kitt, Lena Horne, Ruby Dee and Sammy Davis, Jr. Davis has starred in such movies as *Anna Lucasta, Porgy and Bess* and *A Man Called Adam.*

Sidney Poitier receiving one of his many awards.

Sammy Davis, Jr., and Diahann Carroll.

Sidney Poitier in Porgy and Bess.

Lou Rawls

Ramsey Lewis

Leading musicians of the "pop" jazz and popular music scene include pianist Ramsey Lewis and his group and such vocalists as Lou Rawls, Ray Charles, Nina Simone, Nancy Wilson, Gloria Lynne, Dionne Warwick, and the Supremes.

Pioneers in American dance have been Black dancers Katherine Dunham (author and choreographer of Broadway revues and musicals) and Pearl Primus, an important contributor to modern dance. A leading Black choreographer whose largely Negro

Maxine Brown and Dionne Warwick.

92

The Alvin Ailey dancers

company is one of the leading dance groups today is Alvin Ailey. Ailey's splendid work "Revelations" is often performed by the Alvin Ailey dancers. Black dancer and choreographer Donald McKayle also has an integrated company. Outstanding dancers Mary Hinkson and Matt Turney are with Martha Graham's company. Janet Collins and Carmen de Lavallade have both danced at the Metropolitan Opera. Arthur Mitchell is a star with the New York City Ballet Company.

The Supremes

John Torres. Bronze Dancers. *1962.*

The leading Black American painter of the last two decades is Jacob Lawrence, a powerful recorder of life in the Northern ghettoes. He has produced several series of paintings, among them *The Migration of the Negro* (dealing with the Negro's migration from the rural South to the urban North).

Among artists of the 1930's, 1940's and 1950's are sculptors Elizabeth Catlett and Sargent Johnson, and painters Romare Bearden, Hale Woodruff, Elton C. Fax, Horace Pippin, Charles White, Lois Mailou Jones, John Biggers, Hughie Lee-Smith and Claude Clark.

Artists of the 1960's, many of whom employ an abstract idiom, include sculptors John Torres, Todd Williams and Barbara Chase, and painters Sam Gilliam, Lloyd McNeil, Tom Feelings, David Driskell, Merton Simpson, Archie Jefferson and Raymond Saunders.

Jacob Lawrence. Street Orator. *Gouache. 1936.*

Sam Gilliam. Tempo. *Acrylic on canvas. 1965.*

Black writers of the 1950's and 1960's have been confronted with the dilemma of whether to continue to use racial themes or to concern themselves with the human condition (using either Black or white protagonists).

Outstanding in the latter trend are Ralph Ellison, author of the novel *Invisible Man* (1952), and James Baldwin, novelist and essayist. Baldwin's essays, many of which are collected in *Notes of a Native Son* (1955) and *Nobody Knows My Name* (1961), are among the finest essays of our time. His novels include *Go Tell It on the Mountain* (1953), *Giovanni's Room* (1956) and *Another Country* (1962).

Other writers of fiction include John A. Williams, Robert Boles, Paule Marshall, Lindsay Patterson and William Melvin Kelley.

Perhaps the best-known Black poets of the 1960's are Gwendolyn Brooks and LeRoi Jones. Other recent poets include Robert Hayden, Mari Evans, Ted Joans and G. C. Oden.

James Baldwin

LeRoi Jones with his wife and child.

Jackie Robinson

Jackie Robinson

When Jackie Robinson broke the major league baseball color line in 1947, he officially opened for the Negro the world of major league sports. A fiery competitor, Robinson helped the Dodgers to both Pennants and World Championships and was elected to baseball's Hall of Fame in 1962.

With the door to all major league sports now open, the Negro lost little time in demonstrating to the whole world—not just to minor league and sandlot crowds—his athletic prowess. The names of such stars as Hank Aaron, Ernie Banks, Bob Gibson and, of course, Willie Mays became household words.

Willie Mays

Jim Brown

Sugar Ray Robinson floors an opponent.

Football followed, and soon Joe Perry, Buddy Young, Jimmy Brown and Gale Sayers began to rewrite the record books. In basketball no all-time all-star team would be complete unless it contained Wilt Chamberlain, Bill Russell, Oscar Robertson and Elgin Baylor.

In boxing another Robinson, Sugar Ray, was dominant. In track, Rafer Johnson, Ralph Boston, John Thomas, Bob Hayes (later a football star) and Wilma Rudolph have all excelled. In tennis Althea Gibson and Arthur Ashe were the first Negroes ranked as the top players in the country.

Wilt Chamberlain

Althea Gibson

SECTION II

Two mothers of several jailed Panthers who gathered in New York to protest allegedly poor treatment of prisoners.

Police - Black Panther Conflict

Andrew B. Haynes, Jr.

AFTER INVESTING ten years (1959 to 1969) as a social strategist and political tactician in the Black Movement . . . five as a black nationalist and five as a black powerite . . . I enrolled at Syracuse University to study metropolitan problems, computer applications, and to take a long-needed rest from race problems.

I was in the process of making the difficult transition from the activist to the academic world when two Black Panthers were killed by policemen on December 4, 1969, in Chicago.

For two days after the shooting I received telephone calls concerning the killings. The calls came mainly from the Southeast, where I had worked for five years in operations with a black nationalist group, and the Pacific Northwest, where I spent five years as a black powerite before entering Syracuse University.

The calls came from a cross section of people, but the gist of their questions was similar: What's going on? Do the shootings represent a general policy against all blacks or just the black militants? What should I do if police-Panther conflict spreads to my community? How long will this conflict continue? Who is responsible? Why are they doing it?, etc.

I insisted that I did not have any information on the December 4 Chicago killings, and that I was out of touch with the national grapevine since entering Syracuse University. Most of the callers seemed to disbelieve both responses.

After resenting the disbelief, I became concerned about the degree of alarm reflected in the conversation. Many of the callers were unreasonably paranoiac about the Black Panther killings.

I concluded that the paranoia resulted from an intense desire to get information which seemed unusually scarce, and I decided to provide as many clues to the answers as I could since I had access to information which the callers simply did not have.

I sent out requests for help and made the usual promises to protect information sources. The response from "friends" in the black militant, black nationalist, and law enforcement communities was good.

I am convinced that this report is an accurate overview of the police-Black Panther conflict which in reality was a police-black militancy conflict.

I am responsible for the statements and implications in this report, but I am indebted to others for providing me with a telephone account and discreet information. Without either of those crucial ingredients this report could not have been produced by me.

Report

Black militancy as a vicarious symbol, black power as an ideology, and the Black Panthers as an organization have been effectively decimated. All three will cease to be viable social, political, or para-military forces in America. Except for the natural death throes of the black militants, eulogies and sympathies from elements of the black community, and posthumous diatribes from liberals, black militancy and the Black Panthers are in effect dead . . . for a long time.

Local law enforcement agencies will receive most of the public blame for eradicating the Panthers, but a careful evaluation of the facts indicates that the policemen were simply performing the will of national, local and lay leaders. Furthermore, the policemen's acts were condoned and even welcomed by the general black and white communities.

A hybrid coalition, whose constituents had different reasons for seeking the destruction of black militants, gave the tacit signal for an open season on black militancy.

The target date for the eradication of black militants was 1970; the deadline was 1971.

The tacit but effective coalition consisted of traditional white racists, elements of the Negro middle class, and pragmatic white liberals. As the issues changed and the hybrid coalition developed strength, other parties joined the coalition, but the dominant influence came from the three parties named.

The traditional white racists dislike blacks . . . militant or meek . . . for the usual historical reasons.

The Negro middle class despised most expressions of black militancy, even though they benefited most from early forms of black militancy. The Negro middle class was ashamed of Malcolm X; they despised Stokely Carmichael; Rap Brown made them anemic; and to them Eldridge Cleaver was just another uncommon criminal-turned-crusader.

The pragmatic white liberals decided that black militants had switched from social revolutionaries to successful reactionaries. Furthermore, the liberals felt duty bound to assist in the proper dismantling of the black militants since it was they (the liberals) who had financed the black militants' rise to national significance.

White liberals could have financially starved the black militants out of existence, but the black militants made a quick alliance with the white radical and bought a one- to two-year lease on life. Ironically, the black militants allied with a sinking ship: white radicalism was also under the gun.

One result of the black militant-white radical alliance was a reduction in the amount of anti-white propaganda produced by some of the black militant organizations, especially the ones on the West Coast. It became increasingly difficult to condemn their sole source of support.

Soon after the hybrid coalition began to function, black militancy began its drift into extinction. Men like Gov. Reagan and Dr. S. I. Hayakawa; events like San Francisco State College; Cornell University; South Carolina State College; a few police ambushes; unskilled black militant leadership; and the rise of conservatism sealed the fate of black militants.

The Panthers just happened to be the most visible black militant symbol at the time. However, the dragnets were not limited to Panthers.

White liberals welcomed, and for a while cultivated, black aggression as long as the militancy was verbal and psychological. Liberals viewed black militancy as a vital ingredient in the freedom struggle as well as an effective guilt-purging device. The liberals were correct on both points.

When black militants began to embrace physical violence as a general tactic, liberals began to curtail support for the militants whenever they could do so without appearing to be racists. This in effect meant that most of their anti-black militant policy decisions were discreet.

White liberals further feared that the "law and order" trend in the white community could be driven into virtual fascism by black militant tactics. This fear by white liberals fitted in perfectly with the middle class Negro's fear that the mili-

POLICE—BLACK PANTHER CONFLICT 103

tants were costing them most of their newly won social and political gains made over the last five years. The Negro middle class viewed most of their "instant opportunities" as fire insurance rather than a general reduction of white racialism. The Negro middle class further reasoned that their status was directly dependent upon the rapid taming of black militancy. They were correct.

As long as the activities of the black militants produced "openings" for the middle class Negroes, the militants' tactics were tolerated, but this tolerance was not agreement or support. While the black militants were lambasting the white society, the Negro middle class was grooming itself for white acceptability.

Actually, the Negro middle class had several reasons to welcome the adverse circumstances in which black militants found themselves. Some of the major ones are listed below.

As black militants rose to national prominence, the Negro middle class was displaced from its former monopolistic role of spokesman for the black community—a role which gave the middle class Negroes a type of status in the general community which they did not want to lose. As far as the Negro middle class was concerned, being absorbed into the general white middle class did not compensate for the loss of the position of "Negro Leader."

Black militants and white radicals coerced members of the Negro middle class into a series of Black United Fronts and Black Coalitions in which the Negroes played a minor leadership role and in which they were trapped into publicly endorsing black militancy as an alternative to being branded "Toms." On behalf of social survival, many members of the Negro middle class ate crow and waited for a better day. That day approached as conservatism grew in the white community and as white liberals shifted to safer political positions.

The Negro middle class was also caught in a vocational squeeze. Many of the Negroes entered the middle class through the Great Society programs. When Mr. Nixon won the election, the Negro middle class began to cultivate a capitalist mentality which to black militants meant having a higher regard for property than for people, unless people acted like property.

By July of 1968, both the Republicans and the Democrats were preaching "law and order." The Negro middle class added "justice" to the slogan and joined the conservative chorus. For black militants, this signaled an open season on them since disorder and militancy were synonymous as far as middle class America was concerned.

The Negro middle class always viewed the African culture as uncouth and repulsive, and held black militants directly responsible for the influx of Africanism. Furthermore, Negroes viewed black pride as naked racism and an immediate threat to integration . . . a goal which the majority of the black community want regardless of indications to the contrary.

Finally there was the usual intense class conflict between elements of the Negro middle class and the black militants who usually represented a different class perspective until the militants were co-opted.

Since the white racists, the Negro middle class, and the liberals constituted the base for the bulk of the legitimate and lay social and political leadership, the black militants were totally surrounded by adversaries. Black militants simply did not have the number or the caliber of local or national leaders to escape the collective dragnet. The black militants' problems did not end there.

Between 1965 and 1967 a large percentage of the moderate-to-low-income blacks felt a vicarious identification with black militancy and militant personalities from many of the black militant groups. This empathetic support by the black community for the militants was further boosted when the general white community began to accept or tolerate black militancy; but when it became obvious that the black militants came out on the short end of most police-militant confrontations, the black community began to expect *rhetoric rather than results* from the militants. Henceforth, the militants declined from being psychological shock troops to low-grade entertainers.

By mid-1968 it became obvious that the black militants were doing most of the talking and most of the dying. In most policemen-black militant shoot-outs, the police produced a higher kill ratio than did the militants. In some cases this one-sided kill ratio was desired by black militants.

Furthermore, at least two national events occurred which further increased the disgust the black community had for the reactionary black militants.

One event was the black studies fad which swept the country. White liberals, black militants, and white radicals forced the Afro fad on the black community. The rank and file blacks viewed that fad as a pure waste of money in view of the other needs existing in the black community. Black barbers and beauticians were especially peeved by their financial losses resulting from the "natural" hair fad.

The other event which increased the black community-black militant alienation was the wave of campus disruption climaxed by the Cornell University gun event. The rank and file black viewed the college degree as a sacred key to an escape from the degradation of the ghetto. He had a dim view of black militants throwing away an educational opportunity.

Up to the Cornell University gun event, many moderate-to-low-income blacks were sort of ambivalent toward the black militants' rhetoric. The general feeling was that the militants were ready to do battle and that the obstacle which prevented more black militant-policemen shoot-outs was the fact that the militants were unarmed, and the policemen were armed.

When the Cornell University black militants marched out of the building without firing a shot —this, coupled with the fact that three black protesters died from police bullets in Orangeburg, S.C.—the rank and file blacks began a more serious reevaluation of the sincerity and courage of black militants.

Meanwhile in the ghetto, the Panthers killed and wounded at least twice as many fellow black militants as they did white policemen. Some of the intra-militant political murders were concealed as "usual weekend ghetto brawls" in the police records. However, many street people knew that these conflicts were politically rather than emotionally motivated.

Some local police departments used a self-checking system against black militants. The police would feed factual information to the proper black militant leader or faction and then referee the almost inevitable resulting dispute; then they arrested the "guilty" party for a "cool-off" period. The "cool-off" period usually coincided with the needs of a national *Preventive Policing Program* which existed among big city police departments and federal law enforcement agencies.

In Los Angeles, Newark, and Washington, D.C., the policemen are credited with preventing more intra-black militant deaths than the total number of black militants killed by policemen around the country. For some reason the cultural black militants and the political black militants were unable to generate much brotherly love for each other even in Soulsville.

Although the press portrayed a somewhat different image, the ghetto residents who were in contact with the "street life" knew of these conditions and began to withdraw their empathic support from the militants . . . for the militants failed to live up to the symbols of black masculinity desired by much of the black community.

During the entire black militant era, the pimp remained the "king of the street" in many ghettos while black militants went around throwing anti-honky tantrums in front of white liberal audiences.

On a national scale, the black militants never made a sincere effort to combat the drugs, prostitution, and credit sharking in the black community because the pimps, policemen, and the preachers simply would not permit it.

As an example, one preacher indicated that he made more money as a partner in a bail bonding business than he made as a servant of God. He insisted that members of his flock would pay bail faster than they would pay tithe.

The local police department in conjunction with federal cooperation kept informed of the degree of real or vicarious support in the black community for black militants. Racially sensitive black communities were constantly under surveillance by local and federal officials.

As a matter of fact, the local police departments were usually better informed (in the sense of having current information) about the problems and politics of the ghetto than any other organization inside or outside of the black community. The policeman's access to critical information was the envy of many community organizers.

By mid-1968 the black militants were viewed as reactionaries by the white liberals, as arch-enemies by the Negro middle class, and as loud-mouth trouble makers by moderate-to-low-income blacks. The militants consequently lost all of their political protection from the law enforcement dragnets.

The Negro middle class led the "open season" on the black militants. The Negroes, who could usually get a private audience with elements of the establishment, led the fight against the black militants in a rather subversive manner. The Negroes tried to out-militant the militants in public, and privately assured the politicians that the militants were a serious social cancer which should be eradicated as rapidly as possible.

There is no point in belaboring the enmity which exists between black militants and middle class Negroes. It is sufficient to say that of the three groups—white policemen, black policemen, and the Negro middle class—white policemen were hated less by the black militants than the other two groups.

The total situation strongly suggested that the general black community would not launch a sustained protest against the police for dealing with the black militants. This does not mean that the black community wanted the militants killed; it means that the militants were not politically welcomed in the black community even though the liberal and radical press sometimes suggested otherwise.

Local policemen were aware of the situation in the black community, and moved in a concerted manner to dismantle black militant organizations. The Black Panthers were the most visible as far as the public was concerned. As far as the police—who had been monitoring black militancy from Malcolm X to Eldridge Cleaver—were concerned, the names of the organizations were unimportant, for local hard core militants were usually the same circle of people and floated from one organization to the next depending upon their feelings for the leaders at the time.

The local police department, often acting on information provided by federal or out-of-town law enforcement officials, moved against particular black militants. The police actions were well planned and the militants were carefully categorized into crisis militants, political militants, and hard-core organizers by law enforcement officials. It was the political militants and the hard-core organizers who were the targets of the local and national dragnet.

Although these efforts were usually violent and sometimes fatal, sincere attempts were made by the police departments to limit the casualties to publicly-known hard-core black militants. Further efforts were made to reduce potential violence. Raids were made in the late night or early morning to avoid spectators; summer raids were avoided whenever possible and the vast majority of arrests was made on legitimate or framed criminal charges.

Usually, black policemen were excused or prevented from participating in raids for two reasons. The first reason is that, in general, black police officers would shoot armed or unarmed black militants quicker than white officers would. The second is that a large percentage of the black policemen's families lived in black communities and were vulnerable to reprisal from black militants through the national ripple.

One can expect a certain amount of hypocriti-

Panthers await charges of conspiracy to commit murder, conspiracy to commit assault on police officers and illegal possession of firearms after police raided their Los Angeles headquarters.

Bobby Seale in San Francisco to fight an extradition order to face murder charges in Connecticut.

Robert F. Williams awaiting extradition to North Carolina to face eight-year-old kidnapping charge.

Eldridge Cleaver lashes out at presidential candidates at Stanford University before the 1968 elections.

Stokely Carmichael and H. Rap Brown join blacks protesting Columbia University's "racist policies."

Roy Wilkins, NAACP; Mesia Hewitt, Black Panthers; Rev. Ralph David Abernathy, SCLC, and Roy Ennis, CORE, represent four of the nation's leading black spokesmen.

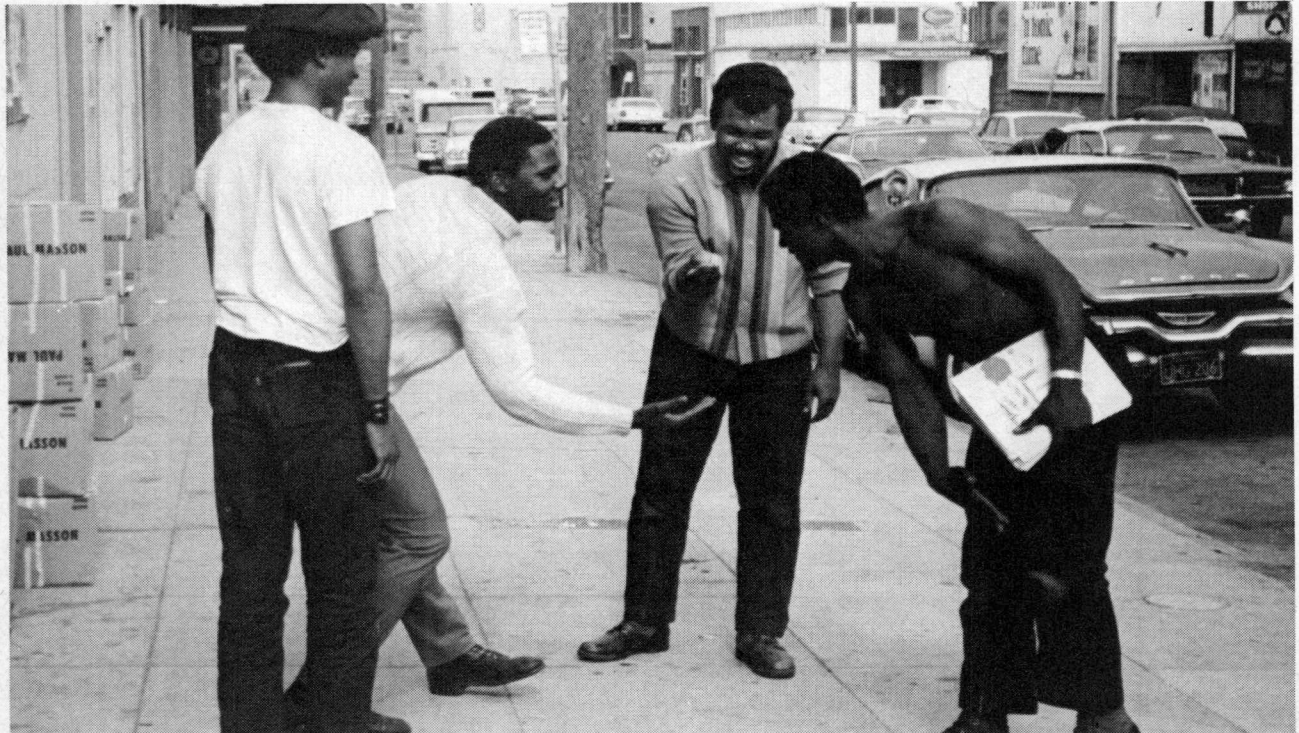

Panthers slap each other's palms in party salute, widely recognized throughout the nation.

Rory Hithe and Landon Robert Williams, suspected of the torture-murder of a fellow Panther in Connecticut.

Student at University of California at Berkeley displays literature asking support of Black Panther Party.

Larry Clayton Powell and wife Jean tell Senate Investigation Subcommittee of their experiences as Panthers and of Panther attempt to kill Powell.

Des Moines Panthers E. C. Smith, Mike Harris and assistants tell press conference they blame police for disturbance in which 15 persons were arrested.

cal diatribes from the Negro middle class and the white liberals condemning the policemen's treatment of Panthers in particular and militants in general. The fact is the policemen were simply carrying out orders which had been cleared through all necessary social, political, and legal channels. The black militants were in effect fingered by the black community and white liberals. The police don't have to worry about being convicted of murder. Even a randomly selected jury of black nationalists would acquit policemen for killing Panthers.

Of course the public statements and the legal ritual will be enacted according to customs, but neither emotional pronouncements nor legal rituals have proven to be effective tools for resurrecting slain black militant leaders.

Police bullets, jail "holds," and interstate and international flight have effectively stripped black militancy of its leadership. The black militancy of the late sixties is dead, and the chances of it reappearing within the next decade are slim.

Claims that the police intimidation of black militants is increasing support for the Panthers or other militants are simply false. There is not much support in the black community for anything but personal survival at present.

Most militant organizations are either dormant or their leaders are converting to black capitalism just as fast as they can throw together a self-help proposal for government funds.

In conclusion, the policemen have practically completed their job. By 1972 it will be a miracle to find a live and free black militant with a high-powered microscope.

Efforts to determine who ordered the eradication will result in nothing but a run around. The militants were the victims of community rejection; consequently, the decision to eradicate the Panthers and the militants was in effect a corporate decision. It is difficult to find the responsible person under such circumstances.

The black community now has the job of coping with the personalities who would have been attracted to the black militants. Many of the potential militants will release their frustra-tions within the confines of the ghetto and help to make the ghetto a worse place to live.

If the potential militants would forgive the black community for doing what it had to do they could then lend their energies to positive community efforts, but they are relatively young and are unlikely to forgive the black community's helping in the destruction of their revolution.

Appendix

It is felt by some ranking members of the black militant and black nationalist communities that the major anti-black militant force in America between 1965 and 1968 was the Defense Department.

According to persons holding this belief, young black draftees from ghetto environments were deeply affected by the domestic black militant indoctrination. The black militant teachings plus the reality of racism in the military generated a variety of problems with the new breed of blacks which did not exist with previous inputs of Negroes who felt the military gave them opportunities which a Negro could not get in civilian life.

The Pentagon officials reasoned that it was wiser to use their influence to get the situation corrected at its source rather than divert time and energy from the military effort to accommodate this relatively new race problem.

The Pentagon officials made it known that domestic black militancy was an impediment to efficient military operations and therefore a threat to national security, and left the correction of the problem to the civilians.

After I did some investigation of this claim it became obvious that I did not have the cooperation or the resources to evaluate this claim within the time allotted for the completion of this report.

I decided to produce the report without discussing the influence of the Pentagon's interest in domestic black militancy. My reason is given below.

If there is a loss due to the omission of the Pentagon's interest in black militancy, the loss is quantitative not qualitative; for the Pentagon force would have been one more force allying with other forces which had ample power to destroy black militancy. Since the eradication of black militancy was done through the domestic machinery, domestic decision makers and influences which were evaluated would have received the greatest attention even if the Pentagon's interests were discussed.

Throughout the development of this report, I was convinced that the Pentagon omission did not distort this overview.

Index of Recent Racial Disorders

The following is a breakdown by state of race-related civil disturbances occurring between January and June 1969, compiled by the Lemberg Center for the Study of Violence of Brandeis University. The disturbances ranged from small street scuffles to large-scale, vicious confrontations between demonstrators and law enforcement agents; the violence was sometimes instigated by blacks, sometimes by whites, and sometimes by a coalition effort of blacks and whites together, protesting what they considered to be blatant racist policies; the issues at stake ran the gamut from disagreements over water-fountain privileges in a high school to arguments concerning control of a university's administrative and academic policies. The demonstrators were a mixed group—ranging from students with leftist leanings protesting racial inequality to parents with rightist leanings protesting racial integration—but they all had in common one underlying motivational factor: racial tension. For the period of January–June 1969, the Civil Disorder Clearinghouse at the Lemberg Center recorded a total of 381 disorders, 73.2 per cent of which involved schools. More specifically, 168 involved pre-colleges, 110 involved colleges or universities, and one involved a university and a high school together.

ALABAMA
Anniston 4/5
Birmingham 4/21
Mobile 4/21
Mobile 5/2–4
Montgomery 3/29; 5/5
Selma 4/7
Selma 6/22
Tuscaloosa 2/18–26

ARIZONA
Tucson 4/18

ARKANSAS
Forrest City 3/20
Forrest City 6/12
Little Rock 2/25, 27
North Little Rock 5/2

CALIFORNIA
Claremont 2/27
Culver City 3/12
Long Beach 5/28
Los Angeles 1/15
Los Angeles 3/7–19
Los Angeles 3/17
Los Angeles 5/11
Los Angeles 5/28
Menlo Park 4/20
Monrovia 3/26, 28
Oakland 5/20
Pacoima 5/26
Palo Alto 2/20
Pasadena 4/29, 30; 5/12
Redding 5/25
Richmond 4/30; 5/1–7
Riverside 4/1, 3
Riverside 5/12
Sacramento 6/15–16
San Diego 4/11–14
San Francisco 1/22–27
San Francisco 2/20; 25–26
San Francisco 2/25
San Francisco 3/3
San Francisco 3/5
San Francisco 4/28
San Francisco 5/1
San Mateo 4/16–17
Santa Ana 3/11–12
Santa Ana 6/29
Walnut 5/9

COLORADO
Boulder 3/3–7
Denver 1/10–2/1
Denver 3/20

CONNECTICUT
Hamden 1/24, 27
Hartford 5/26
Hartford 6/2–7
Middletown 2/21
Middletown 2/24–28
Middletown 6/26–7/1
New Britain 5/6
New Haven 2/20
Waterbury 6/26–28; 7/1
West Haven 5/6

FLORIDA
Bradenton 3/17–21
Fort Pierce 3/18
Gainesville 4/11
Goulds 4/16
Homestead 4/17
Leesburg 4/1
Miami 1/30; 2/10
Miami 4/2–7
Miami 4/16
Miami 4/30–5/8
Ocala 4/21–24
Orange County 2/27, 28; 3/20, 21
St. Petersburg 4/21–23
Sarasota 5/4

GEORGIA
Atlanta 2/25
Atlanta 3/12
Atlanta 4/18, 19
Columbus 2/8
Vidalia 4/8
Waycross 4/7–11
Waycross 5/18–19
Zebulon 4/23–5/16

ILLINOIS
Cairo 3/31; 6/17, 24
Champaign 5/25, 26
Chicago 1/15
Chicago 2/11
Chicago 2/12–21
Chicago 2/26
Chicago 2/26; 3/20
Chicago 2/27
Chicago 3/19
Chicago 3/27
Chicago 4/3

Chicago 4/16
Chicago 4/17, 18; 5/5
Chicago 4/21
Chicago 4/22, 23
Chicago 4/24–26
Chicago 4/25
Chicago 4/28; 5/8
Chicago 5/1–6
Chicago 5/4–5
Chicago 5/6–8
Chicago 5/7, 8, 14
Chicago 5/12
Chicago 5/16–21
Chicago 5/16, 21
Chicago 6/14
Chicago 6/24–25
Chicago Heights 3/14, 17, 26, 27
Chicago Heights 3/19
DeKalb 3/22
East St. Louis 3/10
Edwardsville 2/10
Evanston 2/25–26
Evanston 3/4–6
Kankakee 6/2, 3, 4
Madison 6/17–18
Palos Hills 5/30
Peoria 3/5
Rockford 3/17, 24
Springfield 2/15, 17
Summit 3/25
Venice 6/24
Zion 3/21, 26

INDIANA

Bloomington 5/10
Ft. Wayne 6/29–30
Gary 5/17
Indianapolis 2/25–27
Indianapolis 4/23
Indianapolis 6/5–6
Kokomo 6/26–27
Marion 6/27–28

IOWA

Des Moines 4/13
Des Moines 4/27
Des Moines 5/8, 14
Waterloo 3/3

KANSAS

Lawrence 3/14
Wichita 6/27–7/1

KENTUCKY

Louisville 4/30; 5/1
Louisville 5/1
Louisville 5/23
Louisville 6/8

LOUISIANA

Baton Rouge 5/13
New Orleans 1/17–31; 3/7
New Orleans 4/9; 5/5
New Orleans 4/28

MARYLAND

Annapolis 3/14–18
Baltimore 4/3–4
Baltimore 4/20
Baltimore 6/4
Baltimore 6/7
Hagerstown 3/14
Pasadena 3/13–19

MASSACHUSETTS

Boston 4/23, 24
Boston 5/29
Boston 6/27
Cambridge 4/9–18
Springfield 5/14
Waltham 1/8–18; 2/25; 3/10–11
Williamstown 4/5–8
Worcester 2/20

MICHIGAN

Big Rapids 2/27–28; 3/5
Big Rapids 5/15–19
Detroit 2/19
Detroit 2/25
Detroit 3/11, 18
Detroit 3/29
Detroit 4/22–5/20
Detroit 4/30
Detroit 5/23
East Lansing 4/7
East Lansing 4/28–30
Flint 4/3
Flint 5/1
Highland Park 5/1–2
Jackson 5/1–2
Kalamazoo 4/3
Niles 5/19–21
Pontiac 2/7, 14; 3/6
Saginaw 5/21
Ypsilanti 2/20

MINNESOTA

Minneapolis 1/13–15
Minneapolis 2/27
Moorhead 4/16–20
St. Paul 4/3

MISSISSIPPI

Cleveland 3/10
Itta Bena 2/7–12
Leland 2/26
Lorman 4/1
Port Gibson 4/19
Tunica 2/25

MISSOURI

Forrest Park 2/21
Jefferson City 5/9–12, 19
Kansas City 6/2
St. Louis 1/13–17
St. Louis 2/2, 6
St. Louis 2/3–4
St. Louis 3/23
St. Louis 4/13
St. Louis 4/25–5/9
St. Louis 4/28
Springfield 5/1
Warrensburg 2/20

NEBRASKA

Omaha 6/25–28

NEVADA

Las Vegas 1/31

NEW JERSEY

Camden 5/6–8
East Orange 5/7
Franklin Township 5/13
Freehold 5/19–20
Glassboro 5/15–18
Haddon Heights 4/7–10
Linden 4/25–30
Neptune 3/5, 10
Newark, Camden, New Brunswick 2/6; 3/14
Newark 5/15
Newark 5/19
New Brunswick 3/14, 27
New Brunswick 4/18
Orange 3/18; 4/7
Passaic 3/6–8, 10, 17
Paterson 1/22
Paterson 3/10–18

Piscataway Township 3/19
Plainfield 3/12
Princeton 3/11
Red Bank 6/20–7/1
Trenton 3/7
Trenton 3/12
Trenton 5/12–13
Trenton 5/28
Trenton 6/12–13
Wayne 5/6–8

NEW YORK

Bronx 3/3
Bronx 5/5
Bronx 6/1
Bronx 6/17
Brooklyn 1/10; 5/8
Brooklyn 1/16
Brooklyn 2/20–3/4
Brooklyn 3/7–11
Brooklyn 4/22; 5/5
Brooklyn 5/5, 6
Brooklyn 5/8–29
Brookville 5/22–29
Cedarhurst 1/6
Central Islip 5/6–8
Freeport 4/18–28
Glen Cove 4/16–22
Hamilton 4/25–28
Hempstead 5/6, 27
Huntington 5/6, 27
Huntington 6/9
Ithaca 4/12–20
Long Beach 1/15; 5/9
Long Beach 5/3
Malverne 3/17, 20; 5/13
Manhattan 1/16
Manhattan 3/7
Manhattan 4/11; 5/1
Manhattan 4/14–18, 30
Manhattan 4/15–30
Manhattan 5/6–7
Manhattan 5/10
Manhattan 5/12
Manhattan 5/14–17
Mt. Vernon 2/5
Newburgh 3/28, 31; 4/24
New Rochelle 3/28–29
New York City 4/21
Queens 1/3–5/2
Queens 2/27, 28
Queens 5/19
Rochester 2/24, 25

Rochester 3/2–20
Rochester 3/4–10
Roosevelt 4/25
Syracuse 4/18
Utica 6/13–16
Yonkers 4/22

NORTH CAROLINA

Belmont 4/29–5/6
Burlington 5/16–19
Chapel Hill 3/4
Durham 2/13; 3/11
Elizabeth City 3/19
Fayetteville 2/21
Greensboro 2/17, 13
Greensboro 5/21, 22
Greenville 4/1
Hillsborough 6/30
Laurinburg 4/8, 9
Raleigh 4/14
Raleigh 4/25, 26
Raleigh 5/5–7
Roxboro 6/8–15
Wilmington 2/27
Winston-Salem 4/27–29
Winston-Salem 5/13–16

OHIO

Akron 5/23–30, 6/12
Alliance 6/12
Cincinnati 5/20, 21
Cleveland 1/31; 2/25–26;
    3/6
Cleveland 4/25–28
Cleveland 5/3
Cleveland 5/15–17

Cleveland 5/26–28
Cleveland 6/3–9
Columbus 2/24
Dayton 1/29–31
Lorain 3/6–26
Middletown 2/10
Middletown 6/30
Oberlin 5/22
Springfield 1/18
Steubenville 5/16
Toledo 3/11
Wilberforce 1/14–28

OREGON

Eugene 5/19–20
Portland 2/26–27; 3/1
Portland 3/13
Portland 5/20–23
Portland 6/14–19

PENNSYLVANIA

Carlisle 4/8–10
Chester 1/16
Harrisburg 2/19
Harrisburg 5/30
Harrisburg 6/23–30
Levittown 4/2–8
Oxford 5/21
Philadelphia 2/21
Philadelphia 3/10–11
Philadelphia 6/12
Phoenixville 3/28–31
Pittsburgh 1/9–10; 2/17–
    18

Pittsburgh 1/15–16
Pittsburgh 1/24
Pittsburgh 2/12; 6/5
Pittsburgh 4/3–16
Pittsburgh 6/19
Reading 3/20–27
Roxborough 6/17
Swarthmore 1/9–16
Wilkinsburg 5/26
York 4/6–5/14

RHODE ISLAND

Providence 2/3–6
Providence 4/18
Providence 5/9–15
Providence 5/21

SOUTH CAROLINA

Blacksburg 5/31
Charleston 4/25–6/22
Columbia 2/14
Denmark 4/28, 29

TENNESSEE

Chattanooga 5/14–22
Chattanooga 5/24
Jackson 2/27; 3/12
Memphis 4/4
Memphis 4/23–28
Nashville 5/21, 22

TEXAS

Beaumont 4/10
Beaumont 5/4–7
Dallas 4/29; 5/2

Denton 5/26
Houston 3/17
Marshall 2/18–25
San Antonio 4/21
West Dallas 6/23

VIRGINIA

Hampton 4/23–26
Portsmouth 5/1–5
Williamsburg 4/25

WASHINGTON

Colfax 1/15; 3/1–2
Seattle 4/18, 21
Seattle 5/26
Tacoma 5/11–12

WASHINGTON, D.C.

2/21
2/25–26
3/15
4/7
4/28
5/28
6/6–9

WEST VIRGINIA

Charleston 5/23, 24

WISCONSIN

Beloit 2/6; 3/11
Madison 2/10–21
Madison 4/18
Madison 4/22
Racine 4/23–25

Note: Each entry in the above listing is for a single disorder. In some cases, additional disorders occurred in the same city while the initial disorder was still in progress. These additional disorders are listed separately; for example: "Los Angeles 3/17" is listed separately even though the entry "Los Angeles 3/7–19" would encompass that date.

The Index of Recent Racial Disorders is courtesy of the Lemberg Center for the Study of Violence, Brandeis University, Waltham, Mass.

Charles Evers is sworn in as mayor of Fayette, Mississippi, by Justice of Peace Willis Thompson.

Kenneth Gibson, accompanied by his wife, acknowledges the cheers of the crowd after his victory over incumbent Hugh Addonizio in Newark's mayoral election.

Points of View

RICHARD M. NIXON was elected President in November 1968, having attracted, it was estimated, less than 10 per cent of the Negro vote. At one of his first news conferences in February, the new President conceded that he was not regarded "as a friend by many of our black citizens," but said he hoped "by my actions as President" to rectify that.

At the end of his first year in office, several Negro leaders and others tried to assess the extent to which the President's hope had been realized. Their appraisal was in general a gloomy one. Clarence A. Mitchell, Washington director of the National Association for the Advancement of Colored People (NAACP), told a Washington *Evening Star* reporter late in December that Negroes felt the administration had accomplished "just about what they expected. . . . The Nixon administration is doing us in." He pointed out that there were "no Negroes in the Cabinet, but a few in second-tier jobs, and they make it look like that's progress." He conceded that the President's actions were not the sign of any real "animus against Negroes. He just makes use of all weapons. He is making use of racism and reverse racism." Mitchell said the President regarded Negroes as "a vote we haven't been able to get," but put more important emphasis on keeping his own supporters happy. The all-white Cabinet, Mitchell said, was a "serious step backward."

The assistant executive director of the NAACP, Dr. John A. Morsell, described the administration's first year as "a mixed bag," with "more negative than positive aspects" for Negroes. He counted the Philadelphia Plan, a federal program to set hiring goals for black workers and apprentices in the construction industry, and the proposed minimum income guarantee for poor families among the positive efforts. But among those he listed as not in the best interests of the black community were the nomination of Judge Clement F. Haynsworth, Jr., to the Supreme Court; the scuttling of the 1965 Voting Rights Act instead of extending it for five years; relaxation of some school desegregation guidelines; and approval of defense contracts with textile industries having a long record of hiring discrimination. "I don't think this administration feels the Negro voter is as vital to its success as white voters," Dr. Morsell concluded. "I think this is a mistake."

Mrs. Martin Luther King, Jr., speaking in September on the CBS program "Face the Nation," said that the Nixon administration "is really asking for trouble unless it changes its policy" toward the black community. Negro Nobel Prize winner Ralph Bunche, appearing on the ABC program "Issues and Answers" in December, confessed that he shared the views of black leaders who "do not have confidence in the commitment of the administration to move forward in any bold or imaginative way." The January 1970 issue of *Ebony* magazine summed up 1969 as "a year of marking time," and remarked that the new administration's first year "has not inspired substantial black support."

Tom Wicker of the *New York Times* discussed the administration's record and concluded that the President's hope to rectify the view that he was not a friend of the black community was, at the end of 1969, "only narrowly rescued from oblivion" by his lobbying efforts on behalf of the Philadelphia Plan and a White House proposal to bring cheap or free lunches to millions of poor children.

In defense of the administration, Attorney General John N. Mitchell told Fred P. Graham of the *New York Times* that "the Nixon administration has made impressive gains for Negroes but Negro leaders refuse to admit it publicly because their constituency is predominantly Democratic." Mitchell said he had met privately many times with Negro leaders and found them well satisfied with the administration's programs, only to have the same spokesmen go out and make public statements denouncing these efforts. Other defenders of the administration's policies pointed to Nixon's ideas about black capitalism, to federal tax aid for ghetto industries, and to the fact that "there has been little effort to publicize the administration's role for blacks."

Monroe W. Karmin, writing in the *Wall Street Journal,* pointed out that "emerging Nixon policy means [Negroes] have to share federal help more—not only with other minorities, such as Puerto Ricans, Mexican-Americans, and Indians, but with poor and blue collar whites, many of whom are resentful of Negro gains. Increasingly, federal administrators talk of seeking 'a better balance' of beneficiaries." Defenders of the administration's policy point out that in his inaugural address Mr. Nixon promised to "bring us all together," and that the "better balance," while helping blacks, also softens racial antagonisms by assisting others with their problems. Karmin quotes a presidential adviser as saying, "Let's face it, the more you appear to be helping just one group, the more you set other groups against it."

Richard Strout of the *Christian Science Monitor* concluded, however, "that whatever the object, the Nixon policy is accompanied by a striking increase of support in the South." He commented further, "The breach between President Nixon and the blacks has not perceptibly narrowed . . . and it may have widened."

Blacks in the Administration

Robert H. Finch, President Nixon's nominee for Secretary of Health, Education and Welfare (HEW), made light of the fact that the administration had come to office with so little Negro support. He promised a "new kind of candor and realism" in the drive for racial equality, because no political debts were owed to the "black establishment." And black leaders, although confessing to misgivings, adopted a "wait and see" attitude about the administration in its early days. But most were intensely disappointed when the President appointed no black cabinet member.

However, the administration defended its action. Several Negroes, including Republican Sen. Edward Brooke of Massachusetts, were offered posts but declined them, according to Secretary Finch, often because they feared being labeled Uncle Toms, but also because most Negroes are Democrats, and would be reluctant to serve a Republican administration. Columnist Marquis Childs charged in February that Nixon recruiters were "inept and overcautious" in their approach to prominent Negroes.

The President urged his cabinet members to choose their top aides from "a very broad prospect in terms of geographical area, ethnic groups, and representatives of a basic cross section of the population." The result was that some distinguished Negroes were appointed to sub-cabinet rank. There is a black assistant secretary in virtually every department, and two in Housing and Urban Development (HUD). Administration sources contend that at this level blacks are making a stronger contribution to policy deliberations than ever before.

James Farmer, founder and for a long time director of the Congress of Racial Equality (CORE), was given considerable publicity when he was appointed assistant secretary of HEW. He is serving in this post as liaison with militant young Negroes who feel estranged from the Nixon administration. Farmer said that black students across the nation advised him to accept the appointment in order to help effect changes. Farmer claimed that he still remained "militant" but that this meant "firmness of principle" and not "approval of violence." He said the situation today pointed to a growing separation of the races in the United States and that he intended to counter it as best he could to "prove the American system works and that it can include those who have always been excluded."

Robert J. Brown, the first Negro appointed to President Nixon's staff, was named special assistant for business development, specifically to seek ways of developing black capitalism. "We're not making any grandiose promises," he said, "but we want action." He said he would solicit ideas from the black community on ways to develop black capitalism. He is also a member of the board of the Southern Christian Leadership Conference (SCLC), a lifetime member of the NAACP, and has worked for various housing, urban renewal, and law enforcement agencies. He was head of his own public relations firm of B & C Associates, located in High Point, N.C.

Samuel C. Jackson and Samuel J. Simmons were selected to fill the third and fourth highest positions in HUD. Jackson was named general assistant secretary with specific responsibility for metropolitan development. A former director of the NAACP, he was one of the five original presidential appointees to the Equal Employment Opportunity Commission in 1965. He is also vice president of the American Arbitration Association. Simmons was named assistant secretary for equal opportunity. He has been prominent in the NAACP and for the prior four years had been director of the field services division of the U.S. Civil Rights Commission. He was charged with enforcing the Fair Housing Law of 1968.

Arthur A. Fletcher, the new assistant secretary of Labor, was given authority for wage and labor standards. His major responsibility is manpower development and liaison with mayors and local governments. Before his appointment he was the special urban affairs aide to Washington State's Lt. Gov. Daniel J. Evans, and in 1968 he had been the Republican nominee for governor of the state.

Ronald B. Lee was the first Negro named to a top job in the Post Office Department. He is assistant postmaster general in charge of directing a new bureau of planning, marketing, and systems analysis. A West Point graduate, he had previously been assistant provost and director of the Center for Urban Affairs at Michigan State University.

James E. Johnson was chosen as the associate Republican member of the Civil Service Commission. He was a career Marine officer and recent director of the California Department of Veterans Affairs under Gov. Ronald Reagan. The Senate Civil Service Committee hesitated before approving the nomination because of his suspected association with ultra-conservative groups in California, including the John Birch Society. Johnson also was under questioning for a directive to his California department's employees that they adhere to Gov. Reagan's conservative political philosophy. Johnson denied a link with the John Birch Society, saying he did not know that a group to whom he once gave a speech was a John Birch affiliate.

Benjamin F. Holman was appointed director of the Community Relations Service in the Justice Department. The CRS assists in resolving disputes stemming from racial discrimination, especially in the inner cities. A former CRS assistant director, Holman was working as a producer and reporter for an NBC news series on social issues in the Washington, D.C., area at the time. He had previously reported for the *Chicago Daily News,* WBBM-TV in Chicago, and CBS News in New York.

Two distinguished women appointees were Elizabeth Koontz, a North Carolinian and president of the National Education Association, who was named director of the Women's Bureau in the Labor Department, and Marjorie McGowan, an attorney from Detroit, who was the first high-level woman appointee at HUD.

A prominent lawyer, James Washington, Jr., former dean of the Howard University Law School and former chairman of the District of Columbia Public Service Commission, was appointed general counsel of the Department of Transportation.

Something of the attitudes and philosophy of the top black administration officials (i.e., the assistant secretaries) surfaced in an article by James M. Naughton in the *New York Times* in September, written on the basis of interviews with nearly all of them. Discussing reasons for joining the Republican administration, one declared, "It dawned on me how unfortunate it was everybody with a commitment to civil rights was quitting the government. Somebody had to stay inside to make the case." In talking about their relations with the black community as a result of taking office, the officials declared they had met with little hostility, although one had been booed at a meeting of a Negro group, and another noted "some uptightness in our ranks." All appeared confident that the time was right for a shift in civil rights focus to the equal employment arena, and they expressed confidence in the Nixon administration emphasis on economic betterment of the whole community: "A rising tide lifts all boats." Arthur Fletcher of the Department of Labor endorsed the stress on providing job opportunities. "This administration . . . is going to concentrate on economic opportunities. We got so hung up on the idea that civil rights was a social problem that we failed to see the connecting links. We've got to talk economics."

The officials commented on "a quietness, almost stealth, about getting things done," even to the extent that few people were aware of how many blacks were in office, since there had been

relatively little publicity about their appointments. As one said, "If the White House is 'using' me, they're not getting much capital out of it." This "quietness" was seen by some as a pragmatic approach, avoiding confrontation and despair and achieving results by subtlety and avoidance of tense situations. "Courtrooms and conference rooms are to be the arenas for civil rights battles," it was said. The point was made that this quietness was compatible with the so-called Southern strategy, widely believed to be administration policy, that is, to win over the support the South gave to George Wallace in 1968. The blacks in the administration expressed their firm conviction, however, that "civil rights is not on the back burner of this administration. We may be quiet but we intend to get results."

Equal Employment

Democrat Clifford L. Alexander, a Johnson appointee, resigned as chairman of the Equal Employment Opportunity Commission (EEOC) when the White House indicated in April that he would be replaced by a Republican. William H. Brown III, also a Negro, succeeded him, but the episode contributed to the anxieties of those black Americans who questioned the administration's commitment to civil rights enforcement.

The announcement of Alexander's dismissal came just the day after the late Sen. Everett Dirksen of Illinois, then Senate Minority Leader, had accused him of harassing businessmen in carrying out what Alexander considered his legitimate duties at EEOC. Dirksen objected to EEOC hearings at which firms with few black workers were more or less called on the carpet, and he had threatened to have Alexander fired. The timing of the White House announcement, therefore, was considered unfortunate.

Concern was intensified when Deputy Defense Secretary David Packard was discovered to have awarded $14 million in contracts to three Southern textile mills despite their failure to fulfill government requirements for fair employment practices. Packard had relied on their verbal assurances that they would employ more Negroes. When Transportation Secretary John Volpe revised the requirements to be met by highway contractors in establishing equal employment opportunity, he encountered criticism from Sen. Edward M. Kennedy of Massachusetts that the rules were for the convenience of the construction industry, and from Herbert Hill, NAACP's national labor secretary, who agreed with the senator.

William Brown of EEOC at first endorsed and then withdrew support for a bill introduced by Sen. Jacob Javits (R-N.Y.) and Sen. Harrison Williams (D-N.J.) which granted cease and desist powers to EEOC. He felt that an administration bill introduced in early August by Sen. Winston Prouty (R-Vt.) enabling EEOC to take job discrimination complaints directly to a federal district court if voluntary conciliation failed, was more effective. He said the cease and desist procedure could take four to six years to be enforced while the administration measure ensured speedy action. Brown was criticized by Clifford Alexander and others—"They are making the enforcement of employment rights second class," said civil rights advocate Joseph L. Rauh—and Brown did not continue the public hearings on discrimination by employers which Alexander had begun.

However, the administration's commitment to equal employment opportunity was evidenced by the President's strongly worded executive order of August 8 directed at abolishing job discrimination in the federal government. Called by one reporter "probably the most sweeping of its kind ever made by a President," the order states: "This policy of equal opportunity applies to, and must be, an integral part of every aspect of personnel policy and practice in the employment, development, advancement, and treatment" of U.S. workers. Another new rule for the General Services Administration laid down by the administration was that building sites on space leased for government offices must be situated within reasonable proximity to low- and moderate-cost housing. One federal department was reportedly so conscious of the need to funnel federal funds to minority groups that it required "affirmative action" to bring in black consultants for its projects, and required explanations when they were not hired.

Perhaps the clearest illustration of the administration's methods of securing equal employment opportunity was the Philadelphia Plan, which was to require bidders on federally-financed projects in Philadelphia to work toward minority hiring goals in six skilled construction crafts in the city. The Chicago and Pittsburgh plans, involving voluntary union minority hiring quotas, soon followed, and the prospect of Labor Department action against exclusionary contractors in other Northern cities and in the South, where there are large federal contracts, may produce more "city" plans—which the administration would welcome—for the beautification of the country.

Under Arthur Fletcher, the Labor Department was said to be formulating percentage goals for minority hiring in all the metropolitan districts across the nation, with the added aim of equalizing earnings of black and white workers. While administration policy was largely aimed at discrimination practiced by unions, the Labor Department was quietly bargaining with company presidents for voluntary programs to hire minority craftsmen. In addition, the Justice Department filed lawsuits charging employers and unions with discrimination in the following states: Maryland, New Jersey, California, and Kansas.

At the same time the administration's anti-inflation policy has necessitated a cutback of federal construction programs. The cuts will inevitably have a serious effect on unemployment figures and exacerbate competition between blacks and whites for available jobs, probably intensifying labor union opposition to Philadelphia Plan requirements. In November one congressman was claiming that anti-inflationary measures had cut out 350,000 jobs since January.

Black Capitalism

Black capitalism, often talked of during the 1968 election campaign, was broached once the Republicans were in the White House. Secretary of Commerce Maurice H. Stans explained in February that since the administration wished to include other minority groups such as Mexican-Americans, Puerto Ricans, American Indians, Eskimos, and Aleuts in the concept, the term was to be changed to "minority enterprise." In March an Office of Minority Business Enterprises (OMBE) was set up in the Labor Department by presidential order and was headed first by Thomas Roeser and then by Abraham Venable, one of his black aides. Philip Pruitt, a black investment broker, was appointed assistant administrator in March, but resigned after four months. He was apparently upset by criticism from Negro leaders at the NAACP convention in August and was dissatisfied with the progress of the project.

The intention was that OMBE should encourage minority groups to enter business not only as workers, but as managers and owners. Secretary Stans pointed out that whereas the various minorities constitute 15 per cent of the population, they own only 3 per cent of the businesses, generally small ones at that. OMBE was assigned the task of developing new business opportunities and mobilizing financial and other resources, both public and private, by providing leadership at the local level and removing commercial obstacles such as the unavailability of credit insurance and technical assistance.

Vice President Spiro T. Agnew, in a hard-hitting speech in March to representatives of the nation's biggest corporations—meeting under the auspices of Plans for Progress, a voluntary national business organization formed to ensure equal employment—urged that big business should help the minorities set up their own businesses even if this meant creating competition for themselves. "Let him [the black man] have the collateral assistance we have," Agnew said. "Let him have the same public relations we have, led by a black man to sell his product on competitive markets like we do."

OMBE is also to coordinate the efforts of other government departments in this field—no negligible task with about 114 programs scattered throughout the government. Perhaps the most important underlying aim of the whole OMBE and black capitalism concept is, as Stans put it, "to give inspiration and ambition to others who want to engage in business activity" and as one commentator put it, "to give Negroes something to shoot for." Further, it should help provide more jobs for ghetto residents, an important part of the idea.

The scheme did meet much criticism during the year from black leaders who appear either to mistrust the validity of the idea, disliking and fearing the possibility of black separatism, or to be dissatisfied with its rate of implementation. The inquiry of the House Select Committee on Small Business into administration efforts to stimulate business ownership by minority groups in July was the occasion for these comments— Roy Innis, director of CORE: "Another one of those public relations type operations. Black capitalism has fallen into disrepute in the black community"; Dr. Walter Cooper, chairman of the Small Business Administration's National Advisory Council for Black Business and Economic Development: "We are disappointed in the lack of progress of minority entrepreneurship programs"; Floyd McKissick, former head of CORE, felt that the administration had failed to back up black capitalism campaign rhetoric with commitment. Perhaps one of the most telling comments was that of Howard J. Samuels, former administrator of the Small Business Administration under President Johnson: "There is no reason to doubt that President Nixon is sincere when he states his desire to encourage minority development. But it is frustrating . . . to know that the legislation, the resources, and the tools are there, and yet are not being properly used."

Nevertheless, as *Ebony* points out, the Nixon administration has "announced plans to make up to $500 million available by next June to finance black business opportunities." Secretary Stans "revealed 18 large and small corporations had pledged a minimum of $150,000 each" to sponsor a small business investment company "which in turn would finance business projects of members of minority groups. The funding will be on a 2 to 1 basis, with the government doubling the amount pledged by each corporation."

In September President Nixon asked a group of top-level corporation executives, educators, labor leaders, and foundation managers to help minorities get involved in American business, and named them to a new Advisory Council for Minority Enterprise in the Department of Commerce. At the same time he confessed that he was "keenly aware" of skepticism about the value of the council, but stressed his commitment to the idea of black capitalism and asked the leaders to give minorities "a new hope . . . the chance that you had, and that I had." He said: "Six months ago I pointed out in creating the Office of Minority Business Enterprise that this effort is neither a panacea nor a substitute for other efforts, to create more and better job opportunities for all Americans. We want to create new opportunities and foster the pride of accomplishment in both the management and work force of the nation." As we have seen, the President also appointed Robert J. Brown, a Negro, to serve as a liaison between the White House and OMBE.

But on December 29, with Negro leaders still critical of the concept of black capitalism, a further blow was dealt by Andrew Brimmer, the only Negro member of the Federal Reserve Board, in a paper he helped prepare for the American Economic Association. Brimmer's thesis was that black capitalism "may retard the Negro's economic advancement by discouraging many from the full participation in the national economy with its much broader range of challenges and opportunity." He declared that the ghetto constituted a poor economic environment for business, and that even economic advancement within the Negro community may not improve prospects, but merely increase competition with national firms seeking an expanding Negro market. He pointed out that setting up small scale businesses is contrary to the national trend, and that self-employment "offers a low and rather risky payoff." It may be difficult to ignore such cogent criticism of administration policy of such direct relevance to blacks and other minorities, especially when such a policy will take time to show results.

President Nixon's appointment of Daniel P. Moynihan as his special assistant in the Cabinet on urban affairs, and as the executive secretary of his Urban Affairs Council, received mixed reactions. A sociologist specializing in race relations, author of *Beyond the Melting Pot* and the controversial "Moynihan Report," and a Democrat, he was considered a leading authority in the Cabinet on Negro affairs and problems. As such he was criticized by Dr. Nathan Wright, chairman of the Black Power Conference, who felt that only a Negro could successfully advise the President on these subjects. Nevertheless, his appointment, because of his influence in the White House and his collaboration with HEW Secretary Finch on the problems of the poor, on malnutrition, and on the cities, is of great importance to minority groups and to the underprivileged generally. (His elevation in November to the rank of counselor to the President was thought to indicate a somewhat diminished role for the Urban Affairs Council.)

OEO

In his first substantive message to Congress after his inauguration, Mr. Nixon announced that he would retain the Office of Economic Opportunity (OEO), but would turn over its Head Start and Job Corps programs to HEW and the Department of Labor, respectively, the former to be strengthened by its association with "a wide range of other early development programs," and the other to produce "a more integrated and coordinated manpower effort." His emphasis on the importance of government innovation in efforts to help the poor, on the lack of solid information about poverty and its remedies and the need for comprehensive programs reassured many who had feared the President might take a harder line toward the poor, and perhaps attempt to dismantle the anti-poverty agency entirely. He pledged that he would correct inefficient management practices in the anti-poverty programs—"When programs are ineffectively administered, those hurt most . . . are the poor."

The President had declared the Job Corps "a failure" in campaign speeches, and his Secretary of Labor, George Shultz, announced in April that 59 of 113 Job Corps centers would be closed by July 1 in a move to shift from rural residential centers to urban training. This policy touched off the administration's first battle with Congress, where many members sought to preserve existing camps and called the policy a "potentially disastrous course." The Job Corps budget was cut by $100 million, while promises were made of reaching more hard-core young people through training programs. But the moves were called a 'trick' by Sen. Jacob Javits (R-N.Y.) and Sen. Walter Mondale (D-Minn.).

On May 23 Donald Rumsfeld, 36, a Republican congressman from Illinois, was confirmed by the Senate as OEO director, giving up one of the safest seats in Congress for "one of the most important [and] controversial agencies in the entire government," according to President Nixon. Rumsfeld, said the President, saw his agency as an "innovating agency, an incubator of new programs." Rumsfeld was made an assistant to the President with Cabinet rank to strengthen his hand in directing the agency.

The President committed himself in February to extending OEO for a year beyond its scheduled expiration, which had been June 30, 1970, a commitment he overhauled in June, when he asked Congress to renew the anti-poverty program for two years and asked for an additional $100 million for the agency's fiscal year 1969–70. Nevertheless, the absence of any new anti-poverty programs caused Rep. Augustus F.

Hawkins (D-Calif.) to accuse the administration of "misleading" the poor with "beautiful phrases." When Rumsfeld, at a House Education and Labor Committee hearing, emphasized that the two-year request "is not a commitment simply to continue present programs" but "a commitment to find out what works and what does not, to review the performance of these programs and utilize new knowledge," Hawkins declared that it sounded as though OEO was "going into hibernation to conduct additional studies." The President's request for the extension of OEO without major change ran into further opposition in Congress, led by Rep. Edith Green (D-Ore.) with the aid of Republicans and Southern Democrats, who wanted to turn over control of OEO to the states. In the crucial vote on December 12, this legislation was passed, although civil rights leaders criticized the administration's lack of strategy and willingness to compromise on what they considered vital issues.

In August President Nixon announced "new directions" and a reorganization of OEO to enable it to concentrate on "social pioneering" and act as a research and development agency for the government's social programs, and to "concentrate its energies on causes rather than symptoms." Its programs were to be reassigned to government departments, but it would continue to operate Volunteers in Service to America, Neighborhood Legal Services, Neighborhood Health Centers, family planning, emergency food, rural, older persons, Indian, and migrant programs. The Community Action Program, which had aimed through maximum feasible participation to involve the poor in their own program and had led to militant demonstrations in some areas, was to be considerably trimmed, with a 15 to 20 per cent cutback in funds. Critics said the administration had sounded the death knell of OEO and commented that Rumsfeld—who in May had said he intended to put OEO in the forefront of federal anti-poverty efforts—had suffered a major setback. They pointed out that he could attract no Negroes to high OEO posts, that he had lost the support of the more aggressive local anti-poverty leaders by playing down OEO's advocacy of more help for the poor, and had invited hostility from local officials by pledging to cut off federal funds from ineffective Community Action Programs. Yet his defenders pointed out his necessary preoccupation with the political uncertainties of OEO, and credited him with guarding the agency "from the right" and with providing "the kind of buffer it needs to get on with its most critical work." "He has at least ended OEO's isolation from the White House, its predicament during much of the last administration," said one commentator.

Hunger

In April the President sent to Congress a tax reform package which included a plan to remove from the tax rolls all those officially defined by the government as "poor." The government definition of poverty was set in early December at an income of $3,600 for a non-farm family of four. Thirteen per cent of the population are classed as poor, including one-third of all Negroes. It was estimated that tax reform would remove about two million people from the tax rolls.

The nation was shocked in the spring by revelations of rural and urban malnutrition, mainly, but not solely, concentrated in the South. Senate hearings and congressional investigators turned up evidence of acute starvation which jolted the nation's conscience. In May, declaring that hunger in America was "embarrassing and intolerable," the President proposed a billion-dollar-a-year increase in the federal food aid programs, and appealed for early action to improve and expand the food stamp program. He asked that poor families of four get a minimum of $100 a month in stamps, that the stamps should be free to the very poor and cost no more than 30 per cent of the income of other needy persons. The distribution of food stamps was to be improved, and the whole program was to be seen as complementary "to a revised welfare program." A supplemental food program for needy pregnant women and mothers with infants was to be started, a food and nutrition service to be set up to administer the federal food programs under the Urban Affairs Council, and a subcommittee of that council was to promote coordination between food and nutrition programs and other health, education, and anti-poverty programs.

OEO was at that time to expand its food, health, and sanitation services in depressed neighborhoods, and budget provision was made for $15 million to hire food aides to advise the poor on buying the most nutritious foods. The President declared, "More is at stake here than the health and well-being of 16 million American citizens who will be aided by these programs. . . . Something like the very honor of American democracy is at stake. The moment is at hand to put an end to hunger in America itself for all time."

The White House Conference on Food, Nutrition, and Health, which the President had also promised would advise on how to improve the nutritional status of all Americans, was held in Washington in December and chaired by Dr. Jean Mayer, a Harvard University nutritionist, who is special consultant on hunger to the President. The conference was the scene of radical demands by militants, but also of hard work by more moderate delegates. Together they produced a far-reaching, expensive, five-point program—a blueprint that could, as the President said, "put an end to hunger and malnutrition due to poverty in America." The calls for a massive emergency assault on hunger, for a guaranteed annual cash income of $5,000, and for the declaration of a national hunger emergency, were accompanied by a sheaf of detailed proposals to be sent to the President on the technical problems of hunger, health, and food delivery systems. Some bore almost immediate fruit.

At the end of the year came news of new White House action on school lunch regulations, which would permit private food companies to bring airline-style meals into certain public schools, increasing by late 1970 the number of children receiving free or reduced-price lunches from 3.4 million to 6.6 million. Critics pointed to profits that will be made for private food companies, but, nevertheless, thousands of poor black children are bound to be among those who will get better food than they otherwise would have. In his statement announcing the new scheme, Dr. Mayer outlined all the administration efforts to end hunger, noting that all counties in the United States will have food programs by June 30, 1970, and claiming, "I have no hesitation in saying that this administration has done a great deal more than any administration in history to fight hunger." Sen. George McGovern (D-S.D.), noting the doubling of food stamp funds and the pledge for their redoubling in the next fiscal year, praised the administration's achievement but asked that 1970 see the end of hunger in America.

On August 8 President Nixon announced in a national radio and television address a complex proposal for the reform of the welfare system. The bases of his proposals were "first, a complete replacement of the present welfare system; second, a comprehensive new job training and placement program; third, a revamping of OEO; and fourth, a start on the sharing of federal tax revenue with the states." He amplified his proposals in messages to Congress containing specific measures to put them into effect.

The welfare reform plan involved the abolition of the existing welfare system and the setting up of a family assistance program with a minimum standard of federal aid for every needy family with children. Except for disabled adults and mothers with pre-school children, the poor would be required to accept "suitable" employment or participate in a government training program to be eligible for relief. Aid would be available to the working poor. The unpopular and controversial program—called Aid to Families with Dependent Children—that many thought encouraged men to desert their families so that their children could receive payments varying from $39 a month in Mississippi to $263 a month in New Jersey, was scrapped. The new program was to rest on three principles:

equality of treatment across the nation, a work requirement, and a work incentive. A family of four anywhere with no other income would receive a federal minimum of $1,600 a year, and could earn $720 a year with no loss of benefits. Beyond that, aid would be reduced 50 cents for each dollar until the family's wages reached $3,920. Each recipient would have to register at an unemployment office and take "suitable" work or job training, and the states could supplement the federal aid. A minimum payment of $65 a month would be made to the disabled, blind, and aged, with the federal government contributing the first $50 and sharing in payments above that amount. As the President said, "The new approach would end the blatant unfairness of the welfare system." Administration officials said they expected the welfare rolls to increase from ten million to a total of 22.4 million.

Closely related to the welfare proposals were the President's proposals on manpower training. He asked for a "complete overhaul" of the manpower training services which he called "a terrible tangle of confusion and waste." He proposed decentralization of job training administration, "a flexible funding so the federal money would follow the demands of labor and industry and flow into those programs that people most want and need," equalization of standards of eligibility, and a computerized job bank to match job vacancies to job applicants. The incentives to welfare recipients to accept job training and the expanded day facilities recommended were of most immediate importance to the poor.

The OEO changes announced at that time have already been discussed, and it was the administration's proposals for federal revenue sharing which received most widespread criticism from the black community. The proposal was for a proportion, eventually 1 per cent, of the federal income taxes to be remitted directly to the states. There would be a minimum of federal restrictions on their use, except for the requirement that a percentage be rechanneled to local governments. The President announced that "this start on revenue sharing is a step toward what I call New Federalism. It is a gesture of faith in America's state and local governments and in the principle of democratic self-government."

What looked like a return to states' rights alarmed some blacks. The Institute of Black Elected Officials expressed virtually unanimous disapproval when they met in Washington in September, voicing their apprehension that more money and authority in the hands of local officials would bring a return to "tyranny" against poor minorities. Ruby Martin, former director of the Office of Civil Rights at HEW, stated at the conference, "I wish the Nixon administration had spent more time studying what happens to black people when authority is turned over to states and localities." She quoted the example of Title I of the Elementary and Secondary Education Act of 1965, saying it provided billions of dollars for disadvantaged children but had been widely misused in the hands of local officials. The opinion in the black community was said to be that unless specified uses were laid down for federal money, the states might well not use them for the purposes intended. This is a special danger in the South where, even with specific requirements laid down, federal officials are reportedly unable to enforce them. Secretary Finch defended the proposals at the conference on the grounds that the channeling of money and authority to the states would bring more immediate and flexible aid to the blacks and the poor by reducing red tape.

The Cities

"The basic issues President Nixon is tackling with his new job and income program for the poor are the drift toward racial isolation between slums and suburbs in the United States, and the fiscal breakdown this has caused in the cities and states. . . . His goal is to end the poverty and isolation of the American Negro," commented Richard Critchfield in the Washington *Evening Star*.

Daniel Moynihan, head of the Urban Affairs Council (the setting up of which was the President's first official act of government), is credited by many with being the driving force behind this long-term goal. His own stated view is that the real problem of the Negro family is that it is living in a "state almost of demographic siege," and with an increasingly high birth rate the most explosive problem of the cities—the underemployment of black teenagers—will get increasingly worse. The crisis can only be mitigated by ending the American Negro's "social isolation," by moving poor minorities from slums to suburbs. The voluntary dispersion of black families from the ghetto is reportedly to be achieved by raising economic levels. The welfare reform and revenue-sharing proposals are the administration's tactics for pumping money into the cities to achieve this.

The Model Cities program had been the route the Democrats had chosen to funnel federal aid to cities, and although HUD Secretary Romney continued to support the idea in public statements, White House insiders are said to regard the program as an "administrative nightmare." Federal spending on the cities, originally budgeted for $540 million for the year beginning July 1, 1969, was revised down to $300 million, and of 75 cities scheduled to receive funds by June 30, 1969, only 53 actually had received them by December. Anti-inflationary budget restrictions have taken their toll. *Ebony* magazine had this to say: "Under the Model Cities program affecting six million mostly black people in 150 cities, blacks had hoped for a key role in 'resouling' their slum neighborhoods—a role built into the 1966 law. But Romney, in effect, ruled out grassroots self-determination in his April announcement that "Model Cities planning would be controlled by city hall."

The disillusioned tone of the comment is unmistakable, but efforts were made by the administration to include low-income and minority group representation in area-wide planning organizations. A directive issued in September required extensive citizen participation throughout the planning process and a guarantee of equal employment opportunity practices, on pain of loss of HUD funds for water and sewer projects and open space planning.

In April the President earmarked $200 million in an effort to clean up the rubble left from the riots of 1968. The funds were to come from money already appropriated to HUD but not yet spent, and were to be divided among 20 cities and used for rehabilitation. Where this was not possible, it was earmarked for a program of parks, playgrounds, and recreation centers.

Conditions in Washington, D.C., were of obvious importance to the President. He named Walter E. Washington to a second term as mayor of the nation's capital and at the same time pledged special federal support for the city and support for home rule as a necessary ingredient. His concern that the city had become the "crime capital" of the nation was evidenced by his recommendations for more policemen, public prosecutors, and judges, and his endorsement of the proposal to tighten the bail law so that hard-core criminals could be denied bond while awaiting trial on new charges. "The rapidly mounting urgency of the crime crisis in the District makes immediate, direct, anti-crime measures as the first priority task," said the President. By the end of the year, none of Mr. Nixon's 13 pieces of anti-crime legislation had been passed by Congress, and no action had been taken on his home rule proposals.

Civil Rights

Civil rights enforcement is widely considered the area in which the Nixon administration's record in 1969 has been least satisfactory to blacks. It has been the administration's strategy to avoid confrontation and tension on issues such as open housing, voting rights, and school desegregation, and to concentrate on opening up the job market. As early as April, writing a joint letter of protest about Sen. Dirksen's attack on the EEOC, eight of the nine Negroes in the House of Representatives complained of an "emerging pattern of relaxed enforcement of civil rights laws."

School desegregation policies have been foremost in controversy. In a statement on July 3, Secretary Finch and Attorney General John Mitchell announced that the 1969–1970 deadlines set by the Johnson administration for complete desegregation were "too rigid to be either workable or equitable" and that districts with "bona fide educational and administrative problems" would be allowed "additional time" beyond the fall of 1970 for school integration. At the same time the administration pledged itself unequivocally to the goal of ending segregation in schools, and officials later said that fewer than 20 districts would probably be allowed further delays.

Civil rights leaders reportedly saw the softening of the desegregation guidelines as a payoff for Southern votes the President had received in the election, and some Southerners saw the policy announcement as a green light to delay desegregation. Roy Wilkins, executive secretary of NAACP, said, "The abandonment of rigid desegregation deadlines was almost enough to make you vomit." The NAACP national convention declared it "a cowardly retreat." Several Northern congressmen expressed their concern at the move, with Sen. Javits calling it "potentially disastrous." The move was attacked by the National Education Association, and Joseph Rauh of the Americans for Democratic Action said that "President Nixon has overpaid his debt to his Southern followers at the expense of Southern children."

In contrast, Sen. Strom Thurmond (R-S.C.) considered it "an improvement over past policy," though not much of one, and a Louisiana judge, Ben C. Dawkins, Jr., called it "a sort of new breath of fresh air" and used it as grounds for rejecting desegregation plans for 37 Louisiana school districts and ordering milder desegregation proposals from HEW.

On July 7 a federal court was asked to order the end of segregation in teacher assignments in

Madison County, Ill.; lawsuits were filed by the Justice Department against five school districts in the South; and federal aid was cut off from three Southern school districts in Florida, South Carolina, and Georgia. On July 8 Waterbury, Conn., was warned of court action unless it changed alleged segregationist policies; on July 9 Chicago's board of education was warned that its schools weren't integrated enough; and the entire state of Georgia was given 15 days to provide a plan to desegregate its 194 school districts or be sued. On July 10 the Attorney General announced suits against school districts in Mississippi and Arkansas.

The actions illustrated two aspects of the administration's policy: racial discrimination is a national problem, not a regional one necessitating prosecutions initiated beyond the South; and enforcement was to be shifted from HEW to the Justice Department where feasible.

The Johnson administration had effected school desegregation largely by proceeding under Title VI of the Civil Rights Act of 1964, and by cutting off federal funds to districts practicing racial discrimination. It had used the courts in a complementary role.

The Nixon administration's policy was to defer more to the courts, with HEW acting as their advisor in drafting desegregation plans. A Justice Department official was quoted as reasoning, "What good does it do to cut off federal funds if a district still continues to segregate? Some of these school districts would rather do without the money than integrate. But a court order will compel their officials to act—or face contempt of court charges." Critics of the policy pointed out that while court action against districts already cut off from federal funds was useful, action where funds have not been cut off —as in statewide actions like that against Georgia—could mean years of delaying desegregation while court action dragged on. In addition, once a district is under a court order HEW cannot withdraw funds; should there be a hard-to-enforce statewide order, then districts within the state already cut off would apparently get a

reprieve, in the form of reinstatement of their funds. The fear was that school districts might maintain segregation while fighting a long-drawn-out rear-guard action in the courts and that the Justice Department was too understaffed to process all the recalcitrant districts through the courts.

In August the administration successfully requested the Fifth Circuit of the U.S. Court of Appeals to grant a delay in integration until at least December 1, 1970, in 33 Mississippi school districts. Finch explained that desegregation plans had been too hastily prepared and had not been reviewed before they were filed in court. "Chaos and confusion" would result unless time were allowed for drawing up a workable plan, he claimed. Another explanation given was that a run of natural disasters in the state had put such a strain on social resources that immediate desegregation would hurt both blacks and whites.

The most vehement reaction came from within the Justice Department itself, with a protest reportedly from more than half the lawyers in the Civil Rights Division, demanding reassurances that civil rights laws would be vigorously enforced by the administration. Assistant Attorney General Jerris Leonard was reported to have summed up to the dissidents the administration's approach as one of "speak softly and carry a big stick."

The NAACP Legal Defense Fund took action by taking the issue to the Supreme Court, and won the historic ruling that "all deliberate speed for desegregation is no longer constitutionally possible. . . . The obligation of every school district is to terminate dual school systems at once."

Weary of 15 years of ingenious litigation, delay, and outrageous resistance—which, *Ebony* magazine claimed, yielded only 262 desegregated school districts out of 1,129 in nine Southern states—the Court ordered that the Mississippi districts must "begin immediately to operate as unitary school systems."

The Nixon administration reacted to the decision, which virtually erased its "flexible" policy, by giving assurances that "the administration will carry out the mandate of the Court and will enforce the law." The Court's decision was expected to have implications not only for Mississippi, where the ruin of the public school system was widely predicted, and the South as a whole, but for the North also where racial imbalance in schools often is caused by residential patterns rather than administrative decisions at the local level.

In October the White House published a strong defense of its desegregation policies. "It is a fact that September of 1969 produced more newly integrated school systems than any other school opening since 1954." In 1968 there were 171 districts desegregating, in September 1969 there were 336. Though many were holdovers from the Johnson administration, the Nixon administration claims credit for maintaining momentum. Under President Nixon 77 school districts have been told that federal funds will be cut off if they do not desegregate, compared with 81 under the previous administration in the same period. As to postponements, Civil Rights Commissioner Stephen Horn noted that 67 desegregation plans in the South were delayed until 1970 under Mr. Johnson. Under Mr. Nixon 50 plans have been put off until 1970. The statement quotes Robert Finch's promise that the desegregation accomplished in the next two years "will exceed the accomplishments of the previous 15 years put together." A top official of the Justice Department was quoted as telling a private conference of government lawyers in early December that the Nixon administration intended to eliminate virtually all dual school systems in the South by September 1970.

Nevertheless, criticism of the administration's policies, however good the intentions, came from two authoritative sources. In September the U.S. Commission on Civil Rights, chaired by Rev. Theodore M. Hesburgh, criticized the July 3 softening of desegregation guidelines and the shift from HEW cutoffs to court action as slowing the pace of desegregation. The Commission accused officials of using statistics in such a way

as to give "an overly optimistic," "inaccurate" picture of progress and particularly criticized Finch for his delay in speaking out against a House-passed amendment that would effectively force HEW to accept "freedom of choice" desegregation plans.

In a report published December 13 covering much of the same ground, the Southern Regional Council charged the administration with slowing the pace of desegregation in Southern schools, and fostering defiance of the law in augmenting the "Southern strategy" of the Republican Party by giving hope to "segregationists that the law of the land would not have to be obeyed." The report cited examples of milder desegregation being allowed after the intercession of Republican senators in Tennessee and Florida. It criticized the President for lack of leadership on the issue, saying that without the President's support, even the Supreme Court's ruling will have little impact on school desegregation in the South.

One facet of the Nixon policy in this field is, as we have seen, that it should be national and not regional in application. Secretary Finch has conceded that Sen. John Stennis (D-Miss.) has a "valid point" in his argument that federal law appears to condemn school segregation in the South but condones it in the North and West, where residential patterns are responsible ("de facto segregation"). Figures at the year's end showed that 23 per cent of the six million Negro pupils go to integrated public schools. About half of the six million are in the South, and there the integrated percentage is only 18. Nevertheless, the de facto segregation of the urban North is increasingly a cause for concern. "Can we any longer fail to acknowledge that the federal government is attempting to create in the rural South conditions that cannot in the foreseeable future be attained in large or medium urban centers in the South or the rest of the country?" asked Alexander Bickel in *The New Republic*. "The government is thus seen as applying its law unequally and unjustly, and is, therefore, fueling the politics of George Wallace. At the same time, the government is also putting itself on a collision course with the aspirations of an articulate and vigorous section of Negro leadership," he added.

Declaring that "I cannot support what amounts to regional legislation," Attorney General Mitchell announced the administration's opposition to a five-year extension of the 1965 Voting Rights Act, which had been largely responsible for enrolling 800,000 new black voters in the South. The administration proposals and their progress are discussed in some detail later. However, whatever the motives, the administration's action on this issue was extremely alarming to civil rights leaders, for although the substitute measure made the ban on literacy tests nationwide, the elimination of the key provision that requires Southern states to clear any new voting restrictions with the Justice Department or a U.S. court in Washington seemed to many to invalidate the whole bill. The NAACP's Clarence Mitchell commented that the administration's policy was "a sophisticated but nonetheless deadly way of thwarting the progress we have made." Republican Rep. William McCulloch of Ohio commented, "The administration creates a remedy for which there is no wrong, and leaves grievous wrongs without adequate remedy." Rep. Emanuel Celler (D-N.Y.) said that the government's approach was "like saying because you have a flood in Mississippi, you've got to build a dam in Idaho."

While commenting that "Perhaps no single act of the Nixon administration has seemed more insensitive to the black viewpoint than the proposal to abandon the Voting Rights Act of 1965," Tom Wicker of the *New York Times* pointed to the evidence of a letter from the President to House Minority Leader Gerald Ford (R-Mich.) showing that the President's real interest appears to be in obtaining a ban on literacy requirements in all 50 states and in easing residency requirements for voting. He said the letter is supposed to have opened the possibility that the President might agree to retain the strongest provisions of the 1965 act and work out a compromise. If this were to happen, black

and liberal criticisms of the administration on this issue might be effectively met.

Mr. Nixon's nomination of Judge Clement F. Haynsworth to sit as an associate justice of the Supreme Court provoked furious opposition. Roy Wilkins, speaking as chairman of the Leadership Council on Civil Rights, urged the Senate to reject the nomination and in so doing "affirm our national commitment to an equal and unified society." Wilkins pointed to Judge Haynsworth's "clear opposition to desegregation" and said his appointment "would strengthen the forces working to block full equality." Eight Negro congressmen told the Senate Judiciary Committee that the nomination was "ominous" for Negroes, and a "mockery of law and order." Haynsworth was called a "laundered segregationist" whose work on the Fourth U.S. Circuit Court of Appeals was subtly but effectively segregationist.

The defeat of the nomination, regarded as a stunning political setback for the President, was ascribed chiefly to the efforts of Senate liberals goaded by an activist alliance of labor and civil rights groups.

Significant Elections

Apart from the November elections (dealt with under a separate heading in this book) there were several local elections which were important and newsworthy in 1969.

One of the most exciting—and for liberals disappointing—elections of the year was the mayoralty race in Los Angeles in May. Black Democrat Thomas Bradley started out as one of twelve contenders trying to oust two-term incumbent Mayor Sam Yorty. In the primary, however, backing from a coalition of blacks (18 per cent of the Los Angeles population), Mexican-Americans, and liberal whites gave Bradley 42 per cent of the vote against Yorty's 26 per cent.

As the run-off approached, interest in the election mounted, with Bradley running a dignified campaign based on the backlog of city problems accumulated under Yorty. Until the last moment

Bradley looked likely to win. Yorty, claiming that his opponent was running a "racist campaign," linked Bradley with "black militants and anti-police elements," and made an all-out effort to win.

Yorty's 6 per cent majority was attributed by some commentators partly to the effect of charges linking Bradley to disreputable elements. His victory proved yet again that for Negroes seeking big city office, the problem of campaigning for black and white votes is immense. As Dr. Kenneth B. Clark put it in 1967, "Too much stress on race may lose a black candidate the white vote because of the racism inherent in America." Throughout, the unflappable and widely respected Bradley refuted Yorty's racially oriented charges against him and enlisted broader white support than any other Negro politician in the country, except Sen. Edward Brooke of Massachusetts. Councilman Bradley, clearly, in the words of one analyst, "is going to continue to make his voice heard in the political arena—and his voice will speak for conscience and reconciliation."

In a June election in Compton, a largely black suburb of Los Angeles, however, a Negro was elected for the first time. Douglas Dollarhide, a moderate city councilman, made Compton the largest city west of the Mississippi to be headed by a black mayor. The election showed how far toward Negro government the city had come since 1963, when Dollarhide became the first Negro councilman. The city has a 65 per cent Negro and a 10 per cent Mexican-American population.

Chapel Hill, N.C., which is 90 per cent white, elected Negro Howard Lee mayor in May by 2,367 votes to 2,167. The significance of the election was symbolic rather than real, because the position of mayor is largely a figurehead role in Chapel Hill. The victory was ascribed in part to the liberal influence of the University of North Carolina community at Chapel Hill, but Lee's campaign pledge to make town government "responsive to all the people and not just to a powerful few" also won support. Lee said of his

election: "At least it will give some people an opportunity to see a Negro operate in this high office. Also it may open the eyes of those who think all Negroes are militantly destructive and not law abiding."

Another significant election, which brought the total number of black mayors in the South up to 14, was that of Charles Evers as mayor of Fayette, Miss., where black voters outnumber whites by 386 to 255. Evers, field secretary for the NAACP, pledged that whites and blacks would be equally treated by his administration, and that violence would not be tolerated. One of his first acts was to make it illegal for citizens to carry guns or knives longer than two inches, and his first task after election was to try to attract industry to Jefferson County.

Five other Negroes were elected to the city council, giving Fayette the first all-black government of a bi-racial municipality in the South since Reconstruction. Perhaps the greatest significance of Evers' election lies in the fact that it provided him with a political base from which to operate. The election established Evers as a statewide power, for he also organized and led a statewide campaign by blacks for office.

The drive Evers spearheaded in May, aimed at capturing municipal offices in 48 Mississippi communities, marked the first time in 94 years that Negroes had organized sustained campaigns. About 200 Negroes ran for office in May and June. Twenty-four won posts in 11 small towns, largely in heavily black towns such as Fayette.

The impact of the victories is greater than the number of offices won would indicate. The Mississippi elections were the first statewide municipal elections held since the Voting Rights Act of 1965 enfranchised some 200,000 Negroes, and they established the black vote as a major force in Mississippi politics. It was known in advance from registration figures that the contest would be hopeless for many black candidates. "A lot just ran to let the white community know they were there and to make them aware of their needs," said one observer, and the greatest impact of the black vote is and will be on the tactics and performances of white politicians, who increasingly will have to appeal to black voters. In the sense that black voting power simply failed to materialize as expected in many areas, the elections were significant in showing the difficulties still in the way of the black voter. The Civil Rights Commission reported harassment and misinformation at the polls, fraud, and intimidation of voters despite the presence of federal observers. The report said, "Not one black candidate in a county where federal observers were present believed the election would have been run in an honest manner were it not for the presence of the observers."

Elections in May in North Carolina won municipal office for 24 blacks. There was a stirring election victory in Tallulah, La., in a special election ordered after a February 1968 election was declared invalid by a district court. Zelma Wyche was elected marshall (police chief) and declared he would use his influence to secure repeal of laws designed to intimidate black people. Eleven Negroes, including four incumbents, won Louisiana municipal offices in April, and blacks achieved key positions and control of county offices in Hancock County, Ga.

The election of six Negroes to public office in Greene County, Ala., in July was hailed as a "giant political step for Alabama and the South." White control of the county government was yielded to blacks for the first time since 1816. In the election, Negroes won the four county commission seats at stake by a four to one majority, and the two school board seats at stake by a three to one edge. Blacks outnumber whites in Greene County 10,000 to 3,000. The significance of the victory is considerable.

The encouragement to Southern Negroes to wield ballot box power is important, since taken with the other Southern victories, it portends a more assertive role by the Negro voter and Negro officeholders in the South. The Southern Christian Leadership Conference spearheaded the registration drive in Greene County and was said to have demonstrated its vitality more forcefully in doing so than at any time since Dr.

Martin Luther King's assassination. The National Democratic Party of Alabama, a largely black splinter group claiming to be the only legitimate Democratic entity in the state, demonstrated its potential in politics by its part in the campaign.

Despite the setback in the Los Angeles mayoralty contest, elections in 1969 continued the advancement of black power at the ballot box, even before the major elections in November. The increasing number of black elected officials, especially in the South, not only had the tangible effect of making black influence a fact of life, but also provided encouragement to those blacks who had never before voted and who could now see the potential of their own votes.

The Fall Elections

Some political trends already apparent earlier in 1969 were thought to be confirmed by the results of the November elections, while others seemed checked. The stability of the political parties seemed to be in decline as personalities and issues rather than traditional party loyalties increasingly won over votes. The Negro vote was used with sophistication and an accelerating trend since 1965, and an increasing polarization of votes along social and economic lines was apparent.

The Democratic Party seemed to be in danger of losing its grip in the inner city areas, and yet because of its identification with those areas, it lost votes to Republicans in the suburbs. The Republicans ended the year with control of 32 state houses, their best showing since 1952 and the Eisenhower era. At the same time, however, where Republicans had been in power they were often thrown out. In Connecticut, for example, after elections in 156 towns and cities, 20 municipalities switched from Republican to Democratic and 16 from Democratic to Republican. There seemed to be general disaffection with whatever party was in power.

In Cleveland, Mayor Carl B. Stokes was reelected by almost twice the majority he had won in the last election. It was still, however, a narrow margin over Republican Ralph Perke. Stokes won almost solid black support, 90 to 95 per cent (in a city 35 per cent black), and 24 per cent of the white vote (as opposed to 19 per cent in the previous elections), mainly from upper-income districts. However, he was the only one of seven Negro candidates to win a mayoral election in a major city, although there was an unprecedented number of Negroes standing for lesser offices throughout the country, many of whom were elected to city councils, school boards, and state legislatures.

In a closely watched election in Detroit where Richard H. Austin, the Negro candidate, had been thought to have a strong chance of winning, Sheriff Roman S. Gribbs defeated him by a narrow margin of 35,000 votes. Detroit is about 40 per cent Negro and Austin polled 80 per cent of the Negro vote while Gribbs polled 19.5 per cent. In the white districts Gibbs polled 82 per cent and Austin won 17.2 per cent. This was seen by many as a reflection of the racial tension in Detroit and indicative of the racial polarization elsewhere. Austin's defeat brought little bitterness, however. Negro State Sen. Coleman Young considered the election "a positive base for progress," and another observer, William Patrick, head of New Detroit Inc., said, "I even get the feeling that there has been a victory won. Here's a man who came from relative anonymity, a prohibitive underdog, and with another week or two he might have won." *New York Times* reporter Jerry Flint argues that there may even be less racial polarization in the future as a result of the election because "the city's Negroes have been to the mountaintop and seen that they can win in Detroit." A liberal city council was elected, including three Negroes out of the nine officials elected.

In Buffalo, N.Y., Mayor Frank A. Sedita, a Democrat, won an unprecedented third term defeating Republican "law and order" candidate Mrs. Alfreda Slominski and a Negro candidate, Ambrose I. Lane, by 20,000 votes. The Buffalo race was considered the one that most clearly defined the debate over crime and civil disorders. The election was thought to be an example of the sophistication of the Negro voter—since the Negro candidate did not have a chance of winning, the black vote went mostly to the white candidate who best represented black interests— Sedita. Had Lane been given solid Negro backing, he still could not have won, and Sedita, without black support, would have lost to Mrs. Slominski.

In Dayton, Ohio, Mayor P. Davis Hall was reelected by a three to one margin in a non-partisan contest in which he was opposed by Lawrence Nelson, a Negro.

In Waterbury, Conn., Democrat Edward D. Bergin upset Republican Mayor George Harlamon and defeated two other candidates, including a Negro, who came in last.

In Hartford, Conn., incumbent Republican Mayor Ann Uccello narrowly won re-election against three other candidates, including Negro Wilbur Smith, who came in third.

Earlier in October, popular and liberal Ivan Allen was succeeded as mayor of Atlanta by young, liberal, and Jewish Sam Massell, who defeated Dr. Horace Tate, the black candidate in the primary, and Republican Rodney Cook in the run-off, despite controversy over the collection of funds by his brother from night clubs in company of a policeman. Massell owed his election to Negro votes, and will work with Maynard Jackson, who became the first Negro elected vice mayor of Atlanta. Nine blacks in all were elected to office in Atlanta, more than ever before.

A young state senator, Curtis M. Graves, a Negro, ran for mayor of Houston, the first time a Negro had ever done so, and won 32 per cent of the November vote against one other candidate and incumbent Mayor Louie Welch, who was re-elected. A local analyst calculated that Graves got 10 to 11 per cent of the white vote, whereas Welch got less that 6 per cent of the vote in the Negro wards. Graves, who said he viewed his campaign as "anti-establishment," may well run again in the next election. Mayor Welch acknowledged the importance of the vote for Graves: "I have heard this vote and sympathize with it. It is my sincere hope that during the next two years I will be able to let these people know that their problems represent the problems of the entire community."

Luiska J. Tuyman, a Republican and the first Negro to be elected a mayor in Kentucky, won in Glasgow, which is predominantly white.

The most widely publicized contest, inevitably, was the race for mayor of New York City, an election which typified the voting trend apparent against traditional party allegiances and machines. Mayor John V. Lindsay stood essentially as an independent, having been defeated in the Republican primary, and won re-election against Democratic and Republican rivals. Democrat Mario Procaccino and Republican John J. Marchi split 58 per cent of the vote against Mr. Lindsay's 42 per cent. Their vote, it seems, came mainly from the middle-income groups, whereas Lindsay's came from a coalition of the poor—largely the blacks and the Puerto Ricans—and the rich—mainly Manhattan-oriented liberal whites. A widely held attitude was expressed on election day by former Mayor Robert Wagner, a Democrat who nonetheless voted for Lindsay: "I think Lindsay is the least of three evils." Certainly the other two candidates lacked Lindsay's poise and charisma. In fact, one commentator noted that Lindsay employed "an old-fashioned but deadly political weapon called charm." There is no doubt of the crucial importance of the Negro vote to Lindsay's success, and should he, as has been suggested he might, set up a permanent independent liberal coalition party or switch allegiance to the Democrats, black support will continue to be vital.

The two gubernatorial elections in New Jersey and Virginia were regarded as tossups. Republicans won handsomely in both states, although there did not seem much difference between the rival candidates in either state—all were "respected, experienced, middle-of-the-road politicians." In Virginia, the breakdown of the Democratic party machine and the voting patterns resulting in Linwood Holton's victory were seen as the beginnings of a political realignment, with the Democrats moving to the left and the conservatives joining the Republicans. The Democrats retained control of the state legislature, with a Negro—Dr. William P. Robinson of Norfolk—elected to the state assembly for the first time, and the Republicans making gains in the suburbs and around the District of Columbia. William Cahill's win in New Jersey was ascribed in part to dissatisfaction with 16 years of Democratic rule. The President's active support for Cahill (and for Holton) was credited with winning votes.

It was widely held that the fall election results provided encouraging evidence that the anti-Negro, anti-liberal backlash, manifested in big city elections like that in Los Angeles earlier in the year, had been checked. The "law and order" slogan was not the success widely expected, and though crime was an issue in the big cities, it was discussed on the whole without rancor. The widely predicted blue-collar revolt, one observer noted, in which white working class voters were expected to unload their resentments on politicians who had befriended the black minority, did not materialize, and the campaigns appeared to turn away from expressions of racial hostility.

Blacks in Office

Those black leaders elected to office or appointed at the major metropolitan, state, or national levels are, for the most part, sophisticated men, experienced in public affairs, often with a professional background and prestigious educational qualifications. Yet these men are only part of the total number of blacks in office.

It is noted in the voting section that in the South blacks holding office—mainly at the local level—have increased in number from 72 to 528. The following chart, compiled by the Voter Education Project (VEP) of the Southern Regional Council in December 1969, details the distribution:

NUMBER OF BLACKS HOLDING ELECTED OFFICE IN SOUTH

State Legislators	City Officials	County Officials	Law-Enforcement Officials	School Board Members	Total
0	41	8	27	7	83
0	13	0	4	37	54
1	30	1	2	1	35
14	15	6	0	7	42
1	22	10	22	9	64
1	33	20	18	6	78
1	45	1	1	10	58
0	24	4	4	2	34
8	8	6	5	3	30
3	10	0	0	9	22
2	18	2	6	0	28
31	259	58	89	91	528

This is only part of the picture, for although the South encourages publicity of such statistics, the largest number of elected blacks are in New York, Michigan, California, and New Jersey.

Many of the newly-elected officials—perhaps from poor rural communities, or only recently aware of black political potential, perhaps only recently able to seize the opportunity to seek office—take office less well-equipped than their more privileged white contemporaries. Nevertheless, they may encounter more serious problems, both because of racist attitudes in the general constituency and unrealistic expectations in the black community.

Whatever their capabilities, their influence can be desperately important to blacks. As the only Negro sheriff in the South sees it: "I think it is more significant for a Negro to be a sheriff than to be a congressman," because blacks "dealing with the nitty gritty" as local public officials can do as much for their race as those who hold high office. "It's a lot different being in Congress with a lot of white liberals than it is on the local level where you deal with the most intense aspects of segregation," he points out.

In the all-too-recent past, energies were concentrated mainly on getting blacks registered and enabling them to vote. As that stage is passing, election of blacks is becoming more of a reality, though not without problems. While Harvey Smith of the Russellville, Ky., city council points out that whites are coming to feel that "the time

has come for the Negro to step in and do his share," Charles Evers, mayor of Fayette, Miss., and a leader of the black man's struggle for equality, points out that "there are so many ways a black man can lose an election in the South."

The U.S. Civil Rights Commission continues to find examples of fraud, intimidation, and even violence at the polls. The contemporary black attitude to such affronts is one of determination. In the words of Eddie Davis, a county commissioner in West Feliciana Parish, La.: "We had no voice in the courthouse; we didn't have a choice in anything we undertook to do. All days were the white man's day; the Negroes had no voice in anything. We just had to do what the white man said. I made up my mind that whenever I got power, got to be a registered voter, I would run for election. After I registered and voted, there came up an election, and I decided I would run for something. It didn't make any difference what it was; if it was something I could manage, I was going to run, whether I won or lost. I was doing it to let the white man know that Negroes wanted their rights. Not for what I could get out of it; I wasn't running for that. I was only running to develop my race, so I decided to run."

Once elected, racist attitudes can cause black elected officials great problems, as Charles Evers' first months in office illustrated (see City Government). His experiences were not unique.

When Mrs. Geneva Collings took office as chancery clerk in Mississippi's Claiborne County, the two-member white staff quit. Dan Nixon, a magistrate in Brownsville, Tenn., was never informed of the date for the swearing-in ceremony after his election and had to seek out a local judge to be formally installed in office.

Griffin McLaurin, a constable in Tchula, Miss., says of the white justice of the peace: "When I bring someone in on a traffic charge, if it's a white man, he'll let him go. But if it's a Negro, he'll fine him." In several Southern states local officials are paid on the "fee" system, according to the number of cases they handle. In towns where there is more than one justice of the peace, white officers can choose the official to whom they will bring minor offenders for hearings. William Childs, a justice in Tuskegee, Ala., charged that the white justice in his district averages 300 to 400 traffic cases a month while he gets no more than 20.

In Benton County, Miss., the only black school board member cannot even gain entrance to the "white" school buildings. And most issues are allegedly decided by the white majority before they get to official board meetings.

Open hostility from white Southerners still occurs periodically. Moses Riddick, a member of the board of supervisors of Suffolk, Va., had a cross burned on his lawn after winning a primary. James Jolliff, a black constable in Walkinson County, Miss., was arrested on charges of impeding and intimidating officers and was temporarily suspended from his office when he stopped alcoholic beverage commission agents from searching a black cafeteria without a warrant.

It takes experience, insight, and patience for black officials to cope with such situations.

Attempts are being made on several fronts to share knowledge with and impart administrative skills to the increasing number of black officials around the nation. A network of contacts is being established to enable the neophyte official to feel he has resources at hand in his first, inexperienced months in office.

The Voter Education Project, for one, organized the Southwide Conference of Black Elected Officials in December 1968. It was attended by 200 delegates. The officials—including men from virtually all-black cities such as Roosevelt City, Ala., from rural counties where federally-supervised voting put blacks in an electoral majority, and from the black wards of large cities like Atlanta and Jacksonville, Fla.—discussed how best to improve their effectiveness in the face of lack of cooperation from racist elements; and heard advice on subjects ranging from school administration to law enforcement to revenue and taxation matters, including dealing with the complexities of obtaining federal

funds. Speakers included Georgia State Sen. Julian Bond, the then U.S. Attorney General Ramsey Clark, Mayor Richard G. Hatcher of Gary, Ind., Dr. Kenneth B. Clark, and Rep. Shirley Chisholm (D-N.Y.).

Mrs. T. L. Banks, a lawyer who is director of the Mississippi Center for Elected Officials at Tougaloo College, feels that the principal task of black elected officials is to improve the economic status of their communities.

A second plan, this one to help black legislators increase their effectiveness, was started by Illinois State Sen. Richard H. Newhouse of Chicago, supported by 50 black legislators from several states. The idea is to set up a national black legislative "clearing house" to share legislative ideas and programs and to exchange information and tactics on given issues.

The plan, which has some foundation support, originated two years ago. Sen. Newhouse explained: "We [blacks] have problems that won't wait, and we want to bring black legislators to political maturity as soon as possible. This means, for example, knowing how to make a bill likely to attract white support, mobilizing interest groups and choosing witnesses to testify at hearings." The "clearing house" can also serve as a means of preparing more blacks for public service.

A conference partly aimed at encouraging grassroots political participation was conducted in March for the benefit of Beaufort and Jasper Counties in South Carolina by James Felder of the Scholarship, Education, and Defense Fund for Racial Equality. The Fund has been called the nation's major leadership training organization of the civil rights movement.

The two counties had been chosen by HEW as experimental locales for the liberalization of the federal food stamp program. Beaufort County is a collection of large islands at the southeastern tip of the state, where black people constitute about 40 per cent of the 30,000 residents and nearly one-half of its registered voters, and where in the last three years Negroes have been elected to the board of education, the

Boce W. Barlow, Jr., Connecticut state senator

Mervyn M. Dymally, California state senator

Julian Bond, Georgia state senator

Clarence Mitchell III, Maryland state senator

Clovis Campbell, Arizona state senator

William Lucas, sheriff of Wayne County, Michigan

William L. Clay, Missouri state senator

Freeman Hankins, Pennsylvania state senator

Arthur Shores joins other members of the Birmingham, Alabama, city council after his election to a council seat.

Los Angeles Councilman Thomas Bradley and family during bitter mayoralty campaign which he subsequently lost.

Richard H. Austin concedes victory to Wayne County Sheriff Roman S. Gribbs in Detroit's mayoralty race.

Clifford L. Alexander, Jr.

Clarence Mitchell, Jr.

Samuel Z. Westerfield, U.S. Ambassador to Liberia

county and city councils, and magistrates'offices. In nearby Jasper County, the population is predominantly black but there are no Negro elected officials. Felder believes it is because black leadership in the community has been both ineffective and fragmented. "The purpose of this conference is to get them together," he said.

Even specific problems were discussed, including the situation of Peter Smith who with two other Negroes was elected to the five-member Grand Coteau, La., governing board in 1964. As a majority, they hired a consulting engineer to draw plans for sewers, paved streets, a reliable water system, and a natural gas network to permit town growth. The engineering plan was sent to the Department of Housing and Urban Development with an application for 80 per cent federal financing and 20 per cent local matching funds.

For three years, the board corresponded with HUD's regional office in Austin, Tex., and with Washington, but Grand Coteau could not get a clear response from the federal agency, Mr. Smith said. There was talk of a shortage of funds for small towns but apparently the department found nothing wrong with the plan itself. Mr. Smith said that the city of Lafayette, 12 miles away, received a $55,000 grant to air-condition its bus system and that he was getting discouraged. Advisers at the conference arranged for an investigation of the case.

At the conference, VEP disclosed plans to establish service centers to provide continuing basic training for black leaders. By June 1969 five centers had been set up at Southern University and A & M College in Baton Rouge, La.; Clark College in Atlanta; Tougaloo College in Tougaloo, Miss.; Talladega College in Talladega, Ala.; and Miles College in Birmingham, Ala.

The centers at the campuses are equipped to give advice and aid on legislative matters such as research and preparation of bills, to refer inquiries to technical and legal experts, and to hold workshops on particular problems, among other services.

A further purpose was to train local black leaders and to mobilize the black communities of the two counties to make maximum use of the new food stamp experiment. Felder said, "We believe in politics and the power it can transfer to our people."

The largest and most prestigious gathering of black officeholders from all over the nation, the Institute of Black Elected Officials, met in September under the sponsorship of the Metropolitan Applied Research Center, Inc. The center is a social research organization headed by Dr. Kenneth Clark, and the meeting had the support of several foundations, the Urban League, the Republican and Democratic National Committees, the VEP and the Urban Affairs Institute. The meeting was attended by one-third of the more than 1,200 black officeholders in the U.S., ranging from justices of the peace to a U.S. Senator. Militant and moderate viewpoints were represented and administration speakers included Health, Education and Welfare Secretary Robert H. Finch, Labor Secretary George Shultz, and Office of Economic Opportunity director Donald Rumsfeld.

Dr. Clark listed major problems: "The challenge will be for Negro elected officials to insist that they be taken seriously as public officials. . . . Too often the racist status quo prevails and Negro elected officials are treated as second-class officials while the private interests and public interests of the white majority make common cause in the legislatures of this country." As to the sometimes unrealistic demands made on black officials by their constituents, Clark has this to say: "These demands will increase as the number of Negro officials increases because the residents of the ghetto will perceive their election as evidence of real power to change." The problem, in a sense, is the same for all politicians— "how to find realistic ways to meet the needs of their constituents, and how to be responsive to the emotional and often non-rational demands of the people upon whom they depend for election."

The conference led to the announcement by

several officials that they intended to establish a permanent organization to help black candidates get elected. The group said it intends to "screen" black candidates and then channel money and talent into the campaigns of those it endorses. Mayor Hatcher proposed the organization on the premise that "we must organize black! " He said, "We have a constituency of 21 million people who look to us for leadership. They are unrepresented in Washington as well as unrepresented and ill-represented in the city halls and state governments all across this country. We must organize to give them a more powerful voice that cannot be ignored. . . . It is necessary to develop a unified fund raising apparatus to provide the necessary financial support for our efforts in political organizations."

The effects of such conferences as these should not only be measured in terms of how useful they are to the participants, important though that is. Lester Levine, director of the Political Research Institute of Florida State University, said of one such meeting held at Tallahassee in November: "We accomplished much in terms of public awareness of the black elected officials and public recognition of them."

Public awareness of the role of the black official significantly increased in 1969 and much potentially successful groundwork has been laid to help the officials themselves act more effectively in the face of problems not encountered by most of their white colleagues.

City Government-Black Mayors

Being mayor of any U.S. city is universally acknowledged to be a tough job. And big-city mayors, particularly, are tending more and more to decline to seek re-election because of the strains of the office and the sheer size and complexity of the problems they face. According to Cleveland's Mayor Carl Stokes, 17 mayors declined to run for re-election in 1969.

Money is one serious problem. Stagnant tax bases, ever-increasing demands for municipal services, a plethora of federal grant programs not only wrapped in red tape but requiring matching funds from the locality, delays in implementation of revenue-sharing plans and lack of aid from rural- and suburban-controlled state governments—all are factors holding back funds from decaying inner-cities that desperately need investment.

Insufficient funding of critical local projects such as schools, housing, welfare, and the like often exacerbates racial and ethnic tensions, which in turn can lead to serious backlash within the community. And the mayor takes brickbats from all sides as he tries to bridge the gap.

Richard G. Hatcher, first Negro mayor of a major American city, has been on the public hot seat since his election in Gary, Ind. Hatcher himself is the great-grandson of a Georgia plantation slave; he is a dapper, reserved bachelor who is confronted by the problems of a sprawling, grimy steel town with a 60 per cent black population. Gary epitomizes all the problems of urban America: it has a town center which is mostly black with decayed ghettos and a high unemployment rate surrounded by a white middle-income suburban belt.

Hatcher is credited with turning more federal and foundation money to his city than all previous Gary administrations combined. He reorganized the police department, changing Gary from a center of prostitution and numbers rackets to a city where crime and rackets are no longer ignored. He has constructed the first low income housing in twenty years and "made the blacks in his city feel like first-class citizens," in the view of one observer. There is no doubt that this has played a part in preventing major disturbances there. One of his great campaigns, showing dividends in 1969, has been to get the U.S. Steel Corporation, the economic backbone of the city, to play a bigger role in helping Gary solve its problems. Money is of the essence in this respect, and the mayor is involved in litigation to increase U.S. Steel's taxes by as much as $30 million a year.

That Gary is still a deeply divided city with

increased racial polarization was demonstrated this year by the attempt of Glen Park, a white suburb, to disassociate itself from the city and set up its own incorporated community. Racial feeling certainly played a part in stimulating this move, but so have other factors. The money Hatcher has been pouring into inner-city projects was lost to and thus resented by the white suburb. The gang warfare—black v. black—in the inner-city has caused great alarm, and Hatcher, who has tried to put the gangs to work on "worthwhile" projects, has been criticized for "coddling" militant groups and youth gangs. There was a much-publicized incident in May when demonstrators disrupted a banquet honoring GOP Gov. Edgar D. Whitecombe, and charges of "a reign of terror" in Gary were made. In August a walkout in a wage dispute by firemen, who not only refused to fight a lumberyard blaze but also turned away volunteer and out-of-town firefighters, was a severe test of the mayor's control of the city. It also provided white separatists in Glen Park with arguments that public services would be more effectively administered locally than from city hall.

The big issue Mayor Hatcher has had to face has been whether he can prevent his city from further disintegration, faced as it is with overwhelming social and economic strife. His answer: "We must do more. If the problems of urban America cannot be solved in Gary, they cannot be solved anywhere."

Cleveland is a deeply troubled city, having "languished for a quarter of a century under a succession of caretaker mayors." The only expansion has been in the black community, which has increased from 16 per cent of the total population in 1950 to about 40 per cent in 1969. The ethnically-oriented population, descendants of recent European immigrants, at best has shown little sympathy for the problems and aspirations of the Negroes, and at worst has provided a hard-core bigot vote that the city's politicians calculate at 20 to 25 per cent of the electorate.

Dynamic, attractive, popular Mayor Carl B.

Stokes, a high school dropout who became a lawyer, state legislator, and mayor of the eighth largest city in America, pursued in 1969 his aim of "getting things started." The editor of the *Cleveland Plain Dealer* declared: "I cannot believe the things taking place in this city compared with two years ago; I just can't."

He was referring to the continuing success of the "Cleveland Now" program, an ambitious 10-to-12-year program of civic betterment that Stokes initiated. A total of $4.3 million has been collected to use as seed money in a program eventually involving $1.5 billion in all. It is being spent on such disparate projects as housing, planning, day care centers, arts festivals, and children's camps.

Enthusiasm and inspiration continue to be the keynotes of the mayor's highly personal administration, but he was not without problems in 1969. He has a running feud with his police department, a legacy of the Glenville shoot-out of July 1968, when the mayor ordered the police out of the area so that it could cool off. He has aroused some opposition among whites, embittered because of his spending money on the black East Side. The trickiest issue of 1969 probably was the furor over the granting and withholding of McDonald's Hamburger franchises. Alleging racism after the murder of a black applicant for a franchise in Cleveland, a boycott of McDonald's by the black community was organized by Operation Black Unity, a group which made demands labelled "extortion" by the white community. Stokes avoided fully committing himself on the issue. One analyst commented: "Carl Stokes is in some ways his own worst enemy—a fiercely ambitious, highly complex black man, whose charismatic charm and real dedication alternate with a cold imperiousness that has alienated some of his friends and splintered his political organization."

Robert B. Blackwell was elected mayor of Highland Park, Mich., a three-square-mile town completely surrounded by Detroit, in November 1968. Blackwell, a former labor leader, was the first black appointee of HUD Secretary Romney, who made him executive secretary of the Michigan State Labor Mediation Board. Blackwell has been a long-time political associate of Mr. Nixon.

As the only full-time Republican black mayor, Blackwell's requests for funds have fallen on friendly ears. In May the town received $1.7 million in Model Cities money, in June it received $10 million for the government's neighborhood development program (Detroit itself only asked for $8 million), "and we hope to get another $5 million," according to Blackwell. Despite the fact that it has the highest suburban crime rate for a place of its size in the whole of the United States, Blackwell says his town will become "a model of what federal suburban cooperation can do."

Charles Evers of Fayette, Miss., elected mayor in May 1969, entered office pledging to enforce laws "without distinction or discrimination due to the color of skin or beliefs of persons," and to the accompaniment of rumors that all white citizens of the town would move away, and that all white city employees would quit.

Evers immediately came to grips with the problems of his new administration. And they were many. Fayette has been called "a dying Southern town," with a Negro majority. About two-thirds of the population were on welfare, and a third of the rest unemployed. Evers' first task was to try to bring industry to the town, and his wide and powerful countrywide connections, notably with the Kennedy family, seemed a hopeful augury. All the white city employees did in fact quit, except for an elderly part-time fireman and a lady city attorney, though there was no mass white exodus from the town.

The greatest problem, however, was shortage of cash—such a shortage that Evers felt obliged to pay his first year's salary back to the treasury. In July came the bombshell from an accountant checking city finances that the previous administration had overspent the budget by $8,000 and that funds would not last until the new fiscal year. The new mayor was forced to seek financial help for the town from friends around the country to tide the city over. He got a good response, even to the supplementing of the town's police car complement of two old patrol cars by one new one, donated by generous Negroes on the east coast.

In September there were reports of arrests of alleged Ku Klux Klansmen conspiring to assassinate Evers, who was tipped off about the conspiracy by white friends. In October it became known that Evers was fighting a decision by the Illinois Central Railroad to abandon freight service and tracks between Fayette and Natchez, a move which would inevitably knock the bottom out of all the mayor's efforts to bring industry to the town. He succeeded in rallying the opposition of the Mississippi Public Service Commission, and joined with it and the railway labor unions in persuading the Interstate Commerce Commission—where proposals to abandon track are very seldom opposed—to hold hearings on the abandonment plan.

Howard Lee's progress since his election as mayor of Chapel Hill, N.C., has been consistent and steady. He is working toward having the state legislature change the mayor's position and functions, for the formation of a black and white commission to improve living conditions in Chapel Hill, and for the establishment of guidelines to prevent zoning decisions being influenced by considerations of wealth or race. Overwhelmingly, he is concerned with improvements that will benefit blacks and whites equally.

The man who has been doing exactly that in Washington, D.C., since 1967 is Mayor Walter E. Washington. He was reappointed to a second term by President Nixon after proving himself and his team popular, efficient, and tactful in dealing with the manifold and considerable problems of governing the Nation's Capital, despite few real powers and little freedom of action. The reappointment met criticism from Republican Negroes who felt that Republican supporters should benefit from the President's patronage (Mayor Washington is a Democrat), but elsewhere was widely welcomed. The mayor has continued to make himself and his office the bridge between the black and white communities, and has met some success in making city hall more approachable to the ordinary citizen and more efficient as well.

Mayor Washington himself can take personal credit for many achievements in the District in 1969, and was praised for his handling of the student disturbances at Howard University, his tact in dealing with the fall Vietnam Moratorium rallies and the federal government's preparations to meet it, and his securing luxury housing for elderly public-housing tenants. Mayor Washington, reconciling as he does the often conflicting forces of Congress and the city government, of the administration and his own Democratic party, of the black residents (a 70 per cent majority) and the white, must surely qualify for the title of one of the most able diplomats in Washington.

State Governments

State governments are not generally regarded as initiators in advancing the cause of civil rights. Federal civil rights legislation was enacted mainly because of state power misused by racists in Southern states. States of the North, the Midwest and the West, while considered somewhat less discriminatory, nevertheless have taken relatively little meaningful action to ease the way for Negroes and toward civil rights for all.

As a result, in the great civil rights crusades of the last decade or so, state governments have been relegated to the background of the "action" as the federal government monopolized attention by moving, often forcefully, to enforce the newly-written law of the land.

But as the founding units of American government, retaining powers not delegated to Washington, D.C., under the Constitution, the states are immensely important. They charter cities; shape their governments; grant or deny taxing authority, land use, and zoning powers; set landlord-tenant relations, educational standards, state and local civil service criteria, and the professional licensing requirements that influence employment patterns. States write voting laws and they often determine community participation in many federally-funded programs.

Regardless of these powers, the states have "slept through" the urban crisis which embraces many of the most critical concerns of black people, according to John A. Hamilton of the *New York Times*. Their administrative structures are usually outdated and they often are controlled by rural and suburban interests which are usually embedded in the power system.

The Advisory Commission on Intergovernmental Relations has stressed the importance of reforms at the state level. It has urged states to buy into federal programs aiding cities, thus adding state funds to federal funds; but it reports that only 11 states contribute to urban renewal, only 10 to mass transit, only eight to water and sewage facilities. Of all state aid to localities, only 4.5 per cent goes to supplement new and innovative federal programs.

State legislatures balk at giving cities either the tax resources or the taxing powers they need to raise revenues on their own. New Jersey's legislators recently heard lame-duck Gov. Richard Hughes proclaim Newark "sick, sick unto death," then refused to enact an urban aid program. Exceptions are Delaware and New York, which have shown far more awareness of the urban crisis than most states.

In Atlanta, Lt. Gov. George T. Smith condemned the 1968 Georgia General Assembly for failing to offer state help for city problems, declaring that out of 3,185 measures in the past two legislative sessions, "not one bill was passed to bring relief to our urban areas." He continued, "We scream about states' rights. We damn the federal government for infringing upon our sacred territory. But so far the state has taken no action or responsibility to prove it is capable of righting its past wrongs of omission. Instead, the state has just turned its head the other way. The federal government has instigated more than 450 programs, each designed to help cure some municipal malady." Although 70 per cent of the population of Georgia lives in cities, the assembly killed all bills that were offered to help urban areas.

On the other hand, Illinois has begun to improve communications with its cities. Gov. Richard B. Ogilvie created a state department of human resources in February to direct the social policies of his administration to urban and community problems. He appointed three leading Negroes to head the department. This adds Illinois to the list of twenty states which have recently created offices for urban affairs.

The New Federalism and the States

With the advent of the Nixon administration, the focus of federal action was the transferral of administrative power to the states. Mr. Nixon termed this policy a "New Federalism." The most important proposal espoused by the administration was a federal revenue tax-sharing plan whereby given amounts of federal revenues would be directly rechannelled to the state governments. No specifications were attached except the assumption that some of the money would be directed to the cities. In addition, Mr. Nixon's plan included the delegation of federal programs such as manpower training to state and local management, a consolidation of overlapping grants-in-aid programs,and reform of the welfare system with the federal government bearing a greater share of the cost. Restructuring of administrative responsibilities has already begun but Congress must still pass the revenue-sharing plan.

The New Federalism concept was received critically by black leaders who predicted that the states would not allocate a fair share of the money for black and urban concerns. Cleveland's Mayor Carl Stokes, in a speech asking that the federal government maintain its direct relationship with the cities, said that the state's tax distributions to cities were "inequitable." "The cities are going to be at the mercy of unwilling, inefficient state governments that have heavy rural interests and inadequate resources,"

he said. Under the Johnson administration, the federal government had established a strong relationship with city mayors that bypassed the states in such major areas as the poverty program and urban renewal.

One view holds that the New Federalism can be read as an effort to return to the people directly affected a large measure of the decision-making responsibility in local issues. The concept of returning authority to local governments has been endorsed by a wide range of interests from right to left.

The Governors

At the 1969 National Governors Convention in September, the 50 governors pulled close together in bipartisan support of a welfare policy proposed by Gov. Nelson A. Rockefeller of New York and a national compulsory health insurance program.

The welfare policy statement they adopted asked the federal government to assume the full cost of welfare programs within five years. It urged Mr. Nixon to go beyond his proposal of a national minimum income standard for the poor. They praised his welfare proposal of Aug. 8, but felt that since his proposal covered the entire welfare expenses of 20 states, it should fund all 50. As the welfare proposal stands now, the federal government would help those states, including Southern states, which give the smallest welfare benefits, but it fails to give significant help to those states that carry the major burden. According to Pennsylvania Gov. Raymond P. Shafer, about half the national caseload of Aid to Families with Dependent Children—the most expensive welfare program—is centered in New York, California, Illinois, Ohio, and Pennsylvania. The governors' welfare proposal, according to Gov. Rockefeller, would cost the federal government $15 billion as compared to the $4 billion Mr. Nixon has proposed to spend. When Rockefeller first proposed this policy months before the governors' conference, Mr. Nixon and his administration gave it a very cool reception.

The governors ended the conference with dismayed grumbling over a surprise announcement by Vice President Agnew that Mr. Nixon would attempt to curtail inflation by taking most of the federal funds out of all new public construction projects. The governors' disapproval came because of the great need, as they saw it, for public works such as highways and state buildings. They also objected because the cutback would create higher unemployment and hurt the construction industry.

A few governors urged reforms at the state level. Massachusetts Gov. Winthrop Sargent, proud of his state's recently enacted administrative reorganization law, counseled other states to get "updated." Wisconsin Gov. Warren Knowles, who called a special session of his legislature to restore deleted urban aid funds, suggested "education" for parochial state lawmakers. Nevertheless, the governors refused to vote on a resolution by Rhode Island Gov. Frank Licht that called for a "massive intensification of efforts to solve the urban crisis."

Within the 50 state delegations to the conference, there was only one Negro, even though some governors had brought four or five assistants. Mrs. Ava Jackson, the urban affairs director for Delaware, saw the absence of blacks as reflecting a gubernatorial lack of concern for urban problems. She charged that most governors "simply had not gotten involved" and she worried about the Nixon administration's emphasis on state governments for implementing domestic policies. "Just as the Negro has learned to use the electoral process and to make his vote felt in the cities, the action shifts to the state," she said.

The Role of Blacks in State Legislatures

"Like a lily white island in a sea of black" is a description of the Virginia state capitol complex in downtown Richmond by a Virginia civil rights leader; it is a description which can fit state capitols in many states. No black has yet been elected to a governorship and only a few Negroes have been elected to state legislatures, although these "breakthroughs" have increased in number in recent years.

Most of the new black legislators are concerned with gaining a foothold in state government for their black constituents. James Dean, one of four blacks elected in 1968 to the Georgia legislature, said he came to the legislature not supporting new roads or more industry or lower taxes, but with a promise that the American system will work for urban Negroes. Several of the 14 other black legislators in the Georgia Assembly echoed Dean's promise that they make their role in the legislature work for the people who elected them.

In state legislatures where there are several black representatives, informal coalitions have formed. The coalition that exists among black legislators in the Georgia General Assembly was cited by a member of that group as an example of politics being the only meaningful type of black power. In some states, such as Colorado, black legislators have teamed up with other minorities such as the Mexican-Americans and American Indians to push through legislation of mutual concern.

As a group, black legislators are the primary watchdogs for inimical racial legislation. They must be constantly alert, not only for hostile bills, but also for detrimental clauses and miscellaneous wordings that can appear as "sleepers" in any piece of routine legislation. Another function generally assumed by the black lawmakers is that of chief sponsor for major civil rights legislation. The black lawmakers are not necessarily the sole sponsors of bills dealing with black issues, but they are generally the sponsors of the bills having the most acceptable black approach to a problem. In addition to the special responsibilities black senators and representatives assume and have thrust upon them by virtue of their special relationship to the black community, each must perform the regular functions of an assembly member and the duties owed to his particular party.

Southern States

The annual Southern Governors' Convention was held in September in Williamsburg, Va. James T. Wooten of the *New York Times* said the session was dominated by the spirit of George Wallace. Resolutions by Gov. Albert P. Brewer of Alabama and Gov. Lester Maddox of Georgia to eliminate pupil assignments to specific schools and the use of busing to achieve racial balance in public schools were proposed. Brewer asked the governors to remind the President of his campaign promises to avoid busing and to insure the control of local school systems by local officials. Vice President Agnew, in his address to the governors, announced his disapproval of busing as a desegregation technique. The 16 governors rejected the resolutions of Brewer and Maddox and endorsed instead a substitute resolution of Gov. Mills E. Godwin of Virginia urging "restraint and good judgment" in the use of busing. Alabama, Georgia, and Mississippi were the only states voting against Godwin's resolution.

The Legislature

There are 10 Negroes in the 91st Congress, nine Democratic Representatives and one Republican Senator—"hardly an explosion of black political power," as *Ebony* commented, but an increase of a third over the last Congress. Despite particular constituency demands, the widespread interests and enthusiasms of strikingly different personalities, and indeed, of generations, it goes almost without saying that all 10 are concerned with furthering the best interests of their race, even if they have different ways of doing this.

Legislators in national office are necessarily extremely active in many fields. Nevertheless, their common concern for equality of opportunity in every field, their interest in alleviating hardship by increasing welfare funds and extending social security benefits (often at the expense of cuts in defense spending), their concern to see the black man take his rightful place in American life, are apparent in their collective and individual actions in Congress. Thus, the 10 have formed a loose-knit organization to work out their attitudes and policies on issues of mutual concern.

Of the three freshmen (first-term) congressmen who showed their mettle on the Hill in 1969, Mrs. Shirley Chisholm of New York is perhaps the most eye-catching, not only because she is the only black woman in Congress, but also because of her distinctive political style. She won the endorsement of the 12th Congressional District in New York in a straight contest with Republican James Farmer, receiving substantial Negro support as well as the majority of the non-Negro vote.

She made her mark in Congress soon after she arrived when she protested vigorously against her committee assignment (to a subcommittee of the Agriculture Committee), an almost unheard-of move. In a typically trenchant manner, she commented: "Apparently all they know here in Washington about Brooklyn is that a tree grew there. I can think of no other reason for assigning me to the Agriculture Committee." She continued: "I realize that I'm a freshman and that seniority is the rule. I did not come here expecting to get what I wanted every time I asked for it. But only nine black people have been elected to the House, and those nine should be used as effectively as possible." Her reassignment was to the Committee on Veterans Affairs, which, with a Veterans Administration Hospital in Brooklyn, she finds more relevant. Mrs. Chisholm is a distinguished, dynamic figure who believes that "the black man must step forward, but that does not mean black women have to step back."

In her maiden speech in May, Mrs. Chisholm pledged her opposition to every defense money bill "until the time comes when our values and priorities have been turned right side up again." The priorities for her are jobs, housing, and education for disadvantaged Americans. In 1969, with other black representatives, she supported bills to create a commission on Afro-American history and culture, to broaden the powers of the Department of HUD, and to create a Cabinet-level department of consumer affairs. She rallied black support in Congress against rumored welfare cuts, and in support of the repeal of provisions in the Social Security Act, which would result in expanding welfare payments to dependent children. She also has appealed for abortion law reform.

Another freshman was Louis Stokes, Ohio's first black representative, a lawyer and brother of Mayor Carl Stokes of Cleveland. He has been a hard-working member of the House, advocating tax reform, protesting tax inequalities, and taking a particular interest in how the taxing of charitable foundations would affect voter registration drives. He strongly protested from the floor of the House the administration's apparent slowdown of school desegregation in the South, and was an ally of Mrs. Chisholm in advocating the repeal of the freeze on aid to families with dependent children. He has introduced bills on family planning services and public health and welfare, on occupational safety and health, on consumer protection, and on equality of job and educational opportunities. Supported by two other black congressmen, Stokes introduced a bill to abolish the sugar quota for South Africa on the grounds that it was not in the interest of the United States to provide official support for a country whose racial policies are "anathema to the conscience of the world." He has, of course, worked closely with his brother to try to bring federal funds and support to Cleveland for a variety of local projects.

The third freshman is William Clay, the first black man to represent Missouri on Capitol Hill. Only 37, and looking "more like a graduate student than a congressman," according to one reporter, Clay had a remarkably successful career as a powerful local figure in St. Louis for ten years, with views ranging "from liberal to radical." As a member of the House Committee on Education and Labor, he introduced a bill

amending the Civil Rights Act of 1964 that would implement the U.S. Commission on Civil Rights' recommendations to assure equal job opportunities to members of minority groups in state and local governments. He and his co-sponsor pledged an all-out fight to prod the federal government into assuming leadership in withholding funds from any government agency practicing discrimination. He, Stokes, and Rep. Augustus Hawkins also introduced legislation to give the Equal Employment Opportunity Commission power to issue "cease and desist" orders instead of being restricted only to "conciliation and education" activities.

With Mrs. Chisholm and Rep. John Conyers, the Missouri Democrat sponsored legislation to abolish the draft and set up an all-volunteer army. "Too many American boys from too many families have witnessed discriminatory, un-American practices which have found fertile ground in an unjustly imposed and ill-managed conscription policy," he declared. With Reps. Charles C. Diggs, Hawkins, Conyers, and Chisholm, he proposed an office of defense review to oversee Defense Department procurement costs and policies.

He strongly supported the Vietnam Moratorium days. "The adverse social, economic, and political impact of this war on American life is a most cruel result of our involvement," Clay said. He opposed direct presidential election proposals put forward as electoral reform measures, feeling they would hurt minorities. Clay also tried to widen the operation of the Food Stamp Act and sponsored legislation dealing with drug abuse.

One of the five other members of longer standing in Congress, Augustus Hawkins of California is a much-respected legislator, who served 14 terms in the California legislature before going to Washington in 1962. He took a firm line opposing the extension of the income surtax. "While big businesses are being excluded from the hardship of excessive taxation, the poor should not be made to suffer while the elite continue to profit at their expense," he said. He spoke out against "doubletalk" in the administration's education policy, criticizing its attitude toward desegregation in the South and its cuts in federal education budgets.

Rep. Charles C. Diggs, Jr., of Michigan was elected to Congress in 1954. As a member of the House Foreign Affairs Committee and chairman of its subcommittee on Africa, and a member of the House Committee on the District of Columbia and chairman of its subcommittee No. 2, he is thought to have "established a reputation for satisfying the problems of the underprivileged and other citizens whose difficulties might otherwise go unattended."

Eighty-two-year-old William L. Dawson of Illinois was first elected to the House in 1942, and wields enormous potential and real power as chairman of the House Government Operations Committee.

A third long-term black representative is Robert C. Nix of Pennsylvania, first elected in May 1958. Nix supported legislation to promote equal employment opportunities, and to provide increases in Social Security benefits for elderly and disabled pensioners. His new committee assignment in the 91st Congress has been to the House Select Committee on Crime.

John Conyers of Michigan, first elected in 1964, has been consistently and actively opposed to the draft and to the Vietnam War. "Let us end the Vietnam War and start building America," he says. One of the best-known and most active black congressmen, his record of attempts to "build America" included, in 1969, legislative efforts to broaden the social security umbrella (with Mrs. Chisholm), to promote a full Equal Employment Opportunity Act intended to create new jobs and to strengthen the EEOC (with Mrs. Chisholm, Clay, and Stokes), and to establish a national living income program, a detailed plan "to combat more effectively the grievous blight of poverty."

Rep. Adam Clayton Powell's activities continued to bring him much publicity in 1969. The Supreme Court ruled on June 16 that the House had acted unconstitutionally when it barred the Harlem pastor from taking his seat in 1967 on grounds of alleged misconduct. Despite the expulsion, on his re-election in November 1968 Powell had been allowed to take his seat without seniority as a freshman congressman after payment of a fine. Since the Supreme Court's ruling left open the question of whether its ruling entitled Powell to restoration of his 24 years' seniority, his chairmanship of the Education and Labor Committee, and $55,000 salary, Powell sought from a U.S. district court restoration of "rights, privileges, and emoluments of the office to which he was duly elected" just as if the "unlawful exclusion had not occurred." He also claimed an additional $25,000 as restoration of the fine he paid as a condition of being reseated.

The specter of a struggle within Congress, which has always insisted on its right to conduct its own affairs, was raised when House lawyers opposed Powell's move and indicated that the House might not pay over any money, even if ordered to do so. "The House believes that the decision and mandate of the Supreme Court constitute an unwarrantable action inconsistent with the separation of powers provided by the Constitution," House lawyers declared in court. The judge ruled that Powell would have to refute charges that he misappropriated $46,000 in congressional funds before he could claim his $55,000 back pay, and refused to rule on the question of seniority or the fine. Powell's lawyers took the case to the Supreme Court, which is expected to rule sometime in 1970. Meanwhile, the Internal Revenue Service began an investigation of Congressman Powell's financial dealings.

The only black Republican in Congress is also the only black U.S. Senator. Edward Brooke of Massachusetts has been concerned with cutting expenditures on defense projects and transferring the funds to welfare projects. He welcomed the President's welfare proposals, and his concern for the underprivileged was further reflected in his support for the Housing and Urban Development Act of 1969, and in his testimony in support of the Philadelphia Plan before the Senate Judiciary Committee.

The informal Negro coalition in Congress took a united stand against the administration's Voting Rights Act, against the nomination of Clement F. Haynsworth to the Supreme Court (because of his civil rights record), against the administration's attitude toward school desegregation in the South, and in support of increased welfare payments to the poor.

However hard and impressively the black legislators work on the Hill, they would be better able to achieve their common aims if their numbers increased. Their numbers are not proportionate to the black population in the U.S., but if black voting trends continue to develop as the power of the ballot box is increasingly realized by Negroes, informed observers reckon that there will be as many as 25 black legislators in Congress by 1974. They will join a distinguished and hard-working group.

Black Organizations

To speak of civil rights organizations alone in 1969 is largely inaccurate, since many of those associations which started with the simple aim of achieving equality of rights have often developed and gone on to different goals as their immediate aims have been achieved or frustrated.

Perhaps the most noticeable—and indeed the saddest—feature of the organizations in 1969 was the fragmentation of leadership, the splintering and decline of once powerful groups, and the lack of unity of method and aim among them all. One writer talks of "black activism where leaders streak across the horizon like meteorites and soon disappear," commenting further that "a score of organizations have been born and have died." John Herbers, writing in the *New York Times* as early as March, summed up the situation as follows: "The consensus here is that Negroes probably constitute a stronger force nationally than they ever have, but because of the fragmentation and decline in the national organizations and the racial polarization of the country, their influence in the national govern-

ment may be at its lowest ebb since the Supreme Court's desegregation decision of 1954." Herbers concludes: "Only the Urban League and the NAACP have retained both stability and their contacts with the government."

What follows is a brief account of some of the trends in major black organizations in the U.S.

National Association for the Advancement of Colored People (NAACP)

The year 1969 was, to some extent, a year of respite after the stormy strife the NAACP experienced in 1968. Membership climbed to 450,673 and NAACP income totalled $3.4 million (although the operating deficit hit a record total, too).

What some commentators have called "the widening chasm between the NAACP and other black groups" because "almost alone among the nation's civil rights groups the NAACP has refused to adopt the strident rhetoric and alienated tone of Black Power," was underlined early in the year when Roy Wilkins, executive director, threatened court action to block black student demands for racially separate academic departments and dormitories in colleges and universities across the country. He called such programs reverse segregation: "We have suffered too many heartaches and shed too many tears and too much blood in fighting the evils of racial segregation to return in 1969 to the lonely and dispiriting confines of its demeaning prison." The statement drew an impassioned rebuke from Roy Innis, national director of the Congress of Racial Equality, and from other activists.

The traditional "legalistic, non-violent, assimilationist" approach of the NAACP was also mirrored in the protest Wilkins made to CBS about the series on Negro history called "Black Heritage." He called it "hopelessly flawed" because it showed only a single interpretation—that of "the contemporary left-of-center black militant minority view, liberally garnished with the thrust for a new apartheid."

Yet bridges across the "chasm" were attempted. Wilkins announced a willingness to meet the Black Panthers and other militants "to beat out a kind of strategy or procedure." Together with other Negro leaders, Wilkins chided President Nixon for moving too slowly on some critical racial issues. At the annual convention of the NAACP, leaders expressed to newspapermen their dissatisfaction with the administration on two issues in particular—school desegregation and the extension of the voting rights law. On another occasion, with 13 other civil rights leaders, Wilkins joined a statement giving NAACP support to the campaign to get recognition for the Negro Hospital Workers' Union in Charleston, S.C. At the NAACP convention, too, the "Young Turks" who struggled for power in 1968 pledged their "respect and allegiance to the organization," thus healing the breach they opened last year. In return, NAACP leaders forecast a more militant civil rights role for the organization.

The NAACP could be seen, as one commentator noted, "moving to recapture for its programs momentum it concedes was lost after the successful legal and legislative battles of recent years." Urban program directors were recruited in major cities to step up efforts in the ghettos and to intensify recruitment and training of leaders. The Rockefeller Foundation granted $100,000 to the Nationwide Leadership Development Program. Local branches were allowed to sponsor low-income housing. An attempt was made to break what labor director Herbert Hill called "organized labor's racial stranglehold" on housing practices; the Model Cities program was the first target. A list of minority contractors able to participate in the Model Cities program was compiled and efforts made to get them bonding and insurance without which large jobs would be inaccessible to them. Suits may be filed, and demonstrations called to dramatize the issue unless more minority workers are employed in the program.

The Legal Defense Fund filed suit against three top administration officials, charging that

they granted contracts illegally to three Southern textile firms accused of job discrimination. The National Office for the Rights of the Indigent, a division of the Defense Fund, has expanded to include in its operations legal problems involved in student demonstrations as well as in schools, community relations, and consumer welfare.

At the end of the year the NAACP announced a policy of challenging suburban zoning laws in federal courts beginning with a case against Oyster Bay, Long Island, N.Y. It will ask that federal funds be withheld from areas of the nation that "use their power to zone as a screen for preserving lily-white neighborhoods."

Despite what critics call a "conservative and middle class oriented" approach, NAACP is still at the forefront of the civil rights movement.

National Urban League

The National Urban League defines its role today as a "voluntary community service agency of civic, professional, business, labor, and religious leaders, dedicated to the removal of all forms of segregation and discrimination based on creed or color."

The president of the traditionally biracial League, elected for a second term at the annual conference in July 1969, is James A. Linen, a white, who is also president of Time, Inc. But the powerful figure in the organization is still Whitney M. Young, the executive director since 1961, who is credited with expanding the League's goals from social work and enlightened charity to the "dimension of the bread and butter, meat and potatoes work of finding jobs."

The momentum given to the League by this "new thrust" initiated in mid-1968—in essence an attempt to return to original principles and to work more closely with the black community—was accelerated in 1969 with the "Ghetto Power" drive, launched in January with the creation of a special National Field Services Department directed by Sterling Tucker. The 62 Ghetto

Power programs throughout the country are intended to build greater self-determination in poor communities, or, as Whitney M. Young put it, "to ensure that the black ghetto has a major responsible voice in decisions that affect it, and that black people have the power to build decent, prosperous communities." Laurance S. Rockefeller, chairman of the Rockefeller Brothers Fund which gave a $250,000 grant to further the action programs, commented: "What is significant and promising is that the program gives support to projects that the people in the communities involved themselves see as their way to dignity and equal opportunity."

Other financial support for the ghetto programs has come from the Alfred P. Sloan Foundation ($250,000 over two years), the Ford Foundation ($1,050,000), the Rockefeller Foundation ($300,000), the Richard King Mellon Foundation, and the Alfred Rockefeller Fund.

The League announced plans in July for the formation of a national housing foundation to provide about $1 million seed money over a year to community-controlled housing groups in 12 cities.

The League's Fellowship Program, run since 1965 under the auspices of a $100,000 yearly grant from the Carnegie Foundation to recruit and train potential professionals for employment in the League's affiliates in every field, continued to award scholarships to promising students for graduate study.

In a 51-page memorandum on the urban crisis entitled "Call to Action" and sent to President Nixon on Inauguration Day, the League detailed a long list of "dangerous and challenging" problems "posing a serious threat to the nation's stability." The document described welfare programs as "obsolete, punitive, ineffective, inefficient, and bankrupt" and recommended a guaranteed minimum income and a $2 per hour minimum wage, and investigation of friction between police and Negro communities and of the "rapidly deteriorating climate in the Armed Services."

The League found the administration's actions on the memorandum disappointing and Whitney Young strongly criticized the administration in July for "not moving forward" much more rapidly on domestic issues: "We seem to be moving backward to an age of indifference and repression."

The League's "Call to Action," together with demands of other organizations, appeared, however, to have some effect on the administration's attitude toward welfare. The Nixon "Family Assistance Plan" was announced in August, the first major initiative for welfare reform announced in three decades. It proposed a minimum federal benefit of $1,600 for a family of four and later added grants of $720 in food stamps.

Young also criticized the administration in early January, despite persistent rumors that he himself had refused a Cabinet-level position, for failing to appoint more Negroes. "Either Mr. Nixon doesn't want to appoint any Negroes to his administration or else he is being sabotaged by some key members of his staff," he said. Other outspoken pronouncements carrying the weight of the League's authority were made by Young on anti-Semitism: "religious prejudice has no place among people who have been victims of racial prejudice"; and on the handicapped, when he called for a "coalition of concern" linking the handicapped and disabled with the black civil rights movement.

Despite being one of the traditionally-oriented civil rights organizations, the Urban League's 59th Conference had a strong element of militant protest, provided largely by student summer workers for the League. During the conference Whitney Young outlined "an economic security program" to "erase poverty," and noted new activities such as voter registration drives and housing corporations to be set up in local communities.

The mood of the Urban League in 1969 was summed up by Young in his statement at the conference that "there is still time, but I have moved from cautious optimism to cautious pessimism."

Southern Christian Leadership Conference (SCLC)

SCLC is the only national civil rights organization with strong ties to the militant groups which still honors non-violence and integration as its aims. Its president, Rev. Ralph David Abernathy, does not underestimate the difficulties of the organization's position at a time—the "most difficult period," as he calls it—when clear-cut issues like state segregation laws are no longer the target, but "the whole economic system" and "the most powerful institution in the world, the federal government"; and when SCLC also faces stiffening white resistance and the competition of more aggressive black action groups.

The annual convention concluded that "nationwide protests are no longer feasible in the current mood of the nation, and under the Nixon administration." Plans were made to concentrate national efforts on voter registration and education, political activities, and labor organizing. Rev. Abernathy reaffirmed at the convention his pledges to organize the working poor across the South following the successful precedent of the Charleston hospital workers' strike, which he claimed as the major civil rights achievement of SCLC in 1969. He set out a plan to create a draft resistance counselling service within SCLC —one of the organizations which has adopted an antiwar attitude—and also planned a campaign in the South for voting rights for 18-year-olds. Rev. Andrew Young, executive vice president, cites as the organization's most significant victories in 1969 the hospital workers' strike and the black victories in the elections in Greene County, Ala.

In May Rev. Abernathy led his Poor People's Campaign to the White House to a meeting he called his "most disappointing and fruitless," and to a series of attempts to meet Cabinet members in which he was "rebuffed" and "humiliated," it is said, because the administration did not believe he had wide support among Negroes generally.

As a result of these experiences, SCLC charged in August that the Nixon administration had "written off" the non-white population, and included President Nixon on a list of opponents of blacks and of SCLC. At the time, Abernathy declared, "I do not know how much longer non-violence can be effective in this country," and he described the civil rights movement as "a human rights movement against war, racism and poverty—the triple evils."

On the anniversary of Dr. Martin Luther King's assassination, a series of demonstrations was organized around the country. Mrs. Coretta King, his widow, began to take a more active part than before in SCLC campaigns in April in marches in Memphis and Montgomery which were the beginning of the "second phase" of the Poor People's Campaign which had begun in Washington. Her participation was aimed partly at offsetting rumors that Mr. Abernathy's position as Dr. King's successor was shaky and partly consolidating SCLC leadership generally. Mrs. King also played a leading role in the hospital workers' strike in Charleston.

There appeared early in the year to be a division of opinion between Rev. James Bevel, head of SCLC's non-violent education and direct action wing, and Rev. Abernathy, when the former declared James Earl Ray innocent of murdering Dr. King and offered to defend him. Dr. Abernathy first gave Bevel his support, then withdrew it, and later publicly censured his lieutenant. The incident may be seen as symptomatic of some of SCLC's problems and the way the organization is still "groping for direction" 18 months after the untimely and tragic death of Dr. King.

There have been reports, too, of divisions between Rev. Abernathy and Rev. Jesse Jackson, who runs Operation Breadbasket, which was started to obtain jobs for Negroes. It was extended by Rev. Jackson in 1969—by the use of threat of boycotts—to include obtaining agreements with white merchants to store merchandise manufactured by Negro-owned companies, to patronize Negro banks, to employ Negro building contractors, and to use the services of Negro professionals. Rev. Jackson's spectacular successes in creating economic power in the black community have won him wide notice and respect.

The annual conference of SCLC was believed to have solidified Abernathy's leadership. Ben Franklin wrote in the *New York Times* on Aug. 16 that the conference ended speculation about "his continued leadership of the organization and the loyalty of its staff. He was in charge. He received tributes and ovations. He was told publicly that 'it is not a relevant question any more whether he can take Martin Luther King's place.' "

In a December 24 interview from a jail cell in Memphis—where he was confined after refusing to pay bond set on charges of contributing to the delinquency of minors by encouraging them to stay away from school in protest against the absence of Negroes on the city school board— Abernathy confessed that he and his organization were "tired, really, very tired." While the SCLC's 1969 income was at a high of $1.6 million, a deficit of $400,000 was incurred due to increased expenditures on expanded projects. At least one financial worry was somewhat alleviated, however, when the Justice Department accepted $10,500 as settlement for the $71,795 bill tendered SCLC and NAACP for the cost of Resurrection City during the Poor People's Campaign in Washington, D.C., in 1968.

As Andrew Young pointed out, the effects of 10 years of constant pressure were beginning to take their toll on staff members: "We're not healthy. We're an exhausted organization right now." His pessimism was deep. "We're not really strong enough to take on any national issues like Birmingham or Selma," he added, though he did say that by spring (1970) "we should be in good shape again. We're going to concentrate on political action campaigns and voter registration drives."

This, then, is the kind of activity to be expected from the Southern Christian Leadership Conference in the near future.

National Welfare Rights Organization (NWRO)

George A. Wiley set up NWRO in 1966, convinced that the activities of other rights organizations were "frustrated by financial problems and lack of agreement on long-range objectives." His experience at CORE—where he became associate national director in 1964, but was subsequently squeezed out in one of the leadership struggles of recent years—may have played a part in his reaching this conclusion. His idea was to set up an organization for a specific, limited objective, and to avoid becoming involved with other goals that might prove divisive. The narrow objective is, simply, increased public assistance to the poor.

So effective has the idea proved, and so astute has been Wiley's leadership, that while most other rights organizations have been splintering on the rocks of dissension, NWRO has been quietly growing and consolidating. Latest available figures showed 35,000 members in 186 cities and 46 states. Most members are Negroes, though the organization is open to the people of all races.

Demonstrations against stores throughout the country—particularly against branches of Sears Roebuck & Co.—for extension of $150 worth of credit to welfare recipients, have had some effect in liberalizing credit facilities, not only at Sears but also at other stores.

In 1969, for the first time, Wiley and NWRO were granted an interview with high administration officials. Robert Finch, Secretary of Health, Education and Welfare, acknowledged after the interview that welfare mothers were an important constituency of HEW. The year 1969 saw, too, the first demonstration by NWRO members at the National Conference on Social Welfare, and a donation and an acknowledgment from the NCSW president that he believed in NWRO.

At the second biennial conference of the organization in August, 600 delegates, mostly Negro welfare mothers, approved a militant program for the next two years—a "spending the rent" project. It is aimed at disregarding local welfare directives on spending on basic needs, so that the rent share of welfare payments would be spent on other basic items. To protest meager welfare allowances for other specific living expenses, delegates approved a plan to withhold utility bill payments. A campaign for "wage supplements" for the working poor from state and local general assistance programs was approved, and the campaign started with a drive in New Bedford, Mass.

The organization approved Mr. Nixon's welfare proposals with faint praise—"He did have the initiative to get started . . . but the basic failing is just not enough money." Wiley attributed the President's proposals in part to the success of the organization's pressure in demonstrations and lobbying.

NWRO representatives appeared before the House Ways and Means Committee considering the administration's welfare proposals to ask for a higher guaranteed annual income plan than that presented by Mr. Nixon. They proposed minimum incomes from $1,900 annually for an individual to $14,100 for a family of thirteen persons.

Joining the attack on the "establishment" from another angle, Wiley represented his welfare mothers at the November 15 Vietnam Moratorium in Washington, speaking to the assembled crowd at the Washington Monument about the need to end the war, which was taking such a toll among the poor and black.

The President's three-day conference on Food, Nutrition and Health, held in early December in Washington, was the scene of an attempted demonstration by Wiley, when he tried to stage a sit-in during the closing moments of the conference. He, together with many others at the conference, felt very strongly the need for drastic and emergency measures to tackle the hunger crisis in the U.S. His protests were supported by Rev. Abernathy, who denounced the President's opening speech to the conference and criticized lack of action to reduce the price of food stamps and to extend the whole program.

Congress of Racial Equality (CORE)

The Congress of Racial Equality has, as John Herbers, veteran civil rights reporter, put it, "undergone several splinterings in the continuing struggle over what is relevant to the Negro community and what is not."

The major concern of CORE Director Roy Innis has been to work with the Nixon administration to promote a community self-determination bill. The bill provides for community control of public institutions within incorporated areas, with residents sharing profits from community-owned businesses.

Innis urged, in May 1969, the creation of autonomous black communities in the U.S. emphasizing the need for separatism. The first practical application of the community control idea is incorporated in plans announced for CORE to help in setting up a community corporation to run the public hospital and health facilities in Harlem.

Innis reacted strongly to Roy Wilkins of NAACP when the latter criticized demands by Negro students for separate and all-black studies departments on campuses. The CORE leader rejected NAACP policy: "We are against the policy of integration and assimilation being offered by Mr. Wilkins. We say the civil rights movement is dead."

A former CORE leader, James Farmer, was named assistant secretary of the Department of Health, Education and Welfare. He was the only civil rights activist to obtain a high position in the Nixon administration.

Student Nonviolent Coordinating Committee/Student National Coordinating Committee (SNCC)

The Student Nonviolent Coordinating Committee continued the decline in membership and influence—so apparent in 1968—into 1969. It is no longer a national organization, having "splintered away in ideological and personality struggles." The ranks of its paid organizers, once numbering more than 200, have shrunk, and funds have dwindled.

In July it changed its name, substituting "National" for "Nonviolent" to fit its militant character after the Senate Permanent Investigation Subcommittee had heard testimony that the organization was no longer nonviolent, and had closed its ranks to white members. H. Rap Brown assumed the chairmanship at the time of the name change and outlined a new program for SNCC, including a People's Medical Center for free medical care and a People's Sewing Center "to build the concept of black people controlling their own productive forces." Attempts have been made, too, to forge an alliance of "black liberation movements" in the U.S. with links to revolutionary groups in Asia, Africa, and Latin America.

National Black Economic Development Conference

The National Black Economic Development Conference is sponsored by the Interreligious Foundation for Community Organization (IFCO), composed of 23 national religious agencies and community groups. Spokesman for the conference is James Forman, until mid-1969 a key figure in SNCC and a leader in the development of the civil rights movement.

The conference and its director burst into the headlines when Forman disrupted the Communion Service at New York's interracial interdenominational Riverside Church and demanded, in a speech from the altar area, that U.S. churches and synagogues pay $500 million as "reparations" to Negroes for past "exploitation." Included in the list of demands, based on the so-called Black Manifesto made public on April 25 at the Detroit Conference of IFCO, was that Riverside Church give 60 per cent of its income from various sources to the conference, and that the organization be given office space and telephones at the church and have unrestricted use of the church's radio station. Other proposals in the manifesto were for Negro industrial, educational, and cultural programs to be set up, financed by religious institutions.

Forman declared that his organization had as its goal the creation of "huge industrial combines which will be cooperative ventures, with the money going back into the black community and not into the hands of a few wealthy individuals."

Many churches have agreed to pay reparations through IFCO, whose executive director, Rev. Lucius Walker, Jr., is under fire in some quarters for allegedly supporting "militant and disruptive organizations." He vehemently denies this, however; these organizations promote black awareness and identity.

Republic of New Africa

This is a Detroit-based group founded in March 1968, aiming at creating an independent all-black nation in the United States. It has targeted Louisiana, Mississippi, Alabama, Georgia, and South Carolina, as well as parts of Cleveland and Detroit, as the area where a powerful free black nation will be built.

The group is an amalgamation of militant black groups and individuals who contend it is impossible for blacks and whites to live together. The organization held a convention in August in Washington, D.C., attended by about 100 delegates, reportedly mostly from the urban North, who worked out the way the republic is to be governed. Their president, elected *in absentia*, was, until December, Robert F. Williams, who had fled the country in 1961 after being charged with kidnapping. He has preached revolution by black Americans from refuges in Cuba, China, North Vietnam, and Tanzania. He returned to the U.S. from China after the convention to face court proceedings, because, he said, "The struggle of black people was developing to such a point that I felt it my duty to come back." His experiences in China deeply impressed him, but he protested, "I am not interested in promoting ideologies or philosophies. I am interested in justice and freedom."

Of his own future, he said, "I didn't come back to America with the idea of leading anybody. If the people want me I will be at their service, but if I am to lead it will have to be toward the goal of a selfless society—we have to instill into our people that they have to build a selfless society, a collective society."

Republic of New Africa is the inspiration of two brothers, Milton and Richard Henry; Milton acts as vice president of the organization. Williams' presidency had been hailed by the Black Nationalists and Black Panthers, but he is on record as saying before his return to America, "The world is not ready for a militant black nationalist colony yet."

His resignation as president was not, then, totally unexpected, but with the loss of his leadership and personality, the movement inevitably suffered something of an identity crisis and its future has yet to be worked out.

LeRoi Jones is a minister of culture in the organization; H. Rap Brown is secretary of defense; Malcolm X's widow, Betty Shabbazz, is second vice president.

Black Panther Party for Self-Defense

The Black Panthers are a radical and militant socialist organization with a national but comparatively small membership which operates under constant police surveillance. The year 1969 saw a change in the image of the party. Violence of all sorts around the country has been laid at the door of the Panthers, with 21 Panthers indicted for conspiracy to bomb several Manhattan department stores. Bobby Seale, the party's chairman, was arrested on a charge of murder after the torture-slaying in Connecticut of a former Panther suspected by the party of informing on the bombing plot.

FBI Director J. Edgar Hoover has called the Panthers a national threat, and the Justice Department has set up a special task force to investigate them. A Senate investigating committee heard evidence—from former Panthers—of violence and debauchery, which was hotly denied by the party.

At the same time, in order to achieve the socialist revolution, the tactic of allying with radical white groups has been adopted, with a consequent toning down of extreme attitudes, at least in public. Hence, Don Tax of the Oakland chapter was able to say, "It is not black against white, it is the oppressed against the oppressors. You don't fight racism with racism." A national conference against fascism was held jointly with white radicals in Oakland, Calif., in July, and a Panther rally in September attracted members of the white "Young Patriot" group.

A drive was started to establish more community programs in cities throughout the country, and the Panthers themselves took part in "feed the children breakfast" campaigns in Kansas City, San Francisco, and elsewhere.

The end of the year saw what seemed to many to be an all-out campaign by the authorities to crush the Panthers. The national leadership already was in considerable disarray. Seale, in addition to previous charges, was arrested and charged with conspiracy to provoke a riot at the Democratic National Convention in Chicago in 1968. At the trial, Judge Julius Hoffman ordered Seale bound and gagged in an effort to stop his disruptive outbursts.

Huey Newton, the defense minister, was serving a 2-to-15-year jail term for voluntary manslaughter.

David Hilliard, Panther chief of staff, was arrested Dec. 3 on charges of threatening President Nixon's life in a speech before more than 100,000 antiwar demonstrators in San Francisco on Nov. 15.

Eldridge Cleaver, minister of information, wanted for parole violation in California, spent part of the year in exile in Cuba, moved to Algeria for the Pan-African Conference, and from there was reported in late December to be trying to secure reentry to the United States to come to the aid of his beleaguered party.

These confrontations resulted in local Panther leaders throughout the country finding themselves in jail on charges ranging from illegal weapons possession to resisting arrest. More spectacularly, on Dec. 4, 14 Chicago policemen raided Panther headquarters. The resulting shoot-out ended with two Panthers dead: Illinois chairman Fred Hampton, 21, and Mark Clark, 22. Four Panthers and one policeman were wounded. The raid aroused considerable controversy and a strong backlash of sympathy in favor of the Panthers.

The Justice Department set up an official investigation into Panther charges of police murder in the incident; an unofficial citizens' committee was organized to investigate clashes between the police and the Panthers; and an unofficial congressional hearing on the incident was held in Chicago by five black congressmen.

In Los Angeles, a few days after the Chicago shoot-out, more police raids on Panther centers throughout the city led to the arrest of more than a dozen Panthers and to confiscation of a formidable arsenal of weapons.

The result of such a bleak year for the Panthers is difficult to predict. One federal law enforcement official observed, "The Panthers can't survive these arrests, these costs, and the loss of their leadership. The movement is bound to fade away." Another commentator's viewpoint is that "if past history is any indication . . . [it] will likely mean new posters, more contributions, and an increased sense of unity and determination for the Panthers."

Revolutionary Action Movement (RAM)

Organized in Detroit in 1963, RAM is said to be dedicated to the overthrow of the capitalist system in America and the installation of a socialist system modeled on Red China's interpretation of Marxism-Leninism. It has been described as typical of the extreme militancy developing among some blacks. Robert F. Williams, former president of the Republic of New Africa, is credited with being leader of RAM, and certainly the organization follows his teachings.

The operations of RAM members are kept secret, but the FBI claims RAM members have been involved in long-range plans to assassinate high officials, and on a different level in a plan to assassinate policemen by placing cyanide in station house coffee urns. The return of Williams from China to the U.S. to active leadership of RAM may prove significant to future activities of the organization.

Student Afro-American Society

This is a black student organization, with the reported aim of "forcing compliance with such demands of Negro militants as a new curriculum of black studies, the rights of blacks to dictate hiring and firing of professors, and, as at Cornell University, separate black colleges within university systems."

While university officials said early in the year that there was no central black student organization, other societies such as the Black Students Union, active in the San Francisco State College disorders, and the Black Liberation Front, were reported to be in constant touch across the country with other extremists on arms, methods, and tactics.

At the convention of the National Student Association (NSA) at El Paso in August, however, an organization called the National Association of Black Students (NABS) was born. The first effort of black college students to organize nationally, NABS is to serve as a communications center, with ambitious plans for a legal rights program, visiting lectureships, advisory aids for black studies, and scholarships. It was described by one of the leaders as "the sort of thing we have been looking for for years." The organization plans to work closely with NSA, but feels a black-oriented organization can best promote the interests of black students and give them priority. The group was promised

$50,000 from NSA. NABS has supported the Vietnam Moratorium days and anti war protests planned by white groups, but the character of the group has not yet been seen to be militantly extremist.

A hopeful view of the fragmentation of leadership noted in this section was voiced by Dr. Kenneth B. Clark, director of the Metropolitan Applied Research Center, at the conference of black elected officials in Washington in August: "Elected Negro officials are now the only civil rights leaders who are representatives of the aspirations, desires, and the quest for answers posed by their constituents. The time has passed when self-appointed individual leaders, however genuine their commitment, can speak for the masses of American Negroes."

It is true, it seems, that just as it is no longer possible for politicians to depend on whites to interpret the needs and views of Negroes, it is also no longer possible for them to rely on a few black leaders to interpret and represent the differing and varied interests of an increasingly mature and sophisticated black community.

"Black America is no monolith," as Thomas Johnson noted in the *New York Times*. It is no longer a question of "who speaks for the black community," but of "who represents which section of the black community." Indeed, why should one man be expected to speak for black people when no one man speaks for whites? As Roy Innis declared, "Harlem will speak with one voice when the city council, East New York, Scarsdale, and Syosset speak with one voice."

Voting

George W. Crockett, Jr., a black Detroit judge, voiced a common opinion when he said black power's "most potent manifestation thus far has been at the ballot box in the election of black public officials. If this trend continues . . . racism in the administration of our laws will soon be a thing of the past."

The trend itself started with the 1965 Voting Rights Act, expiring in mid-1970, which is credited with being responsible for the registration of some 800,000 black voters—almost double the pre-1965 total—and indirectly responsible for the election of nearly 500 black officials in the South, where there were only 72 before the act. The act was passed after a shocked nation, perhaps largely ignorant of the real truths of Southern politics, saw white mounted policemen in Alabama brutally attacking Negroes seeking the vote in Selma. The act is aimed at the Southern states, and the key provisions making black voter registration possible are those suspending literacy tests before registration, giving the Attorney General power to send federal examiners and observers to oversee registrars' activities, and requiring affected states to submit any new voting laws to the Attorney General at the federal district court in Washington, D.C.

Examiners have been sent to only 64 of the 556 counties in the South, but the threat of their attendance and of federal intervention enabled the Voter Education Project (VEP) of the Southern Regional Council to register many otherwise disenfranchised blacks. (The council, a non-denominational and non-political organization founded in 1944, has long been concerned with the problems of the South as a region and with mobilizing people to work toward solving them.)

The key issue in 1969 has been, then, whether the Voting Rights Act would be extended beyond the summer of 1970, or allowed to be extinguished by what one commentator called a built-in "self destruct" mechanism in the act.

The Supreme Court ruled in June 1969 on a case concerning literacy tests in Gaston County, N.C. The Court held (*Gaston Co., N.C.* v. *U.S.*) that as long as segregated and inferior education exists, literacy tests cannot be applied with equal fairness to all registrants, black and white. The tests are therefore unconstitutional. Although some Southern states such as Alabama, Louisiana, South Carolina, and Mississippi still maintain literacy laws on their books, they are barred from reinstating the tests as

such, but it is conceivable that states and counties covered by the act could order complete re-
registration, as South Carolina did in 1967.

Without the possibility of federal protection
under the act, together with the deep (and often
justifiable) dread many Southern blacks hold of
officialdom, the task of re-registering those black
voters already on the books would be formidable, especially in the face of obstruction by hostile registrars. Moreover, localities at present
covered by the act could adopt laws and election procedures to disenfranchise Negroes and
remove thereby the electoral base of the 528
black elected officials in the South.

The administration proposed—in place of
extension—changing the act by making the literacy tests national until January 1974; eliminating residency requirements for voting in presidential elections; extending the federal right to
send examiners and observers to include every
state; giving the Attorney General power to
review state election laws and file suits against
discriminatory laws; and creating a presidential
advisory committee to study voting discrimination and other "corrupt practices."

Supporters of a straight five-year extension,
although seeing some desirable features in the
proposals, charged the administration with "fog-
ging the issue." The administration's reply was
that the existing legislation could not be
extended because it was "regional legislation,"
and that the right to vote was "no longer a
regional issue" but was "a national concern."
This last point was borne out in evidence to the
House Judiciary Committee in May showing that
no fewer than 13 non-Southern states still
demanded literacy as a condition of the franchise.

In view of the controversy, the vote of the
House to reject extension of the tough 1965 bill
and replace it with the Nixon administration bill
on Dec. 12 came as a shock to civil rights workers who saw it as the civil rights movement's first
defeat in the House since Congress began passing modern civil rights legislation in 1957.

Clarence Mitchell of the National Association

for the Advancement of Colored People called it
"the most scurrilous attack on constitutional
rights I have ever seen." Former Attorney General Ramsey Clark called the House action "terribly unfortunate" and there was sharp criticism
for the vote from commentators and civil rights
activists on the grounds that with the enactment
of the administration bill the South would
"revert" to its old practices. What Clark called
"the most effective civil rights law in history and
one of the most effective techniques of making
democracy work" would thereby be invalidated.

It falls to the Senate in 1970 to consider the
administration's bill and possibly to amend it.
Sen. Birch Bayh (D-Ind.) predicted a filibuster
"one way or another." Senate instructions to the
Judiciary Committee that the bill be reported
back by March 1, 1970, insured the measure
would reach the floor.

Other threats to black ballot box power
became apparent in 1969. The Voter Education
Project's achievement in the South has been
remarkable, not only in helping to register black
voters and thus affecting profoundly the direction of Southern politics; not only in running
leadership training conferences, but also in keeping in close touch with the field workers; and
documenting and publicizing the frustrations
would-be voters meet. VEP in 1969 continued to
receive reports of registrars maintaining short or
irregular hours and of their arbitrarily closing
their offices without notice, and of tricks being
used to mislead Negroes or to keep them from
voting. Economic reprisals are still threatened if
blacks register. They may find themselves being
fired, evicted, losing terms of credit, or being put
off welfare rolls. Even violence and confrontation still crop up.

The projects run by VEP stood endangered by
proposals included by the House and the Senate
in the Tax Reform Bill. The House passed a proposal limiting the support voter registration organizations could receive from one foundation to
25 per cent of the total funding. VEP gets virtually all its financial support from foundations,
notably the Ford Foundation, which also funded

the voter registration drive before the Cleveland mayoralty election of 1967 when Carl Stokes was first elected mayor.

The importance of this tax reform provision, its implications for black voter registration, and thus black ballot box power, are readily apparent, even though the House bill was apparently designed to except the VEP specifically. However, the Senate Finance Committee voted in late October to flatly prohibit foundations from supporting voter registration activities at all. Vernon E. Jordan, Jr., director of VEP, went to Washington and in a strong protest branded the provision as "punitive" and "racist in its effect." As one commentator said, "More than a million Southern Negroes have become registered voters as a result of foundation-supported voter registration. To shut down VEP now not only jeopardizes the future of black political participation in the country, but conveys to blacks the ugly message that they cannot make it in the system."

Senate and House versions of the proposals in the Tax Reform Bill affecting foundations and voter registration projects were finally settled in conference. The bill signed by the President contained restrictions on foundations close to those first proposed in the House: organizations involved in voter registration campaigns can receive a maximum of 25 per cent of their funding from any one foundation. Those groups involved in registration projects totally dependent on foundation support thus need the backing of at least four foundations, none of which can have any interest in the political outcome of the drive. Voter registration organizations must now operate in at least five states, another requirement attempting to restrict undue foundation influence.

The bill as it became law was received as the least of several evils and occasioned no immediate criticism or praise from the organizations most affected.

The effectiveness of the Negro vote, once registered, is still subject to dilution, both in the North and South. In Greene County, Ala., Negro voters outnumbered whites by two to one after the Supreme Court ordered a new vote because Negroes had been left off the ballot. A clean sweep by Negroes was predicted, but victory margins were unexpectedly narrow. Observers said that fear of reprisals kept many with low-paying jobs from exercising their right to vote.

In a significant case in Indianapolis, a three-judge federal court ruled on a case involving the constitutionality of keeping a predominantly Negro inner-city section of a county from having its fair share of power in electing state legislators. The judges found in Marion County that the Negro precincts were joined with other sections choosing a group of legislators to speak for the district. Since 1960 a white township in the county has been able to control many more seats in the 23-member county delegation than has the more populous Negro inner-city. The court ordered the delegation redistributed by population strengths, and the Supreme Court is likely to receive the case and give a ruling on the legality of such racial gerrymandering. One commentator declared, "Until this issue is finally resolved, Negro neighborhoods, particularly in the core areas of major cities, cannot be sure of their power at the polls."

The Southern Christian Leadership Conference in 1969 backed a campaign in Louisiana, North Carolina, and South Carolina against full slate voting laws, where a person must vote for a candidate for every post vacant to have his vote for any office counted. This can be a subtle form of diluting the vote because the laws have the effect of making it more difficult for minority groups to muster all their strength (the "single shot" vote) behind one candidate for an office.

The debate on the Voting Rights Act extension was the major congressional civil rights battle of 1969 and one of the most significant events in the civil rights field during the year. According to one commentator, "Nothing less than the political future, and with it much of the social and economic future of Southern Negroes, was at stake."

Members of Black Construction Coalition in Pittsburgh show new Black American Symbol representing black power.

In Chicago, blacks and whites end brief battle over alleged racial discrimination in construction industry.

THE COUNCIL OF ECONOMIC ADVIS-
ORS estimated during the Johnson administration that discrimination against blacks in the
job market had cost the United States more than
$30 billion in unrealized gross national product.
Since then, small inroads into that bleak estimate
were made as more kinds of jobs gradually
opened up to black Americans.

By the end of 1968 both the general unemployment rate and that of the nation's ghettos
had dropped to a 15-year low. Well into 1969
black workers were still finding jobs, although
the total ghetto labor force appeared to be
declining. Economists said the drain of the Vietnam war on the country's work force was partly
responsible.

By midsummer, general unemployment was
up to the 1967 level and the gap between black
and white employment had widened. Harold
Goldstein, assistant commissioner for labor statistics, reported "some slowing up in the rate of
demand for labor" as a result of the Nixon
administration's policy to curb demand with
higher taxes and tighter money.

Labor leaders warned the administration that
union campaigns to find jobs for blacks might be
hindered if anti-inflation drives were stepped up.
By the end of the summer more men were
finding jobs, but blue collar workers were still
having a hard time. The unemployment rate for
blacks was still twice that of whites. In the ghettos, two-thirds of the unemployed were Negroes.

A sudden rise in unemployment in September
was widely read as evidence of a slowdown in
economic activity. But within two months, the
rate fell sharply and some felt it showed that
businessmen were continuing to expand their
operations despite higher interest, wage, and
supply costs.

Dr. Andrew Brimmer, a black member of the
Federal Reserve System's board of governors,
said in 1969 that inflation could not be controlled without an "unfortunate and unwelcomed
by-product" of rising unemployment. He called
for new programs to cushion the blow of unemployment, including increased unemployment
compensation benefits and improved job training,
and said the government should "find some way
of providing income directly" to those hardest
hit. He suggested that the government might
guarantee a job to those unable to find employment.

Earlier in the year, Brimmer had noted that
among whites the gap between best-paid and
least-paid workers was narrowing, while among
blacks it was widening. "A basic schism has
developed in the black community," he said,
"and it may be widening year by year."

In a May survey, the Gallup Poll found that
white Americans' attitudes toward their jobs and
incomes had not changed substantially in three
years: 88 per cent were satisfied with the work
they were doing and 67 per cent thought their
incomes were adequate. Among black Ameri-

cans, 76 per cent approved of their jobs, an increase of 7 per cent. The number who were unsatisfied with their family incomes, 44 per cent, had not changed.

The Government Grapples with Its Own Laws

As Defense Secretary Clark M. Clifford ended his term of office he made a number of moves toward helping the nation's disadvantaged. He increased amounts in defense contracts awarded to employers hiring in ghetto areas from $120 million to $165 million. He put experts to work researching the problems of urban redevelopment, mass transportation, and low-cost housing.

In January Clifford L. Alexander, chairman of the Equal Employment Opportunity Commission (EEOC), announced that there had been a marked trend in the hiring of minority workers at all levels by major drug companies. He said the gains were the result of the joint efforts of his agency and the Food and Drug Administration. He noted, however, that blacks still only made up about 5 per cent of the drug companies' work force.

The Nixon administration pledged early to help the nation's disadvantaged find jobs. George P. Shultz, the new Secretary of Labor, listed increased employment of non-whites high on his "action program." "How can the large number of black citizens and others who have not shared in the bounty of America be brought more effectively into jobs that are useful to society and that have a potential for personal and economic growth?" he asked.

A task force of 17 university economists headed by Dr. John T. Dunlop of Harvard was set up to advise the Labor Department. It suggested consolidating manpower services into a single comprehensive program. The group cautioned against substituting tax incentive plans in place of federally-assisted services to the poor and said it was opposed to cutbacks in manpower spending as a means of curbing inflation.

Late in January the Labor Department set up a nine-member advisory committee to investigate testing programs used by federal contractors for selecting new employees. The committee was asked to help revise standard tests geared to whites, often a hindrance to black employment and promotion.

The Defense Department stirred up domestic trouble for itself in February when it awarded contracts totalling $9.4 million to three Southern textile companies, Dan River Mills, Inc., Burlington Industries, Inc., and J. P. Stevens & Co., Inc. Immediately Sen. Walter F. Mondale (D-Minn.) urged Deputy Defense Secretary David Packard to hold up the contracts because the companies had been charged earlier with discriminating against black job applicants. Packard said he had approved the contracts on the basis of "assurances of affirmative action" from the companies that they would move toward ending any racial discrimination in their mills. The Labor Department's Office of Federal Contract Compliance (OFCC) had expressed doubts the month before about the companies' employment policies and it also found that company-owned housing for employees was segregated. Few black women were ever hired, the investigators said, and black men were rarely promoted. The OFCC recommended that the firms be barred from federal bidding.

Roy Wilkins, chairman of the Leadership Conference on Civil Rights, asked President Nixon to review the contract awards. James Hamilton, chairman of the conference's Committee on Compliance and Enforcement, asked Packard to hold up the Defense contracts until "crystal clear proof" was shown that the textile companies had revised their hiring practices. Hamilton pointed out that the Defense Department would be violating a 1965 Executive Order requiring companies with records of racial discrimination in employment to adopt "affirmative action programs" in order to qualify for government contracts of $1 million or more. At the same time, Sen. Strom Thurmond (R-S.C.), Rep. Mendel Rivers (D-S.C.), Sen. John Stennis

(D-Miss.), and Robert Stevens, former Secretary of the Army and president of J.P. Stevens & Co., complained that the fair employment demands were "unreasonable."

The awards were granted. Packard said he had a "gentlemen's agreement" with the companies that they would shape up and he insisted there was advancement for blacks in the arrangement. "We are considerably ahead of where we would have been on any of the other courses recommended to me," he explained.

In March Sen. Mondale was joined by Sen. Edward Brooke (R-Mass.) in his demand that Labor Secretary Shultz cancel the contracts Packard had awarded the month before. The NAACP Legal Defense Fund charged that the government had awarded the contracts illegally.

The political battle grew. Sen. Everett Dirksen (R-Ill.) threatened to go to the "highest authority" to fire EEOC chairman Alexander for "harassing" Southern textile firms. This ultimately led to Alexander's resignation (see Politics), although the EEOC had little to do with this particular issue. Sen. Edward M. Kennedy (D-Mass.), chairman of the subcommittee investigating racial policies of the Nixon administration, called Dirksen's warning a "great disservice to [Alexander] and the American people." Thurmond and Dirksen kept up the attack on civil rights officials while Kennedy and Sen. Philip A. Hart (D-Mich.) attempted to document a charge that the Pentagon had eased compliance procedures for awarding contracts.

Then came word from the White House that Alexander would be replaced even though his appointment was effective until July 1972. Alexander, who resigned as chairman but stayed on the Commission, insisted that he had been enforcing the law, not harassing businessmen. He lashed out at the administration for its "crippling lack" of support for his campaign against institutionalized bigotry. William H. Brown III was named EEOC chairman to replace Alexander.

Shultz came to Packard's defense at this point. He said "intensive mediation" was the key to gaining compliance with the nation's anti-dis-

crimination laws, not hard-nosed cancellation of contracts. "I will insist that all federal contractors take affirmative action wherever we find deficiencies in equal opportunity," Shultz said. He said he would implement a number of structural changes to strengthen the OFCC to coordinate its activities with those of the EEOC and the Justice Department.

In March 1969, Transportation Secretary John A. Volpe announced major changes in the equal employment program for federally-aided highway construction. Contractors no longer had to pass tests of non-discrimination before being allowed to bid on big highway contracts. Under Volpe's plan, standard non-discrimination clauses would be included in the specifications for new highway jobs costing $500,000 or more when they came up for bid. Clarence Mitchell, head of the Washington office of the National Association for the Advancement of Colored People (NAACP), called Volpe's action "spineless capitulation" to the road builders. "It just proves that the big powerful highway contractors, by use of their muscle, have forced the federal government to backtrack in fair employment," he charged. Volpe argued that the changes were "in no way a lessening of our determination to establish equal opportunity . . . as a way of life."

President Nixon urged the National Alliance of Businessmen to widen their search for jobs for the hard-core unemployed in 1969 by looking to the nation's smaller towns and cities. But at the same time his administration was pressuring business to curb inflationary spending. "Inflation must be checked," Andrew Brimmer had noted, "even at the inevitable cost of higher unemployment in black ghettos of the nation's cities."

Within the government itself, minority hiring continued to be slow. Interior Secretary Walter J. Hickel said the percentage of non-whites in his department was disappointing, "shamefully low," and unacceptable. He set about establishing surveillance teams to see that equal employment practices were "really being followed."

The House Agriculture Appropriations Subcommittee reported, about the same time, that some black employees of the Agriculture Department were earning $10,000 a year or more. Black professionals everywhere were finding it much easier to locate jobs. It was the labor unions, and in particular the building trades, that continued to resist change in 1969. Their resistance came to a head about the time the Labor Department announced what came to be known as the Philadelphia Plan.

The plan was to promote black employment in construction trades by insisting that certain quotas of non-white craftsmen be hired to work on federally-funded projects costing more than $500,000. It would begin in Philadelphia and later extend to other metropolitan areas as a means of implementing a provision of the Executive Order that established the OFCC. It was to apply to six crafts, including iron workers, plumbers and pipefitters, sheet metal workers, steamfitters, electrical workers, and elevator constructors.

Labor unions and others cried foul. Sen. Dirksen was quick to pressure President Nixon to hold up the plan on the grounds it would violate an employment section of the 1964 Civil Rights Act. However, Assistant Attorney General Jerris Leonard countered that the plan was "consistent" with the 1964 law. It was eventually ordered into effect in September after several months of argument within the government and negotiations with officials and organizations in nine cities.

The immediate goal for minority employment was four per cent, and the plan stipulated that it was to rise to 26 per cent within four years. Unions and builders in New York, Boston, Chicago, Detroit, Los Angeles, Pittsburgh, St. Louis, San Francisco, and Seattle would have to comply eventually.

Delegates at the AFL-CIO convention in September passed a resolution denouncing the Philadelphia Plan, as was expected. They argued that it was illegal under the 1964 law and insisted that it was not needed because the unions were making progress on their own. They claimed that more and more black apprentices were being hired and they insisted that membership rolls were open to all qualified members of minority groups. C. J. Haggerty, head of the organization's construction and building trades department, said the AFL-CIO was "100 per cent opposed to a quota system, whether it be called the Philadelphia Plan or whatever." AFL-CIO President George Meany said that while there was room for improvement, the construction unions had done a better job of hiring blacks than the Nixon administration, Congress, or the banking and newspaper industries.

It was time, Assistant Labor Secretary Arthur A. Fletcher said, to "quit looking at the civil rights movement without looking at the unemployment rate. . . . We are using contract law to achieve a social end." Some officials of the Nixon administration were soon predicting it would go further on job equality than ever before.

EEOC Chairman William H. Brown III charged that utility companies were among the "poorest performers" in abolishing discrimination. He said blacks hold only 4.8 per cent of the utility jobs and 2.8 per cent of the white collar positions. Less than .5 per cent of the utilities managers and professional employees are Negro, Brown said.

The U.S. Civil Rights Commission charged in May that the government had subsidized racial discrimination in hiring by cooperating with firms known to be violating the 1964 Civil Rights Act. It cited a Brookings Institution report calling for action against those companies and recommending that all fair employment problems be handled exclusively by the EEOC.

The U.S. Civil Service Commission came up with a plan for resolving discrimination complaints from federal employees. Beginning July 1 employees were told they could first discuss their problem with an EEOC counselor who would attempt to resolve it, then file a formal complaint for the worker if the attempt failed. The filing procedure has proved to be a lengthy one in the past.

In late July, Sen. Birch Bayh (D-Ind.) introduced legislation that would aid black construction companies. The bill provided for 90 per cent federal guarantees against loss to private surety companies, acceptance of certifications of competency in lieu of bonding for some federal projects and establishment of a national construction task force to provide technical instruction and counseling to small contractors.

In August the President called for a new manpower training act—the President's idea of a "New Federalism"—that would consolidate previous manpower legislation, the Job Corps, and the community work and training program of the Economic Opportunity Act into one system. He said it would unify control of state and municipal manpower programs. Eventually, all manpower funds would be channeled through the states. The plan provided for a "trigger mechanism" to release 10 per cent in manpower funds whenever the national unemployment rate hit 4.5 per cent or more for three consecutive months. The President said this act would "bring order and efficiency to a tangle of federal programs. . . . By placing greater reliance on state and local elected officials the day-to-day planning and administration of manpower programs will become more responsive to individual job training needs."

A fight had grown out of his earlier plan to transfer the Job Corps and Head Start from OEO to other departments. Rep. Carl D. Perkins (D-Ky.), chairman of the House Education and Labor Committee, said the President's proposed shift of the Job Corps to the Labor Department was an attempt to camouflage an intention to kill it altogether. Perkins said the plan would eliminate more than half of all Job Corps centers and affect 17,000 of the 35,000 youths learning trades there.

In April the administration said it planned to close 59 of the 113 centers and open 30 small ones in city slums. The Job Corps budget was cut by $100 million. Fifteen senators and 11 congressmen wired the President to protest the plan. They argued that it would be bound to spread discouragement among recruits whose training would be terminated. Perkins' committee estimated the closings would cancel out millions of dollars worth of effort already made.

Pollster Louis Harris reported that "blacks can make it" in spite of the "paralyzing" environment they live in and can earn almost as much as whites when given the chance. In overall wage comparisons, annual earnings for Job Corps graduates increased by about $1,000 after training. Gains were greater for graduates of conservation centers than for those of urban centers. He found, however, that after leaving the Job Corps blacks were falling behind. He said this might be an indication the Corps had no "staying power" or that the "old pre-Job Corps world" is quick to intrude on the graduate's life.

Congress, which had not been consulted about the Job Corps order, was critical. Senate Majority Leader Mike Mansfield pledged support to those urging the Nixon administration to suspend Job Corps cutbacks until a congressional review could be made.

The Senate passed the President's plan in June, and in July the Job Corps was moved to the Department of Labor. Labor Secretary Shultz said every enrollee would be given a chance to transfer if his center closed. "We do not anticipate the demise of the Job Corps," he said. "Rather we seek to improve its quality and relevance to the realities of the labor market."

Applying the Laws

The Equal Employment Opportunity Commission is the arm of the government charged with helping to lessen traditional prejudices and discriminatory practices that have kept blacks out of work or in low-paying jobs. Title VII of the 1964 Civil Rights Law prohibits job discrimination based on race, color, religion, sex, or national origin. Since its inception, the EEOC has been attempting to change the lives of many black Americans both by opening up new job opportunities and by chipping away at the old abuses: rock-bottom wages and dead-end jobs.

When Clifford L. Alexander was chairman of the commission he observed that one of the commission's biggest and most difficult jobs was informing people of their rights. He said that part was vital because the law only allows the commission to act after a complaint is filed by an individual.

In 1969 the EEOC's powers were still fairly limited, but in conjunction with the Justice Department and civil rights attorneys, court dockets were showing more and more anti-discrimination cases.

In January the Justice Department charged the Georgia Power Co. and local unions with discrimination in hiring and promotion. It charged that dual job classifications based on color were being maintained because blacks held only the lowest paying jobs and those with the least possibility for promotion. Whites were often hired over blacks, the government charged.

In a unanimous decision written by Associate Justice Hugo L. Black, the U.S. Supreme Court said that black members of the Brotherhood of Railway Carmen of America in Alabama had the right to take complaints of racial discrimination to federal court without following grievance procedures required by their union. The black carmen had charged their union and the St. Louis-San Francisco Railway Co. of Birmingham, Ala., with maintaining segregated job classifications. The case was sent back to the U.S. district court, where the original decision was later overturned.

The EEOC found "clear evidence" of a pattern of racial discrimination in the movie production industry and recommended that the Justice Department file a suit against all motion picture and television film companies and the movie industry craft unions.

Cannon Mills Co. of Kannapolis, N.C., was the target of the Nixon administration's first civil suit against a major Southern textile company. The suit, filed under the Fair Housing Act and the Civil Rights Act, charged Cannon Mills with holding black employees to "menial and low-paying job categories on account of their race or color," and with renting blacks company-owned houses in "physically separate areas" where services and facilities were inferior.

In July a U.S. district court, in a precedent-setting decision, upheld the Newark, N.J., school board's appointment of black administrators, despite the eligibility of whites with more seniority. Judge Anthony T. Augelli ruled that the board had not violated the civil rights of white teachers when it assigned blacks to 20 of the 55 available administrative posts.

Roy Wilkins, NAACP executive director, and Herbert Hill, director of NAACP's labor programs, announced that the association was launching a series of legal actions to try to stop work on government-financed construction programs until qualified black workers were hired. "It is clear that the Nixon administration has failed in its legal obligations to satisfy the statutory requirements of the Model Cities Act in relation to employment," Hill said. "It is the intention of the NAACP to prevent the continued use of federal and state funds to directly subsidize racial discrimination in the construction industry."

One of the suits, aimed at the Charlotte, N.C., Model Cities program, charged the Department of Housing and Urban Development with failure to implement requirements prohibiting racial discrimination in a federally-assisted program. Two other federal court suits were filed, one seeking injunctions to prevent federal, state, and local officials from proceeding with projects in Buffalo, and the other in Chicago.

The Washington Urban League and Julius W. Hobson, a local activist and statistician for the Department of Health, Education and Welfare, asked the U.S. district court in Washington to order broad reforms in the federal civil service system's hiring policies. They charged that the tests used for applicants were administered by whites and were designed around white standards. The suit charged that the tests measured cultural differences rather than intelligence.

The American Civil Liberties Union charged

that a "systematic pattern of racial discrimination in hirings and promotions" existed in the District of Columbia government.

A federal judge permanently enjoined Cone Mills Corp. from practicing racial discrimination at its Hillsborough, N.C., plant when a black woman filed suit claiming she was denied employment in favor of white women.

One employment agency in Los Angeles—Nancy Nolan, Inc.—was enjoined by the state of California from discriminating against applicants because of race, color, ancestry, or national origin. The agency had been charged with false advertising and with failing to consider applications of blacks or Spanish-Americans.

The steamfitters local in Los Angeles was ordered by the federal court to stop discriminating when it was discovered that the union had only one black apprentice out of a total of 160.

In New York State, discrimination charges were filed against the Westchester Fairfield Electrical Apprenticeship Committee, its six industry and labor members, and the president and business manager of Local 501 of the International Brotherhood of Electrical Workers.

In New York City, two black musicians accused the New York Philharmonic of discrimination because they were denied employment.

Maryland's Human Relations Commission charged that the state's own employment agency discriminates against its black employees. The commission's study showed that the Department of Employment Security discriminated in recruiting, promoting, and training of blacks and excluded them from top level staff meetings. The report recommended hiring a full-time equal employment opportunity executive to establish an affirmative action program and standards for hiring and promotion.

Businessmen Get Involved

An Equal Employment Opportunity Commission study released in 1969, based on a three-year-old study of 63,000 employers and 26 million workers, for the first time documented in detail the pattern of employment discrimination in each of the nation's major cities and industries. The EEOC concluded that discrimination is a "profound and pervasive condition in the American economy" and noted that "greater progress by Negroes brings forth progressively stronger discrimination against them."

Discrimination was found to be strongest in those industries that have a high proportion of Negro employees, where Negro and white employees have at least a high school education, and where both are employed in well-paying positions. In other words, if a large number of blacks have jobs in one industry, fewer can expect promotions; if a high number of blacks in an industry are better educated than white co-workers, the bias against them will be greater.

A study by William G. Shepherd, former economic assistant to the head of the Justice Department's antitrust division, found there was no essential difference between hiring patterns in the North and South. The companies hiring the lowest percentage of blacks were airlines, law firms, utilities, and cigarette makers. Those hiring the most blacks were beauty parlors, clothing stores, and restaurants.

But businessmen, to a great degree, were looking for solutions to unemployment in 1969. "Business alone cannot resolve the racial issue and government has been unable to," said Eli Ginzberg, editor of *Business Leadership and the Negro Crisis*. "It is up to business to open the opportunities to Negroes so that they can share in the jobs and the income which is controlled by business."

This theme had been sounded at the National Association of Manufacturers' 73rd Congress of American Industry the previous December. A. Wright Ellicott, National Alliance of Businessmen vice president for urban affairs, said, "There is no single solution, nor is there even a single sector in our society today that is capable, acting unilaterally, of resolving the complexity of problems that confront us. . . . We must be ingenious enough to convert social problems into market opportunities, if we are to activate the total resources of business in this crucial effort."

Dr. Charles F. Jones, president of Humble Oil and Refining Co., suggested that business has sound reasons for trying to alleviate the urban crisis. "Business should harness the enormously effective force of self-interest and put it to work in the social market place," he said. Jones also felt there should be "more direct eyeball-to-eyeball contact between the business community and those at the bottom of the economic barrel."

W. Armin Willig, former president of the Louisville (Ky.) Chamber of Commerce, said much the same thing. "Amid all this wealth," he observed, "let's not wait for these people to burn down the barn to get a little roast pork. We cannot become so immersed in the sea of details of our routine business affairs that we are unable or unwilling to use our enormous ingenuity toward improving the vital quality of our community existence."

Private businesses, frequently armed with Labor Department grants, joined government efforts and in some cases led the way to open up job opportunities for blacks in 1969.

The National Alliance of Businessmen (NAB) continued to play a significant role in finding jobs for the hard-core unemployed in larger cities. The NAB had been called together by President Johnson the year before to cooperate with the government in a combined effort to hire the jobless. The goal was set at 100,000 jobs by June 1969, and another 400,000 by mid-1971.

Government agencies located the jobless men and paid for part of the costs of hiring and training. But there were problems. The new workers were apathetic, frequently absent from their new jobs, and in many cases, illiterate. Veteran employees often resented the newcomers and in at least one case, that of the Miami Community Relations Agency, a discrimination charge was filed against an employer who hired a black man instead of a Puerto Rican.

The turnover rate among the new workers was 45 per cent. Commuting to suburban industries

was difficult and relatively few newly-recruited workers were able to take advantage of those openings. The shortage of day care centers continued to be a factor that prevented many employable black mothers from entering the job market, a problem shared by white women as well.

Arguments arose within industry over whether there should be pre-training programs, additional education offered by the companies, or special counseling given the new recruits. Firms with more than 5,000 employees did a good job of hiring because they were big and well-known, but in many instances smaller industries did not have this success.

A federal study of the NAB program called Job Opportunities in the Business Sector (JOBS) showed that by fall of 1969 only about a fourth of the anticipated jobs had been found. Under the program, General Motors Corp. provided nearly a fifth of the jobs, more than half to blacks, and managed to keep two-thirds of its recruits. Although most of the corporation's hiring was in Michigan, some took place at its plants in California, Kansas, Ohio, Missouri, and New York. GM also had an "affirmative action program" that ranged in activities from on-the-job training to evening classes in the three R's. Ford Motor Co. and the Chrysler Corp. also participated in the NAB program, bringing the auto industry's total to nearly one-third of those jobs placed by the NAB.

The Louisville, Ky., JOBS Now program contracted to train and place 1,400 men over a two-year period. In Los Angeles 15,900 men were placed through JOBS and in Chicago more than 12,000 were hired.

Many individual businesses and suburban industries responded by establishing guidelines and setting up training programs on their own. Aerospace Industries, one of the largest manufacturers in the U.S., provided more jobs for blacks, but under pressure from the federal government. A private company, Bonanza International, Inc., started construction on a new plant in the all-black community of Boley, Okla., that will produce pressure cookers for hickory-smoked meats. In Atlanta, Ga., the Southern Christian Leadership Conference teamed with the Chrysler Corp. to establish both an auto mechanic training program and a program to help set up new car dealerships.

In addition, RCA started an 18-month program to train men in four cities to become television repairmen. The "Four Cities" program included a review of basic education courses and intensive vocational training. All recruits were paid while they studied. The B. F. Goodrich Co. and the Progress Management and Economic Development group, a branch of Opportunities Industrialization Centers of America, began a joint program to train managers for Goodrich retail stores.

A cooperative program for training ghetto youths was started on Wall Street by a number of brokerage firms and banks. It was carried out in conjunction with Sponsors for Educational Opportunity, a non-profit organization that searches out young men with potential. The youths are sponsored and guided through high school and college, placed in jobs on Wall Street during vacation breaks, and encouraged to try for careers at all levels in the investment field.

A few companies and institutions—Chase Manhattan Bank, the New York Telephone Co., and Consolidated Edison—specially trained their supervisors in the psychology of dealing with the new black recruits. Businessmen of downtown New York attended seminars in minority hiring at the New School for Social Research, a new program sponsored by the Rockefeller Brothers Fund.

Allen T. Demaree wrote in *Fortune* magazine: "The leaders of American business have been trying valiantly to go beyond the mere rhetoric of social commitment—to really 'do something' about the snarl of problems that have come to be called the urban crisis. With characteristic enthusiasm, they have charged out into unfamiliar territory, charting courses in many directions. They have built plants in slums, assisted black entrepreneurs to get started in business, provided jobs for men previously considered unemployable, 'adopted' slum schools, and refurbished slum dwellings.

"If urban problems will yield to private enterprise solutions, they will do so only when businessmen apply to them the same dispassionate analysis they apply to the other aspects of their business. . . . For as Kenneth Clark, the Negro sociologist, has said, 'Business and industry are our last hope,' because 'they are the most realistic elements of our society.' Business 'must neither promise too much nor underestimate the magnitude of the task.' "

While some businesses steamed ahead with new programs of fair hiring, others resisted.

Congress of Racial Equality (CORE) officials criticized white businessmen in the San Francisco area for their "unfortunate response" to a CORE proposal to develop black capitalism. "It only proves that in the Bay area, as elsewhere, white people react to Negro demands only in crises," one CORE official said bitterly. The chapter had mailed out 800 invitations to white businessmen to attend a meeting to discuss the goals of a CORE offshoot, CORE Enterprise Corp. (CORENCO). Only 30 businessmen replied; 20 said they would attend.

In New York, the City Commission on Human Rights said that the advertising and broadcasting industries were continuing to discriminate against blacks in their hiring. "It is hard to use even the word 'tokenism' in describing the minority group participation in the advertising and broadcasting industries," commission chairman William H. Booth observed. The commission recommended that the Federal Communications Commission cancel or at least suspend the licenses of stations or networks maintaining discriminatory practices. It also asked that the industries stop requiring prior experience of prospective employees and initiate recruitment and training programs for blacks.

A report by the University of Miami's Center for Advanced International Studies accused the white community of Miami of not living up to its promises to black residents. "It is the black youth of Miami, as elsewhere, who feel deprivation and inequality with a burning indignation," the report said. "This feeling has been fed by well-meaning promises of jobs which did not materialize and by red tape in job applications."

A study for the Atlanta Community Relations Commission pointed out that businessmen failed to sign even one affirmative action agreement with JOBS Creation Atlanta, a project funded by EEOC to find jobs for black Atlanta residents.

Roy Innis, national chairman of CORE, came uninvited to demand $6 billion from the U.S. banking industry for "past injustices" at a meeting of the Bankers Conference on Urban Problems. The money, he said, would be used to start a Black Urban Coalition which would aid black banks, finance black businesses, and develop a risk capital pool for economic development programs. Innis did not set a timetable for payment, but threatened violence if his demands were not met.

At a later meeting, Floyd McKissick, former chairman of CORE, backed the demand. "America owes the black man something," he told the bankers, "and I think $6 billion is a good start." McKissick said he held the banking industry responsible for the black man's position. "There are 14,000 commercial banks in the United States with over $300 billion in loanable funds," he said. "Of that, black-controlled banks command only about $300 million." If they were really concerned about solving problems in the ghetto, McKissick told them, they must invest money there.

The efforts of some businesses were laudable, however.

The NAACP gave Humble Oil and Refining Co. a merit award "in recognition of outstanding and unusual contributions toward better race relations and the achievement of equal opportunity without regard to race." In 1968 about 30 per cent of Humble's employees were non-white. The majority of Negro employees were white collar workers and professionals.

Also notable were the integration efforts of the Allied Radio Corp., which stressed in its advertising that it was an equal opportunity employer. The corporation's work force is now about 60 per cent black.

Blacks and the Unions

A growing number of black union members challenged white labor leadership in 1969, demanding an end to discrimination in both union membership and organization. Herbert Hill, national labor director of the NAACP, said that black power was finally challenging the traditional system of racial control by whites over blacks in labor.

The noisiest, angriest, most bitter of all the Negro groups pressuring for change were the young black revolutionaries, wrote Harry Bernstein in the *Los Angeles Times*. "It is the revolutionaries who are ready to tear down the old structure of unions and corporations because, they charge, the progress which has been made in race relations is meaningless," he observed.

James J. Matles, secretary-treasurer of the United Electrical, Radio and Machine Workers of America, saw a "really tremendous ferment in the rank-and-file of the mass production industries. . . . The young workers, especially—white and black—feel terribly hard-pressed economically, and they are disgusted with the complacency of the union leadership," Matles said. In his opinion,

> the black caucuses in the unions are an outgrowth of the failure of unions to meet the problems of the black workers. . . . Blacks want to be an integral part of the leadership of the union. . . . Until these needs are met by union leadership, not only are we going to have black caucuses within existing unions, but we're going to have black unions in America, and that, in our judgment, would be a very serious development, threatening the possibility of gains both of the white workers and the black workers.

The pressure was applied most heavily on the

auto and building trade unions, but others also felt the heat in 1969.

The Taylor Law, enacted in 1967, opened the way for employees to join any union of their choosing and required state and local governments to bargain collectively with organizations that represent a majority of workers. Seeds of discontent within unions historically dominated by whites flowered into strikes against both unions and industries where union members worked.

Of the country's 18 million union members, nine per cent were black. Few held top union or highly skilled jobs. The black revolt already being felt by cities and college campuses demanded decent working conditions, equal wages, a stronger black voice in labor decisions, and more black plant managers, foremen, and union representatives.

Within the automotive industry, which led in the hiring of hard-core unemployed, small groups of black militants were able to disrupt production by demonstrating or striking. Racial trouble erupted on the lines. Revolutionary organizations began sprouting in the spring. In September 1968 a black caucus had formed within the United Automobile Workers (UAW) to demand equal pay and treatment. The group, the National Ad Hoc Committee of Concerned Negro UAW Members, started at the Ford Motor Co.'s Rouge Works in Dearborn, Mich. It charged that only 7.5 per cent of the UAW's international representatives were black and said blacks held only 7 per cent of the key staff jobs in the union. The movement spread to other plants. As one revolutionary pamphlet put it:

Something is happening in the ranks of American labor and neither the bosses nor the union bureaucrats are pleased. . . . It is one of today's most significant struggles. . . .White supremacy in the unions and the working class must be attacked as the basis for developing class consciousness and the solidarity necessary to battle the ruling class. . . . How can there be togetherness, for instance, when a 20 per cent, across-the-board wage increase or seniority rights mean one thing to the white worker and quite another to the black, who is paid less for similar work; who is the last hired, first fired; who is rarely promoted; who is forced to live in a ghetto; who is systematically miseducated; who is discriminated against in every aspect of life?

The organized revolutionaries in the auto industry were estimated at 500, a fairly small number, in June 1969. The number of sympathizers, however, was incalculable. Production in plants was halted for short periods in June by black-led strikes and demonstrations. Products and production machinery were sabotaged. White workers' reaction to this was sometimes violent.

A union spokesman reported outbreaks of trouble in Detroit, including knifings, physical assault, and arson. "These people do scare me," a union official said of the black revolutionaries. "I admit it. But I'll be damned if I will back away from the UAW position that there is just no such thing as a black solution to problems any more than there is a white solution. We have to work together." A revolutionary countered, "Unions and companies have kept us jammed up in this 'black and white unite and fight' nonsense too long now." The UAW, a promoter of brotherhood for 30 years, "probably could not get a white majority for neighborhood integration," said Mardellius Ivory, the first black UAW regional director. But, he insisted, "we have achieved a large measure of on-the-job democracy."

Later in the summer the building trade unions exploded with trouble and Chicago and Pittsburgh felt the brunt of it. As Rev. Jesse Jackson, head of SCLC's Operation Breadbasket, explained it, "Black people were in a despair a couple of years ago over welfare and warfare and so they could think of nothing to say except 'burn, baby, burn.' Now when we realize that plumbers are making $15,000 and $16,000 a year we decided to change our slogan to 'build, baby, build.' "

But George Meany retorted that there could be "no basis for cooperation with so-called militant groups who pretend to represent these minority people who threaten violence. Nor can the training of skilled mechanics be turned over to people who are completely without competence in this industry."

"Nowhere in America are the patterns of prejudice more stubborn . . . than in the craft-union hiring halls," wrote Lyn Shepard in the *Christian Science Monitor*. He went on:

> The blacks want jobs and training as extensively and as rapidly as possible. Craft unions retort that there can be no such thing as 'an instant craftsman.' Troubles are localized, for the most part in Chicago and Pittsburgh, but the problem is a national one. And, the issue—the blacks' charge of racist practices and closed doors for minorities in the construction industry—is hotly controversial and probably will continue to be explosive. . . . A showdown looms between white construction workers and blacks who want to join them.

In Chicago in mid-July 17 young blacks from the new Coalition for United Community Action seized the office of the president of the Chicago Building Trade Center. The coalition, an alliance of 61 black organizations, demanded at least 9,000 on-the-job training positions for blacks within 90 days on $80 million work of urban renewal and federally-aided Model Cities construction projects. They also asked that blacks with four years of construction experience be made foremen on construction jobs in black communities, that construction in black areas be approved by the community, and that the union hall referral system of assigning jobs be abolished. The following weeks were marked repeatedly by demonstrations, many of which turned into violent clashes with police.

Construction on 20 projects was halted by young blacks who stormed onto the sites and ordered workers off the job. An Illinois state court injunction against demonstrations failed to halt encounters between pickets and union men in August. When negotiations between the blacks and the industries and unions were reopened

in September, construction sites also were reopened.

Little progress was made in the negotiations. Leaders of the building trades rejected black demands with the argument that contractors should not be forced to hire unqualified workmen. They said earlier attempts to interest young black workers in apprenticeships had failed.

The head of the black coalition, the Rev. C. T. Vivian, met with the Chicago Building Trades Council and representatives of the Building Construction Employers Association. He said their offer of 1,000 journeymen jobs and training programs to boost further minority employment was unrealistic. "The paper presented to us by the two groups is not a response nor a complete program," he said. "It is not just, not serious, nor does it deal with our needs. We would not be in control of our own program. We must reject it."

Building trades officials later charged that the coalition leader had "walked out" of the meeting. Arthur F. O'Neill, president of the builders association, said his group was "terribly disappointed" and thought the coalition was making "a terrible mistake in summarily turning down our proposal."

There were more demonstrations. Rev. Ralph David Abernathy and Rev. Jesse Jackson of SCLC came to support the movement. Labor Department officials intervened in hopes of selling a "Philadelphia Plan" to the bickering parties. That plan, introduced earlier in the summer, required builders working on government contracts to hire a certain quota of black workers.

A team from the Department of Housing and Urban Development also investigated the Chicago situation to determine if the building industry had violated federal requirements calling for recruitment of minority workers. Mayor Richard Daley offered to mediate the dispute, but was turned down.

A tentative agreement was worked out by the two parties under which the unions would hire 1,000 blacks for skilled construction jobs immediately, and an additional 3,000 within a year. At the last moment, the coalition rejected the idea because control of the training would be left entirely in union hands. The coalition organized a "Black Monday" demonstration in September and 4,000 supporters rallied, marched, and demanded jobs for blacks. Several days later more than 2,000 angry white construction workers swarmed through downtown Chicago to protest federal plans to withhold funds until minimum quotas for hiring blacks were established.

On the third day of demonstrations by white workers, fighting between protestors and police erupted when the workers attempted to block Negro leaders from entering the U.S. Customs House where hearings on discrimination were being conducted by the Labor Department. Several demonstrators and policemen were injured and Labor Department officials were forced to close the hearings after the second day. An appeal for renewed negotiations was made, but when Mayor Daley called a meeting to try to settle the dispute he failed to invite black coalition head C. T. Vivian. The minister charged that the mayor had bypassed the coalition deliberately.

The labor trouble in Pittsburgh had begun in mid-August when demonstrators shut down construction on 10 projects worth more than $200 million. Members of Pittsburgh's Black Construction Coalition, claiming the support of all black groups in the city, demanded more jobs.

A study by the Mayor's Commission on Human Rights had shown that 2,200 men or seven per cent of Pittsburgh's building and trade union members were black. About a quarter of the Teamsters' Union was black, as was nearly a half of the Construction General Laborers Union. But in four unions—the International Brotherhood of Electrical Workers, Asbestos Workers, Bridge and Iron Workers, and Elevator Constructors—there were no blacks at all.

In 1968 Operation Dig-in, a project backed with Labor Department money, had trained 67 black workers in Pittsburgh. The next year plans for an Operation Dig-in II to train 110 men were rejected by the Pittsburgh Master Builders Association. As a result the Black Coalition was organized to fight for more training programs. The renewed demand was for a minimum of 1,130 jobs in one year and a minimum of 40 per cent black membership in each craft union within two years. In addition, the Coalition wanted training programs to be limited to eight months and asked that a fifth of the trainees be recruited from detention facilities in Western Pennsylvania.

The first day of organized protest was peaceful. But on the second, policemen and demonstrators clashed and there were mass arrests. The Coalition rejected an early offer by the Pittsburgh Building Trade Council for a program of apprentice training for 100 unskilled blacks. The U.S. Steel Corp. was singled out as one major target when it refused to halt construction on its new headquarters building—a maneuver sought by blacks to put pressure on white unions. Contractors finally agreed to suspend work at major construction sites for five days in hopes that the negotiations could settle the differences. In return the Coalition agreed to cancel further protests while the talks were going on.

As soon as the demonstrations were halted, white construction workers began their own organized protest to demand work, pay, and "Wallace for '72!" The truce with the Coalition made the white workers increasingly bitter as payless days mounted. They stormed Mayor Joseph Barr's office to demand payment of wages lost because of the shutdown.

"In closing down the construction projects, maintenance of the peace was the primary consideration," Barr said in his own defense. "I recognize that there is justification for protest on both sides, but in the final analysis, as mayor, I must consider the safety and well-being of the entire community."

"If whites are outraged at a two-day stoppage," Roy Wilkins of the NAACP countered, "Negroes are outraged at a stoppage that for them has lasted all their lives." "Either black men work or nobody works," said the NAACP's labor director, Herbert Hill. "We are not going to allow billions of dollars of federal, state, and municipal funds to be used to subsidize racial discrimination in the construction industry." Hill said the NAACP would file suits to stop all construction being undertaken with federal money to back up demands that more blacks be admitted to craft unions.

The negotiations were described as "fruitless," but they continued. After more demonstrations in September, federal negotiators finally had to come to Pittsburgh to try to help out. Black leaders charged that the union was using stall tactics and called for a summit meeting of civil rights groups in eight cities.

The AFL-CIO continued to back the Pittsburgh locals by quoting statistics of its own. The executive council of the AFL-CIO building and construction trades department said the Apprenticeship Outreach program begun in 1967 had signed up a record 1,537 black youths in skilled trades between January and June 1969. "Ninety-three per cent of the total number were indentured in the building and construction trades, although these trades represent 56 per cent of the total registered apprentices in all industries," the council said. "We make the flat and unqualified recommendation to local unions throughout the United States that for a stated period of time they should invite the application of qualified minority journeymen for membership . . . provided they meet the ordinary and equally administered requirements for membership."

The AFL-CIO declared itself "unalterably opposed" to the quota hiring system set up in the Philadelphia Plan, which was perhaps the most significant and most fiercely debated labor development in 1969.

By the end of 1969 the fledgling Philadelphia Plan survived a major attack when an appropriations bill rider to block the plan's implementation was defeated in both houses of Congress. The rider, backed by a curious alliance of liberal Democrats, the AFL-CIO, and racial conservatives, specified that no funds could be spent on any program or contract that the controller general said contravened a federal law. The issue splintered the civil rights coalition and divided the ranks of congressional liberals. "The only brownie points you get for supporting the Philadelphia Plan are in Heaven," one prominent Senate Democrat told *Washington Post* writer Laurence Stern. One House liberal told Stern that "the pressure is just murderous. If I vote against the plan, that's bigotry. If I vote for it, these unions will want to kill me." Four Senate civil rights liberals dependent on union support in upcoming campaigns for re-election voted against the Philadelphia Plan. They were Albert Gore (D-Tenn.), Thomas Dodd (D-Conn.), William Proxmire (D-Wisc.), and Ralph Yarborough (D-Tex.).

The Nixon administration announced soon after the defeat of the rider that it would follow up the Philadelphia Plan with more drastic steps to reduce the wage disparity between white and black workers on a nationwide basis. Arthur Fletcher said the administration also would attack discriminatory hiring practices in Southern states such as Mississippi, Alabama, and Louisiana, which depend a great deal on large federal contracts. He said his office of contract compliance would formulate percentage goals for minority hiring in cities all over the country. Goals applied to federal contractors would be governed by the overall non-white percentage of the local labor market, with a minimum level for most job categories of 11 per cent. In some cities, where blacks comprise 25 to 30 per cent of the total work force, contractors would be told to apply a standard close to that percentage.

The Chicago and Pittsburgh outbursts of 1969 were the most spectacular of the year, but there were major strikes against the building trade unions in other cities, too.

Twenty-six city construction contracts totaling more than $6 million had been held up in New York in November 1968. The previous May, Mayor John V. Lindsay had ordered all contractors working on city-financed projects to hire a certain percentage of blacks and Puerto Ricans. Unions were slow to comply, however. Local 28 of the Sheet Metal Workers, for one, with 3,000 members, remained all-white.

Elsewhere, a dispute over the hiring of blacks stalled work at the University of Buffalo in New York and at Amherst College in Massachusetts. Officials in Buffalo announced that no contracts would be awarded for campus construction until agreement was reached on a program for a racially-integrated work force on all phases of the project.

The Minority Coalition in Buffalo was selected to screen the unemployed for training and for jobs. In September the Construction Industry Employers Association, the Building and Construction Trades Council of Buffalo and Vicinity, and the Minority Coalition agreed on a program to recruit, train, and employ nonwhites in the construction industry. The agreement ended the moratorium on construction of the $650 million Buffalo campus. The plan provided for a 10-man board of directors, composed of builders and members of the unions and minority coalition, to hire a training staff, arrange for facilities for training, and place the new workers in jobs. Their goal the first year was 350 to 500 trainees.

Seattle, Wash., was hit by a building trades strike in September. The Building and Construction Trades Council there rejected a plan to put unskilled black men to work on four public building projects. However, the Associated General Contractors agreed to hire one unskilled black worker for every four white workers on the jobs. The city and county agreed to increase the costs of the building project by a fifth to fund the program. Later in the month 200 demonstrators, one-third of them black, lined up on the runway at Seattle-Tacoma International Airport to protest the shortage of the construction jobs. They succeeded in closing a building project.

Major trouble was averted in Peoria, Ill., when trade unions and contractors agreed to place 75 blacks in skilled building trades within 60 days at full journeymen's pay.

The building trades were not the only ones that faced racial trouble in 1969. The South Carolina locals of the International Ladies Garment Workers Union struck the Wentworth Manufacturing Co. in October. It began after Wentworth tried to impose a double standard wage agreement. It had proposed that workers in the Florence plant, most of whom are black, receive lower wages under a new contract than workers in the Lake City plant, most of whom are white. The union refused. The picket lines went up and SCLC launched a national boycott of Wentworth products. There was great cooperation between black and white strikers; the picket lines were integrated during the four months the strike lasted.

The National Labor Relations Board said it was filing a formal complaint against the company for violating provisions of the National Labor Relations Act. It was charged with refusing to sign a contract after a first, substantial agreement had been reached in negotiations. After settlement, the strikers were reinstated with full job and vacation rights, expanded medical and hospital insurance benefits, and work guarantees.

Black unionists threatened to walk out of the New York City Central Labor Council in November 1968, saying they would not support the teachers' strike because it went against the black community. They demanded that the council head, Harry Van Arsdale, Jr., try to end the strike and they charged Albert Shanker, president of the teachers' union, with racism. They accused him of trying to crush school decentralization efforts.

A garbage workers' strike in Macon, Ga., went on for two weeks in March 1968 and was settled after the SCLC, NAACP, and AFL-CIO had met with the city's mayor. This new agreement clearly guaranteed the men better working conditions.

Retail workers in New York severed ties in April with the AFL-CIO, charging that the organization had failed to provide "aggressive and progressive" leadership for black and Puerto Rican workers. The retail workers' leader, David Livingston, said, "To say you're for civil rights is not enough any more; everybody is for civil rights. The oppressed want power and some share of responsibility and they have not generally found relevance in the labor movement." He announced that his union would work with the alliance of the United Auto Workers and the Teamsters in an attempt to organize workers in light manufacturing, wholesale trades, direct mail, and corrugated box industries. The local union was granted an interest-free loan of $120,000 from Walter P. Reuther, president of the UAW.

In September garbage workers in Charleston, S.C., struck after their requests for wages of $3 an hour, improved benefits, and union recognition were denied. The SCLC and the National Council of Distributive Workers of America backed the marchers when they renewed their demands at city hall. Charleston was also the scene of a major hospital workers strike that drew nationwide support of officials and civil rights leaders.

"Threatened on one side by the racist and semi-racist rumblings of Wallace supporters," Carl Shier wrote in *Dissent,* "and challenged on the other side by black workers who in their understandable anger sometimes succumb to a form of black nationalism that can slip into anti-unionism, we in the trade union movement are going to have our hands full these next few years. If unions are to survive in this country at all, we will have to find ways, in the day-to-day unglamorous life of the white and black workers, of creating the kind of solidarity which only a few decades ago gave birth to industrial unionism."

The Black Graduates

While the job situation for the hard-core waxes and wanes as the economy shifts, and although only about one per cent of industry's managers are black, there were not enough black college graduates in 1969 to satisfy industry demands. Black graduates at major and minor colleges were wooed by eager companies and recruiting on black college campuses hit an all-time high.

Florida A & M is one example. The placement director there reported that until recently 18 to 24 companies regularly sent recruiters to the Tallahassee campus. In 1969, however, representatives from about 500 firms came looking for graduates to fill jobs "right across the board in business and industry." Southern industries, however, were still under-represented.

One manifestation of the demand for black graduates was the rise in the number of personnel agencies finding jobs for skilled and professional blacks in industry.

San Diego community relations specialist Carroll W. Waymon spoke for many, however, when he described the darker implications of the increased demands for black graduates. "I feel that I cannot be a man, just a man, and a Negro at the same time," he said. He continued,

> To me, being a Negro or a black man is to play a role. And it's this perception of me that causes me to have to play that role because of my blackness that I resent most. . . . This dichotomy that one lives with . . . I think is the core of the reaction of the black man. He cannot, for example, be just another bum, just another criminal or saint or good man. He must be a Negro or a black man. He must be a Negro doctor, or a Negro principal, or a Negro reporter instead of just being a reporter, a doctor, a man.

Black Youth

New York's Neighborhood Youth Corps ran into trouble in January about the time its director, Willie J. Smith, lost his job in a reorganization shuffle. The city's four-year-old Human Resources Administration, the agency that controls the Corps, had been investigated for alleged corruption. The investigators found evidence of mismanagement and fiscal irresponsibility within the administration in general and the Neighborhood Youth Corps in particular. Smith charged that he was being dismissed by the administration to cover up for the mistakes of other administrators.

The General Accounting Office of the federal government told a congressional task force investigating New York City's antipoverty programs that at least $2.7 million had been embezzled from the Neighborhood Youth Corps during the two previous years.

Federal investigators also charged that the Youth Corps was "low on equal opportunity" because almost all its members were black. A spokesman for the Manpower and Career Development Agency defended the local Corps by explaining that it had been "designed not as an experiment in integrated education, but as a project specifically to provide work and work experience for teenagers living in poverty. In New York City most such teenagers happen to be black." A team of federal officials and private management consultants was appointed to oversee the Youth Corps and to determine whether the Human Resources Administration should continue to sponsor it.

A report by the Office of Economic Opportunity in February on the country's 1968 summer programs for youth pointed out that the programs had fallen short of their goals. "Nothing could be clearer than the fact that teenagers and target area residents ranked summer jobs first in importance," the report said. "But too often, the community did not listen to, or did not heed the wishes of program beneficiaries."

In June District of Columbia officials and inner-city leaders told congressmen that federal help would be needed to get the city's summer job program off the ground. The officials praised the private sector for what had already been done, but noted that it was too expensive and too risky for businesses to handle on their own. The Metropolitan Washington Board of Trade later completed its successful campaign for summer jobs for area youths 24 per cent over its goal.

A survey of summer jobs programs in a number of major American cities showed a

degree of progress in race relations. The Neighborhood Youth Corps made the largest effort nationally, finding jobs for 338,000 young people. It operated under an appropriation of $136 million.

The summer jobs survey noted that "almost everyone agrees that a big part of the effort to find jobs stems from a desire to keep peace in the cities, but they say much more than that is involved. Although a number of black militants scorn the effectiveness of the programs," the report went on, "they are generally better received in the black communities than the many antipoverty efforts. The main complaint is that there are not enough jobs to go around."

"We feel that young people for a long time have been left out in the cold, but young people can be successful," said Joseph Gant, manager of a Gulf service station in Washington, D.C., where members of Youth Enterprises, Inc., work. The group was organized by the city's antipoverty agency and funded by the Department of Health, Education and Welfare. "The whole idea," one youth said, "is to get guys trained to learn the whole operation from the bottom up and to encourage young people to go out and get their own businesses."

Toward the end of the Johnson administration, Assistant Secretary of Labor Stanley H. Ruttenberg called on directors of Apprenticeship Information Centers to stimulate in minority youth the desire to be skilled craftsmen. Ruttenberg said the skilled trades offer as promising a future as other careers. He asked information centers and school systems to "make sure that the curriculum is at least adequate enough to insure that the individual acquires the basic education necessary to prepare for apprenticeship."

In Los Angeles a Watts Labor Community Action Committee was set up by 11 international trade unions with federal funds to give jobs to young people. It has been successful in placing dropouts and "unemployables" from the depressed and riot-torn areas of Los Angeles.

In March Labor Secretary Shultz reported that apprentice training programs as of January

1969 were at a 20-year high, with minority groups showing a gain of 19 per cent over the previous year.

Enterprise

Blacks, who represent 12 per cent of the American population, own one per cent of the nation's businesses. During his 1968 campaign Richard M. Nixon often spoke of the need to encourage black capitalism. "We have to get private enterprise into the ghetto," he would say. "But at the same time we have to get the people of the ghetto into private enterprise—as workers, as managers, as owners." Nixon promised to make black capitalism "the federal central target" in his administration's attack on ghetto problems. After his election he announced that "the thrust of my program is to provide incentives to move capital into the ghetto, to develop local initiative and encourage local control, to provide the necessary training and encouragement, and thus to build pride and establish opportunity." So it began.

Reg Murphy wrote in the *Atlanta Constitution* in November 1968 that "one of the stated aims of the Nixon administration is to promote 'black capitalism.' The President-elect has said, 'It will cost little or no government money. . . . ' In the long run, Nixon may be wrong; it may be necessary for the government to help finance black capitalism."

In January Jeanne R. Lowe in the *Saturday Review* disagreed with that concept:

> To concentrate industry's and government's technical asistance efforts, cash, and loans on creating "black capitalists" in the ghetto where risks are highest and consumer incomes lowest, suggests a dangerous short-sightedness, racist cynicism, or both. The white businessmen who are trying to help aspiring black capitalists would do better to assist those entrepreneurs to go where the action and consumer dollars are — in the suburban growth areas, where they can command conventional insurance, serve a more affluent

middle-class market, and compete on equal terms. Sooner or later, the ghetto-improvers will have to admit what the Kerner Commission emphatically stated in its report's conclusion: "A Negro society largely concentrated within large central cities . . . will be permanently relegated to its current status, possibly even if we extend great amounts of money and effort trying to gild the ghetto." Black power will not become green power in the slums.

"There can be a partnership with business that will save time and be productive both for the country and for business," Richard A. Neeneman wrote in the *Christian Science Monitor*. He added:

> There is a lot to be changed to bring America's poorest 10 per cent into the 1970s. Think of it: slums to be rehabilitated or rebuilt; nurseries and schools to be built; many new inner-core transport systems; workers to be educated to minimum levels of mathematical and language proficiency and then trained for specific skills that will be needed in the 1980s and '90s (not for the jobs that will be phased out in the '70s). . . . Black capitalism will cost money.

On Capitol Hill legislators of both parties pushed legislation to set up a system of national, federally-aided, community-controlled development corporations.

Bayard Rustin felt that "there has to be a move on the part of Negroes to develop black institutions and a black image, and all this has to go on while they are going downtown into integrated work situations, while they are trying to get into the suburbs, if they can, while they are doing what all other Americans do in their economic and social grasshopping." Rustin concluded that President Nixon's plan to help blacks through black capitalism was as unrealistic as proposals to establish a separate black nation.

Dr. Karl Deutsch, a professor of government at Harvard University, observed: "What Negroes gain in building their self contained economy might be significantly better than what they could gain through more integration."

A study prepared for the Urban Coalition by Joseph M. Kircheimer, a Wall Street investment banker, said that too much emphasis was being placed on lending to small ghetto retailers restricted to segregated, low-income markets. He noted that the overwhelming majority of black businesses are eating places, beauty parlors, clothing stores, liquor stores, and second-hand shops. Most employ fewer than five people. Threats of racial violence, outrageous insurance rates, poor municipal services, and inadequate transportation into the ghetto all combine to make life for businessmen, black and white, increasingly difficult. And the ghetto entrepreneur, who accounts for less than one-half of one per cent of all retail outlets, is bucking an economic trend toward fewer retail businesses. Kircheimer also recommended greater efforts to establish "supplier companies" that would be helped by a parent corporation. After an initial period, direction of these supplier companies and controlling shares would go to black businessmen.

In March Rev. Ralph D. Abernathy, president of the Southern Christian Leadership Conference, renewed his call for "black socialism" in lieu of black capitalism. He said he would rather see federal aid to ghettos than the intrusion of capitalistic methods. Fellow SCLC official Rev. Jesse Jackson said black capitalism was "divisive."

"The term widens the gap between the poor black and his black brother," Mr. Jackson argued. "Blacks who have been exploited understandably reject the term as a cruel and cynical hoax imposed from without upon a powerless black people." George Meany of the AFL-CIO agreed. He said black capitalism offered no hope for economic advancement for minorities because the overwhelming majority belong to the working class. Some observers argued that the union leaders didn't want black ownership in industry, especially construction, because it would open up membership for greater numbers of blacks in the skilled construction trades, which have been closed to them in the past.

Georgia legislator Julian Bond of Atlanta said he was disenchanted with capitalism, and didn't like the idea of black capitalism either. Stokely Carmichael said the President's suggestions were so ridiculous it was a waste of time to discuss them.

"Black capitalism seems to imply the 'old fashioned' idea of building businesses through tedious time-consuming work," Roland Black wrote, "in contrast to some militants' plans for 'instant' prosperity based on violent revolutionary protest." Black continued:

> While there have been outstanding Negro businessmen, comparatively few black people derive their incomes from Negro-owned firms. The term "black capitalism" has a segregated sound that some people don't like. They note that capitalism implies free markets, while "black capitalism" seems to connote a restricted market. Another charge is that "black capitalism" would be a means by which the federal government could manipulate the black community's economy, leaving black people, as ever, in a dependent situation.

Roy Wilkins and Whitney Young endorsed President Nixon's proposals in principle, although they refused to back him completely. Berkeley G. Burrell, president of the National Business League, had always felt that black capitalism was a reasonable objective. "Criticism of the concept results from a failure to recognize the nature of . . . inequities which are the result of racism," he said in an interview. He continued:

> Black capitalism has as its objective the elimination of these racial inequities as they affect black participation in ownership and management. The solution to this problem is in bringing about change in the economic system which will effect equitable distribution of income and wealth and eliminate poverty. Businessmen provide the real leadership in our country. Our politics, our economy and virtually all other aspects of our existence come under the influence of capitalists and entrepreneurs. If, in our current system, black people hope to acquire real influence and assert relevant responses to our needs, we must

acquire the tools of influence. Those tools are land, labor, capital, and business enterprise.

"Concentrating mainly on jobs will doom the black," former Congress of Racial Equality official Ken Scott said. "There must be a massive effort at economic development to change the ghetto to producers . . . ultimately leading to a greater sovereignty."

Black leaders told Columbia University's 35th American Assembly in April that they wanted a change in the system. "The business community controls the country," they said. "We want a piece of that control. . . . We want a new concept of the American economic organization. . . . We want opportunity. . . . We want subsidy." CORE national director Roy Innis spoke of a "new political unit" that would "regulate the flow of goods and services across our borders." Generally the group stressed the need for government's assurance that economic opportunities would open for blacks, and they said as much in a formal report of the meeting to the Nixon administration.

Marion Barry, program director of Washington's Pride, Inc., spoke in support of the black capitalism concept in May, saying it was "a fraud to delude us into moving politically rather than economically." Black people, Barry said, are "consumers of everything and producers of hardly anything." He added that once black people have economic power, "we can take political power."

At a June meeting of the American Management Association, economic consultant Dunbar McLaurin said "economic racism" practiced subconsciously by most white businessmen was at the root of the problem. He cited as an example the fact that only one company in *Fortune* magazine's 500 top companies has a black board member. At the same meeting, Howard Samuels, former head of the Small Business Administration, charged that the administration had downgraded black capitalism after raising the black community's expectations during the election campaign.

For the record, a survey in Indiana revealed that in most cases the most successful black businessmen were churchgoers, had stable family lives, had high school educations or more, and were either born in the North or had moved from the South when they were young. Only 8.6 per cent of those surveyed had received loans from the SBA.

It also seems "N-ach" may be an important ingredient in a successful businessman, said Harvard professor David C. McClelland to black businessmen speaking on the theory of the "need to achieve," or "N-ach." "Years of research have enabled us to pinpoint quite precisely the thoughts and actions which have to be learned if a person is to have a stronger need to do better all the time," he told them. He claimed that two years after taking part in training programs, the trained men generated nearly three times as much new capital and created twice as many new jobs as their untrained counterparts.

The Government and Black Capitalism

In November Joseph E. Danzansky, chairman of the Mayor's Committee on Economic Development, proposed that five shopping centers be built in the areas damaged in Washington, D.C.'s April 1968 riots. Danzansky said the idea was "to put black businessmen in first class facilities serving the black community. . . . We are determined to build a success syndrome into black entrepreneurship," he said. "A business advisory program is one way to do it." The plan calls for clusters of leased department stores, each shop to be run by an independent merchant who would get security, advertising and bookkeeping services from the development corporation. The Department of Commerce granted the committee an initial $300,000.

In Los Angeles the Economic Development Administration of the Department of Commerce has established the Economic Resources Corporation, a nonprofit agency set up to build an economic base in south-central Los Angeles. ERC makes loans and trains managers.

Another Los Angeles group, the South Central Improvement Action Council headed by Charles Knox, plans to build Ujima Village, a 115-acre development with 600 units of federally-financed housing and commercial enterprises. The organization has a grant from the Department of Commerce for business development and $3.5 million from HUD. "All the business of social programs is not making inroads," Knox said. "We need to expand the capital base in the black community from conventional dominance by whites . . . to sharing control . . . to eventual total black control."

The Economic Development Administration approved three grants in January totaling $1,032,488 to help establish small businesses in ghetto areas of 20 cities. The recipients—the National Business League, the National Urban League, and the Interracial Council for Business Opportunity—are giving management and technical aid and are opening up job opportunities to inner-city residents.

Black business and civil rights leaders were unsuccessful in seeking a "commitment" by the Nixon administration on black capitalism, and were unhappy with the results of meetings with the SBA.

In February James Farmer, newly appointed assistant secretary for administration in the Department of Health, Education and Welfare, said he had "every expectation" the Nixon administration would support a $1 billion-a-year legislative program endorsed by CORE to promote black capitalism. The plan called for establishment of a national Community Development Bank to float loans to local banks which would in turn finance new black businesses in slum areas.

Andrew F. Brimmer of the Federal Reserve Board said in an interview in March that he did not believe that minority businessmen could achieve a viable solution to the problems of urban development unassisted. "I look on the basic problem of the cities primarily as one of jobs," he said. "The key is expansion of job opportunities and upgrading positions within

businesses and primarily within the larger corporations."

President Nixon established an Office of Minority Business Enterprise (OMBE) under the Commerce Department to promote and expand business ownership by minority groups. The President said the new office would be "the focal point of the administration's efforts to assist the establishment of new minority enterprises and expansion of existing ones." He said one of the "priority aims of this administration" would be to encourage minority group business.

Secretary of Commerce Maurice H. Stans said the new office, staffed by 10 experts in various fields, would in no way interfere with established agencies. "They will still run their own programs," insisted Stans. He added, "The money in OEO will stay there and the money in the SBA will stay in the SBA." Walter Rugaber of the *New York Times* quoted one observer as saying that not much had changed. "It still means that if OEO wants to make grants to black business in Watts or Bedford-Stuyvesant it must check with Stans. It's just another layer of clearance."

Washington's Redevelopment Land Agency gave approval to Pride Economic Enterprises in April for a multi-purpose auto service center in the District of Columbia and found an inner-city site for Control Data Corporation's new computer components plant. Both organizations intend to offer training and new jobs.

In June the President's National Advisory Council on Economic Opportunity reported that "black capitalism cannot produce large numbers of wealthy black Americans in any short period of time." The report said while such a program may be valuable in developing racial pride and confidence, it would not involve large numbers of the poor and would not reach those most seriously in need in the city ghettos. "There is a serious question as to whether the separatist idea should be allowed to be stated as an official part of the nation's domestic policy," the council added. President Nixon passed the report on to Congress without comment.

The Senate Select Committee on Small Business held hearings to investigate the administration's programs for black capitalism. Sen. Robert J. Dole (R-Kan.) was the only defender of Nixon's program. The committee's chairman, Sen. Alan Bible (D-Nev.), blasted the administration's black capitalism program, saying the proposals were empty rhetoric backed by very little money. Small Business Aministration chief Hillary Sandoval, Jr., said SBA was not making direct loans, but depended on banks to make conventional high-interest loans. Sen. Mark O. Hatfield (R-Ore.) accused SBA of fabricating its forecast that banks would increase loans to businessmen. He said he feared the program would be axed when it failed to meet its unrealistic goals.

Secretary of Commerce Stans announced the first steps taken by OMBE to help blacks and other minority groups get "a piece of the economic action." In July a $200,000 grant from OEO was made through SBA in the National Bankers Association (a group of black bankers). The grant established a credit pool to provide loan guarantees and equity capital. A grant of $200,000 from the Office of Education was given Howard University in Washington, D.C., to establish a National Institute for Minority Business Education. SBA and the Economic Development Administration made a $650,000 grant to Rev. Leon Sullivan of Philadelphia to train shopping center developers in 13 important cities.

The National Association of Black Consultants and Urbanologists charged the federal government with "collusion and white favoritism" in the awarding of contracts to consulting firms. Association chairman Ford Johnson said he vigorously opposed the "prevailing plantation psychosis in the federal government that only white experts, white consultants, and white urbanologists are able to program the economic, educational, and social growth of the black community." Johnson estimated that only about one per cent of the $500 million allocated by the government for consulting services would go to black-

owned firms. Robert J. Brown, President Nixon's special assistant for black capitalism, said the charges would be investigated.

The Small Business Administration (SBA), set up in the Eisenhower Administration to help small merchants compete in the market place, underwent some changes in the hands of the Nixon administration.

Howard J. Samuels, SBA head under President Johnson, had said inner-cities would decay unless blacks were encouraged to take over the management of businesses there. He said SBA's Project Own, which can guarantee up to 90 per cent of direct loans made by banks to potential businessmen, was one way to development of the inner-cities. "I'm trying to make bankers fill an obligation they should fill," Samuels said. "Compensatory capitalism" is "the most economic and moral way I know to resolve the issue of great injustice to our minorities, to rebuild the inner-cities and to improve race relations," he said.

In November 1968 SBA announced it was setting up an Action Construction Team (ACT) with the means to create 70,000 minority-owned construction contracting firms during the 1970s by underwriting performance bonds.

A Black Economic Development Council was set up the next month to advise SBA on the problems of the nation's cities. Council members —representatives from 40 black organizations —included Rev. Ralph D. Abernathy, head of the SCLC; Sen. Edward W. Brooke (R-Mass.); comedian Dick Gregory; Mayor Richard G. Hatcher of Gary, Ind.; playwright LeRoi Jones; Roy Wilkins of the NAACP; and the Urban League's Whitney M. Young.

"Minorities in the inner-city are like the inhabitants of an underdeveloped nation," Samuels noted. "They can be aided—just as we did in our foreign aid programs, by applying a similar approach to problems of investment."

One major loan arranged through Project Own under Samuels was for Cornelius Pitts, owner of a Washington, D.C., motel, who borrowed $335,000 from the Industrial Bank of Washington. Pitts, a black man, had been unable to get regular financing through normal channels.

Washington Post columnist William Raspberry observed soon after Nixon's election that the Pitts loan "may have been a swan song for . . . Samuels. Samuels may become the first victim of the reaction of President-elect Nixon's selection of an all-white cabinet." Raspberry correctly predicted that Hilary Sandoval, Jr., a Mexican-American, would become the new director of SBA.

David P. Malone, acting SBA regional director in Philadelphia, said his office would loan more than $2.5 million to black businessmen in 1969. He said that during the first six months of fiscal 1969 half of all the loans granted in the Philadelphia area had gone to members of minority groups.

In New York loans to minority businessmen increased dramatically. Most of the gain, according to Samuels, was due to the acceptance by commercial banks of the idea of "compensatory capitalism."

Project Own ran into trouble in March. It was reported that in order to meet its goal of creating 10,000 businesses a year, the project would have to increase its loan rate to meet even half that number. Of the industries SBA counted on to provide managerial and technical help, only one national trade association, the Menswear Retailers of America, had committed itself to the program. Samuels insisted there were "30 industries" waiting in the wings and added, "They'll come in once they see a well-organized program to participate in."

During fiscal 1968, SBA's loss rate was nearly 12 percent of its loan disbursements. The future of SBA in 1969 was clouded and there was talk of budget cuts, despite the President's campaign promises to revitalize black capitalism.

Commerce Secretary Maurice H. Stans was given the job of coordinating all minority ownership programs for the new administration. Stans said he planned to leave Project Own in SBA but said he would see that it was coordinated more closely with other governmental efforts.

SBA's new head, Hilary Sandoval, said they would be "extremely careful" not to raise false hopes. "We don't want to be misunderstood," he said. "We will not set unrealistic goals, nor play a numbers game by starting any people off in business when by every sound standard, the odds are against them. It would be easy to make many loans and boast of our program, although at the same time we knew many were doomed to failure."

Phillip Pruitt, assistant SBA administrator for minority enterprise, said in May that there would be some changes in emphasis: the SBA would concentrate more on management assistance when loans were given and concern itself less with the number of minority loans it was making.

The Black Economic Development Council charged Sandoval with systematically undermining President Nixon's stated commitment to black business. It also accused him of slashing the goals of Project Own and of failing to move fast on black capitalism programs.

In July Pruitt resigned in "disgust and frustration." He said the President "just didn't support the program. Rhetoric, rhetoric, rhetoric, but no support. And it was more . . . it was the failure to back us up on the Hill."

Commerce Secretary Stans defended the administration and said that the new Office of Minority Business Enterprise the President had set up in March in the Commerce Department would soon show concrete achievements. Stans emphasized, however, that the office would coordinate programs of existing agencies and would have no power to make loans or grants.

By the end of November 1969 SBA reported that it had made 4,383 minority loans totaling $105.5 million over the first 11 months of the year. It said this compared with 2,389 loans totaling $46.6 million in 1968. It also reported that from September through November 1969 it had made 58 per cent of its loans to minority racial or ethnic groups. It said this was the highest percentage of minority loans for any three-month period.

Around the country, organizations and private groups also continued to lend their support to potential black entrepreneurs.

Floyd B. McKissick, former national director of CORE, started his own economic development corporation in October. He said his aim was to create new firms and to aid black businesses.

Rev. Jesse Jackson of SCLC's Operation Breadbasket organized a "Black Christmas Shop-In" in Chicago in 1968. He urged the black community to do its Christmas shopping at a black-owned shopping center that year. He said the shop-in, which proved enormously successful, was not an economic boycott but rather recognition of black priority and an affirmation of black people. Jackson promised Chicago children that Santa Claus, "a fat black man from the South Pole," would show up that year. When he did come, Santa wore a dashiki.

Nationally the Negro Industrial Economic Union, a nonprofit organization, continues to assist potential businessmen with training and financial backing. Jim Brown, the former Cleveland Browns fullback, is its president. The Union has offices in Los Angeles, Kansas City, Cleveland, Washington, and New York.

The Bedford-Stuyvesant Development and Services Corporation, created at the urging of the late Sen. Robert F. Kennedy, reported that it had doled out $5 million in low-interest loans from a pool of $100 million pledged by 80 banks in its initial year. The group had also begun work on a block of new apartments with a community center for its own headquarters and started a project to rebuild existing brownstone houses. Local black residents were hired to do the construction work. The corporation also persuaded New York authorities to build a $34 million community college in Bedford-Stuyvesant. The college is being financed partially with $7 million from the Department of Labor and with foundation grants.

In 1969 a New York newspaper ad such as the following found a backer right away. "Wanted immediately," it read, "$25,000, 10-year, 7 per cent loan for new personnel agency specializing in the placement of disadvantaged professional and technical minority group members." Similar agencies were springing up across the country.

In Detroit in 1969 the Inner-City Business Improvement Forum raised $2 million in loans and grants to start black businesses in the city's riot-torn slum areas and to advise new owners once they got started. The resulting black-owned businesses included a plastics firm, a supermarket, and a computerized accounting and management center that would provide services free to small businesses. Clothing stores, small groceries, restaurants, a cosmetics franchise, small building contractors, and a black-owned freight airline also were assisted.

In New Jersey, Ebony Business Men's Association, a nonprofit corporation, was set up to help existing minority businesses and to create new enterprises and jobs.

In 1968 the 180th General Assembly of the United Presbyterian Church had authorized its Presbyterian Economic Development Corp. to make a large share of its unrestricted investment funds available for loans to businesses and low-income housing projects owned and managed by minority businessmen or groups. The corporation reported later that it had approved 19 applications for a total of $2.1 million in loans.

New York City businessmen also are being assisted by Capital Formation, a volunteer organization of bankers and investment brokers who use their business connections to help potential businessmen obtain loans. They provide advice after the businesses are started.

In Washington, D.C., Charles Williams, chairman of the National Business League, urged black businessmen to take over retail liquor stores in the inner-city. Williams thought it would be an ideal project, because "there are more liquor stores in ghettos than anything else" and whites were eager to sell out. Ghetto residents, however, had been telling Washington's planners they would like to see fewer liquor stores in their neighborhoods. However, Williams was able to persuade the SBA to drop its policy of not lending to liquor stores and secured several loans for new businessmen. The new owners attended a series of workshops to learn methods of business practice.

In New York the Association to Assist Negro Business, Inc., also was helping finance aspiring black businessmen. The Association matches a candidate with a business that needs a new owner and then provides the necessary training. More than 24 major corporations and individuals have each pledged $10,000 to help the black-run association guarantee bank loans. Each recipient must agree to channel some of his firm's profits into a loan pool for 10 years to help other beginning businessmen.

The Urban Coalition's Coalition Venture Corp., in New York reported in August that it had lent more than $1 million to prospective businessmen since November 1968.

In Los Angeles the Black Economic Union announced in August that it had launched a campaign to find financing for freshman black businessmen.

In November the Ford Foundation gave grants totaling more than $1 million to the National Urban League in order to further economic, political, and social programs in slum areas nationwide. Whitney M. Young, the League's executive director, said the money would be used to build "ghetto power" in 25 cities by helping blacks buy and operate their own businesses and franchises.

In March the Ford Foundation also passed along $935,000 to a fund to develop black- and Puerto Rican-owned construction companies in Boston, Cleveland, Oakland, Calif., and New York. The New York Urban Coalition announced that its subsidiary, Coalition Venture Corp., would lend the new companies $150,000; the Commerce Department's Economic Development Administration approved a grant of $129,025, and the New York Model Cities Committee said it would provide the fund with $120,000. After local groups made their contributions, the fund amounted to $2.9 million. It

was earmarked for construction performance bonds and administered in conjunction with the United Contractors of America in New York.

Across the country workshops and courses were designed to help fledgling businessmen and to help their communities foster new business.

Nat Welch, director of the Atlanta, Ga., Community Relations Commission, remarked that many businessmen there wanted to help alleviate problems of their city but didn't know how to get involved. He said the city's new workshop on black entrepreneurship would be one way to start. Welch singled out a number of businesses he thought would be most promising for blacks. They included many traditional ventures and one or two new ones: automobile dealerships, service stations, carry-outs, small contracting firms, dry cleaning shops, clothing stores, food catering services, groceries, self-service laundries, and small manufacturing plants.

Northeastern University held a "Money Retreat" conference late in 1968 to introduce small businessmen to the techniques of raising capital to finance business ventures. The conference was held in cooperation with the Roxbury Businessmen's Association in Boston and the Small Business Development Center.

And at Chicago City College, a new adult education course was offered—"Soul Food as a Small Business."

Major Black Businesses

By 1969 black capitalism no longer just meant mom and pop stores or carry-outs that opened one month and closed the next. Black entrepreneurs were branching out into the big time.

In October Progress Plaza, the nation's first major shopping center owned and operated by blacks, opened in North Philadelphia. Its organizers began with pledges of $10 monthly from 650 members of Rev. Leon Sullivan's Zion Baptist Church who said they would support it for three years. Sullivan, a man of great energy, also obtained a $400,000 grant from the Ford Foundation. Working with his Opportunities Industrialization Center, Mr. Sullivan saw that the center was built in the ghetto area.

Winston-Salem, N.C., now is the first city in the nation with a black-owned transit system serving the entire community. The city's Safe Bus Co. had originally served only black neighborhoods. When Winston-Salem's bus system dropped its franchise, Safe Bus picked it up and now has routes in all areas. A $360,000 loan to the company was backed by SBA.

Jonco Laboratories, Inc., reportedly the first black-controlled pharmaceutical company in the country, was begun in Ohio. In Los Angeles, Progress Laboratories, Inc., was started with the help of International Rectifier, Inc.

In November 1968 the American Dream Soap Co. opened in Cleveland, Ohio, to produce its own brand of soaps and detergents.

In Memphis, Tenn., the international headquarters of the Mahalia Jackson Chicken System, as well as the first franchise of the company, opened for business. It was the first national fast-food chain under complete black management.

Soul singer James Brown started his own food franchise, Gold Platter, Inc., to set up a chain of restaurants "dedicated to the objective of providing investment and job opportunities for members of minority races." Its headquarters is in Macon, Ga. Brown also acquired his third radio station—WEBB in Baltimore—by the end of 1969.

Harlem Freedom Associates bought an F.W. Woolworth Co. building for $2 million and then leased it back to the company. The association is a limited partnership of Harlem citizens.

H. G. Parks, Inc., a Baltimore producer of sausage and scrapple, offered shares of common stock in January, reportedly the first public stock offering on a national scale by a black firm.

A new East Harlem furniture cooperative helped sponsor itself by selling shares to community residents for $5 each. It was the brain-

child of Stephen Press, who interested the Office of Economic Opportunity in his project and used the $242,000 it gave him to establish the New York Institute for Consumer Education and Development. The Institute founded the Cooperative Association of East Harlem and loaned it $35,000, which was to be paid back by selling $5 shares to community residents.

Inner City Industries, Inc., a black-owned investment company in Chicago, bought the Swift and Co. ice cream plant and then leased it to the newly-organized Park Manor Ice Cream Co.

In a riot-wrecked section of Palo Alto, Calif., the Black Business Coalition developed Nairobi Village, a center with a restaurant, three stores, and the Coalition offices. The project is being underwritten by SBA. The Unoja Construction Co., which employs young blacks, some with police records, was contracted to do most of the building.

Citywide Distributors, Inc., the first black-owned-and-managed distributor for Carling Brewing Co., opened in Cleveland. It was assisted by the Cleveland Business League, the Southern Christian Leadership Conference, and the Black Economic Union.

In New York Douglas Staten went into business with his own line of Afro-American greeting cards.

In Baltimore a second Super Jet Market, part of a national chain directed by a group of black ministers, opened for business. Another Super Jet also opened in Cleveland.

The "community relations" firm of Ford-Walters-Freeman and Associates opened offices in Mt. Vernon, N.Y. Among its clients are governments, businessmen, and individuals.

The nation's first predominantly black computer analysis firm, Scientific Analysis Consulting and Programming Support Co., opened an office in Washington. Its first contract was with the District of Columbia to study, design, and implement a data processing system. The company was backed by 15 black investors who each put in $200. The founder, Napoleon Rhodes, said, "The response was so beautiful I wanted to cry."

A group of five black businessmen, Community Associates, Inc., became the country's first black bowling entrepreneurs when they bought Detroit's Bowler-O-Drome building. The National Bank of Detroit loaned the men $350,000 on the strength of an SBA guarantee negotiated by Project Own officials.

The Black and Brown Trading Stamp Corp., owned by singer James Brown and former professional football player Art Powell, opened an office in San Francisco. The stamps picture Brown and are distributed by gasoline stations, groceries, furniture stores, and other businesses in the San Francisco Bay area.

Reuben J. Patton, president of Uptown Products Corp., announced that his firm had been contracted to distribute products of the Tom Huston Peanut Co., a subsidary of General Mills, in New York City.

Texas legislator Curtis Graves of Houston set up one of the country's first soul food franchises, Soul Food Houses, Inc.

A joint venture of seven black manufacturers in Chicago, United Distributing Cooperative, began selling their products, produced and packaged in Chicago by blacks, to Cleveland, Ohio, markets.

In the 12-month period ending in June, 14 blacks had opened car dealerships and were selling cars made by American Motors, Ford, and Chrysler.

In Nebraska, Time-Out, Inc., is building carryouts for black businessmen. Time-Out's president, Floyd Collins, said that one key to "making this kind of operation possible is the development by our company, working with an architect and manufacturer, of an attractive drive-in building which can be erected on the site in about 75 days using prefabricated sections. The cost saving permits us to offer a franchise in some instances for as little as $7,500 cash for a business whose total investment is more than $100,000."

And there were other new black businessmen

in 1969, some who had really been running businesses for other men or practicing their trades for years.

Albert Corley, a 30-year veteran of New York's garment district, finally was able to set up his own business, Corley Originals, to manufacture designs for misses sportswear. With the help of the Bedford-Stuyvesant Restoration Corp., a federally-funded program, he obtained a loan of $50,000. The corporation recommended two marketing experts as advisors to help Corley show and sell his dress designs. As one adviser said, "His forte is silk screen printing. He's an artist. But he knows nothing about selling or putting on a show. I can advise him on producing and financing."

In March a new menswear store, Charles Grey, Ltd., was opened in New York by Charles Conway, a salesman for 15 years, who got a loan through the Menswear Retailers of America and SBA. The retailers have pledged to help black entrepreneurs find store sites, set up shop, and select merchandise as well as extend long-term credit to the new businessmen.

Jackson Auto Parts, the first such black-owned store in Atlanta, opened for business in March. Its owners, Ira Jackson and Freddie Johnson, invested $40,000. The McGuire Tire Recapping Co. in Atlanta was the first black business set up by Operation Mainstream.

The first black-owned new car franchise in Philadelphia, Vassall-McClenton, Inc., was partially financed by a loan guaranteed by SBA.

All Pro Chicken, Inc., the first inner-city fried chicken outlet in Bedford-Stuyvesant, opened in May with SBA-guaranteed loans from the First National City Bank of New York, the Urban Coalition, and the Bedford-Stuyvesant Restoration Corp.

In New York Dunhill Personnel System sold six franchises to black men in the metropolitan area. The franchises were financed by loans from the Chase Manhattan Bank.

A cosmetic boutique selling Merle Norman products opened in Washington's elegant new shopping center, L'Enfant Plaza. Phyllis A.

Mann, a black woman, opened the shop with an SBA-guaranteed loan of $25,000.

Shepherd D. Roberts opened Shep's Household Products in Brooklyn, N.Y., with an SBA-guaranteed bank loan and another from the Bedford-Stuyvesant Restoration Corp. The products, Roberts' inventions, include vibrator back rests, baby training seats, combination brushes, and sponge scrapers.

And Washington, D.C., got its first female-owned-and-operated investment company in September when Millicent V. Bouey launched her Bouey Investment Co.

Troubles that plague white businessmen also plague black men who open businesses. They are robbed, beaten, and killed with the same distressing frequency.

"There is agreement that the big city ghettos, with ready markets and white merchants made uneasy by urban rioting, are a logical place to develop these black businesses," columnist William Raspberry wrote in the *Washington Post*. "But one fact has become painfully clear: You can burn a white man out of business, but you can't burn a black one in."

In September, in Fort Lauderdale, Fla., civil disturbances damaged several black businesses. The New Breed Afro Shop was one that was wiped out. Owner Benny Lacue said it was not a race riot. "They just did it to get their loot," he said bitterly. "We are Negroes. Why would they want to get us?" He said he would not rebuild. "By the time we recover some of the loss," he reasoned, "they'll have another riot anyway."

One 10-store shopping center in Delaware, the state's first venture into black capitalism, closed after hoodlums broke into it 16 times in one year and its insurance was cancelled.

The problem of keeping insurance was almost as bad as the problem of looting. Insurance companies become nervous when a business is constantly threatened by vandals. Premium rates are excessive and troubled areas aren't the only ones who pay. Neighboring businesses find their rates going up as well.

In December 1968 companies that insure buildings and businesses in the Washington, D.C., areas hit by the 1968 riots asked the courts for relief from the pressure of city officials. They said the demands of Mayor Walter E. Washington and Superintendent of Insurance Albert F. Jordan that they offer broader coverage were unreasonable.

Ohio set up a "fair plan" to aid inner-city residents whose insurance rates have nearly doubled in the past year. By January so many residents had applied that officials reported it would take a minimum of two months from the time they were contacted to determine if an applicant could be covered. Under the plan the state would reimburse all losses in riots up to 5 per cent of the total amount of fire insurance sold each year in Ohio. Anything over the 5 per cent would be paid by the federal government.

Fifteen black Illinois state legislators demanded that fire insurance rates be lowered in Chicago's black communities in February. They said existing rates were exorbitant and charged that the city's "fair plan" was mismanaged. State Rep. Lewis A. H. Caldwell said ghetto residents were being charged double and triple the normal rates, and he asked Illinois House Speaker Ralph T. Smith to find a way to lower the rate.

Before the "fair plan" was adopted owners either were not able to get insurance or had to pay up to six times the normal rates in Chicago's inner-city.

At about the same time, a committee of the Chicago Cosmopolitan Chamber of Commerce filed its criticisms of the insurance industry with the Illinois Insurance Placement Facility. The committee asked James Baylor, director of the state department of insurance, to make sure the insurance laws were being applied equally in the inner-city.

Dempsey J. Travis, a Chicago real estate man, told the Senate Antitrust and Monopoly Subcommittee in Washington that insurance companies were using the threat of race riots as a subterfuge to deny coverage at standard rates to automobile and property owners in ghetto areas. Dempsey said that riots were "simply a new excuse for denying or surcharging insurance in the black ghettos." "Some major companies have found black business profitable," he said, "because they can collect larger premiums for less risk in the black community. There is no other explanation for this type of exploitation."

Subcommittee chairman Philip A. Hart introduced legislation later to create an agency that would examine insurance firms and protect the interests of policy holders. He asked that the agency be financed by assessments on the companies themselves.

In Illinois, State Rep. Otis G. Collins introduced a bill in March to create an Insurance Advisory Commission to review departmental programs and prepare adequate legislation for ghetto neighborhoods. Collins questioned the logic of charging higher rates in riot areas. "What's odd," he said, "is that all the riots in the country over the past two or three years haven't cost what two or three" natural disasters have.

In New York the state insurance department fined the Royal Globe Insurance Companies in April for dropping Negro policy holders. The companies were charged $20,600—$100 for each policy canceled in Harlem and Bedford-Stuyvesant. The department ordered the policies reinstated, but Royal Globe said it would appeal to the courts.

Intermittently during the summer and fall McDonald's Systems, a chain outlet of carryout restaurants, had to close one inner-city franchise in Cleveland, Ohio, when a coalition of black organizers seeking black ownership demonstrated against four McDonald's hamburger stands. The Black Unity group demanded $10,000 and two per cent of the sale price to support community programs. McDonald's suffered from the economic boycott thrown up by the coalition and Negro Mayor Carl B. Stokes' hopes for re-election were almost dashed against the law and order issue raised by the city's whites. Just before election day Stokes announced that negotiations for the sale of the four restaurants to black groups would begin. The coalition withdrew its picket lines. Stokes was re-elected.

The Black Banks

A survey by United Press International showed that there were at least 20 black-owned banks in the United States in 1969, banks in which the total assets had grown more in the past five years than in the preceding 60. Birmingham, Ala., had a black-owned savings and loan company, opening in the downtown section in March with assets of $9.8 million.

Andrew F. Brimmer of the Federal Reserve Board said that "partly because of the legacy of racial discrimination and segregation in this country, very few Negroes have had an opportunity to acquire the experience called for in bank operations." He urged blacks not to hire other Negroes only because of the "skill gap" that could drag the banks down.

Large corporations were discovering that one way they could support the black community was to bank with these new institutions, as a relatively painless way to encourage economic development.

When the Chrysler Corp. started a program to encourage black economic development, it decided to deposit $100,000 in tax money every month in Atlanta's black-owned Citizens Trust Bank. Chrysler also opened accounts at the black-owned Bank of Finance in Los Angeles and at a bank in Detroit's black community. Olin Mathieson Chemical Corp. said in April it would deposit payroll withholding tax deductions averaging $600,000 a month in treasury accounts in six black-controlled banks, and another $400,000 of its working capital in six other black banks. Pepsico deposited $25,000 in the Allied Federal Savings and Loan Association in New York. The Glen Alden Corp. said it would deposit $1 million in various member banks of the National Bankers Association.

The National Conference of Christians and Jews opened a $25,000 account in the Freedom National Bank of New York in May. NCCJ president Sterling Brown said that "improvement in relations demands improvement in employment, housing, and education for all of our people. This modest step should be taken as a symbol of the commitment of NCCJ to cooperation, to integration, and to brotherhood."

One division of the Amalgamated Transit Union invested $45,000—over half their annual budget—in the Independence Bank of Chicago, the Illinois Federal Savings and Loan Association, and the Service Federal Savings and Loan Association. Consolidated Edison opened a $1 million account in June at the Freedom National Bank of New York to make credit refunds to customers in New York City and Westchester County.

M. Conrad Martin, educational program officer for the National Bankers Association, said of the black banks, "It probably is accurate to say that Negro banks as a group show little or no profit. But that's a false picture of the future if you consider that most of the assets are involved in the banks organized since 1963, and if you consider that new banks aren't supposed to make money for three to five years."

In some cases white banks started programs to help their local black communities. The Citizens & Southern National Bank in Savannah, Ga., pledged $5 million in March to clean up slum neighborhoods, increase the level of home ownership, and stimulate ghetto business growth.

In May the urban development division of the Hyde Park Bank and Trust Co. reported it had loaned more than $1 million to businessmen and housing developers in slum areas of Illinois. Bank president Ronald Grzywinski credited State Treasurer Adlai Stevenson III, who had channeled state money to the project, with getting it off the ground.

Twenty-two banks across the nation announced in September that they were starting programs to train blacks for middle-level management jobs.

Transitions

As the professional world continued to open up for black men and women and as the new

administration moved into its first term, these names were making news:

In October 1968 Roger W. Wilkins was appointed program officer in charge of the social development section of the national affairs division of the Ford Foundation. Wilkins is responsible for developing and monitoring programs to improve the economic and social status of blacks and other disadvantaged minorities. A former assistant attorney general in the Justice Department, Wilkins began his new job in February.

Anita Mack was appointed to the newly-created position of regional management training officer for the Department of Labor's bureau of work-training programs. She is responsible for setting up and coordinating training projects for the bureau's staff in seven of the mid-Western states.

William D. Joyner, a building maintenance expert, was named executive housekeeper of the Washington Hilton Hotel, the first such appointment for a black man in the chain's history.

In Chicago Victoria Lynn Sonders, the city's first black female stockbroker, was hired to work for Glore Forgan, William R. Statts, Inc.

Eastern Airlines made Fred White supervisor of personnel. He had been Eastern's equal employment opportunity officer.

James H. Lovett was named to head the human resources department of the Illinois State Chamber of Commerce. Lovett, formerly with Project Upgrade in Chicago, helps businessmen arrange to train and employ blacks.

Blanch Calloway, a former entertainer and radio broadcasting executive, was named president of Afram House, a national mail order business in Miami, Fla.

RCA named Willis Nummerdor to direct their service company's program to train hard-core unemployed in Chicago.

John H. Patterson became Lockheed-Georgia's personnel programs specialist in urban government affairs. An employee of Lockheed for 17 years, he had been an equal employment opportunity coordinator.

Marion A. Bowden was appointed by the

Atomic Energy Commission to help coordinate their equal employment programs.

Owen C. Fraser was appointed administrator of Chrysler Corp.'s program to assist public schools in Detroit. Fraser had been an employee services representative in Chrysler's personnel department.

Howard Bryand, owner of Home Suburban Realty in Flint, Mich., became the first black member of the city's multiple listing exchange.

Thomas C. Smith, who started with the Manhattan Savings Bank in 1952 as a guard, was named executive assistant in 1969.

Joe Black was named vice president for special markets for the Greyhound Corp. He had the same job with a corporation subsidiary, Greyhound Lines, Inc.

In Cook County, Ill., a Chicago assistant state's attorney, Walter Parris, was named to head the county's fraud and complaint division.

Anderson M. Schweich was elected executive vice president and treasurer of the Chicago Metropolitan Mutual Assurance Co. Schweich had been with the firm for 17 years and was a vice president and controller.

Kenneth L. Hawthorne, Pennsylvania Turnpike supervisor for the Gulf Oil Co., was appointed special representative to industry for urban programs.

Economist Clifton R. Wharton, Jr., vice president of the Agricultural Development Council, was elected a director of the Equitable Life Assurance Society.

John Procope, Jr., was named director of marketing of the Slant/Fin Corp., manufacturers of baseboard heating products. He had previously been advertising sales manager for the New York *Amsterdam News*.

Christopher K. Chisholm was named personnel manager of Kenyon & Eckhardt, a New York advertising agency. Chisholm had been program director in New York of management education for the American Management Association.

Harry E. Polk, director of Far Northeast Community Services, an antipoverty program in Washington, D.C., became a contract compliance specialist in the equal opportunity office of the U.S. Treasury Department. He works primarily with banks, credit unions, and home loan associations to make sure they comply with equal opportunity law.

Sherrill D. Luke, program development director for the city of Washington, was appointed to head the newly-created urban affairs department of the Aetna Life and Casualty Co.

Gerald M. Peterson, an assistant secretary of the group insurance division of Aetna Life and Casualty, was appointed vice president for operations of the National Alliance of Businessmen.

One of the scientists chosen to conduct tests on the lunar material brought back by Apollo 11 was George Reed, a senior scientist with Argonne National Laboratories and a research associate with the Enrico Fermi Institute of the University of Chicago.

Singer James Brown was named "Businessman of the Year" by the National Business League.

Society National Bank of Cleveland hired Donald R. Murphy, formerly with Chemical Bank, New York Trust, to be an assistant cashier with responsibilities in the bank's community relations, public service, and advertising departments.

The National Urban League named a new deputy executive director, Harold R. Sims, former assistant to Sargent Shriver at the Office of Economic Opportunity.

New York youths protest racial discrimination in schools.

The Direction of Education

THE EDUCATIONAL PROCESS in America has traditionally failed to provide its black citizens with skills and abilities to make their way in society, a situation that has fostered political, economic, and social helplessness for black Americans. Black people are educated in second-class institutions within school systems structured to meet the needs of the white majority. The result is the general inability of blacks to adapt to American school systems. These systems cry out for new approaches to educate black children, for education is the method by which society coordinates and perpetuates its cultures and its values.

From the black man's point of view, the system fails to provide equal education, sets up tests that take advantage of cultural differences, and preaches about the bootstrap approach to its failures.

Dr. Price M. Cobbs, co-author of *Black Rage,* has said that the black man has really been changing all along. Now, he says, it's the white man's turn. "We must ask the well-meaning, good, white people to change, to preach love and to pay their dues," Cobbs says. "They have to— or this country is going to blow up."

Behind much of the student unrest on campuses throughout the nation is an apparent deep desire to infuse education with a philosophy and curriculum more related to the current swing to black consciousness and race pride. Black people today are interested in developing their own sense of "peoplehood" and they know one of the best ways of achieving this is through education. Black studies classes and programs have opened up on many campuses. Some institutions offer degrees in African and Afro-American culture, and increasingly this sense of racial awareness has filtered down to the secondary and elementary levels. Administrators and textbook publishers know they must make sure that curricula include accurate representations of the black man's role in society.

The federal government has also made it clear to schools that they face a loss of funds if black studies courses are not open to all students and if teaching positions are closed to certain races. Antioch College was one of the first colleges ordered to integrate its segregated Afro-American Studies Institute, which was operating exclusively for 120 black students. The college was warned that it could lose about $1.5 million in federal funds.

The Decentralization Crisis

Genuine decentralization is a dilemma now faced by all major cities. The issue of local control is one of power, involving the breakdown of traditional lines of authority. In a predominantly black community, local control calls for participation, but does not necessarily exclude whites who share community goals. Local control in the newer sense is far different from the segregationist demand to control schools in the South; black parents want to influence their children's schools within the framework of the law. Community control is also viewed as a chance to revise the theory that a child's academic deficiencies stem from a "culturally deprived" environment rather than inadequate instruction in the classroom.

Community control was first tested in New York in 1966 when Intermediate School 201 opened in East Harlem. The city's board of education also set up "demonstration units" to test community control in Ocean Hill-Brownsville and on the Lower East Side. Blacks in New York had demanded a new system, shifting decision-making powers from the bureaucracy to local boards and community-approved field supervisors and local principals to help promote close school-community ties.

Albert Vann, acting principal of Intermediate School 271 in New York, feels that people who have children in schools are closest to the educational process and ought to have something to say about it. Vann says that parents ought to be able to determine who teaches and what is taught. If they do not have the expertise on their non-professional board to develop the curriculum, Vann feels, they will seek the needed counsel.

In Washington, D.C., a group of black parents persuaded their city's school board in 1967 to let them elect their own local school board. The Adams Elementary School became Washington's first experiment in community control; the city itself did not win the right to elect its own school board until the next year. The Adams-Morgan project was initiated jointly with a team of Antioch College educators and in 1968 a second school, Morgan, was added. During 1969 the schools functioned independently of each other, with separate councils and administrators. Local control is now being tried in other sections of the city.

Boston had five community-controlled schools in 1968–1969, but as in many other cities, parents there simply worked around the public system. The Liberation School was one of the newest, a privately-owned institution begun by parents in September 1968. The school was formed after parents were rebuffed in their attempts to talk to the principal of Gibson School about staff appointments. When the principal refused to bargain with them, the parents gathered 160 pupils and started their own school.

There is growing support for decentralization —as an ideal. But because it disperses authority, local control breeds conflict. Decentralization cannot succeed without a great deal of cooperation between national and local groups. In New York, the Congress of Racial Equality (CORE), along with several black activists, educators, and political figures, is setting up an independent school system for Harlem. In Chicago the Urban League has conducted a seminar on community control of schools.

On the national level the human relations council of the prestigious National Education Association has endorsed community control of schools "with due process guarantees for civil and human rights of all concerned."

MATERIALS AND TEXTBOOKS

The quality of education offered by ghetto schools is diminished by use of curricula and materials poorly adapted to the life-experiences of the students. Designed to serve a middle-class culture, much educational material appears irrelevant to the youth of the racial and economic ghetto. Until recently, few texts featured any Negro personalities. Few books used or courses offered [related] the harsh realities of Negroes to the country's culture and history. This failure to include materials relevant to their own environment has made students skeptical about the utility of what they are being taught. Reduced motivation to learn results.

—Report of the President's Commission on Civil Disorders

"Despite new approaches to racial reality," historian Lerone Bennett has noted, "the textbook world is still white, middle class, and antiseptically unreal." Bennett also pointed out that evidence has shown that both the morale and reading ability of black children are adversely affected by white-oriented books; far worse is the fact that most black children are taught to despise themselves. According to Bennett, poor children are not the only ones whose education suffers because of distorted pictures of history and society in textbooks: white, middle class children reading these books are given a false sense of superiority and a distorted impression of the structure of American society.

In April 1969 members of the College Language Association issued a statement condemning the publishing industry for hastily producing books, especially textbooks, simply to cash in on the growing need for multi-ethnic materials. As a result, the members charged, many of the multi-ethnic publications have suffered in quality. The Association's *Interracial Books for Children* recommends that black men and women of various talents and experiences be used to enhance the quality of new materials. Many publishers have been attacked because they published hastily-assembled multi-racial textbooks for specific school districts and continued to print the standard edition for the majority of the Southern school districts.

Robert McNamara, Jr., of Scott, Foresman and Co., said in defense of the industry that there was a "fear that if a company lined itself up on the side of fair treatment of minorities, *none* of its books would be purchased in the very large geographical area" of the South. McNamara felt this was the reason for publishers not producing adequate material about minorities over the years. He pointed out, too, that the 1954 school desegregation decision and what has transpired since has served to "liberate" publishers so they feel free to publish material about all races. John Hines, owner of New Dimensions Publishing Co., Inc., in New York, said he wants to give children something of their own to identify with

when they read school materials. He said he is trying to give children a visual as well as educational experience. New Dimensions produced a series of black-oriented textbooks for the 1969–1970 school year.

Curriculum Changes

School officials nationwide have spent hours debating whether to include black history and multi-racial material in the general reading and textbooks. The board of education in Washington, D.C., now retires all school books that are not "multi-racial" in nature. Georgia State Rep. Ben Brown submitted a bill to his state legislature which would have required the Georgia education department to order publishers of textbooks which "do not correctly portray" the role of minority groups to stop peddling their books to Georgia school systems. Brown urged state legislators to defeat prejudice "rather than tie the state to ignorance of the past." Brown's bill lost in the House by a small margin. State Rep. Walstein Parker of Sylvania, Brown's fellow member of the Georgia house education committee, said it would be a "dangerous precedent" for the legislature to "legislate curriculum."

But textbooks are only one tool for teaching. Audio-visual materials are being used in greater variety by teachers to supplement lessons and these materials are being examined more critically than previously.

While looking through film strips to use with sound tapes, school librarian Katherine Heylman of Cleveland found they were glaringly outdated and even incorrect, particularly in their treatment of black people. One film on the Civil War explained that some masters had really treated their slaves very well. "These masters gave their slaves time off for fishing and fun," said the caption accompanying a picture of several barefoot, smiling blacks. "These slaves were happy," it continued. Mrs. Heylman feels it is up to the educators who buy the materials to put pressure on the companies to create worthwhile, up-to-date audio-visual material. Mrs. Heylman called the available materials a waste of money and of children's time.

People who want to see America's history books more balanced are working for legislation to set up a commission on Negro history and culture. Sen. Hugh Scott (R-Pa.) and Rep. James H. Scheuer (D-N.Y.) co-sponsored a bill to set up an 11-member commission with a $500,000 budget. It would coordinate efforts to fill in missing chapters in the history of the black man in America. Charles H. Wesley, a prominent scholar and executive director of the Washington-based Association for the Study of Negro Life and History, told the U.S. House Education and Labor subcommittee that continued lack of understanding of Negro history can be equated to suppressive "law and order" actions "against Negroes who seek to be Americans in history and fact." He said he has felt for some time that the black American's African ancestors are an important part of America's heritage and must be included with the Pilgrims and other forebears. The contributions and accomplishments of blacks should be included in such courses as civics, economics, and science, as well as history, he said, and libraries should buy up-to-date materials on minorities. Supplementary materials such as paperbacks are needed to compensate for the deficiencies in some of the texts currently being used in schools.

The Finances of Education

American education got a financial boost in 1969 when Congress voted to spend $4.2 billion on school aid—$1 billion more than President Nixon had sought. Despite massive federal aid, however, many school systems and institutions spend below the norm on students, teachers, and facilities because of tremendous jurisdictional disparities in the amount of money allotted for public education. These disparities are most apparent when cities are compared with suburbs. One study found that in the 37 largest metropol-

itan areas the average per capita expenditure for education by city governments is $82, while the average per capita expenditure in the suburbs is $113. The study found that actual expenditure per student was $449 annually in the cities, on the average, and $573 in the suburbs.

Former Health, Education and Welfare Secretary Wilbur Cohen pointed out that social progress in America has not kept pace with the growing needs of the people, and he cited as an example the disparity between New York State, which spends $912 per child annually on education, and Mississippi, which spends $335.

Washington, D.C., along with other cities, shows inequities in funding among schools. Elementary school averages range from nearly $800 per pupil in one special school to $306 in an overcrowded school. The average spending for all elementary schools in Washington was $404 for the school year 1968–1969.

Some states have experienced a financial squeeze that threatened school districts depending on state aid with shutdowns. East Gary, Ind., was the first school system in that state which actually faced the prospect of closing its schools. In Los Angeles, Calif., the Enterprise School District located in the heart of the black community between the sections of Watts and Compton had run out of funds, forcing it to turn to state and federal assistance.

This country has spent $1 billion annually since 1965 on education for disadvantaged or low-income children. The funds have gone for work-study programs, remedial reading, health services, tutoring, teacher education, summer sessions, and free lunches and breakfasts. The Office of Education estimates that the $1 billion breaks down to $108 for every student assisted.

Inadequate funds have also lessened the effectiveness of the Teacher Corps, whose recruits work in inner-city schools and work toward graduate degrees in colleges. In fiscal year 1968, the Corps was allocated $18 million; the next year, when it asked for $31.1 million but received $20.9 million, the Ford Foundation stepped in to give financial assistance to about

900 applicants who had been turned down for lack of funds.

A report of the National Advisory Council on the Education of Disadvantaged Children said that federal Title I funds for disadvantaged students, while spent for entirely worthy purposes, have "simply failed to achieve the overall purpose of the legislation." States depend greatly on federal funds to balance inequities in spending between jurisdictions. One example is Colorado, where schools in one district have received $935,250 in federal grants for educationally disadvantaged children. The state cooperates by approving school district projects which have received the funds and making sub-allocations of funds to school districts below the county level.

Black colleges and universities look to the federal government as their greatest source of financial assistance to upgrade faculties and facilities. The Higher Education Act of 1965 provided $32 million under Title III, and black colleges received the largest grants because they met the requirements of being "development institutions." In the past, private black colleges have raised half of their incomes from student tuition and a fourth from endowment earnings, earnings of auxiliary enterprises, and federal grants. Private gifts and grants made up the remaining 25 per cent.

In the summer of 1969 presidents of 31 black colleges charged the federal government with misunderstanding the role of the nation's black colleges and misdirecting funds that were supposed to help disadvantaged students. The charges were made at a three-day conference in July in Mobile, Ala., sponsored by the U.S. Office of Education. The administrators wrote to President Nixon, charging that the government, instead of funneling money into black colleges which historically have trained most of the nation's black teachers, had seemed to favor white colleges, which have "no deep understanding and appreciation" for the problems of the disadvantaged minority student. "We are appalled and outraged," they wrote, "at the inadequate understanding of our problems and the weakness of the proposed solutions." Dr. Don Davis, associate commissioner of the Office of Education, promised that $3 million of $13 million appropriated to pay for extra training for slum teachers would be allocated to black Southern colleges in 1969.

Leaders of the National Medical Association asked the Department of Health, Education and Welfare for grants of $8 million to help Howard University and Meharry Medical School, which graduate three-fourths of the nation's black doctors. Assocation President Dr. James Whittico said the appeal to HEW stressed the problems of 13 medical schools in the U.S. that are in the same financial predicament as Howard and Meharry.

In 1968, the United Negro College Fund's 25th year of fund-raising, it distributed over $100 million to its 35 private and fully accredited member institutions. Dudley Dowell, chairman of the fund's board, announced in May that the 1969 goal had been set at $7.5 million, the highest ever sought.

Although private gifts and federal funds provide the bulk of assistance to private black colleges, black educators have been asking industry to take an interest in them also. Dr. Robert L. Owens III, president of Knoxville College, remarked that "a new philosophy of interplay between industry and education is needed in the United States. Black colleges will be the greatest beneficiaries because they are the poorest." Dr. Owens said that of the $300 million donated by industry in 1967 to higher education, only 6 per cent, or less than $18 million, trickled down to the nation's 120 black colleges. This averaged out to about $150,000 per institution. One knowledgeable source, Prince Wilson, executive secretary of the Atlanta University Center Corp., feels this is too high an estimate because data on contributions from industry and foundations is scattered and incomplete.

The Plans for Progress organization has a college-industry "cluster" program almost two years old which seeks to improve vocational guidance and recruitment by industry at black colleges.

Over 200 companies have pledged to aid 44 minority colleges with a combined student enrollment of over 95,000. The largest grant—$390,000—was made by R. J. Reynolds Industries, Inc., to Winston-Salem State College in North Carolina.

In the United States today, black studies programs or courses dealing with Afro-American culture head the list of curriculum innovations at most colleges. The changes mean more funds will be needed to assist individuals and programs in this area. The Danforth Foundation has committed $6,000 over three years for post-graduate fellowships in black studies. First year funding, however, is being used to improve libraries of black institutions.

Backed by the federal government, banks have assisted many students by loaning college tuition money at low interest rates, usually if the student is already a customer, and the Ford Foundation, the nation's largest private foundation, went one step further in 1969 by granting money to several colleges and universities to enable them to admit more black students.

Fifteen public and private universities organized a consortium, the Higher Education Coordinating Council of Metropolitan St. Louis. The consortium is using one $300,000 grant to help finance the locally-based Project AHEAD (Associated Higher Education Assistance for the Disadvantaged).

Seven small, independent, predominantly white liberal arts colleges belonging to the Higher Education Coordinating Council in St. Louis have formed a separate organization, the Missouri College Consortium. A $200,000 Ford grant will enable them to expand their efforts to recruit, admit, and retain black students. Another program, which received $86,000 from the Ford Foundation, has been created to assist predominantly black colleges and universities.

Other institutions awarded special Ford Foundation grants for programs to help meet the changing needs of black college students in 1969 were:

- Texas Southern University, granted $550,000 for additional faculty members, library expansion, scholarships, and student and faculty recruitment at its school of law;
- Duke, Howard, Emory, Tulane, and Vanderbilt Universities and Tuskegee Institute, which received a total of $298,000 to finance summer programs for students from black colleges who want to go to graduate schools;
- The Teachers College of Columbia University, granted $112,000 to aid black students seeking special programs at white colleges;
- The Southern Regional Education Board, given $150,000 to aid twelve black colleges in revising their curricula;
- The Atlanta University School of Library Service, which received a grant in December 1968 to conduct a series of workshops and internship programs designed to contribute to the improvement of libraries in black colleges.

A number of fellowships and grants were established and awarded in 1969 specifically for black studies. These were programs sponsoring studies for college graduates, many of them designed to lead to higher degrees.

The Afro-American Newspapers and the Virginia Council on Human Relations sponsored a year-long project to train and place 15 young black men and women in journalism with a $123,000 grant from the Ford Foundation. Applicants were sought at colleges and prisons, in ghettos, and among servicemen, Job Corps men, Vista volunteers, and returning Peace Corps volunteers.

The Graduate School of Arts and Sciences at Washington University in St. Louis, Mo., awarded ten fellowships to black students who wanted to begin or continue graduate study leading to doctorate degrees. Stipends ranged from $2,000 to $2,500, in addition to tuition.

At Morehouse College in Atlanta, six outstanding students received Merrill European Travel Study Grants for the academic school year 1969–1970.

The Scholarship, Education and Defense Fund for Racial Equality awarded 60 Eleanor Roosevelt Scholarships to students throughout the United States who demonstrated leadership ability, but did not qualify for conventional assistance. The scholarships were for varying amounts up to $1,500. Since it was begun in 1963 the fund has supported about 145 black students.

Morehouse also received a $100,000 grant from the Field Foundation in memory of Dr. Martin Luther King, Jr., a Morehouse alumnus, to study the problems of the inner-city and its possible relations with the college.

The National Endowment for the Humanities approved a $24,410 grant to the University of Texas for a six-week summer institute in black studies for 30 university faculty members.

In addition, scholarship awards to black students on the undergraduate level were numerous. Some of the programs were already in existence, while others were newly established in 1969.

On the high school level the National Merit Scholarship Program designated 340 outstanding black students for college scholarships. About 110 winners received four-year achievement scholarships of $250 to $1,000 a year. The other 230 students were awarded one-time non-renewable scholarships of $1,000 under a new program begun in 1969. More than 38,000 students in 36 states were in competition for these awards. The national achievement scholarship program is now five years old and has awarded 1,041 scholarships to black students.

At least three scholarships were created in the names of slain black men. Shimer College at Mount Carroll, Ill., created the Martin Luther King Scholarships for students demonstrating leadership. The scholarships pay up to one-half the tuition costs at Shimer. The first two recipients were both third-year students selected by the faculty committee. Drexel Institute of Technology established an undergraduate scholarship in the name of slain black nationalist Malcolm X. The scholarship is for $2,000 and was donated by Albert J. Nesbitt, a Philadelphia industrialist. In Washington, D.C., the Herman L. Clifford

Memorial four-year college scholarship was set up by the PTA of Cardozo High School in memory of an assistant principal slain Jan. 24 in a robbery at the school bank.

The Educators

Teachers and administrators throughout the nation have recently been caught in the middle of unprecedented controversy over problems that range from wage disputes to charges of racism. And increasingly, they seem to be more concerned, more militant, and more human. Frank W. Barr, superintendent of schools in Fairview Park, Ohio, says this militancy is not for higher pay—"It's for taking part in developing educational policies, trying to have something to say about what education is going to be."

As the complexities of education increase for educators generally, teachers who deal with black children face even greater problems. An editorial in *Ebony* remarked that "the children of the slum ghetto face almost all the problems of the white middle class child plus those that accompany being poor and black. As problems multiply for the ghetto child, they multiply for the teacher." It added that the ghetto teacher starts out with two strikes against her—the pupils have more problems and the teacher has to handle larger classes.

The roles of educators in both teaching and administrative capacities are changing: one ghetto teacher in Chicago complained that she had to be social worker, psychiatrist, big sister, pal, mother, and counselor to the children she taught. Most teachers are primarily concerned with the quality of education. Evidence of this is the refusal of black teachers in Chicago to support a teachers' strike that would close schools. They demanded that the Chicago Teachers Union make quality education for black children a first priority in 1969 contract negotiations.

When the 1969–1970 fall session began it was quite evident that as dual black and white school systems were being eliminated throughout the

Southern states, many black educators were being transferred, demoted, and dismissed in an obviously racial pattern.

"The numbers are not great, but the decline continues," Leon W. Lindsay wrote in the *Christian Science Monitor*. "And the feeling persists that only a few black teachers in integrated classrooms will be tolerated."

The Georgia Teachers Education Association has compiled data which show that since state schools moved to desegregate, the number of black teachers has decreased by 27 per cent. The association's figures show that a similar decline is evident in other Southern states, while the number of white teachers is increasing in the same systems. In areas of Louisiana figures show that only two out of 10 black teachers were retained when schools were desegregated. In Texas a committee to study equal employment opportunities in public schools found that the majority of black teachers were not rehired when black schools were closed. "We are greatly concerned that a proposal being considered in Austin to cut the number of school districts from 3,000 to 1,000 will greatly jeopardize the future of the black instructors in Texas," said Rev. V. T. Thompson, committee chairman. The Georgia Association says that if the present rate of dismissal continues, in five years 144 blacks will lose their jobs in 30 Georgia school systems alone—a loss of $3 million a year in purchasing power.

The ramifications of such declines go beyond the personal level: the education of black children is directly affected. Clifton J. Haynes of the Louisiana Education Association cited a study of pass-fail records which discloses that only about 30 per cent of the black students passed compared to 90 per cent of the white students. He contends that one factor behind this statistic was the lack of black teachers in the schools.

Leon Lindsay concludes that "black educators —long regarded as some of the most conservative, satisfied, and integration-minded members of the Negro community—are beginning to think and talk militant."

Black principals are falling victim to Southern desegregation, too. White school officials feel that white Southerners don't want their children to go to schools run by blacks. "When there is a choice between keeping a black man or a white man with similar qualifications in a principal's job," Lindsay says, "it appears the white man usually gets the job. Black men are usually transferred to 'less sensitive' positions such as supervisor of transportation." Lee County, Miss., had five black principals. After integration there were none. In Paris, Tex., a black principal was reassigned as a school bus driver after his job was taken away. J. K. Haynes, a black educator, remarked that in nearly every instance the assumption is that a black high school principal is inferior.

Meanwhile, teachers refused to remain silent any longer. In Washington, D.C., 40 teachers at Eliot Junior High School walked out to protest a temporary school board ruling banning student suspension. Parents had claimed that teachers misused their authority. Teachers claimed that relaxing of regulations by the school board made their job more difficult. The Chicago Teachers Union threatened a city-wide strike for higher pay and job security during 1969 summer programs. A coalition of black teachers refused to support the strike unless critical problems of the black community were considered along with teachers' demands.

University administrators—black and white —were under more fire from their students in 1969 than ever before. Nearly 300 campuses across the nation were looking for a "new breed" of man to fill the office of president. Dr. John Calfrey of the American Council on Education described this man as one who "gets along with the police, has a thick skin, and lives in a fort." The new college president is expected to be a mediator, politician, and interpreter. Those 300 colleges are an eighth of America's colleges, universities, and two-year institutions. Many are new schools, but at a number of the established colleges vacancies are partly attributable to campus disorders.

Dr. Robert D. Cross resigned as president of Hunter College to replace Swarthmore College president Courtney Smith, who died of a heart attack during student demonstrations there. James Cheek, 36-year-old president of Shaw University in Raleigh, N.C., resigned to replace Dr. James M. Nabrit, 67, president of Howard University. Nabrit retired after almost a year of conflict with Howard's more militant students. He had taught and administered there 39 years. Cheek had been president of Shaw University since 1963, and during that time had brought the institution back from the brink of bankruptcy. Howard students seemed to feel that Nabrit was a symbol of times past and stood in the way of moving Howard ahead.

William Miller, managing editor of the *Chronicle of Education,* said that the pressures of being a college president are so great that the job isn't worth it. He contends there's a lot more money and a lot less tension in teaching. Dr. Roger Howell, president of Bowdoin College, said that college administrators are being "boxed in by students, by faculties, by governing boards, and by public opinion to the point that they can no longer function properly."

Also, there is the "black brain drain," defined by Dr. Vincent Harding, chairman of the history department at Spelman College. "Black faculty members are being mercilessly tempted by offers of greatly increased salaries, prestige, and opportunities for research and publication from Northern as well as Southern white institutions—most often in response to the militant, urgent, and often threatening demands of their black students." Dr. Harding further states that these white schools are taking the best black teachers they can find—the ones most needed on black campuses.

The March 1969 issue of *Progress* magazine cited the vicious cycle of inferior black education. Black colleges, starved for funds, turn out poorly educated black teachers for colleges and secondary schools. These teachers then turn out a product in their images, the article said. This cycle, if unbroken, will condemn Southern blacks to decade after decade of inferior education.

In an attempt to increase the ranks of qualified Negro professors, the Ford Foundation awarded 45 Ph.D. fellowships for black students.

Officials on Southern black campuses say that the demands of black instructors to teach new courses in black history and culture will be granted. One solution to the drain of black teachers, they suggest, would be the development of a dozen centers for black studies across the country.

Dr. Harding describes this present trend as "cultural deracination," and offers the suggestion that white institutions establish more visiting professorships for black teachers. This way, he says, the institutions would obtain the services of capable instructors without any permanent loss of talent to the black colleges.

Desegregation

Fifteen years after the May 17, 1954, order of the U.S. Supreme Court to end desegregation in public schools, the vast majority of the nation's schools were still segregated. In fact, racial imbalance in schools in most parts of the country had increased. Growing school populations, along with increasing racial polarization between central cities and suburbs, has made school systems even more segregated.

Robert H. Finch, Secretary of Health, Education and Welfare, promised that the Nixon administration would move against public school segregation in the North as well as in the South. "The law is on the books, and we're going to enforce it nationally, not just in the South," Finch declared. "You've got de facto segregation in every part of this country," he said, "and we're going to go after it." Most federal enforcement activity thus far has been concentrated in the Southern states. "A major problem in dealing with segregation in cities such as New York and Los Angeles," Finch said, "lies in the fact that their large school districts appear statistically to be integrated. Actually these systems contain large all-black and all-white enclaves."

In March 1969 Finch informed Congress that his agency's school desegregation enforcement staff in the North exceeded the number of personnel in Southern states. Finch said that 53 staff members were assigned to compliance efforts in the North and West as of March 1; 51 staff members were assigned to 17 Southern and border states. In 1968 Congress had ordered HEW to put as much money and manpower in Northern civil rights enforcement as in the South.

One target of HEW's investigation was California. Of 48 districts under investigation nationally, 12 were in California. The others were scattered among a dozen states.

The desegregation of Southern public schools was greatly stepped up in 1969. During the 1968–1969 school year, one-fifth of the black children in the South attended integrated schools. HEW reported that the figure had doubled when schools opened in September 1969, and William J. Page, Jr., HEW's regional director for the Southeast, said it was clear that the South was moving significantly beyond tokenism in school integration. But at the same time, he cautioned that more than 2,000,000 black children in 11 Southern states are still being educated in segregated classes.

"The Nixon administration's school desegregation policy—if indeed such a policy exists—has been swallowed up in a fog of confusion born of high level contradictions," the *New York Times* editorialized in September. It went on to list numerous "zig-zags" in the administration's actions, including the delay of desegregation in Mississippi; the lessening emphasis on HEW guidelines set down in the 1964 Civil Rights Act; Vice President Spiro Agnew's attack on busing as a means to achieve desegregation. These vacillations have been interpreted by civil rights leaders as an attempt to appease Southern politicians to retain their political support. Anti-desegregation forces seems to take the government's

uncertainty as an invitation to further political pressure. As in many of his administrative policies, Nixon claimed to be seeking a "middle course" on desegregation between "those who want instant desegregation and those who want segregation forever."

Desegregation took these turns in school districts of 11 Southern states when schools opened in September:

• *Alabama*—Most of the state's 118 school districts were still operating under freedom-of-choice plans. Consequently, almost all of them were involved in court suits over desegregation when classes reconvened. Twenty-five districts were under court order to desegregate as a result of Justice Department action taken during 1969. During the 1968–1969 school year, one of every 15 black children attended integrated schools. This figure was expected to be one in every three, or approximately 30 per cent, during the 1969–1970 school year.

Former Gov. George Wallace appealed to President Nixon in September to fulfill his campaign promises regarding desegregation. Wallace said that federal judges, who had ordered most Alabama school districts to use zoning to integrate schools, were "the biggest law breakers in the country." Zoning methods would require busing students, closing schools, and other means, of which Wallace claimed Nixon had shown disapproval during his campaign.

• *Arkansas*—Fifteen years after the violent integration of Little Rock's Central High School, desegregation in this state was being achieved relatively quietly. In September 272 of the state's 390 school districts had desegregated, another 49 had promised to, and 11 were involved in court suits. Eleven districts had had their funds cut off and another 11 were in the cut-off process; 36 districts still had to be dealt with.

• *Florida*—Only 12 of the state's 67 school districts were segregated in September. One of every five black students had attended an integrated school the previous year. Of the remaining 55 districts, 21 were appealing to the courts,

16 had promised to desegregate, four had lost federal aid, and 10 were under review. White parents protested the assignment of their children to predominantly black schools, particularly in the Tampa area.

● *Georgia*—One month before the beginning of the 1969–1970 school year, the Justice Department filed a major suit aimed at ending the dual school system throughout the state. This suit marked the first time the federal government had initiated a desegregation suit against an entire state school system. Officials felt that this case was an important test of the Nixon administration's new policy of relying more heavily on broadly-aimed desegregation suits and less on cut-off of federal school aid to individual districts.

At least 17 school districts reneged on promises to desegregate, but another 17 kept their word despite Gov. Lester Maddox's polemics. He charged that integration methods in the state lead to "hardship, confusion, chaos, disorder, and financial and physical harm" for Georgia's pupils. Only 33 of the state's 195 school districts were fully desegregated, an increase over the 14 per cent integration of the previous year, but a greater number, 36, had lost federal funds.

● *Louisiana*—According to HEW, none of Louisiana's 66 school districts was desegregated. Desegregation in 1968 amounted to 8.8 per cent. Thirty-seven districts were under court order to give up freedom-of-choice plans.

Protest over desegregation enforcement was widespread during September among both whites and blacks. Schools were boycotted and picketed, and in one instance federal marshals were called in. Parents imposed an almost total boycott of newly-integrated schools in Ascension Parish and attendance was 60 per cent below normal when schools were reopened. They were reopened only under threat of a court contempt citation for attempting to close classes. In the town of Thomas, federal marshals were ordered in to protect five black teachers who integrated the local high school's faculty. The teachers were escorted past a line of angry white parents and

ultimately the school was closed. In New Iberia, police used tear gas to disperse about 300 black students demonstrating in front of the local high school. The students fought police with sticks and bottles. Throughout the area school attendance was down by half. Black students protested the closing or transforming of previously all-black schools.

● *Mississippi*—"Chaos and utter turmoil" was state school superintendent Garvin Johnston's description of Mississippi's desegregation situation. Only seven of 149 school districts were considered by HEW to be desegregated. Half of the state's districts were under court order to revise their policies.

In August the Justice Department asked for a delay in desegregation of 33 school districts. According to HEW Secretary Finch, the delay was needed to prevent "chaos, confusion, and catastrophic educational setback." The action set integration in those districts back by at least a year and greatly angered the NAACP Legal Defense Fund and the U.S. Civil Rights Commission. NAACP attorneys filed an objecting motion, but it was promptly denied. By allowing 222 schools in those districts to open under freedom-of-choice plans, the court-ordered delay reversed a July 3 order to initiate new plans in the 1969–1970 school year. Mr. Nixon denied reports that Mississippi Democratic Sen. John D. Stennis had won the reprieve for the school districts by threatening not to defend the administration's controversial military spending bill.

● *South Carolina*—In September it was reported that concessions on desegregation had been made by the Nixon administration to almost all of the 92 school districts in the state. South Carolina's Republican Senator, Strom Thurmond, had campaigned throughout the South in 1968 for Nixon, promising Southerners that the candidate would uphold "freedom-of-choice" desegregation. About 15 per cent of all black students had attended integrated schools during the previous school year. Twelve school districts that had sought court relief were given another year to desegregate. Twenty-six promised to desegregate, leaving 10 predominantly black districts still to be dealt with.

In previous years in Ridgeville, S.C., three school systems had been operated separately, much like several South Carolina counties. There was a system for whites, one for blacks, and one for dark-skinned children of obscure racial origin called "brass-ankles." Four Holes Elementary School for "brass-ankles"—the last of its type in the state—was slated to be closed during the 1970–1971 school year. Victoria Delee, a Four Holes teacher, demanded that the school be closed immediately, claiming that it was inadequate in every aspect. She wanted the pupils enrolled in Ridgeville Elementary School, where blacks were enrolled for the first time in 1969, but school officials claimed the school was already overcrowded.

• *Tennessee*—More than 100 of Tennessee's 151 school districts had desegregated, according to HEW. Most cities in the state are under court order to desegregate.

• *Texas*—Most of the state's 1,265 districts had desegregated and exclusively white and exclusively black schools were unusual. The major problems were found in larger cities such as Houston, which was challenged in court in February to void its freedom-of-choice plan—the latest development in a 12-year court battle over desegregation in that city.

• *Virginia*—The 1968–1969 school year saw a fourth of the state's schools integrated. The percentage was expected to double during the 1969–1970 term. A proportionate increase is anticipated in the state's private school movement. Five districts in the Southside and Tidewater areas had their federal funds cut off and only 65 of Virginia's 135 districts were considered desegregated in September 1969. Staff writer Peter Milius summed up the Virginia situation in the *Washington Post:* "White Virginians have hardly come to relish the prospect of desegregation. But massive resistance is long gone, and Virginia seems to be approaching a state of Massive Resignation."

The Colleges Face Desegregation

The National Association of State Universities and Land Grant Colleges, the Southern Education Reporting Service, and the Southern Education Foundation made a survey of integration in the nation's colleges and universities. It showed that in public institutions desegregation "has been slight—far out of proportion to the ratio of whites to Negroes in the population." According to the study, less than two per cent of the students at leading state universities—North and South—are black. The study found that in the 80 predominantly white state universities, with a combined enrollment of 1,222,382, there were 23,630 or 1.93 per cent black students.

But the study also found that there had been an increase in educational opportunities for black Americans in recent years. Half the black students in predominantly white state universities in 1969 were freshmen.

The Department of Health, Education and Welfare has accused several states of operating racially segregated college systems. States like Maryland, Louisiana, and Arkansas have been told to submit desegregation plans for state-run colleges or lose federal funds for construction, student loans, and various faculty and equipment grants.

Student protest at the University of California at Berkeley, San Francisco State College, Duke University, and elsewhere has included demands for black studies departments. In HEW's opinion, the legality of such programs hinges on how segregated black studies departments make themselves. An HEW memorandum to college officials warned that they risk loss of federal funds if they "sanction housing, social activities, or academic courses that exclude any race."

In general the cry for community control of education in the schools and student power in higher education has pointed to a relatively unheralded fact: many black people reject desegregation. They intend to achieve quality education on their own.

Racism—A Continuing Institution

An independent study following up the 1968 report of the National Advisory Commission on Civil Disorders found that the United States was a year closer to having two increasingly separate and unequal societies—black and white. The follow-up study added that the year 1968 had not seen even a serious start toward the changes in national priorities, programs, and institutions suggested by the "Kerner Commission Report."

Many people believe strongly that education will obliterate racism. But others such as Father James Groppi charge educational institutions and organized religion with "perpetuating the evils of racist society." Father Groppi, a militant priest in Milwaukee, told delegates to the Georgia Teachers Education Association conference in March that public education in America is white and middle class oriented, and tends to make black children ashamed of their "color, features, culture, and heritage." The *Atlanta Constitution* reported that Groppi felt the most important job confronting educators today is the problem of trying to develop "black identity" among black children. "The education system in America is a tool of the status quo," Groppi was quoted as saying. "Black children are victims of non-education and mis-education."

One novel approach to racism has been tried by the Belleville, Ill.,Catholic Diocese, which has been transferring racially prejudiced girls to the integrated St. Theresa Academy.

Innovations in Education

- *Head Start*

As early as February 1969 critics in the new Republican administration were suggesting that the Office of Economic Opportunity (OEO) be dissolved because it administered its programs badly. President Nixon said OEO "has been a valuable fund of ideas and enthusiasm" and would continue "as an initiating agency" in the anti-poverty program, but he transferred the Job Corps to the Department of Labor, and Head Start to the Department of Health, Education and Welfare.

The President said the change would help Head Start and strengthen the administration's "commitment to providing all American children an opportunity for healthful and stimulating development during the first five years of life."

Testimony presented to the House Education and Labor Committee about the efficiency of the Head Start program was inconclusive. The American Academy of Pediatrics concluded that Head Start provided an exceptionally rewarding experience for children from both health and educational standpoints. However, Head Start children lost headway once they entered the "deadening atmosphere" of regular public schools, most educators found.

In April President Nixon created an Office of Child Development to take over the Head Start program and directed HEW to begin thinking about revamping the program to new scientific findings which show that in the "process of learning, how to learn begins very, very early in the life of the infant child." Modern science, said the President, confirmed that the child of impoverished parents can suffer "lasting disabilities" and that this can lead to "the transmission of poverty from one generation to the next." The President called this process a "most ominous aspect of the urban crisis" and indicated that Head Start should redirect its efforts from the preschool playground to the crib. Among the proposals: double the number of parent-child centers for infants and toddlers three years old and under; encourage communities to redirect funds marked for summer programs to programs involving a smaller number of children on a year-round basis; spend more money on follow-through programs in elementary and secondary schools to help children retain advantages gained in Head Start.

A study made public in April reported that the effects of Head Start were "insignificant." Westinghouse Learning Corp. and Ohio University's study argued that any federal attempt to break the poverty cycle could have only limited success if programs are "not part of a child's environment for long periods of time." The report recommended total change of environment for disadvantaged children, which would include helping the father find a job, the family find housing, and teaching the mother about child development. HEW implemented the study's recommendations at their experimental parent-child centers.

Independent educators spoke up for Head Start, saying federal reports depended "excessively on paper and pencil tests of achievement and intelligence." Dr. Robert A. Dentler, director of the Center for Urban Education, said, "Preschool programs like Head Start have been evaluated by educational researchers for more than 20 years." Such programs "make their greatest contribution to the enhancement of the social skills and social growth in children," he said. Dr. Bernard Mackler, associate professor of urban affairs at Hunter College, described a Harlem Head Start program he studied in 1967 as having "tremendous behavioral" gains. Others around the country defended the program. However, Dr. Howard G. Madow, a statistician at Stanford University who had been a consultant to the Westinghouse study, refused payment for his work and asked to have his name removed from the report because he considered the research design and conclusions incorrect. Dr. Verne S. Atwater, president of Westinghouse, defended the study as "a reliable statistical scanning of the entire universe of Head Start," and said it did need further analysis.

● Black Studies on the Elementary Level

Many school systems are beginning to change their curricula to reflect the role of the black man in American history. In the Dade City, Fla., elementary schools, for example, black history has been interspersed with other social studies in kindergarten through sixth-grade classes. The new curriculum includes African heritage, and emphasizes the contributions and cultural achievements of the black man. It presents a general overview of blacks in America.

The Washington, D.C., school board adopted a plan in June to meet the needs of black students with an experimental program in black history limited to seven elementary schools. Other schools were encouraged to set up their own programs. Seattle has also incorporated minority history into social studies classes in its elementary schools.

● Language

Language arts is another field that is controversial and changing in light of revitalized black pride. In inner-city classes, like those of Washington, D.C., teachers must try not only to teach children to read, but how to speak English as it is spoken in white society. Many black pupils in urban schools speak a language that is not considered standard English or even American English. Language researchers contend that a separate communication system exists for these children. It is sometimes described as "nonstandard English," black dialect, or "soul talk." Some researchers now feel that language can be considered acceptable on two levels—formal and informal. The response of school administrators to this particular language problem has been called inadequate by a number of critics.

Some administrators have attempted to revise their programs, but others have refused to change traditional teaching methods. Dorothy L. Vaill, head of the Washington school system's department of speech, said that urban language research is not relevant to her department's programs. As a reaction to the traditional attitude toward language, Speech Therapists for Human Dignity was organized in Washington with the aim of preserving rather than changing black dialect. They have asked administrators to scrap the present program. "Speech therapy is designed for children who lisp, stutter, or have physical defects," the group maintains. The therapists argued that remedial speech in the schools "attempts to destroy what the child already has —a language system which he should be proud of."

"Language programs in inner-city schools

should be built on the language the children bring to school," says Kenneth R. Johnson, an authority on black dialect. Negro dialect is sometimes more complicated than standard English and in some cases is more "correct" than standard English, he argues. Johnson talked about black subculture at a Milwaukee workshop in March that was organized to prepare some 90 teachers to teach other educators how to work more effectively with black children. He told them they had to understand that black dialect is a variety of English, much as standard English itself is a variation of the classical English language.

● *Innovative Programs in a Traditional System*

Individually Prescribed Instruction (IPI) is a program originally developed at the Learning Research and Development Center of the University of Pittsburgh. Its emphasis is on the pupil working on his own, even though he is nominally part of a group. Some instruction is given on a group basis.

Richland Elementary School, Bucks County, Pa., was a pilot school for IPI math in the 1966–1967 academic year, and IPI reading was introduced there the following year. Math, reading, social studies, and spelling were experimented with in the spring of 1969, while another school worked with the science program at the same time.

A year-long study conducted in Urbana, Ill., compared a group of IPI students in math and reading with a control group. Both groups were in the same ungraded school's primary program. The results showed that IPI pupils at nearly every IQ level scored higher than the others.

Although test results of all the IPI programs are not yet available, Philadelphia researchers are convinced that the program is on the right track. IPI will be field-tested and refined by a federally financed educational research lab in Philadelphia, Research for Better Schools, Inc.

The Potential School for Exceptional Children, a chartered and non-profit organization in Chicago, offers instruction for emotionally disturbed and mentally retarded children as well as bright "gifted" children. The school, which enrolls children from ages 3 through 12, emphasizes the building of self-esteem, individual responsibility, and awareness. The children receive individual and group instruction. The Potential School has been financed entirely in the past by the black community.

The Tri-School project in Washington, D.C., received national recognition early in 1969 when it received an Aerospace Education Foundation award as one of the 10 most innovative schools in the country. Three neighboring elementary schools operate as one, with children of each grade level attending classes together in the same facility. The theory behind the project is that poor and affluent parents can unite to pressure school boards into providing equal facilities for children in all neighborhoods. In the Tri-School's three years of operation, integration is no longer an issue; "Southern Education Report" wrote in March that parental concern centers mainly around quality education.

One inter-school program in the Cleveland, Ohio, area has helped foster friendships and understanding among children of varying backgrounds from 11 elementary schools in the Cleveland Heights-University Heights school system and nine in Shaker Heights. Educators there are emphasizing development of children's respect for each other as individuals rather than as members of a specific group. Some classes meet for a joint music program; others take trips together and visit each other's classrooms.

Secondary Schools

Black junior and senior high school students today are demanding more of their schools than ever before. An article in the *New York Times* pointed out that these students have been sold the idea that there are no limits to freedom. After studying student unrest at a White Plains, N.Y., school, one research team concluded that the black power movement and "its pride of race and heritage" is mainly responsible for racial unrest in high schools. Dan W. Dodson, a New York University sociologist, contends in this report that "a switch from apathy to militancy by black students will force the schools to adapt or face the certain future prospects that the militant . . . Negro will demand local control of the schools."

All across the country, student unrest intensified after the April 1968 assassination of Dr. Martin Luther King, Jr. In New York City many black students continued to press demands for changes in school rules and increased student power, more black teachers, and more courses in black studies. During the teachers' strike in the fall of 1968 in New York City, black students took up the demands of many adult Negro groups for community control.

In Chicago more than 30,000 black students boycotted high school classes during October 1968. One of their demands was for the inclusion of black history in textbooks. In February 1969 students in Washington, D.C., threatened to disrupt proceedings at a board of education meeting if steps were not taken to set up ad hoc committees to deal with their demands. The board subsequently adopted a student "bill of rights" including the right to attend classes in black studies.

At many junior and senior high schools, students clashed with administrations over threatened expulsion for wearing "natural" hairstyles. A list of demands was drawn up by black students at De La Salle Institute in Chicago calling for an immediate halt to intimidation of students wearing "ethnic" hairstyles.

Curricula in many school systems were revised to accommodate student and community demands. In Dade County, Fla., a bi-racial team of six Dade teachers and Dr. Leedell Neyland, dean of Florida A & M University's school of arts and sciences, compiled a secondary curriculum that covers race and culture, African heritage, slavery, reconstruction, contributions of the Negro, and the "new Negro mood."

In Washington, D.C., high schools began offering black history, Swahili, and African studies in the summer of 1969, and junior high schools began to include black history courses in their fall curriculum. Eastern High School Freedom Annex, the only student-run auxiliary high school in the country, was formed in November 1968. It offers courses not covered by the Washington school system, including black history, contemporary problems, community organization, black philosophy, black literature, and black art and drama. Students shaped the curriculum, selected the teachers, and arranged the classrooms.

In Alexandria, Va., a black studies course is being offered at three high schools during the 1969–1970 school year. One course traces black culture from Africa to the contemporary civil rights movement.

Louisville, Ky., high schools are offering an elective one-semester course in black history and culture in addition to American history. The state board of education passed a resolution in 1969 calling for the inclusion of black and other minority group history. The new course is intended for students who want to learn more about black history than can be included in a broad survey course like American history.

Seattle, Wash., has introduced elective black history courses at most high schools and has incorporated "minority" history in social studies classes in its junior high schools. Seattle's Garfield High School offers the most comprehensive black studies program in the city. It includes black history, black art history, African dance, Swahili, and an anthropology class on the origins of the black race.

Milwaukee, Wis., junior high schools offer a seventh grade course emphasizing racial differences and similarities and one in eighth grade covering the black heritage. In most Milwaukee high schools a book on black history, *The American Negro,* serves as supplement to the regular text in American history. Milwaukee schools also use their publication, "The Negro in American Life," which offers a brief résumé of black contributions to American life.

Students who took over library at Voorhees College, Denmark, S.C., in demand for black studies program (above) are sustained by outside supporters. Southern University, Baton Rouge, La., students (below) show expended tear gas casings after hassle with state police.

Mother of a Brandeis University, Waltham, Mass., student searches for her son who had joined other blacks in barricading a building to force the establishment of an autonomous black studies department.

James Cheek, president of Howard University

Walter L. Walker, vice president for planning,
University of Chicago

Arnold Mitchem, director of a special program for the
culturally distinct student, Marquette University

Samuel D. Proctor, professor of education,
Rutgers University

Clifton R. Wharton, Jr.,
president of Michigan State University

Lionel H. Newsom, president of
Johnson C. Smith University

Manford Byrd, Jr.,
deputy superintendent of schools, Chicago

Benjamin Quarles, professor of history,
Morgan State College

College and University Recruitment

Ivy League colleges, spurred by their own black undergraduates, stepped up efforts to recruit new black students during 1969. Other schools followed suit, and although blacks account for only 3 to 4 per cent of the country's undergraduates, their numbers are increasing.

The most noticeable change has been at the better women's colleges on the East Coast. Until recently, several refused to reveal how many black students they had enrolled, but it was obvious that they lagged behind the prestigious men's schools of the Ivy League.

In 1969 these prestigious colleges—the Ivy League and the Seven Sisters—claimed black enrollments of 13 per cent or better, giving them a higher proportion of blacks than the nation's population.

The acceptance of more black students reflects the mounting pressures felt by colleges and, to some extent, their new commitment.

Wellesley College is an example. Eighty-seven black students—more than three times the previous year's number—were accepted for the 1969–1970 school year. These students, who made up 17 per cent of the freshman class, were recruited partly by the efforts of Wellesley students who raised $5,000 for the campaign and accompanied college recruiters to 20 cities.

At Princeton, 160 black students were admitted in the fall of 1969, almost twice as many as were enrolled the fall before.

It was evident, however, that student unrest the year before had had a dampening effect on total applications. Several schools, including Columbia and Barnard, which were wracked by some of the worst disturbances, reported that the number of applicants had declined by as much as 13 per cent or more. But some, such as Radcliffe, Brown, Smith, and Wellesley, noted that there had been extraordinary increases in the number of black applicants.

Other colleges and universities made increased efforts to recruit black students in 1969, sometimes at the urging of their own undergraduates and sometimes at the urging of the federal government.

At Manhattanville College in Purchase, N.Y., a special program, Project Share, brought 27 black and Puerto Rican graduates of slum high schools three years ago. In 1969 Share students were able, in turn, to recruit 25 more blacks and Puerto Ricans for this Catholic women's college. At their urging, the college also hired a black student adviser and set up a black studies program.

Officials at Rutgers University, New Brunswick, N.J., decided to recruit 700 disadvantaged youths for enrollment in the fall 1969 semester; the recruits were admitted to classes at three urban campuses of the university in an attempt to upgrade their skills.

George Washington University in Washington, D.C., allotted 40 places for inner-city youths in their 1969–1970 school year, a number equal to the quota of students it finances under its regular scholarship program. Other predominantly white colleges in Washington, including American, Catholic, and Georgetown Universities, are recruiting blacks with varying degrees of success.

Student pressure and warnings from the U.S. Department of Health, Education and Welfare led officials of University of Maryland campuses to recruit more black students in an attempt to desegregate what the government termed its "racially segregated" institutions.

Trustees of the University of New York decided in the summer of 1969 to try to admit all city high school graduates to some type of college program in 1970, provided the necessary funds were available.

A Ford Foundation survey of 105 arts and sciences graduate schools found that less than two per cent of their total enrollment by January 1969 was black. Less than one per cent of all doctorates were awarded to blacks: only 300 of the 40,000 doctorates in the United States in the past five years have gone to blacks.

Although the enrollment of undergraduate schools has increased, that of graduate schools has not. Several factors limit black post-graduate degrees. One is the lure of industry; another is lack of motivation. Andre Beaumont of the Ford Foundation's College Placement Service says a vast number of black students are afraid the white world will not accept them or they suffer from undue pressure from their parents.

The Ford Foundation, in a move to correct this imbalance, awarded 104 grants to black faculty members for advanced graduate study during the 1969–1970 academic year. The grants, ranging from $6,400 to $14,015, were made to teachers at 70 universities and colleges.

Among other innovative graduate programs were these:

• In the spring of 1969 the Ford Foundation also financed summer study for students—from predominantly black colleges—at the graduate schools of Duke, Emory, Howard, Tulane, Vanderbilt, and Yale Universities.

• The New York State University Center initiated a program in 1969 to recruit black graduate students from areas and backgrounds usually not seriously considered for admission to graduate schools.

• The Office of Economic Opportunity and the Council on Legal Opportunity set up a nationwide program to encourage and assist eligible minority-group college graduates at eight law schools.

• The University of California at Los Angeles established a special program in 1963 to encourage qualified minority students to do post-graduate work. A large grant in 1967 from the Danforth Foundation helped set up a Master's Opportunity Fellowship Program. Of 75 applicants in 1969–1970, 27 were accepted.

• Washington University in St. Louis launched a training program in the summer of 1969 in an attempt to alleviate the shortage of black economists in this country. According to estimates, there are only about 74 Negro economists with Ph.D.s in the United States. Under the plan, 10 black college juniors were given a $500 stipend plus room, board, and traveling expenses. Their summer was spent preparing for graduate study in economics. Those who completed

the summer successfully earned six college credits toward a degree.

• The Woodrow Wilson National Fellowship Foundation awarded a new grant to begin a major drive to make the Martin Luther King program a large source of backing for black veterans of military service who plan careers in service to the nation. The 50 new fellowships were to cover graduate and professional school costs.

Student Protest

On a number of campuses black studies has replaced the war in Vietnam as the major issue at the center of student protest. Throughout the 1968–1969 school year black students were able to command the attention of much of the public as well as that of college administrations. By moving quietly to set up programs in black studies, administrators at Harvard, Yale, and Stanford Universities showed concern that kept the issue from becoming a matter of public grievance.

At large universities like Harvard and Yale, black students were too widely dispersed to unite. Loud protest was heard at smaller colleges where black students are an obvious minority. It was on these campuses that black students began to unite around the common cause of black studies. Sympathetic students from the white majority were drawn over to the cause of the blacks, particularly at schools with liberal traditions such as Swarthmore College, Brandeis University, and San Francisco State College.

Howard University, Morehouse College, and other predominantly black colleges had their share of problems, too. There students demanded more scholarships as well as black studies.

Public officials used a wide range of tactics to deal with campus disorders, which have sometimes resulted in property damage and personal injury. In the case of San Francisco State, California Gov. Ronald Reagan has actively sought public confrontation with the black students. In

May U.S. Attorney General John H. Mitchell said that "the time has come for an end to patience." He called on university and law enforcement officials to order arrests and prosecutions of "professional militants" behind campus disorders. Vice President Spiro Agnew urged Congress to cut off aid to militant students and to colleges that fail to keep protest "within the limits of permissibility."

However, despite this public posture of hard-line condemnation, the Nixon administration remained seriously divided on the best response to student disorders. Health, Education and Welfare Secretary Robert H. Finch, for one, did not spring to denounce the activists. He reportedly believed that tough rhetoric on the part of the administration might actually inflame campuses rather than settle them.

Rep. Shirley Chisholm (D-N.Y.), the House of Representatives' only black congresswoman, told graduating Howard University students that they couldn't "tear down everything and build everything new at once. You can learn this from men and women who have, in their own best conscience, fought the same fight before you." Mrs. Chisholm appealed to the older generation as well for understanding, alliance, and cooperation with young people. "The fierce clarity of the moral vision of the young is beautiful, and it is true. But it is not often matched by practical wisdom to make that vision real," the congresswoman told them.

A partial chronology of student unrest in 1969 included these developments:

• January 8—In a surprise move, 15 members of the Afro-American Society at Brandeis University seized the campus communications center to press demands for an African studies department (and power to hire and dismiss its teachers); year-round recruitment of Negro students by black undergraduates under the leadership of a Negro director; immediate hiring of Negro professors in various departments; and establishment of 10 full scholarships for Negro students.

• January 15—Nearly 150 black and white students held control of the University of Minnesota administration building while counter-demonstrators protested the occupation.

• January 23—Police encircled a crowd at an unauthorized strike rally in the center of the San Francisco State College campus and arrested 380 persons. One of the prisoners was Dr. Nathan Hare, head of the school's embryonic black studies department. Student demand that the department and an ethnic studies college be operated by non-whites—with complete autonomy—was one of the major unsettled issues of the student strike that began the previous November. The mass arrest this day was the biggest in San Francisco's history. It took three hours for the 380 to be searched, photographed, and loaded into paddy wagons and a sheriff's bus for 17 separate trips to the city jail.

• January 24—A fire of undetermined origin destroyed the Student Union at Wilberforce University in Ohio. Damage was set at $90,000. Students had boycotted classes the previous week to protest disciplinary procedures and the expulsion of 75 students for academic reasons.

• February 9—About 150 Mississippi highway patrolmen broke up a student protest at the all-black Mississippi Valley State College in Itta Bena. Fifteen students were arrested. William Joseph, president of the Student Government Association, said the students were demanding courses in black history, the addition of books by black authors to the library, courses in remedial math, extension of the women's curfew hours, and lectures by prominent Negroes.

• February 24—Students at Howard University in Washington, D.C., occupied the law school building. Early the next morning, U.S. Marshal Luke C. Moore, an adjunct professor at the school, read a temporary restraining order obtained after Patricia Harris, law dean at the time, was unable to get the students to relinquish control of the building. The faculty accepted a long list of demands from the students during the occupation.

• February 27—Six University of Wisconsin students were charged with vandalism after 150 persons stormed through six classroom buildings tossing stink bombs and breaking windows. The campus had been in periodic tumult since Feb. 7, when a group of about 200 black students boycotted classes to dramatize their demand for a black studies program. National Guardsmen had been called in to keep the peace.

At the University of Chicago, where students had occupied the school's administration building for 16 days, stink bombs were thrown into six classroom buildings and the library after students were expelled for taking part in earlier sit-ins.

Black students at the Newark campus of Rutgers University ended a sit-in and claimed victory in winning demands that more black and Puerto Rican students be admitted.

Students at Stillman College in Tuscaloosa, Ala., also ended a sit-in but vowed to continue their fight for student power.

At Clark University in Worcester, Mass., where students had occupied the administration center six days before, university trustees agreed to establish a scholarship fund for Negro students.

Dr. Andrew Cordier, acting president of Columbia University, recommended that the university abandon the gymnasium construction project that had helped touch off the student rebellion the previous spring.

Twelve persons were arrested during a club-swinging melee between students and police at the University of California at Berkeley. Among those arrested were student strike leader Manuel Delgado, and Ysidro Macias of the Third World Liberation Front.

The executive committee of tiny Wiley College in Marshall, Tex., which was closed after nine days of student boycotts and demonstrations, voted to reopen the college Mar. 12 and to set up a committee to hear student demands for an improved faculty and a new president.

Several thousand students attended rallies supporting opposing sides of a dispute at Oregon State University involving the athletic department. One thousand students heard Olympic runner John Carlos of San Jose College urge support for a class boycott because of the football coach's order that a black team member shave. Three thousand students came to another assembly to hear the coach say he would continue to ban beards on the team.

• March 10—A melee broke out after students from North Carolina A & T College marched in support of a strike by cafeteria workers in Greensboro, N.C., Three persons were injured—two by gunshot—and 18 students were arrested.

• March 13—North Carolina Gov. Bob Scott ordered 350 National Guardsmen into Durham, N.C., to enforce a curfew after groups of students from Duke University and North Carolina College at Durham broke 40 store windows in the Five Points area of downtown Durham. The outburst came after a rally to discuss the announcement by 25 Negro students that they were withdrawing from Duke in a dispute over black studies courses.

• March 14—Classes were cancelled for the fourth day at the Southeastern campus of Chicago City College because of student demonstrations for a degree-granting black studies department and for an investigation of charges of racism in the school's nursing department.

Rutgers University President Mason W. Gross ordered the class suspension on the Newark campus because of what he termed "serious" threats of violence from dissident Negro students.

• March 26—For the second year in a row, black students at the University of Maryland staged a walkout during a spring convocation talk by President Wilson H. Elkins at Cole Field House. They crashed a hall where a reception was being set up for Elkins and forced its cancellation.

• April 16—Students boycotted classes at predominantly black Southern University in New Orleans to dramatize demands by the Afro-American Society for a department of black studies.

• April 19—Black students armed with guns

seized Willard Straight Hall, the student center at Cornell University, and yielded the next day only after amnesty was granted to those who seized the building. The dean of faculty, Robert D. Miller, promised the blacks he would urge the faculty to nullify disciplinary action against five black students for their part in campus disorders the previous December and January. The faculty rejected this agreement, but reversed itself two days later.

The university's Afro-American Society, in explaining its seizure of the building, accused members of the white Delta Upsilon fraternity of having "perpetrated assault and battery against nonviolent black people, who have yet to engage in any kind of violent action on this campus." The night before the seizure a cross was burned outside the Wari Co-op.

• April 28—About 75 students, armed with guns and knives, took over the library-administration building at Voorhees College, Denmark, S.C., proclaiming it "the liberated Malcolm X University." They issued a list of 14 demands, including establishment of a black studies program leading to a degree in Afro-American studies.

• May 6—Howard University in Washington, D.C., was closed "indefinitely" after students seized six buildings and sealed off the entire campus. Trouble at Howard spread after a small group of militants refused to obey a court order to surrender buildings they had seized earlier in the week. The militants were demanding an equal voice in decision-making and curriculum changes.

The City College of New York came close to a riot when white and Negro students engaged in bloody fighting when the school reopened. The South campus had been closed since April 22 when Negroes and Puerto Ricans occupied buildings in support of demands for a separate school of black and Spanish studies and the admission of more minority students.

• May 23—Students and snipers barricaded in a dormitory at North Carolina A & T University were driven from the campus by about 500 National Guardsmen armed with rifles and tear gas. The trouble had started when students of the all-Negro Dudley High School objected to administrators taking a popular young militant out of the race for student government president. A & T students had taken up the cause and the disturbances increased.

• October 2—The Black Student Union at the University of Maryland was granted $6,040 by the student government after 75 blacks, several of them carrying bicycle chains, broke up a government meeting and prevented leaders from leaving the room. The next day, several dozen white students applied for membership in the Black Student Union to test whether it was open to all students.

• October 28—About 450 black students from Langston University in Langston, Okla., brought the Oklahoma state legislature to a standstill by filling the halls of the state capitol to protest the firing of their school president. Dr. William H. Hale, Langston president, had been fired by state regents allegedly because of immoral conduct.

Yale University law students said a boycott of classes at Yale's law school to protest campus police harassment of black law students had been about 60 per cent effective. The strike organizers, most of whom were white, demanded that the university stop disciplinary action against four black students involved in disruption of some classes Oct. 20 to protest the attitude of campus police. The blacks claimed they are regularly accosted by police and asked to present student identification cards.

• October 30—Black coeds at Vassar College barricaded themselves into part of the college's administration building to demand a separate black studies program and dormitory. The occupation was ended three days later.

• November 7—Black and white students at Tufts University continued their boycott of classes to press demands that minority workers be hired for construction of a women's dormitory. The Afro-American Society demanded that at least 25 black workers be employed.

• November 19—A Harvard dean was held captive and two others were harassed during the occupation of an administration building by black and white radicals demanding increased employment of blacks at the university.

• December 10—Black students took over the administration building at the University of Akron, demanding more black studies. National Guardsmen were mobilized, but the demonstrators left the building before they were deployed on campus.

Partial List of Colleges and Universities Which Are Doing Extensive Recruiting of Black Students

Institution	Location	Affiliation
American University	Washington, D.C.	*
Barnard College	New York City	*
Boston University	Boston, Mass.	*
Brown University	Providence, R.I.	*
Bryn Mawr College	Bryn Mawr, Pa.	
Columbia University	New York City	*
Cornell University	Ithaca, N.Y.	*
Dartmouth College	Hanover, N.H.	*
Duke University	Durham, N.C.	*
Fordham University	New York City	*
Frostburg College	Frostburg, Md.	*
Georgetown University	Washington, D.C.	*
George Washington University	Washington, D.C.	*
Harvard University	Cambridge, Mass.	*
Illinois, University of	Urbana and Chicago, Ill.	Stat
Louisville, University of	Louisville, Ky.	Municipal
Maryland, University of	College Park, Md.	State
Mount Holyoke College	South Hadley, Mass.	*
New York University	New York City	*
Pennsylvania, University of	Philadelphia, Pa.	*
Princeton University	Princeton, N.J.	*
Rochester University	Rochester, N.Y.	*
Rutgers University	New Brunswick, N.J.	State

Institution	Location	Affiliation
Sarah Lawrence College	Bronxville, N.Y.	*
Smith College	Northampton, Mass.	*
Trinity College	Washington, D.C.	*
Tufts University	Medford, Mass.	*
Vassar College	Poughkeepsie, N.Y.	*
Vermont, University of	Burlington, Vt.	* and State
Virginia, University of	Charlottesville, Va.	State
Wellesley College	Wellesley, Mass.	*
Yale University	New Haven, Conn.	*

* Private

Partial List of Colleges and Universities Offering Black Studies

Institution	Courses	Department, Center, or Programs	Degree Granted
American University	X		
Antioch College		X	
Atlanta University *		X	
Brown University	X		
Catholic University	X		
Central State College *	X		
City College of New York		X	
Claremont Men's College		X	
Columbia University *		X	
Cornell University		X	
Dayton, University of	X		
Denver, University of	X		
Duke University		X	
Franklin and Marshall College	X		
Georgetown University	X		
George Washington University	X		
Georgia, University of		X	
Goucher College		X	
Harvard University			X
Harvey Mudd College *		X	
Howard University			X
Hunter College		X	
Illinois State University	X		
Indiana University		X	

Institution	Courses	Department, Center, or Programs	Degree Granted
Johns Hopkins University		X	
Lafayette College	X		
Lincoln University		X	
Maryland, University of	X		
Merritt College			X
Morgan State College		X	
Mount Holyoke College		X	
New York State College		X	
Oberlin College		X	
Ohio State University	X		
Pennsylvania State University	X		
Pitzer College *			
Pomona College *			
Princeton University	X		
Roosevelt University		X	
Sacramento State College		X	
San Francisco State College		X	
Scripps College*		X	
Southern Illinois, University of	X		
Swarthmore College	X		
Syracuse University	X		
Vassar College		X	
Yale University			X

* Consortium.

A Partial List of Predominantly Black Universities and Colleges in the United States

Institution	Location	Control
ALABAMA		
Alabama A & M	Normal	State
Alabama State	Montgomery	State
Daniel Payne Junior College	Birmingham	Ame
Miles College	Birmingham	Cme
Oakwood College	Huntsville	Sda
Selma University	Selma	Mbc
Stillman College	Tuscaloosa	Pc
Talladega College	Talladega	Ucc
Tuskegee Institute	Tuskegee	Pr

Institution	Location	Control
ARKANSAS		
Arkansas Agricultural, Mechanical & Normal	Pine Bluff	State
Philander Smith College	Little Rock	Mc
Shorter College	Little Rock	Ame
DELAWARE		
Delaware State	Dover	State
DISTRICT OF COLUMBIA		
District of Columbia Teachers College	Washington, D.C.	Dg
Federal City College	Washington, D.C.	Fg
Howard University	Washington, D.C.	Fg
FLORIDA		
Bethune-Cookman College	Daytona Beach	Mc
Edward Waters College	Jacksonville	Cg
Florida A&M University	Tallahassee	State
Florida Memorial College	St. Augustine	Abc
Volusia County Community College	Daytona Beach	State
Washington Junior College	Pensacola	State, Cg
GEORGIA		
Albany State College	Albany	State
Atlanta University	Atlanta	Pr
Clark College	Atlanta	Mc
Interdenominational Theological Center	Atlanta	Pr
Morehouse College	Atlanta	Pr
Morris Brown College	Atlanta	Ame
Spelman College	Atlanta	Pr.
Fort Valley State College	Macon	State
Paine College	Augusta	Mc
Savannah State College	Savannah	State
KENTUCKY		
Kentucky State College	Frankfort	State
LOUISIANA		
Dillard University	New Orleans	Ucc
Grambling College	Grambling	State
Southern University	Baton Rouge	State
Xavier University	New Orleans	Rc

Institution	Location	Control
MARYLAND		
Bowie State College	Bowie	State
Coppin State College	Baltimore	State
Maryland State College	Princess Anne	State
Morgan State College	Baltimore	State
MISSISSIPPI		
Alcorn A & M	Lorman	State
Coahoma Junior College	Clarksdale	State
Jackson State College	Jackson	State
Mary Holmes Junior College	West Point	Up
Mississippi Industrial College	Holly Springs	Cme
Natchez Junior College	Natchez	Pr
Okolona College	Okolona	Pec
Piney Woods County Life School	Piney Woods	Pr
Prentiss Normal & Industrial Institute	Prentiss	Pr
Rust College	Holly Springs	Mc
Saints Junior College	Lexington	Cc
T. J. Harris Junior College	Meridian	Mg
Tougaloo College	Tougaloo	Ucc
Utica Junior College	Utica	Dg
MISSOURI		
Lincoln University	Jefferson City	State
NORTH CAROLINA		
A & T College of North Carolina	Greensboro	State
Barber-Scotia College	Concord	Up
Bennett College	Greensboro	Mc
Elizabeth City State College	Elizabeth City	State
Fayetteville State College	Fayetteville	State
Johnson C. Smith University	Charlotte	Up
Livingstone College	Salisbury	Amez
North Carolina College of Durham	Durham	State
St. Augustine's College	Raleigh	Pec
Shaw University	Raleigh	Nbc
Winston-Salem State College	Winston-Salem	State
OHIO		
Central State College	Wilberforce	State
Wilberforce University	Wilberforce	Ame

Institution	Location	Control
OKLAHOMA		
Langston University	Langston	State
PENNSYLVANIA		
Cheyney State College	Cheyney	State
Lincoln University	Oxford	Pr
SOUTH CAROLINA		
Allen University	Columbia	Ame
Benedict College	Columbia	Abc
Claflin College	Orangeburg	Mc
Friendship Junior College	Rock Hill	Abc
Mather Junior College	Beaufort	Abc
Morris College	Sumter	Sbc
South Carolina State College	Orangeburg	State
Voorhees College	Denmark	Pec
TENNESSEE		
Fisk University	Nashville	Pr
Knoxville College	Knoxville	Up
Lane College	Jackson	Cme
Le Moyne College	Memphis	Ucc
Meharry Medical College	Nashville	Mc
Morristown College	Morristown	Mc
Owen College	Memphis	Gar
Tennessee Agricultural & Industrial State University	Nashville	State
TEXAS		
Bishop College	Dallas	Abc
Butler College	Tyler	Sbc
Huston-Tillotson College	Austin	Mc
Jarvis Christian College	Hawkins	Pr
Paul Quinn College	Waco	Ame
Prairie View A & M	Prairie View	State
St. Phillip's College	San Antonio	Dg
Southwestern Christian College	Terrell	Cc
Texas College	Tyler	Dc
Texas Southern University	Houston	State
Tyler Junior College	Tyler	State
Wiley College	Marshall	Mc
VIRGINIA		
Hampton Institute	Hampton	Pr
St. Paul's College	Lawrenceville	Pec
Virginia State College	Petersburg	State
Virginia Theological Seminary	Lynchburg	Pr
Virginia Union University	Richmond	Abc

Institution	Location	Control
WEST VIRGINIA		
Bluefield State College	Bluefield	State
West Virginia State College	Institute	State

Dc	Disciples of Christ
Dg	District government
Fg	Federal government
Gar	General Association of Regular Baptist Churches
Mbc	Mennonite Brethren Churches of North America
Mc	Moravian Church in America
Nbc	National Baptist Convention, U.S.A.
Pc	Presbyterian Church in the U.S.
Pec	Protestant Episcopal Church
Pr	Private Organization
Rc	Roman Catholic
Sbc	Southern Baptist Convention
Sda	General Conference Seventh Day Adventists
Ucc	United Church of Christ
Up	United Presbyterian Church in the U.S.A.

Control Symbols

Abc	American Baptist Convention
Ame	African Methodist Episcopal Church
Amez	African Methodist Episcopal Zion Church
Cc	Church of Christ
Cg	County government
Cme	Christian Methodist Episcopal Church

A Partial List of Available Scholarships

Grantor & No. of Awards	Who May Apply	Value of Awards	Where to Query
AMVETS National Foundation	Children whose fathers are deceased or totally disabled as a result of military service	Varies	AMVETS National Foundation 1710 Rhode Island Ave., N.W. Washington, D. C. 20036
American Fund for Dental Education	Pre-dental undergraduates in their junior year	$2,500 for student's final year of undergraduate pre-dental study and $2,500 for each of the four years of regular dental school	American Fund for Dental Education 211 East Chicago Ave. Chicago, Ill. 60611
American Newspaper Publishers Association Foundation Journalism Scholarships	Negro college students study journalism	Varies	American Newspaper Publishers Association Foundation 750 Third Ave. New York, N. Y. 10017
Babson Institute of Business Administration (male Negro students only)	Male Negro students at Babson Institute	Full-tuition scholarship at Babson Institute	Financial Aid Office Babson Institute of Business Administration Babson Park, Mass. 02157
Carleton Student Association Scholarship	Preference given to North American Indians and Negro students (must apply to Carleton as a student first)	Two 4-year $550 scholarships annually—renewable	Carleton College Admissions Office Room 4, Leighton Hall Northfield, Minn. 55057
Catholic Scholarships for Negroes, Inc.	High school seniors (not limited to Catholics)	Number and value depend on yearly donations	Mrs. Roger L. Putnam, President 254 Union Street Springfield, Mass. 01105

A Partial List of Available Scholarships (cont.)

Grantor & No. of Awards	Who May Apply	Value of Awards	Where to Query
The Cooperative Program for Educational Opportunity Eligibility	High school seniors; major part of program focuses on Negroes	Admitted students receive necessary amount of financial aid	Cooperative Program for Educational Opportunity 17 Hillhouse Ave. New Haven, Conn. 06520
Elks National Foundation Scholarship Awards (32)	High school seniors or college undergraduates (not college seniors)	From $800 to $1,500 a year	ENFSA Mr. John F. Malley, Chairman 40 Court Street Boston, Mass. 02108
General Motors Corporation Scholarship Plan	High school seniors	From $200 to $2,000 a year	General Motors Corp. General Motors Building Detroit, Mich. 48102
John Hay Whitney Foundation (number available varies)	Primarily for racially or culturally deprived students; must be college senior about to begin graduate work	$3,000 a year	John Hay Whitney Foundation 111 W. 50th Street New York, N. Y. 10020
Higher Education Act of 1965 "Educational Opportunity Grants"	All undergraduates	Up to $800 a year	Financial aid office at one of participating colleges
Martin Luther King Memorial Scholarship at the University of Southern California	Negro students	Tuition plus several hundred dollars for books, fees, other expenses	Financial Aid Department University of Southern Calif. Los Angeles, Cal. 90007
Martin Luther King, Jr. Scholarship Fund at New York University; unspecified	For minority group students, both graduates and undergraduates	Varies according to financial need	Office of Admissions and Financial Aid New York University 13 University Place New York, N. Y. 10003
R. R. McCormick Charitable Trust Scholarships for Journalism Students	High school students applying at Notre Dame	Varies	Financial Aid Director Notre Dame University Notre Dame, Ind. 46556
Manhattan College Scholarship for Negroes	Negro students at Manhattan College	Up to tuition costs each year	Financial aid office Manhattan College Bronx, New York, N. Y. 10471
Minority Groups Scholarship Program	High school seniors at any of seven specified colleges or universities	Varies	Admissions office of particular member college: Antioch, Carleton, Grinnell, Oberlin, Occidental, Reed, Swarthmore
National Achievement Scholarship Program for Outstanding Negro Students (200)	High school seniors	$1,000-$6,000 scholarships for four years	National Achievement Scholarship Program 990 Grove Street Evanston, Ill. 60201

A Partial List of Available Scholarships (cont.)

Grantor & No. of Awards	Who May Apply	Value of Awards	Where to Query
National Honor Society Scholarship Program (231)	High school members of National Honor Society	$500-$6,000	Take preliminary scholastic aptitude test (PSAT) in October; indicate on answer sheet where candidacy is desired
National Scholarship Service and Fund for Negro Students (Supplementary Scholarship Fund)	High school seniors who have been counseled by this organization	Up to $600	Write *early* in junior year to: NSSFNS 6 East 82nd Street New York, N.Y. 10028
New York State Regents College Scholarship (1700)	High school seniors who are residents of New York	$250-$750 annually	State Education Department Regents Exam. and Scholarship Center New York, N.Y. 10013
The Newspaper Fund Journalism Scholarship	Students with interest in journalism	$100-$1,500	Journalism Scholarship Guide % Paul S. Swensson The Newspaper Fund P.O. Box 300 Princeton, N. J. 08540
Pfeiffer Research Foundation Scholarships in Medicine for Negro Men	Students going into pre-med program at Wesleyan University	$500-$3,000 a year	Dr. John C. Hoy Dean of Admissions Wesleyan University Middletown, Conn. 06457
Polytechnic Institute of Brooklyn, Huber Scholarships for Negroes (10)	Students working on degree in electrical engineering	Tuition and maintenance costs	Huber Scholarship Financial Aid Office Brooklyn Polytechnic Institute Brooklyn, N. Y. 11201
RCA Scholarships (34)	Undergraduates in one of the specified schools in the program	$800—renewable	Financial aid office of specified school. Write the college at which you have been accepted.
Eleanor Roosevelt Scholarship Program	Undergraduates actively involved in the Civil Rights Movement	Up to $1,500 a year	CORE SEDF 150 Nassau Street Room 1312 New York, N. Y. 10038
Roosevelt University (Edward A. Filene Good Will Fund)	Negro and Indian students wishing to study in the College of Business Administration	$1,500 a year	Roosevelt University 430 South Michigan Ave. Chicago, Ill. 60605

A Partial List of Available Scholarships (cont.)

Grantor & No. of Awards	Who May Apply	Value of Awards	Where to Query
Alfred P. Sloan Foundation	Male high school seniors going to major Negro colleges and universities	Varies	Financial aid office of specified school. Write the college where you have been accepted.
Student Opportunity Scholarships	Preference given to minority group students	Determined by need	Student Opportunity Scholarships, Room 1140 475 Riverside Drive New York, N. Y. 10027
Texas Southern University School of Business Scholarships (15)	High school seniors interested in business	Four-year full payment grants	Have guidance counselor write to Texas Southern University for you
United Negro College Fund	High school seniors and college undergraduates	Varies	United Negro College Fund 22 East 54th Street New York, N. Y. 10022
War Orphans Education Program	Children of servicemen who died serving in armed forces; must be between ages 18-23	$130 a month	Local Veterans Administration Office
Westinghouse Science Talent Search (40)	High school seniors	From $250-$7,000	Have science teacher write to Science Clubs of America 1719 N Street, N.W. Washington, D.C. 20006
Westinghouse Education Foundation Scholarships	High school seniors	$6,800 for four years	Director of Admissions Carnegie-Mellon University Pittsburgh, Pa. 15213

A Partial List of Fellowships

Grantor, Value & No. Offered	Purposes	Where to Query
AMA African Studies Grant; unspecified	For black American graduates of American Missionary Association and other accredited colleges	President of AMA 287 Park Ave. South New York, N. Y. 10010
Atlanta University, School of Library Service Fellowships; up to $1,000 a year; 10	U. S. citizens with outstanding scholarship records	Dean of School of Library Science Atlanta University Atlanta, Ga. 30314
American Council of Learned Societies; up to $7000; 40.	For research in specialized fields including foreign area studies	American Council of Learned Societies 345 E. 46th St. New York, N. Y. 10017
Bollingen Foundation; $1,200 to $3,600	For research and writing in anthropology, archaeology, comparative religion, cultural history, mythology, philosophy, psychology	Bollingen Foundation 140 E. 62nd St. New York, N. Y. 10021

A Partial List of Fellowships (cont.)

Grantor, Value & No. Offered	Purposes	Where to Query
University of Chicago, Graduate School of Business—Special Intern Plan; varies	Plan set up by several business firms with expressed interest in hiring Negro graduates	Dean of Students Graduate School of Business University of Chicago 5836 S. Greenwood Ave. Chicago, Ill. 60637
Columbia Law School Scholarship for a Negro; max. $3,000	Young Negro man interested in studying law at Columbia	Dr. Frank Waler Assistant to the Dean Columbia Law School 435 W. 116th St. New York, N. Y. 10027
Danforth Foundation, Inc.; varies.	For college graduates under 30 years of age with no previous graduate study	Danforth Foundation, Inc. 601 N. Grand Blvd. St. Louis, Mo. 63103
Edward A. Filene Good Will Fund for Negro and American Indian Students; $1,550 per year	Negro or American Indian students wishing to study business administration	Roosevelt University 430 South Michigan Ave. Chicago, Ill. 60605
Fulbright Act Grants; cover cost of living and study in foreign countries	For study abroad	Fulbright Fellowships 809 United Nations Plaza New York, N. Y. 10017
Howard University Foreign Service Careers Fellowships; $4,000 per year	For members of minority groups, especially Negroes, who are interested in foreign service careers	Financial Aid Office Howard University Washington, D. C. 20001
Howard University Law School Fellowships; $1,500 per year	For needy students who qualify for admission to law school	Office of the Dean The Law School Howard University Washington, D. C. 20001
Ford Foundation Doctoral Fellowships for Black Students; 40 full tuition and fees plus allowance of $200 for books and supplies plus a monthly stipend to help pay the Fellow's living costs	Students just beginning graduate work	Doctoral Fellowships for Black Students Ford Foundation New York, N. Y. 10017
Herbert Lehman Education Fund; varies	For graduate students continuing education in such fields as law, teaching, medicine, engineering, government, ministry, agriculture, social work, nursing, or others	Herbert Lehman Education Fund 10 Columbus Circle Suite 2030 New York, N.Y. 10019
Martin Luther King, Jr., Fellowships; 50 free tuition and fees plus $270 a month for living expenses	Negro veterans pursuing graduate or professional training for careers of service to the nation and to their communities	Martin Luther King, Jr., Fellowships Woodrow Wilson National Fellowship Foundation 32 Nassau St. Princeton, N.J. 08540
National Medical Fellowships, Inc.; $150-$200 per month; 10	For male Negro students who are U. S. citizens and who are studying medicine	National Medical Fellowships, Inc. 951 E. 58th St. Chicago, Ill. 60637
National Foundation Research Fellowships; up to $8,000; about 30	For students in areas of science related to medicine	Dept. of Professional Education The National Foundation 800 Second Ave. New York, N.Y. 10017
National Science Foundation; varies	For study in the mathematical, physical, medical, biological, and engineering sciences (U.S. citizens only)	National Science Foundation Division of Scientific Personnel and Education Washington, D.C. 20025
Opportunity Fellowships Program; max. $3,000; 50	For study in this country and abroad for minority group students	Opportunity Fellowships John Hay Whitney Foundation 111 West 50th St. New York, N.Y. 10020

A Partial List of Fellowships (cont.)

Grantor, Value & No. Offered	Purposes	Where to Query
Protestant Fellowship Program; tuition and maintenance expenses; 30	For outstanding Negro ministerial candidates	Rev. C. Shelby Rooks Fund for Theological Education, Inc. 136 Nassau St. Princeton, N.J. 08540
Russell Sage Foundation; up to $5,500; about 10	For post-doctoral work in sociology, social psychology, and anthropology	Dr. Donald Young, President Russell Sage Foundation 505 Park Ave. New York, N.Y. 10022
Southern Education Foundation; varies; 50	For college teachers at colleges listed below: George Peabody, and the Universities of Ala., Fla., Ky., N.C., Okla., Tenn., Tex., Va.	Financial aid offices of the schools listed.
U. S. Office of Education; $2,000 to $2,400 plus $400 for each child; 1,500	For use at those institutions whose proposed programs have been approved	U. S. Office of Education Washington, D.C. 20025
Washington Journalism Center Fellowship	For black college graduates who are interested in training for careers in journalism	Washington Journalism Center 2401 Virginia Ave., N.W. Washington, D.C. 20037

A Partial List of Available Loans

Grantor, Value & No. Offered	Stipulations	Where to Query
American Leaders Foundation; amount varies according to individual need	Student should have at least one year of college and cannot be over 28 years old	American Leaders Foundation % Northeastern Pa. Bank and Trust Co. P.O. Box 937 Scranton, Pa. 18503
Bergen Foundation Nursing Loans; usually covers tuition costs	High school graduate girls already in nursing school	The Bergen Foundation 6536 Sunset Blvd. Hollywood, Cal. 90028
Disabled American Veterans Educational Loan Fund; up to $200 a year	Children of parents who have been members of Disabled American Veterans and its Auxiliary for at least one year	Mrs. Eunice Bluestein 130 63rd St. South St. Petersburg, Florida 33707
Eddy Student Loan Fund; up to $1,500 a year	College juniors and seniors or any student who has completed two years of work at an accredited college	Eddy Student Loan Fund % Thomas and Thomas 504 Broadway Suite 1016 Gary, Ind. 46402
Education Funds, Inc.; from $700 to $14,000 over a four year period	Graduating high school seniors and college students	Education Funds, Inc. 10 Dorance St. Providence, R.I. 02901
Entre Nous Club of Detroit Student Loan Fund; max. $200 per quarter	Must be a student at Wayne State University; preference given to Negroes	Office of Scholarships and Financial Aid Wayne State University Detroit, Mich. 48202
Friends Education Fund for Negroes; varies	Must be used at Indiana colleges and universities	Mr. A. J. Palmer, Treasurer FEFFN 1004 State Office Building Indianapolis, Ind. 46204
Funds for Education, Inc. Loans; from $350 to $2,500	Any school, college, or university	Funds for Education, Inc. 319 Lincoln St. Manchester, N.H. 01201
The Tuition Plan	Loans regardless of school location	The Tuition Plan 410 N. Michigan Ave. Chicago, Ill. 60611

A Partial List of Available Loans (cont.)

Grantor, Value & No. Offered	Stipulations	Where to Query
National Association of Colored Women; varies	Vary	National Association of Colored Women 1601 R St., N.W. Washington, D.C. 20009
The National Defense Student Loan Program; up to $1,000 a year	Student must carry at least one-half the normal full time academic work-load (as determined by the university)	Director of financial aid at one of the participating colleges or universities (most major schools are participants in this program)
Azalia P. Oberg Foundation, Inc.; varies	Renewable; no restrictions	Thomas and Thomas Azalia P. Oberg Foundation, Inc. 504 Broadway, Room 1016 Gary, Ind.
Pickett and Hatcher Educational Loan Fund; varies	Restricted to students in the field of liberal arts	Pickett and Hatcher Educational Loan Fund P.O. Box 2128 Columbus, Ga. 31902
Henry Warren Roth Educational Fund; from $500 to $1,500	All undergraduates	Financial Aid Office Thiel College Greenville, Pa.
Hattie M. Strong Loan Foundation; from $800 to $1,500 a year	Graduating high school seniors	Hattie M. Strong Loan Foundation 409 Cafritz Bldg. 1625 Eye St., N.W. Washington, D. C. 20006
United Student Aid Funds, Inc. Loans; up to $1,000	Graduates and undergraduates at any of the 700 participating schools	United Student Aid Fund 845 Third Ave. New York, N.Y. 10022

Additional Sources of Information:

Financial Aids for Undergraduate Students, available free from the Office of Education, U.S. Department of Health, Education and Welfare, Washington, D.C. 20025

How To Get Money for College, by Benjamin Fine and Sidney A. Eisenberg; $2.50

The New American Guide to Colleges, by Gene R. Hawes, published by New American Library (a Signet paperback edition is available); 95¢

The New American Guide to Scholarships, Fellowships and Loans, by John Bradley; published by the New American Library (a Signet paperback edition is available); 95¢

The Foundation Directory, edited by A. D. Walton and M. O. Lewis; published by the Russell Sage Foundation; $12

The Cost of Four Years of College, available from the Career Information Service of the New York Life Insurance Co., Box 51, Madison Square Station, New York, N.Y. 10010

The National Defense Student Loan Program (OE-550001-62), available free from the Office of Education, U.S. Department of Health, Education and Welfare, Washington, D.C. 20025

Need A Lift?, compiled and published by The American Legion Educational and Scholarship Program, Americanism Division, Indianapolis, Indiana 46206; 25¢

College Opportunities for Southern Negro Students, compiled by the University of North Carolina, Scholarship Information Center, YMCA-YWCA Human Relations Committees, Chapel Hill, North Carolina 27514; free to high school students and only 25¢ for others

Higher Education Opportunities for Southern Negroes, compiled by the Southern Education Foundation, 811 Cypress Street, N.E., Atlanta, Georgia 30308; free upon request

Federal Aids for College Students, compiled by the U.S. Department of Health, Education and Welfare; free copies upon request from the Division of Student Financial Aid, Bureau of Higher Education, Washington, D.C. 20202

Occupational Outlook Handbook, compiled by The Bureau of Labor Statistics; copies available from the Supt. of Documents, Washington, D.C. 20402; $4.25

The face of a boy and the face of a building—a challenge to the nation to live up to its promise.

Welfare

WITH THE ADVENT of the Nixon administration and its general disillusionment with the War on Poverty, dissatisfaction in both liberal and conservative circles with the present system of welfare helped make 1969 a year of reappraisal. In the new administration, the general consensus was that anti-poverty programs had promised too much and yielded too little. It also was generally acknowledged that the present system of relief, developed in the 1930s, was no longer relevant to the needs of poor people and was actually impeding their progress toward economic self-sufficiency. But 1969 saw no real agreement on how the system should be changed.

While there is little opposition to present welfare programs aiding the aged, the blind, or the disabled, the major program, Aid to Families with Dependent Children (AFDC), which provides income to 5.6 million people, has been a source of tremendous controversy. The general public finds it difficult to understand why, in a time of relative prosperity, almost 8.5 million Americans are on the dole. They ask, too, why welfare costs—$5.3 billion in 1968—keep rising. But others are frustrated by the fact that the present system simply fails to help 18 million Americans who live in poverty.

AFDC is the biggest sore spot. It is the AFDC rolls which are always spoken of as "spiralling," and of which blacks constitute an ever-increasing percentage. Half of all AFDC recipients are black, compared to 22 to 31 per cent of the aged, blind, and disabled welfare recipients.

The often-quoted solution—"take people off relief rolls and put them on the payrolls"—is not as easy as it might seem. Of the 1.4 million families on AFDC, *The New Republic* reported, not more than 60,000 are living with fathers who are physically able to work. Most families headed by women often face a breakdown of some sort if, as some regulations require, the mother is forced into training or work programs as a condition of receiving relief benefits. On the other hand, self-sufficiency is hardly encouraged by deduction of family earnings from welfare allotments.

The Johnson administration was concerned in its final days with reappraisal and reform of the system. Wilbur Cohen, Secretary of the Department of Health, Education and Welfare during 1968, felt that the welfare system had to be totally restructured. He believed the system humiliates recipients and angers unconvinced taxpayers. In January 1969 he recommended a guaranteed income for the poor, possibly by means of a negative income tax. Under this arrangement, the worker whose deductions and exemptions exceed his earnings would be paid part of the remainder in government money. This method would have to be supported, Cohen felt, by strong mechanisms to encourage the recipient to get off relief and by much improved work training programs. He predicted, however, that before a guaranteed income system could prove practical, the present number of poor people—22 million—would have to be reduced by nearly half.

This possibility has been the subject of much study under both the Johnson and Nixon administrations. President Johnson instituted the Commission on Income Maintenance in January 1968. The Nixon administration had a task force working on the same problem. With the concern and time spent on this issue, there was evidence of a new attitude toward public assistance. It was voiced in one form early in February by the new White House expert on urban problems, Dr. Daniel P. Moynihan: "We are the only industrial democracy in the world that in the last 25 years has allowed the levels of unemployment we have," he said. Once the child of poor parents himself, he objected strongly to the common characterization of welfare payments as a "handout." "It's not a handout," he insisted. "It's an investment in the human resources that ultimately determine whether or not this is a healthy, stable, prosperous, happy country."

Even if these were not the specific views of the administration, there was official agreement that very basic changes would have to be made in the welfare system.

Many ideas were generated by the dialogue in and around the White House. The *Wall Street Journal* saw the ideas developing along three major lines: help for the poor, fiscal help for the states, and the attempt to slow migration from the rural South to the urban North.

In the first area, establishing a national minimum for relief payments was one major proposal directed toward erasing the discrepancy between average monthly AFDC payments, which ranged from $8.50 in Mississippi to $63 in New York. In the simplest terms, federal money would aid the unnoticed poor in Mississippi and at the same time assist the state government in New York, which had already assumed much of its own welfare burden. Establishing a national minimum standard, however, would raise the problem of compensating for variations in cost of living across the country. Administration advisers hoped that this plan would help cut down migration to the North, because they felt higher welfare payments were a lure to the Southern poor.

Day care centers, payments to families with unemployed fathers to discourage desertion, job training and job creation programs were among other proposals considered. But the priorities were hard to set. In the view of the *Wall Street Journal,* the more critical choices were between emphasis on aid to Southern poor or on fiscal aid to the wealthier states; between increased aid to the poorest recipients, those on AFDC, or to the aged, blind, and disabled; between increasing expenditures in the more popular health and education areas, or in the area of welfare.

The major obstacle to the reform of the welfare system was the conservative House Ways and Means Committee. Democrat Wilbur Mills, its chairman, traditionally has favored limiting public assistance rather than increasing its benefits and scope.

All these plans began to take more definite form in April when the administration announced plans to make a specific study of the proposal for instituting a guaranteed annual income. President Nixon had been solidly opposed to such a plan during his campaign, but HEW requested funds for fiscal 1970 for the purpose of experimenting with guaranteed annual income and children's allowance in selected Model Cities areas.

About 1,000 families were included in a guaranteed income pilot project in New Jersey. The experiment is attempting to discover how a family will use such funds—"for bread or booze," one HEW source was quoted as saying —and how the funds will affect their work habits and motivation. The department also hopes to find out if a guaranteed annual income will have any effect on social patterns such as birth and marriage rates, educational performance, and family structures. Payments are being made to both welfare and non-welfare families, and to both white and black families, to test its practicality.

By late April it was more or less official that the welfare plan under consideration would provide some form of subsidy for the working poor. This plan would, in effect, pay the family to stay together, and pay the father to seek training and employment; it was described as the boldest domestic proposal under consideration at the White House.

By this time, the proposal for a negative income tax was being given increasing public and private scrutiny, although it had no real commitment from the administration. From the beginning the White House had considered it an extremely radical measure. Author James Daniel pointed out that such a system would encourage the poor to earn more money and that under such a system no needy person would be without aid, as is presently the case. Currently, two-thirds of those Americans whose incomes fall below the poverty level receive no government assistance. Economist Milton Friedman, a strong supporter of the negative income tax plan, predicted that the proposal could be paid for by the $9 billion now being used for welfare and by $3 billion borrowed from other anti-poverty programs, now costing $50 billion. He pointed out the advantages of ending much of the humiliation inherent in the old system's requirement for close supervision. The new system would also nearly eliminate the need to pay 110,000 government employees for distributing and administering the aid.

Reports in early summer indicated the President might forego revamping or substantially dilute the welfare system, acting against pressure within his administration for a national income maintenance plan and a centralized manpower training and placement service, among others. A proposal developed by presidential counselor Arthur F. Burns would have scratched more far-reaching ideas, such as those of Robert H. Finch, Secretary of Health, Education and Wel-fare, in favor of retaining the present welfare system but adding numerous new features. Burns favored retaining the various categories of welfare aid as well as some form of revenue-sharing with the states. His plan would not have included the "working poor" or those families headed by marginal wage earners in the relief program.

On Aug. 8, in a televised address to the nation, Nixon proposed a drastic overhaul of the welfare system that would set a national standard payment of $1,600 a year to every family of four below poverty level. In outlining his plan, which was widely regarded as his most courageous proposal of 1969, the President proposed a guaranteed basic income of $1,600 for the working poor with reduced assistance in graduated steps for families earning up to $3,920, and set a minimum national standard of $65 a month for the aged, blind, or disabled in all states (subsequently raised to $90). The sweeping changes, which would scrap the controversial AFDC program in favor of family assistance for all needy families with children, and which provided supplementary aid above the federal minimum to be paid mostly by the states, also involved more funds for job training and day care. Mr. Nixon estimated that the family assistance program would cost $4 billion the first year.

In outlining his plan, the President said it was "designed to correct the condition it deals with" by providing "equality of treatment, a work requirement, and a work incentive." He stressed that the new system would establish "a direct link between the government's willingness to help the needy, and the willingness of the needy to help themselves."

Reaction to the welfare reform proposals was immediate and mixed. On Capitol Hill, Republicans generally praised the speech for offering a new departure from an unsatisfactory system. But some, such as New York's Republican Sens. Jacob K. Javits and Charles E. Goodell, had reservations because the greatest portion of fed-

How long must the millions wait . . . and wait . . . and wait . . . ?

Rev. Ralph D. Abernathy and Hosea Williams at Cape Kennedy protest from the steps of a mockup of a lunar module.

White welfare organizer Father James Groppi leads demonstrators from the Madison, Wisc., state capitol building.

Some find hope in slogans, some in prayers and some spend their lives seeking what others assume are rights.

eral aid—50.1 per cent—would go to the South, the area that has shown the least concern for its poor. Similarly, New York Gov. Nelson A. Rockefeller and John V. Lindsay, mayor of New York City, vowed to seek changes in distribution formulas.

In Democratic ranks, Rep. Wilbur D. Mills of Arkansas, chairman of the House Ways and Means Committee, which passes on the kinds of legislation that would carry out the President's proposals, said he supported the general concept of the plan but had reservations about its cost. He agreed with other congressional leaders that there was no chance for final passage of the bill in 1969.

Two Senate liberals were less than enthusiastic about the Nixon proposals. Sen. George McGovern (D-S.D.) called the plan "disappointing and misleading" and Sen. Walter F. Mondale (D-Minn.) expressed fears about budgetary aspects of the proposal, although he did say he thought some portions of the program would be warmly received.

Organized interest groups damned the plan with faint praise. The National Welfare Rights Organization (NWRO), the nation's largest association of the poor, commended Nixon for taking the "initiative" in reforming the welfare system. But Johnnie Tillmon, NWRO chairman, said the plan itself was "insufficient" and just didn't call for enough money. George A. Wiley, NWRO executive director, said the White House and the Department of Health, Education and Welfare had failed to keep a promise to consult with the poor before drafting the plan.

John R. Kramer, executive director of the National Council on Hunger and Malnutrition, charged that millions of people would lead even worse lives if forced to exist with the cash allowance instead of welfare benefits and food stamps. The administration, which had called earlier for an increase in food stamps, did reconsider its stand on this issue. By October, after substantial "internal jockeying," it was decided to dovetail food stamps into the welfare reforms, so that in addition to $1,600 a year in cash a family of

four could get $750 in food benefits. In December major improvements in the scheme were announced, under which any participating family of four would get $106 worth of food stamps a month for a minimum of $10 cash outlay, or a maximum of 25 per cent of its income.

The Urban Coalition praised the President's initiative, but suggested an increase in minimum income levels to help the large cities that "are being crushed by the spiraling welfare burden."

Wilbur J. Cohen, one of the principal architects of the welfare system in America, charged that Nixon was merely trying to give an established program a new name.

But long-term dividends were forecast for the President by Washington columnists Roscoe and Geoffrey Drummond, who felt that his proposals came at a time when "the political spin-off will most aid the Republican cause" by moving power, initiative, and financing from Washington to state capitols. Thirty of the country's 50 governors in 1969 were members of the Republican Party.

A Harris Survey in October found that while only one out of three Americans was aware of the President's proposals, those who were familiar with them favored the welfare recommendations by a margin of 47 to 17 per cent.

As the year ended, H.R. 14173—the Family Assistance Proposal—was thought to have relatively favorable chances for passage in the second session of the 91st Congress. Public hearings on the bill by the House Ways and Means Committee in the fall had produced criticism from Democrats and social welfare leaders, who said the minimum income guarantee was too low. Labor leaders said they feared the bill's work requirements could be used to subsidize cheap labor. But Rep. John W. Byrnes of Wisconsin, ranking Republican on the committee, said he was committed to the concept of helping the working poor that had been outlined in the President's bill. The committee scheduled executive sessions early in 1970 to hammer out its version of Mr. Nixon's most ambitious piece of social legislation in 1969.

The Courts

The Supreme Court made several decisions in 1969 that were sensitive to the needs of the poor, but it sidestepped questions of constitutional guarantees for low-income citizens. It ruled that tenants of low-income housing are entitled to know *why* they are being evicted before they are evicted, that landlords in Washington, D.C., can't evict tenants simply because they complain about housing code violations, and that unpaid rent can't be collected in the District of Columbia on property that violates housing code requirements. But each of these cases was directed to local or federal law rather than to constitutional issues.

However, the court's decision in June invalidating welfare residency requirements in 40 states and the District of Columbia was made on clearly constitutional grounds. The requirement that a needy person live in a given state for a year before receiving welfare was ruled a violation of the citizen's constitutional right to move freely through the country. The decision was thought to have added considerable weight to the administration's proposal to help states bring their welfare payments up to minimum standards.

A New York State federal court granted a temporary injunction in early August to three partially disabled women against new state welfare legislation which had set welfare payments for aged, blind, and disabled residents of counties surrounding New York City at $4 to $5 less than in the city. The women appealed to the constitutional right to equal treatment under the law. The court's opinion noted that "to an indigent person now receiving approximately 90 cents per day for food, an additional 15 cents per day can hardly be described as 'de minimus.'"

Other significant reappraisals of the welfare system have been made with the support of foundations and by local governments in recent years.

Late in 1968 the Ford Foundation announced that it was granting $830,000 for 10 projects aimed at public assistance reform. The grants went largely to educational institutions for study of the income concept, work incentives, and the relation between welfare and the labor market.

One study in New York City by its department of social services found that three-fourths of the welfare recipients who had been rated employable were actually not work-ready because they were in need of education or medical or psychiatric care. Welfare mothers often wanted to work, it was argued, but the shortage of day care facilities kept them from taking jobs. People who wanted to set up day care centers found it extremely difficult to find facilities that met all health, education, and fire safety standards. No mention was made of the conditions to which the same children would be subjected were they not placed in day care centers.

These mothers and their children made up about three-fourths of the total welfare enrollment of New York City.

Fighting City Hall

The need to reform the welfare system and an increasing awareness of his rights on the part of the welfare client have outdistanced the response of those in power. The poor are increasingly less willing to compromise. Welfare is coming to be viewed not as a privilege, but a right.

In New Orleans, late in 1968, 22 mothers were arrested and their children taken into custody for invading a welfare office to protest a 10 per cent cut in Aid to Dependent Children payments. A federal court issued a temporary restraining order blocking the cuts for a matter of days but the state welfare commission argued that it was running out of money. It said it wouldn't be able to make welfare payments in 1969 unless checks were reduced by 10 percent.

The New York Citywide Coordinating Committee of Welfare Groups organized demonstrations at three of the city's 35 welfare centers in December. The protesters—mostly women and children—argued that newly-revised clothing allowances did not provide enough for children's winter clothing.

About the same time, 44 welfare mothers in Cleveland disrupted welfare offices to demand special payments for their children's winter clothing. After a nine-hour sit-in police were summoned and the protesters arrested. The county welfare director claimed their demands would cost the county $26,000 it did not have. An editorial in the *Cleveland Call and Post* claimed that welfare payments to the mothers constituted only "83 per cent of their determined needs." This was increased to 93 per cent as of Jan. 1, 1969.

The National Welfare Rights Organization, the spirit behind a great many of the demonstrations, met to plan policy in Jackson, Miss., in February. Workshops were also held to train Southerners to fight their region's welfare policies.

In March about 30 mothers of the Citywide Welfare Council in Washington, D.C., temporarily occupied the D.C., welfare office to demand added payments for furniture. They were eventually turned out. Two days later the same women, joined by a group of 50 welfare mothers from South Carolina, returned to the welfare department's offices. Their leader explained that because many of them were unable to afford enough beds, their families had to sleep in shifts, some spending alternate nights on the floor. The deputy director of the welfare department told them that while their demands were reasonable and "justifiable," there was simply not enough money. "They have money to put men on the moon, but no money to take our children from the floor," the mothers jeered. The group moved on to the Old Senate Office Building and later staged three more demonstrations. While welfare officials were not able to grant them funds for furniture, the department urged Washington's mayor to increase the furniture stipend in the 1971 budget.

A quiet group of about 175 children, mothers,

and aged persons protested the proposed federal freeze on AFDC payments in Atlanta one day in March. They supported the move under consideration at the state capitol to make up the difference with state funds. Georgia Gov. Lester Maddox told them, "This is not a state problem, this is a decision made by Congress. . . .I'm for helping the children all I can, but there are adults out there that should be working."

In May the proceedings of the National Conference on Social Welfare meeting in New York were disrupted by young representatives of national welfare rights organizations, who prevented delegates from leaving the first session to ask for contributions to the NWRO. The demonstrators complained that the conference was not answering the needs of the poor. The keynote speech by former HEW Secretary Arthur Flemming was very much in sympathy with the views of the protesters and they were given a half an hour to air their opinions. During the conference a new group, the Social Welfare Workers Movement, was formed to give social workers another forum besides the National Association of Social Workers, which was alleged to perpetuate a "cast system" within the profession.

On the third day of the conference, proceedings were brought to a halt by a new group, the National Association of Black Social Workers, which refused to let the regular agenda continue until certain demands were met. One of these was providing $35,000 to send 250 members of the NWRO to the Social Welfare Conference of 1970.

On June 11, 1969, the National Welfare Rights Organization staged a "people's hearing" in an HEW auditorium before 500 welfare and federal officials to point out that the subsistence level existence had been reached by the welfare system. "Look around," one leader said, "you'll see a lot of healthy, fat ladies, but they feel bad. They have to eat the wrong kinds of foods, some days they don't eat and when they do eat, they overeat. . . . We have to live like the lowest creatures on earth."

Floyd B. McKissick receives encouragement from attorney T. T. Clayton and former Secretary of Agriculture Orville Freeman for his plan to build a new town in rural "Black Belt" of North Carolina.

Urban Development

The Poor

"THOUGH there still is too much poverty in the black community, there is a major change," Reg Murphy of the *Atlanta Constitution* observed. He continued, "Where a total of 56 per cent of the blacks were classified as poor in 1961, that total now has fallen to 33 per cent. . . . [Census Bureau] figures do not say that poverty has been eliminated. They do not say that all Americans get enough to eat and enough medical attention. In fact, there still are 24.5 million who are in the grisly grip of poverty." A third of these Americans are black.

About poverty, people say, "Yes, the children are innocent and need to be fed; but no, we cannot coddle people. Yes, there is plenty of misery around; but no, special favors simply cannot be granted. Yes, some people really do need help; but no, the only help we ought to get has to come from God and our own exertions," Robert Coles noted in *The New Republic*.

Derrick A. Bell, a professor at Harvard, said, "An economic double standard in this country . . . presents a serious handicap to our efforts to correct domestic problems of race and poverty . . . but the real substantive problems—economic and educational inequalities—and the racism that continue to pervade the land go on taking their toll."

"All the planning and all the money on earth won't provide the ultimate solutions to our prob-

lems unless we're prepared to make personal and moral changes in our attitudes and practices," said Atlanta Mayor Ivan Allen, Jr. "Many of us feel a certain longing for the past, for the simplicity of life in the days when everyone and everything had a place and generally stayed in it. . . . Ever since slavery was abolished in the South, we have tried to invent new ways to keep black people in servitude. We have been very successful. The median income of a white Georgian is $2,500, but the same measure of income for a black Georgian yields only $1,000."

In recent years the rising crime rates, the boggle of jammed streets and skies, the soaring cost of living, housing shortages, decaying neighborhoods and schools, and the white flight to the suburbs—leaving a narrowed tax base to fight the problems in the cities—have come to be known as the urban crisis.

"By all the standard measurements of human troubles in the city, the ghetto has always been with us—it has tragically endured. . . . Despite continuing efforts to effect radical reform, little has been accomplished that permanently improved the fundamental conditions of life of most Negroes, nor has any ideology or program radically bettered the tone of race relations in the North if the largest city (New York) is a suitable model," said Prof. Gilbert Osofsky of the University of Illinois.

Cleveland Mayor Carl B. Stokes said he felt that "things are going to get somewhat worse in this country before they get better, until the country is painfully aware of the need for its maximum involvement. It is only at that point that the country will turn its great resources, imagination and inventiveness, to solving poverty. . . . It is a war. These cities have become a battleground. I don't mean a battleground exclusively in the sense of people with guns. That's just part of it. It's a battleground for survival. The people have flocked to these big cities for a chance to live—not for freedom like the Negro migrated 20 years ago to try to find."

David Rockefeller said that "the problem of our cities, our urban areas," would be the biggest domestic problem to confront President Nixon. "A major aspect of it has been the migration of Negro agricultural labor from the South into the great urban areas of the North over the past 20 or 25 years," Rockefeller said. "This has caused a basic change in the population composition of the core cities and has resulted in a large portion of the middle-income white population moving out into the suburbs. That created many new problems. . . . This has reduced the cities' tax take and at the same time increased the requirement for all kinds of services, including schools and hospitals, police and sanitation. . . . I believe it's going to require a certain amount of reorganization of governmental structure, bringing together in larger groupings a variety of existing units. One possible out is for the federal government to pay to the states and the local governments a larger amount of revenues which are raised without specific allocation."

Ronald P. Smolin wrote that "in poverty neighborhoods, businessmen who usually live elsewhere own and manage virtually the whole economy. . . . Millions of dollars a year in profits are taken out of and do little to bolster economic growth of an impoverished community. . . . This continued hemorrhaging of capital is a contributing factor to the economic sickness of slum communities and, of course, to the poverty of individual families."

Areas with small populations were also having problems. "Not only are small cities growing into big ones with problems of housing, education, revenues, and race, but their officials have recognized that federal aid is both necessary and complicated," Robert L. Asher wrote in the *Washington Post*. "Local officials are the best people to decide what should be done in their areas, the mayors of suburban communities argued, adding that they are doing all they can to squeeze out more taxes."

Former Secretary of Health, Education and Welfare John W. Gardner, now head of the Urban Coalition, said that "fragmentation" of American cities has made them breeding grounds of fear and hostility. "This generation will not accept solutions that are precooked in the back rooms of the Establishment. People want to have their say," he added.

Richard Goldfarb agreed. "What blacks want is to bring the voice of the black community into programs which can effect permanent institutional change. They want white men to hear directly from those who live in the black world's tenements, work at its deadened jobs, attend its chaotic schools. They want white men to learn first hand what the black man's fury is all about," he wrote.

Dr. Kenneth B. Clark said that community action programs such as those sponsored by the Office of Economic Opportunity (OEO) have failed and have "contributed significantly to the fuel of urban conflagration." According to Clark, community action, designed to get at the heart of poverty by involving the poor, has delivered verbal promises but has made little noticeable change in the predicament of the poor. Unkept promises add "to the restlessness, the alienation, and the sense of hopelessness of the deprived," he said. Clark's study was done in 1965 and 1966, the first two years community action was implemented, and covered 51 poverty programs in 12 cities. "Politicians, social workers, social scientists, community actionists, and some indigenous workers have all benefited to one degree or another from anti-poverty programs. The poor seem to have benefited less," Clark observed. Daniel P. Moynihan, urban affairs adviser to President Nixon, was also a leading critic of community action.

But a three-year study financed by the Ford Foundation defended such programs. The director of the study, Sar A. Levitan, said OEO "must certainly be judged an innovative agency which gave the poor their first social and political role."

One "master plan" for New York City advised, "We must provide more opportunity for the low income residents of our ghettos. This is without question the gut issue in the urban crisis. The urban poor feel more trapped and deprived today than ever before because they live in the most affluent of nations in the most affluent of times. The pressure is building up. The cities will explode unless the poor find ways to participate fully in American life."

The Healers

The Urban Coalition was formed by private citizens in August 1967 in the wake of severe riots. The Coalition aimed to bring about greater federal efforts to provide jobs, adequate incomes, decent housing, and improved education for the poor. John W. Gardner believes, however, that the Coalition has failed at the community level. "We have talked a great game of community leadership, but we haven't lived up to it," he said. "The federal government can only give the communities the pieces [grants and programs] and it is up to them to put the pieces together."

In Chicago major businesses, prompted by Gardner, agreed to contribute $815,000 to the Coalition for United Community Action to underwrite the first stage of a plan to improve conditions for black citizens. The First National Bank and Sears Roebuck and Co. led the way in supporting the Coalition and in soliciting financial aid to establish a center for training blacks in community development.

The American Jewish Congress promoted anti-poverty programs in the Bronx and Boston areas where it sponsored meetings to form inter-faith and interracial community councils to improve neighborhoods. In Washington, D.C., the Congress helped transfer businesses from Jewish to black ownership. On Long Island's North Shore, it helped set up a College for Mature Adults Foundation at the Nassau Community College to prepare adults for college. The Congress also sponsored a housing project for black families on Long Island.

The Los Angeles City Council and the Community Redevelopment Council okayed a project to revitalize the riot-devastated Watts area with shops, housing, and schools. But as one local doctor pointed out, "Urban renewal means Negro removal, no matter how you put it. There are renters in Watts who can't pay $60 a month. How are they going to pay $225?"

"We know we won't fit into the redevelopment plan," another Watts resident argued. "We would like to be left alone—to help ourselves."

East St. Louis, Ill., one of the most critical urban areas in the state, is hungering after federal money. Industry has left the city; housing has been deteriorating for years; crime is on the rise. East St. Louis is part of the Model Cities Program and looks to that for salvation. "Everything is hanging on Model Cities," said city planner Will McGarghy, Jr. "If it doesn't go, we will really have a ghost town."

Walter L. Thomas, a Watts civic leader, declared, "We are going to turn the corner by utilizing the young blood we have here. With young vigor meshed with experience on the other side of the generation gap, we are going to make it. But we must realize that, to do it, we must come through—and soon. We must deliver on our promises or we are in for some very difficult times."

A recent report on urban blight in California pinpointed Southern California's expanding freeway system as one of the causes of slums and deterioration. The report by the Southern California Research Council said the freeways "made it possible for those who had established themselves [in the cities] to abandon rundown housing, rather than maintaining and improving it. . . .

Many land speculators build homes in a hurry, neglecting adequate provision for schools, roads, and other necessary public services. The buildings themselves were shoddily constructed by quick-profit entrepreneurs, creating 'instant slums' that were built so cheaply they were virtually unmaintainable."

Richard Reeves reported in the *New York Times* that a master plan for New York City, approved by the City Planning Commission, "outlines an over-all development strategy that includes a 10-year, $19 billion program to create a new middle class out of the three million poor, the establishment of 'community hospitals' where physicians would be assigned to every family in a neighborhood, and the placing of limits on the number of automobiles permitted into midtown Manhattan." Most of the money was to come from the federal government, not the city.

Housing

The 1968 Housing Act requires a coordinated approach to urban renewal programs, not only on a citywide basis, but regionally. The Model Cities section of the act put more control of funds in the hands of state and local governments, but 1969 saw no great boom in housing for the poor.

"Contributing to the problem [of urban renewal] are delays and a philosophical argument about whom urban renewal should house and how," Bill Amlong observed in the *Miami Herald*. "There is also a debate raging about whether urban renewal's first purpose should be to house the poor it removed from the slums in 'gilded ghettos' of public housing, or whether it should provide for neighborhoods containing an 'economic blend' and preferably a racial mix, too. Meanwhile the poor persons who need housing are sitting in squalor. . . ."

One legal consultant to the National Commission on Urban Problems suggested three ways to curb urban sprawl: compensatory regulations— payments to owners whose property falls under highly restrictive zoning; public land assembly —extending the power of eminent domain to assemble large tracts of land in underdeveloped areas; and planned development zoning—extending special regulations for large tracts of land planned as a single unit.

Clarence Funnye, director of urban planning for the National Committee Against Discrimination in Housing in New York, described antipoverty programs such as the war on poverty and Model Cities as having "all the fury of two giants dueling with powder puffs." Funnye proposed a "de-ghettoization" process that would open the way for city and state university systems to enroll a great many more blacks and Puerto Ricans by 1970. He also called for the integration of towns outside the central cities and for construction of at least 400,000 subsidized housing units each year for 10 years, giving subsidy priority to new towns for housing, sewer, water, and transportation improvement.

The Hungry Americans

The most dramatic and poignant fact about people who are poor is that they are hungry— most of the time.

"From time to time during the past few years, there has come to public attention the jarring news that a great many Americans do not get enough to eat because they are too poor," said one commentator. "The words 'starvation,' and 'hunger,' and 'malnutrition' have all been used to describe the phenomenon. Each of these conditions is difficult to isolate, or even describe, or to separate from related diseases, because there has been little scientific or official interest in the problem. Yet it is generally agreed, even among government circles, that at a minimum, ten million Americans are malnourished and some of these are chronically hungry, even starving, because they are poor. The failure of the Johnson administration to make substantial progress toward feeding the poor is viewed by many as its most serious domestic failure."

Senate subcommittees have been studying the problem of hunger for years. But the problem had not received wide public attention until a 1968 CBS broadcast, "Hunger in America," helped make it an issue. Sen. George S. McGovern (D-S.D.) and his Senate Select Committee on Nutrition and Human Needs set about investigating the depth of the crisis of hunger in the United States.

People generally pay about 18 per cent of their income for food but the poor must spend from 30 to 50 per cent. To help poor people supplement their diets, the government has two basic programs: food stamps (sold at a price lower than the value of the food the stamps would be traded for) and distribution of "surplus commodities." Each county decides on one or the other method—or neither. The list of commodities from the Department of Agriculture includes 22 items. Most officials—and grocers—prefer the food stamp program over commodity distribution. But the big problem is that families are required to buy their food stamps at one time each month. Many simply cannot come up with the lump sum of cash at the crucial time. In many areas, food prices are raised on stamp sale day.

Whitney Young, executive secretary of the Urban League, was one of many who said the food stamp program would have to be revised. "Unless the new administration wants America to be known as a land of hunger and illness, it will have to move fast to correct this national scandal," he said. "Prices for the stamps are often too costly and the allotments too low to provide an adequate diet." He said free stamps should be provided to the poorest families.

Anthropologist Margaret Mead told McGovern's subcommittee that almost 10 million Americans were not getting adequate nourishment and that "many of these are on the verge of starvation. . . . The American people are less well-nourished, as a whole, than they were 10 years ago."

In the Mississippi delta, one health center out to provide free medical diagnoses and treatment found that the most crucial item needed to improve the health of many of the patients was food.

In January outgoing Secretary of Agriculture Orville L. Freeman estimated it would cost an additional $1 billion a year to close the nutritional gap and end hunger in the United States. In his farewell speech, he pointed out two obstacles: the refusal of Congress to appropriate sufficient funds and the reluctance of more conservative counties to participate in federal food programs.

In an official study of nutrition, Dr. Arnold E. Schaefer of the Public Health Service surveyed over 30 developing nations and found severe hunger in many of them; when he investigated American poverty areas he found surprisingly similar conditions. Schaefer's statistics showed one-sixth of the nation to be ill-fed. He reported cases of goiter, rickets, night blindness, and kwashiorkor—severe malnutrition often found in African children. "We found a few cases of diseases we didn't think even existed in the United States," he said. "Evidence suggested that mental as well as physical retardation often resulted from the chronic malnutrition. "Youngsters with hemoglobin counts below 10 grams will never reach their full potential for physical growth," Dr. Schaefer noted, "and there's a good chance they will never fulfill their mental capabilities. . . . What we would find often was that infants would start off within the normal growth curve and then their growth would taper off after about six months. . . . The crucial period seems to be between the time they stop breast feeding and the time they're old enough to eat scraps off the table." The survey found that most of the people with serious nutritional problems were members of minority groups; 55 per cent of those studied were black.

Dr. Mark Hegsted, Harvard nutrition professor and chairman of the Food and Nutrition Board of the National Academy of Sciences; Dr. Charles U. Lowe, scientific director of the National Institute of Child Health and Human Development and chairman of the Food and Nutrition Council of the American Academy of

Pediatrics; Dr. David B. Coursin, research director of St. Joseph Hospital Research Institute in Pennsylvania and a leading investigator of birth defects, all agreed that there is a chain effect of inadequate nutrition that can lead to permanent brain damage. They told the Senate subcommittee that poverty leads ill-fed pregnant women to bear ill-fed fetuses that fail to synthesize proteins and brain cells at normal rates. For these babies there is a high rate of premature births and early deaths. Those who survive are fed a diet lacking necessary vitamins and proteins and the result is permanently stunted brains and bodies.

In February the Senate Rules Committee cut the budget of the subcommittee studying hunger from $250,000 to $150,000. Sen. McGovern said it was "a sad day for hungry people."

Robert L. Gnaizda, deputy director of the federally-financed California Rural Assistance League, took on a case to test whether hungry Americans have a constitutional right to food. The U.S. Department of Agriculture moved to have the whole case tossed out of court, but a three-judge federal court instead issued a temporary order to set up federal food programs in all California counties. Some had refused the programs, claiming either that they had no poverty-stricken residents or that they opposed the concept of federal help to the poor.

Some senators went out in search of collective hunger. Sen. Ernest F. Hollings (D-S.C.) toured South Carolina and reported, "There's no question about the hunger and malnutrition. I've seen it." Sen. Strom Thurmond (R-S.C.) denounced the claim and implied that the Democratic senator's trip had been political.

Dr. Aaron Shirley, a Jackson, Miss., pediatrician and civil rights leader, said of the blacks living in the Mississippi Delta: "They aren't starving, really, but they are undernourished as hell." This was denied by the white establishment. The state's governor, Paul B. Johnson, Jr., is said to have talked of blacks he had seen as "fat and shiny."

Health, Education and Welfare Secretary Robert H. Finch said he was troubled about the possibility of mental retardation and learning difficulties that were a result of bad nutrition in infancy and early childhood. He ordered an expansion of the national nutrition survey.

Secretary of Agriculture Clifford Hardin said he was hoping to move every possible resource to wipe out malnutrition and he approved a pilot project to send free food to two South Carolina counties. At McGovern's request Hardin declared an emergency and shipped food to the counties where people couldn't afford to buy even the lowest priced food stamps. Hardin used an appropriation of $50 million to supplement existing food programs for the poor. Other members of Congress were quick to ask about free food for their states.

Researchers at the University of South Carolina who studied preschool black children in Beaufort County found that 73 per cent had roundworms, whipworms, or both. The worms grow a foot in length and consume what little food the children manage to get. Many of the children were eating only 800 calories a day, "certainly not enough to support the child—and rarely enough to support the worms," said Dr. James P. Carter of Vanderbilt University.

McGovern felt the pilot program in South Carolina was a breakthrough that could lead to a nationwide program of food distribution to those poor who could not afford to pay a 50 cent token fee.

Toward the end of February, the issue of human hunger was taken up in the Senate. McGovern got back the $100,000 that had been stripped from his subcommittee's budget and no one complained about the overturning of the Rules Committee's decision. One reason the money had been cut originally was that Southerners controlled the Rules Committee; the South had been reluctant to admit that it could not feed its people.

In the South Carolina counties, a group of about 60 black members of the Welfare Rights Union threatened to charter a bus to go to Washington to protest the "narrow scope" of the free food stamp program. Union leaders said the stamps were a "gimmick" and only a token gesture that would aid few families. They said they wanted a broader program. When stamp distribution began in March to families of four or more whose incomes were under $30 a month, few turned out to pick them up. The poor response was felt to be partly a problem of communication—people did not know about the free stamps—and partly a Union-inspired boycott. Soon, however, the boycott lessened and people began to collect their free stamps.

McGovern also asked Hardin to distribute free food stamps to the poor in Washington, D.C., in a trial plan. "We can end hunger in this country in two to three years. This is one part of the war on poverty we can win and we can win it at a modest cost," McGovern said.

Even Sen. Herman E. Talmadge (D-Ga.) requested free food stamps for his state, a move that surprised political observers. "I don't want to see those kids go to school hungry because of default of their parents," was Talmadge's reasoning.

In early March, 40 members of the Welfare Rights Union came to Washington to meet with Agriculture Department officials. The group charged the officials with murdering and crippling children by holding back on food programs. Agriculture officials promised to consider the delegation's recommendations.

Dr. Kenneth Aycock, a state health officer for South Carolina, announced a pilot program to supplement the free food stamp program for expectant mothers and preschool children in two South Carolina counties. A dozen federal commodities of high nutrient content were chosen for distribution.

The Senate subcommittee investigating hunger found that in Lee County, Fla., the local director of Commodity Food Distribution, Robert Craft (dubbed "Mr. Crab" by the poor) was humiliating any persons seeking food. Although free food was available, it was not reaching the needy. McGovern commented that "most of the cattle and hogs in America are better fed and sheltered than the families we have visited."

During the tours and the investigations, seemingly limitless families were found to be living in shacks, with little or no income but plenty of children. Filth and disease were found to be rampant. Repeatedly, the same story and scenes were presented, but those who were there reported words or photographs could not convey the wretched smells and conditions.

In mid-March the Agricultural Committee of the National Planning Association recommended a revised food stamp program and suggested the program be transferred from the Department of Agriculture to HEW. "Food aid policies should be considered entirely as programs of help for poor people and not as farm programs," the association said. The proposed program would allow families to spend what they could afford to feed their children, with the difference made up by the variable cost of stamps. It would eliminate the problem that most often discouraged families from participating in the current food stamp program: the prohibitive cost of having to buy an entire month's supply of food stamps at one time. The association also called for increased federal control to protect poor residents of states with indifferent administrations.

Hardin told President Nixon that funds to fight the hunger in America should be increased by about $1 billion over the next four years if the program was to work. He wanted to authorize more food stamp money to give a greater subsidy to low income families, to make stamps available at food stores rather than at county welfare offices and to permit families to buy stamps more often than once a month.

Talmadge proposed in April that food stamps be distributed by post offices (relieving county governments of responsibility) and that poor people not be required to pay more than 25 per cent of their income for food stamps. Talmadge toured Georgia to determine the degree of actual continuous hunger. Talmadge said that feeding children so they could study properly was "the only way we will end this cycle of welfare cases."

Sen. William B. Spong, Jr. (D-Va.) toured

his state's mountain regions and reported that "these people couldn't get along without the [federal food] programs." Spong was surprised to find hungry people in Fairfax County, a suburb of Washington, D.C.

Gov. Lester Maddox of Georgia took up the cause by urging support of "Martha's Day"—a day of prayer and fasting to dramatize the plight of "Martha" and other hungry children of Atlanta. Maddox asked also for contributions to a milk fund for hungry school children.

The Senate subcommittee heard that children in Arkansas were so undernourished they could no longer walk, talk, or even eat; a New Mexico family ate nothing but the chipmunks and wild birds they were able to catch. Many of the poor did not know of the food program; many who had heard of food stamps did not believe they would really receive food.

McGovern proposed that families with monthly incomes under $80 receive free food stamps and that eligibility standards be lowered. He said it would cost the government $1.8 billion to feed 8 million people the first year—5 million more than were currently being served.

At the end of April Hardin said there was not enough money in the national budget to end hunger—and that the White House knew it. The President had decided that top domestic priority would go to stopping inflation.

In May the President announced that he had been able to juggle the federal budget to allow an extra $1 billion for an expanded food stamp program. He said it was a moment to act with vigor toward ending hunger. McGovern called the $1 billion "inadequate." The President established a new federal agency, the Food and Nutrition Service, to administer all food programs. In some areas, under a new project, pregnant women and mothers of infants could redeem vouchers for infant formulas and other special foods.

Finch told the Senate subcommittee that "over the longer run, a more basic answer to the problem of malnutrition—as with the other problems associated with poverty—must be found in reform of our public assistance and employment programs. Cash income—not a succession of payments in kind—best preserves the dignity and freedom of choice of the individual to meet his own needs."

Dr. Charles U. Lowe, scientific director of the National Institute of Child Health and Human Development, told the subcommittee that "unmistakable scientific evidence" had conclusively linked infant malnutrition with mental retardation. There was no longer any doubt, he said.

The Southern Christian Leadership Conference's Operation Breadbasket, along with black Illinois legislators, launched an anti-hunger campaign in Illinois. Rev. Jesse Jackson, head of Operation Breadbasket, led 3,000 persons on a "hunger march" on the Illinois state capitol in Springfield, and Gov. Richard B. Ogilvie withdrew his proposal to slash Illinois' public aid budget by $25 million. State Treasurer Adlai Stevenson III said the state could put an end to hunger immediately. He was highly critical of priorities that allow millions to be spent for county fairs, race horses, and roads, yet allocates only a few thousand dollars for food programs in Illinois.

In September a massive increase in the food stamp program was authorized by the U.S. Senate. The bill, introduced by McGovern, was designed to allow families to use stamps for things like soap, and to permit poorer families to buy less than their full allotment. The bill would also permit stamps to be sold at post offices and to be mailed to recipients. Local non-profit organizations or federal agencies would operate stamp programs in areas where state and local governments had refused. The government food distribution program would be operated at the same time where necessary.

The Fight to End Hunger

On farm cooperatives in the South men have begun to grow food instead of cotton. They pool their land and labor and use modern farm equipment. The crops they grow feed some of the hungry poor as well as their families, and a few farms have done well enough to market surplus produce.

The extent to which agricultural cooperatives can aid the Southern poor remains to be seen. Thus far the successful ones have been financed by the government or foundations. Many have had political and managerial problems. Al Ulmer, in a report for the Southern Regional Council, concluded, "Strengthened and expanded and subsidized on a long-term basis, co-ops can make an economic impact on the lives of the rural poor. Moreover, properly decentralized to insure democratic control, they would stand ready as channels for a greatly needed rehabilitation effort in the rural South."

Dr. H. Jack Geiger, head of the Tufts University Delta Community Health Center, has urged poor blacks in Mound Bayou, Miss., to utilize their own rich delta. Geiger helped form a cooperative farm with a grant from OEO that was able to feed 12,000 people in one county. Geiger feels migration to city slums must be reversed because "the big cities tend to crush those over 30 and make the young wild." Co-worker John Hatch, a Negro, said, "I can't imagine anyone living on this land, the richest in the nation, and starving."

The Southern Cooperative Development Program provides management assistance to 38 poor people's co-ops and credit unions operating in Alabama, Louisiana, Mississippi, and Tennessee with a $578,000 grant from the Ford Foundation. More than 25,000 black farmers in 11 Southern states have pooled their land, farm machinery, and produce to form the Federation of Southern Cooperatives. They no longer have to sell individually. Farmers in St. Francis County, Ark., increased production of vegetables and their gross incomes when they formed the St. Francis County Vegetable Growers Cooperative Association. The co-op was aided by the Department of Agriculture's Farmers Home Administration.

The Right to Health

A survey by *Medical Tribune* reported in November 1968 that federal money and civil rights laws were slowly improving the status of Negro doctors, while providing better medical care for black Americans. The progress came, not from a change of heart, but from fear of punitive action or loss of federal money, the report stated.

Dr. Paul B. Cornely, head of the Department of Preventive Medicine and Public Health of Howard University's College of Medicine, said medical care and health services for the nation's poor amounted to "exploitation." "Too often the poor are victimized by a system that may require a person to sit for hours in a bleak waiting room of a large clinic or hospital," noted one magazine, *Progressive Architecture*. "Under these conditions it is not surprising that 30 per cent of the children from poor families have never seen a doctor and that 60 per cent have never seen a dentist. Adults in poor families have four times more disabling heart disease, six times more mental, and 10 times more visual impairments than do adults in families that are not poor. The poor are likelier to be sick and the sick are likely to be poor."

Health specialists and physicians attending a July Conference on "Medicine in the Ghettos" sent a telegram to the President urging him to pressure for reorganization and reform of medical school curricula, health care centers, and hospitals. "To date you have not announced a healthy policy directed at these needs of the nation, and particularly of the poor," the conferees wired. "Your administration has not introduced health legislation to cope with the crisis in medical care."

In March a bill was introduced in the California legislature to provide "pre-paid preventive health care" for low-income people. Its sponsor, State Sen. Mervyn M. Dymally, said, "Current practices are wasteful, and it should prove obvious that a concept of total health care and preventive medicine will save lives and money."

Also in March the National Health Council urged that the poor be given representation on the boards of most major health agencies. The Council, a group of private and public associations, also endorsed a national health insurance program and special training of slum residents for paraprofessional medical jobs. In Chicago, four blacks were among nine persons selected for the County Hospital's governing commission.

The Black Doctor

Dr. Paul Cornely commented on his fellow Negro medical professionals: "The black doctor has been excluded from many of the ghetto programs; only recently, by virtue of the stimulus given by the National Medical Association [an organization of black physicians], is the black doctor getting part of the action."

The American Medical Association, at its 22nd annual Clinic Convention late in 1968, acted to bar racial discrimination by member societies. An enforcement system was set up under which local societies would be ousted for repeated discrimination. It was the first such step ever taken by the conservative AMA, although the association had previously argued that it was opposed to discrimination.

Dr. Alfred Haynes, director of the National Medical Association Foundation, said that in the United States there is little equal treatment for black doctors. Haynes said the chances of a black becoming a doctor were one-tenth those of a white man. Black men who make it through medical school often run into prejudice and are denied hospital privileges, he said.

"By and large, American medicine has provided one of the most shocking examples of discrimination against minority groups our society has witnessed," notes Gary, Ind., Mayor Richard Hatcher. "Today's shortage of black physicians is critical." The shortage is the result of "years of traditions in white medical schools, which either admit minority groups on a quota basis or not at all," Hatcher said.

Dr. Julius W. Hill, new president of the National Medical Association, admits there is "constant frustration" among Negro physicians. He applauds Medicare and Medicaid programs, but comments that he becomes "so disgusted when I submit a bill and am treated like a suspect or criminal. . . . The biggest problem facing a black physician is his constant frustration at being on the ground floor of projects and policy making, and the fact that when he is taken into a program, it's almost a token thing." The ghetto doctor "is not getting the pay he deserves," Hill said, "so that what he is doing is almost a labor of love, and he is treating an average of 60 patients a day. This is too many. You can't attract doctors to the ghetto when they don't get the pay they should."

Physicians to the Poor

The National Medical Association Foundation, a black doctors' organization, broke ground for a nursing home and comprehensive health center late in 1969 for inner-city residents of Washington, D.C. Foundation President Lionel F. Swan said the center would be a step toward "ending current discrimination against the poor in the delivery of health care." The center is the first of several planned nationwide and is one of the first such projects attempted by an organization of private doctors in an urban ghetto. The Equitable Life Assurance Society, under a Federal Housing Administration guarantee, loaned the doctors $2.6 million. Another group of black physicians set up a medical clinic to serve residents of the slums of South Jamaica, Queens, N.Y.

In Chicago black doctors said they planned a nationwide campaign to pressure state and local officials into arranging for federally funded health programs for the poor. Dr. Andrew L. Thomas, president of the Cook County Physicians Association, said, "There is an obvious gap between the black community and the federally funded programs out of Washington to major metropolitan cities. The money never gets down to the grassroots level, to the black communities where you have people dying for lack of food." The doctors planned to recruit blacks into the biomedical sciences and pressure state and local agencies to both plan effective programs for black communities and revamp welfare programs.

Care for Black Americans

Doctors at the Watts Extended Health and Family Planning Group, Inc., said they feared that a federally administered birth control program might be used to keep America's black population in check. This view has been denounced by Jerome H. Holland, chairman of Planned Parenthood-World Population. Holland, who is black, said the real problem was that the non-white infant mortality rate is double that of whites in the United States. "Black babies and black mothers die because medical service is denied," he said.

At the convention of the Association of Chest Physicians, a subsidiary of the American Medical Association, members of the black National Medical Association disagreed with one of the recommendations concerning organ transplants. The NMA did not want the identity of donors kept secret. Said Dr. W. Montague Cobb, "Nobody likes to entertain the thought of genocide, but the action of the chest physicians has inevitably raised suspicions. . . .The withholding of the names of donors as policy should be scrutinized with greatest care. . . . Minority and impoverished groups would be the most likely to be affected by this policy of anonymity."

A new diagnostic test for a blood disorder found mainly in blacks was presented at the annual meeting of the American Society of Clinical Pathologists in October. The test, described as a practical method for routine diagnosis, was presented by Dr. L.W. Diggs, Goodman professor of medicine at the Tennessee College of Medicine; Dr. Julian B. Schoor, associate clinical professor of pathology at Albert Einstein College of Medicine; Dr. William Q. Ascari, director of diagnostic clinical research; and Dr. Alice Reiss of the Ortho Research Foundation.

In December the New York City Health Department reported that in black and Puerto Rican areas the number of reported rat bites had been cut by 50 per cent over a five-year period.

Dr. James C. Wallace, Jr., president of the National Dental Association, said that nationally "the ratio of dentists to population is about one for every 2,000 persons. In the black community, however, the ratio is one dentist to every 15,000, and this ratio is steadily dropping each year." Dr. Wallace said that almost 100 per cent of the ghetto population suffers from dental decay.

In Washington, D.C., doctors at Children's Hospital reported a significant increase in an eye disorder in black newborns caused by gonorrhea in the mothers.

Alice Scott, a student at Cornell University, won the right to be re-examined by a black psychiatrist after being observed by a white university psychologist and placed on compulsory medical leave. Miss Scott challenged the competence of white psychiatrists and psychologists to judge the mental fitness of blacks. Dr. George Miller of the Cornell Mental Health Clinic said the real questions are whether a white person can understand a black person and if the concept of mental health is different for different races.

In April the results of a five-year study of Manhattan children, directed by Dr. Thomas S. Langer, an associate professor of psychiatry at the New York University School of Medicine, were reported at the annual convention of the American Orthopsychiatric Association. Only 12 per cent of the children studied were found to be mentally healthy. Twelve per cent were described as disturbed, an additional 34 per cent as "moderately" impaired. The rate of illness which the researchers found to be related to poverty was more than twice as high for blacks and Spanish-speaking persons as for whites. For whites and Spanish-speaking people, the risk of mental illness was found to decrease as the parents' education and income increased, but this was not true for blacks. "Our current impression is that Negro children start at age six to nine on an equal footing with white children with regard to impairment," Langer said. "The picture changes dramatically at ages 10 to 13, when the proportion of markedly impaired Negro children starts to exceed those of whites."

In May Dr. Augustus F. Kinzel, a teacher of psychiatry at Columbia University's College of Physicians and Surgeons, reported the results of his studies at the United States Medical Center for Federal Prisoners in Springfield, Mo. He found that men who have been imprisoned for crimes of violence appear to be far more sensitive to the physical closeness of others than prisoners convicted of crimes against property. He said it was one possible explanation of the high number of violent crimes in overcrowded slums.

In June the Chicago Board of Health reported that the rate of deaths for non-white infants, although still higher than that for whites, was declining. The city's health commissioner, Dr. Morgan J. O'Connell, said the change may have been due to improved prenatal care for non-white babies.

In contrast to the report from Chicago, Dr. H. Jack Geiger, director of the Tufts Delta Health Center in Bolivar County, Miss., told a Senate subcommittee that the mortality rate for black infants there had risen to as high as 100 per 1,000 births, compared to a national average of 20.6 per 1,000.

A report on suicides among blacks for the National Institute of Mental Health by Dr. Herbert Hendin, associate professor of psychiatry at Columbia University, stated, "The high frequency of suicide among older whites has led to the misconception that suicide is a 'white' problem, obscuring the fact that among younger adults, particularly in urban areas, it is actually more of a black problem. . . . For example, [suicide is] twice as frequent among New York Negroes between 20 and 35 as it is among whites

of the same age. . . . It is perhaps most apparent that the murderous rage and self-hatred that mark their suicide attempts are an integral part of their racial experience and form part of the burden of being black in America."

Strikes

The largest and longest strike against any hospital in 1969 was in Charleston, S.C. The strike began in March. Twelve nonprofessional workers at Medical College Hospital presented the president of the hospital, Dr. William McCord, with a list of grievances that claimed the workers received substandard pay and were discriminated against. The hospital workers demanded union representation by the National Hospital and Nursing Home Workers Union and pay equal to that of the white workers. McCord fired the twelve: "I am not about to turn a $25 million complex over to a bunch of people who don't have a grammar school education." Charleston County Hospital workers struck eight days after the Medical College workers, and between the two, 200 workers walked off their jobs.

Demonstrations were organized and 44 hospital workers marched willingly into police vans to protest the hospital's actions. In the first five days of the strike, over 100 demonstrators were arrested.

A circuit judge moved to bring the hospital workers' union up for contempt action. Mr. William Huff, a vice president of the Medical College Hospital, said, "We don't plan to talk to anyone who represents a union." Huff asserted that hospitals could not deal with union wage demands because the salaries were set by legislative appropriation.

The strike was supported nationally by an alliance of labor and civil rights leaders. They agreed Charleston was a proving ground and perhaps would be a turning point in the civil rights movement. Mrs. Coretta Scott King, Rev. Ralph David Abernathy, president of the Southern Christian Leadership Conference, Roy Wilkins, executive secretary of the NAACP, Whitney M. Young, Jr., executive director of the National Urban League, Roy Innis, national director of the Congress of Racial Equality, Bayard Rustin, executive director of the A. Philip Randolph Institute, Dorothy I. Height, president of the National Council of Negro Women, George A. Wiley, executive director of the National Welfare Rights Organization, Representative Shirley Chisholm, Democrat of Brooklyn, Rep. John M. Conyers, Democrat of Detroit, Mayor Richard G. Hatcher of Gary, Ind., Mayor Carl B. Stokes of Cleveland, Julian Bond, member of the Georgia House of Representatives—all gave the strikers their full approval. The group issued this statement: "We cannot fail to recall that the right of workers to be represented by a union is precisely the same issue that led to the tragedy in Memphis last year," referring to the murder of Dr. Martin Luther King, Jr. Mrs. King said, "If the black people of Charleston are defeated, the tragic polarization in our nation will intensify."

During April about 500 to 600 workers left their jobs. There were demonstrations and intermittent reports of false fire alarms and some windows broken, but no serious damage was done. The strikers organized boycotts of all stores, except food and drug, to put pressure on businessmen. Hospitals remained open offering limited service.

At the end of April about 2,000 marchers led by Mrs. King paraded through the town singing and clapping past posted National Guardsmen. Strikers and Guardsmen collided. Over 350 persons were arrested, including Rev. Abernathy. A 9 PM curfew was set for Charleston.

In May George Meany, president of the AFL-CIO, called on the federation's millions of members to "help win the most important struggle to achieve basic economic and human rights through donations of money to assist strikers or, when possible, by joining the Negro strikers on picket lines."

The pace quickened. Abernathy summoned his troops: "In view of the unyielding position of the state of South Carolina, I am today issuing a national call to some of our supporters to escalate this movement beginning with a mass Mother's Day march." They did. Nearly 7,000 people marched on May 11. The group was led by United Auto Workers' President Walter Reuther, Abernathy, Conyers and Charles Diggs of Michigan, Allard Lowenstein and Edward Koch of New York, and William F. Ryan, plus other nationally prominent figures. Reuther gave Local 1199B a check for $10,000 and pledged $500 a week in support of the strikers.

In an unexpected move, the Department of Health, Education and Welfare, in a letter dated June 5, directed the South Carolina Medical College Hospital to return the original 12 workers to its staff with back pay or face the loss of $12 million in federal funds. The timing was coincidental. HEW had been investigating the hospital since July 1968 to see if federal standards were being met. The HEW investigation revealed that all physicians at the hospital were white and that non-paying patients, mostly black, received inferior treatment compared with the treatment for paying patients, mostly white. And, "Employment patterns clearly suggest stratification of employees with regard to race: i.e., administrative and professional positions are occupied by whites; non-whites are concentrated in service and nonskilled categories." HEW ordered the hospital to develop an "affirmative program in equal employment opportunity" that included the recruitment and development of minority-group persons in job categories where they are not represented. Huff, speaking for the hospital, said, "We have the whole question under advisement and we are not taking it lightly." He said the workers could have their jobs back: "All of them who want to can probably come back to work when this thing is settled." The hospital had previously stated that the workers would definitely not be reinstated.

In June the state of South Carolina had quietly announced a rise in wages for state employees from $1.30 to $1.60 an hour, relieving the hospitals of having to act on the higher wage demands by strikers.

A tentative agreement was approved. The fighting continued, becoming political. A note was sent to the strikers saying, "Please be advised that the offer to employ the 12 discharged workers made on June 9 is now withdrawn as of Thursday, June 12." Meanwhile, Sen. Strom Thurmond (R-S.C.) and Rep. L. Mendel Rivers (D-S.C.) protested HEW's strong ruling against the hospital and HEW Secretary Robert H. Finch said the rehiring proposal was subject to review. Democratic Gov. Bob E. McNair was told voters would hold him accountable if the 12 workers were rehired. At the hospital some doctors and nurses threatened to resign if the 12 were rehired. Pickets protested in Washington, demanding Finch act decisively to end the strike.

There were outbreaks as the town grew more tense. Abernathy called for non-violence but said, once again, "I am fearful of what could happen." More arrests were made, this time including that of Abernathy.

It took another month of marches, boycotts, and curfews before the strike was settled. Presidential aide Harry Dent hinted to the hospital that if the strikes were not ended, the $12 million worth of federal funds might not be forthcoming, despite Thurmond and Rivers' protests. Toward the end of the strike, the dockers offered to shut down the city port.

The workers were reinstated in their hospital jobs with raises granted by the hurriedly passed minimum wage increase.

Perhaps the most significant facet of the Charleston hospital strike was the new cooperative effort between the civil rights movement and organized labor toward a single goal.

And, there were other strikes.

In November Council 50 of the State, County and Municipal Employees struck in New York against four state mental hospitals. About 60 per cent of the workers in the state's 35 mental hospitals and schools for the mentally retarded are non-white. The council reported over 17,000 out of 50,000 psychiatric attendants, nurses' aides,

laundry, food, and dietary workers, and maintenance and other employees had agreed to join the strike.

In February service employees at Walther Memorial Hospital in Chicago "stood up to be counted for the democratic right to unionize the hospital." The Teamsters Union, Local 73 of the AFL-CIO, and the Hospital Employees Labor Program (HELP) gave full backing to the striking service workers who were seeking higher pay and better treatment and working conditions.

New York's Adelphi Hospital's non-professional workers went on strike. Congresswoman Shirley Chisholm, head of the Citizens Committee to Support the Adelphi Hospital Workers, called for a "sweeping investigation of the hospital, run on taxpayers money, [that] had ignored the people of the community and failed to appoint any black or Puerto Rican members to the board of trustees or to the medical staff."

In July approximately half the registered nurses and surgical technicians at Michael Reese Hospital in Chicago walked off their jobs. The protest was against "discrimination in work responsibilities." They charged the hospital gave housekeeping duties to trained black personnel. Before striking, the group first presented their demands to the director of nurses. The hospital charged the strikers with "attempting to dictate hospital policy."

In August Mrs. Coretta Scott King met with non-professional employees at Johns Hopkins Hospital in Baltimore and urged them to join the National Organization Committee of the Hospital and Nursing Home Employees Union (AFL-CIO). The union was successful in gaining representation for the hospital workers in Charleston. Mrs. King talked of "soul power and union power."

In addition to hospital strikes, there were other troubles.

March was the month of the Harlem Hospital showdown. The medical board of the hospital voted to shut down the 800-bed public facility because of severe shortages of personnel resulting from Gov. Rockefeller's 1969–1970 budget cutback. The medical board said, "We are no longer willing to assume the responsibility for trying to provide hospital care with the inadequate facilities here." The hospital suffered from chronic overcrowding and acute shortages of nurses and auxiliary personnel. The city refused to grant an additional $4.9 million for personnel and ordered a cut in spending. However, the hospital had been successful in attracting all the American-educated interns it had sought. Dr. Herbert Cave agreed the hospital added "oodles of new services," among them family planning clinics, community psychiatry, methadone research, epidemiology, and health education. The closing was called "an obvious Lindsay ploy," "a lack of state aid in general, not hospital aid in particular," "a conspiracy between the hospital staff and Columbia University's College of Physicians and Surgeons."

A few days after the threat to close the hospital, the medical board, reiterating that it could not operate with a curtailed budget, agreed to hold off the closing. Hospital Commissioner Joseph V. Terenzio persuaded the board to declare a 10-day moratorium.

There was a street rally to protest the closing of the hospital. Dr. Cave said, "We have got to force the city [to grant more funds to the hospital] and we call upon community leaders for the kind of support that is necessary for us to do that." The Lincoln Hospital in the Bronx and Metropolitan Hospital in Manhattan followed Harlem's example and announced they would not trim their budgets and threatened to terminate all services. Other hospitals followed suit. Eventually the city found funds for the hospitals.

The Black Consumer

High-pressure salesmanship and easy credit combine to snare poor Americans into buying on terms of exorbitant interest rates and unreasonable contracts. "Reasonable" department stores generally turn down black residents of the inner-city when they ask for credit, and so these people must often buy from the ghetto merchants who offer "easy terms" with hidden charges. There is nowhere else to go.

In October 1968 the Washington Urban League called for special credit cards for the poor. The League's acting executive director, John E. Jacob, asked the subcommittee on financial institutions of the Senate Banking and Currency Committee to consider a plan to extend consumer credit to all Americans.

Jacob said that in the two years since the Urban League's Armstrong Credit Union had been in operation a total of $118,301 had been loaned and only 1.2 per cent of that had to be charged off as a loss. Jacob concluded that there was no valid reason why ghetto residents should not share in America's credit card economy. Under the existing system, he said, they pay two and three times as much as middle-class consumers for the same goods.

In an attempt to crack down on specific profiteering operations, the Federal Trade Commission charged one jewelry company in Washington, D.C., with using false advertising and deceptive sales tactics. The jewelry store claimed it was selling eyeglasses for $7.50 complete. According to the FTC, no sales records were found for either $7.50 glasses or the $12.50 eye examination-and-glasses deal the store was offering. Of the glasses sold, 72 per cent cost more than $39, and 17 per cent cost more than twice that. The interest rates, advertised as 1.5 per cent a month, amounted to 42 per cent a year.

Slum real estate profiteering also came under attack in the District of Columbia.

The American Bar Association, in an analysis of the Federal Trade Commission, said the FTC "has not done what it could with the resources that have been available to it. . . . Notwithstanding the great potential of the FTC in the field of antitrust and consumer protection, if change does not occur, there will be no substantial purpose to be served by its continued existence."

The NAACP Legal Defense and Educational

Fund began a legal campaign against fine-print clauses in installment contracts and loan agreements that deprive consumers of the right to defend themselves. "Poor consumers, both black and white, are routinely cheated and used by merchants and creditors. We are using every available legal device to protect these buyers and borrowers because such merchants contribute significantly to keeping poor people poor," an NAACP spokesman said.

Even privately, people were organizing to protect themselves.

One local official wrote, "A fair profit and no more has become more than a slogan for us at Neighborhood Consumer Information Center. . . . We look to whether the merchant's policies on warrantees and guarantees, credit plans, and the distribution of quality merchandise and good services are equitable—and by all considerations ethical. . . . Let us now forget the sloganizing which essentially has worked only to exchange a white businessman in the ghetto for a black one. Instead, let us concentrate on the harsh realities of what the black community must do for itself if it is to survive and, hopefully, prosper."

The Concerned Clergy—40 Atlanta area ministers—picketed Buehleris Super Markets in November 1968 demanding that the inner-city food chain lower prices, improve sanitation, eliminate discriminatory employment practices, and improve salaries.

Late in 1968 the Better Business Bureau of Harlem took steps to end deceptive advertising and to eliminate consumer abuses in the furniture industry. The bureau gathered testimony of professional shoppers who reported that high pressure salesmen kept them in stores to try to sell them poor quality furniture at high prices. If furniture was damaged when it was delivered, the merchants refused to take it back. The bureau worked out advertising guidelines that banned "rooms of furniture" ads, deceptive price and credit offers, bait-and-switch advertising, and the practice of button-holing shoppers in the store.

In Washington, D.C., a pilot money management class for low income families was directed by the National Foundation for Consumer Credit and sponsored by Central Charge, Woodward and Lothrop, Hahn Shoes, Sears Roebuck, J. C. Penny, Montgomery Ward, Julius Lansburgh's, and the Hecht Co. The class took field trips to supermarkets and studied "grocery economics." When the course ended, all of the students were eligible to apply for charge accounts at the sponsoring stores.

A bus boycott was organized in Chicago when the transit authority announced a 10-cent fare increase; in March, two Washington consumer groups, the United Planning Organization Consumer Action Program and the D.C. Citywide Consumer Council, announced plans to fight a proposed increase in the cost of electricity.

The National Welfare Rights Organization called for a nationwide boycott of Sears Roebuck & Co. stores because of Sears' alleged reluctance to extend credit to welfare recipients. The group demanded credit with maximum monthly repayments of not more than $8 for welfare clients bearing letters of reference from welfare rights groups. The organization's executive director said people on welfare "need Sears stores because their prices are fair and their merchandise is good. Poor people living in the ghetto get taken by stores with high prices and cheap merchandise with sky high credit charges."

A study by the task force on public aid of the Church Federation of Greater Chicago reported food prices are higher in poor neighborhoods than in more affluent areas. The inner-city stores argued that they had to charge higher prices because of the theft problem and the higher cost of insurance in poor neighborhoods.

After a week-long boycott robbed them of business, Better Foods, Inc., a Los Angeles food chain, said it would hire black managers, train and upgrade black employees, and provide quality merchandise at equitable prices. The Coalition of Community Groups had sponsored the boycott and issued the demands.

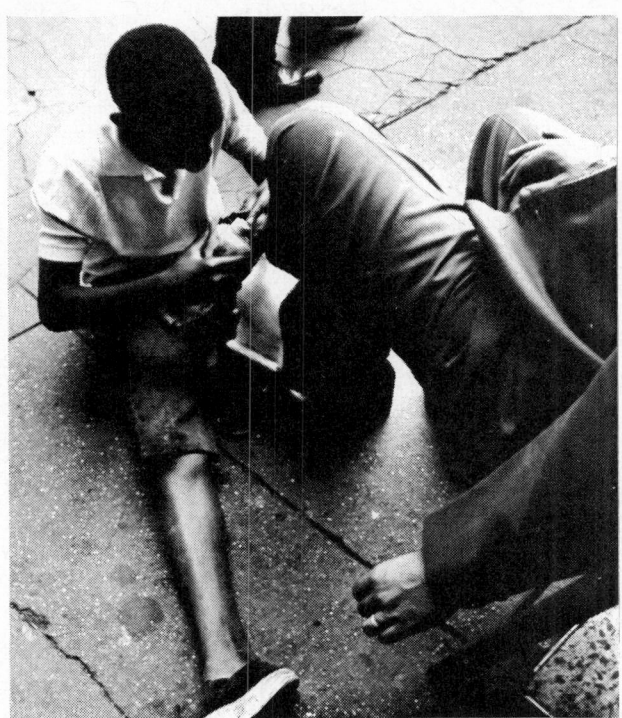

Starting at ground level can have its rewards, as Millicent Bouey, first black woman in the U.S. to own and operate her own investment company, would probably testify.

Roy Innis appears uninvited at a bankers conference to demand funds as payment for past "exploitation" of blacks.

Housing

The realization of a decent home and a suitable living environment for every American family was made a national goal by the Housing Act of 1949. By 1969, the country was not much nearer to fulfillment of this goal than it was 20 years ago.

Available statistics indicate that the housing problem has reached crisis proportions. The 1960 Census revealed that 12.6 million, or 24 per cent, of all occupied dwelling units can be classified as deteriorating, dilapidated, or sound but lacking some or all plumbing facilities. The census definition of substandard housing, however, does not include deteriorated dwellings with sound plumbing, overcrowded dwellings (defined by the census as more than 1.01 persons per room), rent gouging practices (defined as a household spending in excess of 25 per cent of its income for rent), and environmental deficiencies, whose virulent ramifications, in effect, transform a standard dwelling into one that is substandard. Taking these factors into consideration, far more than 24 per cent of all occupied dwelling units can be classified as "substandard."

The axiomatic relationship between housing and income was underscored in 1969 by the squeeze on the national economy wrought by inflation and the measures taken to combat it. Record-high interest rates brought about a money squeeze at all levels. The construction industry was unable to obtain the financing it needed, even as a "preferred customer" of banks. High- and middle-income families encountered the same difficulty in obtaining home financing, or were priced completely out of the market by interest rates; and low-income families, who represent more than 25 per cent of the nation's households, had all the more difficulty finding sale or rental units at prices which were within their means.

A report issued in 1968 by the National Commission on Urban Problems, headed by former Sen. Paul H. Douglas of Illinois, offers some incisive observations concerning the relationship between poverty and housing:

1. For the whole United States, 19 per cent of all housing units were substandard in 1960. Of the units occupied by poor households, 36 per cent were substandard.

2. Of all owner-occupied units in the United States, 11 per cent were substandard. Of those whose owners were poor, 30 per cent were substandard.

3. Of all renter-occupied units in the United States, 23 per cent were substandard. Of those whose renters were poor, 42 per cent were substandard.

4. For all SMSAs (Standard Metropolitan Statistical Areas), 11 per cent of all housing units were substandard in 1960. Of those units occupied by poor families, 23 per cent were substandard.

5. Of all owner-occupied units in SMSAs, 5 per cent were substandard; of those whose owners were poor, 14 per cent were substandard.

6. Of all renter-occupied units in SMSAs, 16 per cent were substandard; of those whose renters were poor, 30 per cent were substandard.

Approximately 30 million persons live below the poverty level, which is defined by the Department of Health, Education and Welfare as a family of four whose income falls below $3,200 per year. Of this group, 68.3 per cent were white while 31.7 per cent were nonwhite. (The nonwhite group consists almost entirely of Negroes, but also includes persons of Puerto Rican, Mexican, and Indian descent.) Proportionately, however, the incidence of poverty is approximately three and a half times higher for nonwhites than whites, according to the figures provided by the 1960 Census.

Housing Conditions in Urban Poverty Areas, a report made to the Douglas Commission, found that poverty areas in the central cities of SMSAs with populations greater than 250,000 harbored 79 per cent of all housing units occupied by nonwhite families. Additionally, this study revealed that these areas contained:

33 per cent of all the cities' housing units

76 per cent of the substandard units

54 per cent of the overcrowded units

45 per cent of the vacant housing units

41 per cent of the units in structures over 20 years old

42 per cent of the units in multi-unit structures

44 per cent of the renter-occupied units

19 per cent of all city owner-occupied units

As indicated by another presidentially appointed group, the Kaiser Commission, the average American family spends 15 per cent of its annual income on rent. Based on the generally accepted rent formula, a family may spend a maximum of 25 per cent of its annual income on rent without sacrificing other necessities, such as food and clothing. Poor families who are not the occupants of substandard housing can, then, be presumed to pay an excessive amount of rent. This dilemma was dramatized by the Douglas Commission as follows:

1. Of renters with incomes between $2,000 and $3,000 in 1960...63 per cent pay 25 per cent or more of income for rent, and of these...31 per cent pay 25 to 35 per cent of income for rent; 32 per cent pay 35 per cent or more of income for rent.
2. Of renters with incomes between $6,000 and $7,000 in 1960...6 per cent pay 25 per cent or more for rent; 1 per cent pay 35 per cent or more for rent.
3. Of renters with incomes over $8,000 in 1960 . . . 1 per cent pay 25 to 35 per cent of income for rent; 0.5 per cent pay 35 per cent or more of income for rent.

Poor families who live in standard housing find little solace. In fact, in many instances poor families pay excessive rent and still occupy substandard housing.

Both the National Commission on Civil Disorders and the National Commission on Urban Problems urged against the increasing separation of races that is currently taking place. When it comes to substandard housing there is no separate and equal dwelling. The Douglas Commission observed:

1. In metropolitan areas in 1960, 23.5 per cent of all poverty households, white and nonwhite, lived in substandard housing.
2. In the same areas in the same year, 41.6 per cent of nonwhite households below the poverty line lived in substandard housing.
3. In other words, within the poverty category, the proportion of Negroes and other nonwhites in substandard housing was more than twice the proportion among whites. Race, therefore, seems to be a factor in bad housing.

Discrimination in housing takes other forms, too. The National Commission on Civil Disorders describes how Negroes often pay the same rents as whites but receive less for their money, or pay higher rents for dwellings of equivalent quality. In Chicago, the Commission found that units rented by nonwhites were:

1. Smaller (the median number of rooms was 3.35 for nonwhites versus 3.95 for whites).
2. In worse condition (30.7 per cent of all nonwhite units were deteriorating or dilapidated units versus 11.6 per cent for whites).
3. Occupied by more people (the median household size was 3.53 for nonwhites versus 2.88 for whites).
4. More likely to be overcrowded (27.4 per cent of nonwhite units had 1.01 or more persons per room versus 7.9 per cent for whites).

On the other hand, the Negro is subjected to another type of discrimination. Frequently, the black family pays more for housing. George Sternlieb, author of *Tenement Landlord,* argues that nonwhites pay a "color tax" in excess of 10 per cent in the Newark, N.J., ghetto.

Fair Housing Legislation

The first substantive open housing laws of national scope were set out in the 1968 Civil Rights Act and the Supreme Court's decision in *Jones* v. *Alfred H. Mayer Co.* concerning the 1866 Civil Rights Act. The effects of these laws were becoming evident in 1969.

The Civil Rights Act, 1968

The Civil Rights Act of 1968 went into its second stage of implementation in 1969. The first stage, which took effect upon enactment last April, covered only housing units accepting federal financial assistance (about one million units). The second stage went into effect Jan. 1, 1969 (covering an additional 17.5 million), and it forbids racial and religious discrimination by apartment owners, homebuilders, and mortgage lenders. The last stage takes effect Jan. 1, 1970, and at that time owner-occupants of single-family homes can no longer discriminate by race if the sale of the property is handled by a real estate broker. (It is expected to cover an estimated 34.9 million units.) The law leaves uncovered private homeowners who sell their own property without the aid of any type of a sales agent.

The second stage contains the following specific provisions: it forbids the denial of loans or the setting of excessive interest rates in real estate lending by banks, building and loan associations, insurance companies, or any other business enterprise involved in making commercial real estate loans; it bans discrimination against black real estate brokers by other brokers, such as by refusing Negroes membership in brokers' organizations and access to lists of houses for sale in multiple listing services; an anti-block-busting provision forbids anyone "for profit, to induce any person to sell or rent any dwelling by representations regarding the entry or prospective entry into the neighborhood of a person or persons of a particular race, color, religion, or national origin."

Furthermore, the law lists specific remedies available to blacks who believe an apartment owner or housing developer is discriminating

against them because of their race. For example, a person can sue for an injunction in a federal court compelling sale or rental of the unit and for money damages; responsibility rests on the plaintiff to prove that the original refusal was racially motivated. The statute also authorizes the Department of Housing and Urban Development to mediate complaints of housing discrimination, to hire people to enforce the law, and to publicize the provisions and procedures for making restraints.

Enforcement of the law by HUD has been handicapped by the budget cutbacks instituted to fight inflation. HUD did formally notify real estate dealers, apartment house owners, and others of the second stage. Teams of attorneys were sent to six selected cities to investigate compliance. Several cases of discrimination were uncovered but suits were not filed because the parties agreed out of court to guarantee open access to their housing. According to assistant Attorney General Jerris Leonard, the astronomical number of potential law suits makes "clear that, in the long run, equal opportunity in housing will be made available only by voluntary compliance with the law."

Nevertheless, there were several court cases in 1969 as a result of the law. The first enforcement suit was filed in July 1968 against six Baton Rouge, La., real estate firms using federally guaranteed mortgages for refusing to sell a home to Paul J. Brown in three of their subdivisions. However, a federal judge in a U.S. district court dismissed the suit in April 1969 because the particular houses which Mr. Brown had attempted to buy had not been built with federal monies.

The first suit to be filed under the second section of the act charged the "committee on admissions" of the Ontario Apartments, a cooperative apartment in Washington, D.C., with refusing to allow several of its owners to sell to otherwise qualified Negroes.

In April a case in Chicago involved Mrs. Nadine Byars, who charged G. Dette Realty Co. with attempting to prevent her from occupying the apartment in which she now lives because of her race. She filed the lawsuit under the Civil Rights Acts of 1968 and 1866. (The 1866 law is described below.) The U.S. district court awarded her four months free rent and a monthly rent reduction as settlement.

In June Attorney General John Mitchell filed suit against the owners of a luxury apartment building in Washington, D.C., for falsely telling prospective black tenants there were no apartments available.

In August the Justice Department filed its first housing discrimination suit on the West Coast in Sacramento, Calif., against Mr. and Mrs. Leo A. Schalich, apartment house owners who allegedly refused to rent to blacks because of their race. They also were cited for imposing harsher terms and conditions on the only black tenant to have lived in the building than on white tenants.

The Civil Rights Act of 1866

Two months after the Civil Rights Act of 1968 became law, the Supreme Court upheld a nearly forgotten open housing law passed in 1866. This act upheld the right of Negroes to own property. It was based on the 13th Amendment, which abolished slavery—discrimination by a private group was a "badge of slavery," according to the original lawmakers.

In *Jones* v. *Alfred H. Mayer Co.*, the High Court held that the law applies without exception to today's housing market. The law had not been used by the federal government for many years because it was thought that jurisdiction prohibiting discrimination must come from the state rather than the national government—the policy of states rights. The 1968 Supreme Court decision allows blacks to go directly to federal court with allegations of discrimination. The 1866 law is broader than the 1968 Civil Rights Act in that it forbids all property owners, including those private home owners who do not engage real estate company assistance, from dis-

criminating. It is also easier to enforce than the more recent act because it is based on a Constitutional amendment. The 1968 Act requires criminal proceedings and, therefore, more complete proof.

Several cases in 1969 relied on the 1866 law. The 1866 Act was invoked in January when the Charles J. Dancik firm of Downers Grove near Chicago was forced to pay $1,000 damages to Mr. and Mrs. Charles Tyler, a racially mixed couple, for refusing to show them its houses for sale. Lawyers believe it is the first time damages will be paid under the 1866 law.

The act was used against a hitherto-uncovered area of discrimination—owner-occupied duplex apartments—in a case in Massachusetts between Mr. and Mrs. Roland Harris (black) and Mr. and Mrs. Jonathan Jones (white). In February 1969 Mrs. Jones refused to rent a duplex apartment to the Harris couple on the grounds that she wanted a middle-aged couple. Later she was willing to rent to a young white graduate student. Owner-occupied duplex apartments are not covered by the Housing Act of 1968 or by Massachusetts law, but U.S. District Judge Andrew Caffrey ruled that the Joneses must lease the upstairs apartment to the Harris couple for one year on the basis of the 1866 Act. A lawyer of Fair Housing, Inc., a neighborhood legal service, stated, "This Massachusetts case will be a breakthrough for us because in . . . any town where there are duplexes it is hard for blacks to move in."

Another case in April showed that the 1866 law can be used in cases also covered by the 1968 Civil Rights Act. Housing in an apartment building for two Lexington, Ky., blacks was made available in a consent court order filed in a U.S. district court under the 1866 statute.

A second case in April in Biloxi, Miss., was filed on the basis of the *Jones* v. *Alfred H. Mayer Co.* case. The federal district court ordered a white real estate firm, Southern Homesites Corp., to sell a lot in its Gulf Coast development to Johnie Lee, just as it had advertised in a letter sent to Lee previously. The firm admittedly had refused to sell to Lee because of a no-Negro policy. The court admonished the real estate dealers for illegally discriminating under both the fair housing laws of 1866 and 1968.

"Blockbusting"

"Blockbusting" is a practice of real estate agencies that has created racially segregated housing in cities and involves excessive and fraudulent prices for prospective black home buyers. The device works this way: first, a real estate agent selects a neighborhood where residents are all or almost all of a single race, usually a middle class white area. Second, he conducts a scare campaign warning residents that the ghetto is taking over and that they should sell their houses and move out quickly— at this point the agent obtains the houses for much less than the market value due to panic selling; and third, he resells the homes to Negroes at prices above the market value.

Since black purchasers often have few financial resources and frequently have difficulty getting housing loans through normal channels, they turn to land contracts. Land contracts are made with the real estate agent or a contract developer. The arrangements are usually vague, providing for a system of installment payments through which title to the house does not pass to the occupant until the final payment. Extra costs and conditions are often concealed in the intricate legal contracts. The contract purchaser receives no equity and may lose his home if he misses a single payment. He often makes payments on insurance on which the developer is the beneficiary, pays for home repair services which are nonexistent, and frequently pays for the same services a number of times. In a single blockbusting arrangement, the real estate agent often makes from $10,000 to $20,000 profit.

Major attempts at restricting this practice, prevalent in many cities across the country, were made in 1969. Blockbusting is prohibited under the second stage of the 1968 Civil Rights Act. It is also a violation of the Civil Rights Act of 1866, which covers all areas of selling and renting to Negroes. The Civil Rights Division of the Justice Department, according to Jerris Leonard, believes "the way to stop blockbusting is to take the profit out of it." He means to accomplish this by obtaining court decisions under the aforementioned laws.

The government response was prompted by a case begun in 1968 in Chicago—*Contract Buyers League, et al.* v. *F & F Investment, et al.*

The Contract Buyers League, a Westside group of black homeowners, filed two suits in January 1969 against 91 real estate and investment companies. They charged that their rights were violated by discriminatory contracts that created residential segregation in ghettos and exploited the buyers by excessive selling and lending prices. The group filed a class suit on behalf of all black buyers who had purchased a home on such installment contracts since 1952. They based their complaint on the 13th and 14th Amendments, the federal civil rights acts, the federal anti-trust laws, the federal securities laws, and Illinois statutes. Richard L. Strout of the *Christian Science Monitor* called the case "a test proceeding . . . that is one of the most remarkable in years."

The League had organized in February 1968. It first attempted to re-negotiate contracts, went on to a series of picketing marches, and began withholding contract payments in December. In January the League filed suit. At the end of January it won a court victory when a countersuit brought by one of the land contract sales agents, Hamilton Corporation, to make three League members continue their payments, failed. Several other countersuits were pending.

In March the League gained government support when the Justice Department filed a "friend-of-the-court" petition asking the court to rule that the homeowners are entitled to attack residential "blockbusting" as a violation of the 1866 Civil Rights Act. Attorney General Mitchell said the landmark petition was the federal government's "first effort to break massive Northern housing segregation."

Court hearings and discussions centered on whether black home buyers could legally be called an identifiable class and which defenders should be held legally liable within the definition of the class. The discussion of remedies concerned whether punitive damages should be awarded or whether the contracts should simply be re-negotiated on the same ground used for white people.

If the federal district court decides in favor of the League, the case will have:

> said that it is against the law for real estate speculators and investors to take advantage of racial segregation to gouge black home buyers;
>
> established that the practice of blockbusting is a concrete example of institutional racism as spelled out in the Kerner Report;
>
> opened the door for potential savings of at least $60 million for an estimated 7,000 black homeowners in Chicago who are represented in this suit;
>
> established a legal principle which could be used to provide relief for black home buyers who are exploited all over the nation;
>
> provided an effective means of putting an end to blockbusting in real estate; and
>
> handed down a landmark precedent which would help root out one of the worst racist practices in the country,

according to Sheryl Fitsgerald of the Chicago *Daily Defender*.

Government efforts to stop blockbusting continued after the Chicago case. Leonard said, "There is some evidence of blockbusting in almost every major city in the North that has had a Negro area or de facto segregation." The department began investigation in seven cities: Detroit; Baltimore; Washington, D.C.; New Orleans; Fort Worth; Buffalo; and Kansas City.

Housing and Urban Development regional officials advised a group of DeKalb County, Ga., homeowners who were concerned about block-busting attempts in their neighborhood to file a private suit against the real estate agents in March. It became the first blockbusting suit filed by the original private homeowners. U.S. district judge Sidney O. Smith, Jr., issued an order forbidding blockbusting activities on the part of the DeKalb real estate company, commenting that although no actual damage was done, attempts to use blockbusting tactics to sell property are just as illegal as successful efforts.

In September, the state of New York ordered investigations into reports of blockbusting in the East Flatbush area of Brooklyn. Apparently, panic selling had been common in the area since 1966. The investigation led to charges against four Brooklyn real estate brokers for blockbusting and against three other brokers for obtaining fraudulent mortgage loans. Subsequently, the investigation by the New York secretary of state also spread to other counties in the New York metropolitan area where patterns of collusion among real estate agents were evidenced.

State and Local Fair Housing Laws

When Congress passed the Fair Housing Act in 1968, about 62 per cent of the U.S. population was already covered by some form of local or state fair housing law. Twenty-two states and 293 local governments now have open housing laws, according to HUD statistics. The number of local ordinances is increasing rapidly; in May 1968 there were only 155.

The relationships between the federal, state, and local laws show different degrees of effectiveness. The federal laws were originally sought primarily because local and state laws had proved ineffective. However, litigation based on state and federal laws generally consumes more time and effort than local laws, where authorities are close at hand. Consequently, local laws have become preferred. This is one reason for the large increase in local fair housing laws.

A complaint must first be filed under the local law if there is one, secondly under the state law if there is one, and finally under the federal law. The 1968 Civil Rights Act applied only if there is no local agency to handle the complaint. HUD, which enforces the law, can step in only if the local agency does not act within 30 days after a complaint is filed. On the other hand, the 1866 Civil Rights Act is of a general nature covering areas left out of state and local laws; therefore, appeals under this law can often go directly to federal court and prosecution is easier due to the nature of the law.

The greater effectiveness of local housing ordinances over state and federal laws was noted by Mrs. Margaret Fisher, associate executive director of the National Committee Against Discrimination in Housing. She cited the following reasons:

A local law enables a person with a complaint to go to a nearby agency such as the local human rights commission or village, town and country attorney, where often he can get immediate action. The office of the federal and state agencies are usually in major cities and a complainant from an outlying area can lose several days' pay travelling back and forth.

The mere threat of jail sentences and fines provided in most local laws that are enforced in local courts are often enough to bring about settlement of complaints without trial. Under state law, the threat of penalties and jail sentences usually does not come into play until after civil proceedings, which can last up to six months.

The enforcement of open housing laws by state agencies, such as the New York State Division of Human Rights, has been disappointing. The state agencies often have inadequate budgets and are short-staffed and the procedure for dealing with complaints is slow.

State and local laws generally cover public, publicly assisted housing, and private multiple housing units controlled by one person or firm. Extending coverage to the private market has proved difficult.

The following developments on the state and local scene in 1969 are listed by alphabetical order according to state; local and city ordinances are dealt with under the individual state.

California—In San Diego, Eloise Brown was refused the opportunity to rent an apartment because of her race by the resident manager of an apartment building. The California Fair Employment Practices Commission found the apartment building owner and his agent guilty, ordered them to "cease and desist" such practices, and ordered the agent to pay $500 damages to Mrs. Brown. This was the eighth case under the California Fair Housing Law to reach public hearing and award damages. Over 1,000 cases have been received by state FEPC since the law passed in 1963.

In a second case in San Francisco the state FEPC ruled that a real estate firm and one of its salesmen must pay $500 damages to a black teacher discriminated against in an apartment rental.

Delaware—An open housing law for Delaware was passed in April 1969 after five years of legislative efforts and a one-vote majority decision in the state house of representatives. The bill prohibits discrimination in housing on the grounds of race, color, religion, or national origin. Two exceptions to the bill are for owner-occupied dwellings with four or fewer living units, and for non-commercial dwellings operated by a religious organization. Enforcement goes through the state human relations commission which receives complaints and attempts conciliation. Further recourse is through the court of chancery for injunctive relief, or the attorney general for prosecution. Maximum penalties for violations are a $500 fine, 90 days in jail, or both.

Illinois—The state senate refused to pass a strong open housing law for Illinois amid angry protests from various senators. The series of fair housing bills had been proposed by Rep. Harold Washington "in order to avoid the invoking of a federal statute (the 1968 or 1866 Civil Rights Acts) within the state of Illinois." Illinois is the only Northern industrial state without a comprehensive fair housing law. Proponents of the law wanted an affirmative commitment to fair housing in the state in addition to the right of enforcement. However, opponents believed the

1968 and 1866 laws made it unnecessary for the people of Illinois to take such a stand.

The Chicago Housing Authority in February was condemned for racial segregation by federal judge Richard B. Austin. American Civil Liberties Union officials called it a landmark decision. The CHA, which builds and controls all public housing in Chicago, was found to have segregated its housing projects. Judge Austin commented: "The disparity between the low number of Negro families in these projects and the high number of Negro applicants indicates the Chicago Housing Authority has imposed a Negro quota."

In another case in Chicago, the Commission of Human Relations took two steps to strengthen its fair housing enforcement procedures and to speed up the resolution of discrimination cases. It was the first reorganization of the enforcement machinery since Chicago's fair housing ordinance was passed in 1963. The reforms were 1) the commission can now seek federal court injunctions under the law of 1866 when necessary to keep homes and apartments off the market until complaints are resolved, and 2) it can use subpoena powers during investigations if needed to gain access to records of real estate brokers. These actions were taken because so few people who file complaints of housing discrimination ever get the home or apartment originally sought. Last year only 26 out of 185 litigants obtained the home over which they brought suit.

Maryland—Montgomery County's open housing law, one of the strongest in the nation, was upheld by the Maryland court of appeals. The ordinance passed in May 1968 bans discrimination in the sale or rental of most houses and in the granting of home loans, and blockbusting. It is stronger than the 1968 Civil Rights Act and most state laws. The court's decision rejected arguments by the Montgomery Citizens' League that the council was not legally in a legislative session when the ordinance was adopted.

The Montgomery County Fair Housing Authority charged the management of two Bethesda apartment buildings with discrimination against blacks in May. The charges are the first to be brought under the county's open housing law. The charges were the result of 26 "tests" conducted by the fair housing group whereby both black and white volunteers were sent to rent houses and apartments. The county attorney advised that the charges could not be maintained because the victims did not actually intend to rent.

The first complaint to be filed under the county law was made by Noel Myricks, an instructor from Federal City College, against a Silver Spring real estate agent for not renting him a house. Later he decided not to rent because of an unreceptive community atmosphere.

New York—Gov. Nelson A. Rockefeller asked the state legislature for additional fair housing legislation. His proposals would include under the new anti-discrimination law two-family owner-occupied housing, boarding houses or owner-occupied houses which lease three or more rooms, and, most importantly, a provision hitting at the economic roots of blockbusting.

A local fair housing ordinance was proposed for Nassau County in June. Strong support was voiced at a series of public hearings. The proposed ordinance provides for a maximum fine of $500 and 25 days in jail.

Scarsdale Village adopted its own fair housing ordinance in March, enabling the village government to take action locally.

Ohio—A lawsuit filed in Akron four years ago advanced to the Supreme Court this year and was hailed by many civil rights leaders as advancing the case of fair housing. The Supreme Court ruled in the case of Mrs. Nellie Hunter that cities, like states, cannot enact ordinances or charter provisions which have the effect of establishing discrimination in housing. Mrs. Hunter, a local housewife, had filed a complaint with city hall asking the protection of a 1964 ordinance banning housing discrimination. Officials told her that local real estate interests had successfully staged a drive to amend the charter, nullifying the ordinance, and requiring that any future fair housing proposal be approved by a vote of the people. After a series of appeals, the Supreme Court decided in an eight to one vote that the Akron referendum placed an unusual stumbling block to blacks by requiring them to win a popular referendum before a fair housing law could be restored. Associate Justice Byron R. White, in stating the majority opinion, said, "The state may no more disadvantage any particular group by making it more difficult to enact legislation in its behalf than it may dilute any person's vote or give any group a smaller representation than another of comparable size." The court's decision nullifies the charter amendment and reverses the unsuccessful results of an effort which took place in November 1968 to repeal the amendment.

Virginia—The Alexandria city council passed a local housing law in February, the last major governing body in the metropolitan area of Washington, D.C., to do so. The law is almost identical to the federal legislation. It takes effect Jan. 1, 1970. Criticism of the law centered on the need for stronger enforcement machinery since the housing board to be set up will not have subpoena powers nor the right to initiate investigations.

Wisconsin—The Milwaukee common council strengthened the city's open housing law by removing all exceptions to the ordinance. The action passed smoothly in contrast to the bitter controversy in April 1968, when the open housing law was first passed. The new ordinance removes exemptions in rentals for owner-occupied dwellings with one or two units and in sales for owner-occupied single family dwellings.

Effects

Fair housing coverage of most of the population is in effect now. What are the tangible results?

Public policy is committed to fair housing; private attitudes and behavior are not so easily changed and committed. No rapid move of black families into all-white neighborhoods is expected. Instead, the trend of black families taking over the older and lower-income neighborhoods is expected to continue.

Roger N. I. Bailenson, a vice president of a non-profit corporation that helps blacks find and finance homes in New York, said the anti-discrimination laws were only the first step in helping blacks find housing in white communities. The next step needed is economic assistance. Now the laws mainly benefit affluent blacks who can afford to move into suburban areas. In addition to local housing laws, he declared, local governments must also take advantage of state and federal programs to build middle-income and low-income housing. "Until that happens," he added, "all open-housing laws have only a limited significance."

Another detriment of fair housing laws is that they do not affect the motivation of black people. The majority of blacks are not familiar with the law nor can most afford to buy, says John Robertson of the Arlington, Va., Community Action Program. In addition, it requires a great deal of initiative for a black person to enter a hitherto all-white community. Besides the resistance he might encounter, it is a different type of a community system in which he is an outsider.

The major impact of the fair housing laws appears to be psychological. Public discussion of fair housing improves the general climate for acceptance of black families in white neighborhoods. Upper and middle class whites seem increasingly disposed to accept black neighbors of similar socio-economic status, according to Lynn W. Eley, a leading proponent of the local housing bill in Ann Arbor, Mich. White families can use the law as a reason not to flee from an integrated neighborhood. On the other hand, the laws put a psychological restraint on extremists who might try to intimidate black families moving in. The laws also give psychological security to the potential buyer, the rental agent, and the white family selling.

A fair housing law sets the standard for equal opportunity, but provisions are not necessarily explicitly enforced. Mrs. Alfred J. Denny, of the Arlington Fair Housing Board, says, "There are many subterfuges and ruses available to the renter or seller. It is difficult to prove someone has been discriminated against." In many cases, landlords can point out that they have rejected whites for the same reasons they use to reject blacks.

Although real estate operators are basically hostile to open housing laws, some agents have joined together in efforts to adhere to fair housing practices. In Cleveland, a community campaign was staged to convince real estate brokers that the public will support open housing. The campaign wants to identify brokers who are privately sympathetic but fear a loss of business if they deal with Negroes. In Philadelphia, six real estate operators signed consent orders pledging not to discriminate in order to avoid further litigation after investigation disclosed violations. Such compliances with the law after being warned or asked to comply are fairly common. Quite often, complaints are informally settled. In Miami, realtors were urged by the Community Relations Board to "accept the responsibility of finding an answer to the problems of the black community." More positive action is lacking, however.

Lynn W. Eley said, "We confront a situation in which a majority of the people of the United States probably oppose integrated housing for any statistically significant number of blacks, though on a legal and policy level much of American government has been at least partially converted to the cause of integrated housing. What Daniel P. Moynihan has called 'the ethnic disarray' of most of our cities and the hostile attitudes toward Negroes in working class and ethnic neighborhoods severely limits the possibility for open housing. So do the tokenism of the upper-class suburbs and the thrust toward black separatism in the Negro ghettos."

Urban Renewal

In metropolitan areas around the country the pattern is much the same: the core of the city is a work center for white collar residents of outlying areas, while the suburban regions provide work for new blue collar workers as more and more large industries and employers relocate where space is not at a premium.

But for the black worker the move to the suburbs, both to find work and a place to live, has been slow. Nearly 3 million black Americans lived in the suburbs in 1960 and that number is expected to double by 1985, but the same holds for white Americans, whose numbers in the suburbs in 1960—52 million—will also double.

For America's black workers, locked out of the suburbs except as commuters, transportation has become a major obstacle to finding work.

In the past, proposals to use mass transit to unsnarl traffic congestion, revitalize downtown business districts and relieve urban disorder were hailed by some city planners but generally ignored by the public. But increasingly, planners and the commuting public have come to believe that efficient public transit systems are a key to solving many of the social and physical ills of metropolitan areas.

In a country where nearly 90 per cent of the families classified as non-poor own cars, only 57 per cent of those earning less than $4,000 annually are car owners.

The pressing transportation needs of the poor were pointed out in a report by Project Labor Market at the New York University Graduate School of Business Administration. It noted that even though residents of poor neighborhoods are far more dependent on transit systems than residents of middle class sections, those systems serve them less well.

Prospects

The 1968 Federal Housing and Urban Development Act called for construction or rehabilitation of 26 million housing units by 1978. But a year after passage, faint progress had been made toward that goal. Building was harder to finance and interest rates for buyers continued to soar. Ada Louise Huxtable, architecture critic of the *New York Times,* said much construction was being thwarted by a lack of funds, "construction techniques and practices that hold down productivity and a lobster quadrille of bureaucratic buck-passing from federal to state to local levels."

John W. Gardner, head of the Urban Coalition, suggested that the Department of Housing and Urban Development make grants—of all types—only to those communities that are "providing adequate housing for low and moderate income families.

"It must be recognized," he added, "that higher density housing for low and moderate income families may result in lower per capita tax receipts and higher costs for public services —schools, playgrounds, welfare and social services—that must be borne by the locality in which the housing is located." Communities often cited this problem as a reason for not building low and moderate income housing.

Clarence Funnye, director of planning for the National Committee Against Discrimination in Housing, suggested that it might be better to move blacks out of the ghetto rather than to try to improve the neighborhoods in which they lived. "Ghettos are nothing but updated Southern plantations," he said, "and the highly publicized urban programs such as Model Cities and the community development corporations will only perpetuate these monochromatic preserves."

Former Secretary of Agriculture Orville Freeman is among those who feel that "new towns" are one good alternative to urban renewal. "While working with and for existing communities in developing opportunity in rural America," Freeman said, "our planners should consider moving ahead on a seventh concept for a new America: that of new towns. Columbia, Md., is such a town. Planned from the outset as a completely new city to accommodate some 100,000

people, it was designed for people and to serve people's needs. The natural landscape carefully preserved can be enjoyed by all. The basic public facilities are in place. Provisions have been made for schools, churches, libraries, theaters, hotels, medical services, shopping, and jobs." The Government and Housing report to the U.S. Commission on Civil Rights charged that the federal government has contributed to discriminatory housing patterns. The report said that in Washington, D.C., for example, blacks are locked into the city while the surrounding suburbs become populated by more and more whites.

President Nixon insisted in March that "problems of the city will be on the front burner in this administration," but within the month, HUD's budget was cut in what officials called an attempt to stunt the growth of inflation. "The Nixon administration is formulating a long-range urban policy aimed at moving poor minorities from slums to suburbs," wrote *Evening Star* reporter Richard Critchfield. "The underlying assumption is that the voluntary dispersion of black families from the ghettos is the only way to solve the educational, housing, employment, crime, and environmental problems of the American cities. As one White House aide explained it, 'The idea would be to create a whole spirit of incentives in government. If there are lots of houses for sale and lots of Negroes with money to buy them, you build natural incentives and normal operations into the system.' "

In September, John A. Volpe, Secretary of Transportation, ruled that future highway projects involving the displacement of people would not be approved "until adequate replacement housing has already been provided for and built." A new program to provide $30 million for housing rehabilitation was announced by the Government National Mortgage Association in October. It was set up to provide special financing for renovating housing to be rehabilitated for purchase by low-income families.

The National Opinion Research Center found that, in 1969, 36 million Americans in 11 million households—one fifth of the total population—live in integrated neighborhoods. Toward improving that percentage, the Ford Foundation granted $300,000 to the Housing Opportunities Council, made up of leaders of suburban open housing groups in the Washington, D.C., area, to help speed the rate at which blacks move to the suburbs. "If some civil rights enthusiasts really believed the 1968 Open Housing Act would quickly squelch discrimination against Negroes in the U.S. housing market, they have been sadly disappointed," one writer observed. "Today, in most parts of the country, Negroes are still hitting serious roadblocks when they seek to buy or rent a place to live." Among the roadblocks: the Village Board, the elected body of Scarsdale, N.Y., vetoed construction of subsidized low- and middle-income apartments as a means of integrating its community of expensive homes; voters in Austin, Tex., rejected a proposed open housing ordinance. In Silver Spring, Md., a plan to build a 51-unit low-income housing project was attacked by local residents who feared the project would become a ghetto and bring down property values in the area.

Floyd McKissick said one alternative to the housing crisis was new black towns, and he announced plans to build "Soul City" in North Carolina's Warren County. "The roots of the urban crisis are in the migratory pattern of rural people seeking to leave areas of economic and racial oppression," McKissick said. "The black man has been searching for his identity and destiny in the cities. He should be able to find it in Warren County."

The Rev. David Hird organized another such project, Miracle Village, in upstate New York. Blacks, using their own money and skills, are building the village of approximately 25 to 30 homes to escape from housing in the inner-city.

Model Cities

The Model Cities program was proposed by Robert C. Weaver, the first Secretary of Housing and Urban Development, and enacted under President Johnson in 1966. Its original purpose was to inspire city mayors to improve their own slum areas. Model Cities was to sponsor preliminary development of ideas for urban restoration and it would show how a decayed area could be revitalized through a combination of federal, state, and city services. Standards would be set by the federal government, but local governments and citizens would share control. Elected Model Cities commissions in 150 municipalities would work with all agencies to marshal available public and private money for a massive attack on urban problems. A small number of blighted neighborhoods—covering up to 10 per cent of a city's population—would be singled out for the programs. These showcase cities would demonstrate what could be accomplished by concentrated efforts to improve housing, social services, education, employment, health, crime control, and recreation.

Weaver said he would be looking to those cities that appeared to be arriving at solutions that were not just "the same old problems," and he said he wanted to insure that the residents of Model Cities neighborhoods had a major role in developing those solutions. Special emphasis was placed on using black contractors.

Seattle, Wash., was the first city to move its Model Cities program out of the planning stage. Planners there announced late in 1968 that they intended to use $2.5 million the first year to set up the administrative machinery for a low-cost housing corporation, a development land bank, and neighborhood organizations to direct rebuilding.

HUD officials predicted that the nation would not be able to see a real demonstration of the worth of the Model Cities plan until 250 U.S. cities completed at least one phase of their reconstruction.

During 1969, two-thirds of the 75 "first round" cities received supplemental grants totaling $300 million. They ranged from $788,000 for Winooski, Vt., to $65 million for New York. But of the total, HUD officials estimated, only

$15 million was spent in 1969 for actual projects because of the time lag in setting up administrative machinery.

In January, George Romney was named Secretary of HUD and Floyd H. Hyde, mayor of Fresno, Calif., was appointed to administer the Model Cities program. A study group appointed by President Nixon was quick to point out that the Model Cities concept contained philosophies embraced by Nixon during his campaign: decentralization of federal services, citizen participation, and block grants.

"The partnership between city and neighborhood is fragile and skepticism is great" in the majority of Model Cities areas, Romney was told by his assistants. "In some cities," one assistant reported, "citizen participation has been pro forma; in others, there has been conflict and there continues to be great distrust . . . In almost every Model City, there is a relationship and a planning dialogue between the city and the community. It can, and must, be nurtured."

In March the HUD budget was cut by the administration in an effort to stem inflation. Romney said low-cost housing would fall victim to the budget cut. "We are losing ground every year," he said. "In the last three years, the unmet need has grown by 1,000,000 housing units. There is not one major aspect of this problem that is not going in the wrong direction at the present time—land costs, cost of money, materials and labor, fragmentation of the market, building trades practices."

Romney advocated extending the Model Cities program from failing neighborhoods to entire cities and he asked for greater cooperation among all agencies involved in channeling funds and technical support to the program.

Late in April the administration followed through by announcing that money for Model Cities could be spread throughout poor neighborhoods and no longer had to be confined to specific target areas. Romney said that local officials would be given greater latitude in drawing program boundaries to conform to local conditions. Direct responsibility for federal involvement in the revenue sharing program was assumed by the Council for Urban Affairs. Programs were delayed in some areas because officials were unable to decide on a target area.

Describing his hopes for Dayton, Ohio, which had more than $1 million in projects going by the end of 1969, Model Cities Planning Council chairman Robert Prear said, "We're going to do it meticulously, brick by brick, structure by structure, street by street, rehabilitating where we can and rebuilding where we must. But it's much more than a brick-and-mortar project. People want to be treated as individuals, and we'll pay special attention to each family's wishes. We want a revitalization and rehabilitation of the human factor. We're going to relate everything together—and at the same time—education, employment, housing, social and health services, recreation. We want to develop human values, pride through involvement. There will be some gleaming new buildings and homes because urban renewal money is part of it, but we want more to instill the self-reliance to give the black community freedom of movement and freedom of self-improvement."

Model Cities has been a difficult program to propel. The complex programs involve many groups of people who must meet, plan, research and decide about plans that affect many lives. Coordination is hard because federal funding systems are so diverse.

In Atlanta, there was a battle for control of the multi-million-dollar program between federal officials and city hall, which wanted to decide which neighborhoods to include. Alex Coffin reported in the *Atlanta Constitution* that Atlanta officials weren't the only ones fighting for power in their own city. "City hall officials all over the country fear that the federal government, through the U.S. Department of Housing and Urban Development, will slowly emerge with more power over municipal affairs because of such programs as Model Cities," he wrote.

Many cities suffered from a binding profusion of local and federal red tape. There were problems about the degree of citizen participation and there were the complications of planning for a city's future. Model Cities information centers in general were short on practical guidance in these matters.

The Chicago program ran into trouble when dissident citizens there began charging that the planning council was a rubber stamp group that was not representative of the community. The citizens charged that the council violated federal guidelines calling for widespread citizen participation in the planning of rehabilitation. The protest gained momentum in April when the Coalition for United Community Action Against Consumer Injustice acted to stop the planning until the grievances were resolved.

In the District of Columbia, where the program threatened to run short of funds, citizen groups accused the local Model Cities commission of being antagonistic toward voluntary services.

By the end of the year, Peter Braestrup reported in the *Washington Post,* the Nixon administration had begun a major reappraisal of the "slow-moving, embryonic, $1 billion Model Cities effort at urban uplift. . . ." Braestrup wrote that, for different reasons, Nixon and his liberal critics were dissatisfied with Model Cities.

"It boils down to middleclass blacks giving money and jobs to middleclass blacks," one White House official complained. Other officials charged that the federal government had simply failed to live up to its promises for the program. They told Braestrup they felt the program has been "over-regulated" by HUD and "under-supported" by other federal agencies. Lack of an over-all manager with authority to force coordination has led to "delay and frustration all around," the *Post* reporter wrote.

The theory that every dollar of Model Cities money was supposed to generate six dollars in funds from other federal programs had fallen considerably below the mark. Critics were ready to note that there was no guarantee that state and local bureaucrats could do any better than their federal counterparts in improving the neighborhoods of America's inner-cities.

Fred (Ahmed) Evans arrives at Ohio penitentiary after being found guilty of first degree murder in Cleveland for the slaying of three policemen and a civilian.

ONE WHITE POLICEMAN was killed, another wounded, and five Negroes were injured during a weekend exchange of gunfire at a church . . . . A meeting of the New Republic of Africa had just adjourned."

Four Negroes inside the church were shot and wounded; another suffered a broken leg. Police had stormed the building.

"Police said the dead officer . . . was shot seven times in the head and chest when he and his partner tried to question about a dozen Negroes carrying rifles and carbines outside the church."

An incident such as this may have been the exception in the past. But the present conflict which exists between the police and the community has as its focal point the question of the exact function of law enforcement agencies. As defined by society, that function is the maintenance of public peace and order, the enforcement of laws, and the prevention and detection of crime. However, the consensus among blacks is that the police department is a government agency established by the white power structure to suppress the ghetto; they see the police officer as an oppressive agent of the establishment, rather than as a protector. According to Robert L. Carter, former general counsel of the National Association for the Advancement of Colored People, who supports this point of view, the experience of black people in the United States "has been one of callous indifference, and accepted brutality, brutalization, and inhumanity." The result is that blacks see the police department as a threat to their day-to-day life patterns.

Why do blacks feel the way they do? Aren't the police necessary for the protection of black people as well as white people? While the opinion of one man—Carter—may not be enough to justify the hostilities toward the police that exist within the black community, numerous events have occurred that tend to substantiate allegations made by blacks against the police department. The Detroit *Free Press* conducted a survey in the summer of 1968 which showed that the major single cause of the 1967 riot was police brutality. A more recent survey reveals that Negroes are complaining more than ever about police brutality, and that 71 per cent of the inner-city Negroes interviewed said that police brutality would have a great deal to do with a future riot. The survey went on to say that the rise in the number of complaints appears to be less a reflection of an actual increase in police brutality than it is a willingness of black people to speak openly about it.

In March 1969 the Report of the President's National Advisory Commission on Civil Disorders—usually called the Kerner Report—was released. According to the Kerner Report the deep hostility which exists between police and ghetto communities has been a major source of grievance, tension, and ultimate disorder. "Negroes firmly believe that police brutality and harassment occur repeatedly in Negro neighborhoods. This belief is unquestionably one of the major reasons for intense Negro resentment against police." According to a report submitted to Commissioner Howard R. Leary of New York by the police department's Civilian Complaint Review Board, 21 per cent more complaints had been filed against the police department in 1968 than in 1967. Figures showed that the board reviewed 1,549 complaints in 1968 and 1,281 in 1967. In 1967 the board dismissed 811 cases for lack of identification of either the policeman or the complaint, and in 1968 only 126 cases were dismissed. Out of the total number of complaints 612 were made by blacks. The largest category of complaints, totaling 839, involved the alleged use of unnecessary force by policemen. The next largest categories were discourtesy, which drew 434 complaints, and abuse of authority, which drew 211. Manhattan had 618 complaints, the largest number filed in the city; Brooklyn had 425; the Bronx, 240; Queens, 220; Staten Island, 23; and 23 others were made in unidentified precincts.

A sampling of police brutality charges made by black neighborhoods in 1969 serves both as illustration of and substantiation for the conclusions drawn by such surveys and reports.

During October 1968 the Passaic County grand jury charged individuals of the Paterson, N.J., police department with vandalism, brutality, and intimidation in quelling a week of racial disorders during the month of July. The jury also declared it had evidence that the police had resorted to "terrorism" and "goon squad" tactics in putting down the disturbance. The following is a statement made by the grand jury expressing its opinion of the incident: "This grand jury states its abhorrence and dismay at the actions of a relative handful of misguided officers who, while sworn to uphold the law and provide protection for life and property, chose instead on this occasion to break the law and destroy private property, including that of private citizens not involved in any way with the disturbances."

In November, off-duty Detroit policemen attending a dance sponsored by the police officers'

wives were accused of attacking and beating a group of black youths. According to the officers the teenagers provoked the attack by making obscene gestures to the wives. Mayor Cavanaugh ordered an immediate investigation of the incident, but investigating procedures were hampered by the establishment of a "blue curtain" of police secrecy. Eventually, though, Detroit's police commissioner, Johannes F. Spreen, said the investigation showed that the charges made were correct "in varying degrees" and that some of the attackers had been identified. As a result of the investigation, warrants were issued charging one officer with felonious assault for hitting a youth with a gun, and another with assault and battery. Nine policemen, including the two charged, were suspended from the police department.

Two instances of police ill-treatment of blacks in custody occurred during November in Newark, N.J. Arrested for fighting in the street, a Negro woman was taken to a medical center, where she claimed she was repeatedly "stomped" by a policeman while changing her clothes in the restroom. The other incident described in the same report involved a Negro male who had been arrested for drunkenness and was reported to have been in good physical condition when he arrived at the police station. The next morning the prisoner was found in his cell lying unconscious in a pool of blood.

During February an 18-year-old Vietnam-bound black soldier was viciously beaten by police officers in a Greyhound bus station in Chicago. The attack was not provoked, according to the victim and his brother, who was accompanying him at the time. The brother testified that police officers took them into a small room, and once inside began kicking the soldier. Several minutes later a second policeman came into the room and joined the melee. After the beating the victim and his brother were taken to military police headquarters where it was later discovered that the victim had a clean military record.

Dr. William K. Allen, a prominent dentist of Columbus, Ohio, earlier this year charged that police had beaten him and broken his nose for no apparent reason when he inadvertently stepped behind the counter of a restaurant in downtown Columbus. Dr. Allen intends to take his case to federal court for a complete redress of the deprivation of his constitutional rights.

An excerpt from Paul Chevigny's book *Police Power* serves as an excellent illustration of police brutality, in this case arising from a misunderstanding between a ghetto resident and his wife and the police.

> On the wife's night off, they were having drinks in a bar where she worked, and at the end of the evening, she went out to hail a cab. A policeman, mistaking her flashy clothes for those of a prostitute, ordered her to move on. A vituperative argument ensued, and the wife was knocked down with a punch in the eye. When the husband ran out of the bar with a friend to protest, he was also knocked down. The wife was charged with assault and the husband with disorderly conduct.

In many incidents involving ghetto residents and the police this type of situation is common. In Chicago a black security guard was severely beaten by two members of the police department's task force unit. The victim, Edward Shanks, was stopped by the officers for a minor traffic violation. The officers discovered a pistol in his possession, and then proceeded to arrest him for unlawful use of a weapon. Shanks protested and produced his identification. As a result of his attempts to defend his rights he was beaten. Shanks was admitted to a hospital where the resident physician said that "a major operation must be performed. He must remain hospitalized for at least three weeks. . . . He was lucky to survive."

Don Wright, a black community leader in Venice, Calif., was beaten by a group of policemen while attempting to stop a fight between two juveniles on the street. When police asked Mr. Wright to step back, he obeyed, but was still handcuffed and arrested. Wright testified later that his handcuffs were removed at the police station and he was led into a room where he was

beaten and kicked by several officers. The charge brought against Wright was interference with a police officer in the act of performing his duty.

Members of the student government at North Carolina A & T University have charged that police shot and killed a Negro youth as he pleaded for his life during violence that occurred at the predominantly black school in May. Vince McCullough, president of the student body, said, "It was cold-blooded murder." Police later denied that a policeman deliberately shot the Negro youth, but said the youth was shot in a crossfire between officers and snipers. They also added the fact that police officers did not carry .32 caliber ammunition — the type of ammunition that was found in the bullet-ridden body of the youth. McCullough later stated that some of the police officers were carrying their personal weapons.

According to the Kerner Report the intensity of black community feelings about police misconduct may even be exceeded by the conviction that black neighborhoods are not given adequate police protection. This belief is founded on two basic types of complaints. The first is that the police carry on a much less rigorous standard of law enforcement in the ghetto than elsewhere. They are tolerant of dope peddling, prostitution, and street violence. The second is that police, in many instances, are negligent in answering complaints and calls for help from black areas.

David Hardy, staff member of the New York *Daily News,* has said: "To put it simply, for decades little if any law enforcement has prevailed among Negroes in America, particularly those in the ghettos. If a black man kills another black man the law is generally enforced at its minimum."

A report of a New Haven community group also adds some light on this situation: "When calls for help are registered, it is all too frequent that police respond too slowly or not at all. . . . When they do come they arrive with many more men and cars than are necessary . . . brandishing guns and adding to the confusion."

The Kerner Report goes on to say that studies

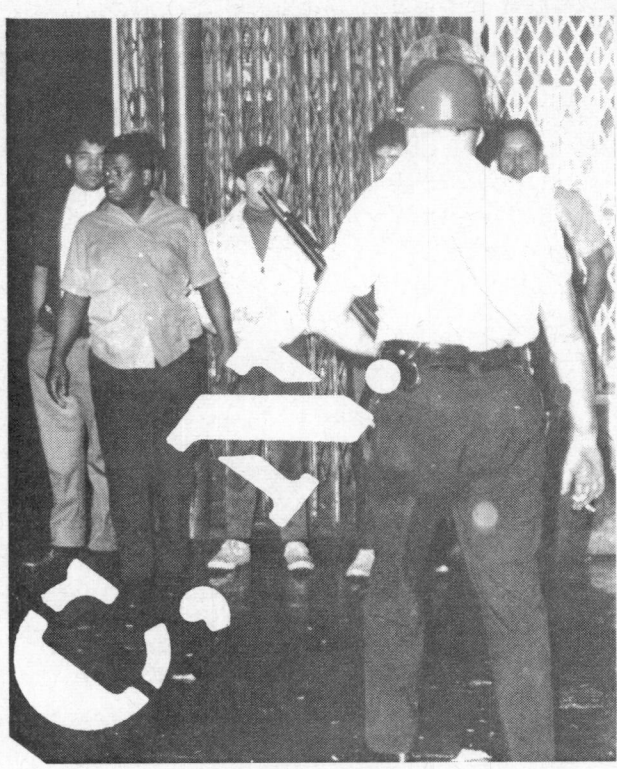

have substantial documented evidence which
vividly illustrates the inadequacies of police response in ghetto areas. For example, a *Yale
Law Journal* study of Hartford, Conn., found
that "the residents of a large area in the center
of the Negro ghetto are victims of over one-
third of the daylight residential burglaries in the
city. Yet during the daytime only one of Hartford's 18 police patrol cars and none of its
11 foot patrolmen are assigned to this area.
Sections in the white part of town about the
same size as the central ghetto area receive
slightly more intensive daytime patrol even
though the citizens in the ghetto area summon
the police about six times as often because of
criminal acts."

A recent survey conducted by the Detroit *Free
Press* showed that two-thirds of those interviewed
said they were dissatisfied with police protection.
One of the most frequent complaints was that
"if you call the police, they most likely don't
even come, or they show up after everything's
over."

Robert Pearman suggests in "Black Crime,
Black Victims" that the most often overlooked
problems in policing ghetto areas are deficiencies in investigation, public interest, public cooperation, and prosecution. Found in almost
every major city in the country, such problems
parallel high crime rates, abortive prosecution,
and danger for the people who live within the
community. Pearman also indicates that there
are fewer solutions, less prosecution, and shorter
sentences for offenses committed by blacks
against other blacks. Harold Holiday of the
Missouri legislature comes right to the point:
"People tend to spend time and energy on things
they think are important. And the police don't
think that crime in our neighborhood is important."

President Johnson's Commission on Law Enforcement and the Administration of Justice said:
"The inner-city has always been hard on whoever
is living in it. . . . Not long ago there was a
tendency to dismiss reports on all but the most
serious offenses in slum areas and segregated

minority group districts. They were left to take
care of their own problems. The ghetto, the very
neighborhood that needs protection most, is
often explosive. There is much distrust, especially
among boys and young men . . . the people
the police most often deal with."

The apathy of many police departments toward black communities is related to both their
misunderstanding of the life patterns of the black
community—patterns which frequently differ
from those of the establishment—and their
racist attitudes. Into the life of the black community comes the police officer—an instrument
of the white power establishment and a symbol
of law enforcement. For eight hours or more he
is thrust into the role of keeping the peace. If he
is white he lives in another section of town or
in the suburbs, and finds it very difficult to relate to or understand the life patterns of the black
community. More often than not this becomes an
incredibly tense, nerve-wracking, and possibly
even fearful experience. If the police officer is
black he is faced with the dilemma of conflict
between professional duty and racial allegiance.
First, he is irrevocably a part of the black community; secondly he is a servant of the system
that employs him, and according to L. F. Pal-
mer, Jr., he may find himself "overreacting"
against black people in a desperate attempt to
prove his objectivity, his "professionalism," his
ability to shut out the haunting knowledge that
"though he is a cop, he is also a black man."

The Kerner Report expresses the feeling that
the factor which serves as a catalyst in shaping
police-community relationships is the way a
police officer handles himself in day-to-day encounters with the citizens of the community.
These encounters must involve a considerable
amount of discretion on the part of the police
officer, or he can create needless tension and contribute to community grievances. Therefore, the
Kerner Commission suggests that it is the responsibility of the police to draft guidelines for
dealing with police-community problems within
the ghetto. Police research and planning units
should be fully used in identifying problem areas,

performing the necessary studies, and resolving problems.

"Going by the Book," an article by Hillard J. Trubitt, asserts that an outstanding cause of such misunderstandings is the officers' high regard for procedural regularity. Trubitt says that "a great majority of the situations in which policemen intervene are not, or are not interpreted by police to be, criminal situations in the sense that they call for arrest. . . . A common kind of situation . . . is the matrimonial dispute, which police experts estimate consumes as much time as any other single kind of situation." He feels that in these situations the officer's actions or inactions will tend to produce the malaise which in turn creates, or is rationalized as the basis for, community tension. Through all of this misunderstanding the law enforcement agent continues to perform his duty, unaware that he is missing the mark, and insisting that he is fulfilling his duty as an officer of the law "in the proper manner."

Many policemen openly express attitudes about blacks that psychologists would consider racist or prejudiced, although few white policemen would agree with that description. A study conducted by the President's commission on crime revealed that 72 per cent of the white policemen and 18 per cent of the black policemen in four inner-city precincts were prejudiced against black people. Attitudes that would most often be categorized as racist by some people are just common sense to others. For instance, a policeman in Boston, Mass., was quoted as saying, "What is a ghetto? I grew up in Roxbury [now Boston's largest black neighborhood]. I woke up in the morning and saw frost on the inside of the window. We didn't have any electric furnace. We had Momma and Poppa and God."

Many white policemen feel this way. Another Washington police officer, describing Pride, Inc., a federally supported, black-run employment and self-help organization, said: "The only thing they are doing out there is taking that money, they are going out and housebreaking, they are rob-

bing banks. . . . You find out most of them are involved in rapes." He was asked if he knew this to be a fact. "I would have to check the records for you," the officer replied, "but I can guarantee you they are there."

George Edwards, former Detroit police commissioner and presently a federal judge, estimates that 90 per cent of the Detroit policemen are bigoted, and that dislike for blacks is continuously manifested in both their verbal and physical abuse.

Abuse of police power also causes tension between the ghetto community and the police department. According to the Kerner Commission, "formally, the police officer has no discretion; his task is to enforce all laws at all times. Formally, the officer's only basic enforcement option is to make an arrest, or to do nothing. Formally, when a citizen resists arrest the officer's only recourse is to apply such reasonable force as he can bring with his hands, nightstick, and revolver." If a police officer deviates from this in any way, then he is abusing the police power which society has invested in him. In *Police Power,* mentioned above, Chevigny discusses many instances in which policemen have abused their authority. Chevigny believes that many times the apparently irrational and provocative behavior of police in street confrontations may be a deliberate encouragement of violence or disorderly behavior from a troublemaker in order to show that he really is an offender and to provide grounds for removing him from the streets by arrest. He goes on to say that the worst abuse of police power is not physical abuse, but rather that the police officer often lies in order to secure an arrest. Once a person has been arrested,

lying becomes an inevitable part of the procedure of making [an incident] . . . look like a crime, and thus the lie is the chief abuse with which we must come to grips. If the police simply hit a man and let him go, there would be an abuse of the authority conferred by the uniform and the stick, but not the compound abuse of hitting a man and then dragging him to court on criminal charges, really a more serious injury than a blow. One's head heals up, but a criminal record never goes away. There is no more embittering experience in the legal system than to be abused by the police and then be tried and convicted on false evidence.

This type of experience is responsible for feeding the impulse to riot; once respect for the legal process is gone, it seems the only avenue of expression is through violence.

The Kerner Report prophesied that America was gradually developing into two distinct societies—black and white—with the policeman caught up in the middle. To attempt to remedy this, the Kerner Report called for more black police, black-white patrol units, the screening of officers to assure that those assigned to minority group areas know and understand the problems there, a reassignment of officers with bad reputations among members of minority groups, the same standard of law enforcement for all communities, and a community relations program designed to help with community problems, not just to improve the police image.

The city of Detroit provides graphic examples of the difficulties faced by citizens, police, and the government throughout much of the United States.

Detroit *Free Press* reporter William Serrin wrote in an article called "God Help Our City" that "abysmal police-Negro relations [in Detroit] are a symbol of all that is wrong with the city: a teetering war on poverty, shoddy schools, an inhuman urban-renewal program, polluted air and water, an archaic tax structure, and, for the most part, its unconcerned politicians, business leaders, and citizenry." Rev. Robert Morrison of St. Joseph's Episcopal Church in Detroit also supports this dismal point of view: "The cops are the greatest organizer of militancy in the black community. . . . The cops' attitude, and maybe they're right, is that every black person is a potential enemy. You cannot assume the police want a solution; they are committed to the *status quo,* to the maintenance of law and order.

More and more, the police are the hated symbol of authority, and as they become more repressive black anxieties will increase."

One of the great problems in Detroit is the question of who controls the Detroit police—the citizens or the police themselves. The Detroit Police Officers Association (DPOA) openly thwarted Mayor Cavanagh in his efforts to amend strained police-community relations. In an editorial in its newspaper, *Tuebor,* the president of the association explained DPOA's position:

> Frankly, we would rather not get involved in politics. We believe we have a far more important job to do of working toward our goal of professionalism of the police. But until such a time as proper bargaining procedures can be made effective, we will not abandon the political arena, and [will] campaign in behalf of police causes and resist every attempt at "union-busting."
>
> The DPOA believes . . . the charges of police brutality are part of a nefarious plot by those who would like our form of government overthrown. The blueprint for anarchy calls for the destruction of the effectiveness of the police. Certainly it must be obvious that every incident is magnified and exploited with only one purpose. A lot of well-meaning people, without realizing their real role, are doing the job for the anarchists.

In 1969 Detroit's police department made efforts to manifest its authority as a law enforcement agency and in the process helped spawn a number of incidents that have exacerbated the city's racial mood.

One of the most serious incidents was a shoot-out at the New Bethel Baptist Church in March between two white police officers and members of the Republic of New Africa. The immediate result of this confrontation was the death of one white patrolman and the injury of the other, as well as injuries of some of the black people inside the church. A prominent black judge, George W. Crockett, Jr., presiding at the recorder's court, was later informed that police had arrested 142 persons, and were holding them incommunicado at the precinct station without recourse to counsel. By the next morning Judge Crockett had released all but eight of the prisoners. His actions caused a racially polarized upheaval. The black community rallied overwhelmingly behind Judge Crockett, the whites overwhelmingly against him.

The DPOA picketed recorder's court, and the Guardians, a black policemen's group, counter-picketed. DPOA president Carl Parsell accused Judge Crockett of giving people "a free license to shoot policemen," and then went on to demand his impeachment.

Political involvement by the DPOA has caused many blacks to feel that the police are attempting to organize politically against them. Substantiation of this opinion can be found in a statement made by a group of 15 reporters who participated in a seven-city inner-city tour sponsored by the National Urban League in an effort to give them a view of urban problems from the viewpoint of black neighborhoods: "Despite the efforts in many cities to improve community re-

lations with police departments, police hostility remains the number one complaint. In cities like Detroit, the blacks expect the police to organize politically against them for control of the local governments."

Although faced with much opposition, Mayor Cavanagh has made attempts to implement some of the recommendations made by the Kerner Commission. Infuriated by the police department's obstinacy against hiring more black recruits, Cavanagh ordered Police Commissioner Johannes F. Spreen late in 1968 to hire blacks at a rate of 4 to 1 over whites, until the number of blacks on the force—now at 412, proportionately one of the lowest in America—began to approach 40 per cent. Many of the high command officers disregarded Cavanagh's order, and some went as far as accusing him of "reverse discrimination." Richard V. Marks, head of Detroit's commission on community relations, said, "Even the white bigots want black officers on the police force. The only guys that don't are the white cops themselves."

Soul Singer James Brown

Theater

THE YEAR 1969 was decidedly a year that witnessed more plays by and about blacks than ever before. An enormous upsurge of black theater was reflected both on and off Broadway and throughout the country. Doris E. Abramson's *Negro Playwrights in the American Theater* noted that although black dramatists were creating plays long before the advent of the civil rights movement and although black theater is not a new phenomenon, not until 1969 was widespread attention given to black theater. In the past black writers failed even to find a producer interested in their work; in 1969 there were opportunities for blacks on and off Broadway, in regional theaters, and, significantly, in uniquely black institutions. The sheer volume of plays produced in 1969—whether directed toward a mixed audience or toward an exclusively black one—was impressive. In January alone at least six plays by black playwrights appeared both on and off Broadway.

But black theater as viewed by major black playwrights including LeRoi Jones, Ed Bullins, Ossie Davis, Ron Milner, and Lonne Elder, III, had come to mean, by 1969, more than the Broadway success hailed by white critics. In the view of these playwrights, successful and productive black theater was essentially a body of work and experience that, although prepared for the stage, could be performed in streets, bars, pool halls, churches, and warehouses. No longer primarily concerned with achieving success in the white man's eyes, black theater received its strength from its attempts to reflect the attitudes, desires, condition, will, and spirit of black people. These black playwrights suggested that it failed only when the "brothers" remained insensitive—when the set went black but the audience didn't.

Two successful approaches to black theater were created in Washington, D.C., one through Howard University and the other at Federal City College. Howard University's assistant professor of drama, Paul Carter Harrison, felt the customs, culture, and habits of blacks are unique enough to warrant an independent theatrical form, and thus he organized a theater troupe oriented toward a black audience watching a "black experience." James Garrett, director of black studies at Federal City, had ideas not unlike Harrison's. His play, "And We Own the Night," was performed by Federal City's company.

Black playwrights of 1969 recognized the opportunity the stage offered for the propagation of their ideas. They used the theater as a platform to voice the black community's aspirations and philosophies.

The National Black Theatre, founded in October 1968 in New York City, conducted acting classes and symposiums in 1969 in which prominent political and cultural figures participated. The purpose of both is to develop actors and actresses who, independent of accepted theater standards, learn both to act with an awareness of black life styles and to become attuned to black "inner pride." Director Barbara Ann Teer created the program in order to establish a "black art standard." According to Miss Teer, the black theater today cannot copy white theater guidelines and models because they haven't satisfied the needs of black people. She suggests that the artists who attend her classes learn to be not merely good actors but "black liberators," fully equipped to lead black people toward a greater awareness of self.

The Living Stage '69 seeks to make theater more relevant to inner-city youths by using improvisation as a tool to speak to the issues that concern young blacks. The group of actors traveled around the country in an attempt to create interest and stimulate response from young people in ghetto areas. One such appearance was made at the Police Boys Club in Washington, D.C. When the youngsters in the audience were asked to suggest some situations they were concerned with, they provided everything from disinterested schoolteachers, sex, police brutality, and drunken fathers to corrupt black cops and gambling. The troupe improvised the situations suggested and attempted to give solutions to some of the problems mentioned. After the performance a discussion session revealed many of the thoughts and fears of the youths and it was said to have helped both them and the members of Living Stage '69 to gain insight into some of the problems of the inner-city.

The Inner-City Cultural Center of Los Angeles began its second season in 1969. Located in the urban center of the city, the theater group's prime objective is to bring the arts into the lives of people who have had little or no contact with them. The company is one of three educational laboratory theater projects established with support from the federal government, through the National Arts Endowment and the Office of Education, and from local and county educational authorities. The ICCC presented an unusual cast in its production of Thornton Wilder's "Our Town" late in 1968. Emily Webb, the girl, was played by a Negro, her father by an Apache Indian, her mother by a Russian-American and her brother by a Mexican-American. Her sweetheart was portrayed by a blond Caucasian, his father by a Japanese-American, his mother by a Negro and his sister by a Chinese-American. The multiracial company was not a matter of chance but a direct effort by the ICCC to provide a new perspective in casting for producers. It was the Center's hope that by showing this type of casting to be productive and lucrative, other producers would begin using talented persons of minority groups more frequently.

In an effort to develop an interracial theater and an interracial audience, the Arena Stage of Washington, D.C., opened its 1969 season with one-third of its 24-member company composed of Negroes. Many of the black actors were included with the assistance of a $250,000 Ford Foundation grant designed to develop Negro involvement in the theater. Arena gave its black performers roles that normally would have been associated with white actors, a plan similar to that used by the Inner-City Cultural Center. Arena also attempted to produce the plays in such a way that the inclusion of the blacks in the cast would heighten the impact of the performances. Among the plays produced during the season were "The Threepenny Opera," "Six Characters in Search of an Author," and "King Lear."

The Negro Ensemble Company, located in New York City, was by mid-1969 wavering between becoming an affectionately regarded community theater and a genuinely professional ensemble. Until that time it had been successful as a community workshop geared to involve non-professional young black talent. With the outstanding reviews of their production of "Ceremonies in Dark Old Men," and with an invitation from London to participate in the "World Theater Season," the Company was able to measure its success. Robert Hooks, star of ABC-TV's "N.Y.P.D.," helped establish the Company two years ago with a $434,000 grant from the Ford Foundation. The purpose of the Ensemble has been to give blacks a chance to grow in the theater.

Lonne Elder, III, author of "Ceremonies in Dark Old Men," and a member of the group, worked 10 years on "Ceremonies." The story of a decent Harlem family caught up in rackets, the play is a realistic interpretation of the experiences of ordinary black people. According to many reviewers it was the most exciting play yet produced by the Company.

Other productions were Ray McIver's "God Is a (Guess What?)" and a group of one-act plays: "Contribution," by Ted Shine; "String," by Alice Childress; and "Malcochon," by Derek Walcott. Following the run of "An Evening of One Acts," the company offered a workshop festival involving the acting, dancing, technical, play writing, and directing skills of the group. In May the company appeared in London as part of the "World Theater Season," visited Rome for a week, and returned to New York City to present Earl Hill's "Man Better Man," a musical set in the West Indies.

Playwright Lanford Wilson's "The Gingham Dog" had its premiere at the Washington Theater Club, Washington, D.C., in October 1968. The play deals with a racially mixed couple in the process of separation because of incompatibility arising from the racial difference. Critics agreed the play was smoothly structured, but suggested its plot was unoriginal and the script cliché-ridden.

"The Great White Hope" was considered by many critics the most brilliant play of the 1968–1969 season, a judgment reinforced seven months after its October 1968 opening, when the play was named the best drama of the year and its star, James Earl Jones, named best actor, at the 23rd annual presentation of the Antoinette Perry awards. Howard Sackler's drama, which also won a Pulitzer Prize and the New York Drama Critics Circle award, is based on the career of Jack Johnson, the first Negro heavyweight boxing champion, and the uproar his career caused. According to Del Carnes, *Denver*

Post drama critic, it was "the great hope of Broadway." A movie version is planned with James Earl Jones again playing the leading role.

On Dec. 8, 1968, "Big Time Buck White," a satire of black and white power by Joseph Dolan Tuotti, opened in New York City after playing nearly three years in California. Called both funny and powerful by critics, the play's form is original: beginning humorously, its tone changes almost immediately with the arrival of Big Time Buck White. The audience is brought from the happy world of the melon-grinning shoeshine boy to the real world of black aspiration and revolutionary black power. Later the jokes made by the black cast are reversed and the audience is directed into participation when Buck asks for questions and responses. Critics praised the play's strength.

A new off Broadway play by Yabo Yablonsky, "Americana Pastoral," is the story of a poor Southern village confused and disgusted when it learns a wealthy black Yankee will be establishing a cotton mill there. It received mixed reviews from the critics who had reservations about the validity of the characters and the ability of the actors.

The 1961 musical "Carnival" became for the first time an interracial love story when it was performed at the New York City Center on Dec. 12, 1968. Victoria Mallory, a white, and Leon Bibb, a black, starred. Bibb explained how he felt about the casting: "People may be attracted to the interracial love in the play. I don't knock it—but it isn't the most important thing. To cast black actors in roles where they can bring an extra dimension to the story is important."

Ed Bullins' play. "In the Wine of Time," presented "a slice of black life as it is actually lived," according to Lindsay Patterson, editor of the *Anthology of the American Negro in the Theatre*. The play, which premiered in New York City, tells of the life of a ghetto family, distorted and hurt by its place in society. According to Patterson the play is relevant not only to the black experience but to all experience. He added, "It has that quality called universality."

At 29, Lorraine Hansberry achieved fame with her first play, "A Raisin in the Sun." In 1965, at the age of 34, she died of cancer during the Broadway run of her second play, "The Sign in Sidney Brustein's Window." Left behind were plays not yet produced and unpublished writings. From this material her husband, Robert Nemiroff, created the play "To Be Young, Gifted and Black," which opened Jan. 2, 1969, at the Cherry Lane Theater in Manhattan. The play focuses on her fight for people in the battle against ignorance, stupidity, and simple-mindedness. The title comes from a speech Miss Hansberry made to a group of young black student writers; she was referring not to herself but to them. It is a message play, and according to *Time* magazine, something of a milestone in the current black-white confrontation: "It is suffused not only with hot anger at indignity and injustice but with a glowing concern for men and women as men and women. . . . [It] is a moving reminder of how much the young, gifted, and black Miss Hansberry is to be missed."

"The Blacks," a controversial two-act play by French playwright Jean Gênet, was produced by the Karamu Arena Theater in Cleveland in January. Critics called the play everything from stimulating to an avant-garde clown show and, in general, no one seemed to understand what its point was. According to the director, playwright Gênet felt that all whites interpret all blacks as children and he therefore wrote his shocking play as a stylistic children's game. The plot revolves around the re-enactment of a make-believe murder crime—the victim is a white woman. Cleveland *Call and Post* critic Roland Forte called "The Blacks" a highly effective pornographic play with sociological significance.

The Mark Topper Forum of the Los Angeles Music Center opened March 20 with a play adapted from George Bernard Shaw's novel, *The Adventures of a Black Girl in Her Search for God*. Playwright Christopher Isherwood did the adaptation for the stage. Isherwood selected Shaw's theme that in an age of power, only the idea of God as universal love can save the human race. He estimated that although changes in movement and action were made, the bulk of the dialogue was Shaw's. The Forum conducted after-play seminars to involve the audience in discussion about the value of the play.

Garret Robinson, resident playwright, director, and designer of Roger Furman's New Heritage Repertory Theater in Harlem, wrote a play which was presented by the repertory group. Entitled "Hamhocks," the play is the story of a Southern couple who migrated to a typical Harlem slum dwelling. "Hamhocks" is significant in that no play has been written about Harlem and shown there since Langston Hughes' "Simply Heavenly," 10 years earlier.

"The Perfect Party" opened off Broadway at Tambellini's Gate Theater in New York City. Charles H. Fuller's play is a study of five husbands and five wives who organize a village for integrated couples like themselves. It raises a number of questions about interracial marriage as a realistic solution to the problems of blacks and whites in American society and attempts to answer some of these questions. Critic Lawrence Van Gelder of the *New York Times* praised Mr. Fuller's smoothly written dialogue and deft characterizations but suggested that the play falls victim to a quick, weak ending. He added that he felt Mr. Fuller "has permitted his blacks and whites to integrate but has barred them from an opportunity to blend."

Playwright Leonard Spigelgass drew on his own experiences as a tenement house owner for the play "The Wrong Way Light Bulb," which opened in March at the John Golden Theater in New York. It is the story of a young Jewish liberal who inherits a tenement and turkish bath in Brooklyn from his grandfather. He is warned of the problems involved in ownership—racial tension, vandalism, rising maintenance costs—but feels these things can be overcome. He decides not only to keep the tenement, but to live in it; inevitably, he becomes bitterly disillusioned. *New York Times* reviewer Clive Barnes suggested that playwright Spigelgass presents attitudes rather than characters and that the play faces racial issues in a dangerously oversimplified, superficial way.

The play "Someone's Comin' Hungry" which opened off Broadway is long, according to critic Mary Campbell, and gives little food for thought. It deals with an interracial couple's problems—their failure to understand each other and her mother's refusal to recognize their marriage. It was written in a first collaborative effort by McCrea Imbrie and Neil Selden.

The Ebony Showcase Theater in Los Angeles staged "The Roar of the Greasepaint—The Smell of the Crowd" in April. Both leads were played by black men, and according to critic Dan Sullivan of the *Los Angeles Times,* the portrayals added freshness to the 1965 musical.

"We Righteous Bombers" opened April 18 at the New Lafayette Theater in New York City. Written by Kingsley B. Bass, Jr., the play's theme involves violence, mystery, and love. Artistic director Robert Macbeth utilized practically the entire company and engaged live musicians who performed "new sound" with a variety of instruments rarely seen or heard today.

"Trumpets of the Lord," an adaptation by Vinnette Carroll of James Weldon Johnson's *God's Trombones,* which was originally produced in 1963, reappeared at Ford's Theater in Washington, D.C., and at the Brooks Atkinson Theater in New York. The setting of the play is a country church and the occasion is a gospel meeting conducted by the pastor of the church and two visiting ministers. The show, which combines the spoken word with gospel singing, starred Theresa Merritt, Lex Monson, Bernard Ward, and Hilda Simms in both productions.

Black playwright Charles Gordone's "No Place To Be Somebody" opened early in May at the New York Shakespeare Festival's Public Theater. The play centers around Johnny Williams, who has made it out of Harlem to Greenwich Village, where he owns a bar. He is awaiting the release from jail of Sweets Crane, crook and father figure, with whom he wants to make the big time. But Sweets comes out a dying and reformed man, a change which Johnny cannot

accept. Critics were divided in their appraisal of the story. John Simon, writing in *New York* magazine, suggested that although the play is interesting, it is essentially a "typical protest play." Walter Kerr of the *New York Times,* however, said he saw in Gordone the most astonishing new American playwright to come along since Albee.

All-black casts performed four one-act plays by black playwrights Ed Bullins, Ben Caldwell, Evan Walker, and Jimmy Garrett at the Performing Arts Society of Los Angeles in June. "Clara's Ole Man" by Bullins opened the program. The play centers around young, attractive Clara, her college boy friend, and the variety of distasteful persons they must contend with in her ghetto apartment building. Ben Caldwell's "Top Secret" shows the President and his Cabinet wearing white-face and discussing at huge length a macabre "final solution" for the "Negro problem." Walker's "The Message" foresees a police state with a concentration camp for blacks. The final play, "And We Own the Night," by Jimmy Garrett, is a confrontation between a mother and her mortally wounded son during a riot. Critic Fredric L. Milstein suggested in his review of the four plays that "The Message" was the most convincing and powerful.

During June and July, Washington, D.C.'s Smithsonian Institution presented "The Ballad of the Black Dragon," written by Gaye Williams and based on four orations by Frederick Douglass covering a period of 60 years in his life. Williams explained that he wrote the play "because I want to get at the philosophy and soul of Douglass." He added that Douglass' words are as important and significant to the 20th century as they were in Douglass' era.

Films

In December 1968 Sidney Poitier was named "Star of the Year" by the National Association of Theater Owners. It was later announced—and came as a surprise to no one—that Poitier had also attained the ultimate recognition from the public—he was the number one box-office attraction in 1968. This suggested to observers that in the motion picture industry a positive and open atmosphere toward all races finally was becoming a reality.

The number of films written, produced, directed, and acted in by blacks in 1969 was also encouraging in this respect, although dissatisfaction was still apparent among both black and white film figures. Hollywood film writer Sterling Silliphant, Academy Award winner for his screenplay "In the Heat of the Night," suggested that the rising tide of racial themes in motion pictures could have dangerous repercussions because of what he labeled "an unrealistic portrayal of an everything-is-right world" in films. Silliphant explained: "God knows we neglected the Negro for so many years in our films—unless we showed him carrying our bourbon or showed his knees knocking as he passed a cemetery—that we have every reason now to smother him in the rush to compensate and atone. But instead, I fear, there's more tokenism than atonement; more exploitation than compensation." He added that this exploitation—involving hastily assembled productions lacking much insight—will mislead the vast white middle class which has limited daily contact with black people as well as frustrate minorities and the underprivileged who know they are a long way from the "happy ending" depicted. "What is needed," said Silliphant, is to tell it like it is, by showing blacks first and foremost and always as human beings, not as black types; to look at them in stories not as a product of biology, but of history and sociology."

Actors Paul Newman, Sidney Poitier, and Barbra Streisand echoed Silliphant's suggestions when they announced in June plans to form a new motion picture company called First Artists Productions. Said Poitier at the time of the announcement, "The motion picture industry is moving. . . . We are creating new opportunities not only for ourselves but for many new, young, and diverse talents in the country from all ethnic and minority groups."

Whether produced purely for entertainment or to give honest insight into the "black experience," film makers offered many films of particular interest to the black public in 1969.

Photojournalist Gordon Parks made his autobiographical novel, *The Learning Tree,* into a film of the same title. The hero is a black boy in his teens who learns about racial hatred when a redneck sheriff murders a black man. He learns about sex in a brief scene with an older woman and about love from a young girl. He learns about faith and how to face death from his deeply religious mother, and in the courtroom scene which climaxes the film, he learns about bravery and justice. The film is set in the farmlands of Cherokee Flats, Kans., in the 1920s.

Philip Langner, the producer of "Slaves," explained that he discovered no one had ever made a film that dealt honestly and extensively with slavery in the United States, so he made that film to try to fill the void. The screenplay by John O. Killens and Alida Sherman concerns a Christian slave who thinks God will lead his people out of bondage, until he literally gets sold down the river. His new master is harsh and soon demonstrates that the slave will need more than God's help to win the freedom his previous master had promised. Ossie Davis portrays the slave, Dionne Warwick the slaveowner's mistress. Harry MacArthur, drama critic for the Washington *Star,* felt that although the producers had their hearts in the right places, the film they created gave the overall effect of a class-B "Uncle Tom's Cabin." The film was similarly panned by other critics.

"The Lost Man" marked a new portrayal for Sidney Poitier. It is the story of an embittered young black man swept up in the demands of a changing society. He sees the fruitless non-violent efforts of his friends and decides upon an alternate solution, that of organizing a gang to steal funds to aid families harassed, hospitalized, or jailed by the police. Over 50 per cent of the movie crew was black. Poitier made this possible through a request to Universal Studios that black persons be utilized in the production wherever possible.

The film "100 Rifles" made the headlines in 1969 for two reasons. The first was the picketing of the gala benefit premiere in Washington, D.C., by Pride, Inc., a black self-help organization that provides job opportunities for local residents. Pride program director Marion Barry complained that neither the cocktail party nor the premiere was held at a black establishment. Jeff Mitchell, D.C. director of the Black Economic Union, the group for which the benefit was held, responded to the charges by saying, "I think Pride is missing the boat in what we are trying to accomplish. We have made a major breakthrough in getting 20th Century Fox to put on this premiere tonight as a benefit for a black cause."

The second controversy arose over dialogue in a love scene in the picture in which Raquel Welch and Jim Brown were scantily clad. Barry charged, "The promotion of a fund-raising affair for the Black Economic Union should not include pictures on the theater ticket which shatter racial pride. Black people in 1969 do not need a half-naked black buck-white sex goddess image." The film itself is a fast-action western in which Brown plays a sheriff in search of a hold-up man. Critics generally agreed the production contained more action and violence than it did dialogue. Drama critic Harry MacArthur of the *Washington Star* felt that "it is hardly the sort of thing that merits a gala world premiere. It might have been smarter of 20th Century Fox, in fact, to allow it to escape rather than to release it."

Noted actor-playwright Ossie Davis made his debut as a director in "Cotton Comes to Harlem," a movie based on the novel by Chester B. Hines. The film starred Godfrey Cambridge, Raymond St. Jacques, and Calvin Lockhart. It is the story of two detectives and their search for $87,000 stolen at a "Back to Africa" rally. It was filmed on location in Harlem and about 200 extras were recruited from the area. Davis

explained the purpose of the film is "to show there is something different going on in Harlem" that other film makers haven't seen: "the community's colorful, exciting, life style and wit."

"Uptight" was one of the first attempts by a major motion picture company (Paramount) to deal with a doubly touchy subject. Directed by Jules Dassin, the film is the story of an alcoholic steelworker rejected by both his white employers and his black power companions. When one of his militant friends murders a man during a holdup, the alcoholic turns him in for the $1,000 reward money. Later he is shot for his disloyalty. "Uptight" was filmed in the Cleveland ghetto and starred Raymond St. Jacques, Ruby Dee, Roscoe Lee Browne, and Julian Mayfield. Movie critic Roger Ebert called the film "a forthright treatment of black militancy. . . . The passions and beliefs of black militants are presented head-on, with little in the way of comfort for white liberals."

Toka Films, a non-profit all-black concern, provided funds for five young men to travel 72,000 miles across the United States to attempt to capture on film the essence of the black man on the American continent. Titled "Black Man," the film tries to depict black reality. The purpose of the picture, according to Ahmad Akbar, an executive of Toka, is to provide the American people with a clear, unbiased, in-depth picture of the black American. "When black people can see themselves on the screen they, too, will gain increased knowledge of themselves and will find a more complete black identity," explained Akbar.

"Riot" confirmed Jim Brown's success as a movie star in 1969. He played the leading role in the motion picture based on a novel written in prison by former convict Frank Elli. Filmed within the walls of the Arizona State Prison, it is the story of a tough, laconic loner who finds himself leading a prison riot he did not start. Critics were moderately favorable in their reviews of the film. Said Vincent Canby of the *New York Times,* "It is not a great movie, but it is a respectable one."

Pearl Bailey was back in films for the first time in 10 years in the movie "The Landlord." Based on the Kristin Hunter novel, the comedy is about a well-to-do young man who buys a brownstone in a ghetto area with the intention of using it himself, but ends up becoming involved with the tenants. Also starring in the film is Diana Sands, who portrays one of the tenants. Local residents of Brooklyn, where the film was shot, were recruited as extras.

Art

An exhibition of paintings, graphics, and sculpture by 30 black artists traveled across the country in November 1968 from its home at the Minneapolis Institute of Art. The tour visited Atlanta; Flint, Mich.; Syracuse and Rochester, N.Y.; Providence, R.I.; and San Francisco. It included the works of Romare Bearden, Emma Amos, Benny Andrews, Betty Blayton, Peter Bradley, Floyd Coleman, Emilio Cruz, and Avel de Knight.

At the same time a group of more than 30 black artists picketed a Whitney Museum exhibit in New York City, protesting what they described as the exclusion of Negro artists from the Whitney's exhibition entitled "The 1930s: Painting and Sculpture in America." Henri Ghent, director of the Brooklyn Museum's new Community Gallery, explained that the group was not saying the exclusion was deliberate; however, they did feel that the white establishment refuses to acknowledge the black artist's work. The protesters felt the title of the exhibit was inaccurate and wanted to point out that black artists were very much a part of America in the 1930s.

In response to the protest, John I. H. Baur, director of the Whitney, explained that he felt the black artists had every right to picket but stressed that the museum has followed a policy of selecting art for its artistic value alone—without regard to race. Baur said, "I have deep sympathy with the black artist's struggle to find a place for himself in our civilization, but I think he has to be judged on the same basis as any other artist—on the quality of his work." A museum spokesman pointed out that the works of many Negro artists, including Jacob Lawrence, Romare Bearden, Charles Alston, and Charles White, were among the Whitney's permanent collection. He said the museum had exhibited the works of many Negro artists previously and that it intended to include the works of four Negro sculptors in a forthcoming show. The protesting group of black artists then organized a counter-show entitled "Invisible Americans: Black Artists of the Thirties." Exhibited at the Studio Museum in Harlem, the show included the works of Lawrence, Bearden, William Hale Woodruff, and Ernest Chrichlow. Many of the works for the counter-show were lent by the National Collection of Fine Arts of the Smithsonian Institution in Washington, D.C., and the Schomburg Collection of the New York Public Library.

One month later, in January 1969, another controversial show opened at New York City's Metropolitan Museum of Art. "Harlem on My Mind: Cultural Capital of Black America (1900–1968)" drew reactions from every conceivable source and was undoubtedly the most controversial exhibit of the year. C. Allon Schoener, director of visual arts of the New York State Council on the Arts and coordinater of the exhibit, wrote in his introduction to the show's catalogue that it was conceived "as a communications environment—one that parallels our daily lives in which we are deluged with information stimuli. Images and sounds—documentary in character—have been organized into a pattern of experiences recreating the history of Harlem as it happened. . . . From all this information available from a variety of sources, each person selects what he wants for himself and reacts to it."

The controversy began before the opening of the show when the Harlem Cultural Council complained that it was not sufficiently consulted in the preparation and withdrew its endorsement of the show. It charged the organizers of the exhibit with being more concerned with "show business" techniques than with the actual content. Donald Harper, associate research and media director of "Harlem On My Mind," explained that he felt "show business techniques were not necessarily bad and that the show, in his opinion, was valid.

Another criticism was that although the show was subtitled "Cultural Capital of Black America" and presented the works of poets, writers, and musicians, it entirely avoided the work of Harlem artists. Schoener argued that the show was never meant to be an art exhibit but an exhibit of cultural documents related to information techniques, and that painting would be contradictory to those techniques. Schoener added that he felt painting is no longer a valid means of expression in the 20th century.

The show was organized with a basic staff of five—Robert Malone, exhibit designer, Harper, A'Lelia Nelson, community research coordinator, Martin S. Moskof, exhibition graphic designer, and Reginald McGhee, director of photographic research. Mr. McGhee selected more than 30 per cent of the photographs used from a shop in Harlem owned by James Vanderzee, a photographer who has been taking pictures of Harlem for the past 50 years. McGhee and Harper were criticized as being unsuited for their positions because they were not from New York City. McGhee explained that the jobs were open. He felt the appointment was fair: "I applied for a job, was qualified for a job, and I got a job."

More animosity developed when New York City Mayor John V. Lindsay said he felt that a portion of the show's catalogue expressed anti-Semitic feelings. Lindsay urged that the catalogue be withdrawn immediately. His statement came in response to a complaint from the American Jewish Committee that a five-paragraph segment taken from a 17-year-old Harlem girl's high school term paper was racist. Candice Van Ellison said in her paper that blacks in Harlem are exploited by Jews through high prices and exorbitant rents. This exploitation led to anti-

Semitic feelings in the black community. According to Miss Van Ellison, this black contempt toward Jews involves blacks in a national prejudice, with the ironic result that anti-Semitism makes blacks feel more completely "American." Director Hoving answered the charges by saying, "I'm fully convinced that this personal observation by a sensitive and talented 17-year-old girl is not racist, is not bigotry, is not slander . . . . It represents the personal account of a sensitive, observant girl looking out upon what was not and is not a very pleasant world." In an effort to clear the issue, the museum inserted a disclaimer in the catalogue. Written by Miss Van Ellison, it said, "In regards to the controversy concerning the section in my introduction dealing with intergroup relations, I would like to state that the facts were organized according to the socio-economic realities in Harlem at that time and that any racist overtones which were inferred from the passages quoted out of context are regrettable."

After the exhibit had been open for several weeks, the three co-chairmen of the Black Emergency Cultural Coalition of 75 Negro and white artists charged that "Harlem On My Mind" was so full of distortions and misrepresentations that it should be closed immediately. Benny Andrews, Henri Ghent, and Edward Taylor, co-chairmen of the Coalition, said the exhibit conveyed "the white man's distorted, irrelevant, and insulting" view of Harlem. In contrast, New York City Human Rights Commissioner William H. Booth, a Negro, called the show "well-rounded" and added, "I believe that both the ups and downs of Harlem are shown. . . . I don't agree that there are no signs of hope in this exhibition. I think there are both the good side and the seamy side of Harlem shown." Booth also mentioned that he felt the introduction to the catalogue written by Miss Van Ellison simply demonstrated the fact that its author is a "product of her society" and that "race hatred" does exist in this country.

Of the consequences resulting from the controversy, saddest of all perhaps was the defacement of 10 of the museum's paintings, including a Rembrandt. An unknown vandal scratched an H into the corners of the canvases, presumably to stand for either Hoving or Harlem. Although the damage was repaired, the act shocked museum officials and protesters alike. Hoving labeled the damage "poisonous mischief" and the Harlem Cultural Council voiced equal dismay.

Reaction within the Metropolitan Museum reflected hopelessness and despair in the face of the widespread criticism and hostility toward the exhibit. One Met official explained, "We thought there would be criticism but we never anticipated anything like this." Despite adverse reactions, public response was good. One Sunday in February the museum announced it had had 9,500 visitors, many of whom had to be turned away at closing.

Despite the criticism of "Harlem On My Mind," Met officials presented a major exhibit of primitive art from Oceania, Africa, and the Americas in July and August. Shown were nearly 1,000 bronzes, stone and wood carvings from Africa, stone and ceramic sculpture, precious objects of gold, jade and shell, rare wood carvings, ancient textiles and feather hangings from the Americas, and painted masks, ceremonial boards, drums, and carved figures from Oceania. It was the first comprehensive exhibition of primitive art—spanning a period of 3,000 years—ever shown in the New York City museum.

The Lee Nordness Gallery in New York City opened its exhibit entitled "1969: Twelve Afro-American Artists" in late January. The show displayed, among others, the works of sculptor Jack White, and painters Norman Lewis, Felrath Hines, Carroll Stockwell, Alma W. Thomas, and Russ Thompson. *New York Times* critic Hilton Kramer praised the artists' works highly but suggested the exhibit proved the futility of categorizing contemporary works of art according to the racial origin of the artists. In his opinion the show projected a mixed, confusing picture that detracted from the sensitivity and creativity of the artists.

On Feb. 7, Kent State University, Kent, Ohio, sponsored a weekend black arts festival entitled "Shades of Black." Sponsored by the Black United Students, the festival presented three plays, readings from Negro poets, Afro-American music, and a display of black arts.

During the month of February a special exhibit of sculpture and painting by African and American black artists was shown in the Chicago area suburb of Kingston Green. The works were loaned to the New Horizions Development Corporation, the builders of Kingston Green, from the Museum of Afro-American History in Chicago. More than 900 families viewed the works. The exhibit aimed to encourage viewers to frequent the museum in Chicago.

The Shepherd Gallery of New York City displayed in February and March the works of Captain William Buck, a white British naval officer who in the 1840s participated in the British Royal Navy anti-slavery patrols. Captain Buck recorded on canvas the unusual life of the patrolmen and the injustices he witnessed while chasing down and seizing slave ships and crews. The significance of Buck's paintings was cited by Michael Teague in the February issue of *American Heritage*. Mr. Teague is the owner of the collection. He said, "One thing conspicuously scarce in historical records of the slave trade is illustrative material; the camera was hardly available while the traffic lasted, and few men involved in the business had any aesthetic sensibilities. A rare exception has recently come to light in the curious personage of Capt. William Buck."

"One Man's Anguish," an exhibit of abstract paintings by Cuttie William Bacon III opened at Chicago State College on Feb. 17. The artist is a graduate of Kentucky State College and at the time of the exhibit was studying for an M.S. degree in education at Loyola University in Chicago. Bacon has taught art classes, coordinated art fairs, and led discussions at numerous Chicago community centers. Bacon's works characterized his moods and feelings while he was working for the war on poverty. He explained,

"Many days after 12 or more hours on the job I would come home to express the misery and pain I had witnessed on canvas. Though I used the abstract approach, my paintings represented my anger and provocation."

Fourteen Atlanta artists exhibited their works for the "28th Annual Exhibition of Paintings, Sculpture and Prints by Negro Artists." The show opened March 30 and was held at Atlanta University.

On April 4 the Southern Christian Leadership Conference opened its art exhibition in memory of Dr. Martin Luther King, Jr. A $1.5 million display of oil paintings was presented to the public at the Ebenezer Baptist Church in Atlanta. Previously, the SCLC, together with the Museum of Modern Art in New York City, had coordinated an exhibit there to honor Dr. King. Numerous prominent American artists sent their works to be shown and sold for the benefit of the SCLC Fund. Among the artists were Alexander Calder, Adoph Gottlieb, Jacob Lawrence, Robert Rauschenberg, George Segal, Romare Bearden, Norman Lewis, Daniel Johnson, Vivian Browne, Richard Mayhew, William Majors, and Faith Ringgold.

The Sixth Biennial National Religious Art Exhibition, the nation's largest all-faiths religious art show, presented two works by black artists during the month of April. The works of Romare Bearden appeared along with the paintings of the late Ernest Hardman. Bearden's canvas, "The Multitudes," was selected for a $500 prize.

The Frederick Douglass Institute of Washington, D.C., in collaboration with the National Collection of Fine Arts, presented a major one-man show displaying the works of Henry O. Tanner during July and August. The exhibit traveled to the Cleveland Museum of Art, the McNay Art Institute in San Antonio, Tex., the Delgado Museum of Art in New Orleans, and Brandeis University, Waltham, Mass. Warren M. Robbins, founder-director of the Douglass Institute and the Museum of African Art, selected the works to be displayed. In the foreword to the

catalogue accompanying the exhibit Mr. Robbins stated that the show provided the first real opportunity for the American public to become acquainted with Tanner's work.

On July 31 the Smithsonian Institution sponsored a preview of its exhibit entitled "Contemporary Black American Artists." The preview was a benefit at $25 per person for the NAACP; nearly $3,000 was raised. The ten black artists given the opportunity to display their works were Nathaniel Knight, Alma Thomas, Luther Stovall, Charles McGee, Arthur Copedge, Felrath Hines, Norman Lewis, Arthur Smith, Russ Thompson, and Walter Williams. Kenneth Young, a 34-year-old Washington painter, was asked to participate in the showing, but refused because he said he didn't believe in the concept of a show by black artists exclusively.

Chicago's Roosevelt University sponsored a six-day art show in late July entitled "Contemporary Black Art." A number of Chicago's promising black artists were featured, including Keith Morrison, Al Tyler, Lester Lashley, Joseph Bryce, Wadsworth Jarrell, Elliott Hunter, Robert Lewis, Sherman Beck, Jose Williams, Leo Williams, David Bates, Joyce Bowen, John Crenshaw, Sharon Williams, and Kush Bey.

A two-week exhibit by members of the Confederation of Black Artists of Toledo was presented in the University of Toledo's Student Union in August. The show included stone sculpture, beaten copperwork, oil and acrylic painting, chalk and charcoal drawing, and wood block prints. Among the featured artists were Johann Nichols, Marvin R. Vines, Richard Rogers, and James L. Boyd. The Confederation of Black Artists was established two years ago to increase the awareness of the entire community —black and white—of the contribution made by local contemporary black artists in the fields of painting, sculpture, dance, theater, music, and writing.

During the latter part of August the nation's capital hosted an African-Soul Celebration on the grounds of abolitionist Frederick Douglass' home. The exhibit was a living black studies pro-

Ron Nichols

TV producer Lionel J. Monagas

TV newsman Gil Noble

Marc Copage, of TV series "Julia"

Comedian Bill Cosby

Kyle Johnson, star of motion picture
"The Learning Tree"

Comic Flip Wilson

Photographer Gordon Parks, author and director
of "The Learning Tree"

Temptations

Modern Jazz Quartet

Booker T. & the M.G.'s

Rosey Grier

Stevie Wonder

John Lewis

B. B. King

Frederick O'Neal, president of
Actors Equity Association

Playwright Lonnie Elder III

Charles Hobson, TV producer

Musician Les McCann

Teresa Graves

Chelsea Brown

Ramsey Lewis Trio

King Curtis

Leslie Uggams

Johnnie Taylor

Wilson Pickett

· Don Mitchell

Betty Blayton

"Transcendence"

"Sweet Charity" by Benny Andrews

Benny Andrews

Reggie Gammon

"Paul Robeson" by Reggie Gammon

A.C. Hollinsworth

"The Prophet"

Jacob Lawrence

"Northbound"

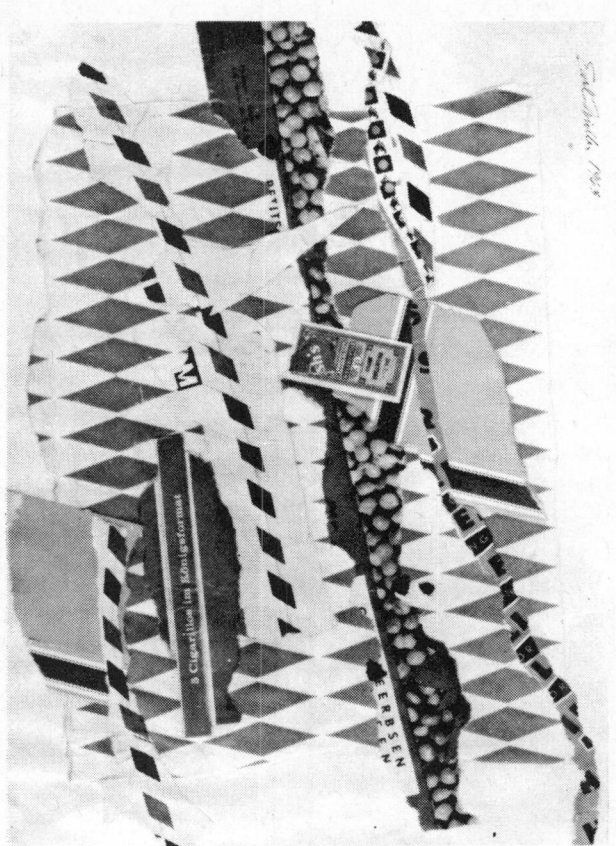

"Blue Diamond Munich" by Earl Miller

Earl Miller

Sam Gilliam

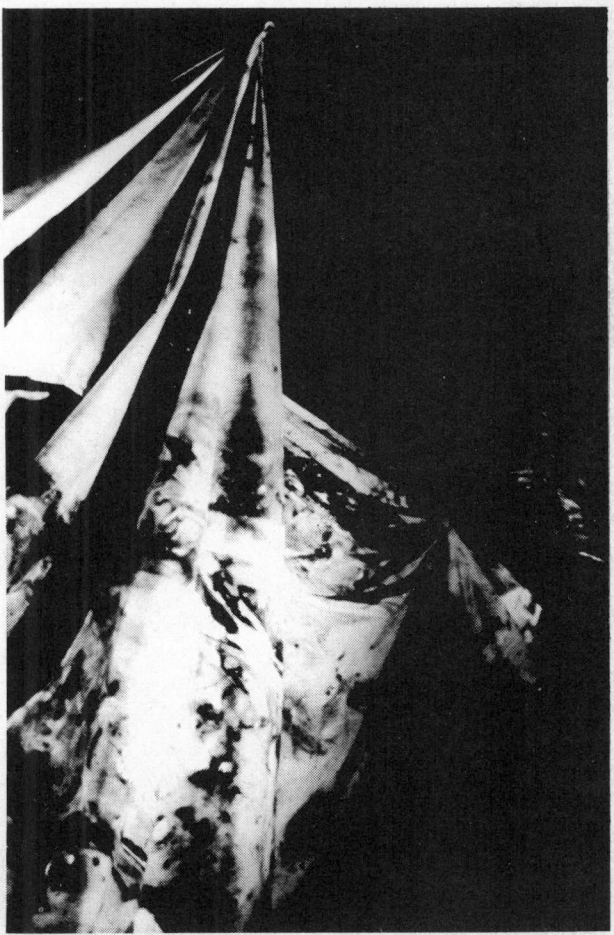

"Perpendicular Extension" by Sam Gilliam

gram that gave American blacks the opportunity to taste African food, learn African games, and see African hair styles. The Celebration sponsored a sewing workshop, a display of African tribal sculpture from Washington's Museum of African Art, a presentation by Black Drama Inc. of the play "You Member," and a music festival which featured gospel and jazz groups.

The second annual "Festival in Black" highlighted contributions made by Afro-American culture. It was held in Los Angeles' MacArthur Park Aug. 22–24. The festival, sponsored by the City Recreation and Parks Department, featured an exhibit of 50 works by local black artists, a jazz-rock concert, and a song and dance pageant depicting the history of American blacks.

The National Center for Afro-American Artists opened in May 1969 in Boston. Established to aid black Americans in achieving their goal of self-knowledge and to add a new dimension to the emphasis on Afro-American art, the organization is divided into three sections: a drama center, a school for the performing arts and a museum featuring works of black artists. Elma Lewis, director of the School of Fine Arts in Boston, initiated the project after a successful summer activities program with Boston's black community.

Studio Watts Workshop, a non-profit fine arts institution incorporated in California, attempted to create new opportunities for many ghetto youths in Los Angeles in 1969. Through its master-apprentice program the talents of many young persons are encouraged; the instruction and materials for painting, sculpture, and pottery making are provided at no cost to students. James M. Woods, founder-president of Studio Watts, explained that "the basic aim of the organization is to emphasize the process of creating, rather than the final product. . . . Studio Watts gives the individual a place to express himself. We utilize art as an element or tool to enable the individual to examine his relationship to the environment, thereby introducing change, but it's not up to us to tell the individual how to change." The workshop is supported by individu-

als and foundations. In 1969 it received a $75,000 grant from the Ford Foundation and used the money for expansion.

During the summer of 1969 Chicago's famous Hull House sponsored art and music camps which sent Chicago youths to camps in southern Wisconsin. The youngsters put on plays, took part in orchestra concerts and dance programs, painted, and worked in ceramics. A science camp for children interested in math, physics, and chemistry was instituted and was held in collaboration with the arts program.

There was a movement among many of America's larger city museums in 1969 to increase their appeal to inner-city youths. Recognition of the ghettos surrounding many of their institutions apparently led museum officials to ask themselves, "What are we doing to justify our existence?" Kyran McGrath, director of the American Association of Museums in Washington, said that during their national convention one-fourth of the time was devoted to this question. The Detroit Institute of Arts opened its sculpture court for free neighborhood dances during the summer and the Oakland, Calif., City Museum purchased a 40-foot van to carry Negro artifacts to churches and redevelopment centers in black areas. The Smithsonian Institution opened a storefront museum in one of the District of Columbia ghetto areas, and organized a black theater group that presented several plays, including "Ballad of the Black Dragon," based on the life of Frederick Douglass.

During 1969 black artists became increasingly involved in the black arts movement—a movement which, according to Washington, D.C., writer Larry Neal, "is radically opposed to any concept of the artist that alienates him from his community." According to Neal, "Black art is the aesthetic and spiritual sister of the Black Power concept [and] as such, it envisions an art that speaks directly to the needs and aspirations of black America."

Early in 1969 the *Washington Post* published an article by James O. Gibson, a staff associate of the Potomac Institute in Washington, explaining the need for a black arts movement and describing the black institutions in Washington seeking to fulfill this need. The black artists of this new movement are saying, according to Gibson, that their "thing" is not the same as the white, Western-oriented "thing." Gibson added that white cultural institutions have often worked to the detriment of the black man by ignoring black contributions to the arts and denigrating black art as worthless or alien.

Gibson found a dichotomy in this situation. He explained in his article that in several instances support for the Washington black arts movement has come from white "establishment" organizations such as the Anacostia Neighborhood Museum (an offshoot of the Smithsonian) and from special exhibits sponsored by the Corcoran Gallery of Art.

Totally black art in Washington, however, has come from the New School of Afro-American Thought, also located in the District. Blacks work only with other blacks at the school and, apart from a large program of summer park and street concerts, the New School receives no outside support.

Gibson explained that he felt the dichotomy was best exemplified in two key figures of Washington's black arts movement: poet Gaston Neal of the New School and urban designer Colin (Topper) Carew of an organization called The New Thing. In contrast to the New School, The New Thing has white board members, staff members, and participants, and has white financial backing. While allowing and encouraging white support, "making it black and beautiful" is the purpose, according to founder-director Carew. Gibson added that The New Thing may be described as "separatist" insofar as it seeks to acknowledge, through black art, that blacks want something better for themselves than American society presently has to offer. Although the organizations differ in their acceptance of white participation, Gibson suggested in his article that both are successfully increasing awareness and knowledge among blacks about their African heritage, and both are struggling to incorporate black art and culture into the black community as a whole.

The black arts movement, to judge from the Washington situation, has caused a dilemma for many black artists. It has, in some instances, urged the artist to diverge for the time being from his original non-ethnic purpose and intent in order to help attain the goals blacks are fighting for. Vinnette Carroll, director of the Ghetto Arts Program of the New York State Council of the Arts, said he saw the need for black artist participation in the present movement in order to achieve a worthwhile working environment in the future. Mr. Carroll explained:

> An artist cannot fully develop in an apartheid society. Only in peace, in peace, in mutual trust, sharing and respect, is the work excellent. . . . The deprivation imposed by the white community on the black artist is not only crippling to the Deprived, but also to the Depriver . . . . It is incumbent upon the Black Artist to separate racial pride from racist ignorance; to integrate without assimilating; to realize that it is as important to recognize his friends as it is to recognize his enemies; to eliminate race as a peg on which to hang his neuroses and inadequacies and to be ruthless in his pursuit of excellence.

These black artists have recently been in the news:

Charles Alston (Painter)

Charles Alston is a black painter who does not believe in "black art" as a separatist movement. Alston feels that blacks have unique experiences but explains that these experiences are also American. He suggests that black artists want to be and should be in the mainstream of American life, and has spent his life pursuing this goal. At the age of 61, the painter-teacher held his first show in eight years in December 1968. Exhibited at the Gallery of Modern Art in New York City, his work was divided into six categories ranging from pure abstraction to near realism.

The subjects of Alston's paintings have always been black, and his style has reflected a sophisticated distortion of African sculpture. One of

Alston's better-known paintings, "Family No. 4," has been on view at the NAACP National Office in New York City. The work shows a faceless couple sitting on a bench because, as Alston expresses it, "faceless . . . is the way whites see Negroes."

The winner of many prizes and awards, Alston is associate professor of art at the University of the City of New York, and is instructor at the Art Students League. He has also taught painting at the Museum of Modern Art and the New School for Social Research.

Dana Chandler (Painter)

A native of Boston, Dana Chandler in 1969 contributed to his community, along with colleague Gary Rickson, two wall-size murals covering an old brick building in the heart of Boston's South End section. Chandler created his paintings to be relevant to blacks. Included within his "wall of respect" were the words, "Say it Loud, I'm Black and Proud."

Several of Chandler's paintings have been criticized for an over-emphasis on violence. Ten of his works were destroyed during private showings, but despite criticism he maintains an even attitude and continues to paint. He denies any over-emphasis on violence by asserting, "Violence is already here . . . [and] is being dealt to us every day."

William C. Fenderson (Print-maker)

William Fenderson has become well-known in the field of print-making. A teacher of painting and drawing at the Pontiac Cultural Center in Pontiac, Mich., Fenderson became involved in the field because he felt the traditional art forms limited his ability to produce a quantity of excellent art. Print-making enables the artist to reproduce many images of the original work, thus allowing more time for creativity, he feels.

Fenderson received his bachelor's degree in fine arts from Alabama State University and a master's degree from Cranbrook Academy of Art in Bloomfield Hills, Mich. His work has been exhibited on black college campuses throughout the country and he was the single participant in a recent print-making exhibit at Ohio University.

Dorothy Hayes (Graphic designer)

A graduate of both Alabama State College and Cooper Union, Dorothy Hayes has penetrated the inner circle of a field requiring exceptional talent. In 1969 she received recognition for her abilities in graphic design with the inclusion of her work in the July-August issue of *Print* magazine. Miss Hayes, operating in her own studio in New York City, also coordinated an exhibition of black designers, illustrators, and photographers for Gallery 303 in New York.

Richard Hunt (Sculptor)

Richard Hunt is one of the most distinguished American sculptors. In 1969 he participated in the Minneapolis Museum of Art's exhibit entitled "30 Contemporary Black Artists." His work has also been exhibited at the Whitney Museum and the Museum of Modern Art in New York City, and at the Art Institute of Chicago. He is a former Guggenheim Fellow and a Tamarind Artists Fellow (awarded by the Ford Foundation).

Douglas Staten (Painter)

In January an original line of greeting cards aimed for the Negro market was introduced in New York City. Stanita designs, developed by artist Douglas Staten, proved to be a profitable investment. Staten, educated at the Art Institute in Chicago, owned an art gallery in Greenwich Village and worked in sculpture and papier-mâché before turning to greeting card design.

The messages on the cards stress humor and happiness rather than political activism or protest messages. He explained, "My first idea for my cards is that they give a sort of uplift to any black person who looks at them." He suggested that he tried to represent blackness without stereotyping and explained, "If I have any message at all, it's a message of hope." The first run of cards produced birthday, get-well, and friendship messages and the company plans to create a line of Christmas cards for the 1970 season.

Television

A 1965 monitoring survey of the three major networks showed that three blacks were likely to be seen on television in a five-hour period—two of them for less than a minute. In 1969 major television networks produced at least 14 evening programs featuring blacks in prominent roles. Among them were "Outcasts," with Otis Young; "Julia," starring Diahann Carroll and Marc Copage; "Laugh-In," with Chelsea Brown; "Cowboy in Africa," with Gerald Edwards; "Mission Impossible," with Greg Morris; "Star Trek," with Nichelle Nichols; "Land of the Giants," with Don Marshall; "Mod Squad," with Clarence Williams III; "Hogan's Heroes," with Ivan Dixon; "Ironside," with Don Mitchell; "N.Y.P.D.," with Robert Hooks; "Lawrence Welk Show," with dancer Arthur Duncan; "Peyton Place," with Percy Rodrigues, Ruby Dee, and Glynn Turman; "Mannix," with Gail Foster; and the now defunct "Daktari," with Hari Rhodes.

These programs have been praised as well as criticized by both blacks and whites. Some say the programs in themselves show tremendous advances and are worth viewing for that reason, regardless of the content. Others criticize the programs for creating false images of black life-styles and for making these life-styles a duplicate of white thoughts and actions. NBC's "Julia" has been severely criticized for its saccharine portrayal of life in a high-priced integrated apartment building and for its heroine's wardrobe, which a nurse probably could not afford. Many have criticized the fact that larger racial issues are ignored. Diahann Carroll's reaction to such criticism is intense. She feels that black life—whether in a banal setting or not—is at least being viewed. According to Miss Carroll, the fact that the show went on the air at all is a plus and a plus long overdue. Why not attack the fact that it's taken so long, she asks, and adds that *this* is the real outrage. The program, according to Miss Carroll, has been judged mistakenly as a documentary or a social tract rather than for

what it is—a situation comedy that is about as true to life as are other TV series.

Clarence Williams, III, "Mod Squad" star, feels this may not be the proper year to evaluate the situation. He explains that few persons in television at this time can honestly tell until several seasons have passed if improvement is being made. "Hogan's Heroes" star Ivan Dixon explains that as yet white producers and directors do not fully comprehend black life, and consequently project a false image.

Programs during the fall season appeared to be continuing to improve. NBC selected Leslie Uggams to replace the "Smothers Brothers Comedy Hour" after cancellation of the latter because of a censorship dispute. "The Leslie Uggams Show," according to one critic, benefits from "the lovely Miss Uggams," and has everything but "a large audience." On the other hand the "Bill Cosby Show" placed third in the third national Nielsen ratings in October and it was quite favorably reviewed. Cosby was also featured in several one-hour specials and two half-hour animated specials based on characters conjured up from Cosby's childhood.

Singer Della Reese became the first Negro hostess —in fact the first hostess—to appear regularly on a nighttime talk show.

Former Los Angeles Rams tackle Roosevelt (Rosey) Grier hosted his own Saturday entertainment program over KABC in Los Angeles. Grier also joined the cast of "Daniel Boone."

Programs such as "What's It All About World?" and "Laugh-In" added humor to the television season while creating an atmosphere of good feeling between blacks and whites. Jokes were aimed at the NAACP, Ku Klux Klan, and black militant students. "Laugh-In included a sketch in which all members of the cast appeared in minstrel-style blackface except Chelsea Brown, the only Negro in the group. She was in whiteface.

Criticism of these programs has been limited. Digby Wolfe, a former writer for "Laugh-In," does warn, however, that the "here-come-de-judge" syndrome can be very dangerous because it is apt to convince white audiences that Negroes are, after all, "just kidding." The programs' producers point out that, no matter how limp the humor, the jokes are still basically satire.

Various continuing series offered an occasional significant weekly segment. "Bonanza," which placed second in the October Nielsen ratings, aired an episode entitled "The Wish," written and directed by Michael Landon, one of the show's regular actors. Ossie Davis and George Spell starred as father and son, with Harry Page and Barbara Parrio as the two younger children of the family. Landon explained that he wrote the show to "help cool white backlash" and to "get across to white people why black people are angry."

Many heretofore unknown talented blacks were given opportunities in 1969 to display their abilities through the broadcast media. Kenneth Washington played his first comedy role in CBS's "Petticoat Junction" series. As a result of that appearance he was awarded roles in several "Daktari" segments, "Adam 12," "My Friend Tony," "Name of the Game," and the "Red Skelton Show." "Laugh-In" added Teresa Graves to the cast as a replacement for Chelsea Brown, the show's first Negro comedienne, and Gloria Calomee became a permanent member of "Days of Our Lives," a daytime dramatic series on NBC. Scoey Mitchell and Gerri Granger were thrust into the spotlight on ABC's "What's It All About World?" Mitchell had previously appeared with "The Smothers Brothers" and on the "Ed Sullivan Show."

Familar faces appeared throughout the year on specials and as guests on weekly programs. Aretha Franklin guest-starred on an Andy Williams Special and Ella Fitzgerald appeared with Bing Crosby on "Hollywood Palace." Pearl Bailey joined Carol Channing in a two-woman show in March, singing favorites from Broadway muscials, and comedian Godfrey Cambridge appeared on "The Jackie Gleason Show" in June.

Efforts were made by major networks and local stations to program meaningful, creative specials. CBS network taped and televised in 13 cities (for the first time) the third annual Harlem Cultural Festival. The program featured gospel, blues, jazz, and Caribbean music, and reflected the diverse Harlem culture. Appearing were the Fifth Dimension, George Kirby, the Edwin Hawkins Singers, Abbey Lincoln, Max Roach, the Chambers Brothers, and Olatunji and his African dancers and drummers.

In February of 1969 "NBC Experiment in Television" presented a drama dealing with a problem arising from World War II interracial marriages. "Color Me German" was the story of a German-born Negro youth, the child of a German mother and an American Negro GI, raised by his mother despite her family's refusal to accept him. The play, written by Manya Starr, was filmed in Munich and featured James Edwards.

NBC contributed more throughout the year with a series of three news programs dealing with the problems of the city, entitled "White Paper: The Ordeal of the American City." The second of the series, appearing in January, attempted to set the theme of the documentary by quoting from Shakespeare's *Coriolanus*, proposing the concept that the city is only what the people believe it to be.

In December 1968 "CBS Playhouse Drama" focused on the black child in the ghetto in its production "Saturday Adoption." In the play a 14-year-old boy, portrayed by Eric Laneuville, is tutored every Saturday by a white college youth and, because of this, is torn between accepting the realities of the ghetto or the bright picture of the future painted for him by his tutor. The author of the drama, 23-year-old Ron Cowen, is the youngest writer ever commissioned for a major drama by one of the TV networks.

Westinghouse Broadcasting Company produced through its facilities at station KDKA a special with actress Paulene Myers, entitled "Where's the Back of the Merry-Go-Round?" Televised in February, the program utilized the poems of Langston Hughes (the title was taken from a Hughes poem) and Paul Laurence Dunbar. Miss Myers presented their work in dramatized form using a minimum of props. According to Hazel Garland of the *Pittsburgh Courier,* the picture Miss Myers presented of black people was one of drama, comedy, and pathos, with little despair. Miss Garland highly praised Miss Myers' artistic ability.

Local television stations have created worthwhile programs focusing on problems and solutions particular to their individual areas. KBTV in Denver, Colo., in association with the communications commission of the Colorado Council of Churches, instituted a monthly program focusing on Negro-white community projects. In New York City, WNBC-TV sponsored a series of phone-in shows that ran from June 29 through Aug. 31, 1969. Hosted by Simon Golar of the city's human rights commission, the program's aim, according to Golar, was to disseminate information, dispel fears, and report accomplishments. Entitled "Open Circuit," the viewer-participation program addressed itself to the problems confronting the black and Puerto Rican communities at the time of each broadcast.

Early in 1969, Chicago television station WTTW created "More from My Life," a soap opera depicting the life of a black family in the ghetto—a concept new to television. Made possible through a Ford Foundation grant, the serial, according to the directors, was aimed at examining the social and economic problems of black people in the ghetto and to suggest some solutions to these problems.

"Black Heritage: A History of Afro-Americans" was created by WCBS-TV in association with Columbia University and ran as a series of 108 daily programs in the New York City area. The broadcast of educational lectures presented the views of black people and their history from Africa to today and was aimed at "telling it like it is," according to Dr. Vincent Harding, the program's advisory committee chairman. Black lecturers and historians representing various disciplines and a wide range of viewpoints from many parts of the country participated.

The "Black Heritage" series became the center of controversy when NAACP leader Roy Wilkins accused the program of being biased and hopelessly flawed. Wilkins suggested the series attempted to interpret history from a single point of view—the contemporary left-of-center black militant view, and said he was disappointed that no spokesman for the NAACP had been asked to participate in the series. Ralph Daniels, vice president and general manager of WCBS-TV, responded to the charges immediately. Daniels said he regretted the fact that Wilkins had passed judgment after having viewed only the first two of the series' 108 programs. Daniels felt that a highly qualified panel had prepared the programs and he did not think it was flawed in the way Wilkins had charged.

Later in the year John Henrik Clarke, editor of *Freedomways* magazine and a member of the "Black Heritage" advisory board, attempted to clarify the genesis and the promise of the TV series. According to Clarke, the opening of the prospectus (the basic guide in preparing the series) stated that the intent of the series was to present a new and creative approach to the history of blacks and that the programs were to be aimed at a broad general audience of Americans with the assumption that the information presented, properly used, would benefit all Americans and would help to clear up many of the misconceptions relating to blacks and the role that they have played in shaping the history of the Americas. Clarke added that the committee that planned the series realized from the beginning that there was a need for a total re-examination of both African and Afro-American history and that a new frame of reference was necessary. The committee promised to take a new look, with major emphasis on the plight of black Americans. As to the charge of separatist tendencies, Clarke suggested that separatism has been around for quite some time and that the planners of "Black Heritage" did not invent it.

According to Clarke, the separatism struggle is as old as the struggle for human dignity in America.

National Educational Television's comprehensive program "Black Journal" focused on three areas of black involvement: economics, politics, and community control. The program as originally conceived by NET's public affairs programming department was to have been solely concerned with ghetto problems. After the assassination of Dr. Martin Luther King, Jr., the format was changed to a continuing series. The objective, according to William H. Kobin, NET's vice president for programming, was to provide a real alternative for the Negro viewer as well as for the white viewer, and was to reflect faithfully the temperament and the personality of the black community. The series has been made possible through grants from several major corporations, including the Polaroid Corporation and the Coca Cola Company.

In the first "Black Journal" program of 1969, the past year was reviewed. Mrs. Kathleen Cleaver, communications secretary of the Black Panther Party and wife of Eldridge Cleaver, appeared on a panel with poet and playwright LeRoi Jones; Andrew Young, executive director of SCLC; Bill Strickland, former executive director of the Northern Student Movement; Robert Johnson, managing editor of *Jet* magazine; and Alexander Allen, eastern regional director of the Urban League. A second panel consisted of Claude Brown, author of *Manchild in the Promised Land;* Daniel Watts, editor of *Liberator;* Julian Mayfield, co-author and star of the film "Up Tight"; and Richard Moore, author and historian.

A second program appearing Jan. 27 presented what *Liberator* editor Watts considered the challenge to the black community posed by the Nixon administration. The program invited leading black spokesmen to discuss 1969 in the areas of politics, economics, and social control. During the broadcast, militant leader Ron Karenga called 1969 the year of self-determination, self-respect, and self-defense, and proposed the

need for political coalitions—rather than alliances—with whites. Kathleen Cleaver voiced skepticism about the validity of the franchise, while Rev. Albert Cleage expressed optimism in this area by citing the emergence of Georgia legislator Julian Bond as a national political figure. Cleage suggested this emergence could offer new direction for many blacks.

During a March broadcast, "Black Journal" probed black anti-Semitism and white racism with an experiment in group dynamics. This technique, called sensitivity training, involves several hours of discussion and confrontation in order to break down personality facades that enable one to prevent disclosure of any unpleasant feelings (in this case prejudices). After 11 hours of conversation the barriers were down and the issues were squarely faced. The result was two hours (edited) of candid and sometimes shocking conversation that, according to panel members, accomplished a great deal without coming to any major conclusions. Understanding, communication, and mutual respect became the goals of the telecast.

For another broadcast the "Black Journal" crew spent two months in the South, touching on some rural communities and working in what many officals call the "New South Cities" of Atlanta, New Orleans, and Houston. The first half of the program was devoted to black art and included an interview with artist-teacher Dr. John Biggers of Houston. The second half made clear the point brought out many times before that despite scattered efforts to alleviate the poverty problem, it still exists.

National Educational Television station WQED created an interesting off-beat black history series (which alienated itself from the normal history course format). Entitled "Black Blues, Black!" the program stressed survival and revival of African culture in America. Actress Maya Angelou presented the course through multiple means including songs, dances, and poetry. Although the series addressed itself to the black community, WQED urged white audiences to view it in order to gain greater understanding and insight into the black man's history and culture.

A new field of televising was introduced when Washington, D.C.'s educational station WETA broadcast the Lincoln Day concert from Constitution Hall. Mrs. Martin Luther King, Jr., delivered words of Abraham Lincoln and Aaron Copeland conducted the National Symphony Orchestra. In a review of the performance Bernie Harrison of the *Washington Evening Star* suggested that television's general lack of interest in the entire area of serious music is regrettable, and said he feels that the possibilities to do more are enormous.

Television has continued to struggle purposefully but often unsuccessfully with the difficult problem of incorporating the black American into drama, adventure, and comedy realistically. It was generally agreed that during 1969 the networks deserved commendation for effort in this respect, yet that their achievement was far from spectacular.

Although the fall season had blacks in starring or leading roles in 14 series—a slight gain over the previous season—two Michigan State University researchers reported that, to judge from previous seasons, the roles, dress, and language of blacks on television are still very white. The report concluded that "television feels a need to project black images, but really doesn't know how."

An Associated Press report noted that the networks are not likely to offer any realistic portrayals of black roles soon, either. Television, it was noted, has never been a pioneering medium and with the controversy caused in 1969 over "violence and sex" on the airwaves, the industry has clearly decided to lay low for a while in all areas.

In addition, Bill Cosby has noted, "I think the reality of what happens in the news is depressing enough. A show about a black man on a walk through life wouldn't last 13 weeks."

A problem for television is how involved it should become in racial conflict and what responsibilities it should take. After the National Advisory Commission on Civil Disorders cited white racism as the major cause of black suppression in modern America, it was generally agreed that the medium could play an important role in re-educating Americans and could serve as an instrument of action. The problem has been how best to undertake such a task.

Misunderstandings in this area came into the public eye in 1969 as certain radio and television stations came under attack for alleged abuses. In September, Washington, D.C., television and radio station WTOP was charged with violating the fairness doctrine laid down by the Federal Communications Commission in which different viewpoints must be adequately represented in programming. A member of the D.C. Federation of Citizens Associations charged in a separate petition to the FCC challenging the renewal of the station's licenses that WTOP news coverage helped, among other things, to create the "background and environment" triggering the April 1968 rioting in the nation's capital.

Three weeks before, a Negro group challenged the renewal application of another D.C. television station, WMAL, contending that it had not been adequately responsive to the needs and interests of the black community.

Boston's WPIX-TV came under fire for allegedly using stale film in a report of a ghetto riot in Boston and student demonstrations at San Francisco State College.

In the *Columbia Journalism Review* (Winter 1968/1969) Lawrence Pinkham discussed in his article "Television for the Black Community" how the medium could and should become relevant to the black community. Pinkham cited the proposals for media improvement listed in the National Advisory Commission on Civil Disorders report—among them assignment of newsmen on a regular basis to the ghetto, regular use of Negro broadcasters on television, and workable guidelines for responsible ghetto coverage—but suggested that even if these proposals were put into effect, they would not be sufficient to make a serious impact on the deep national crisis. He stressed in his article that if real results are to be obtained, the role of television must be approached with the same sense of urgency that the Commission report stressed was needed with employment, housing, and welfare. There is a growing school of thought, according to Pinkham, which feels that the use of all media is a public right guaranteed by the First Amendment, but that in practice, service to the public has been narrowly defined. For the medium to make a contribution to the betterment of the black community and to work toward the transformation of society as a whole, television must devote large amounts of time to programming of, by and for the black community. This programming must be on a scale proportionate to the size of the Negro community in the nation's population. Pinkham stated that this would amount to ten per cent of all programming on all networks on a national level. Pinkham also stressed that the programming must be controlled by residents of the black community themselves.

An interesting development in light of these proposals was the surfacing of a presidential task force report recommending establishment of a new federal department of communications. The report had been kept under wraps by both the Johnson and Nixon administrations, but Rep. Lionel Van Deerlin (D-Calif.) in April called for its release. Other recommendations included the use of low-powered television channels to meet the needs of the ghetto. Specifically, the report proposed a four-channel, low-powered television system to be used in a ghetto such as the Watts section of Los Angeles. The system, which would cost an estimated $750,000, would be "devoted to job information and training; to both in-school and at-home instruction tailored to the special needs of ghetto children; to the presentation of programs created by and for the local community"; and to "public health, adult education, and literacy training," according to the version of the report published in the *Washington Post*.

Pinkham concluded that even a moderately accelerated programming improvement plan will be unable to meet the needs of the nation. He said it was unfortunate that the Kerner Commission Report had failed to attach to public broadcasting, specifically television, the same importance given the housing, welfare, and employment problems.

Radio

A relatively new concept has emerged in the field of radio in recent years and by 1969 had become a successful form of communication with the black community. "Soul Radio" has proved meaningful and relevant to blacks because its music, advertisements, and social commentary are aimed specifically at black interests. There is ample evidence of the success of "Soul Radio."

Milwaukee, Wis., has two black-oriented stations, WNOV and WAWA. Both, according to audience surveys, can claim the majority of black listeners in the Milwaukee area as listeners. The stations consider themselves spokesmen for the black community and have instituted numerous public services. Last year WAWA spent $30,000 to involve 60 teenagers in a massive clean-up, paint-up campaign that enabled them to improve 21 inner-city houses. It reported spending $2,000 taking 500 children to day camps and $3,000 more for summer dances attracting 30,000 teenagers. In addition, the station has built a basketball court and has sponsored basketball clinics and Little League teams. O. C. White, a disc jockey for WAWA, says that one of the station's objectives is to help youngsters. WNOV disc jockey Cecil Hale reflects the same sentiment by urging his listeners to "stay in school." Both feel the function of Soul Radio is to stress the idea of one black "brother" helping another black "brother" become independent and through this independence show the world that he can do greater things. During the Milwaukee disturbance in 1967, WAWA was able to help "cool" the community and earned praise for its broadcasting from the Federal Communications Commission.

Soul station WABQ ("Tiger Radio") in Cleveland also played a helpful part in the crisis after Dr. Martin Luther King's assassination. The station remained on the air 24 hours and during that time instituted a talk program that enabled more than 10,000 listeners to air their views. For five days WABQ held a "memorial" to Dr. King.

WAWA, WNOV, and WABQ, along with more than 100 other black radio stations, and about 200 more that broadcast to the black community on a part-time basis, have achieved new respectability. Nicholas Johnson of the Federal Communications Commission stated recently at a black disc jockey convention that "today, minority stations have an important role to play. No other institution inside or outside government can match their power to administer day-in, day-out therapy to the root cause of the worsening malaise of our cities."

Of significant note in 1969 was the presentation of a "Salute to Soul Disc Jockeys" from the Fair Play Committee of New York City. The FPC, an independent community action group working on a national level to create equal opportunity employment for qualified blacks in the field of communications, presented the salute April 3 in an attempt to recognize some of the contributions black disc jockeys have made to their communities. According to the FPC, Soul Radio has done much to create internal cohesiveness and constructive dialogue within the black community.

Several programs created in 1969 have attempted to involve the black community in matters of concern to it. Radio station WWRL in the Queens area of New York produced a weekly "Tell It Like It Is" series where all varieties of Negro opinion are voiced on subjects bothering black communities in the large cities. WNJR in Union City, N.J., uses the same format on its program "The People Speak." Controversy and anger are the essence of both programs, where arguments emerge about anti-poverty programs, jobs, health, housing—the bread and butter issues of slum life.

Black cultural and historical programs also have emerged this year. Columbia University created the "Black Encyclopedia of the Air," a series of 28 segments on black culture sent to black radio stations throughout the country. Produced by the Black Identity Project at Columbia, the programs reflected the purpose of the research project: to help blacks become more aware of their past and to give them a stabilizing sense of self-identity and pride. Dr. Alan Lomax, director of the project, explained that "Black Encyclopedia of the Air" meant to get this information to the man in the street by showing him the power and the extent of African influence. The project was made possible by a Ford Foundation grant and John Henrik Clarke, the noted black historian and editor of *Freedomways* magazine, supplied the historical research.

Early in February, station WGRT in Chicago featured Jackie Robinson, the first black baseball star to enter the major leagues. Robinson presented short surveys about Negroes who have made valuable contributions to the history and progress of America in a special salute to National Negro History Week.

On February 13, Atlanta station WSB aired a special program entitled "Which Side?" The program used the recorded voices of Robert Kennedy and Dr. Martin Luther King, Jr., and songs by Judy Collins, Dion, and Pete Seeger to raise the question, "What can the individual do to live more in harmony with his neighbors?"

Ernie Ladd, using his 297 pounds as successfully here as he did with the Kansas City Chiefs, applies a headlock to force his opponent, Gorilla Monsoon, to yield.

A real study in contrast, NFL Rookie of the Year Calvin Hill spends many of his off hours studying theology at Perkins School of Theology at SMU.

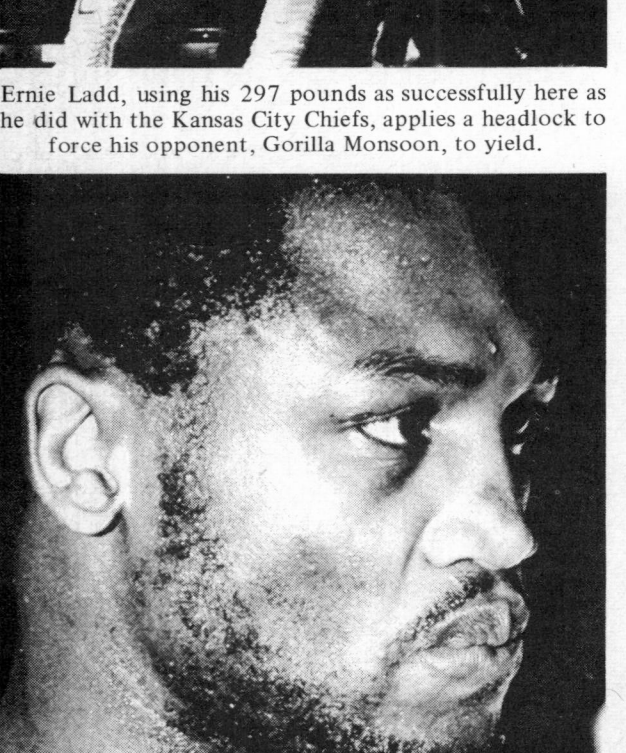

Powerful features and grim determination go hand-in-hand with powerful fists and make Joe Frazier the recognized heavyweight champion of the world.

Warren Armstrong, ABA Rookie of the Year, drives for a shot despite the efforts of Dallas' John Beasley (44) and Cincy Powell.

Pro Football

NO ONE EVER DOUBTED that the Kansas City Chiefs had talent. Year in and year out the Chiefs dazzled the American Football League with their size, speed, and raw ability. But somehow they got the reputation for achieving less than they should and there was always the humiliation they lived with for having lost the first Super Bowl to Green Bay by the embarrassing score of 35–10.

Well, KC got its vindication in the '69 season. Finishing second in the West during the regular campaign with an 11–3 record, the Chiefs whipped first-place Oakland (12–1–1) for the AFL title, 17–7, and then destroyed favored Minnesota, 23–7, in the Super Bowl game.

The KC defense played no small part in the drive to the world championship. Up front, 6–7, 287-pound tackle Buck Buchanan and 6–5, 265-pound end Aaron Brown kept fearsome pressure on rival quarterbacks and 6–1, 265-pound tackle Curley Culp joined them in sealing off the running plays thrown against them. Said Minnesota's quarterback Joe Kapp after the Super Bowl: "The Kansas City defensive line looked like a redwood forest." Indeed, the charge of the Chiefs dumped Kapp three times and had a lot to do with the three interceptions the team came up with.

Linebackers Bobby Bell and Willie Lanier—both All-Stars—blitzed, plugged holes in the line, and dropped back to help in pass coverage. Lanier made an interception against the Vikings. Cornerbacks Emmitt Thomas and Jim Marsalis limited Minnesota's best receiver, Gene Washington, to one catch and Thomas came up with an interception, too. During the regular season, Thomas had picked off nine interceptions to lead the league.

On offense, Kansas City got its best mileage from explosive receivers Otis Taylor and Frank Pitts and tough little runners Mike Garrett, Bob Holmes, and Warren McVea. Taylor beat the Vikings for six catches and 81 yards, including a 46-yard touchdown play on which he broke one tackle, faked another man out of position, and then turned on his outstanding speed. Garrett was the leading rusher in the Super Bowl with 39 yards and scored once on a five-yard bolt off left tackle. Mike had finished 4th in the AFL in rushing (732 yards) and 8th in pass receiving (432 yards) in regular season play.

But for the Super Bowl the Vikings (12–2) put together a sensational season. They were known as a physical team. They did nothing fancy; they just hit hard and executed cleanly. The cornerstone of the club was the rugged front-four unit on defense, and that gang included tackle Alan Page and All-Pro ends Carl Eller and Jim Marshall. Split end Gene Washington was the Vikings' primary deep threat and showed how he could break open a game in the NFL title game against Cleveland. On the first series he raced up the left sideline under a Joe Kapp bomb and outfought defender Walt Sumner for the ball. That play carried from the Minnesota 33 to the Browns' 24 and the Vikings took it in from there. Later, Washington took a Kapp pass and went all the way for a 75-yard touchdown play. Minnesota won, 27–7.

Oakland, the loser in the AFL title game, also had a standout season. Until that decisive loss to Kansas City, the Raiders had dropped just one game (and had beaten the Chiefs twice). Among their All-AFL players were defensive backs Willie Brown and Dave Grayson, defensive end Ike Lassiter, wide receiver Warren Wells (who led the league with 14 touchdown passes), and offensive guard Gene Upshaw.

NFL runner-up Cleveland got excellent running from Leroy Kelly (817 yards, despite time out with injuries) and fine receiving from Paul Warfield.

In both leagues, the season was notable for the emergence of some spectacular rookies. In the NFL, Dallas's fullback Calvin Hill was Offensive Rookie of the Year. Hill, 6–3 and 230 pounds, hit with power inside and turned the corners with a blend of speed and agility. Until an injury slowed him down, he was leading the league in rushing and still finished second with 942 yards for a 4.6 yards-per-average. Joe Greene, a 6–4, 270-pound tackle for the Pittsburgh Steelers, was Defensive Rookie of the Year. He stepped right in and aggressively knocked quarterbacks and runners around all season long.

Carl Garrett, the Boston Patriots' third draft choice, won the AFL Rookie of the Year award. Garrett, a running back out of New Mexico Highlands, gained 691 yards and tallied five touchdowns for a losing ball club. Houston receiver Jerry Levias, who finished ninth in pass receptions and third in punt returns, and O. J. Simpson of Buffalo, who was sixth in rushing, were among the top rookies in the AFL.

One of the success stories of the year turned out to be the way Chicago's Gale Sayers came back from knee surgery. Though not breaking

away for any long runs, Gale still rolled for 1,032 yards to take the rushing crown in the NFL. First-year man Larry Brown of Washington finished fourth (with 888 yards).

In the pass-receiving department, Charlie Taylor of Washington (71 catches) and Roy Jefferson of Pittsburgh (67 receptions) ranked second and third respectively in the NFL. Other NFL men having top years were Deacon Jones, Los Angeles' great defensive end; Bob Brown, LA's powerful offensive tackle; Lem Barney, Detroit's All-Pro defensive back; Herb Adderley and Willie Wood, Green Bay defensive backs; Dave Robinson, Packer linebacker; Jimmy Johnson, San Francisco cornerback; and Mel Renfro, Dallas safetyman.

Among the AFL's other outstanding performers in '69 were running backs Jim Nance of Boston (2nd in the AFL in rushing) and Floyd Little of Denver (5th in the AFL), defensive end Rich Jackson (Denver), linebacker George Webster (Houston), offensive tackle Winston Hill (New York), receiver Al Denson of Denver (3rd in the league with 53 catches), and defensive backs Butch Byrd (Buffalo), Booker Edgerson (Buffalo), Miller Farr (Houston), Ken Houston (Houston), and Ken Graham (San Diego).

Baseball

Toast the '69 baseball season with a hearty "bottoms up." For the perennial bottoms, those New York Mets, came *up* all right—and kept soaring skyward until they were nigh out of sight. First it was the Eastern Division title in the National League, then the National League championship, and, finally, the whole thing—victory in the World Series. Were there further worlds to conquer out there in the cosmos, who would have wagered against this team of destiny?

For there always seemed to be someone there to deliver the key hit or make the clutch catch or perform the necessary miracle. Take, for example, centerfielder Tommie Agee. A hapless hitter and erratic fielder in 1968, he suddenly burst forth in '69 as the team's money hitter and began to range all over the field making acrobatic catches. Though batting lead-off, he led the Mets with 26 homers and 76 runs-batted-in.

The purest single showcase of his all-around skills came in the third game of the World Series. Baltimore and New York had split the first two games and the Mets got off to a 3–0 lead in the third contest. But with two outs and two on in the fourth, the Orioles appeared ready to strike back. Elrod Hendricks ripped a long drive to left center that seemed a sure extra-base hit. Agee, shaded into right center, however, would concede nothing. Breaking with the crack of the bat, he flew across the outfield, reached far across his body, and made a spectacular backhand catch two steps from the wall. Three innings later, Baltimore loaded the bases and, crack, there was another line drive, this time into right center—a potential triple. Again the swift Agee erupted in pell-mell chase and just when the ball seemed to zoom past, he dove to his glove-hand side and intercepted it. In all, Agee saved five runs on defense and contributed one on offense with a homer as New York won, 5–0.

The big bat in the Series, of course, belonged to first baseman Donn Clendenon. Though he got into only four of the five games, he struck three homers for a Series record and won the classic's Most Valuable Player award. This was the same Clendenon who had quit baseball at the start of the year and then had unretired to start the season indifferently with expansionist Montreal. Most of his regular-season 16 homers and 51 RBIs were hit for the Met cause.

The most consistent hitter in the great Met turnabout had to be leftfielder Cleon Jones. Not a power man (he hit only 12 home runs), Jones nonetheless drove in 75 runs and ranked fifth in the league with his .340 average.

It was merely a super Baltimore team that the Mets outclassed in five games. The Orioles spurted out in front of their division by 10 games as early as June and the race was all but over. And after they routed Minnesota in three straight for the American League flag, they were installed as Series favorites.

Who could argue? For they had, among others, such accomplished hitters as Frank Robinson (.308, 100 RBIs, 32 homers), Don Buford (.292, 64 RBIs), and Paul Blair (.285, 76 RBIs, 26 homers). But the boom in the Baltimore bats went silent before the parade of strong Met pitchers.

The greatest non-performance of the year came from Philadelphia Phillies superstar Richie Allen. Manager Bon Skinner suspended his moody slugger for missing a twi-night doubleheader and Richie, on his own, extended it to a 26-day leave of absence. He was fined $11,700 on his return, grumpily finished out the season (.288, 89 RBIs, 32 homers), and was traded to St. Louis in the off-season.

While Allen was underproducing, hulking Willie McCovey of the San Francisco Giants was getting maximum sock out of his work. He crashed 45 home runs (tops in the National League), drove in 126 runs (also tops in the league), averaged .320 and won the league's MVP award. His two homers helped the National League win the All-Star game 9–3, but all his heroics couldn't quite bring off what he wanted most—a pennant for the Giants. San Francisco finished second to Atlanta in the National League's Western Division.

What carried Atlanta to the top in the West was the force of its hitting, and the two big men were Hank Aaron and Rico Carty. Hank was in his customary home-run groove—he had 44 in '69—and he drove in 96 runs. His average was .299. And though his Braves lost the National League play-offs to the Mets in three straight, Aaron continued to hit with power and consistency. What was particularly admirable about his play-off performance was the fact that he had accidentally sliced his hand in a home mishap and played the whole series with stiches in the wound. Carty, plagued recently by tuberculosis and assorted injuries, came on strongly as the Braves made their late drive for the pennant.

Though a sore shoulder kept him from throwing very well from the outfield, Rico more than made up for it with his bat. Spraying clutch hits all over the place, Carty wound up with a .342 average and knocked in 58 runs (he had 16 homers).

Over in the American League, the major challenger to the Oriole club was slugging Minnesota and two major Twins contributors were Rod Carew and Tony Oliva. Carew's quick bat made him the league's number one hitter—at .332—and his flying feet enabled him to establish a league record. Rod stole home seven times to break the mark of six set by both Ty Cobb and Bob Roth. A natural at the plate, Oliva was fourth in the league with his .309 and demonstrated his strength with 24 homers and 101 RBIs.

Among the also-rans in the American League, Oakland and its exciting young Reggie Jackson made something of a splash. The A's started impressively and Jackson had the baseball world agog with his early home-run pace. On June 14 he hit two homers against Boston and drove in 10 runs in that one game. On July 2 he collected three homers in a game with Seattle. On July 20 he was leading both leagues with 36 home runs and everyone was talking about records. But the pitchers started giving him the star treatment—knocking him down frequently and throwing him as few strikes to hit at as they could manage. With these problems, plus an illness, plus the law of averages, Reggie had to settle for 47 home runs (.276 average and 118 RBIs). Harmon Killebrew (49) and Frank Howard (48) were the only major-leaguers with more homers. Oakland got some excellent pitching from righthander Blue Moon Odom (15–6, 2.94 ERA).

The Red Sox struggled along without good pitching, but got an excellent year from outfielder Reggie Smith. He ran, he threw, and he hit. His .309 was third-best in the league and he had enough punch to drive 25 homers and account for 93 RBIs.

Chicago and New York struggled without no-table success, yet each club had two men who seemed to reach maturity as batters. The White Sox' Walt Williams, an energetic little outfielder, finished seventh in the league with his .304 average, while teammate Carlos May, just a rookie, hit for distance (18 homers, 62 RBIs) and average (.281). May's season—and perhaps career—was cut short when an accidental explosion during his Army reserve stint damaged his fingers. For the Yanks, outfielder Roy White emerged as a solid pro with his .290 average and 74 RBIs. New York second baseman Horace Clarke gave his club tight defense and consistent hitting (.287).

Willie Horton, the big gun when Detroit won the pennant in '68, faded just a bit—as did his ball club. Willie got off slowly, jumped the club at one point because of personal problems, and then came on with some substantial swinging. He connected for 28 home runs, 91 RBIs, and a .262 average.

Over in the National League, the Chicago Cubs got some fine individual efforts despite their late-season collapse. They led most of the season until the Mets overtook them, and Billy Williams, Ernie Banks, and Ferguson Jenkins had much to do with that success. Williams averaged .293 (with 21 home runs and 95 RBIs), Banks drove home 106 runs (23 homers and a .253 average), and pitcher Jenkins went 21–15.

The league's supposed super team, the St. Louis Cardinals, stumbled from lack of pitching and consistency, but righthander Bob Gibson fanned 268 batters to become the first National League pitcher to strike out 200 or more batters for seven seasons. Gibson was 20–13 with a 2.18 ERA, yet was not so overpowering as he had been in previous years. Lou Brock (.295) and Curt Flood (.285) had good, if not spectacular, years at the plate.

Pittsburgh and Cincinnati had the hitting clubs. The Pirates got their offensive oomph from Roberto Clemente (.345 and 91 RBIs), Matty Alou (.331), and Willie Stargell (.307, 92 RBIs, 29 homers), among others. The Red sluggers included Alex Johnson (.315 and 87

RBIs), Bobby Tolan (.306, 21 homers, 93 RBIs), Tony Perez (.294, 123 RBIs, and 37 homers), and Lee May (38 homers and 110 RBIs).

Out on the West Coast, the Los Angeles Dodgers got good years from Manny Mota (.320), Willie Davis (.311), and Maury Wills (.274). Wills was traded back to his old team from Montreal and fired up a young Dodger squad with his spirited, poised leadership. Backing up McCovey on the Giants were aging superstar Willie Mays (.283, 58 RBIs, 13 homers) and promising youngster Bobby Bonds (.257, 32 homers, 90 RBIs). Bonds became the fourth player in history to hit at least 30 homers and steal at lease 30 bases in the same season. And for San Francisco, Juan Marichal had his usual outstanding season on the mound (21–11 and 2.10 ERA).

Jimmy Wynn of Houston supplied what little hitting the Astros had with his 33 home runs and 87 RBIs (he averaged .269).

Off the field, former Dodger catcher Roy Campanella, three times the National League's Most Valuable Player, was elected to baseball's Hall of Fame. An ex-Yankee, Hector Lopez, was named manager of Washington's Triple-A club at Buffalo. Lopez is believed to be the first Negro to manage a team in organized baseball in the United States. That situation notwithstanding, Hall of Famer Jackie Robinson had bitter words with former Cleveland pitcher Bob Feller over what Jackie called the lack of opportunities for Negroes in baseball's executive jobs. "Robinson has always been bush," said Feller. "I don't think baseball owes colored people anything. I don't think colored people owe baseball anything either." "Feller has had his head in the sand," replied Robinson.

Boxing

Without so much as a swing in anger, Muhammad Ali-Cassius Clay kept boxing in the headlines in 1969 while less stylish men like Joe Frazier and Bob Foster methodically knocked down everything they saw in the ring.

Ali, already in trouble with the U.S. government for refusing induction into the Armed Forces, got slapped down from an unexpected source—his own Black Muslims. Ali had said that if his conviction and five-year sentence were overturned in the courts, he would return to boxing. The money he'd earn, he said, would help pay off debts. But no sooner had he spoken than leader Elijah Muhammad suspended him from the Black Muslims for a year and stripped him of his adopted name, Muhammad Ali. Elijah Muhammad accused him of having "stepped down from the spiritual platform of Islam to go and see if he can make money in the sport world."

In August Clay couldn't resist an invitation from an old sparring partner—and the result again made big news. Clay used to employ Jimmy Ellis to help him sharpen up for his matches and now Ellis, currently World Boxing Association heavyweight champ, asked Cassius to aid him in tuning up. "It would be my pleasure," said Cassius, and the two went at it for three rounds. Clay, still able to move quickly, kept Ellis moving with jabbing lefts and jarring rights. Jimmy landed some good left hooks to the head and body. "He's in good shape," said Clay when it was over. "His left hook works real good." "He's still got his moves," said Ellis of Clay.

If he had the boxing moves in the ring, Cassius didn't seem to have much boxing luck outside it. Toward the end of '69, he kept running into obstacles when he tried to arrange a match with Joe Frazier, heavyweight champion of six states. In the meantime, though, he made some money by performing in a movie and a Broadway play. He personally got outstanding reviews in the play, "Buck White," but it closed after seven performances.

Frazier, of course, was anxious to get a shot at Clay. Said Joe: "I would like to button his big mouth once and for all, knock him out, and get rid of him. What kind of man is this who don't want to fight for his country? Clay's day is over. I am getting awfully tired of him."

Frazier didn't sit idly by waiting for Clay. In the spring he defended his title against Dave Zyglewicz in Houston. Joe knocked Zyglewicz out in 1:36 of the first round. For summer exercise, Frazier took on Jerry Quarry in New York's Madison Square Garden. Joe pounded Quarry and slashed him and won by a TKO in the seventh round.

Arrangements for a Frazier-Ellis bout fell through for late '69, but were finally set for early 1970. Ellis' only scheduled fight in '69—against Gregorio Peralta in Buenos Aires—had been called off because of promotional difficulties.

In other heavyweight activity, ex-champ Sonny Liston saw his streak of 14 straight victories come to an end in Las Vegas. Sonny ran into three crushing punches from Leotis Martin and went down for the full count. Martin paid for his success, though. Leotis suffered a detached retina in the fight and required a corrective operation. His career may well be over.

Much-publicized heavyweight Buster Mathis whipped sturdy George Chuvalo in a Madison Square Garden 12-rounder, but then Mathis flopped dismally against Jerry Quarry. Quarry stalked big Buster and slammed him about with impunity. Mathis showed neither desire nor skill in dropping the 12-round decision.

Promising George Foreman, who won a gold medal as an Olympic heavyweight in '68, knocked out Don Waldhelm in three rounds and later won his eighth straight pro fight with a unanimous decision over Robert Davila of Peru.

In one of the year's oddest bouts, heavyweight Charlie Green paid for a six-dollar seat to watch former light heavyweight champion José Torres try a comeback against Jimmy Ralston—and ended up as Ralston's replacement in the ring when Jimmy couldn't make it. Remarkably, Green dumped Torres twice in the first two rounds, but then José wound up and knocked Green out.

Light heavyweight champion Bob Foster was perhaps the most destructive fighter of 1969. Early in the year, he decked Frankie DePaula three times in the first round to conclude a successful defense of his title. In the spring, he stopped Andy Kendall at 1:15 of the fourth round, but then conceded, "He's the toughest guy I've met. I hit him with everything. Man, he sure could take a lot." Replied Kendall: "I think I'll quit." Late in June, Foster beat Levan Rountree on a fourth round TKO. The decisive blow was a Foster right that opened a cut over Rountree's eye.

Dick Tiger, still fighting strongly at 40, upset middleweight champion Nino Benvenuti in a non-title 10-rounder in New York (Benvenuti said he hurt his hand) and later won an easy 10-round decision over Andy Kendall.

It was a big year for José Napoles, a Cuban refugee now fighting out of Mexico City. José took the welterweight title from Curtis Cokes with a 13th round knockout. His eyes nearly swollen shut, Cokes could console himself with the $80,000 guarantee he earned. And then early in the summer, Cokes took on Napoles to try to win back his title. Napoles again battered Cokes and Curtis didn't come out for the 11th round. Then in October, Napoles put his title on the line again, this time against the formidable Emile Griffith (who had won the welterweight title three times and had twice been the middleweight champ). Napoles took the decision and Emile admitted after the fight: "He is a great fighter. I can't knock him. After all, he beat a good fighter tonight."

Also in '69, Mando Ramos, a 20-year-old from Long Beach, Calif., became the youngest lightweight champion ever with his 11th round TKO win over Carlos Cruz.

The boxing world braced for the worst in June when Joe Louis, one of the greatest heavyweight champions ever, collapsed on the street in New York and was hospitalized with what was first described as a heart attack. Later it was said that he had merely had a physical breakdown ("I just felt faint, was all," said Joe) and within 31 hours he was released from the hospital.

College Basketball

The Alcindor Monopoly cashed in all the chips in '68–'69, ending three seasons of almost total restraint of fair trade in college basketball. Lew Alcindor, 7–1½, wound up his career at UCLA with a typically overwhelming performance. The date was March 22, the opponent Purdue, the stakes the NCAA championship. All Lew did was hit on 15 of his 20 shots from the floor, score a total of 37 points, haul in 20 rebounds, and intimidate Purdue's shooters with his strong defense underneath. With 1:19 remaining in the 92–72 rout, Alcindor jogged off the floor to a deserved ovation. After the game, he cut the net off one of the baskets, draped it around his neck, and went over to shake hands with each of the Purdue ballplayers. Then he just strolled around, waving one finger aloft, shouting, "Number One."

And, indeed, Lew and his mates had been decisively number one during his time at UCLA. Three seasons, three NCAA championships, 88 victories in 90 games. The only losses had been to Houston his junior year and to Southern California in '68–'69 (in a slowdown-style ball game). A fast, alert Drake team had almost upset UCLA in the '68–'69 semi-finals, but the Bruins pulled it out to set the stage for Alcindor's grand finale. When it was all over, he was named the MVP of the tourney for the third straight year, an unprecedented record. And, of course, he made All-America for the third time.

With both the NBA and the ABA bidding for his professional services, Alcindor sat back and listened to the staggering offers. He opted for the Milwaukee Bucks of the NBA. The package deal was for $1.4 million. Before he ever donned his professional uniform, though, Alcindor got involved in an additional discussion over big money. It started harmlessly in a pick-up game in Los Angeles—during which Lew was subjected to a bit of rough play. Lew hit a stuff shot to end the game, reported Dennis Grey, a Los Angeles Stars player and a rival of Alcindor's in that scrimmage. And then, says Grey, Lew hit him—right on the jaw. The jaw proved to be broken, and, though Alcindor later apologized, Grey sued for $750,000. That test for Lew would eventually come up in a court of law. Meanwhile, he moved on to Milwaukee for the most challenging tests of his life—on the courts of the NBA.

A newcomer to college basketball, Spencer Haywood, commanded almost as many headlines as did Alcindor—and for a variety of reasons. First, naturally, there was his basketball skill. A graceful 6-8, he had paced the U.S. Olympic team to its gold medal in 1968. Then came his sophomore year last season for the University of Detroit. And Haywood took hold right away—the sign of the superstar. He rebounded, he blocked shots, and he scored. Haywood's quickness and agility for a man his size are surpassing. By season's end, he was fourth in the nation with his 31.8 scoring average and he was a first-team All-America.

The second reason for bold headlines involved a fit of temper. In a game against Toledo, Spencer drew one technical foul when referee George Strauthers said he had swung at an opponent under the basket—and then got slapped with a second technical when he turned and started punching at Strauthers. Haywood was banished from the game and was suspended for a week (missing two games). Spencer apologized to Strauthers, the Toledo team, and its coach, Bob Nichols.

In August Haywood made the news again, this time with no apologies. He quit the college game to sign with the Denver Rockets of the ABA for a sum allegedly exceeding $250,000. One of 10 children and fatherless, he said that family responsibilities made it impossible for him to continue his college career.

Another of the successful big centers in '68–'69 was 6-11 Bob Lanier of St. Bonaventure. Lanier plays a powerful game inside and proved that he had a deft scoring touch. Up front, forwards Jim McMillian of Columbia and Mike Maloy of Davidson came in for All-America mention. McMillian, 6-5, scored 20.4 points a

Former Brooklyn Dodger catcher, Roy Campanella, is congratulated by (from left to right) Monte Irvin, Commissioner William Eckert and Elston Howard after he was named to Baseball's Hall of Fame this year. During his brilliant career with the Dodgers, Campy was named the NL's Most Valuable Player three times.

Action and surprise were the key words for the recent baseball season. Typical of the action was this driving slide by Montreal Expo's Mack Jones and the powerful longball hitting of Oakland's Reggie Jackson. The surprise, of course, came from the "amazin' Mets" and their stars, Don Clendenon (receiving congratulations) and Tommy Agee, seen here after Clendenon's three-run homer clinched the Eastern Division title for the Mets.

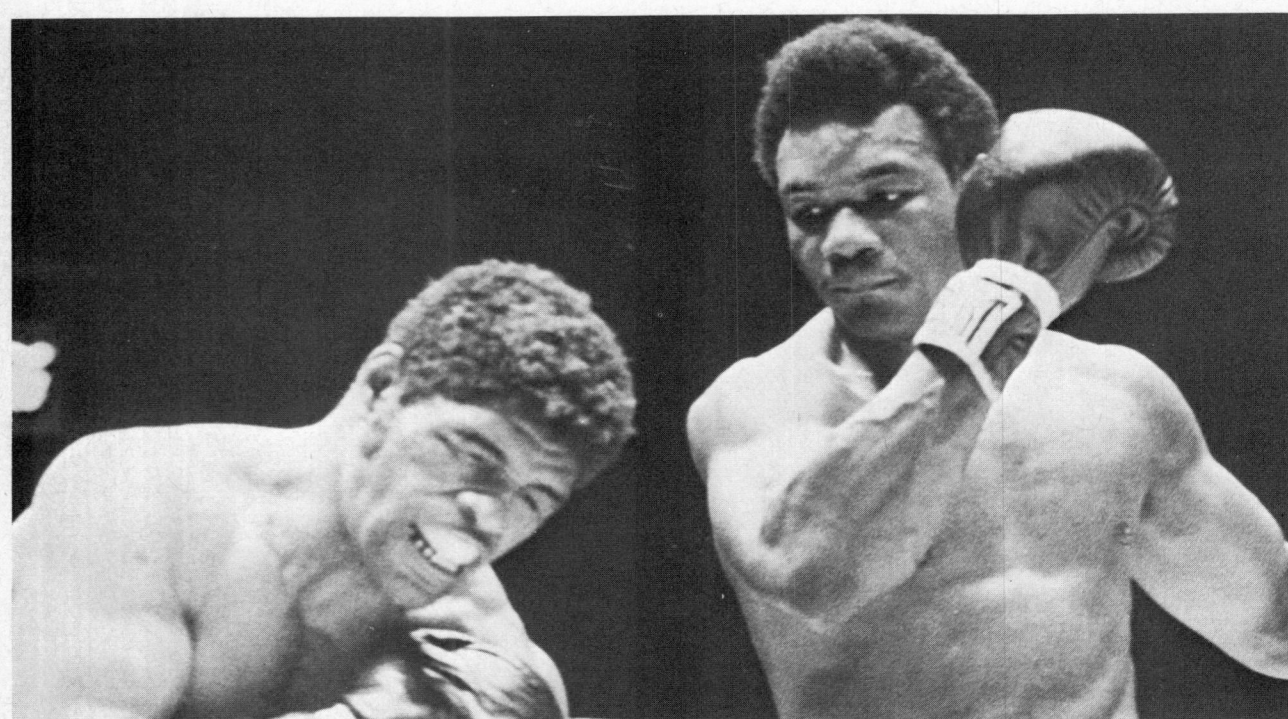

Although the form is the same, the situation is not. Former Olympic Gold Medalist (top) George Forman demonstrates his power with a hard right to the head of Roberto Davila en route to an easy eight-round victory. But Henry Armstrong (below), the only man ever to hold three titles simultaneously, now uses his tremendous energy and ability to work with young boys, as these members of the Herbert Hoover Boys' Club in St. Louis.

Despite being stripped of his title for refusing to be inducted into the Army, Cassius Clay (Muhammad Ali) still remains a center of attraction in boxing circles. He drew a large crowd when he appeared at the Black Arts Festival at North Texas State and used the time to comment on his present position. Although there is a chance he may successfully defeat the government's case against him, he could not fully defend himself in his computerized "superfight" with Rocky Marciano and as a result, suffered the first major boxing defeat in his career.

Ballet is usually performed to sophisticated audiences in refined theaters, but the Knick's Willis Reed (the NBA's MVP in 1970) and the 76er's Archie Clark used this moment to bring that cultural entertainment to the basketball court. Looking on are Dave Stallworth (9), Walt Frazier (10) and Bill Bradley.

Speed and agility were clearly the key words in this years basketball season. A clear example of such speed is illustrated by the Knick's backcourt ace, Cazzie Russell, as he drives up court past Detroit's Terry Dischinger. And for agility . . . Lew Alcindor, the NBA's unanimous Rookie of the Year and the brightest prospect for instant stardom since Wilt Chamberlain, is shown here leaping out of a crowd to score against the Knicks.

But the season was also filled with drama and it ended with a major trade, Cincinnati's Oscar Robertson (left - 14) for Milwaukee's Flynn Robinson. Robertson, the Royal's aging superstar didn't quite fit into the new image being moulded by Royal's coach Bob Cousy and was dealt to the Bucks for all-star guard Robinson.

Using his blazing speed and deft moves, Redskin split end Charlie Taylor leaves Eagle defender Irv Cross in his wake as he makes a spectacular one-handed grab of a perfectly timed TD pass.

Demonstrating to Redskin quarterback Sonny Jurgensen why he was named NFL Defensive Rookie of the Year, Pittsburgh's Joe Greene forces Jurgensen to hurry, resulting in an incomplete pass.

Football, on top of all the on-field action, had plenty of news coverage off the field. (top) Joe Williams (center pointing) speaks out during a student meeting at the University of Wyoming protesting coach Lloyd Eaton's firing of all 14 Negro players from his team. Far from being considered an outside demonstrator, Williams was deeply concerned, since he was a starting halfback and tri-captain of the squad.

It was more tranquil in San Francisco for former All-Pro fullback Joe Perry. "The Jet," as he was known during the 14 seasons he starred for the 49ers, smiles proudly with his family after being named to Pro Football's Hall of Fame. Perry led the All-American Conference in rushing in 1949 and the NFL in 1953 and 1954.

Mattilene Render, running for Tennessee A & I, wins easily as she ties the world indoor record with a time of 8.7 seconds in the 70 yard low hurdle event.

Bob Beamon of the Houston Striders displays his Olympic Gold Metal form as he easily wins the long jump event at the Examiner Meet in San Francisco.

Olympic hurdler Willie Davenport (left) of the Houston Striders narrowly beats off challenger Leon Coleman of the Southern California Striders to win the 60-yard hurdle event with a meet record of 6.9 seconds.

While golfing ace Pete Brown tensely waits for a putt to drop, Tennis star Arthur Ashe was tensely waiting for the South African government to reverse its position and allow him to participate in the South African Open tournament. Ashe was denied entry because the South Africans felt that he was only coming for political reasons.

Despite fears of racial unrest and demonstrations, Charlie Sifford, the first Black to ever play on the PGA tour, refused to boycott the PGA Tournament at Dayton and, instead, turns his attention to keeping his drive in play.

game, checked some of the country's best scorers on defense, and rebounded strongly. Maloy, a quick and aggressive 6-7, averaged eight blocked shots a game in addition to his strong scoring and rebounding.

Among the nation's top backcourt men were 5-10 Calvin Murphy of Niagara, a dynamic little ballplayer who can hit from anywhere on the court; North Carolina's Charlie Scott, a scorer-passer-defender with the knack for producing under pressure; Kansas' Jo Jo White, a cool floor leader and tenacious defender, and Louisville's Butch Beard, a skilled all-around guard.

Pro Basketball

It was not quite ring out the old—for the aging Boston Celtics came through with another championship—but there was certainly plenty of new to ring in during the '68–'69 season. There were two superlative rookies, Wes Unseld and Elvin Hayes, and dazzling second-year man Walt Frazier, who all moved in to challenge the more established stars. And there was a late-starting team, the New York Knicks, that suddenly seemed to burst forth as the team of the future.

No one seriously expected Boston would be a serious contender for the title. Player-coach Bill Russell and Sam Jones were both used up, people said, and, sure enough, after the halfway mark of the season, the Celtics were virtually out of contention for the Eastern Division crown. While Boston was limping in an unimpressive fourth, New York, after a disastrous beginning, caught fire. The Knicks were the hottest team in pro ball as they came surging to the wire in third place. Willis Reed, Dick Barnett, and Frazier were the top New York scorers in the Knick resurgence.

And with the start of the play-offs, New York went right at the Eastern Division champs, the Baltimore Bullets. Baltimore had had a fine year, paced by Earl Monroe's shooting and Unseld's rebounding. But the Bullets proved no match for the streaking Knicks. It was New York in four straight.

Meanwhile, Boston had awakened from its slumber. Russell, Jones, & Company smelled championship money. The Celtics fought past the Philadelphia 76ers, 4–1, and met the Knicks head on. The match-up was a good one, as the young New York squad carried the battle to the veteran Celtics. The count was 3–2 Boston as the series headed into its sixth game and New York hopes were dimmed because Frazier had been slowed down with a groin injury. On came the Celtics, with Jones and Em Bryant sparkling in backcourt and Russell intimidating underneath. It was Boston's game—and series—and Russell walked off the floor with 21 rebounds, 12 points, and a big grin.

Now it was time for the Western champs, the Los Angeles Lakers. That meant Elgin Baylor (who had averaged 24.8 points a game during the season), Wilt Chamberlain, and Jerry West. Boston couldn't stop West, but overall Russell outplayed Chamberlain and Baylor was inconsistent, seemingly showing his age. The result was a dramatic Boston victory in seven games. For Russell, it was his 11th NBA title in 13 seasons—and it enabled him to go out the way he had always been, a winner. Player-coach Russell announced his retirement from basketball during the off-season, leaving behind such records as his 21,721 career rebounds. Jones, too, quit as an active player. He had averaged 16.3 points a game during his last season.

The most surprising individual performance of the season had to come from Unseld. At 6–8 and 245, he was sturdy all right, but didn't seem to have the height to compete favorably with giants like Chamberlain and Nate Thurmond of San Francisco. Even Gene Shue, Unseld's coach, admitted before the season, "Unseld's awfully small to play the pivot, his speed is horrible, his shooting must also be considered questionable."

All Unseld did was take this last-place team from '67–'68 and drive it to the Eastern Division title in '68–'69. Wes went to the boards with a special zeal and immediately picked up the knack of pitching the ball out to trigger the Bullets' fast break. He finished second in the league in rebounds (with 1491), averaged 13.8 points a game, and even picked up 213 assists. For his efforts, Unseld was named not only Rookie of the Year but also Most Valuable Player.

In most other years, the top rookie award would have gone to San Diego's Elvin Hayes. Early in the season, the 6–9 Hayes scored 40 points one night against Chicago and came back the next evening to hit for 54 against Chicago. With a 38 point performance against Chamberlain soon thereafter, Hayes made it clear that there would be no stopping him. He wound up leading the NBA in scoring—with 28.4 points a game—and averaged 17.1 rebounds per game as well.

The third bright young star of the season was Frazier, who took over as quarterback of the New York Knicks' attack. He controlled the ball, penetrated to make the plays (finishing third in the league with 7.9 assists per game), and shot brilliantly (he hit a spectacular 50.7 per cent of his shots from backcourt and scored 17.5 points a game). In addition, he played such superb defense he polled the greatest number of votes in being elected to the NBA's All-Defensive team.

New York's Reed, runner-up in the MVP polling, was another of the year's outstanding players with his 21.1 scoring average, 14.5 rebounds per game, and 52.1 field-goal percentage. Wilt Chamberlain led the NBA in shooting percentage (58.3) and rebounds (1712 for a 21.1 average) and scored 20 points a game as well. Cincinnati's superstar Oscar Robertson had his usual superior season with a 24.7 scoring average, 9.8 assists per game (tops in the NBA), and 83.8 foul-shooting percentage (fifth in the league). Earl Monroe, the second-highest scorer in the league with his 25.8 average, and Seattle's Lenny Wilkens, with 22.4 points a game and 8.2 assists each outing, were other backcourt standouts. Wilkins was hired as player coach of Seattle for the '69–'70 season, making him the second black ever accorded the honor in the NBA.

In the NBA, Oakland (the franchise has since moved to Washington) took the championship and its Warren Armstrong was Rookie of the Year. Mel Daniels of Indiana—with 24 points and 16.5 rebounds a game—won the league's MVP award. Connie Hawkins of Minnesota contributed 30.2 points a game and his usual all-round excellence, then moved on to Phoenix of the NBA for '69–'70. John McLendon was hired as coach of the Denver Rockets, thus establishing himself as the first black to hold such a position in the ABA. Part way through the season, though, he was fired when the Rockets went into a slump.

Tennis

Where 1968 had been a year of triumph for Arthur Ashe (he won the first U.S. Open at Forest Hills and paced the United States as it won the Davis Cup back from Australia), 1969 was distinguished for less exalted athletic achievements. Like helping to break down the color barrier—the color, that is, of what a tennis player wears on the court. Arthur began playing in canary yellow shirts and socks and sometimes varied it with a powder blue ensemble. A women's committee at Forest Hills told him that was "disgraceful."

"I don't wear white any more," he said.

"Is there any significance in that?" someone asked him.

"No," he said, laughing. "I'm not anti-white."

He is also not anti-money, and thus achieved a payment of $50,000 for merely using a particular brand of aluminum-and-fiberglass racquet.

The problem is that he didn't use the racquet with much success. He wasn't swinging with his customary grace because of a problem with his elbow. And without the necessary power for his serve and ground strokes, Ashe didn't have the cunning and consistency to remain a big winner.

He lost to Stan Smith in the finals of the Victoria men's singles tournament (in Australia), to Cliff Richey in the Pacific Coast International Championships, to Bob Lutz in the U.S.

National Tennis Tournament, to Jim Osborne in the Pacific Southwest tennis championships, to Pancho Gonzales in the Howard Hughes Open Tennis Tournament, to Rod Laver in the U.S. Open. True, he was earning decent money—as a competitor in the player category—but Arthur Ashe didn't scare people any more, the way he had in '68.

Nonetheless, when it came time for the Davis Cup matches against Rumania in late September, U.S. captain Don Dell picked Ashe as his number one player. "If there's anyone in America I would want to open with and close with in a Davis Cup match," said Dell, "it would be Arthur Ashe." Ashe, after all, had won 19 of the 21 Cup singles matches he played for America. With cold efficiency, he vindicated Dell's confidence. He went out that first day in Cleveland and disposed of Ilie Nastase, 6–2, 15–13, and 7–5, to lead a U.S. sweep of the competition.

Not surprisingly, given his status as the only major black player in big-time tennis, Ashe made headlines for reasons beyond his winning and losing. He asked two anti-apartheid groups not to picket the U.S. Open even though a South African was tournament director. "I told them," said Ashe, "you'll have to trust me for another year. I said we think we can lick this problem, and that if nothing's done by next year, I'd join the picket line myself."

As '69 came to a close, it appeared as if Ashe might have to back up his threat. For he applied to play in the South African Open in March 1970, and, though approval by the South African Lawn Tennis Union was expected, the South African government indicated it would deny him a visa.

Meanwhile, he was worrying, too, about his decline as a tennis player. He feels it was more than just the bad elbow: "My extremely disappointing form, which shocked a lot of people after my victory in the U.S. championship last season, was partly due to distractions, including my interest in political matters. That is a definite mistake, a shortcoming on my part. I've got to forget the race problem for awhile, forget my

other business commitments for a while. It is possible to be a tennis player first and a black man second. It has to be. If I put the priorities the other way round, I'll be a poor tennis player and therefore a less effective black man. My role as somebody who gives voice on behalf of black opinion hinges on my success as a sportsman and if I stop winning I lose any power I have." Ashe's New Year's resolution for 1970 was for renewed power—for both his tennis and his politics.

Track and Field

This was the first year after the tumultuous Olympics of '68 and the athletes seemed more inclined to compete and less apt to crusade. Sprinter John Carlos was perhaps most representative of this tendency to zero in more on the race than the racial.

Carlos, it will be remembered, was one of two Americans suspended from the U.S. Olympic team in Mexico City for his black power salute on the victory stand. But then Carlos came under the influence of Robert ("Pappy") Gault, the first black man ever to be head coach of a U.S. Olympic team (he ran the '68 Olympic boxing squad) and the athletic director of the Seafarers' International Union.

Gault told Carlos to shave off his beard and mustache; Carlos did. Gault preached self-advancement. Carlos listened. "I still want to do what I can for my people," said Carlos, "but I want to do something for my wife and daughter, too, so I am going to be discreet now. This is my new image."

And it was. Gradually the boos that normally greeted his appearances subsided. And he came on like a winner. Oversized for a sprinter—6–4 and 200 pounds—yet graceful, Carlos stepped out as the 1969 model of the world's fastest human.

At one point during the year, he was named the outstanding performer in six straight meets. He did things like tying the world record for the

100 with a 9.1 in the West Coast Relays. In the Kansas Relays, he took the invitation 100 and 220 events and anchored the winning relay teams in the 440 and 880. He raced a 9.9 100 meters in the Indian Summer Games at South Lake Tahoe—which equalled a world record—only to have the effort disallowed because of a 7.1 mile-an-hour wind. In the Quantico relays in May he had a world record achievement—a 9.0 100—disallowed because of a 15 mile-per-hour wind. "My life," said Carlos, "don't seem to be ruined like some said it would be."

With less fanfare and at least equal measure of talent, hurdler Willie Davenport exercised almost complete dominance of his specialty. During one streak, he reeled off 22 victories in a row. On successive nights in February, he broke two world indoor records with a 5.8 in the 50-yard high hurdles and a 7.8 in the 70-yard high hurdles. He set another indoor world record in the Boston AA meet with a 5.3 for the 45-yard high hurdles. He did all his important running on weekends because during the week he was tied up student teaching at Capitol High School in Baton Rouge, La. "By the time I'm through in track," Davenport said at one point in '69, "I want those hurdling records to have no one's name on them but yours truly." And except for two high hurdles records he shares—the 120 outdoors and the 60 indoors—Davenport has them all to himself.

Track season was not all Davenport and Carlos, however. Lennox Miller of the University of Southern California established a new world indoor record for the 100-yard dash (9.4) during the Astrodome Federation National Relays in Houston. During the outdoor NCAA championships in Knoxville, Curtis Mills of Texas A&M outran Olympians Lee Evans and Larry James to record a new world 440 mark of 44.7. And in the same meet, Villanova's Erv Hall tied the world 120-yard high hurdle record with a 13.2 effort.

His teammate from Villanova, Larry James, enjoyed a successful year, too. Larry did world record time for the indoor 500 (55.4) in the Mason-Dixon Games in Louisville, beat nemesis Lee Evans at 440 yards in the NCAA indoor championships, and also stood out at the Dr. Martin Luther King, Jr., Games and the Penn Relays. Byron Dyce of NYU was named the outstanding athlete at the Penn Relays (he ran a 1:46.8 anchor leg in the two-mile relay) and at the Quantico Relays (where he anchored team victories in the sprint and distance medleys and the college mile relay). One of the dramatic upsets of the year came in the AAU 100-yard dash when little (5–6) Ivory Crockett from Southern Illinois flashed by John Carlos to win in 9.3. Lee Evans' 45.6 in the 440 set a new standard for the same AAU meet and Lee's triumph was his fourth national AAU title in a row.

Among the women, Doris Brown turned in one of the year's best performances when she covered the mile in 4:48.7, a new U.S. women's record.

There was some trouble at Oregon State and Purdue during the year. Two blacks on the Oregon State track team, Willie Turner and Ernie Smith, withdrew from a meet against the University of Washington, saying that Washington black students had warned them that they better not run. At Purdue, star hurdler Eric McCaskill was dismissed from the team for skipping practice while two other blacks, Mel Harris and Jimmy Jackson, were dropped for refusing to shave off their mustaches. Said Purdue athletic director Guy (Red) Mackey: "Purdue has had a good grooming rule for its athletes for more than 20 years. The order for clean-shaven athletes does not apply just to black people. It's in full force for the tennis and swimming teams, which have no Negroes, and for the baseball team, which has only one."

Golf

In terms of pure success for black golfers in 1969, there were Charlie Sifford's smashing victory in the Los Angeles Open and Lee Elder's gallant effort in the Buick Open. The year was marred, however, by some heckling of black stars on tour—and by the failure of a black to break the color line in the Masters.

Sifford was just recovering from the flu when he teed off in the LA Open, the first big tournament of the year. Convalescence must agree with him, for he fired an eight-under-par 63 to take the early lead. Harold Henning of South Africa eventually caught up to Charlie, but on the first hole in the sudden-death playoff, Sifford hit his drive right down the middle, placed his second shot within six feet of the pin, and sank his putt for a birdie three and the championship. It was worth $20,000 to him—and much, much more. "I've been trying to win here for so long," said Sifford, "and I thank God that he gave me the courage to keep trying." The prestigious LA Open is the second-oldest event in the PGA tour and when Sifford's final putt went in, a black lady journalist raced up and kissed him and former Dodger pitcher Don Newcombe hurried over to pump his hand.

For a while, it looked as if Lee Elder would duplicate Sifford's feat in the Buick Open at Flint, Mich. Playing with a borrowed putter, Lee led the second and third rounds of the $125,000 event. But he slipped to an 80 on the last 18 to finish with a 286 to winner Dave Hill's 277.

It was during this time in July that Ted Rhodes, the first Negro to play in a PGA tournament, died. Rhodes had been close to Elder as both a friend and instructor. "I owe everything to Rhodes," said Elder. "He taught me everything I know about golf." Lee had vowed to win the $25,000 first prize at the Buick Open and give $10,000 of it to the Rhodes family. Lee's biggest single purse of the year was the $17,000 he made prior to the Buick Open as runner-up in the Memphis Open.

Like Elder at the Buick Open, Pete Brown got off to a fast start in a big tournament when he led all qualifiers the first day of the Atlanta Golf Tournament. But Pete faded in the later going and settled for winnings of $4,180.

Elder and Sifford both found themselves subjected to racial taunts in some stops on the tour. During the Greater Greensboro (N.C.) Open in April, four white men were arrested for following Sifford around and hollering, "Miss it, nigger!"

"It's very difficult for a Negro to play on the tour," commented Elder in June. "It's not only me but the others (there are 10 Negro regulars on the tour) feel the same pressures from the galleries. It's very hard to concentrate when you hear some of the comments. There are three or four tournaments where I just can't play. I'm tired of being called Nigger or Black Boy. It's just come to a head. I haven't said anything about this before, but I feel I've held it underneath long enough and believe it should be brought out in the open."

None of the blacks was invited to compete in the Masters in '69—not surprising in that no black has ever played in that tournament. Clifford Roberts, who directs the Masters annually, says he'd be happy to let Sifford or anyone else play provided the man meets certain qualifying standards. Indeed there are qualifying criteria, but some players—foreigners, for example—are invited without having to qualify.

College Football

In 1968 two black running backs, O.J. Simpson and Leroy Keyes, were acclaimed as America's two best college players. And they dominated the headlines. In '69 the black players tended to make news in groups—and more for their grievances than for their gridiron achievements.

One of the big stories of the year came out of the University of Wyoming when coach Lloyd Eaton dismissed 14 black members of his team October 17 for wearing black armbands in a protest demonstration. The players had previously made public a letter criticizing the racial policies of the Mormon church and wore black armbands to Lloyd Eaton's office in connection with an upcoming game against Mormon-run Brigham Young University.

In ordering the dismissal, Coach Eaton said he had warned the players that he would not tolerate factions or demonstrations on his team. University president Dr. William D. Carlson backed Coach Eaton's action. The student council and faculty senate called for further investigation.

When the players sought a hearing with the Western Athletic Conference—of which Wyoming is a member—their request was denied. A $1.1 million damage suit was filed in behalf of the 14 players.

Wyoming, undefeated and nationally ranked before the dismissal, went on to beat Brigham Young without the blacks, but subsequently lost several games and dropped from national ranking.

In a related action, Stanford University announced in November that it would schedule no more competitions with Brigham Young.

There was trouble on the West Coast, too, when Jim Owens, coach of the University of Washington, suspended four black players for "failure to express a 100% commitment to Washington football" and to Owens himself. For the next game against UCLA, the eight remaining blacks on the team and Harvey Gayton, a black assistant coach, decided to remain at home. Subsequently, the eight blacks returned to the team, Owens reinstated three of the four suspended players, and Gayton resigned as assistant to Owens.

In action out of the Middle West, Indiana University coach John Pont suspended 10 black players for missing two straight practices without legitimate excuse. At the University of Minnesota, 16 of 18 black members of the team met with coach Murray Warmath and asked for a black assistant coach and a guidance counselor for black athletes.

In what was probably the last expression of dissatisfaction of the season, four black players left the site of the second annual American Bowl game in Tampa, Fla., two days before the game. The four were Ron Shanklin and Glen Holloway of North Texas State, Arthur James of East Texas State, and Ron Gardin of Arizona. The complaint had nothing to do with the coaches or other players.

Shanklin explained that they had spotted a number of people going into a ballroom at the Sheraton Tampa Hotel where the players were staying. "We just walked in, just to see what was going on," said Shanklin. "These guys grabbed us by the arm and started wrestling us out. They didn't come up to us and say, 'This is a private party. You'll have to leave.' We could have resisted and been stupid like they were but we didn't." Shanklin added that employees of the hotel witnessed the situation but didn't explain that the four Negroes were staying at the hotel.

Out on the field, of course, there were some outstanding black players in '69. Two mentioned for All-America honors on offense were slippery running back Charlie Pittman of undefeated Penn State and end Ken Burroughs of Texas Southern, a 6–5, 215-pounder with sure hands and 9.4 speed for the 100. The tough Southern Cal team had two outstanding backs, quarterback Jimmy Jones and tailback Clarence Davis. Jones, swift afoot and hardthrowing, led his team to an undefeated season (there was a tie with Notre Dame) and victory over powerful Michigan in the Rose Bowl. Jimmy completed 10 of 17 passes for 128 yards in the Rose Bowl and threw a 33-yard scoring pass to Bob Chandler that gave the Trojans their 10–3 triumph. Davis, stepping in for the graduated O.J. Simpson, rolled for impressive yardage all year and was the leading rusher in the game against Michigan with 76 yards on 15 carries.

Those mentioned for the defensive All-America squad included ends Al Cowlings (6–5, 250 pounds) and Jim Gunn (6–1, 210 pounds) of Southern Cal, linebackers Don Parish (6–4, 232 pounds) of Stanford and Mike Ballou (6–3, 230 pounds) of UCLA, and back John Tatum (6–0, 204 pounds) of Ohio State.

Gloria Smith, Miss Black America

Personalities

Following are brief sketches of prominent black Americans:

Clifford L. Alexander, Jr., is the first black man to become associated as a partner with the Washington, D.C., law firm of Arnold and Porter. He was formerly chairman of the Equal Employment Opportunity Commission.

Marian Anderson, hailed by music critics as one of the greatest singers of the century, was the first Negro to sing with the Metropolitan Opera. She recently retired with her husband to their farm in Danbury, Conn.

Benny Andrews, a prominent artist whose work is featured in the collections of the Museum of African Art in Washington, D.C.; the Butler Institute of American Art in Youngstown, Ohio; the Joseph Hirshhorn Collection; and many others, was also seen in Exhibition in 1969: "Counterpoint 23" in New York City.

Marvin Arrington, a lawyer, was named student adviser at Emory University in Atlanta. Mr. Arrington, 28, is the first member of his race to hold such a position there.

Arthur Ashe was enabled by the adoption of a Wimbledon tradition to become the first Negro member of the West Side Tennis Club, host of the U.S. Open Championship.

Thomas I. Atkins, Negro city councilman in Boston, was appointed by Wellesley College as a lecturer in political science. Mr. Atkins has been instrumental in leading the fight for city council resolutions urging President Nixon to rapidly reduce the American commitment in Vietnam.

Hugh C. Banks was appointed assistant chancellor of New York University. Dr. Banks is the first Negro in N.Y.U.'s history to become one of the university's general officers. He was formerly special assistant for black affairs.

Annie Mae Bankhead received the 1969 "Woman of Conscience" award from the National Council of Women. It is offered annually for outstanding individual contribution to the realization of an NCW goal.

Romare H. Bearden, the noted artist-writer, exhibited in February and March 1969 at Williams College, Williamstown, Mass. He was instrumental in opening a gallery for young minority artists and in giving young unknowns a chance to exhibit cost-free.

Betty Blayton, an artist and secretary to the board of trustees at the Studio Museum in Harlem, was a consultant to the Counterpoints Guild for the "Counterpoint 23" exhibition at Lever House in New York.

Julian Bond, a Georgia state representative, has inspired a new concept of black political participation in the South. He was the recipient of the 1969 Russwurm Award presented by the National Newspaper Publishers Assn., and is a poet who has had many of his works published in anthologies.

Booker T. and the M.G.s, today's leading exponent of Memphis soul, comprises Booker T., a gifted composer and performer who has played professionally since age 14; Donald Dunn, on electric bass; Al Jackson, drummer; and Steve Cropper, guitarist.

Millicent V. Bouey has the distinction of being the first black woman in the U.S. to own and operate an investment company. Prior to this venture Miss Bouey worked as a real estate broker in the Los Angeles area. A woman of many talents, she was affiliated with the Hal Roach Motion Picture Studio as a fashion designer; she also manufactured her own designs.

Thomas Bradley, a Los Angeles city councilman, was the first black to be nominated for the office of mayor in his city. He ran unsuccessfully against incumbent Mayor Sam Yorty.

Gwendolyn Brooks is a poet and one of the most acclaimed women writers of her time. Her honors date back to 1950 when she became the first—and thus far the only—Negro to win a Pulitzer Prize. She has helped many young writers gain exposure by recommending them for lectures and readings.

Grace L. Brown, founder and pastor of Grace Protestant Chapel in Brooklyn, N.Y., is the first black member of the clergy awarded honorary degrees for outstanding citizenship and the first to lead a group in a prayer retreat at the Capitol in Washington, D.C.

James Brown was presented the Humanitarian Award for 1969 from the Music and Performing Arts Lodge of B'nai B'rith. He has established a scholarship month each October when he will donate his earnings from engagements to help black students stay in school.

William H. Brown, III, an attorney, was appointed chairman of the Equal Employment Opportunity Commission by President Nixon.

Dr. Eugene S. Callender was elected president of the New York Urban Coalition and is responsible for the direction of the 90-man, 30-program organization.

Diahann Carroll was voted best female television star of 1969 by the Hollywood Foreign Press Association for her starring role as widow Julia Baker in the comedy series, "Julia." *Cue* magazine named her "Entertainer of the Year" for her night club appearances.

Matthew G. Carter, first member of his race to be elected mayor of Montclair, a major New Jersey municipality, was presented the 1969 Distinguished Service Award by Bankers National Life Insurance Company on behalf of the citizens of Montclair.

James Edward Cheek, former president of Shaw University, was elected president of Howard University on July 1, 1969.

Shirley Chisholm, the nation's only black congresswoman, represents the 12th District of New York. In 1969 she supported domestic bills relating to the creation of a study commission on Afro-American history and culture and broadening the powers of the Department of Housing and Urban Development. She was a recipient of the 1969 Russwurm Award.

Xerona Clayton, hostess of the television program "Themes and Variations," was selected "Bronze Woman of the Year 1969" in the field of human relations. The widow of Edward L. Clayton, journalist, author, and publisher, is writing a biography of Mrs. Martin Luther King, Jr.

Marc Copage, 7, starring as Corey Baker on NBC-TV's "Julia" series, is both singer and actor. He was the 1969 National Youth Ambassador for the National Christmas Seal Campaign.

Eulalia Corbin was named administrative assistant to Rep. Robert McClory (R-Ill.). She is the first Negro to receive such an appointment under a Republican congressman. Mrs. Corbin is 71 and had been serving as Congressman McClory's executive secretary.

Bill Cosby, who made the transition from stand-up comic to actor in the NBC-TV series "I Spy," and who now has his own show, starred in many television specials and is one of the top comedy recording artists in the U.S.

Alvin Davis was appointed coordinator of the College Discovery Program at Manhattan Community College. He joined the college after serving as executive director of the Lower East Side Neighborhood Association in New York.

Georgia M. Davis is the first black and the first woman elected to the Kentucky state senate.

Charles C. Diggs, Jr., Michigan's first Negro congressman, is a member of the House Foreign Affairs Committee and chairman of its subcommittee on Africa. He has traveled extensively as subcommittee chairman and is considered the leading spokesman in Congress for improving U.S.-Africa relations. Rep. Diggs was the author of many bills in 1969, including measures for providing employment, training opportunities, and housing for low-income and unemployed persons.

Howard Dixon of Montgomery County, Md., was appointed the state's first Negro deputy sheriff.

Mervyn M. Dymally, a California Democrat representing parts of Watts and downtown Los Angeles in the State Senate, serves as chairman of the Senate Social Welfare Committee and is a member of the education, water resources, elections, and reapportionment committees.

Duke Ellington received a standing ovation at his 70th birthday party at the White House, where President Nixon presented him with the Medal of Freedom, the highest civilian award of the U.S. government. The President commented, "In the royalty of American music, no man swings more or stands higher than the Duke."

Roger W. Flood was appointed by Mayor John V. Lindsay to serve until 1973 as a member of the New York City Housing Authority.

John Hope Franklin, a professor and chairman of the history department at the University of Chicago, is a member of the Fisk University board of trustees and chairman of its committee on educational policy.

Addison Gayle, Jr., is an assistant professor of English at the Bernard M. Baruch College of the City University of New York. He edited the anthology, *Black Expression: Essays by and about Black Americans in the Creative Arts,* and is author of *The Sound of Anger,* to be published in 1970 by Horizon Press.

Simeon Golar was appointed chairman of the New York City Commission by Mayor John V. Lindsay. Prior to that appointment he had served the city in various other capacities.

Bertha C. Gordon, former chairman of the department of nursing at Eli Whitney Vocational School in New York, became the first regularly licensed Negro principal of the Morris High School in the Bronx.

Teresa Graves, formerly of the Doodletown Pipers, joined the cast of NBC's "Rowan and Martin's Laugh-In."

William Greaves is executive producer of the television series "Black Journal" for National Educational Television. The program was nominated for an Emmy award in 1969 as an outstanding news documentary program. Mr. Greaves was also the producer, writer, and director of two theatrical release films made for the U.S. Information Agency and films for other public service organizations.

Roosevelt (Rosey) Grier, the great, 300-pound tackle for the Los Angeles Rams, gave up a highly successful football career soon after he was signed to star in his own television show.

Freeman Hankins, elected a Pennsylvania state senator, is the author of a new program to tell the story of the Negro in American history in public schools in his state.

Howard F. Harris was appointed executive director of the Tampa, Fla., Housing Authority, becoming the first member of his race to head a major local housing authority in the Southeastern U.S.

James T. Harris of New Rochelle, N.Y., was appointed to the board of trustees of Newton College of the Sacred Heart in Newton, Mass. He is the school's first Negro board member.

Patricia Harris, former Ambassador to Luxembourg and former dean of the Howard School of Law at Howard University, was a contributor to a report of the National Commission on Violence.

Margaret Haywood, Washington, D.C., city councilwoman, is rapidly developing a reputation as a most effective leader of the District's unrepresented residents.

Joseph S. Hines, appointed one of the first black full professors at the University of North Carolina, has joined the department of sociology and anthropology there. Prior to assuming his new post, he was on the faculty of North Carolina Central University in Durham.

Charles B. Hobson is writer-professor of WABC-Radio's "Like It Is," a lecturer at the New School for Social Research, and a columnist for *Tuesday* magazine. He was formerly production director for WBAI-Radio in New York.

Clarence H. Hunter was named associate director of the Washington Journalism Center. He leads the effort to recruit and train young Negroes for careers in journalism under a $295,000 Ford Foundation grant to the center. Since 1965 Mr. Hunter has been information officer for the U.S. Civil Rights Commission.

Blyden Jackson, appointed one of the first black full professors at the University of North Carolina, specializes in Negro literature as a member of the college's English department. He was formerly dean of the graduate school of Southern University, Baton Rouge, La.

Jesse Jackson, a dedicated Negro leader, has experienced enormous success in increasing economic power in the black community through his direction of "Operation Breadbasket."

Maynard Jackson is an attorney and the first member of his race to be elected vice mayor of Atlanta in its 122-year history. Mr. Jackson, 31, a vice president of the Atlanta NAACP, ran on a platform of enforcing anti-discrimination laws in the Georgia capital's first bi-racial election for mayor and vice mayor.

John L. Johnson was appointed assistant provost for minority group affairs and director of Afro-American Studies at Syracuse University.

Judith S. Johnson was the first Negro appointed by the Alexandria, Va., city government to the position of director of the Economic Opportunities Commission, the city's anti-poverty agency.

Leroy Johnson, the first black man in modern Georgia history to be appointed to a general assembly committee chairmanship, was named head of the senate committee on scientific research.

James L. Jones plans and coordinates summer programs for the youth of the District of Columbia in his role as director of the youth programs unit in Washington, D.C.

Quincy Jones, one of the most sought-after musical composers in the motion picture industry today, was responsible for the musical score of Columbia Pictures' "McKenna's Gold."

Vernon Jordan, Atlanta civil rights leader and attorney, was named "Alumnus of the Year" by De Pauw University's senior class. At 33 he was the youngest person ever named for the honor.

Joe Kershaw, Florida's first Negro state representative in 96 years, was appointed the state's new commissioner on human relations.

John Oliver Killens, noted black writer, was named adjunct professor of writing at the Columbia University School of the Arts. Mr. Killens is a columnist for the Chicago *Daily Defender*.

B. B. King, today's father figure of the blues, has had a major influence on the course of blues history and has gained wide acceptance in recent times.

Marian Anderson

Romare H. Beardon

Gwendolyn Brooks

Dr. Eugene S. Callender

Diahann Carroll

Matthew G. Carter

Georgia M. Davis

Charles C. Diggs, Jr.

Roger W. Flood

Addison Gayle, Jr.

Simeon Golar

William Greaves

Margaret Haywood

Jesse Jackson

James L. Jones

Don L. Lee

Walter B. Lewis

Perry J. Ludy

Keith Morrison

Arthur Statum, Jr.

Verda F. Welcome

Sterling Tucker

Ralph L. William

Eddie N. Williams

Elizabeth Duncan Koontz was appointed director of the Women's Bureau of the Department of Labor. Mrs. Koontz is the first black to hold this position and earlier was the first Negro to serve as president of the National Education Association.

Don L. Lee, poet, essayist, and critic, is currently a lecturer in Afro-American literature and writer-in-residence at Northeastern Illinois State College in Chicago. Mr. Lee is also a book reviewer for the *Negro Digest* and has published three volumes of poetry. He is presently completing a book of criticism on black poets of the 1960s.

Howard Nathaniel Lee was elected mayor of Chapel Hill, N.C. He was the first black to assume the office of mayor in a predominantly white Southern town since Reconstruction.

John Lewis is composer, pianist, and musical director of the Modern Jazz Quartet. He has succeeded in creating a new stream of music from his memorable improvisations, which have found a place in the serious concert world. Other members of the quartet are Milt Jackson, vibraphonist; Connie Kay, drums; and Percy Heath, bass.

Walter B. Lewis, executive director of the Metropolitan Washington Urban Coalition, is a regular lecturer in public administration at American University. He has also lectured at the National War College and at the Brookings Institution.

Tom Lloyd is an artist and instructor at Sarah Lawrence College, Bronxville, N.Y. He has exhibited at the University of California at Los Angeles and at the Phoenix Art Museum in Arizona.

Perry Joseph Ludy, 17, of Oxford, Calif., was the first Negro ever chosen as the Nation's Boy of the Year. The Boys' Clubs of America, which sponsors the award, honored him for superlative service to his home, church, school, community and Boys' Club.

Hollis R. Lynch was named professor of history at Columbia University, where he is focusing his efforts largely on the training of black historians in black culture and history. Dr. Lynch was formerly professor of history and director of black studies at the State University of New York at Buffalo.

W. Philip McLaurin has joined the faculty of Portland State University in Oregon as assistant professor in general studies and director of the experimental black studies program.

Ivan A. Michael was the first Negro named to the New York City Planning Commission.

Earl Miller, an artist and instructor in drawing and graphic design, is acting associate professor at the University of Washington in Seattle.

Clarence M. Mitchell III was the youngest person ever to be elected to the Maryland state senate. He also was awarded the coveted Spingarn Medal for his outstanding contributions to civil rights.

Edward E. Mitchell of Reston, Va., has been named deputy assistant administrator to Robert L. Kunzig, General Services Administration chief. Mr. Mitchell, 55, a retired Army lieutenant colonel, is the highest-ranking Negro at GSA.

Arnold L. Mitchem was appointed to the newly-created position of director of the special program for the culturally distinct student at Marquette University. Mr. Mitchem will continue to hold the rank of instructor in the history department of the university.

Louis M. Montgomery has been appointed to the position of regional administrative assistant for Western Air Lines in San Francisco. An honored athlete, he also received an award for encouraging interracial justice, presented to him by the late Francis Cardinal Spellman, archbishop of New York.

Keith Morrison became the first black man to hold a department chairmanship at De Paul University in Chicago when he was appointed to head the department of fine arts. Mr. Morrison is a well-known artist whose works have been exhibited widely in the U.S., England, India, Liberia, and Jamaica.

Oliver Nelson has mastered most musical instruments and is a much-sought-after music arranger, author of a textbook on jazz improvisation, and owner of a music publishing company. In 1969 the American Wind Symphony, under the direction of Robert Boudreau, presented a special "Tribute to Oliver Nelson," playing three of his serious works along with contemporary and experimental music.

Gil Noble, ABC-TV newsman, started his career as a jazz pianist. He was awarded a "Golden Mike" by the National Association of Television and Radio Announcers, and the National Newspaper Publishers Assn.'s Russwurm Award, both in 1969.

Frederick O'Neal, president of Actor's Equity, is primarily responsible for bringing live performances to the famous Ford's Theater in Washington, D.C. He was also the third Negro to be elected a vice president of the AFL-CIO.

Gordon Parks, a gifted photographer, motion picture director, composer, and writer, was a staff photographer for *Life* magazine for 20 years. In 1969 he directed the screen version of *The Learning Tree,* an autobiographical novel based on his youth in a small Kansas town. Mr. Parks has agreed to direct three more films for Warner Brothers-Seven Arts.

Jeanus B. Parks, Jr., has been named director of the United Planning Organization of Washington, D.C., the city's anti-poverty agency.

Wilson Pickett, a former gospel singer, has written and sung his way to the top of the entertainment ladder in the rhythm and blues field in five years.

J. Ronald Pittman, of Youngstown, Ohio, is executive director of the mayor's Human Relations Commission and the Fair Employment Practice Committee. He has worked to develop the city's anti-poverty program and was chairman of the Youngstown Area Council of Human Rights when it was formed.

Adam Clayton Powell, Harlem congressman, won a Supreme Court decision reinstating him to his seat in the U.S. House of Representatives after he had been excluded for alleged misconduct.

Rogers Priester, a federal program analyst for the U.S. Commission on Civil Rights, was chosen an "Outstanding Young Man of 1969" by the American Foundation.

Samuel D. Proctor is a specialist in the area of Negro life in America. The author of *The Young Negro in America 1960-1980* was appointed professor of education at Rutgers University.

Benjamin Quarles published *Black Abolitionists* in 1969. A professor of history at Morgan State College in Baltimore, he was named chairman of a commission on Negro history and culture by Maryland Gov. Marvin Mandel.

Robert Reid, an artist whose works have been exhibited in many parts of the world, was listed in the 1969 edition of "Who's Who in American Art."

Hari Rhodes, television and motion picture performer, stars on the NBC-TV series, "The Bold Ones." He has also written *A Chosen Few,* based on his Marine Corps experience and now in its second printing.

Carl T. Rowan, noted syndicated columnist and political commentator, was named to the Newspaper Boy Hall of Fame. Mr. Rowan was formerly director of the U.S. Information Agency and Ambassador to Sweden.

Mahler B. Ryder, art instructor for the New York City board of education, held exhibits in Atlanta, New York, and Providence, R.I., in 1969.

Arthur D. Shores is an attorney and the first Negro city councilman elected by Birmingham, Ala., voters. Mr. Shores was one of ten nationwide recipients of the 1969 Russwurm Award. He was selected for his leadership in politics in Alabama.

Benito A. Sinclair, 36-year-old consultant to the Larwin Company, is the first Negro in California to attain the rank of structural engineer, the highest registration for an engineer in the building industry. He is also the head of his own consulting firm, Benito A. Sinclair & Associates.

Gloria Smith was selected Miss Black America in the first nationwide beauty pageant catering exclusively to black women held in New York on August 23, 1969.

Arthur Statum, Jr., All-American end at North Carolina A & T University, was appointed to the athletic department at Lafayette College. Mr. Statum is the first black man to join the Lafayette faculty as a full-time member.

Sterling Tucker was appointed vice chairman of the nine-member District of Columbia city council by President Nixon. The author of *Beyond the Burning* and *Black Reflections on White Power* has served for 12 years as executive director of the Washington Urban League.

Walter L. Walker became vice president of the University of Chicago in 1969. An assistant professor in the school of social service administration, he was also assistant to the president of the university and is currently chairman of a committee on child care there.

Barbara M. Watson is an attorney and administrator of the Bureau of Security and Consular Affairs at the Department of State, where she is responsible for visa and passport matters and special consular services. Miss Watson holds the rank of assistant secretary and is the first woman and the first Negro to hold such a senior position in that agency.

Carroll W. Waymon is executive director of the Citizens' Interracial Committee, the official human relations agency for San Diego County, Calif. Mr. Waymon is a well-known lecturer and activist in race relations and has recently completed a book on the subject.

Verda F. Welcome, a Democrat, is Baltimore's first woman state senator. She sponsored a measure which created a Negro history and culture commission in Maryland and was instrumental in instituting an investigation into discrimination in housing policies at the University of Maryland.

Samuel Z. Westerfield, Jr., was sworn in as Ambassador to the Republic of Liberia in 1969. Since 1967 he had served as deputy assistant secretary of the Department of State for African affairs.

Clifton R. Wharton, Jr., 43-year-old economist, was elected president of 40,000-student Michigan State University. Dr. Wharton thus became the first Negro to head a predominantly white, major American university. Chosen from among 300 nominees, he left his position as vice president of the Agricultural Development Council, Inc., to assume his new post.

Ralph L. William, warden at the Maryland House of Correction in Jessup, Md., is the first black to head a maximum security institution in the state.

Eddie N. Williams was appointed assistant vice president for development and public affairs at the University of Chicago. Mr. Williams was director of the Office of Equal Employment and a special assistant at the Department of State.

Flip Wilson signed a contract with NBC-TV for a comedy-variety special. He was also named the best comic of the year by the Negro Broadcasters Association and has received the Golden Mike Award.

Lawrence B. Wilson, the first Negro cultural affairs officer appointed by the Department of State, was named to the newly-established post of director of urban affairs for the United California Bank.

Olly Wilson is assistant professor of music theory at Oberlin Conservatory. His compositions include classical works, orchestral works, and, most recently, works for the electronic medium. Mr. Wilson was a recipient of the Dartmouth Arts Council Prize for his electronic composition entitled "Cetus." He has completed a piece for chorus and electronic tape in memory of Dr. Martin Luther King, Jr.

Stevie Wonder, 19-year-old recording and television star, received the "Distinguished Service Award" from the President's Committee on Employment of the Handicapped.

Nathan Wright, an authority on the theory of black power, was named professor of urban affairs at Albany State University. Dr. Wright also heads the school's department of Afro-American studies.

Colleges and Universities Attended Predominantly By Negroes

STATE and INSTITUTION	LOCATION and LEVEL	AFFILIATION
ALABAMA		
	(Senior Colleges)	
Alabama A & M College	Normal	state
Alabama State College	Montgomery	state
Miles College	Birmingham	CME
*Oakwood College	Huntsville	SDA
*Stillman College	Tuscaloosa	Presby (USA)
*Talladega College	Talladega	UCC
*Tuskegee Institute	Tuskegee Institute	private
	(Junior Colleges)	
Alabama Lutheran Academy and College	Selma	Lutheran
Daniel Payne College	Birmingham	AME
Lomax-Hannon College	Greenville	Meth
Selma College	Selma	Bapt
ARKANSAS		
	(Senior Colleges)	
Agricultural, Mechanical & Normal College	Pine Bluff	state
Arkansas Baptist College	Little Rock	Bapt
*Philander Smith College	Little Rock	Meth
	(Junior Colleges)	
Shorter College	North Little Rock	AME
DELAWARE		
	(Senior Colleges)	
Delaware State College	Dover	state
DISTRICT OF COLUMBIA		
	(Senior Colleges)	
District of Columbia Teachers College	Washington	city
Federal City College	Washington	federal
Howard University	Washington	private
FLORIDA		
	(Senior Colleges)	
*Bethune-Cookman College	Daytona Beach	Meth
Edward Waters College	Jacksonville	AME
Florida A & M University	Tallahassee	state
*Florida Memorial College	St. Augustine	Bapt
	(Junior Colleges)	
Gibbs Junior College	St. Petersburg	county
Hampton Junior College	Ocala	county
J. W. Johnson Junior College	Leesburg	county
Lincoln Junior College	Fort Pierce	county
Roosevelt Junior College	W. Palm Beach	county
Suwannee Junior College	Madison	county
Volusia County Junior College	Daytona Beach	county
Washington Junior College	Pensacola	state

STATE and INSTITUTION	LOCATION and LEVEL	AFFILIATION
GEORGIA	(Senior Colleges)	
Albany State College	Albany	state
*Atlanta University	Atlanta	private
*Clark College	Atlanta	Meth
The Fort Valley State College	Fort Valley	state
*Interdenominational Theological Center	Atlanta	Interdenominat'l
*Morehouse College	Atlanta	Bapt
*Morris Brown College	Atlanta	AME
*Paine College	Augusta	CME & Meth
Savannah State College	Savannah	state
*Spelman College	Atlanta	Bapt
KENTUCKY	(Senior Colleges)	
Kentucky State College	Frankfort	state
Simmons University	Louisville	Bapt
LOUISIANA	(Senior Colleges)	
*Dillard University	New Orleans	UCC & Meth
Grambling College	Grambling	state
Southern University A & M	Baton Rouge	state
*Xavier University	New Orleans	RC
MARYLAND	(Senior Colleges)	
Bowie State College	Bowie	state
Coppin State Teachers	Baltimore	state
Maryland State College	Princess Anne	state
Morgan State College	Baltimore	state
MISSISSIPPI	(Senior Colleges)	
Alcorn A & M College	Lorman	state
Jackson State College	Jackson	state
Mississippi Industrial College	Holly Springs	CME
Mississippi Valley State College	Itta Bena	state
Rust College	Holly Springs	Meth
*Tougaloo College	Tougaloo	AMA
	(Junior Colleges)	
Coahoma Junior College	Clarksdale	county
J. P. Campbell Junior College	Jackson	AME
Mary Holmes Junior College	West Point	Presby (USA)
Natchez Junior College	Natchez	Bapt
Okolona College	Okolona	PE
Piney Woods Country Life School	Piney Woods	private
Prentiss Institute	Prentiss	private
Saints Junior College	Lexington	Ch. of God
T. J. Harris Junior College	Meridian	city
Utica Junior College	Utica	county
MISSOURI	(Senior Colleges)	
Lincoln University	Jefferson City	state
NORTH CAROLINA	(Senior Colleges)	
Agric. Techn. College of N.C.	Greensboro	state
*Barber-Scotia College	Concord	Presby (USA)
*Bennett College	Greensboro	Meth
Elizabeth City State College	Elizabeth City	state
Fayetteville State College	Fayetteville	state
*Johnson C. Smith University	Charlotte	Presby (USA)
*Livingston College	Salisbury	AMEZ
N.C. College at Durham	Durham	state
*St. Augustine's College	Raleigh	PE
*Shaw University	Raleigh	Bapt

STATE and INSTITUTION	LOCATION and LEVEL	AFFILIATION
NORTH CAROLINA (Cont.)		
Winston-Salem State College	Winston-Salem	state
	(Junior Colleges)	
Kittrell College	Kittrell	AME
OHIO		
	(Senior Colleges)	
Central State College	Wilberforce	state
*Wilberforce University	Wilberforce	AME
OKLAHOMA		
	(Senior Colleges)	
Langston University	Langston	state
PENNSYLVANIA		
	(Senior Colleges)	
Cheyney State College	Cheyney	state
Lincoln University	Lincoln University	private
SOUTH CAROLINA		
	(Senior Colleges)	
Allen University	Columbia	AME
*Benedict College	Columbia	Bapt
*Claflin College	Orangeburg	Meth
Morris College	Sumter	Bapt
S.C. State College	Orangeburg	state
Vorhees College	Denmark	PE
	(Junior Colleges)	
Clinton College	Rock Hill	Meth
Friendship Junior College	Rock Hill	Bapt
Mather College	Beaufort	Bapt
TENNESSEE		
	(Senior Colleges)	
*Fisk University	Nashville	AMA
*Knoxville College	Knoxville	Presby (USA)
*Lane College	Jackson	CME
*LeMoyne-Owen	Memphis	AMA
Meharry Medical College	Nashville	private
Tennessee Agric. & Indus. State University	Nashville	state
	(Junior Colleges)	
Morristown College	Morristown	Meth
TEXAS		
	(Senior Colleges)	
*Bishop College	Dallas	Bapt
*Huston-Tillotson College	Austin	Meth & AMA
Jarvis Christian College	Hawkins	Dis of C
Paul Quinn College	Waco	AME
Prairie View A & M College	Prairie View	state
Texas College	Tyler	CME
Texas Southern University	Houston	state
*Wiley College	Marshall	Meth
	(Junior Colleges)	
Butler College	Tyler	Bapt
St. Philip's College	San Antonio	county or district
Southwestern Christian College	Terrell	Ch of Christ
Tyler District College	Tyler	county
VIRGINIA		
	(Senior Colleges)	
*Hampton Institute	Hampton	private
*St. Paul's College	Lawrenceville	PE
Virginia State College	Petersburg	state
Virginia Theological Seminary	Lynchburg	Bapt
*Virginia Union University	Richmond	Bapt

KEY

Under AFFILIATION

AMA	American Missionary Association, Congregational
AME	African Methodist Episcopal Church
AMEZ	African Methodist Episcopal Zion Church
Bapt	Baptist
Ch of Christ	Church of Christ
Ch of God	Church of God
CME	Christian Methodist Episcopal Church
Dis of C	Disciples of Christ
Meth	Methodist
PE	Protestant Episcopal Church
Presby (USA)	United Presbyterian Church in the United States of America
RC	Roman Catholic Church
SDA	Seventh-Day Adventist
UCC	United Church of Christ

*United Negro College Fund member institution

SOURCES: 1. *The Predominantly Negro Colleges and Universities in Transition,* Earl J. McGrath
2. *American Colleges and Universities and American Junior Colleges,* American Council on Education
3. United Negro College Fund, Inc.

Amidst the chaos a moment of relaxation. Despite the rigors of the war, this Marine finds the time to play with two Vietnamese children during a rest break.

Three faces of war. Above left: Mrs. Beulah Harris happily relates news of her son's escape from communist war camp; Above right: PFC Dan Bullock, youngest American to die in Vietnam; Below: the face of this unnamed soldier seems to ponder the fate that awaits him.

Marine Sgt. Henry Lackey shown here with his wife and children has refused second tour of duty in Vietnam, stating that if necessary he would prefer to face AWOL charges in the U.S. than more fighting in Vietnam.

Gen. Frederic E. Davison, first Negro general to command American infantry, shows his daughters his new uniform.

The widow of Marine Sgt. Rodney M. Davis, who threw himself on a grenade to save the life of his buddies, receives the Congressional Medal of Honor, posthumously awarded to her husband.

The recent passing from the American scene of distinguished black men and women is recorded in the following list. Those selected for inclusion had enjoyed prominence during their lifetimes in their own fields.

Dan Bullock, 17, killed while doing guard duty at a combat base in Quangnam Province, Vietnam, was the youngest American serviceman to die in the war up until that time. A native of Brooklyn, Dan had given a false birth date when he enlisted in the Marines in September 1968. A Pentagon spokesman noted that Dan might have been the youngest American to die in uniform since before World War I.

Frank Buncom, linebacker for the Cincinnati Bengals, died in Cincinnati at age 29. Mr. Buncom, a veteran of eight years in pro football, came to Cincinnati from the San Diego Chargers in the expansion draft when the Cincinnati Bengals entered the American Professional Football League.

Albert I. Cassell, a noted architect, died at the age of 74. His largest project was Mayfair Mansions, a $5 million apartment development in Washington, D.C. Other design credits include schools in the Pennsylvania and Washington, D.C., areas, and international projects in Lagos, Nigeria, and in the Belgian Congo.

Thomas Humes Chase, a jazz pianist who had played with such notables as Thomas (Fats) Waller, Coleman Hawkins, and Duke Ellington, died in Washington, D.C., at age 62. He had played jazz and classical engagements in Europe and North Africa, but in recent years had confined his appearances to local clubs.

Dr. Walter R. Chivers, a distinguished sociologist and retired professor and chairman of the department of sociology at Morehouse College, died in Atlanta. He collaborated with Dr. Arthur Raper in the research and writing of the classic sociological study, *The Tragedy of Lynching,* and with Dr. Gunnar Myrdal in the writing of *An American Dilemma.*

Charles E. Cornish, the first Negro to head a governing body in Maryland and a leader in local civil rights efforts, died at the age of 72 in Cambridge, Md. Mr. Cornish had been president of the Cambridge City Council—and the only Negro on the five-member body—for the past eight years. He had served on the Council for 22 years.

J. Daniel Diggs, 74, one of two Negro members of the New York City Council, died of cancer in New York. At the time of his death, the Brooklyn Democrat was serving his third term on the Council as a representative of the Bedford-Stuyvesant area.

Raymond A. Diggs, a retired army lieutenant colonel and military educator who was cited for heroism in World War II, died in Baltimore.

James Edwards, one of the first actors to break out of the stereotyped roles often given blacks, died at the age of 51. His professional roles included the lead in the touring company of the Broadway play, "Deep Are the Roots," and the lead in "The Home of the Brave."

Thomas (Tommy) Edwards, well-known singer, died at his home in Richmond, Va., at the age of 47. His best known recording was "It's All in the Game."

George (Pops) Foster, 77, a jazz musician, died in San Francisco. He began his career in New Orleans and played with Fats Marabel's Riverboat Band and such stars as Louis Armstrong, Earl Hines, and Sidney Bechet.

Dr. James R. Gladden, chief of orthopedic surgery at Howard University Medical School from 1952 to 1964, died at age 58. He was the first Negro to become a Diplomate of the American Board of Orthopedic Surgeons and was the first black Fellow of the American Academy of Orthopedic Surgeons.

Coleman Hawkins, renowned tenor saxophonist, died of a liver ailment at the age of 64. Hawkins' most famous recording was "Body and Soul," and he was the recipient of numerous honors in his field.

George Hayes, 74, civic leader and attorney, died in Washington, D.C. Mr. Hayes was a senior partner in the law firm of Cobb, Howard, Hayes and Winsor. He was the first Negro elected to the board of directors of the Metropolitan Washington Board of Trade and the first to hold office in the D.C. Bar Association.

Talley R. Holmes, who helped organize the American Tennis Association, died at the age of 70.

Rex Ingram, noted stage, screen, and television actor, died of a heart attack at age 73. Mr. Ingram, who had studied medicine and was one of the first of his race elected to Phi Beta Kappa, began his acting career at the age of 20 when he was cast in the first Tarzan motion picture. He played various stereotyped Negro roles until his starring part in "Green Pastures," and created the role of Crown in the stage play "Porgy," on which the musical "Porgy and Bess" was based. One of his favorite roles was that of Emperor Jones in the stage play of the same name by Eugene O'Neill.

Hilton W. Jefferson, a jazz saxophonist, died at the age of 65. He played through the Big Band era with such well-known bands as Blue Barron's Rhythm Band and McKinney's Cotton Pickers. Mr. Jefferson also worked with Fletcher Henderson and Duke Ellington.

Rev. A. D. Williams King, brother of the late Dr. Martin Luther King, Jr., died in Atlanta at the age of 38. His death in the swimming pool of his home was ruled accidental drowning. Mr. King, who strongly resembled his brother, was active in civil rights causes and had led or participated in civil rights activities in Birmingham, Ala., Louisville, Ky., Washington, D.C., and St. Petersburg, Fla. He became associate pastor of the 4500-member Ebenezer Baptist Church in 1968 and was a director of the Southern Christian Leadership Conference that his brother had headed.

Dolly King, 51, honored athlete and college coach, died of a heart ailment in New York. His athletic prowess in football and basketball was legendary and just before his death he had been nominated for the Basketball Hall of Fame. He was director of Intercollegiate Athletics and Intramurals and professor of Student Life at Manhattan Community College.

Judge William Lovelace, first black municipal court judge in Cincinnati, died at the age of 67. His career of legal service began in 1931. He was elected to the bench in 1965.

Roberta Martin, organizer of the famous Roberta Martin Singers, died at age 57. The renowned gospel personality traveled with her singing group throughout the United States and Europe.

William H. Minor, a Spanish-American War veteran believed to be the oldest living veteran of Theodore Roosevelt's Great White Fleet Voyage of 1908, died at the age of 101.

Joseph C. Parks, 76, noted figure in Maryland politics, died after a long illness. He was the first Negro chairman of the state Human Relations Commission and the first of his race to run for Charles County Commissioner, an election he lost.

Rossetta W. Scott, great-granddaughter of Frederick Douglass, died at age 59 in Washington, D.C.

Henry (Hammerin' Hank) Thompson, former New York Giants third baseman, died in Fresno, Calif., at the age of 43. Mr. Thompson played for nine years in the major league and compiled a lifetime batting average of .267. He and Monte Irvin, the first Negro players to sign with the Giants, joined the club in 1949. Thompson led National League third basemen in double plays in 1950 with 43. He and the more famous Bobby Thompson came to be known as the Tom-Tom Twins because of their long-range hitting. He left the Giants in 1956 when they moved from New York to San Francisco.

Dr. James C. Wallace, Jr., 47, dental director of Chicago's Martin Luther King Comprehensive Health Center, died two days after being inducted as a Fellow of the American College of Dentistry. A past president of the National Dental Association, a primarily black professional organization, Dr. Wallace also was board chairman of Chicago's Halfway House Committee for Unfortunate Girls.

Ivory Deek Watson, 56, an original member and tenor in the Ink Spots Quartet, died in Washington, D.C. Mr. Watson wrote many of his group's greatest hits, including "I Love You for Sentimental Reasons" and "We'll Meet Again." He continued performing after the breakup of the Ink Spots and had been making television appearances with another group before his death.

Carter Walker Wesley, lawyer and publisher, died at age 77. Founder of the 120-member National Newspaper Publishers Association, Mr. Wesley edited and published newspapers throughout the South and in California.

Josh White, famous baritone and guitarist, died of a heart ailment at the age of 61. One of the first folk singers to appear in nightclubs, White had a wide repertoire that delighted cabaret and concert audiences. His best-known songs included "One Meatball," "The Ballad of John Henry," "Jim Crow Train," "Strange Fruit," and "Hard Times Blues." With his recording of the album "Chain Gang" in the early 1940s, his career was launched. In his later years he was a success on the college concert circuit and often performed with his son, Josh White, Jr., and his daughter, Beverly Saunders.

Louis White, bass-baritone singer and actor, died at the age of 66. He was the first Negro given a contract to sing as staff artist on Radio Station WGN in Chicago. Mr. White, who often teamed with his wife in a duo known as "The Singing Whites," sang with her in the original company of "Porgy and Bess."

William Young, 68, former Secretary of Labor and Industry of Pennsylvania, and a well-known athlete in his youth, died in Pittsburgh. A former All-American quarterback who also played baseball and basketball, Mr. Young tutored Roy Campanella and other younger stars. He had been active in Republican activities in the state.

A Selected Annotated Bibliography of Articles

The following list of source materials deals with various aspects of the black experience in nine major areas. This list is in no way meant to be definitive, but only to be representative of the types and quality of articles published.

Black Arts

DIXON, MELVIN. "Black Theater: The Aesthetics," *Negro Digest*, Vol. 18, No. 9 (July 1969) pp. 41-45.
How the black man can apply black aesthetics in the development of an Afro-American tradition. The author's answer—look within the black community first, and externalize that which is internal.

HENDRICKS, JON. "Jazz and Its Critics," *Liberator*, Vol. 9, No. 11 (November 1969) pp. 14-16.
Author suggests that jazz critics do not understand the culture the black jazz musician portrays. He maintains that critics seek to flatter many black jazz musicians and in doing so turn them away from their attempts to portray their culture through their music.

KILGORE, JAMES C. "A Case for Black Literature," *Negro Digest*, Vol. 18, No. 9 (July 1969) pp. 22-25, 66-69.
The value and need of including black literature in school curricula.

SILVERA, FRANK. "Towards a Theater of Understanding," *Negro Digest*, Vol. 18, No. 6 (April 1969) pp. 33-35.
A critique of James Baldwin's play, "The Amen Corner."

Black Capitalism and Business

"Black Capitalism," *Saturday Review*, Vol. 53, No. 34 (Aug. 23, 1969) pp. 15-39, 55-60.
Articles by Whitney M. Young, Nathan Glazer, and others examining the prospects and problems of black capitalism.

HILL, HERBERT. "Employment, Manpower Training and the Black Workers," *The Journal of Negro Education*, Vol. 38, No. 3 (Summer 1969) pp. 204-217.
An analysis of the causes for the present status of black workers and what can be done to upgrade this status.

Black Education

BERUBE, MAURICE R. "Black Power and the Learning Process," *Commonweal*, Vol. 90, No. 4 (April 11, 1969) pp. 98-101.
Maintains that "black power" holds the key to the learning process of the black man in America. Berube cites three studies conducted on the "learning process" and concludes that the attitudes of teachers and school administrators in the black community are expressive of a desire to establish black community control of schools—in essence a "private" school system.

CASS, JAMES. "Can the University Survive the Black Challenge?" *Saturday Review*, Vol. 52, No. 25 (June 21, 1969) pp. 68-71, 83-84.
The challenge black students have presented to colleges and universities, a challenge which in essence poses a functional threat to the university because it strikes at its traditional concept and function.

CLIFT, VIRGINIA A. "Curriculum Strategy Based on the Personality Characteristics of Disadvantaged Youth," *Journal of Negro Education*, Vol. 38, No. 2 (Spring 1969) pp. 94-104.
A technical examination of innovations geared to aid disadvantaged youths.

CUDJOE, SELWYN R. "Needed: A Black Studies Consortium," *Liberator*, Vol. 9, No. 9 (September 1969) pp. 14-16.
A lack of good graduate programs in Afro-American studies results in a lack of continuous flow of competent faculties to continue such a program. One solution is a consortium program where colleges and universities would pool their resources in an effort to build a strong Afro-American studies

program that would continually produce qualified personnel.

GENOVESE, EUGENE D. "Black Studies: Trouble Ahead," *The Atlantic*, Vol. 223, No. 6 (June 1969) pp. 37-41.

The problems which may be created by the establishment of black studies programs in the universities if a complete understanding of the "why" of black studies programs is not answered.

MONRO, JOHN V. "Negro Colleges: Escape from the Dark Cave," *The Nation*, Vol. 209, No. 14 (October 27, 1969) pp. 430-434.

An appeal to readers to support black colleges in an effort to make them stronger and more effective. The example used is Miles College in Birmingham, Alabama.

Black History

ARMAH, AYI KWEI. "Fanon: The Awakener," *Negro Digest*, Vol. 18, No. 12 (October 1969) pp. 4-10.

The life and work of Franz Fanon and the relevance of his works to black people today.

CROWE, CHARLES. "Racial Massacre in Atlanta, September 22, 1906," *The Journal of Negro History*, Vol. 104, No. 2 (April 1969) pp. 150-173.

A confrontation between blacks and whites in Atlanta, Georgia, in 1906, including racial and political implications for today.

D'ELIA, DONALD J. "Dr. Benjamin Rush and the Negro," *Journal of the History of Ideas*, Vol. 30, No. 3 (July-September 1969) pp. 413-422.

FLYNN, JOHN P. "Booker T. Washington: Uncle Tom or Wooden Horse," *The Journal of Negro History*, Vol. 104, No. 3 (July 1969) pp. 262-272.

An examination of the alternative roles that have been attributed to Washington: (1) "Uncle Tom" and (2) Wooden Horse, a role which was assigned to him by a beneficiary of his political manipulations.

GARVEY, AMY JACQUES. "Marcus Mosiah Garvey," *Negro Digest*, Vol. 18, No. 7 (May 1969) pp. 42-75, 79.

Garvey's widow deals with some of the motives which directed Garvey to seek a "nationhood" for black people and the spirit of Garveyism which manifests itself in the goals and aspirations of blacks today.

HARDING, VINCENT. "W.E.B. Du Bois and the Black Messianic Vision," *Freedomways*, Vol. 9, No. 1 (Winter 1969) pp. 44-58.

The black nationalistic tendencies in the works of Du Bois as a black messianism "stretched over the boundaries of humanity."

OFARI, EARL. "The Roots of Black Radicalism," *Negro Digest*, Vol. 18, No. 10 (August 1969) pp. 18-21.

An examination of the historical background of black radicalism in the 19th century suggesting that the current movement is only an extension of earlier ones.

Black Politics

HENNINGER, DANIEL. "Cleveland: Challenge to Mayor Stokes," *The New Republic*, Vol. 161, Nos. 8-9 (August 1969) pp. 12-14.

Stokes' political rivals in Cleveland and their proposed programs of election attack against him.

Black Power

DRAPER, THEODORE. "The Fantasy of Black Nationalism," *Commentary*, Vol. 48, No. 3 (September 1969) pp. 27-54.

An attack on the "myths" of black nationalism.

FRANCOIS, TERRY A. "A Black Man Looks at Black Racism," *Reader's Digest*, Vol. 95, No. 569 (September 1969) pp. 209-214.

A conservative discussion of the manifestations and implications of black racism in America.

SAYRE, NORA. "Black Panthers," *The Progressive*, Vol. 33, No. 7 (July 1969) pp. 20-23.

A sympathetic examination of the Black Panthers, their origin, history, and goals.

STAPLES, ROBERT E. "Black Ideology and the Search for Community," *Liberator*, Vol. 9, No. 6 (June 1969) pp. 8-11.

The interests of blacks and the interests of the American political and economic system are diametrically opposed, and consequently a black ideology must be developed and centered in the black communal experience.

Black Religion

BOYNTON, ERNEST. "Christianity's Black Power," *Church in Metropolis*, No. 19 (Winter 1968) pp. 20-24.

A discussion of the Black Caucus Movement as reflected at the second annual convocation of the National Committee of Black Churchmen in St. Louis, 1968.

The Journal of Religious Thought, Vol. 26, No. 2 (Summer Supplement 1969)

A collection of articles on the black church and black theology. Three articles of particular interest are J. Deotis Roberts, "The Black Caucus and the Failure of Christian Theology"; Rosemary Ruether, "Black Theology and the Black Church"; and Leon E. Wright, "Black Theology or Black Experience."

WILMORE, GAYRAUD S. "The Case for a New Black Church Style," *Church in Metropolis*, No. 18 (Fall 1968) pp. 18-22.

The black church's difficulty in America and black power as a means to understanding its new role.

Black-White Relations

"The Black and the Jew: A Falling Out of Allies," *Time* (Jan. 3, 1969) pp. 55-59.

An analysis of the causes and ramifications of the breach between blacks and Jews.

BARTIMOLE, ROLDO. "Bad Day in Cleveland," *Nation,* Vol. 209, No. 2 (July 14, 1969) pp. 41-45, 61.

A summary of the Glenville shoot-out, the trial of Ahmed Evans, and the possible ramifications of these events.

CROWELL, ERBIN. "Anti-Racism: The New Movement," *Civil Rights Digest*, Vol. 2, No. 1 (Winter 1969) pp. 24-30.

The premise of several new organizations such as People Against Racism that racism is a white problem and that essentially it is up to white people to resolve the problem.

CURTIS, MICHAEL. "Travels with Mr. Charlie," *The Atlantic*, Vol. 224, No. 2 (August 1969) pp. 31-39.

An inspired account of a seven-day, seven-city journey taken by a small group of senior journalists.

ENDICOTT, WILLIAM, and STANLEY WILLIFORD. "Color and Mayhem Uptight in the Armed Forces," *The Nation*, Vol. 209, No. 15 (November 3, 1969) pp. 464-467.

Recent "racial" incidents on military bases and some of the efforts made to alleviate the tensions that cause such incidents. "The laws are there, but the prejudice within the people is still there, too."

JONES, ROBERT A. "Front Against Fascism: Panthers' Conference," *The Nation*, Vol. 209, No. 4 (August 11, 1969) pp. 102-103.

An account of the First Conference for a United Front Against Fascism in America, maintaining that although both the Black Panthers and the Peace and Freedom Party met for unifying purpose, no unity existed.

HAMILTON, CHARLES V. "The Black Revolution: A Primer for White Liberals," *Progressive*, Vol. 33, No. 1 (January 1969) pp. 29-31.

In this article the author discusses the failures of the white liberal establishment in understanding both the methodology and goals of the Black Revolution. While the author says well what he has to say, it has all been said before.

MOLOTCH, HARVEY. "Racial Change in a Stable Community," *American Journal of Sociology,* Vol. 75, No. 2 (September 1969) pp. 226 ff.

Comparison between a Chicago community experiencing racial transition and an all-white area to test the theory that there is a link between transition and instability (i.e., property turnover).

SCHOEN, DEREK. "Racial Crisis in a Small City," *Progressive*, Vol. 33, No. 3 (March 1969) pp. 24-27.

An examination of the racial strife in Waterloo, Iowa, in which the author attempts to pinpoint the causes of racial unrest. This article should be useful to anyone seeking a better perspective of race relations in any U.S. city under 25,000.

Miscellaneous

"Black Decision-Makers," *Library Journal*, Vol. 94, No. 11 (June 1, 1969) pp. 2203-2206.

A survey conducted by the *Library Journal* staff in an attempt to assess the number and percentage of personnel on library staffs throughout the country holding positions that would affect policy-making decisions, particularly in the types of books made available to the public.

"The Black Revolution," *Ebony*, Vol. 24, No. 10 (August 1969) pp. 29-162.

Articles dealing with the status of the black revolution today. Offers insight into dreams lost and hopes to be realized.

LESTER, JULIUS. "To Recapture the Dream," *Liberation*, Vol. 14, Nos. 5-6 (August 1969) pp. 26-30.

Examines the ideologies that shaped and reshaped "the movement," particularly the civil rights-black power struggle during the 1960s. Particularly critical of the black Marxist viewpoint.

LEWIS, W. ARTHUR. "The Black Man's Route to the Top," *Reader's Digest* (August 1969) pp. 157-164.

WOLFRAM, WALTER, and RALPH W. FASOLD. "A Black English Translation of John 3:1-21 with Grammatical Notes," *The Bible Translator*, Vol. 20, No. 20 (April 1969) pp. 48-54.

An examination of the dynamics, implications, and possible uses of ghetto English.

Bibliography of Recently Published Titles

Biography

BLAIR, CLAY, JR. *The Strange Case of James Earl Ray: The Man Who Murdered Martin Luther King.* New York, 1969.

CLARKE, JOHN HENRIK (ed.). *Malcolm X: The Man and His Times.* New York, 1969.

DAVIS, BENJAMIN J. *Communist Councilman from Harlem: Autobiographical Notes Written in a Federal Penitentiary.* New York, 1969.

DECOY, ROBERT H. *The Big Black Fire.* Los Angeles, 1969.

*EBONY PICTURE BIOGRAPHY. *Martin Luther King, Jr., 1929–1968.* Chicago, 1968.

EWERS, CAROLYN H. *The Long Journey: A Biography of Sidney Poitier.* New York, 1969.

FENDERSON, LEWIS H., and STANTON L. WORMLEY (eds.). *Many Shades of Black.* New York, 1969.

FERRIS, LOUANNE (as told to BETH DAY). *I'm Done Crying.* New York, 1969.

FREDERICKSON, GEORGE M. (ed.). *William Lloyd Garrison.* Englewood Cliffs, N. J., 1968.

*HERSCHLER, MILDRED BARGER. *Frederick Douglass.* Chicago, 1969.

KING, CORETTA SCOTT. *My Life with Martin Luther King, Jr.* New York, 1969.

MCKEE, J. D. *Martin Luther King, Jr.* New York, 1969.

NEMIROFF, ROBERT (adaptor). *To Be Young, Gifted and Black: Lorraine Hansberry in Her Own Words.* Englewood Cliffs, N. J., 1969.

*SCHRAFF, A. E. *Black Courage.* Philadelphia, 1969.

THORNBROUGH, EMMA LOU. *Booker T. Washington.* Englewood Cliffs, N. J., 1969.

ULLMAN, VICTOR. *Look to the North Star: A Life of William King.* Boston, 1969.

*ZAGOREN, RUBY. *Venture for Freedom; The True Story of an African Yankee.* Cleveland, 1969.

For juveniles
Textbooks and reprints omitted unless of particular significance to the general reader.

History

ADLER, MORTIMER J., GEORGE DUCAS, and CHARLES VAN DOREN (eds.). *The Negro in American History* (3 vols.). New York, 1968.

AFRICAN BIBLIOGRAPHIC CENTER. *Black History Viewpoints.* (Special Bibliographic Series, Vol. 7, No. 1.). Washington, D. C., 1969.

BERGMAN, PETER M. *The Chronological History of the Negro in America.* New York, 1969.

*BURT, OLIVE W. *Negroes in the Early West.* New York, 1969.

CALLCOTT, MARGARET L. *The Negro in Maryland Politics, 1870-1912.* Baltimore, 1969.

CRAVEN, AVERY. *Reconstruction: The Ending of the Civil War.* New York, 1969.

CRUDEN, ROBERT L. *The Negro in Reconstruction.* Englewood Cliffs, N. J., 1969.

DAVIS, DAVID BRION. *The Problem of Slavery in Western Culture.* Ithaca, N. Y., 1969.

*DOWNEY, FAIRFAX. *The Buffalo Soldiers in the Indian Wars.* New York, 1969.

DROTNING, PHILLIP T. *Black Heroes in Our Nation's History.* New York, 1969.

GENOVESE, EUGENE. *The World the Slaveholders Made.* New York, 1969.

GOODMAN, WALTER. *Black Bondage: The Life of Slaves in the South.* New York, 1969.

HEARD, J. NORMAN. *The Black Frontiersmen: Adventures of Negroes Among American Indians, 1528-1918.* New York, 1969.

JACKSON, MILES M. (ed.). *A Bibliography of Negro History and Culture.* Atlanta, 1969.

KRADITOR, AILEEN S. *Means and Ends in American Abolitionism: Garrison and His Critics on Strategy and Tactics.* New York, 1969.

KUTLER, STANLEY IRA. *Judicial Power and Reconstruction Politics.* Chicago, 1968.

MEIER, AUGUST, and ELLIOTT RUDWICK (eds.). *The Making of Black America: Essays in Negro Life and History* (2 vols.). New York, 1969.

NEVINSON, HENRY W. *A Modern Slavery.* New York, 1968.

News Front EDITORIAL STAFF (eds.). *Pictorial History of the Black American.* New York, 1968.

NOBLE, P. *The Negro in Films.* Port Washington, N. Y., 1969.

QUARLES, BENJAMIN. *Black Abolitionists.* New York, 1969.

ROMERO, PATRICIA W. (ed.). *In Black America—1968: The Year of Awakening.* Washington, D. C. 1969.

ROZWENC, E. C., and T. T. LYONS. *Reconstruction and the Race Problem.* Boston, 1968.

RUCHAMES, LOUIS (ed). *Racial Thought in America: From the Puritans to Abraham Lincoln.* Amherst, Mass., 1969.

SHADE, WILLIAM G., and ROY C. HERRENKOHL (eds.). *Seven on Black: Reflections on the Negro Experiences in America.* Philadelphia, 1969.

SOUTHERN, DAVID W. *The Malignant Heritage: Yankee Progressives and the Negro Question, 1901-1904.* Chicago, 1968.

STAMPP, KENNETH M., and LEON F. LITWACK (eds.). *Reconstruction: An Anthology of Revisionist Writings.* Baton Rouge, 1969.

STERNSHER, BERNARD (ed). *The Negro in Depression and War: Prelude to Revolution.* Chicago, 1969.

TREFOUSSE, HANS L. *The Radical Republicans: Lincoln's Vanguard for Social Justice.* New York, 1968.

WEINSTEIN, ALLEN, and FRANK OTTO GATELL (eds.). *American Negro Slavery: A Modern Reader.* New York, 1969.

WILLIAMSON, JOEL. *Origins of Segregation.* Boston, 1968.

WOOD, FORREST G. *Black Scare: The Racist Response to Emancipation and Reconstruction.* Berkeley, 1968.

Africa and the Caribbean

AFRICAN BIBLIOGRAPHIC CENTER. *African Affairs for the General Reader.* (Special Bibliographic Series, Vol. 6. No. 3.). Washington, D. C., 1968.

———. *Contemporary African Women.* (Special Bibliographic Series, Vol. 6, No. 2.). Washington, D. C., 1968.

———. *Current Themes in African Historical Studies.* (Special Bibliographic Series, Vol. 7, No. 2.). Washington, D. C., 1969.

———. *Upper Volta Today.* (Special Bibliographic Series, Vol. 6, No. 1.). Washington, D. C., 1968.

ANDRESKI, STANISLAV. *The African Predicament.* New York, 1969.

COLLINS, ROBERT O. *The Partition of Africa: Illusion or Necessity.* New York, 1969.

DIEDERICH, BERNARD, and AL BURT, *Papa Doc: The Truth About Haiti Today.* New York, 1969.

DUMOGA, J. *Africa, Between East and West.* Chester Springs, Penna., 1969.

FORSYTH, FREDERICK. *The Biafra Story.* Harmondsworth, England, 1969.

Jeune Afrique EDITORIAL STAFF (ed. & comp.). *Africa 69/70: A Reference Volume on the African Continent.* New York, 1969.

LEE, JOHN MICHAEL. *African Armies and Civil Order.* New York, 1969.

LOGAN, RAYFORD W. *Haiti and the Dominican Republic.* New York, 1968.

DE LUSIGNAN, GUY. *French Speaking Africa Since Independence.* New York, 1969.

MARKOVITZ, IRVING LEONARD. *Leopold Senghor and the Politics of Negritude.* New York, 1969.

MOK, MICHAEL. *Biafra Journal.* New York, 1969.

MOREL, EDMUND DENE. *The Black Man's Burden: The White Man in Africa from the 15th Century to World War I.* London, 1920. Reprint London, 1969.

MORGAN, WILLIAM B., and J. C. PUGH. *West Africa.* London, 1969.

MURPHY, E. JEFFERSON. *Understanding Africa.* New York, 1969.

NKRUMAH, KWAME. *Handbook of Revolutionary Warfare.* London, 1968.

OGOT, BETHWELL A., and J. A. KIERNAN (eds.). *Famani: A Survey of East African History.* London, 1968.

OJUKWU, C. ODUMEGWU. *Biafra: Selected Speeches and Random Thoughts of C. Odumegwu Ojukwu, with Diary of Events.* New York, 1969.

PATTERSON, HORACE. *The Sociology of Slavery: Slave Society in Jamaica.* Rutherford, N. J., 1969.

PROTHERO, RALPH MANSELL (ed.). *A Geography of Africa: Regional Essays on Fundamental Characteristics, Issues and Problems.* New York, 1969.

SKURNIK, W. A. E. (ed.). *African Political Thought: Lumumba, Nkrumah, and Touré.* (Monograph Series in World Affairs). Denver, 1968.

African Culture

ADDO, PETER E. A. *Ghana Folk Tales.* Jericho, N. Y., 1968.

ARMAH, AYI KWEI. *The Beautiful Ones Are Not Yet Born.* Boston, 1969.

BEIER, ULLI. *Contemporary Art in Africa.* New York, 1968.

BEN-JOCHANNAN, YOSEF, et al. *Africa: The Land, the People, the Culture.* New York, 1968.

BURLAND, COTTIE A. *The Exotic White Man: An Alien in Asian and African Art.* New York, 1969.

*D'AMATO, JANET, and ALEX D'AMATO. *African Crafts for You to Make.* New York, 1969.

HEAD, BESSIE. *When Rain Clouds Gather.* New York, 1969.

HURD, PRISCILLA PAYNE. *Chasing Culture with the Brooklyn Museum.* Brooklyn, 1969.

LAURENCE, MARGARET. *Long Drums and Cannons*. New York, 1969.

MBITI, JOHN SAMUEL. *African Religions and Philosophy*. New York, 1969.

MONTI, FRANCO. *African Masks*. London, 1969.

MUTWA, VUSAMAZULU CREDO. *My People, My Africa*. New York, 1969.

PARRINDER, GEOFFREY. *Religion in Africa*. Harmondsworth, England, 1969.

PIETERSE, COSMOS, and DAVID MUNRO (eds.). *Protest and Conflict in African Literature*. New York, 1969

TROWELL, KATHLEEN MARGARET, and HANS NEVERMAN. *African and Oceanic Art*. New York, 1968.

Black Power

BRAZIER, ARTHUR M. *Black Self-Determination: The Story of the Woodlawn Organization*. Grand Rapids, 1969.

BROWN, H. RAP. *Die, Nigger, Die! A Political Autobiography*. New York, 1969.

CONE, JAMES H. *Black Theology and Black Power*. New York, 1969.

DELORIA, VINE, JR. *Custer Died for Your Sins*. New York, 1969.

EDWARDS, HARRY. *The Revolt of the Black Athlete*. New York, 1969.

ELLIS, WILLIAM W. *White Ethics and Black Power: The Emergence of the West Side Organization*. Chicago, 1969.

HARRIS, JANET and JULIUS W. HOBSON. *Black Pride: A People's Struggle*. New York, 1969.

HOLLOWAY, HARRY. *The Politics of the Southern Negro: From Exclusion to Big City Organization*. New York, 1969.

KEECH, WILLIAM R. *The Impact of Negro Voting: The Role of the Vote in the Quest for Equality*. Chicago, 1968.

LADD, E. C., JR. *Negro Political Leadership in the South*. New York, 1969.

LESTER, JULIUS. *Revolutionary Notes*. New York, 1969.
———. *Search for the New Land*. New York, 1969.

MCKISSICK, FLOYD. *Three-fifths of a Man*. New York, 1969.

MARINE, GENE. *The Black Panthers*. New York, 1969.

PINKNEY, ALPHONSO. *Black Americans*. Englewood Cliffs, N.J., 1969.

SCHEER, ROBERT (ed.). *Eldridge Cleaver: Post-Prison Writings and Speeches*. New York, 1969.

SCOTT, BENJAMIN. *The Coming of the Black Man*. Boston, 1969.

SCOTT, ROBERT L., and WAYNE BROCKRIEDE (eds.). *The Rhetoric of Black Power*. New York, 1969.

SLEEPER, C. FREEMAN. *Black Power and Christian Responsibility*. Nashville, 1969.

SULLIVAN, LEON H. *Build, Brother, Build*. Philadelphia, 1969.

TUCKER, STERLING. *Black Reflections on White Power*. Grand Rapids, 1969.

WAGSTAFF, THOMAS (comp.). *Black Power: The Radical Response to White America*. Beverly Hills, 1969.

WALTON, HANES, JR. *The Negro in Third-Party Politics*. Philadelphia, 1969.

Social Issues

BLOCH, HERMAN D. *The Circle of Discrimination: An Economic and Social Study of the Black Man in New York*. New York, 1969.

CARNEY, FRANK J., et al. *Action on the Streets: A Handbook for Inner City Youth Work*. New York, 1969.

CARSON, JOSEPHINE. *Silent Voices: The Southern Negro Woman Today*. New York, 1969.

GELL, FRANK. *The Black Badge: Confessions of a Caseworker*. New York, 1969.

HARE, A. PAUL, and HERBERT H. BLUMBERG (eds.). *Nonviolent Direct Action: American Cases—Social Psychological Analyses*. Washington, 1968.

HENDIN, HERBERT. *Black Suicide*. New York, 1969.

JONES, LEROI. *Home: Social Essays*. London, 1968.

LEGGETT, JOHN C. *Class, Race and Labor: Working Class Consciousness in Detroit*. New York, 1968.

MAYS, BENJAMIN E. *Disturbed About Man*. Richmond, Va., 1969.

THURMAN, HOWARD. *The Centering Moment*. New York, 1969.

WATTERS, PAT. *The South and the Nation*. New York, 1969.

Education

BERUBE, MAURICE R., and MARILYN GITTELL (eds.). *Confrontation at Ocean Hill-Brownsville*. New York, 1969.

COGAN, LEE. *Negroes for Medicine*. Baltimore, 1968.

DECKER, SUNNY. *An Empty Spoon*. New York, 1969.

FUCHS, ESTELLE. *Teachers Talk: Views from Inside City Schools*. New York, 1969.

GRANT, JOANNE. *Confrontation on Campus: The Columbia Pattern for the New Protest*. New York, 1969.

GREENBERG, POLLY. *The Devil Has Slippery Shoes*. New York, 1969.

Harvard Educational Review EDITORIAL BOARD. *Equal Educational Opportunity*. Cambridge, 1969.

HILL, ROSCOE, and MALCOLM FEELEY (eds.). *Affirmative School Integration: Efforts to Overcome De facto Segregation in Urban Schools*. Beverly Hills, 1968.

LARSON, RICHARD, and JAMES OLSON. *I Have a Kind of Fear*. Chicago, 1969.

MAYER, MARTIN. *The Teachers Strike: New York, 1968.* New York, 1969.

ORFIELD, GARY. *The Reconstruction of Southern Education.* New York, 1969.

ROBINSON, ARMSTEAD L., CRAIG C. FOSTER, and DONALD H. OGILVIE (eds.). *Black Studies in the University.* New Haven, 1969.

WISE, ARTHUR E. *Rich Schools, Poor Schools: The Promise of Equal Educational Opportunity.* Chicago, 1968.

Race and Race Relations

BROWN, DOUGLAS. *Against the World: Attitudes of White South Africa.* Garden City, N. Y., 1968.

CANTY, DONALD. *A Single Society: Alternatives to Urban Apartheid.* New York, 1969.

CHICAGO THEOLOGICAL SEMINARY STUDENTS. *Racism and White Christians.* Chicago, 1968.

DALFIUME, RICHARD M. *Desegregation of the U. S. Armed Forces.* Columbia, Mo., 1969.

FRYE, WILLIAM R. *In Whitest Africa: The Dynamics of Apartheid.* Englewood Cliffs, N. J., 1968.

GLOCK, CHARLES Y., and ELEEN SELIGMAN (eds.). *Prejudice U.S.A.* New York, 1969.

GREVIOUS, SAUNDRAH C. *Teaching Children and Adults to Understand Human and Race Relations.* Minneapolis, 1968.

HALSEL, GRACE. *Soul Sister.* New York, 1969.

HELPER, ROSE. *Racial Policies and Practices of Real Estate Brokers.* Minneapolis, 1969.

PATTERSON, SHEILA. *Immigration and Race Relations in Britain 1960-1967.* New York, 1969.

ROSE, PETER I. *The Subject Is Race: Traditional Ideologies and the Teaching of Race Relations.* New York, 1968.

TEAGUE, BOB. *Letters to a Black Boy.* New York, 1968.

VAN DEN BERGE, PIERRE LOUIS. *Race and Racism: A Comparative Perspective.* New York, 1969.

YOUNG, WHITNEY M., JR. *Beyond Racism: Building an Open Society.* New York, 1969.

Civil Rights

CARTER, DAN T. *Scottsboro, a Tragedy of the American South.* Baton Rouge, 1969.

COUSENS, FRANCES REISSMAN. *Public Civil Rights Agencies and Fair Employment: Promise vs. Performance.* New York, 1969.

COX, ARCHIBALD. *The Warren Court: Constitutional Decision as an Instrument of Reform.* Cambridge, Mass., 1968.

HILTON, BRUCE. *The Delta Ministry.* New York, 1969.

HOROWITZ, HAROLD, and K. C. KARST. *Law, Lawyers, and Social Change: Cases and Materials on the Abolition of Slavery, Racial Segregation, and Inequality of Educational Opportunity.* New York, 1969.

NATIONAL ASSOCIATION OF MANUFACTURERS. *Equal Employment Opportunity: Compliance and Affirmative Action.* New York, 1969.

PAUL, ARNOLD M. *The Conservative Crisis and the Rule of Law: Attitudes of Bar and Bench, 1887-1895.* New York, 1960. Reprint London, 1969.

SHAPIRO, FRED. *Whitmore.* Indianapolis, 1969.

U. S. COMMISSION ON CIVIL RIGHTS. *Equal Economic Opportunity for Negroes in Alabama.* Washington, D. C., 1969.

_____. *For All the People . . . By All the People,* Washington, D. C., 1969.

U. S. EQUAL EMPLOYMENT OPPORTUNITY COMMISSION. *Hearings . . . on Discrimination in White Collar Employment.* Washington, D. C., 1968.

WITHERSPOON, JOSEPH PARKER. *Administrative Implementation of Civil Rights.* Austin, Texas, 1968.

Urban Life and Issues

ACADEMY OF POLITICAL SCIENCE, COLUMBIA UNIVERSITY. *Urban Riots: Violence and Social Change.* New York, 1968.

CONOT, ROBERT. *Rivers of Blood, Years of Darkness: The Unforgettable Classic Account of the Watts Riot.* New York, 1968.

DALY, CHARLES U. (ed.). *The Media and the Cities.* Chicago, 1968.

ETZKOWITZ, HENRY, and GERALD M. SCHAFLAUDER. *Ghetto Crisis: Riots or Reconciliation.* Boston, 1969.

HANNERZ, ULF. *Soul Side: Inquiries into Ghetto Culture and Community.* New York, 1969.

HEARD, NATHAN C. *Howard Street.* New York, 1968.

*HOLLAND, JOHN. *The Way It Is.* New York, 1969.

HOWELL, LEON. *Freedom City.* Richmond, Va., 1969.

*JOSEPH, STEPHEN M. *The Me Nobody Knows: Children's Voices from the Ghetto.* New York, 1969.

JUSTICE, BLAIR. *Violence in the City.* Fort Worth, 1969.

MASOTTI, LOUIS H., and JEROME R. CORSI. *Shoot-out in Cleveland, Black Militants and the Police: July 23, 1968.* New York, 1969.

LEINWAND, GERALD (ed.). *The Negro in the City.* New York, 1968.

LIEBOW, ELLIOT. *Tally's Corner.* Boston, 1968.

McCORD, WILLIAM, et al. *Life Styles in the Black Ghetto.* New York, 1969.

*MENDOZA, GEORGE. *The World from My Window.* New York, 1969.

ODIORNE, GEORGE S. *Green Power: The Corporation and the Urban Crisis.* New York, 1969.

OPPENHEIMER, MARTIN. *The Urban Guerilla.* Chicago, 1969.

SCHULZ, DAVID A. *Coming Up Black: Patterns of Ghetto Socialization.* Englewood Cliffs, N. J., 1969.

SUTTLES, GERALD. *The Social Order of the Slum.* Chicago, 1968.

URBAN AMERICA, INC., and the URBAN COALITION. *One Year Later.* New York, 1969.

*VOGEL, RAY. *The Other City.* New York, 1969.

Economic and Labor Issues

BLOOD, ROBERT O., JR. *Northern Breakthrough*. Belmont, Calif., 1968.

CROSS, THEODORE L. *Black Capitalism: Strategy for Business in the Ghetto*. New York, 1969.

COLES, ROBERT, and AL CLAYTON. *Still Hungry in America*. New York, 1969.

FAGER, CHARLES. *Uncertain Resurrection: The Poor People's Washington Campaign*. Grand Rapids, Mich., 1969.

GIBSON, D. PARKE. *The $30 Billion Negro*. London, England, 1969.

HADDAD, WILLIAM F., and DOUGLAS G. PUGH (eds.). *Black Economic Development*. Englewood Cliffs, N. J., 1969.

HOLLAND, JEROME H. *Black Opportunity*. New York, 1969.

KING, CARL B., and H. W. RISHER. *The Negro in the Petroleum Industry*. Philadelphia, 1969.

METROPOLITAN APPLIED RESEARCH CENTER. *A Relevant War Against Poverty: A Study of Community Action Programs and Observable Social Change*. New York, 1968.

MURRAY, JOAN. *The News*. New York, 1968.

WEAVER, R. C. *Negro Labor: A National Problem*. Port Washington, N. Y., 1969.

Literary History, Criticism, and Anthologies

ABRAMSON, DORIS E. *Negro Playwrights in the American Theatre 1925-1959*. New York, 1969.

COOK, MERCER, and STEPHEN E. HENDERSON. *The Militant Black Writer in Africa and the United States*. Madison, 1969.

DABBS, JAMES MCBRIDE. *Civil Rights in Recent Southern Fiction*. Atlanta, 1969.

DENT, THOMAS C., RICHARD SCHECHNER, and GILBERT MOSES (eds.). *The Free Southern Theatre by the Free Southern Theatre*. Indianapolis, 1969.

DODDS, B. *Negro Literature for High School Students*. Champaign, Ill., 1968.

GAYLE, ADDISON, JR. (ed.). *Black Expression*. New York, 1969.

HEERMANCE, J. NOEL. *William Wells Brown and Clotelle*. New Haven, 1969.

JAHN, JANHEINZ. *Neo-African Literature: A History of Black Writing*. New York, 1969.

KEARNS, FRANCIS E. (ed.). *The Black Experience: An Anthology of American Literature for the 1970's*. New York, 1969.

MCCALL, DAN. *The Example of Richard Wright*. New York, 1969.

MAJOR, CLARENCE. *The New Black Poetry*. New York, 1969.

MARGOLIES, EDWARD. *The Art of Richard Wright*. Carbondale, Ill., 1969.

RANDALL, DUDLEY. *Black Poetry: A Supplement to Anthologies Which Exclude Black Poets*. Detroit, 1969.

ROBINSON, WILLIAM H. (ed.). *Early Black American Poets*. Dubuque, Iowa, 1969.

SCOTT, NATHAN A., JR. *Negative Capability: Studies in the New Literature and the Religious Situation*. New Haven, 1969.

TURNER, DARWIN T. (ed.). *Black American Literature: Essays*. Columbus, 1969.

*LESTER, JULIUS. *Black Folktales*. New York, 1969.

LEWIS, SAMELLA S., and RUTH G. WADDY (eds.). *Black Artists on Art*. Los Angeles, 1969.

*MCGOVERN, ANN. *Black Is Beautiful*. New York, 1969.

OLIVER, PAUL. *The Story of the Blues*. Philadelphia, 1969.

OSOFSKY, GILBERT (ed.). *Puttin' on Ole Massa*. New York, 1969.

RAMSEY, FREDERIC, JR. *Been Here and Gone*. New Brunswick, N. J.

Poetry and Drama

BROOKS, GWENDOLYN. *Riot*. Chicago, 1969.

BULLINS, ED. *Five Plays*. Indianapolis, 1969.

CLIFTON, LUCILLE. *Good Times: Poems*. New York, 1969.

ECKELS, JON. *Home Is Where the Soul Is*. Detroit, 1969.

ELDER, LONNE III. *Ceremonies in Dark Old Men*. New York, 1969.

GORDONE, CHARLES. *No Place to Be Somebody*. Indianapolis, 1969.

JOANS, TED. *Black Pow-Wow*. New York, 1969.

JONES, LEROI. *Black Magic Poetry, 1961-1967*. Indianapolis, 1969.

_____. *Four Black Revolutionary Plays*. Indianapolis. 1969.

JORDAN, JUNE. *Who Look at Me*. New York, 1969.

LEE, DON L. *Black Pride*. Detroit, 1968.

_____. *Don't Cry, Scream*. Detroit, 1969.

RANDALL, DUDLEY. *Cities Burning*. Chicago, 1968.

TUOTTI, JOSEPH DOLAN. *Big Time Buck White*. New York, 1969.

Fiction

BECKHAM, BARRY. *My Main Mother*. New York, 1969.

BLUE, ROSE, *A Quiet Place*. New York, 1969.

CORLEY, EDWIN. *Siege*. New York, 1969.

CRUZ, VICTOR HERNANDEZ. *Snaps*. New York. 1969.

FORD, JESSE HILL. *The Feast of Saint Barnabas*. Boston, 1969

GRAVES, WALLACE. *Trixie*. New York, 1969.

GREENLEE, SAM. *The Spook Who Sat by the Door*. London, 1969.

HICKS, JOHN. *The Long Whip*. New York, 1969.

HIMES, CHESTER B. *Blind Man with a Pistol*. New York, 1969.

LEE, AUDREY. *The Clarion People*. New York, 1968.

——————. *The Workers*. New York, 1969.

MacINNES, COLIN. *The London Novels of Colin Mac-Innes*. New York, 1969.

McPHERSON, JAMES ALAN. *Hue and Cry*. Boston, 1969.

MAHONEY, WILLIAM. *Black Jacob*. New York, 1969.

MAJOR, CLARENCE. *All-Night Visitors*. New York, 1969.

MANO, D. KEITH. *Horn*. Boston, 1969.

PHARR, ROBERT DEANE. *The Book of Numbers*. New York, 1969.

PHILIPS, JUDSON. *Hot Summer Killing*. New York, 1969.

REED, ISHMAEL. *Yellow Back Radio Broke-Down*. New York.

VAN DYKE, HENRY. *Blood of Strawberries*. New York, 1969.

VAN PEEPLES, MELVIN. *A Bear for the F.B.I.* New York, 1969.

WILLIAMS, JOHN A. *Sons of Darkness, Sons of Light*. Boston, 1969.

WRIGHT, SARAH E. *This Child's Gonna Live*. New York, 1969.

Black Heritage

*BOND, JEAN CAREY. *Brown Is a Beautiful Color*. New York, 1969.

BONTEMPS, ARNA (comp.). *Great Slave Narratives*. Boston, 1969.

BREWER, J. MASON. *American Negro Folklore*. Chicago, 1968.

CALLAHAN, ED, and JIM HARWOOD (eds.). *Soul Food*. Los Angeles, 1969.

GASKINS, RUTH L. *A Good Heart and a Light Hand*. Alexandria, Va., 1969.

GRIFFIN, HATTIE RHINEHART. *Soul Food Cookbook*. New York, 1969.

HAVERLY, J. *Negro Minstrels: A Complete Guide to Negro Minstrels*. Ridgewood, N. J., 1969.

HEARON, ETHEL B. (ed.). *Cooking with Soul*. Milwaukee, 1968.

JONES, C. E., JR. *Negro Myths from the Georgia Coast*. Detroit, 1969.

LEADBITTER, MIKE, and NEIL SLAVEN. *Blues Records, January 1943 to December 1966*. London, 1968.

Black Press

Black owned and operated newspapers in the United States are illustrative of black capitalism at work and point to its continuing growth over the past one hundred and forty-two years. This list can serve as a research tool for those interested in pursuing studies in black history or in contemporary race relations.

Alabama

BIRMINGHAM WORLD
Emory O. Jackson
312 17th Street North
Birmingham, 35203

MOBILE BEACON
Frank P. Thomas
415 S. Cedar Street
P.O. Box 1407
Mobile, 36603

Arizona

ARIZONA TRIBUNE
Edward Banks
2137 East Broadway Road
Phoenix, 85040

California

THE POST
Edith M. Austin
2999 Shattuch Avenue
Berkeley, 94705

STAR NEWS—THE VOICE
Rowland K. Reblee
Star News Publishing Company
Chula Vista, 92010

LOS ANGELES SENTINEL
Leon Washington
1112 E. 43rd Street
Los Angeles, 90011

CALIFORNIA VOICE
E. A. Daly
814 27th Street
Oakland, 94607

SACRAMENTO OBSERVER
William H. Lee
Box 209
Sacramento, 95801

SAN DIEGO LIGHTHOUSE
N. M. Young
2652 Imperial Avenue
San Diego, 92102

SAN FRANCISCO SUN REPORTER
Carlton V. Goodlett
1599 Post Street
San Francisco, 94109

Colorado

DENVER BLADE
Joe Brown
3224 Downing Street
Denver, 80205

Florida

FORT PIERCE CHRONICLE
C. E. Bolen
1527 Avenue D
Fort Pierce, 33450

FLORIDA STAR
E. O. Simpson
2323 Moncrief Road
Jacksonville, 32209

JACKSONVILLE ADVOCATE
M. J. Greens
7326 Richardson Road
Jacksonville, 32209

MIAMI TIMES
Garth Reeves
6740 N.W. 15th Street
Miami, 33126

FLORIDA SENTINEL BULLETIN
G. Blytha Andrews
2207 N. 21st Street
Tampa, 33605

NEWS REPORTER
James Jackson
1610 N. Howard Avenue
Tampa, 33607

PHOTO NEWS
A. A. Williams
2108½ N. Tamarind Avenue
West Palm Beach, 33407

Georgia

SOUTHWEST GEORGIAN
A. C. Searless
517 Gordon Avenue
Albany, 31701

ATLANTA DAILY WORLD
C. A. Scott
210 Auburn Avenue, N.E.
Atlanta, 30303

ATLANTA INQUIRER
Earnest Pharr
787 Parsons Street, S.W.
Atlanta, 30314

COLUMBUS NEWS
Vernon Mitchell
500 9th Street
Columbus, 31901

Illinois

CHICAGO CRUSADER
Balm E. Leavell, Jr.
7121 E. 45th Street
Chicago, 60637

CHICAGO DEFENDER
John Sengstacks
2400 So. Michigan Avenue
Chicago, 60616

MUHAMMAD SPEAKS
Herbert Muhammad
634 East 79th Street
Chicago, 60619

NEW CRUSADER
Balm L. Leavell, Jr.
6429 S. Park Avenue
Chicago, 60637

EAST ST. LOUIS CRUSADER
John Kirkpatrick
1600 Missouri Avenue
East St. Louis, 62205

THE MONITOR
Clyde C. Jordan
413 St. Louis Avenue
East St. Louis, 62201

VOICE
Dr. L. H. Holman
168 S. Chicago Street
Joliet, 60436

ROCKFORD CRUSADER
Joseph S. Saunders
821 S. Winnebago
Rockford, 61103

Indiana

INDIANA HERALD
Opal Tandy
225 W. 30th Street
Indianapolis, 46208

INDIANAPOLIS RECORDER
Marcus Stewart
518 Indiana Avenue
Indianapolis, 46202

Iowa

IOWA BYSTANDER
James Morris
223½ E. Locust Street
Des Moines, 50309

Kansas

WICHITA ENLIGHTENER
Edwin T. Saxon
2226 Mossman
Wichita, 67214

Kentucky

LOUISVILLE DEFENDER
Frank L. Stanley
1503 S.W. Broadway
Louisville, 40203

Louisiana

NEWS LEADER
J. L. Land
156 S. 15th Street
Baton Rouge, 70802

NEWS LEADER
Samuel Douglas
P.O. Box 1217
Monroe, 71201

LOUISIANA WEEKLY
C.C. Dajois, Jr.
640 S. Rampart Street
New Orleans, 70113

SHREVEPORT SUN
W. L. Collins
1030 Texas Avenue
Shreveport, 71101

Maryland

AFRO-AMERICAN
John and Howard Murphy
628 N. Eutaw
Baltimore, 21201

Massachusetts

BOSTON ROXBURY
   CITY NEWS
Nelson Noble
719 Boylston
Boston, 02116

BAY STATE BANNER
Melvin Miller
25 Ruggles Street
Roxbury, 02119

Michigan

MICHIGAN CHRONICLE
Longworth Quinn
479 Ledyard Street
Detroit, 48201

JACKSON BLAZER
Rollins Greens
479 Ledyard Street
Jackson, 49203

Minnesota

MINNEAPOLIS SPOKESMAN
Cecil Newman
2722 4th Street
Minneapolis, 55422

TWIN CITIES COURIER
Frank C. Kant
322 W. 48th Street
Minneapolis, 55409

Mississippi

JACKSON ADVOCATE
Percy Greens
406½ N. Farish
Jackson, 39202

MISSISSIPPI FREE PRESS
Charles Butt
538½ N. Farish Street
Jackson, 39202

Missouri

KANSAS CITY CALL
Lucille Bluford
1715 E. 18th Street
Kansas City, 64108

PEOPLE'S GUIDE
J. Vaughn Chapman
5927 Easton Avenue
St. Louis, 63112

ST. LOUIS AMERICAN
N. A. Sweets
3608 Cozens Avenue
St. Louis, 63113

ST. LOUIS ARGUS
Frank Mitchell
4595 Easton Avenue
St. Louis, 63113

ST. LOUIS SENTINEL
Howard B. Woods
3000 Easton Avenue
St. Louis, 63106

Nebraska

OMAHA STAR
Mildred Brown
2216 N. 24th Street
Omaha, 68110

Nevada

LAS VEGAS VOICE
Charles I. West
902 W. Bonanza
Las Vegas, 89106

New Jersey

NEW JERSEY HERALD NEWS
Oliver Brown
188 Belmont Avenue
Newark, 07108

New York

WESTCHESTER COUNTY
    PRESS
Algar Adams
61 Pinecrest Drive
Hastings-on-Hudson, 10706

QUEENS VOICE
Kenneth Drew
170-11 Hilside Avenue
Jamaica, 11432

THE VOICE
Kenneth Drew
171-18 Liberty Avenue
Jamaica, 11433

AMSTERDAM NEWS
Jimmy Hicks
2340 8th Avenue
New York, 10027

North Carolina

CHARLOTTE POST
J. S. Nathaniel Tross
219 North McDowell
Charlotte, 28204

QUEEN CITY GAZETTE
Bill Johnson
2224 Beatties Ford Road
Charlotte, 28208

CAROLINA TIMES
L. E. Austin
436 East Pettigrew Street
Durham, 27701

THE CAROLINIAN
R. P. Jarvey
518 E. Martin
Raleigh, 27601

WILMINGTON JOURNAL
T. C. Jarvey
412 S. 7th Street
Wilmington, 28401

Ohio

CINCINNATI HERALD
N. B. Porter
313 Opera Place
Cincinnati, 45202

CLEVELAND CALL AND POST
William D. Walker
1949 E. 105th Street
Cleveland, 44106

DAYTON EXPRESS
Joseph S. Saunders
P.O. Box 911
Dayton, 45401

Oklahoma

BLACK DISPATCH
John Dungee
P.O. Box 1254
Oklahoma City, 73101

OKLAHOMA EAGLE
Edwin Goodwin
123 N. Greenwood Avenue
Tulsa, 74120

Pennsylvania

PHILADELPHIA INDEPENDENT
Robert Williams
1708 Lombard
Philadelphia, 19146

PHILADELPHIA TRIBUNE
E. Washington Rhodes
526 S. 16th Street
Philadelphia, 19146

THE NEW PITTSBURGH COURIER
Eleanor Lofton
315 E. Carson
Pittsburgh, 15219

South Carolina

PALMETTO TIMES
E. Cedric Hart
2022 Taylor Street
Columbia, 29204

Tennessee

CHATTANOOGA OBSERVER
W. C. Robinson
124½ 9th Street
Chattanooga, 37403

THE KNOX COUNTY OBSERVER
William J. Robinson
236 New Avenue, S.E.
Knoxville, 37915

TRI-STATE DEFENDER
Whittier Sengstacks
124 Calhoun Avenue East
Memphis, 38103

Texas

IN SEPIA DALLAS
Tony Davis
2700 Grand Avenue
Dallas, 75215

FORT WORTH MIND
R. L. Milton
805 Bryan
Fort Worth, 76104

FORWARD TIMES
Julius Carter
4411 Almeda Road
Houston, 77004

HOUSTON INFORMER
Doris Wesley
2418 Leeland Avenue
Houston, 77003

SAN ANTONIO REGISTER
W. K. Andrews
207 N. Center Street
San Antonio, 78202

Virginia

NORFOLK JOURNAL AND GUIDE
Thomas Young
719 E. Olney Road
Norfolk, 23504

ROANOKE TRIBUNE
F. E. Alexander
312 First Street, N.W.
Roanoke, 24016

Wisconsin

MILWAUKEE STAR
Kenneth Coulter
2334 N. Third Street
Milwaukee, 53212

Greek Social and Professional Organizations

As A GOOD DEAL of attention within Black society has traditionally been focused on Greek letter societies—professional as well as social—the following list of organizations and their memberships is included.

Name	National Officer	Membership (1968)	Founded
Alpha Kappa Alpha Sorority Social sorority	Dr. Larzette G. Hale	45,000	1908
Alpha Kappa Mu National Honor Society Scholastic honor society	Dr. E. K. Williams	10,593	1937
Alpha Phi Alpha Fraternity Social fraternity	Ernest N. Morial	50,000	1906
Chi Delta Mu Fraternity Medical fraternity	Nolan N. Atkinson, M.D.	600	1913
Chi Eta Phi Sorority Nursing sorority	Leota P. Brown	1,200	1932
Delta Sigma Theta Sorority Social sorority	Frankee M. Freeman	50,000	1913
Eta Phi Beta Sorority Business women's sorority	Annette Clardy	——	1942
Iota Phi Lambda Sorority Social sorority	Mrs. Mahala S. Evans	3,000	——
Kappa Alpha Psi Fraternity Social fraternity	William Davenport	31,000	1911
Lambda Kappa Mu Sorority Social sorority	Mrs. Marie G. Leatherman	500	1927
Omega Psi Phi Fraternity Social fraternity	Ellis F. Corbett	35,000	1911
Phi Beta Sigma Fraternity Social fraternity	Dr. Alvin J. McNeil	13,124	1914
Sigma Gamma Rho Sorority Community service sorority	Lorraine Williams	6,000	1922
Tau Gamma Delta Sorority Business and professional women's sorority	Agnes Fischer	325	1948
Zeta Phi Beta Sorority Social sorority	Mildred Bradham	20,000	1920

SECTION IV

Summary of the Civil Rights Act of 1964

ON JULY 2, 1964, President Johnson signed into law the Civil Rights Act of 1964. The House voted for passage of the bill on February 10 by a vote of 290 to 130. The Senate passed a somewhat amended version on June 19, 1964, by a vote of 73 to 27, a year to the day after President Kennedy sent to Congress his special message on civil rights and transmitted his proposed civil rights legislation. The final House vote, accepting the Senate changes, was 289 to 126.

The impact of this law is direct and simple. It says that voting booths, classrooms, federally assisted programs, public parks, hotels, and other places serving the public shall, in fact, be open to all the public on an equal basis.

More specifically, the eleven Titles of the Act contain the following provisions:

Title I—Voting Rights

Title I reinforces the existing authority of the federal government, under the Civil Rights Acts of 1957 and 1960, to guarantee to all citizens the right to vote in federal elections without discrimination. It does this by forbidding the application of literacy and other tests in such a way as to deny Negroes the right to vote.

In some localities voting registrars make it a practice to reject Negro applicants—even those with college degrees—because of trivial, immaterial mistakes on their application forms or literacy tests, while at the same time they permit white applicants to vote even if they make far more serious errors. The new law specifically prohibits such practices. And, to facilitate proof of discrimination in voting cases in the federal courts, the law also establishes a rule of evidence that a person who applies to vote is presumed literate if he has finished six years of school. Of course, local officials remain free to prove that the applicant is, in fact, not literate. The law does not forbid literacy tests; it simply requires that if literacy tests are used, they must be in writing.

The standards for eligibility to vote remain the responsibility of the state. The federal statute neither establishes voting requirements nor controls the state's right to make determinations of eligibility. Basically, all that the new law requires is that state standards be uniformly and fairly applied to all, regardless of their race.

Title I also expedites the hearing of voting rights cases. Long delays in setting a date for hearings of such cases and the lengthy process of appeals have prevented the actual exercise of the right to vote for months, even years. The new law therefore provides that the more important voting right cases, involving a pattern or practice of discrimination, may be tried before a three-judge court, whose decision can be appealed immediately to the Supreme Court. It also requires the prompt handling of all cases.

Title II—Places of Public Accommodation

Title II of the Act establishes the right of all the public, without regard to race or color, to the full and equal use of certain places of business which are open to the public. The following types of businesses are covered:

1. Hotels, motels, and other places offering lodging to transient guests. Only owner-occupied facilities offering not more than five rooms for rent are excepted.

2. Restaurants, lunch counters, soda fountains, and other facilities principally engaged in selling food to be eaten on the premises.

3. Gasoline stations.

4. Theaters, sports arenas, and other public places of exhibition or amusement.

5. Establishments which are either located within or contain a business listed above and are intended to serve the patrons of such business. For example, in the case of a retail store containing a lunch counter, all the facilities of the store, not simply the eating place, are covered. In the same way, all business facilities located within a hotel for use of its guests are required to give non-discriminatory service, as well as the hotel itself.

Title II prohibits any person from denying any person his right to equal service, from intimidating anyone for the purpose of interfering with that right, and from punishing any person for exercising such right. However, it is only a refusal to serve based upon grounds of race, color, religion, or national origin that is prohibited. A proprietor retains his authority to refuse service to persons who are disorderly, for example, or to decline to provide service for other legitimate reasons. And a proprietor may not be criminally prosecuted for violating the title. The only federal criminal remedy against a proprietor is a criminal contempt proceeding for disobedience of a court order.

In case of violation, the victim may sue for a court order to end the discrimination. Primary reliance is placed on state or local laws forbidding discrimination in places of public accommodation, wherever such laws exist. Public accommodation laws of varying scope presently exist in 31 states and in the District of Columbia. Only if, after a reasonable length of time, local remedies prove futile, may the victim of the discrimination bring a federal court case. If there are no state or local laws forbidding discrimination, the federal court is authorized to refer the complaint to the Community Relations Service, the federal mediation agency established by Title X of the Civil Rights Act of 1964, in order to induce voluntary compliance if at all possible.

The Department of Justice is also granted authority to bring a lawsuit under the title, but it may sue only if the discrimination amounts to a "pattern or practice." As in voting right suits under Title I, provisions are made for expediting such actions, including the use of a three-judge court.

In enacting this legislation, Congress has called upon its constitutional authority to regulate interstate commerce, as well as the mandate of the Fourteenth Amendment forbidding the states to deny their citizens the equal protection of the laws. This title does not infringe on private property rights. It does not apply to private facilities or clubs, to private homes or apartments, or, in general to service or professional facilities. Its aim is to end racial discrimination in public accommodations—in short, to help restore the word "public" to its true meaning.

Title III—Public Facilities

It is well established by many court decisions that the Fourteenth Amendment to the Constitution prohibits racial discrimination in all government facilities—public parks, public libraries, and the like, and of course in public schools. Private individuals have brought numerous suits to assert their rights to equal access to such facilities. Many persons, however, are prevented from obtaining their constitutional justice by financial inability to sue, or by fear of reprisal.

Title III meets these problems by empowering the Department of Justice, on receipt of a written complaint, to bring suit to desegregate the public facility in question when the complaint is meritorious, when the complainants are unable to maintain appropriate legal proceedings, and when the suit would materially further the orderly desegregation of public facilities.

Title IV—School Desegregation

Although ten years have passed since segregated public education was declared unconstitutional, more than 90 per cent of the Negro school-age children, in states formerly requiring segregation, still attend segregated schools.

Title IV aids and speeds school desegregation in two ways. First, it provides for financial and technical assistance to schools attempting to carry out desegregation plans.

Second, it authorizes the Attorney General, upon receipt of a written, signed complaint, to sue in federal court to bring about desegregation, if students or the parents involved are unable to bring suit themselves, and if the filing of a lawsuit would further the orderly achievement of desegregation. Before taking action, however, the Attorney General must notify the appropriate school authorities and allow them a reasonable time to act voluntarily to adjust the conditions alleged in the complaint.

The law makes it clear that the federal government is *not* authorized to deal with "racial imbalance" or to establish racial quotas in schools. No federal official or court is empowered by this law to issue any order seeking to achieve racial balance in any school by requiring the transportation of pupils from one school to another or one school district to another.

Title V—Civil Rights Commission

The Civil Rights Commission was established in 1957 to investigate and report practices of racial discrimination affecting voting rights and other constitutional rights.

Title V extends the life of the Commission for another four-year period. It also gives the Commission new and useful authority to serve as a national clearing-house for information about denials of the equal protection of the laws, and to investigate allegations of fraud or discrimination in federal elections. The Commission has no law enforcement powers.

Title VI—Discrimination in Federally-Assisted Programs

This Title assures that public funds, to which taxpayers of all races contribute, will not be spent on a discriminatory basis.

It is clearly inconsistent with our national policy of fair play and justice if any citizen is excluded on racial grounds from programs or activities receiving financial aid from the federal government. The new law would prevent this from happening.

For example, it offers assurance that hospitals financed by federal money will not deny adequate care to Negroes. It prevents such abuses—and they have actually occurred—as denying food surplus supplies to Negroes while giving these benefits to white persons. It assures Negroes the right to participate in programs of higher education financed by federal money. In short, it assures the right to equal treatment in the enjoyment of all federal funds.

It does not affect federal programs of insurance or guaranty, such as Federal Housing Administration or veterans' home mortgage insurance or guaranties. Moreover, any termination of federal assistance affects only the particular program in which a violation occurs, and federal assistance may be terminated as a last resort after all other measures, including attempts to secure voluntary compliance, have failed. Even then termination can occur only under certain conditions and after careful procedures have been followed. Finally, any termination is expressly made subject to congressional scrutiny and judicial review.

Title VII—Equal Employment Opportunity

The right of a competent worker to equal opportunity in employment, regardless of race, sex, religion, or national origin is basic to our democratic system. Nevertheless, discrimination in employment opportunity does exist. Title VII prohibits employers of more than 25 persons, in industries affecting interstate commerce, from discriminating on account of race, color, religion, sex, or national origin in their hiring practices. It also forbids discrimination by employment agencies in job referrals, and by labor unions in their qualifications for membership or participation in training programs. It does not require racial balance or racial quotas in employment. And nothing in the Title denies an employer the right to hire a person based upon his qualifications for the job.

As a matter of practical convenience—to enable employers, employment agencies, and labor unions to bring their procedures into line with the requirements of the new law—the Title does not take effect until one year after the date of its enactment. Employers of fewer than 100 workers and labor organizations with fewer than 100 members are excluded from coverage for an additional year, those with fewer than 75 have a two-year exemption, and those with fewer than 50 employees or members have a third year before the Title becomes applicable to them.

A bi-partisan Equal Employment Opportunity Commission administers the new law. It is empowered to investigate charges of discrimination, and to attempt, through conciliation, to resolve disputes involving such charges. The Commission has no authority to enter orders directing non-discrimination and is limited to seeking voluntary compliance. If its attempts at conciliation fail, the person claiming to be aggrieved may bring a civil court action. The Attorney General is authorized to intervene in such actions. He also may institute an original action when he believes that a pattern or practice of discrimination exists in violation of Title VII. These legal actions could result in injunctions against future violations, orders for reinstatement or, in appropriate cases, the payment of back wages. No criminal penalty is provided for failure by an employer or a union to afford equal employment opportunity.

Existing state and local fair employment laws, which are now on the books in 25 states, remain in effect, and before action under federal law is taken, the state or local agency must be given an opportunity to handle the problem under state or local law.

Title VIII—Registration and Voting Statistics

This Title directs the Secretary of Commerce to conduct a survey and compile registration and voting statistics by race, color, and national origin. It does not require anyone to reveal how he voted.

The survey, made only in those geographic areas specified by the Civil Rights Commission, is designed to help bring to light all instances of discriminatory voting practices within the United States.

Title IX—Intervention and Procedure After Removal in Civil Rights Cases

The first section of this Title is a technical provision amending existing law to provide for appeals when efforts to remove civil rights cases from state to federal courts are denied.

The second section authorizes the Attorney General to intervene in privately-instituted cases involving the denial of equal protection of the laws because of race, color, religion or national origin.

Title X—Community Relations Service

This Title establishes a federal agency, as a part of the Department of Commerce, which is authorized to assist local communities in voluntarily resolving disputes and difficulties relating to racial problems. It may offer its services either upon its own motion or upon the request of an appropriate state or local official or other interested person. The Service also handles disputes over public accommodations which are referred to it by district courts under Title II of the Act. Mr. LeRoy Collins, the former governnor of Florida, was appointed director of the Community Relations Service.

Title XI—Jury Trial and Miscellaneous

The final Title of the bill makes various provisions concerning criminal contempt proceedings which may be brought against persons who violate court orders issued under Titles II through VII of the Act. Upon demand the accused may have a trial by jury. The penalty may not exceed $1,000 or six months imprisonment. The Title also provides that a person may not be placed in double jeopardy by prosecution for both criminal contempt and a specific federal crime based upon the same deed or omission arising under the 1964 Act.

As former President Johnson stated, the purpose of the new law is not to punish. "Its purpose is not to divide, but to end divisions—divisions which have lasted all too long. Its purpose is national, not regional. Its purpose is to promote a more abiding commitment to freedom, and more constant pursuit of justice, and a deeper respect for human dignity.

"We will achieve these goals because most Americans are law-abiding citizens who want to do what is right. That is why the Civil Rights Act relies first on voluntary compliance, then on the efforts of local communities and states to secure the rights of citizens. It provides for the national authority to step in only when others cannot or will not do the job.

"This Civil Rights Act is a challenge to all of us to go to work in our communities and our states, in our homes and in our hearts, to eliminate the last vestiges of injustice in our beloved America."

Public Accommodations Suits Filed by the United States for Fiscal Years 1965 – 1970

State	Total	1965	1966	1967	1968	1969	1970
Arkansas	1	0	0	0	1	0	0
Alabama	12	2	3	1	0	5	1
Connecticut	1	0	0	0	0	0	1
Florida	6	1	0	3	0	2	0
Georgia	8	2	0	3	0	3	0
Louisiana	31	6	5	4	3	12	1
Maryland	3	0	0	1	1	1	0
Mississippi	23	1	9	12	0	1	0
North Carolina	29	0	1	10	8	7	3
South Carolina	19	1	1	9	4	4	0
Tennessee	3	1	0	0	2	0	0
Texas	8	0	1	5	2	3	2
Virginia	13	0	1	5	2	3	2
Totals	158	14	21	48	24	43	8

Cases Filed by the United States Alleging Discrimination in Housing Practices in Violation of Title VIII of the Civil Rights Act of 1968

United States v. *Knippers and Day Real Estate Co. et al,* Baton Rouge, Louisiana
  (C.A. No. 68–123, E.D. La.)
  Complaint filed: 7/22/68
  Case dismissed: 4/24/69
  Notice of appeal filed: 6/23/69
  Action is against three real estate dealers.

United States v. *Young Men's Christian Association of Columbia, South Carolina*
  (C.A. No. 68-267, D.S.C.) Amended complaint filed: 1/15/69
  The original complaint alleged violation of the public accommodations section of the Civil Rights Act of 1964. The amended complaint added allegations of housing discrimination.

Kennedy Park Homes Association, Inc., and United States v. *City of Lackawanna, New York*
  (C.A. No. Civ.—1968–385, W.D. N.Y.)
  Complaint in intervention filed: 1/17/69
  Action alleges interference, coercion, or intimidation in the exercise of the right to fair housing.

United States v. *The Ontario Owners, Inc.,* Washington, D.C.
  (C.A. No. 142–69, D.C. D.C.)

Complaint filed: 1/17/69
Consent decree: 3/27/69
Action was against a cooperative apartment organization.

United States v. *The Greater Gadsden Housing Authority of Gadsden, Ala., et al*
(C.A. No. 69–36, N.D. Ala.)
Complaint filed: 1/18/69

United States v. *The Housing Authority of the City of Albany, Georgia, et al*
(C.A. No. 1007, M.D. Ga.)
Complaint filed: 1/20/69

United States v. *Anderson County, South Carolina, et al*
(C.A. No. 69–324, D.S.C.)
Complaint filed: 4/4/69
Alleges discrimination in the operation of a home for the elderly indigent.

United States v. *Cannon Mills, Inc.,* Charlotte, North Carolina
(C.A. No. C–65–S–69)
Complaint filed: 4/8/69
This action in part is against the operation of 2,000 company-owned houses.

United States v. *Elaine and Allen Mintzes, d/b/a Castle Realty Co.,* Baltimore, Maryland
(C.A. No. 20698, D. Md.)
Complaint filed: 4/24/69
Order entered: 10/13/69
This action is based on alleged blockbusting.

United States v. *Harry T. Owens, et al, d/b/a "Elmhurst,"* Baltimore, Maryland
(C.A. No. 20900, D. Md.)
Complaint filed: 6/24/69
Alleges discrimination in the sale of lots and the inclusion in each deed of a restrictive covenant forbidding the re-sale of the lots to Negroes.

United States v. *West Peachtree Tenth Corporation,* Atlanta, Georgia
(C.A. No. 12839, N.D. Ga.)
Complaint filed: 6/24/69
Action is against the management which allegedly refuses to rent to Negroes.

United States v. *West Suburban Board of Realtors,* Chicago, Illinois

(C.A. No. 69–C–1460, N.D. Ill.)
Complaint filed: 7/14/69

United States v. *Lakratt Corporation, et al,* New Orleans, Louisiana
(C.A. No. 69–1662, E.D. La.)
Complaint filed: 7/24/69
Consent decree: 8/1/69
Alleges discrimination against the sale of lots to Negroes

United States v. *Tilden Garden Apartments, Inc.,* Washington, D.C.
(C.A. No. 2703–69, D.D.C.)
Complaint filed: 9/24/69
Action alleges discrimination in making apartments available and in the terms, conditions, and privileges of sale or rental at this seven building cooperative.

United States v. *Scott Management Co.,* Suitland and Oxon Hill, Md.
(C.A. No. 21234, D. Md.)
Complaint filed: 9/24/69
Action alleges discrimination in making apartments available and in the terms, conditions and privileges of sale or rental at two developments.

United States v. *Georgia Power Company, Local Union No. 822, Athens, Local Union No. 84, Atlanta, Local Union No. 923, Augusta, Local Union No. 780, Columbus, Local Union No. 896, Macon, Local Union No. 847, Rome, Local Union No. 511, Valdosta, of the International Brotherhood of Electrical Workers,* Atlanta, Ga.
(C.A. No. 12355, N.D. Ga.)
Complaint filed: 1/10/69

United States v. *Owens-Corning Fiberglass Corporation and Glass Bottle Blowers Association of the United States and Canada, Local No. 15,* Anderson, S.C.
(C.A. No. 69–65, D. S.C.)
Complaint filed: 1/17/69

United States v. *The International Union of Operating Engineers, Local Union No. 520; William J. Stuhr, Jr., David A. Gasper, Sr.,* East St. Louis, Ill.

(C.A. No. 69–9, E.D. Ill.)
Complaint filed: 1/17/69

United States v. *The International Brotherhood of Electrical Workers, Local Union No. 309; Robert Camerer, Robert J. Faust,* East St. Louis, Ill.

(C.A. No. 69–10, E.D. Ill.)
Complaint filed: 1/17/69

United States v. *Operative Plasterers and Cement Masons International Association, Local Union No. 90; the Cement Masons Local No. 90 Joint Apprenticeship Committee; Norman Hayes, Dean Turner, Marvin Pennock, Wayne Barber, Jr.,* East St. Louis, Ill.

(C.A. No. 69–11, E.D. Ill.)
Complaint filed: 1/17/69

United States v. *International Longshoremen's Association; South Atlantic and Gulf Coast District, International Longshoremen's Association; and Locals 1367, 1368, and 1372, I.L.A. Brownsville, Texas; Locals 872, 1231, 1271, 1273, 1330, 1331, 1525, and 1581, I.L.A., Houston, Texas; Locals 325, 1306, and 1610, I.L.A., Beaumont, Texas; Locals 307, 329, 851, and 1576, I.L.A., Galveston, Texas; Locals 1224, 1225, 1241, 1245, 1280, 1281, I.L.A., Corpus Christi, Texas; Locals 1723 and 1818, I.L.A., Freeport, Texas; Locals 636, 991, 1405, and 1406, I.L.A., Texas City, Texas; Locals 440, 1029, and 1175, I.L.A., Port Arthur, Texas; Locals 341 and 814, I.L.A., Orange, Texas; Locals 1758 and 1763, I.L.A., Port Lavaca, Texas*

(C.A. No. 69–B–3, S.D. Tex.)
Complaint filed: 1/20/69

United States v. *Cannon Mills Company,* North and South Carolina

(C.A. No. C–65–S–69, M.D. N.C.)
Complaint filed: 4/8/69

United States v. *International Longshoremen's Association; Atlantic Coast District, International Longshoremen's Association; and Locals 829 and 858, I.L.A.,* Baltimore, Maryland

(C.A. No. 20688, D. Md.)
Complaint filed: 4/22/69

United States v. *Gustin-Bacon Division, Certain-Teed Products Corporation; Local 41 of the International Brotherhood of Teamsters, Chauffeurs, Warehousemen, and Helpers of America,* Kansas City, Kansas

(C.A. No. KC–2967, D. Kansas)
Complaint filed: 4/24/69

United States v. *Sheet Metal Workers International Association, Local Union No. 10; the Joint Apprenticeship and Training Committee of the Sheet Metal Contractors Association of Essex and Passaic Counties, New Jersey, and Local No. 10 of the Sheet Metal Workers International Association*

(C.A. No. 487–69, D. N.J.)
Complaint filed: 4/25/69

United States v. *Local 377, International Association of Bridge, Structural and Ornamental Workers; San Francisco Steel, Erection Trade Apprenticeship Committee; Santa Clara Steel Erection Trade,* San Francisco, California

(C.A. No. 51592, N.D. of Calif.)
Complaint filed: 6/24/69

United States v. *Central Motor Lines, Inc., a corporation, and Local Union No. 71, Local Union No. 391, and Local Union No. 710, International Brotherhood of Teamsters, Chauffeurs, Warehousemen, and Helpers of America,* Charlotte, North Carolina

(C.A. No. 2521, W.D. N.C.)
Complaint filed: 8/12/69

United States v. *Lucile B. Keil,* Washington, D.C.
(C.A. No. 2898–69, D.D.C.)
Complaint filed: 10/13/69
Action alleges discrimination at a rooming house, which provides lodging to transient guests and permanent residents. This action was filed also under Title II of the Civil Rights Act of 1964.

United States v. *Charnita, Inc., and Vacation Estates, Inc.*

(C.A. No. 69–409, M.D. Pa.)
Complaint filed: 10/13/69

Action alleges discrimination in the offering of land for sale and in soliciting prospective buyers.

United States v. *Lake Carolina, Inc., et al,* Ladysmith, Virginia

(C.A. No. 432–69–R, E.D. Va.)

Complaint filed: 10/13/69

Action alleges discrimination in the sale of lots and employment opportunities (Title VII of the Civil Rights Act of 1964).

Cases Filed Alleging Housing Discrimination in Violation of Other Federal Statutes

United States v. *Little Rock, Arkansas, Housing Authority*

(C.A. No. LR 68C–239, E.D. Ark.)

Complaint filed: 11/21/68

Consent Order: 12/6/68

The defendants refused to comply with Title VI regulations pertaining to tenant selection and assignment.

Cases Filed Alleging Housing Discrimination in Which the United States Participated as Amicus Curiae in the District Court

Contract Buyers League, et al v. *F&F Investment, et al,* Chicago, Illinois

(C.A. No. 69–C–15, N.D. Ill.)

U.S. became *amicus curiae:* 3/28/69

This action was instituted by private individuals seeking damages for the economic losses that they suffered due to the alleged blockbusting tactics of the various defendants.

Gautreaux v. *Chicago Housing Authority,* Chicago, Illinois

(C.A. No. 66–C–1459, N.D. Ill.)

U.S. became *amicus curiae:* 6/30/69

The district court found discrimination in tenant assignment and site selection.

Cases Alleging Housing Discrimination in Which the United States Participated as Amicus Curiae on Appeal

Jones v. *Alfred H. Mayer Co.*

[392 U.S. 409 (1968)]

The United States Supreme Court in a decision reported that the Civil Rights Act of 1866, 42 U.S.C. 1982, prohibits discrimination in the sale or rental of any dwelling.

Hunter v. *Erickson*

[37 LW 4091 (Jan. 20, 1969]

The United States Supreme Court held in an opinion that an ordinance passed by referendum in Akron, Ohio, was unconstitutional because it purported to make the passage of fair housing ordinances more difficult than the passage of other ordinances.

School Desegregation Cases to Which the United States Is a Party

The headings "Title IV," "Title VI," and "Title IX," are used throughout to refer to the title of the Civil Rights Act of 1964 under which the case was filed. The heading *"amicus curiae"* indicates that the United States participated in the case as *amicus curiae* in the district court.

Alabama

Northern District of Alabama

Title IX:

Brown v. *Board of Education of City of Bessemer*

(C.A. No. 65–366, N.D. Ala.)

Complaint in intervention filed: 6/16/65

Stout v. *Jefferson County Board of Education*

(C.A. No. 65–396, N.D. Ala.)

Complaint in intervention filed: 7/12/65

Boykins v. *Board of Education of City of Fairfield*

(C.A. No. 65–499, N.D. Ala.)

Complaint in intervention filed: 7/30/65

Armstrong v. *Board of Education of City of Birmingham*

(C.A. No. 9678, N.D. Ala.)

Complaint in intervention filed: 4/8/66

Bennett v. *Madison County Board of Education*

(C.A. No. 63–613, N.D. Ala.)

Complaint in intervention filed: 4/12/66

Hereford v. *Board of Education of City of Huntsville*

(C.A. No. 63–109, N.D. Ala.)

Complaint in intervention filed: 4/12/66

Miller v. *Board of Education of City of Gadsden*

(C.A. No. 63–547, N.D. Ala.)

Complaint in intervention filed: 4/12/66

Middle District of Alabama

Title IV:

United States v. *Lowndes County Board of Education*

(C.A. No. 2328–N, M.D. Ala.)

Complaint filed: 1/11/66

Title IX:

Harris v. *Crenshaw County Board of Education*

(C.A. No. 2455–N, M.D. Ala.)

Complaint in intervention filed: 9/12/66

Amicus Curiae:

Carr v. *Montgomery County Board of Education*

(C.A. No. 2072–N, M.D. Ala.)

U.S. became *amicus curiae* and party: 5/18/64

Harris v. *Bullock County Board of Education*

(C.A. No. 2073–N, M.D. Ala.)

U.S. became *amicus curiae* and party: 5/18/64

Southern District of Alabama

Title IV:

United States v. *Wilcox County Board of Education*

(C.A. No. 3934–65, S.D. Ala.)

Complaint filed: 11/22/65

United States v. *Hale County Board of Education*

(C.A. No. 3980–66, S.D. Ala.)

Complaint filed: 2/7/66

United States v. *Perry County Board of Education*

(C.A. No. 4222–66, S.D. Ala.)

Complaint filed: 8/16/66

United States v. *Choctaw County Board of Education*

(C.A. No. 4246–66, S.D. Ala.)

Complaint filed: 8/31/66

Title IX:

Davis v. *Board of School Commissioners of Mobile County*

(C.A. No. 30003–63, S.D. Ala.)

Complaint in intervention filed: 6/14/67

Statewide

Lee v. *Macon County Board of Education* (statewide suit involving 99 school systems and three judicial districts)

This case was originally filed to desegregate the public schools of Macon County. In 1964, the Governor of Alabama, the State Superintendent of Education, and the State Board of Education were named as party defendants and a three-judge court was convened to hear the case. On July 13, 1964, the court enjoined the defendants from interfering with the elimination of racial discrimination in any school district in Alabama. On March 22, 1967, the court issued a decree and opinion requiring that desegregation plans be adopted in Alabama's 99 school districts not yet covered by federal court order.

(C.A. No. 604–E, M.D. Ala.)

U.S. became *amicus curiae:* 7/16/63

U.S. granted leave to intervene: 8/31/66

Arkansas

Eastern District of Arkansas

Title IV:

United States v. *Crawfordsville School District No. 2*

(C.A. No. J-66-C-38, E.D. Ark.)

Complaint filed: 7/8/66

Western District of Arkansas

Title IV:

United States v. *Junction City School District No. 75*

(C.A. No. 1095, W.D. Ark.)

Complaint filed: 2/7/66

United States v. *Bright Star School District #6, et al*

(C.A. No. T-69-C-24, W.D. Ark. Miller Div.)
Complaint filed: 7/10/69
United States v. *Hermitage School District No. 12, et al*
(C.A. No. ED-69-C-33, W.D. Ark.)
Complaint filed: 9/22/69
Title IX:
McGhee v. *Nashville Special School District No. 1*

This action was originally filed against Nashville Special School District #1 and Childress School District #39. As a result of the amended complaint in intervention, filed 3/25/66, three additional districts were joined as parties to the suit, Howard County Training School—District #38, Saratoga School District #11, and Mineral Springs School District #3. The Childress and Howard County Training School Districts have since been consolidated and are no longer in existence.

(C.A. No. 692, W.D. Ark.)
Amended complaint in intervention filed: 6/2/67
Amicus Curiae:
Haney v. *County Board of Seiver County*
(Appeal No. 19404, W.D. Ark. Texarkana Div.)
Complaint filed: 10/3/68
U.S. became *amicus curiae* on appeal to the 8th Circuit: 10/2/68

California

Southern District of California
Title IX:
Spangler v. *Pasadena City Board of Education*
(C.A. No. 68–1438–R, S.D. Calif.)
Complaint in intervention filed: 11/21/68

Connecticut

District of Connecticut
Title IV:
United States v. *The Board of Education of Waterbury, Connecticut, et al*
Complaint filed: 10/13/69

Florida

Northern District of Florida
Title IX:
Youngblood v. *Board of Public Instruction of Bay County*
(C.A. No. 572, N.D. Fla.)
Complaint in intervention filed: 8/16/66
Board of Public Instruction, Palm Beach v. *Cohen*
(C.A. No. 68–1014–Civ-Cf, S.D. Fla.)
Complaint filed: 8/26/68
Board of Public Instruction of Taylor County, Florida v. *Cohen*
(C.A. No. 1440, N.D. Fla., Tallahassee Division)
Complaint filed: 10/15/68
Steele v. *Board of Public Instruction of Leon County*
(C.A. No. 854, N.D. Fla.)
United States became *amicus curiae:* 4/30/66
Case Reinstated: 7/69
Middle District of Florida
Zinnerman and United States v. *Columbia County Board of Public Instruction*
(C.A. No. 64–264, M.D. Fla., Jacksonville)
Complaint filed: 6/12/69
Title IX:
Blalock v. *Board of Public Instruction of Lee County*
(C.A. No. 64–168–Civ. T, M.D. Fla.)
Complaint in intervention filed: 8/16/66
Mills v. *Board of Public Instruction of Polk County*
(C.A. No. 63–150–Civ. T, M.D. Fla.)
Complaint in intervention filed: 3/1/67

Georgia

Middle District of Georgia
Title IV:
United States v. *Board of Education of Ben Hill County*

(C.A. No. 642, M.D. Ga.)
Complaint filed: 4/7/67
United States v. *Board of Education of Decatur County*
(C.A. No. 1800, M.D. Ga.)
Complaint filed: 5/29/67
United States v. *Board of Education of Webster County*
(C.A. No. 646, M.D. Ga.)
Complaint filed: 5/29/67
United States v. *Board of Education of Baldwin County*
(C.A. No. 2329, M.D. Ga.)
Complaint filed: 2/14/68
United States v. *Board of Education of Crisp County*
(C.A. No. 663, M.D. Ga.)
Complaint filed: 2/14/68
United States v. *Board of Education of Lowndes County*
(C.A. No. 785, M.D. Ga.)
Complaint filed: 7/11/68
Title VI:
United States v. *Board of Education of Talbot County*
(C.A. No. 1372, M.D. Ga.)
Complaint filed: 9/8/69
United States v. *Board of Education of Clinch County*
(C.A. No. 821, M.D. Ga.)
Complaint filed: 9/3/69
Southern District of Georgia
Title IV:
United States v. *Board of Education of Johnson County*
(C.A. No. 696, S.D. Ga.)
Complaint filed: 9/8/67
United States v. *Board of Education of Screven County*
(C.A. No. 2293, S.D. Ga.)
Complaint filed: 2/15/68
United States v. *Board of Education of Bullock County*
(C.A. No. 462, S.D. Ga.)
Complaint filed: 7/11/68

United States v. *Board of Education of Lincoln County*
(C.A. No. 1400, S.D. Ga.)
Complaint filed: 7/11/68
United States v. *Board of Education of Glascock County*
(C.A. No. 1442, S.D. Ga.)
Complaint filed: 1/17/69
Title VI:
United States v. *Grimes, et al*

This case is to be dismissed and joined with *United States* v. *Board of Education of Wheeler County.*

(C.A. No. 723, S.D. Ga.)
Complaint filed: 7/25/69
United States v. *Board of Education of Coffee County*
(C.A. No. 679, S.D. Ga.)
Complaint filed: 9/2/69
United States v. *Board of Education of Dodge County*
(C.A. No. 727, S.D. Ga.)
Complaint filed: 9/3/69
United States v. *Board of Education of Emanuel County*
(C.A. No. 787, S.D. Ga.)
Complaint filed: 9/2/69
United States v. *Board of Education of Wheeler County*
(C.A. No. 729, S.D. Ga.)
Complaint filed: 9/2/69
United States v. *Board of Education of Long County*
(C.A. No. 967, S.D. Ga.)
Complaint filed: 9/3/69
United States v. *Board of Education of Telfair County*
(C.A. No. 726, S.D. Ga.)
Complaint filed: 9/3/69
Title IX:
Stell v. *Savannah—Chatham Board of Education*
(C.A. No. 1316, S.D. Ga.)
Complaint in intervention filed: 11/15/65
United States as Defendant:
Bulloch County Georgia v. *HEW*

(C.A. No. 27121, S.D. Ga.)
Complaint filed: 12/26/68

Northern District of Georgia
Statewide
United States v. *The State of Georgia, et al*
    (C.A. No. 12972, N.D. Ga.)
Complaint filed: 8/1/69
Title VI:
United States v. *Board of Education of Jackson County, et al and the Board of Education of Jefferson City, et al*
    (C.A. No. 1287, N.D. Ga.)
Complaint filed: 9/11/69

Illinois

Northern District of Illinois
Title IV:
United States v. *School District 151 of Cook County*
    (C.A. No. 68–C–755, N.D. Ill.)
Complaint filed: 4/25/68

Eastern District of Illinois
Title IV:
United States v. *School District 189 of St. Clair County*
    (C.A. No. 68–134, E.D. Ill.)
Complaint filed: 9/6/68

Southern District of Illinois
Title IV:
United States v. *School District #12 of Madison County*
    (C.A. No. 4422, S.D. Ill.)
Complaint filed: 7/7/69

Indiana

Southern District of Indiana
Title IV:
United States v. *Board of School Commissioners of Indianapolis*
    (C.A. No. IP–68–C–225, S.D. Ind.)
Complaint filed: 5/31/68

Louisiana

Eastern District of Louisiana
Title IV:
United States v. *St. Bernard Parish School Board*
    (C.A. No. 16323, E.D. La.)
Complaint filed: 2/16/66
United States v. *Plaquemines Parish School Board*
    (C.A. No. 6671–A, E.D. La.)
Complaint filed: 7/21/66
Title IX:
Hall v. *St. Helena Parish School Board*
    (C.A. No. 1068, E.D. La.)
Complaint in intervention filed: 6/27/65

On March 17, 1961, the United States became *amicus curiae* in this case for the purpose of enjoining state anti-integration statutes and the closing of schools.

Jenkins v. *City of Bogalusa School Board (Washington Parish)*
    (C.A. No. 15798, E.D. La.)
Complaint in intervention filed: 8/11/65
Banks v. *St. James Parish School Board*
    (C.A. No. 16173, E.D. La.)
Complaint in intervention filed: 1/11/66
Boyd v. *Pointe Coupee Parish School Board*
    (C.A. No. 3164, E.D. La.)
Complaint in intervention filed: 6/6/66
Charles v. *Ascension Parish School Board*
    (C.A. No. 3257, E.D. La.)
Complaint in intervention filed: 6/6/66
Dunn v. *Livingston Parish School Board*
    (C.A. No. 3197, E.D. La.)
Complaint in intervention filed: 6/7/66
Williams v. *Iberville Parish School Board*
    (C.A. No. 2921, E.D. La.)
Complaint in intervention filed: 6/7/66
Smith v. *St. Tammany Parish School Board*
    (C.A. No. 15463, E.D. La.)
Complaint in intervention filed: 8/1/66
Amicus Curiae:
Donald Thomas, et al v. *West Baton Rouge Parish School Board, et al*
    (C.A. No. 3208, E.D. La.)

United States became *amicus curiae:* 9/11/69

Hamond Harris, Jr., et al v. *St. John the Baptist Parish School Board, et al*
  (C.A. No. 13212, E.D. La.)
  United States became *amicus curiae:* 9/24/69

Western District of Louisiana
Title IV:
United States v. *Lincoln Parish School Board*
  (C.A. No. 12071, W.D. La.)
  Complaint filed: 6/8/66

United States v. *Richland Parish School Board*
  (C.A. No. 12169, W.D. La.)
  Complaint filed: 7/21/66

United States v. *La Salle Parish School Board*
  (C.A. No. 12178, W.D. La.)
  Complaint filed: 7/25/66

United States v. *Bienville Parish School Board*
  (C.A. No. 12177, W.D. La.)
  Complaint filed: 7/26/66

United States v. *Red River Parish School Board*
  (W.D. La., Shreveport Div.)
  Complaint filed: 7/8/69

United States v. *Tensas Parish School Board*
  (W.D. La., Monroe Div.)
  Complaint filed: 7/8/69

United States v. *Grant Parish School Board*
  (C.A. No. 12265, W.D. La.)
  Complaint filed: 8/26/66

United States v. *DeSoto Parish School Board*
  (C.A. No. 12589, W.D. La.)
  Complaint filed: 1/11/67

United States v. *Avoyelles Parish School Board*
  (C.A. No. 12721, W.D. La.)
  Complaint filed: 3/2/67

United States v. *East Carroll Parish School Board*
  (C.A. No. 12722, W.D. La.)
  Complaint filed: 3/2/67

United States v. *Catahoula Parish School Board*
  (C.A. No. 14430, W.D. La.)
  Complaint filed: 2/10/69

United States v. *Morehouse Parish School Board*
  (C.A. No. 14429, W.D. La.)
  Complaint filed: 2/10/69

United States v. *West Carroll Parish School Board*
  (C.A. No. 14428, W.D. La.)
  Complaint filed: 2/10/69

Title IX:
Lemon v. *Bossier Parish School Board*
  (C.A. No. 10687, W.D. La.)
  Complaint in intervention filed: 1/4/65

Amicus Curiae:
Joann Graham, et al v. *Evangeline Parish School Board, et al*
  (C.A. No. 11053, W.D. La.)
  United States became *amicus curiae:* 8/28/69

Gwen Boudreaux, et al v. *St. Mary Parish School Board, et al*
  (C.A. No. 11351, W.D. La.)
  United States became *amicus curiae:* 9/9/68

Monteilh v. *St. Landry Parish School Board, et al*
  (C.A. No. 10912, W.D. La.)
  United States became *amicus curiae:* 9/9/69

Dorothy Thomas, et al v. *St. Martin Parish School Board, et al*
  (C.A. No. 11314, W.D. La.)
  United States became *amicus curiae:* 9/9/69

Jones v. *Caddo Parish School Board*
  (C.A. No. 11055, W.D. La.)
  Complaint in intervention filed: 7/19/65

Valley v. *Rapides Parish School Board*
  (C.A. No. 10946, W.D. La.)
  Complaint in intervention filed: 8/6/65

Smith v. *Concordia Parish School Board*
  (C.A. No. 11577, W.D. La.)
  Complaint in intervention filed: 1/24/66

Banks v. *Claiborne Parish School Board*
  (C.A. No. 11304, W.D. La.)
  Complaint in intervention filed: 2/7/66

Johnson v. *Jackson Parish School Board*
    (C.A. No. 11130, W.D. La.)
    Complaint in intervention filed: 2/7/66
Other:
Cameron Parish Police Jury v. *Udall*
    (C.A. No. 14206–LC, W.D. La.)
    Complaint filed: 10/31/68
    Third-party complaint filed: 1/6/69

This case was originally filed against Secretary of the Interior Udall seeking review of an administrative order terminating federal financial assistance to Cameron Parish, pursuant to the Refuge Revenue Sharing Act, because of non-compliance with Title VI requirements for school desegregation. The United States filed a third-party complaint asking the court to order the desegregation of the public schools in the Parish.

Mississippi

Northern District of Mississippi
    Title IV:
United States v. *Aberdeen Municipal Separate School*
    (C.A. No. 6564, N.D. Miss.)
    Complaint filed: 8/26/65
United States v. *Carroll County School District*
    (C.A. No. 6541, N.D. Miss.)
    Complaint filed: 8/26/65
United States v. *Indianola Municipal Separate School District*
    (C.A. No. 6637, N.D. Miss.)
    Complaint filed: 7/14/66
United States v. *Sunflower County School District*
    (C.A. No. 6637A, N.D. Miss.)
    Complaint filed: 7/14/66
United States v. *Greenwood Municipal Separate School District*
    (C.A. No. 6640, N.D. Miss.)
    Complaint filed: 8/1/66
United States v. *Leflore County School District*
    (C.A. No. 6640A, N.D. Miss.)
    Complaint filed: 8/1/66
United States v. *Calhoun County School District*

    (C.A. No. 6632, N.D. Miss.)
    Complaint filed: 8/12/66
United States v. *Humphreys County School District*
    (C.A. No. 6645, N.D. Miss.)
    Complaint filed: 8/15/66
United States v. *Louisville Municipal Separate School District*
    (C.A. No. 6668, N.D. Miss.)
    Complaint filed: 8/19/66
United States v. *North Tippah Consolidated School District*

On August 5, 1968, the United States filed an amended complaint adding South Tippah Consolidated School District as a party defendant.

    (C.A. No. 6641, N.D. Miss.)
    Complaint filed: 9/2/66
United States v. *Iuka Special Municipal Separate School District*
    (C.A. No. 6673, N.D. Miss.)
    Complaint filed: 9/8/66
United States v. *Corinth Municipal Separate School District*
    (C.A. No. 6680, N.D. Miss.)
    Complaint filed: 10/3/66
United States v. *Montgomery County School District*
    (C.A. No. 6720, N.D. Miss.)
    Complaint filed: 6/7/67
United States v. *Tunica County School District*
    (C.A. No. 6718, N.D. Miss.)
    Complaint filed: 7/5/67
United States v. *Pontotoc County School District*
    (C.A. No. 6735, N.D. Miss.)
    Complaint filed: 9/14/67
United States v. *Coffeeville-Oakland Consolidated School District*
    (C.A. No. WC 6957-K, N.D. Miss.)
    Complaint filed: 7/10/69
Title VI:
United States v. *Nettleton Line Consolidated School District*

(C.A. No. EC 6963-K, N.D. Miss.)
Complaint filed: 9/8/69
Title IX:
Baird v. *Benton County School District*
(C.A. No. 6513, N.D. Miss.)
Complaint in intervention filed: 7/16/65

Southern District of Mississippi
Title IV:
United States v. *North Pike Consolidated School District*
(C.A. No. 3807, S.D. Miss.)
Complaint filed: 8/25/65
United States v. *Natchez Special Municipal Separate School District*
(C.A. No. 1120, S.D. Miss.)
Complaint filed: 9/7/65
United States v. *Lauderdale County School District*
(C.A. No. 1367, S.D. Miss.)
Complaint filed: 8/7/66
United States v. *Amite County School District*
(C.A. No. 3983, S.D. Miss.)
Complaint filed: 8/9/66
United States v. *South Pike Consolidated School District*
(C.A. No. 1096, S.D. Miss.)
Complaint filed: 8/9/66
United States v. *Philadelphia Municipal Separate School District*
(C.A. No. 1368, S.D. Miss.)
Complaint filed: 8/18/66
United States v. *Noxubee County School District*
(C.A. No. 1372, S.D. Miss.)
Complaint filed: 8/26/66
United States v. *Kemper County School District*
(C.A. No. 1373, S.D. Miss.)
Complaint filed: 8/30/66
United States v. *Wilkinson County School District*
(C.A. No. 1160, S.D. Miss.)
Complaint filed: 9/8/66
United States v. *Covington County School District*

(C.A. No. 2148, S.D. Miss.)
Complaint filed: 12/12/66
United States v. *Hinds County School District*
(C.A. No. 4075, S.D. Miss.)
Complaint filed: 1/11/67
United States v. *Neshoba County School District*
(C.A. No. 1396, S.D. Miss.)
Complaint filed: 1/11/67
United States v. *Marion County School District*
(C.A. No. 2178, S.D. Miss.)
Complaint filed: 4/3/67
United States v. *Columbia Municipal Separate School District*
(C.A. No. 2199, S.D. Miss.)
Complaint filed: 6/28/67
United States v. *Lawrence County School District*
(C.A. No. 2216, S.D. Miss.)
Complaint filed: 9/25/67
United States v. *Franklin County School District*
(C.A. No. 4256, S.D. Miss.)
Complaint filed: 2/12/68
United States v. *Lincoln County School District*
(C.A. No. 4294, S.D. Miss.)
Complaint filed: 4/26/68
Title IX:
Singleton v. *Jackson Municipal Separate School District*
(C.A. No. 3379, S.D. Miss.)
Complaint in intervention filed: 6/8/65

The United States intervened in this case on appeal in the United States Court of Appeals for the Fifth Circuit.

Anderson v. *Canton Municipal Separate School District and Madison County School District*
(C.A. No. 3700, S.D. Miss.)
Complaint in intervention filed: 6/12/65
Barnhardt v. *Meridian Separate School District*
(C.A. No. 1300, S.D. Miss.)
Complaint in intervention filed: 6/12/65

Alexander v. *Holmes County School District*
(C.A. No. 3906, S.D. Miss.)
Complaint in intervention filed: 7/19/65
Amicus Curiae:
Hudson v. *Leake County School District*
(C.A. No. 3382, S.D. Miss.)
U.S. became *amicus curiae:* 6/28/65
Mason v. *Biloxi Municipal Separate School District*
(C.A. No. 2696, S.D. Miss.)
U.S. became *amicus curiae*
Blackwell v. *Sharkey-Issaquena County School District and Anguilla Line Consolidated School District*
(C.A. No. 1096, S.D. Miss.)
U.S. became *amicus curiae:* 3/4/66
Closed: 8/19/68
Anthony v. *Marshall County*
(C.A. No. WC 6819, N.D. Miss.)
Complaint filed: 7/19/68
Other:
Lee v. *United States* (Forrest County, Miss.)
(C.A. No. 2034, S.D. Miss.)
Complaint filed: 10/8/65
Counterclaim filed: 12/10/65

This case was originally filed by Forrest County School District to challenge the legality of the school desegregation guidelines of the Department of Health, Education and Welfare. The United States filed a counter-claim asking the court to order the desegregation of Forrest County Public Schools.

United States v. *Farrar* (Noxubee County, Miss.)

The United States filed suit to obtain an injunction against intimidation and harassment of Negroes seeking to desegregate public schools pursuant to federal court order.

(C.A. No. 1432, S.D. Miss.)
Complaint filed: 9/11/67
Court Appointed the United States as Defendant:
David Johnson, et al v. *D.R.O.P. Stone, et al and the United States*
(C.A. No. WC 6945-S, S.D. Miss.)
Complaint filed: 6/2/69
Closed: 8/20/69

North Carolina

Eastern District of North Carolina
Title IV:
United States v. *Northampton County Board of Education*
(C.A. No. 1025, E.D. N.C.)
Complaint filed: 4/26/67
United States v. *Bertie County Board of Education*
(C.A. No. 632, E.D. N.C.)
Complaint filed: 6/16/67
United States v. *Jones County Board of Education*
(C.A. No. 732, E.D. N.C.)
Complaint filed: 6/16/67
United States v. *Halifax County Board of Education*
(C.A. No. 1128, E.D. N.C.)
Complaint filed: 6/16/69
Title IX:
Coppedge v. *Franklin County Board of Education*
(C.A. No. C-1796, E.D. N.C.)
Complaint in intervention filed: 1/11/66
Western District of North Carolina
Title IX:
Singleton v. *Anson County Board of Education*
(C.A. No. 2259, W.D. N.C.)
Complaint in intervention filed: 11/29/67
Title XI:
Reginald Hawkins v. *North Carolina Board of Education, et al*
(C.A. No. C-2067, W.D. N.C.)
Complaint in intervention filed: 1/18/66
Case Reinstated: 7/69

Oklahoma

Northern District of Oklahoma
Title IV:
United States v. *Board of Education of Independent School District No. 1 of Tulsa*

(C.A. No. 68-C-185, N.D. Okla.)
Complaint filed: 7/30/68
Amicus Curiae:
Patsy Bohlander v. *Independent School District of Tulsa No. 1*
(C.A. 346–69, N.D. Okla.)
United States became *amicus curiae:* 8/19/69

South Carolina

District of South Carolina
Title IV:
United States v. *Lexington School District No. 1*
(C.A. No. 66–96, D. S.C.)
Complaint filed: 2/7/66
United States v. *Calhoun School District No. 2*
(C.A. No. 66–598, D. S.C.)
Complaint filed: 8/16/66
United States v. *Orangeburg County School District No. 7* (Elloree)
(C.A. No. 67–628, D. S.C.)
Complaint filed: 8/2/68
United States v. *Allendale County School District*
(C.A. No. 68–698, D. S.C.)
Complaint filed: 8/2/68
United States v. *Anderson County School District*
(C.A. No. 68–699, D. S.C.)
Complaint filed: 8/2/68
United States v. *Dorchester County School District No. 1*
(C.A. No. 68–697, D. S.C.)
Complaint filed: 8/2/68
United States v. *Georgetown County School District*
(C.A. No. 69–43, D. S.C.)
Complaint filed: 1/15/69
United States v. *Hampton County School District No. 1*
(C.A. No. 69–45, D. S.C.)
Complaint filed: 1/15/69

United States v. *Saluda County School District No. 1*
(C.A. No. 69–460, D. S.C.)
Complaint filed: 5/16/69
United States v. *Barnwell County No. 45*
(C.A. No. 69–613, D. S.C.)
Complaint filed: 7/7/69
United States v. *Abbeville County School District No. 60*
(C.A. No. 69–615, D. S.C.)
Complaint filed: 7/8/69
Title IV and Title VI:
United States v. *Chesterfield County School District*
(C.A. No. 69–46, D. S.C.)
Complaint filed: 1/15/69
Title VI:
United States v. *Darlington County School District*
(C.A. No. 68–328, D. S.C.)
Complaint filed: 4/15/68
United States v. *Bamberg County School District No. 2*
(C.A. No. 69–44, D. S.C.)
Complaint filed: 1/15/69
Title IX:
Miller v. *Clarendon County School District No. 2*
(C.A. No. 8752, D. S.C.)
Complaint in intervention filed: 2/7/66

Tennessee

Middle District of Tennessee
Title IX:
Sanders v. *Ellington*

This suit seeks the desegregation of Tennessee's university system.

(C.A. No. 5077, M.D. Tenn.)
Complaint in intervention filed: 7/22/68
Western District of Tennessee
Title IV:
United States v. *Crockett County Board of Education*

(C.A. No. 1663, W.D. Tenn.)
Complaint filed: 6/7/66
United States v. *Dyersburg County Board of Education*
(C.A. No. C-66-241, W.D. Tenn.)
Complaint filed: 8/26/66
United States v. *Haywood County Board of Education and Brownsville City Board of* Education
(C.A. No. C-67-30, W.D. Tenn.)
Complaint filed: 2/3/67
United States v. *Hardeman County Board of Education*
(C.A. No. 1926, W.D. Tenn.)
Complaint filed: 7/8/69
Title IX:
McFerren v. *Fayette County Board of Education*
(C.A. No. C-65-136, W.D. Tenn.)
Complaint in intervention filed: 8/9/65
Fayne v. *Board of Education of Tipton County*
(C.A. No. C-65-274, W.D. Tenn.)
Complaint in intervention filed: 1/11/66
Robinson v. *Shelby County Board of Education*
(C.A. No. 4916, W.D. Tenn.)
Complaint in intervention filed: 5/5/66

Texas

Eastern District of Texas
Title VI:
United States v. *Tatum Independent School District*
(C.A. No. 5044, E.D. Texas)
Complaint filed: 9/10/69
Title IX:
Adams v. *Matthews* (Longview Independent School District)

(C.A. No. 3095, E.D. Tex.)
Complaint in intervention filed: 8/18/65
Southern District of Texas
Title IV:
United States v. *Board of Trustees of Crosby Independent School District*
Complaint filed: 8/15/69
Title IX:
Ross v. *Eckels* (Houston Independent School District)
(C.A. No. 10444, S.D. Tex.)
Complaint in intervention filed: 6/2/67

Virginia

Eastern District of Virginia
Title IV:
United States v. *School Board of Franklin County*
(C.A. No. 7111-N, E.D. Va.)
Complaint filed: 11/29/68
United States v. *School Board of Sussex County*
(C.A. No. 6060-R, E.D. Va.)
Complaint filed: 11/29/68
United States v. *School Board of Southampton County*
(C.A. No. 7133-N, E.D. Va.)
Complaint filed: 12/13/68
United States v. *County School Board of Richmond, Virginia*
(C.A. No. 224-69-R, E.D. Va.)
Complaint filed: 6/6/69
Title IX:
Brewer v. *School Board of City of Norfolk*
(C.A. No. 2214, E.D. Va.)
Complaint in intervention filed: 2/15/66
Corbin v. *School Board of Loudoun County*
(C.A. No. 2737, E.D. Va.)
Complaint in intervention filed: 5/9/67

Civil Rights Legislation

T HE LEGISLATIVE CAMPAIGN for the
right to human dignity and equality continues to be waged on all fronts; black congressmen dedicated to an ethic of positive change
persistently voice their demands in an attempt
to affect not just verbal attitudes, but written law.
The following bills represent a sampling of civil
rights legislation introduced in the House of Representatives in 1969. Attacking the whole gamut
of social problems—including the lack of adequate housing, public health, and employment
opportunities—as well as establishing the need
for widespread recognition of the cultural heritage of minority ethnic groups, they represent
only a portion of the extensive legislative efforts
presently being expended in this vital area.

91st CONGRESS
1st SESSION
H. R. 3338

IN THE HOUSE OF REPRESENTATIVES

JANUARY 14, 1969

Mr. CONYERS (for himself, Mr. ANNUNZIO, Mr. BROWN of California, Mr. BURTON of California, Mrs. CHISHOLM, Mr. CLAY, Mr. EDWARDS of California, Mr. FARBSTEIN, Mr. FRASER, Mr. GILBERT, Mr. GONZALEZ, Mr. HALPERN, Mr. HELSTOSKI, Mr. KASTENMEIER, Mr. LOWENSTEIN, Mr. MATSUNAGA, Mr. MIKVA, Mr. MOORHEAD, Mr. PODELL, Mr. REUSS, Mr. ROSENTHAL, Mr. ROYBAL, Mr. RYAN, Mr. STOKES, and Mr. CHARLES H. WILSON) introduced the following bill; which was referred to the Committee on Education and Labor

---

A BILL

To assure to every American a full opportunity to have adequate employment, housing, and education, free from any discrimination on account of race, color, religion, or national origin, and for other purposes.

1   *Be it enacted by the Senate and House of Representa-*

2   *tives of the United States of America in Congress assembled,*

3   That this Act, divided by title and sections, as in the fol-

4   lowing table of contents, may be cited as the "Full Oppor-

5   tunity Act".

I—O

J. 98–001—A——1

TABLE OF CONTENTS

TITLE I—FULL EMPLOYMENT OPPORTUNITY

TITLE II—COMPREHENSIVE MINIMUM WAGE

TITLE III—EQUAL EMPLOYMENT OPPORTUNITY ENFORCEMENT

TITLE IV—FAMILY ALLOWANCES

TITLE V—ADEQUATE HOUSING

TITLE I—FULL EMPLOYMENT OPPORTUNITY

FINDINGS AND PURPOSE

SEC. 101. (a) The Congress finds that—

(1) unemployment and underemployment among those who are able, willing, and seeking work are major problems for the Nation and are of even greater concern among those who are unable to secure employment or who have ceased seeking employment because of lack of basic education, occupational skills, work experience, or transportation, because of excessively long distances

1   between places of residence and employment, or because

2   of artificial and discriminatory barriers to employment

3   and occupational advancements;

4   (2) the lack of full employment opportunities for

5   all Americans is especially serious in particular areas,

6   communities, and parts of communities, and in those

7   places it is reaching crisis proportions and often contrib-

8   utes, at least in part, to social unrest and civil disorders;

9   and

10   (3) the lack of a full employment economy under-

11   mines the Nation's productivity, prevents the Nation

12   from achieving many of its long-sought goals, and is a

13   great burden for Federal, State, and local governments

14   in providing welfare and other special services.

15   (b) The Congress further finds that there is a great and

16   urgent need for increased public service employment in such

17   fields as health; education; recreation; housing and neigh-

18   borhood improvement; maintenance of streets, parks, and

19   other governmental facilities; rural development; beautifi-

20   cation; conservation; and other fields of human betterment

21   and public improvement. This need for increased public

22   service employment far exceeds the total number of indi-

23   viduals who are unemployed or underemployed for whatever

24   reasons.

25   (c) It is therefore the purpose of this title and the policy

1 of the United States to guarantee meaningful employment
2 opportunities for all Americans to whatever extent the pri-
3 vate economy is unable to do so and to contribute to the
4 national interest by fulfilling unmet needs through the crea-
5 tion of public service employment opportunities.

EMPLOYMENT OPPORTUNITY GRANTS

7 SEC. 102. (a) The Secretary of Labor (hereafter re-
8 ferred to in this title as the "Secretary") shall make grants
9 to Federal, State, and local governmental agencies or to
10 nonprofit organizations to provide employment for up to
11 three million individuals. These grants shall provide funds
12 for wages, employment benefits, and other necessary re-
13 lated expenses, including equipment and supplies.

14 (b) To be eligible for employment provided by grants
15 made under this title an individual must—

16 (1) be at least sixteen years of age;

17 (2) be able to receive and benefit from training
18 and be able to work;

19 (3) be unemployed for at least five weeks; and

20 (4) have an annual income of less than $4,000.

21 (c) Employment created or made available under this
22 title may include services and supporting facilities in ac-
23 tivities which contribute to the improvement of the physical,
24 social, economic, and cultural conditions of the Nation and

1 shall, to the extent possible, be concentrated in those areas

2 of public service employment listed in section 101 (b) of

3 this title.

4 EMPLOYMENT OPPORTUNITIES RESERVED FOR "THE

5 UNEMPLOYABLE"

6 SEC. 103. (a) One third of the employment oppor-

7 tunities to be created through grants made under section

8 102 shall be reserved for individuals whose basic education

9 and employment-related training are so inadequate that

10 they are unqualified for any currently available employment.

11 (b) Grants made to provide employment opportunities

12 for individuals described in subsection (a) shall provide

13 such individuals with income and prepare them for employ-

14 ment opportunities which it is reasonably expected will be

15 available for the indefinite future. Programs assisted by

16 such grants shall include appropriate combinations of on-

17 the-job training, basic education, and employment.

18 REQUIREMENTS FOR GRANTS

19 SEC. 104. A grant may not be made unless an applica-

20 tion therefor has been submitted to the Secretary in accord-

21 ance with such procedures as he shall by regulation prescribe.

22 The following conditions shall be enforced by the Secretary

23 as requirements for applicants receiving and continuing to

24 receive grants under section 102:

25 (1) The wage rates and other conditions of em-

1   ployment shall be appropriate and reasonable in con-

2   sideration of such factors as the type of work, the pro-

3   ficiency of the employee, and the prevailing practice in

4   the area, except that in no case shall the wage rate be

5   less than the minimum wage rate prescribed in section

6   6 of the Fair Labor Standards Act of 1938.

7   (2) The applicant for the grant must demonstrate

8   that the program will result in an increase in employ-

9   ment opportunities without the displacement of existing

10   employment opportunities, and shall not impair existing

11   conditions of employment in the area.

12   (3) The normal hours of work for an employee

13   shall not exceed eight per day or forty per week, except

14   that the Secretary may authorize a longer work schedule

15   if he determines that it is reasonable and necessary.

16   (4) The Secretary shall require programs to have

17   adequate internal administrative controls, accounting pro-

18   cedures, personnel standards and policies, evaluation pro-

19   cedures, and other policies as may be necessary to pro-

20   mote and insure the effective expenditure of funds and

21   the implementation of the purposes of this title.

22   The Secretary may withhold any payment under a grant au-

23   thorized by this title when he determines that the conditions

24   under which such grant was made are not being met.

PRIORITY TO BE GIVEN LOW-INCOME AREAS

SEC. 105. (a) In the approval of grant applications, the Secretary shall give preference to those which provide employment for eligible individuals residing in areas which have a high proportion of low-income families and individuals who have severe problems of unemployment and underemployment. The Secretary shall designate such areas without regard to political boundaries.

(b) In the approval of applications for grants for the improvement or construction of physical facilities, the Secretary shall give preference to applications related to facilities located in areas designated under subsection (a).

OTHER PRIORITIES FOR GRANTS

SEC. 106. In the approval of applications for grants under this title, the Secretary shall give preference to those for grants which will be the most effective in fulfilling the purposes of this title, especially those applications which emphasize the use of grants for—

(1) employment of individuals who have been unemployed for thirteen weeks or longer;

(2) employment of individuals who have an annual income of $2,000 or less; and

(3) the payment of wages.

1   TRAINING FOR INCREASED EMPLOYMENT OPPORTUNITIES

2   SEC. 107. (a) The Secretary shall contract with Fed-

3   eral, State, or local governmental agencies or with nonprofit

4   agencies to provide appropriate training programs for per-

5   sons employed through grants provided under this title to

6   prepare them to obtain regular competitive employment in

7   the future.

8   (b) Training and education provided under this section

9   shall be—

10   (1) in addition to that provided under section 103

11   of this title; and

12   (2) coordinated with the education and training

13   programs provided under the Manpower Development

14   and Training Act of 1962, the Economic Opportunity

15   Act of 1964 and with other relevant programs provided

16   by Federal, State, and local governmental agencies and

17   nonprofit private agencies.

18   AUTHORIZATION OF APPROPRIATIONS

19   SEC. 108. (a) For the purpose of carrying out the pro-

20   visions of this title, there is authorized to be appropriated

21    $16,000,000,000 for the fiscal year beginning July 1, 1969;

22    $14,000,000,000 for the fiscal year beginning July 1, 1970;

J. 98–001–A——2

1 $12,000,000,000 for the fiscal year beginning July 1, 1971;

2 $10,000,000,000 for the fiscal year beginning July 1, 1972;

3 $8,000,000,000 for the fiscal year beginning July 1, 1973;

4 $6,000,000,000 for the fiscal year beginning July 1, 1974;

5 $4,000,000,000 for the fiscal year beginning July 1, 1975;

6 $2,000,000,000 for the fiscal year beginning July 1, 1976;

7 and $100,000,000 for the fiscal year beginning July 1, 1977.

8   (b) Sums appropriated under subsection (a) are au-

9 thorized to remain available until expended, or until June 30,

10 1978, whichever first occurs. Any unappropriated portion of

11 the amount authorized to be appropriated for any fiscal year

12 may be appropriated in any subsequent fiscal year during the

13 period beginning July 1, 1970, and ending June 30, 1978,

14 in addition to the amount otherwise authorized to be appro-

15 priated for such subsequent fiscal year.

16 TITLE II—COMPREHENSIVE MINIMUM WAGE

17 FINDINGS AND PURPOSE

18   SEC. 201. (a) The Congress hereby finds that one

19 out of every three American workers receive a wage rate

20 so low that they and their families are living in a condition

21 of poverty. The Congress further finds that in order to

22 fulfill the promise of the Fair Labor Standards Act of 1938

23 (hereafter referred to in this title as the "Act") to provide

24 "the minimum standard of living necessary for health, effi-

25 ciency, and general well-being of workers", the protections

1   of that Act must be extended to every American working

2   man and woman.

3   (b) It is therefore the purpose of this title to assure

4   to every American working man and woman, without excep-

5   tion, the guarantee of a minimum wage necessary to provide

6   a decent standard of living for himself and his family.

7   INCLUSION OF EVERY AMERICAN WORKER

8   SEC. 202. (a) The basic coverage of the Act is ex-

9   tended—

10   (1) by amending sections 2 (a), 3 (s), 5 (a), 6

11   (a), 7 (a) (1), and 12 (c) of the Act by inserting

12   "affecting commerce or" immediately before "engaged

13   in commerce" each place it appears in such sections;

14   (2) by amending section 3 (s) of the Act by strik-

15   ing out "an enterprise which has employees" and in-

16   serting in lieu thereof "an enterprise which has any

17   employee"; and

18   (3) by eliminating the gross volume of sales tests

19   and other restrictions in section 3 (s) of the Act by

20   striking out in such section all after "produced for

21   commerce by any person" and inserting in lieu thereof

22   a period.

23   (b) Agricultural workers are included under the pro-

24   tection of the Act—

25   (1) by amending section 3 (e) of the Act by strik-

1 ing out all after "employed by an employer" the first

2 place it appears in such section and inserting in lieu

3 thereof a period;

4   (2) by repealing section 3 (u) of the Act;

5   (3) by amending section 6 (a) (4) of the Act by

6 striking out "; or" at the end of such subsection and

7 inserting in lieu thereof a period; and

8   (4) by repealing sections 6 (a) (5) and 6 (c) (3)

9 of the Act.

10   (c) Domestic workers and governmental employees are

11 included under the protection of the Act—

12   (1) by amending section 3 (d) to read as follows:

13 "(d) 'Employer' includes any person acting directly or

14 indirectly as an agent of any employer, and such term in-

15 cludes any person employing individuals performing domestic

16 services, the United States, any State or political subdivision

17 of a State, and any labor organization when acting as an

18 employer and any agent of such labor organization.";

19   (2) by amending section 3 (e) (defining the term

20 "employee"), as amended by subsection (b) (1) of this

21 section, by adding before the period the following: ",

22 except members of the Armed Forces of the United

23 States and the National Guards of the several States";

24   (3) by repealing section 6 (e) of the Act; and

25   (4) by amending section 18 of the Act by striking

26 out "(a)" and subsection (b).

1   (d) The various miscellaneous exemptions from the pro-

2 tection of the Act are eliminated by repealing sections 13 and

3 14 of the Act and renumbering the following sections ac-

4 cordingly.

5    $2 AN HOUR MINIMUM WAGE UNIFORM APPLIED

6   SEC. 203. (a) Section 6(a)(1) of the Act is amended

7 to read as follows:

8   "(1) not less than $2 an hour, except as otherwise

9   provided in this section;".

10   (b) Section 6(b) of the Act is repealed, paragraph (1)

11 of section 6(c) of the Act is amended by striking out "sub-

12 sections (a) and (b)" and inserting "subsection (a)", para-

13 graph (4) of section 6(c) of the Act is amended by striking

14 out "or subsection (b)", and section 7(f) of the Act is

15 amended by striking out "or (b)".

16   (c) Sections 6(c) and 6(d) of the Act are redesig-

17 nated as sections 6(b) and 6(c), respectively.

18 TITLE III—EQUAL EMPLOYMENT OPPORTUNITY

19   ENFORCEMENT

20   FINDINGS AND PURPOSE

21   SEC. 301. (a) The Congress hereby finds that the

22 exclusion from coverage under title VII of the Civil Rights

23 Act of 1964 (relating to equal employment opportunity) of

24 various individuals due to their employment by an agency

25 of government, their personal associations, the number of

1 other individuals employed by their employer, or their status

2 as applicants for employment or union membership, and the

3 inadequate provisions for enforcement of those rights, in-

4 cluding the requirement for individuals to initiate court suits

5 to protect their rights, denies to millions of American work-

6 ing men and women adequate protection of the right to be

7 protected against discrimination in employment due to race,

8 color, religion, sex, or national origin.

9   (b) It is therefore the purpose of this title to provide

10 enforceable guarantees of equal employment opportunity to

11 all Americans regardless of race, color, religion, sex, or

12 national origin to every person in America without exception

13 and to provide for full enforcement of these rights by grant-

14 ing the Equal Employment Opportunity Commission (here-

15 after referred to in this title as "Commission") powers to

16 issue orders requiring those found to be in violation of this

17 Act to cease and desist from such practices and to take

18 affirmative action to correct the effects of these practices,

19 both on the complaint of the individual aggrieved and on the

20 basis of information otherwise available.

21 EXTENDING COVERAGE TO ALL EMPLOYEES, EMPLOYERS,

22 EMPLOYMENT AGENCIES, AND LABOR ORGANIZATIONS

23   SEC. 302. Title VII of the Civil Rights Act of 1964 is

24 amended to include within its coverage all employers, em-

25 ployees (including applicants for employment or for labor

1   union membership), labor unions, and employment agencies

2   by—

3   (1) amending section 701 (b) to read as follows:

4   "(b) The term 'employer' means, the United States

5   or instrumentality thereof, a State or a political subdivision

6   thereof, or a person engaged in an industry affecting com-

7   merce who has one or more employees.";

8   (2) amending section 701 (c) by inserting a period

9   after "such a person" and striking everything following;

10   (3) amending section 701 (e) (2) (C) by striking

11   "twenty-five" and inserting "one";

12   (4) amending section 701 (f) by inserting before

13   the period at the end the following: "or applying for

14   employment"; and

15   (5) repealing section 703 (f) and redesignating

16   subsections (g) through (j) as (f) through (i),

17   respectively.

18   FULL ENFORCEMENT POWERS TO THE EQUAL EMPLOYMENT

19   OPPORTUNITY COMMISSION

20   SEC. 303. (a) The powers of the Commission are ex-

21   panded to include the authority to initiate and require

22   affirmative actions to implement the purposes of this title

23   on a broad scale by repealing section 705 (g) (6) of such

24   title and substituting in lieu thereof the following:

25   "(6) to require under sections 706 and 707 of

1   this title that persons subject to this title to initiate

2   affirmative action to fully implement the purposes of

3   this title so as to completely eliminate unlawful em-

4   ployment practices and their effects;"

5   (b) Title VII of such Act is amended to provide for

6   more effective prosecution of valid allegations of unlawful

7   employment practices, and patterns or practices of such vio-

8   lations, by all persons subject to this title, including the

9   United States Government, by providing that the Commis-

10   sion instead of the Attorney General shall conduct all litiga-

11   tion pursuant to this title by—

12   (1) amending section 705(h) by adding at the

13   end thereof the following: "The Commission shall con-

14   duct all litigation to which the Commission is a party

15   pursuant to this title."

16   (2) amending section 707 of such title by substitut-

17   ing "Commission" for "Attorney General" wherever it

18   appears, by striking subsection (a)(1) and renumbering

19   the following such subsections (a)(2) and (a)(3) as

20   (a)(1) and (a)(2) respectively, by amending subsec-

21   tion (a)(2) (as so redesignated) by striking out "he"

22   and inserting "it", and by amending subsection (b) by

23   striking "in his opinion" and substituting "in its opinion."

24   (c)(1) Section 705 of such title is amended by adding

25   at the end the following new subsection:

1   "(k) There shall be a General Counsel of the Commis-

2   sion who shall be appointed by the President, by and with

3   the advice and consent of the Senate, for a term of four years.

4   The General Counsel shall exercise general supervision over

5   all attorneys employed by the Commission (other than legal

6   assistants to Commission members) and over the officers and

7   employees in any State or regional offices which the Com-

8   mission may establish. He shall have final authority, on

9   behalf of the Commission, in respect of the investigation of

10   charges and issuance of complaints under section 706, and in

11   respect of the prosecution of such complaints before the Com-

12   mission, and shall have such other duties as the Commission

13   shall prescribe or as may be provided by law."

14   (2) Section 5315 of title 5, United States Code, is

15   amended by inserting after paragraph (1) the following

16   new paragraph:

17   "(2) General Counsel of the Equal Employment

18   Opportunity Commission."

19   (d) (1) Section 706 of such title is amended to provide

20   that elimination of valid complaints of unlawful employment

21   practices will be the responsibility of the Commission through

22   the issuance of orders to cease and desist and to take appro-

23   priate affirmative action instead of relying on the filing of

24   court suits by the aggrieved individuals for the protection of

1 their rights, by repealing subsections (a) through (j) and

2 inserting in lieu thereof the following:

3   "SEC. 706. (a) (1) Whenever (A) (i) it is charged in

4 writing under oath by a person claiming to be aggrieved that

5 an employer, employment agency, or labor organization has

6 engaged in an unlawful employment practice, or (ii) a writ-

7 ten charge has been filed by the General Counsel where he

8 has reasonable cause to believe that an employer, employ-

9 ment agency, or labor organization has engaged in an unlaw-

10 ful employment practice, and (B) such charge sets forth the

11 facts upon which it is based, the General Counsel shall fur-

12 nish such employer, employment agency, or labor organiza-

13 tion (hereafter in this section referred to as the 'respondent')

14 with a copy of such charge and shall make an investigation

15 of such charge. Such charge shall not be made public by the

16 General Counsel. In the case of a charge made by an ag-

17 grieved person, the General Counsel shall within one hun-

18 dred and eighty days after the filing of such charge deter-

19 mine whether there is reasonable cause to believe such

20 charge is true and shall notify both the aggrieved person and

21 the respondent of such determination. In the case of any

22 charge filed by the General Counsel, or of a charge filed by

23 an aggrieved person which the General Counsel determines,

24 after such investigation, that there is reasonable cause to be-

25 lieve is true, the General Counsel shall endeavor to eliminate

1   any such alleged unlawful employment practice alleged in

2   such charge by informal methods of conference, conciliation,

3   and persuasion. Nothing said or done during and as a part of

4   such endeavors may be made public by the General Counsel

5   without the written consent of the parties, or used as evidence

6   in a subsequent proceeding. Any officer or employee of the

7   Commission, who shall make public in any manner whatever

8   any information in violation of this paragraph shall be

9   deemed guilty of a misdemeanor and upon conviction thereof

10   shall be fined not more than $1,000 or imprisoned not more

11   than one year.

12   "(2) An aggrieved person may institute a civil action

13   against the respondent named in the charge in the appro-

14   priate United States district court, without regard to the

15   amount in controversy, or in any State or local court of

16   competent jurisdiction if, the General Counsel, within 180

17   days after determining that there is reasonable cause to be-

18   lieve the charge is true under paragraph (1) in the case of

19   a charge made by such aggrieved person, or 180 days after

20   filing the charge, in the case of a change filed by the Gen-

21   eral Counsel, has neither issued a complaint nor secured

22   from the respondent a conciliation agreement acceptable to

23   the General Counsel and the person aggrieved. The court

24   may grant any relief which the Commission is authorized

25   to grant under subsection (c).

1   "(b) (1) If the General Counsel determines after at-

2 tempting to secure voluntary compliance under subsection

3 (a) that he is unable to secure from the respondent a con-

4 ciliation agreement acceptable to the General Counsel and to

5 the person aggrieved, which determination shall not be

6 reviewable in any court, the General Counsel shall issue and

7 cause to be served upon the respondent a complaint stating

8 the facts upon which the allegation of the unlawful employ-

9 ment practice is based, together with a notice of hearing

10 before the Commission. No complaint shall issue based upon

11 any unlawful employment practice occurring more than one

12 year prior to the filing of such charge unless the person

13 aggrieved thereby was prevented from filing such charge by

14 reason of service in the Armed Forces, in which event the

15 period of military service shall not be included in computing

16 the one-year period.

17   "(2) Such hearing shall be conducted in accordance

18 with regulations of the Commission. The respondent shall

19 have the right to file a verified answer to such complaint

20 and to appear at such hearing, to present evidence, and to

21 examine and cross-examine witnesses.

22   "(c) If, upon the preponderance of the evidence, in-

23 cluding all the testimony taken, the Commission shall find

24 that the respondent engaged in any unlawful employment

25 practice, the Commission shall state its findings of fact and

1   shall issue and cause to be served on the respondent and

2   other parties an order requiring the respondent to cease and

3   desist from such unlawful employment practice and to take

4   such affirmative action as will effectuate the policies of this

5   Act, including reinstatement or hiring of employees, with

6   or without backpay (payable by the employer, employ-

7   ment agency, or labor organization, as the case may be,

8   responsible for the discrimination). The Commission may

9   also include in its order the awarding of damages to an

10   aggrieved individual, including damages for humiliation and

11   mental pain and suffering, and up to $500 punitive damages.

12   Such order may further require such respondent to make

13   reports from time to time showing the extent to which it has

14   complied with the order. If the Commission shall find that

15   the respondent has not engaged in any unlawful employ-

16   ment practice, the Commission shall state its findings of fact

17   and shall issue and cause to be served on such person and

18   other parties an order dismissing the complaint.

19   "(d) The Commission may at any time, upon reason-

20   able notice and in such manner as it shall deem proper,

21   modify or set aside, in whole or in part, any finding or order

22   made or issued by it.

23   "(e) Enforcement and review of orders of the Commis-

24   sion shall be had in the same manner as is provided for

25   enforcement and review of orders of the National Labor

1 Relations Board under subsections (e) through (i) of sec-

2 tion 10 of the National Labor Relations Act (29 U.S.C.

3 160 (e) – (i)) .''

4   (2) Subsection (k) of section 706 of such Act is

5 redesignated as subsection (f) .

6   TITLE IV—FAMILY ALLOWANCES

7   FINDINGS AND PURPOSE

8   SEC. 401. (a) The Congress hereby finds that the future

9 of this or any other nation depends upon its children. It is

10 essential that they have those necessities of life which will

11 enable them to develop into healthy and useful citizens.

12 Such concern has led many countries to adopt family allow-

13 ances plans as an integral part of their social security sys-

14 tems. The United States, alone among the industrialized

15 nations of the world, does not have this type of program.

16 In spite of the high standards of living enjoyed by many

17 of our citizens, millions of American children are being

18 raised in families whose incomes are such as to afford less

19 than a satisfactory mode of existence. Experience has shown

20 that existing income maintenance and related measures are

21 inadequate to cope successfully with this problem.

22   (b) It is therefore declared to be the purpose of this

23 title to promote the general welfare through the payment of

24 monthly family allowances for the maintenance, care, train-

25 ing, education, and advancement of all American children.

PAYMENT OF FAMILY ALLOWANCES

1

2   SEC. 402. The Secretary of Health, Education, and Wel-

3   fare (hereafter referred to in this title as the "Secretary"),

4   through the Social Security Administration, shall pay, with

5   respect to each eligible child, an allowance of $10 per month

6   on the first day of every month, starting on July 1, 1969,

7   after the registration of such child. The allowances shall—

8   (1) be paid to the mother of the eligible child,

9   unless otherwise provided pursuant to regulation, and

10   shall be applied by the person receiving it exclusively

11   toward the maintenance, care, training, education, and

12   advancement of the child;

13   (2) not serve as a substitute for or result in a reduc-

14   tion in existing benefits paid on behalf of the child by the

15   Federal, State, or local governments under the various

16   titles of the Social Security Act (including title IV

17   relating to aid to families with dependent children),

18   the Railroad Retirement Act of 1937, programs for the

19   benefit of survivors of veterans, or any other federally

20   supported or assisted programs; and

21   (3) be paid for each eligible child regardless of the

22   income or financial status of the parents, but the allow-

23   ances shall be included as part of the taxable income

24   of the person receiving the allowance under chapter 1

1   of the Internal Revenue Code of 1954 and (to the ex-

2   tent provided therein) under any State or local income

3   tax law. However, no allowance shall be subject to the

4   operation of any law relating to bankruptcy or insolvency

5   or be assigned, charged, attached, anticipated, or given

6   as security by or in the interest of the person receiving

7   the allowance.

8   ALLOWANCE CONTINGENT ON SCHOOL ATTENDANCE

9   SEC. 403. (a) The allowance shall cease to be payable

10   if the child does not regularly attend school as required by

11   the law of the State or local community in which he or

12   she resides. In case of children unable to attend school by

13   reason of any mental or physical infirmity, payment may

14   be made in accordance with regulation.

15   (b) In those instances in which a child, otherwise

16   eligible for payments, is no longer required to attend school

17   because the law of the State or local community in which

18   he or she resides does not compel attendance until the age

19   of eighteen, such child shall be eligible only if he or she

20   remains in school or is enrolled on a full-time basis in an

21   educational institution, other than a correspondence school,

22   which provides training or instruction of an educational,

23   vocational, or technical nature to improve the qualifications

24   of enrollees for employment or for carrying on or engaging

25   in a trade, business, profession, or occupation. The standards

1 for such an educational institution shall be prescribed by

2 regulation.

3   DEFINITIONS

4   SEC. 404. As used in this title—

5   (1) the term "eligible child" means any person

6 under the age of eighteen years—

7   (A) who is a citizen of the United States,

8   whether or not he or she is residing in the United

9   States; or

10   (B) who has been a resident of the United

11   States for one year immediately prior to registra-

12   tion, whether or not he or she is a citizen of the

13   United States; or

14   (C) whose father's or mother's domicile was

15   in the United States at the time of his birth and for

16   one year prior thereto, and who has continued to be

17   in the United States up to the date of such registra-

18   tion; or

19   (D) who was born while his father or mother

20   was a member of the Armed Forces of the United

21   States or within twelve months after his father or

22   mother ceased to be a member of the Armed Forces

23   of the United States;

24   but shall not include any person who ceases to be main-

1   tained by a parent, or who marries, or who is in the

2   United States in violation of any of the provisions of

3   the Immigration and Nationality Act;

4   (2) the term "parent" means a father, stepfather,

5   adoptive father, foster father, mother, stepmother, adop-

6   tive mother, or foster mother, or any other person,

7   agency, or institution who (as determined under regula-

8   tions) maintains wholly or substantially, or holds legal

9   custody of, a child; and

10   (3) the term "regulation" means regulations pre-

11   scribed by the Secretary in accordance with this title.

12   PENALTIES

13   SEC. 405. (a) Any person who knowingly—

14   (1) makes a false or misleading statement orally

15   or in writing with the intention of influencing any de-

16   cision with respect to the payment of an allowance under

17   this title either for himself or for any other person, or

18   (2) makes or presents to the Secretary or any agent

19   or employee of the Secretary, in connection with any

20   claim under this title, any statement or document that is

21   false in any material part, or

22   (3) accepts, receives, or converts to his own use

23   any allowance under this title to which he is not en-

24   titled, or

25   (4) being a person to whom an allowance has been

1   but is no longer payable, fails to report that such allow-

2   ance has ceased to be payable,

3   shall be fined not more than $500 or imprisoned not more

4   than six months, or both.

5   (b) Any person who knowingly violates any other pro-

6   vision of this title, or of any regulation, shall be fined not

7   more than $200 or imprisoned not more than three months.

8   (c) No prosecution for any offense under this section

9   may be commenced after the expiration of three years from

10   the commission of the offense.

11   ADMINISTRATIVE AND PROCEDURAL PROVISIONS

12   SEC. 406. (a) The Secretary is authorized to prescribe

13   such regulations as may be necessary and appropriate to

14   carry out the purposes and provisions of this title and such

15   regulations shall include the following:

16   (1) In cases where it is considered necessary and

17   appropriate by the Secretary because of the age, in-

18   firmity, ill health, insanity, improvidence, or other

19   reasonable condition causing the mother of the eligible

20   child to be inappropriate as the recipient of the allow-

21   ance, or because of the failure of whomever is receiving

22   the allowance to utilize it in accordance with the pro-

23   visions of section 402 (1), the Secretary shall provide

24   that the allowance be paid to the person, agency, or in

1 stitution most suitable for the carrying out of the pur-

2 poses and provisions of this title.

3 (2) Any person aggrieved by a decision regarding

4 his right to receive an allowance, or by any other mat-

5 ter arising under this title, shall have the benefit of a

6 hearing and review procedure under the terms of the

7 Administrative Procedure Act.

8 (b) The Secretary shall submit to Congress as soon as

9 possible after the beginning of each session thereof a full

10 report of expenditures and administration in connection with

11 this title during the previous year.

12 AUTHORIZATION OF APPROPRIATIONS

13 SEC. 407. There is authorized to be appropriated to

14 provide for payment of monthly allowances and otherwise

15 carry out the provisions of this title, including administrative

16 expenses, for the fiscal year beginning on July 1, 1969, the

17 sum of $8,600,000,000; for each subsequent fiscal year up

18 to and including the fiscal year beginning on July 1, 1977,

19 the sum authorized for the preceding fiscal year increased

20 by $50,000,000; and for the fiscal year beginning on July

21 1, 1978, the sum of $9,000,000,000.

1   # TITLE V—ADEQUATE HOUSING

2   FINDINGS AND PURPOSE

3   SEC. 501. (a) The Congress hereby finds that—

4   (1) adequate housing, and particularly homeown-

5   ership, greatly contributes to family stability and com-

6   munity and national cohesion;

7   (2) only an immediate and massive increase of Fed-

8   eral assistance will achieve the established national hous-

9   ing policy of the United States of "a decent home and

10   a suitable living environment for every American

11   family", and, to achieve this minimal goal as soon as

12   possible, the Federal Government must annually for the

13   next ten years assist the financing of an additional one

14   million housing units for low- and moderate-income fam-

15   ilies in order that every American family will have the

16   opportunity to obtain adequate housing; and

17   (3) widespread slum housing, and the many social

18   problems related to such housing, particularly for low-

19   income individuals who frequently reside in the center

20   of our cities, is a serious problem which in part has con-

21   tributed to major civil disorders.

1   (b) It is therefore the purpose of this title to establish

2 as an immediate and priority goal the full implementation of

3 the national policy of the United States to provide an oppor-

4 tunity for every American to have a decent home and a suit-

5 able living environment.

PUBLIC HOUSING

6

7   SEC. 502. In order to authorize three hundred thou-

8 sand additional public housing units to be financed each year

9 for the next ten years, section 10 (e) of the United States

10 Housing Act of 1937 is amended by striking out "$150,000,-

11 000 on July 1 in each of the years 1969 and 1970" and

12 inserting in lieu thereof "$275,000,000 on July 1 of each

13 subsequent year up to and including 1978".

RENT SUPPLEMENTS

14

15   SEC. 503. (a) In order to authorize two hundred thou-

16 sand additional housing units to be financed under the rent

17 supplements program each year for the next ten years, sec-

18 tion 101 (a) of the Housing and Urban Development Act

19 of 1965 is amended by striking out "$40,000,000" and

20 everything that follows in the third sentence and inserting in

21 lieu thereof "$175,000,000 on July 1, 1969, and by $175,-

22 000,000 on July 1 of each subsequent year up to and includ-

23 ing 1978."

24   (b) In order to eliminate the various restrictions on

25 eligibility for receiving rent supplements by establishing that

1   the only requirement is that the individuals or families have

2   income levels below that established in the area as the quali-

3   fication for occupancy of a public housing dwelling, section

4   101 (c) of the Housing and Urban Development Act of

5   1965 is amended by striking out everything in the first sen-

6   tence after "been determined" and inserting in lieu thereof

7   "to have an income below the maximum amount which can

8   be established in the area, pursuant to the limitations pre-

9   scribed in sections 2 (2) and 15 (7) (b) (ii) of the United

10   States Housing Act of 1937, for occupancy in public housing

11   dwellings."

12   SECTION 221(d)(3) MULTIFAMILY HOUSING

13   SEC. 504. The section 221 (d) (3) program assisting

14   the creation of multifamily housing is expanded as follows:

15   (a) In order to make the program permanent, section

16   221 (f) of the National Housing Act is amended by striking

17   out the fifth sentence.

18   (b) In order to authorize an increase in the amount

19   of Presidential special assistance funds administered by the

20   Government National Mortgage Association and thereby to

21   enable the financing of an additional one hundred and fifty

22   thousand housing units every year for the next ten years,

23   section 305 (h) of the National Housing Act is amended—

24   (1) by striking out "as limited by" and inserting in

25   lieu thereof "but without regard to the limit of"; and

1   (2) by adding at the end thereof the following:

2   "The total amount of such commitments made after

3   June 30, 1969, with respect to mortgages insured under

4   section 221 (d) (3) shall not exceed $2,500,000,000

5   which amount shall be increased by $2,500,000,000 on

6   July 1 in each of the years 1970 through 1978. The

7   total amount of outstanding authority under subsection

8   (c) shall be reduced by the amount determined by

9   subtracting from $2,170,000,000 the total amount of

10   such purchases and commitments outstanding on

11   June 30, 1969, and such reduction shall be effective as

12   of July 1, 1969."

13   (c) In order to increase the amount of rent supplement

14   funds that may be used in connection with housing provided

15   under the program so as to make housing under the pro-

16   gram available to those with low incomes, section 101 (j)

17   (2) of the Housing and Urban Development Act of 1965

18   is amended by striking out "5" where it first appears and

19   inserting in lieu thereof "25".

20   (d) In order to assure that interest rates under the pro-

21   gram of condominium ownership for low and moderate in-

22   come families are within the means of such families, clause

23   (ii) of section 221 (i) (2) (A) of the National Housing Act

24   is amended to read as follows:

1 " (iii) bear interest at a rate which shall be period-

2 ically adjusted in accordance with regulations of the

3 Secretary (but which shall be not less than zero or more

4 than the highest interest rate permissible under this

5 section and the regulations of the Secretary in effect

6 at the date the commitment was issued for insurance of

7 the mortgage) so that the monthly payment of the

8 mortgagor for principal, interest, taxes, insurance, and

9 mortgage insurance premium does not exceed 20 per

10 centum of his monthly income; and".

11 (e) In order to make local public housing authorities

12 eligible to be sponsors, section 221 (d) (3) of the National

13 Housing Act is amended by striking out " (and which certi-

14 fies that it is not receiving financial assistance from the

15 United States exclusively pursuant to the United States

16 Housing Act of 1937) ".

17 REHABILITATION ASSISTANCE FOR LOW- AND MODERATE-

18 INCOME HOMEOWNERS

19 SEC. 505. (a) In order to provide that rehabilitation

20 grants and loans, which are currently authorized by law to be

21 made available to low- and moderate-income homeowners

22 for use only in certain designated areas, may be used in any

23 area which either is now or gives reasonable promise of be-

1   coming a stable environment, the phrase ", or in an area ful-

2   filling the requirements established in section 221 (h) (3)

3   of the National Housing Act" is inserted—

4   (1) after "in an urban renewal area" in section

5   115 (a) (1) of the Housing Act of 1949, and

6   (2) after "condition of the property" in section 312

7   (a) (1) (A) of the Housing Act of 1964;

8   and section 115 (a) of the Housing Act of 1949 is further

9   amended by inserting "may make grants or" after "the

10   Secretary".

11   (c) In order to allow the Secretary of Housing and

12   Urban Development to make grants and loans to rehabili-

13   tate one hundred and fifty thousand additional housing units

14   every year for the next ten years—

15   (1) section 312 of the Housing Act of 1964 is

16   amended—

17   (A) by striking out "$150,000,000" in subsec-

18   tion (d) and inserting in lieu thereof "$275,000,-

19   000"; and

20   (B) by striking out "June 30, 1973" in sub-

21   section (h) and inserting in lieu thereof "June 30,

22   1979"; and

23   (2) section 115 of the Housing Act of 1949 is

24   amended by adding at the end thereof a new subsection

25   (d), as follows:

1   "(d) There is hereby authorized to be appropriated for

2   the purpose of making grants under this section the amount

3   of $150,000,000 for the fiscal year starting on July 1, 1969;

4   and the same sum for each subsequent fiscal year up to and

5   including the fiscal year starting on July 1, 1978. Amounts

6   appropriated pursuant to this subsection shall remain avail-

7   able until expended; and any amount which is authorized to

8   be appropriated for any fiscal year, but which is not actually

9   appropriated for that year, may be appropriated for subse-

10   quent fiscal years ending before July 1, 1979."

11   (d) The program authorized under section 221 (h) of

12   the National Housing Act, providing low-interest loans to

13   nonprofit organizations to finance the purchase and re-

14   habilitation of deteriorating or substandard housing for

15   subsequent resale to home purchasers, is expanded as follows:

16   (1) In order to permit the interest rate on such

17   loans to be reduced to zero so that individuals with

18   much lower incomes may purchase homes rehabilitated

19   by the program, section 221 (h) (5) of such Act is

20   amended by adding at the end thereof the following new

21   subparagraph:

22   "(G) Notwithstanding subparagraph (B) (ii), any

23   mortgage insured under this paragraph shall bear interest

24   at a rate which shall be periodically adjusted in accordance

25   with regulations of the Secretary (but which shall be not

1   less than zero nor more than the highest interest rate
2   permissible under this section and the regulations of the
3   Secretary in effect at the date the commitment was issued
4   for insurance of the mortgage) so that the monthly payment
5   of the mortgagor for principal, interest, taxes, insurance,
6   and mortgage insurance premium does not exceed 20 per
7   centum of his monthly income."

8   (2) In order to extend the eligibility require-
9   ments for sponsors of housing under the program, section
10   221 (h) of such Act is amended—

11   (A) by striking out "a nonprofit organization"
12   in paragraph (1) and inserting in lieu thereof "an
13   organization eligible as a mortgagor under subsection
14   (d) (3)",

15   (B) by striking out "a private nonprofit corpo-
16   ration or association" in paragraph (2) (A) and
17   inserting in lieu thereof "an organization", and

18   (C) by striking out clauses (i), (ii), and (iii)
19   in paragraph (5) (F) and inserting in lieu thereof
20   "an organization eligible as a mortgagor of a low-
21   income purchaser, approved for the purposes of this
22   subsection by the Secretary".

23   (3) In order to extend the benefits of the program
24   to moderate-income individuals, section 221 (h) (5) (A)
25   of such Act is amended by striking out "specified (with

1   respect to the area involved) in section 101 (c) (1) of

2   the Housing and Urban Development Act of 1965."

3   and inserting in lieu thereof "established pursuant to

4   subsection (d) (3) (iii) (with respect to the area in-

5   volved) for occupants of housing financed under sub-

6   section (d) (3) at below-market interest rates."

7   (4) (A) In order to allow the Secretary to provide

8   assistance under the program to facilitate the rehabilita-

9   tion for resale of an additional fifty thousand housing

10   units per year, section 221 (h) (4) of such Act is

11   amended by inserting after "and outstanding at any one

12   time shall not exceed $50,000,000" the following:

13   ", which limit shall be increased by $135,000,000 on

14   July 1, 1969, and on July 1 of each year thereafter

15   through 1978".

16   (B) In order to provide a similar increase in the

17   amount of Presidential special assistance funds admin-

18   istered by the Government National Mortgage Associa-

19   tion, section 305 (h) of such Act, as amended by section

20   504 (b) (2) of this Act, is amended by inserting be-

21   fore the last sentence the following new sentence: "The

22   total amount of such commitments made after June 30,

23   1969, with respect to mortgages insured under section

24   221 (h) shall not exceed $135,000,000 which amount

1 shall be increased by $135,000,000 on July 1 in each

2 of the years 1970 through 1978."

3 ASSISTANCE FOR HOMEOWNERSHIP BY LOW- AND

4 MODERATE-INCOME FAMILIES

5 SEC. 506. In order to assist one hundred thousand low-

6 and moderate-income families every year for the next ten

7 years in acquiring homeownership, section 235 of the Na-

8 tional Housing Act is amended—

9 (1) by striking out "at the rates of 1 per centum

10 per annum" in subsection (c) (2) and inserting in lieu

11 thereof "at a zero rate"; and

12 (2) by striking out "$100,000,000" and all that

13 follows in subsection (h) (1) and inserting in lieu

14 thereof "$150,000,000 on July 1, 1969, and by $150,-

15 000,000 on each subsequent July 1 up to and including

16 July 1, 1978."

17 FINANCIAL AND TECHNICAL ASSISTANCE TO SPONSORS OF

18 LOW- AND MODERATE-INCOME HOUSING

19 SEC. 507. (a) There is hereby authorized to be appro-

20 priated $100,000,000 per annum starting in the fiscal year

21 beginning on July 1, 1969, to be used by the Secretary of

22 Housing and Urban Development to make grants or loans for

23 organizational and development expenses of nonprofit or

24 cooperative organizations established to provide housing for

25 low- and moderate-income families to be financed under

1 subsection (d) (3), (h), or (i) of section 221 of the Na-

2 tional Housing Act, or to provide housing for elderly or

3 handicapped families to be financed under section 202 of

4 the Housing Act of 1959.

5   (b) The Secretary shall disseminate information relat-

6 ing to programs providing housing for low- and moderate-

7 income families and shall provide technical assistance to

8 organizations sponsoring such programs listed in subsec-

9 tion (a).

10   (c) Assistance under this section shall be in addition to

11 any assistance provided under section 106 of the Housing

12 and Urban Development Act of 1968.

13 LOCAL COMMUNITIES NOT ALLOWED TO OUTLAW RENT

14 SUPPLEMENT AND 221(d)(3) PROJECTS

15   SEC. 508. In order to eliminate the ability of local com-

16 munities to prevent rent supplement and section 221 (d) (3)

17 projects from being located inside their boundaries by failing

18 to present an appropriate workable program for community

19 improvement, section 101 (c) of the Housing Act of 1949 is

20 amended—

21   (1) by striking out "or section 221 (d) (3)" where

22   it first appears; and

23   (2) by striking out " (i) " immediately before "sec-

24   tion 220" in the first proviso, and by striking out ", or

1   (ii)" and all that follows through "or commitment" at

2   the end of such proviso.

3   TITLE VI—FAIR HOUSING

4   SEC. 601. Section 801 of the Act entitled "An Act

5 to prescribe penalties for certain acts of violence or intimida-

6 tion, and for other purposes", approved April 11, 1968 (82

7 Stat. 81), is amended to read as follows:

8   "FINDINGS, POLICY, AND SHORT TITLE

9   "SEC. 801. (a) The Congress hereby finds that discrim-

10 ination on account of race, color, religion, or national origin

11 in the sale, rental, leasing, financing, and occupancy of

12 housing has—

13   "(1) resulted in the denial of the equal opportunity

14   to gain adequate employment, housing, and education;

15   '(2) acted to prevent the equal enjoyment of the

16   rights and benefits sought to be provided by the United

17   States and State and local governments under various

18   programs and laws to all citizens;

19   "(3) been a burden on commerce; and

20   "(4) resulted in the disruption of domestic tran-

21   quillity.

22   "(b) It is, therefore, the purpose of this title, and the

23 policy of the United States, to assure every American a full

24 opportunity to obtain housing for himself and his family free

1   from any discrimination on account of race, color, religion, or

2   national origin.

3   " (c) This title may be cited as the 'Fair Housing Act'.",

4   SEC. 602. Section 803 of the Fair Housing Act is

5   amended to read as follows:

6   "NATIONAL FAIR HOUSING BOARD

7   "SEC. 803. (a) There is hereby created the National

8   Fair Housing Board (hereafter in this title referred to as the

9   'Board'), which shall be composed of five members, not

10   more than three of whom shall be members of the same

11   political party, who shall be appointed by the President by

12   and with the advice and consent of the Senate. One of the

13   original members shall be appointed for a term of one year,

14   one for a term of two years, one for a term of three years,

15   one for a term of four years, and one for a term of five years,

16   beginning from the date of enactment of this title, but their

17   successors shall be appointed for terms of five years each,

18   except that an individual chosen to fill a vacancy shall be

19   appointed only for the unexpired term of the member whom

20   he shall succeed. The President shall designate one member

21   to serve as Chairman of the Board. The Chairman shall be

22   responsible on behalf of the Board for the administrative

23   operations of the Board, and shall appoint such officers,

1 agents, attorneys, and employees as he deems necessary to

2 perform functions under this title.

3 "(b) The Board shall make a report to Congress at the

4 close of each fiscal year.

5 "(c) There shall be a General Counsel of the Board

6 who shall be appointed by the President, by and with the

7 advice and consent of the Senate, for a term of four years.

8 The General Counsel shall exercise general supervision over

9 all attorneys employed by the Board (other than legal assist-

10 ants to Board members). He shall have final authority, on

11 behalf of the Board, in respect to the investigation of charges

12 and issuance of complaints under section 807, and in respect

13 of the prosecution of such complaints before the Board, and

14 shall have such other duties as the Board shall prescribe or

15 as may be provided by law.

16 "(d) The Board may establish such regional or State

17 offices as it deems necessary to accomplish the purposes of

18 this title.

19 "(e) The principal office of the Board shall be in the

20 District of Columbia, but it may meet and exercise any of

21 its powers at any other place.".

22 SEC. 603. Section 804 of the Fair Housing Act is

23 amended to read as follows:

1   "DISCRIMINATION IN THE SALE OR RENTAL OF HOUSING

2   "SEC. 804. (a) It shall be unlawful, because of race,

3   color, religion, or national origin—

4   "(1) to refuse to sell or rent, to refuse to negotiate

5   for the sale or rental of, or otherwise make unavailable

6   or deny, a dwelling to any person;

7   "(2) to discriminate against any person in the

8   terms, conditions, or privileges of sale or rental of a

9   dwelling, or in the provision of services or facilities in

10   connection therewith;

11   "(3) to make, print, or publish, or cause to be

12   made, printed, or published any oral or written notice,

13   statement or advertisement, with respect to the sale or

14   rental of a dwelling that indicates any preference, limi-

15   tation, or discrimination or an intention to make any

16   preference, limitation, or discrimination; or

17   "(4) to represent to any person that any dwelling

18   is not available for inspection, sale, or rental when

19   such dwelling is in fact so available.

20   "(b) It shall be unlawful to induce or attempt to induce

21   any person to sell or rent any dwelling by representations

22   regarding the entry or prospective entry into the neighbor-

1 hood of a person or persons of a particular race, color, reli-

2 gion, or national origin."

3   SEC. 604. Section 805 of the Fair Housing Act is

4 amended by striking out "commercial real estate loans," and

5 all that precedes it and inserting in lieu thereof "SEC. 805.

6 It shall be unlawful for any person", and by striking out the

7 colon and all that follows and inserting in lieu thereof a

8 period.

9   SEC. 605. Section 806 of the Fair Housing Act is

10 amended by striking out "After December 31, 1968, it" and

11 inserting in lieu thereof "It".

12   SEC. 606. Section 807 of the Fair Housing Act is

13 amended to read as follows:

14 "PREVENTION OF DISCRIMINATORY HOUSING PRACTICES

15   "SEC. 807. (a) (1) Whenever it is charged in writing

16 under oath by a person claiming to be aggrieved, or a writ-

17 ten charge has been filed by the General Counsel where he

18 has reasonable cause to believe a violation of this title has

19 occurred (and such charge sets forth the facts upon which

20 it is based) that any person has committed a discriminatory

21 housing practice, the General Counsel shall furnish such

22 person (hereafter referred to in this title as the 'respondent')

23 with a copy of such charge and shall make an investigation

24 of such charge, except that such charge shall not be made

25 public by the General Counsel. Within one hundred and

1 eighty days after the filing of a charge by an aggrieved

2 person, the General Counsel shall determine, after such in-

3 vestigation, that there is reasonable cause to believe that the

4 charge is true, the General Counsel shall endeavor to elimi-

5 nate any such alleged discriminatory housing practice by

6 informal methods of conference, conciliation, and persuasion.

7 Nothing said or done during and as a part of such endeavors

8 may be made public by the General Counsel without the

9 written consent of the parties, or used as evidence in a sub-

10 sequent proceeding. Any officer or employee of the Board,

11 who shall make public in any manner whatever any infor-

12 mation in violation of this subsection shall be deemed guilty

13 of a misdemeanor and upon conviction thereof shall be fined

14 not more than $1,000 or imprisoned not more than one

15 year.

16 "(2) An aggrieved person may institute a civil action

17 against the respondent named in the charge in the appro-

18 priate United States district court, without regard to the

19 amount in controversy, or in any State or local court of

20 competent jurisdiction if the General Counsel, within one

21 hundred and eighty days after determining that there is

22 reasonable cause to believe such charge is true under para-

23 graph (1), has neither issued a complaint nor effected

24 voluntary compliance. The court may grant any relief which

25 the Board is authorized to grant under subsection (c).

1 " (b) (1) If the General Counsel determines after at-

2 tempting to secure voluntary compliance under subsection

3 (a) that he is unable to secure from the respondent a con-

4 ciliation agreement acceptable to the General Counsel and

5 to the person aggrieved, which determination shall not be

6 reviewable in any court, the General Counsel shall issue and

7 cause to be served upon the respondent a complaint stating

8 the facts upon which the allegation of the discriminatory

9 housing practice is based, together with a notice of hearing

10 before the Board. No complaint shall issue based upon any

11 discriminatory housing practice occurring more than one

12 year prior to the filing of such charge unless the person

13 aggrieved thereby was prevented from filing such charges

14 by reason of service in the Armed Forces, in which event

15 the period of military service shall not be included in com-

16 puting the one-year period.

17 " (2) Such hearing shall be conducted in accordance

18 with regulations of the Board. The respondent shall have the

19 right to file a verified answer to such complaint and to

20 appear at such hearing, to present evidence, and to examine

21 and cross-examine witnesses.

22 " (c) If, upon the preponderance of the evidence, in-

23 cluding all the testimony taken, the Board shall find that

24 the respondent engaged in any discriminatory housing prac-

25 tice, the Board shall state its findings of fact and shall issue

1 and cause to be served on such person and other parties an

2 order requiring such person to cease and desist from such

3 discriminatory housing practice and to take such affirmative

4 action as will effectuate the policies of this title. The Board

5 may also include in its order the awarding of damages to

6 an aggrieved individual, including damages for humiliation

7 and mental pain and suffering, and up to $500 punitive

8 damages. Such order may further require such respondent

9 to make reports from time to time showing the extent to

10 which he has complied with the order. If the Board shall

11 find that the respondent has not engaged in any discrimina-

12 tory housing practice, the Board shall state its findings of

13 fact and shall issue and cause to be served on such person

14 and other parties an order dismissing the complaint.

15   "(d) The Board may at any time, upon reasonable

16 notice and in such manner as it shall deem proper, modify

17 or set aside, in whole or in part, any finding or order made

18 or issued by it.

19   "(e) Enforcement and review of orders of the Board

20 shall be had in the same manner as is provided for enforce-

21 ment and review of orders of the National Labor Relations

22 Board under subsections (e) through (i) of section 10 of

23 the National Labor Relations Act (29 U.S.C. 160 (e) –

24 (i)).".

1   SEC. 607. Section 808 of the Fair Housing Act is

2   amended to read as follows:

3   "GOVERNMENT AGENCIES TO AFFIRMATIVELY PROMOTE

4   FAIR HOUSING

5   "SEC. 808. (a) The Secretary of Housing and Urban

6   Development, and all Federal, State, and local governmental

7   agencies, shall administer their programs and activities relat-

8   ing to housing and urban development in a manner to

9   affirmatively further the purposes of this title.

10   "(b) Any violation of the above subsection or of

11   sections 803, 804, or 805 by any such agency or department

12   shall be considered by the Board in the same manner as

13   are any other violations of sections 803, 804, or 805.".

14   SEC. 608. Section 809 of the Fair Housing Act is

15   amended to read as follows:

16   "RESPONSIBILITIES OF FEDERALLY INSURED LENDING

17   INSTITUTIONS

18   "SEC. 809. (a) Every federally insured lending institu-

19   tion shall require legally enforceable assurances to be pro-

20   vided by an applicant for a loan described under section

21   805 of this title that such a dwelling will be sold, leased,

22   rented or otherwise disposed of without regard to race, color,

23   religion, or national origin. Full and faithful conformity with

24   this subsection shall be a condition of receiving and main-

25   taining the status of a federally insured lending institution.

1 " (b) This section shall be administered and enforced

2 by the appropriate agency or instrumentality of the United

3 States Government which has jurisdiction over, or provides

4 insurance for, any lending institution, except that in any

5 order issued pursuant to section 807 of this title, the Board

6 may, in its discretion, make a finding that such an institu-

7 tion shall be denied the status of a federally insured lending

8 institution. Upon such a finding by the Board, such agency

9 or instrumentality of the United States Government shall

10 immediately initiate appropriate action to enforce such

11 finding.".

12   SEC. 609. (a) Section 817 of the Fair Housing Act is

13 amended by striking out "803,".

14   (b) (1) Section 5314 of title 5, United States Code,

15 is amended by adding at the end the following new para-

16 graph:

17   "(53) Chairman, National Fair Housing Board.".

18   (2) Section 5314 of title 5, United States Code, is

19 amended by adding at the end the following new paragraphs:

20   "(90) Members, National Fair Housing Board.

21   "(91) General Counsel of the National Fair Hous-

22   ing Board.".

23   SEC. 610. (a) Sections 810, 811, and 812 of the Fair

24 Housing Act are repealed, and sections 813 through 819 of

1 such Act are redesignated as sections 810 through 816,

2 respectively.

3   (b) (1) All orders, determinations, rules, and regula-

4 tions which have been issued or made by the Attorney Gen-

5 eral, or any court of competent jurisdiction, under any pro-

6 vision of law repealed or amended by this Act, and which

7 are in effect on the date of the enactment of this Act,

8 shall continue in effect according to their terms until modi-

9 fied, terminated, superseded, set aside, or repealed by the

10 Attorney General or, as the case may be, by any court of

11 competent jurisdiction, or by operation of law.

12   (2) Proceedings pending before the Secretary of Hous-

13 ing and Urban Development on the date of enactment of

14 this Act shall be continued before the National Fair Housing

15 Board, and the provisions of the Fair Housing Act shall

16 apply with respect to such proceedings.

17   (3) The provisions of this Act shall not affect suits

18 commenced prior to the date of enactment of this Act by

19 an aggrieved person under section 810 (d) of the Act of

20 April 11, 1968, or by the Attorney General under section

21 813 of such Act, and all such suits shall be continued by

22 such aggrieved person or the Attorney General, as the case

23 may be, proceedings therein had, appeals therein taken, and

24 judgments therein rendered, in the same manner and with

25 the same effect as if this Act had not been passed.

1   ## TITLE VII—MORE EFFECTIVE SCHOOLS

2   FINDINGS AND PURPOSE

3   SEC. 701. (a) The Congress finds that children attend-

4   ing schools in areas where there are high concentrations of

5   children from low-income families are deprived of educational

6   advantages made available to children in more affluent areas;

7   that existing Federal aid for children from low-income fami-

8   lies is designed to provide special educational services which

9   are essentially remedial and noncurricular in nature; and

10   that there is an urgent need for Federal support for programs

11   which make basic and comprehensive improvements in the

12   regular school programs. The Congress further finds that

13   this Nation can no longer afford to delay a national commit-

14   ment to more effective schools for children in low-income

15   families.

16   (b) It is therefore the purpose of this title to assist local

17   educational agencies to carry out programs for more effec-

18   tive schools serving areas where there are high concentra-

19   tions of children from low-income families.

20   PROGRAMS FOR MORE EFFECTIVE SCHOOLS

21   SEC. 702. Local educational agencies (as defined in sec-

22   tion 303 (6) (B) of Public Law 874, Eighty-first Congress)

23   shall be eligible for grants from the Commissioner of Educa-

24   tion (hereafter referred to in this title as the

25   "Commissioner") for planning and implementing intensive

1   programs for more effective schools in areas where there are

2   high concentrations of children from low-income families

3   through—

4   (a) improved utilization of educational personnel

5   designed to achieve a lower and more effective per-

6   student ratio of teachers, counselors, aides, and other

7   educational personnel;

8   (b) training and development programs designed

9   to enable teachers and other educational personnel to

10   continuously improve their training and educational

11   capabilities while carrying out their responsibilities in

12   the schools;

13   (c) comprehensive educational programs designed

14   to meet the particular educational needs of children

15   from low-income families including the development and

16   implementation of new curriculum and instructional

17   methods, materials, and equipment;

18   (d) construction and remodeling programs to assure

19   adequate physical facilities; and

20   (e) procedures for the maximum feasible partici-

21   pation of parents of children served by these schools

22   and the effective use of their services.

23 For purposes of this title, "children from low-income fami-

24 lies" means children counted under section 203 (a) (2) of

25 title I of the Elementary and Secondary Education Act of

1 1965 for the purpose of determining the amount of basic

2 grants made under section 203 of such title.

3   REQUIREMENTS FOR FEDERAL ASSISTANCE

4   SEC. 703. The Commissioner shall make grants under

5 section 702 to local educational agencies for programs for

6 more effective schools only if he determines that—

7   (a) the local educational agency has a workable

8   program of a comprehensive nature for using financial

9   resources from all sources for more effective schools for

10   children from low-income families;

11   (b) schools serving areas where there are high

12   concentrations of children from low-income families will

13   not receive less in expenditures per pupil from State

14   and local sources than other schools administered by

15   the local educational agency;

16   (c) each program for a more effective school will

17   be of such size, scope, quality, and design as to assure

18   a substantial effect in meeting the educational needs of

19   children from low-income families; and

20   (d) any construction or remodeling projects fi-

21   nanced under this title will follow the prevailing wage

22   and labor standards requirements of section 209 of

23   title I of the Elementary and Secondary Education

24   Act of 1965.

1   AUTHORIZATION AND APPORTIONMENT OF

2   APPROPRIATIONS

3   SEC. 704. (a) For the purposes of carrying out the

4   provisions of this title, there is hereby authorized to be

5   appropriated the sum of $1,000,000,000 for the fiscal year

6   beginning July 1, 1969; and for each subsequent fiscal year

7   the same sum increased by annual increments of $500,000,-

8   000 until and including the fiscal year beginning July 1,

9   1976, and for the fiscal years beginning on July 1 in 1977

10   and 1978 the sum of $5,000,000,000. Sums appropriated

11   under this subsection are authorized to remain available

12   until expended, or until June 30, 1979, whichever first

13   occurs. Any unappropriated portion of the amount author-

14   ized to be appropriated for any fiscal year may be appro-

15   priated in any subsequent fiscal year during the period

16   beginning July 1, 1970, and ending June 30, 1979, in addi-

17   tion to the amount otherwise authorized to be appropriated

18   for such subsequent fiscal year.

19   (b) Sums appropriated to implement the purposes of

20   this title for any fiscal year shall be apportioned by the

21   Commissioner among the States in proportion to the num-

22   ber of children from low-income families within each State.

23   Sums apportioned for any particular State beyond that

24   needed for grants to eligible applicants shall be reapportioned

25   to other States on the same basis.

1   TITLE VIII—FULL POSTSECONDARY EDUCA-

2   TIONAL OPPORTUNITY

3   FINDINGS AND PURPOSE

4   SEC. 801. (a) The Congress hereby finds that—

5   (1) the financial costs of postsecondary education,

6   whether in a college or a technical or a vocational insti-

7   tution, are creating an increasingly difficult burden for

8   individual students and their families, educational insti-

9   tutions, and State and local government;

10   (2) it is inequitable and unreasonable that the por-

11   tion of the costs of education appropriately to be borne

12   by the individual students and their families, should pri-

13   marily be paid while the student is enrolled;

14   (3) partly due to the above reasons, millions of

15   Americans are being denied an equal opportunity to ob-

16   tain a postsecondary education or to obtain such an edu-

17   cation at an institution suited to their needs and abilities;

18   (4) a postsecondary education is increasingly nec-

19   essary for citizens to secure adequate employment and

20   further that a much more highly trained labor force is

21   necessary if the American economy is to create the addi-

22   tional employment opportunities to provide full employ-

23   ment opportunities to all;

24   (5) institutions of higher education need to receive

25   increased Federal financial assistance if they are to

1   expand in response to the expected increased demand

2   for education; and

3   (6) the growing and serious shortage of elementary

4   and secondary teachers has resulted in the denial of

5   equal educational opportunities at those levels of educa-

6   tion to millions more of Americans.

7   (b) It is therefore the purpose of this title to—

8   (1) assure a full educational opportunity beyond

9   high school for all Americans through a program of long-

10   term low interest loans to students regardless of financial

11   status and through increased Federal grants to institu-

12   tions for higher education to provide for the necessary

13   expansion of such institutions of higher education to

14   provide for necessary expansion of such institutions; and

15   (2) to encourage a greatly increased number of

16   qualified individuals to teach in elementary and second-

17   ary schools, particularly in low-income areas and in

18   programs to combat poverty, unemployment, or cultural

19   disadvantage.

20   POSTSECONDARY EDUCATIONAL LOAN PROGRAM

21   SEC. 802. The Commissioner of Education (hereafter

22   referred to in this title as the "Commissioner") shall estab-

23   lish and administer a program of loans to students in post-

24   secondary educational institutions. He shall issue reasonable

25   and necessary regulations in furtherance of the purposes of

1 this title. These regulations shall be consistent with the
2 following:

3   (a) All individuals expecting to be enrolled as under-
4 graduate students in postsecondary institutions shall be eligi-
5 ble to apply for loans without regard to the financial status
6 of themselves or their families. The final granting of the
7 loans shall be subject to the actual enrollment of the indi-
8 vidual and the amount of the loans granted shall be for no
9 more than the period for which the individual is certified by
10 the institution as being enrolled.

11   (b) Loans shall be for whatever amount the Commis-
12 sioner determines is necessary to pay for the tuition, other
13 educational expenses, and reasonable living expenses up to
14 a maximum rate of $4,000 per academic year and for a
15 maximum of five full academic years, but the total amount
16 loaned to any individual shall not exceed $15,000.

17   (c) The contract for the loans shall provide for repay-
18 ment over a period ending when the borrower attains the
19 age of sixty-five years.

20   (d) Interest shall accrue on the loans, starting in the
21 first year during which repayment on the principal is re-
22 quired, at the rate of 3 per centum on the unpaid balance.

23   (e) The Commissioner shall establish various and ap-
24 propriate repayment schedules including—

1   (1) equal monthly repayments during the entire

2   term of the loan; and

3   (2) a graduated schedule of increasingly larger

4   payments during the entire term of the loan to be in

5   relationship to the expected increase in the average

6   incomes of borrowers during their income-producing life-

7   span.

8   (f) Borrowers may elect to change from a repayment

9   schedule described in paragraph (1) of subsection (e) to

10   a schedule described in paragraph (2) of subsection (e) at

11   any time during the term of the loan. Borrowers may also

12   pay amounts on the principal and interest of the loan in

13   advance of the schedule without penalty.

14   (g) No payment of the principal shall be required nor

15   shall interest accrue for a period not in excess of five years,

16   while the borrower is enrolled in any postsecondary educa-

17   tional institution, nor for a period not in excess of five years

18   while the borrower is enrolled in any program of graduate

19   or professional education supervised by any postsecondary

20   educational institution, nor during service, not in excess of

21   three years, in the Armed Forces, Peace Corps, or Volunteers

22   in Service to America.

23   (h) The liability to repay any loan shall be canceled

24   upon the death of the borrower, and shall be suspended dur-

1   ing any period of total disability (determined under regula-

2   tions of the Commissioner).

3   (i) As used in this section the term "postsecondary

4   educational institution" shall have the same meaning as an

5   "eligible institution" under subpart B of title VI of the

6   Higher Education Act of 1965 or under the National Voca-

7   tional Student Loan Insurance Act of 1965.

8   LOAN CANCELLATION FOR SERVICE AS A TEACHER

9   SEC. 803. (a) Not exceeding 50 per centum of any

10 loan provided under section 802 shall be canceled for service

11 as a full-time teacher in a public or private nonprofit ele-

12 mentary or secondary school in a State or operated by the

13 Armed Forces of the United States overseas, at the rate of

14 10 per centum of the total amount of such loan for each

15 complete academic year of such service.

16   (b) Not exceeding 100 per centum of any such loan,

17 shall be canceled for service as a full-time teacher in—

18   (1) a school which has a high concentration of

19   children from low-income families in accordance with

20   the criteria used in implementing title I of the Ele-

21   mentary and Secondary Education Act of 1965; or

22   (2) a program of special, including preschool, edu-

23   cation, or training designed to combat poverty, unem-

24   ployment, or cultural disadvantage under the Economic

1   Opportunity Act of 1964 or the Manpower and Devel-

2   opment Training Act of 1962,

3   at the rate of 20 per centum of the total amount of the

4   loan for each complete academic year of such service.

5   EXPANSION OF HIGHER EDUCATION FACILITIES

6   SEC. 804. (a) To provide for the expansion of higher

7   education facilities as will be required by the growing de-

8   mand for higher education, especially as is stimulated by

9   this title, section 401 (d) of the Higher Education Facilities

10   Act of 1963, is amended by—

11   (a) striking the Federal matching share for higher

12   educational facilities of "50 per centum" and inserting

13   in lieu thereof "66⅔ per centum;" and

14   (b) striking the Federal matching share for com-

15   munity colleges of "50 per centum" and inserting in

16   lieu thereof "70 per centum."

17   (b) Section 202 (b) of such Act is amended by strik-

18   ing out "50 per centum" and inserting in lieu thereof "66⅔

19   per centum".

20   AUTHORIZATION OF APPROPRIATIONS

21   SEC. 805. (a) For the purposes of carrying out the pro-

22   visions of this title, except for section 805, there is hereby

23   authorized to be appropriated the sum of $1,000,000,000 for

24   the fiscal year beginning on July 1, 1969; and for each sub-

25   sequent fiscal year the same sum increased by annual incre-

1 ments of $500,000,000, until the fiscal year beginning on

2 July 1, 1977; and for each fiscal year thereafter the sum

3 of $5,000,000,000.

4   (b) For the purposes of carrying out the provisions of

5 section 804 of this title, section 101 (b) of the Higher Edu-

6 cation Facilities Act of 1963 is amended by striking out

7 everything in the first sentence following "$936,000,000"

8 and inserting in lieu thereof "for the fiscal year ending

9 June 30, 1969, and "$1,800,000,000 for the fiscal year

10 beginning July 1, 1969; and for each subsequent fiscal year

11 the same sum increased by annual increments of $300,000,-

12 000 up to and including the fiscal year beginning July 1,

13 1976; and for the fiscal years beginning on July 1 in 1977

14 and 1978 the sum of $4,200,000,000. Sums appropriated

15 under this subsection are authorized to remain available until

16 expended, or until June 30, 1979, whichever first occurs.

17 Any unappropriated portion of the amount authorized to be

18 appropriated for any such fiscal year may be appropriated

19 in any subsequent fiscal year during the period beginning

20 July 1, 1970, and ending June 30, 1979, in addition to the

21 amount otherwise authorized to be appropriated for such

22 subsequent fiscal year."

91st CONGRESS
1st SESSION
H. R. 11550

IN THE HOUSE OF REPRESENTATIVES

MAY 21, 1969

Mr. SCHEUER (for himself, Mr. BUSH, Mr. BUTTON, Mrs. CHISHOLM, Mr. CON-
ABLE, Mr. CONYERS, Mr. DELLENBACK, Mr. DIGGS, Mr. ESCH, Mr. FRASER,
Mr. HAWKINS, Mr. LEGGETT, Mr. MCCLOSKEY, Mr. MIKVA, Mr. OTTINGER,
Mr. PODELL, Mr. ROSENTHAL, Mr. STOKES, Mr. TAFT, and Mr. UDALL) intro-
duced the following bill; which was referred to the Committee on Interstate
and Foreign Commerce

A BILL

To promote public health and welfare by expanding, improving
and better coordinating the family planning services and
population research activities of the Federal Government,
and for other purposes.

Whereas unwanted births impair the stability and well-being
of the individual family and severely limit the opportunity
for each child within the family; and

Whereas over five million American women are denied access
to modern, effective, medically safe family planning services
due to financial need; and

Whereas significant benefits for the family and the community
may be derived from planning including the alleviation of

I

poverty, the reduction of maternal and infant mortality rates, the reduction of the number of premature births, and of crippling and mental diseases in infants;

Whereas research efforts to develop more effective, medically safe methods of family planning are inadequate to meet the need and urgency of the problem; and

Whereas family planning has been recognized nationally and internationally as a universal human right; and

Whereas it is the policy of Congress to foster the integrity of the family and the opportunity for each child; to guarantee the right of the family to freely determine the number and spacing of its children within the dictates of its individual conscience; to extend family planning services, on a voluntary basis, to all who desire such services: Now, therefore,

1   *Be it enacted by the Senate and House of Representa-*
2   *tives of the United States of America in Congress assembled,*

3   DECLARATION OF PURPOSE

4   SECTION 1. It is the purpose of this Act—

5   (a) to make comprehensive voluntary family plan-
6   ning services readily available to all persons desiring
7   such services;

8   (b) to coordinate domestic population and family
9   planning research with the present and future needs of
10 population and family planning programs;

11   (c) to improve administrative and operational

1   supervision of domestic family planning services and of

2   population research programs related to such services;

3   (d) to enable public and voluntary agencies to

4   plan and develop comprehensive programs of family

5   planning services;

6   (e) to evaluate and improve the effectiveness of

7   family planning service programs and of population

8   research;

9   (f) to provide the trained professional, nonprofes-

10   sional, and new careers manpower needed to effectively

11   carry out programs of population research and family

12   planning services; and

13   (g) to establish a National Center for Population

14   and Family Planning as a primary focus within the

15   Federal Government on matters pertaining to popula-

16   tion and family planning, through which the Secretary

17   of Health, Education, and Welfare shall carry out the

18   purposes of this Act.

19   ESTABLISHMENT OF NATIONAL CENTER FOR POPULATION

20   AND FAMILY PLANNING

21   SEC. 2. (a) There is hereby established, within the

22   Department of Health, Education, and Welfare, a National

23   Center for Population and Family Planning (hereinafter in

1 this Act referred to as the "Center"). The Center shall, for

2 administrative purposes within such Department, be placed

3 under the direct supervision of the Assistant Secretary for

4 Health and Scientific Affairs.

5   (b) The Center shall have a Director and a Deputy Di-

6 rector and such regional population and family planning ad-

7 visers of the Center as the Director, with the approval of

8 the Secretary of Health, Education, and Welfare (herein-

9 after referred to as the "Secretary"), may determine.

10   (c) The Center shall establish identifiable units to

11 carry out, at a minimum, the following functions: public

12 information, program planning and development, manpower

13 development and training, supervision of field services, re-

14 productive physiology research, contraceptive development,

15 operational and evaluation research, behavioral research, and

16 grants management (research and services).

17   (d) The Secretary is authorized to provide the Center

18 with such full-time professional and clerical staff and with the

19 services of such consultants as may be necessary for the Cen-

20 ter to carry out its duties and functions.

21   FUNCTIONS OF THE CENTER

22   SEC. 3. (a) The Secretary of Health, Education, and

23 Welfare shall utilize the Center—

24   (1) to administer all Federal laws, over which the

25 Secretary has administrative responsibility, which pro-

1   vide for or authorize the making of special project grants

2   related to population and family planning;

3   (2) to administer and be responsible for all popula-

4   tion and family planning research carried on directly by

5   the Department of Health, Education, and Welfare or

6   supported through grants to or contracts with public and

7   nonprofit agencies, institutions, and individuals;

8   (3) to act as a clearinghouse for information per-

9   taining to domestic and international population and

10   family planning programs;

11   (4) to provide a liaison with the activities carried

12   on by other agencies and instrumentalities of the Federal

13   Government relating to population and family planning;

14   (5) to provide or support training for necessary

15   professional, nonprofessional, and new careers manpower

16   for domestic and foreign population and family planning

17   programs of service and research;

18   (6) to coordinate and be responsible for the evalua-

19   tion of the other Department of Health, Education,

20   and Welfare programs related to family planning and

21   population and to make periodic recommendations to the

22   Secretary as set forth in section 4.

23   (7) to carry out the purposes set forth in subsec-

24   tions (a) through (f) of section 1 of this Act; and

1   (8) to carry out the programs established by the

2   succeeding provisions of this Act.

3   (b) There are hereby authorized to be appropriated

4   for each fiscal year such amounts as may be necessary to

5   meet the administrative expenses of the Center.

6   PLANS AND REPORTS

7   SEC. 4. (a) Not later than six months after the passage

8   of this bill the Secretary shall make a report to the Congress

9   setting forth a plan, to be carried out over a period of five

10 years, for extension of family planning services to all per-

11 sons desiring such services, for research programs, and for

12 training of necessary manpower.

13   (b) Such a plan shall, at a minimum, indicate on a

14 phased basis:

15   (1) the number of individuals to be served, the re-

16 search goals to be reached, and the number and type of

17 professional, nonprofessional, and new careers manpower

18 to be trained;

19   (2) an estimate of the costs and personnel require-

20 ments needed to meet these objectives; and

21   (3) the steps to be taken to establish a systematic

22 reporting system capable of yielding comprehensive data

23 on which service figures and program evaluations for

24 the Department of Health, Education, and Welfare

25 shall be based.

1   (c) On January 1 following submission of the plan and

2   on each January 1 thereafter for a period of five years, the

3   Secretary shall submit to the Congress a report which shall:

4   (1) compare results achieved during the preceding

5   fiscal year for provision of services with the objectives

6   established for such year under the plan;

7   (2) indicate steps being taken to achieve the ob-

8   jective during the remaining fiscal years of the plan and

9   any revisions necessary to meet these objectives; and

10   (3) make recommendations with respect to any

11   additional legislative or administrative action necessary

12   or desirable in carrying out the plan.

13   SPECIAL PROJECT GRANTS FOR FAMILY PLANNING SERVICES

14   SEC. 5. (a) The Secretary is authorized to make,

15   through the Center, grants to public agencies and nonprofit

16   organizations and institutions to assist in the establishment

17   and operation of voluntary family planning projects.

18   (b) Grants under this section shall be made according

19   to regulations promulgated by the Secretary. Funds shall

20   be allocated after taking into account the number of patients

21   to be served, the extent to which family planning services

22   are needed locally, the relative need of the applicant and its

23   capacity to make rapid and effective use of such assistance.

24   (c) Any grant under this section shall be payable in

25   such installments and subject to such conditions as the

1 Secretary may determine to be appropriate to assure that

2 such grant will be effectively utilized for the purpose for

3 which it is made.

4   (d) For the purpose of making grants under this sec-

5 tion, there is authorized to be appropriated $30,000,000

6 for the fiscal year ending June 30, 1971; $60,000,000

7 for the fiscal year ending June 30, 1972; $90,000,000

8 for the fiscal year ending June 30, 1973; $120,000,000

9 for the fiscal year ending June 30, 1974; and $150,000,000

10 for the fiscal year ending June 30, 1975.

11   (e) The acceptance of family planning services pro-

12 vided shall be voluntary and shall not be a prerequisite or

13 impediment to eligibility for or the receipt from other or

14 participation in any other programs of financal or medical

15 assistance.

16 FORMULA GRANTS FOR FAMILY PLANNING PUBLIC HEALTH

17   SERVICES

18   SEC. 6. (a) There are authorized to be appropriated

19 $10,000,000 for the fiscal year ending June 30, 1971;

20 $15,000,000 for the fiscal year ending June 30, 1972; $20,-

21 000,000 for the fiscal year ending June 30, 1973; and

22 $25,000,000 for the fiscal year ending June 30, 1974 to

23 enable the Secretary to make grants to State health agen-

24 cies to assist the States in planning, establishing, maintain-

25 ing, coordinating and evaluating family planning services.

1   The sum so appropriated shall be used for making payments

2   to States which have submitted, and had approved by the

3   Secretary, State plans for a coordinated and comprehensive

4   program of family planning services.

5   (b) From the sums appropriated to carry out the pro-

6   visions of this section, the several States shall be entitled for

7   each fiscal year to allotments determined by the Secretary

8   on the basis of the population and financial need of the re-

9   spective States.

10   (c) For the purposes of this section the term "State"

11 includes the Commonwealth of Puerto Rico, Guam, Amer-

12 ican Samoa, the Virgin Islands, and the District of Columbia.

13   (d) The acceptance of family planning services pro-

14 vided shall be voluntary and shall not be a prerequisite or

15 impediment to eligibility for or the receipt from other or

16 participation in any other programs of financial or medical

17 assistance.

18   TRAINING GRANTS

19   SEC. 7. For the purpose of training the necessary pro-

20 fessional, nonprofessional, and new careers manpower re-

21 quired to fulfill the purposes of sections 4 and 5, the follow-

22 ing sums shall be authorized and appropriated: $2,000,000

23 for the fiscal year ending June 30, 1971; $3,000,000 for

24 the fiscal year ending June 30, 1972; $4,000,000 for the

1 fiscal year ending June 30, 1973; $5,000,000 for the fiscal

2 year ending June 30, 1974; and $6,000,000 for the fiscal

3 year ending June 30, 1975.

4   RESEARCH GRANTS

5 SEC. 8. (a) In order to promote research in the bio-

6 medical, contraceptive development, behavioral and pro-

7 gram implementation fields related to population and family

8 planning, the Secretary is authorized to make grants to

9 public agencies and nonprofit organizations and institutions,

10 and to enter into contracts with groups, associations, in-

11 stitutions and individuals or corporations for the conduct

12 of such research. The Secretary shall utilize the Center in

13 administering the provisions of this section.

14   (b) For the purpose of making grants and entering

15 into contracts under this section, there is hereby authorized

16 to be appropriated $35,000,000 for the fiscal year ending

17 June 30, 1971; $50,000,000 for the fiscal year ending

18 June 30, 1972; $65,000,000 for the fiscal year ending

19 June 30, 1973; $85,000,000 for the fiscal year ending

20 June 30, 1974; and $100,000,000 for the fiscal year ending

21 June 30, 1975.

1 GRANTS FOR CONSTRUCTION OF POPULATION RESEARCH

2   CENTERS

3   SEC. 9. (a) There is authorized to be appropriated

4 $12,000,000 for the fiscal year ending June 30, 1971; $14,-

5 000,000 for the fiscal year ending June 30, 1972; $16,000,-

6 000 for the fiscal year ending June 30, 1973; $18,000,000

7 for the fiscal year ending June 30, 1974; and $20,000,000

8 for the fiscal year ending June 30, 1975, for project grants to

9 assist in meeting the cost of construction and operation of

10 centers for research (or research and related activities) re-

11 lating to human reproduction, sterility, contraception, effec-

12 tiveness of service delivery, population trends, and other

13 aspects of, or factors which affect, population dynamics.

14 Sums so appropriated shall available until expended for

15 payments with respect to projects for which applications

16 have been filed under this part before July 1, 1976 and

17 approved by the Secretary before July 1, 1977.

18   (b) Applications for grants under this section with

19 respect to any center may be approved by the Secretary

20 only if—

21   (1) the applicant is an institution of higher educa-

1 tion or other public or private nonprofit institution which

2 the Secretary determines, after consultation with the

3 appropriate national advisory council or councils, is com-

4 petent to engage in the type of research (or research and

5 related activities for which the Center is to be constructed

6 and;

7 (2) the application contains or is supported by

8 reasonable assurances that (A) for not less than twenty

9 years after completion of construction, the facility will

10 be used for the purposes for which it was constructed;

11 (B) sufficient funds will be available for meeting the

12 non-Federal share of the cost of constructing the facility;

13 (C) sufficient funds will be available, when the con-

14 struction is completed, for effective use of the facility for

15 the purposes for which it was constructed; (D) that

16 in the design and construction, maximum attention will

17 be given to architecture and design; and (E) all labor-

18 ers and mechanics employed by contractors or subcon-

19 tractors in the performance of construction of the center

20 will be paid wages at rates not less than those prevailing

21 or similar construction in the locality as determined by

22 the Secretary of Labor in accordance with the Davis-

23 Bacon Act, as amended (40 U.S.C. 276a—276a-5);

24 and the Secretary of Labor shall have, with respect to

25 the labor standards specified in this clause the authority

1   and functions set forth in Reorganization Plan Numbered

2   14 of 1950 (15 F.R. 3176) and section 2 of the Act

3   of June 13, 1934, as amended (40 U.S.C. 276c).

4   (c) In acting on applications for grants, the Secretary

5 shall take into consideration the relative effectiveness of

6 the proposed facilities in expanding the Nation's capacity

7 for research (or research and related activities) in the field

8 of population dynamics and such other factors as he, after

9 consultation with the appropriate national advisory council

10 or councils, may prescribe by regulations in order to assure

11 that the facilities constructed with such grants, severally and

12 together, will best serve the purpose of advancing scientific

13 knowledge related to population dynamics.

14   (d) (1) The total of the grants with respect to any

15 project under this section may not exceed 75 per centum of

16 the necessary cost of the project as determined by the

17 Secretary.

18   (2) Payment of grants under this section shall be made

19 in advance or by way of reimbursement, and in such install-

20 ments (consistent with construction progress) and on such

21 conditions, as the Secretary may determine.

22   (e) If, within twenty years after completion of any

23 construction for which funds have been paid under this

24 section—

25   (1) the applicant or other owner of the facility

1   shall cease to be a public or private nonprofit institu-

2   tion, or

3   (2) the facility shall cease to be used for the pur-

4   poses for which it was constructed, unless the Secretary

5   determines, in accordance with the regulations, that

6   there is good cause for releasing the applicant or other

7   owner from the obligation to do so,

8   the United States shall be entitled to recover from the appli-

9   cant or other owner of the facility the amount bearing the

10   same ration to the then value (as determined by agreements

11   of the parties or by action brought in the United States dis-

12   trict court for the district in which such facility is situated)

13   of the facility, as the amount of the Federal participation

14   bore to the cost of the construction of the facility.

15   (f) Except as otherwise specifically provided in this

16   section, nothing contained in this section shall be con-

17   strued as authorizing any department, agency, officer, or

18   employee of the United States to exercise any direction,

19   supervision, or control over, or impose any requirement or

20   condition with respect to, the research or related activities

21   conducted by, or the personnel or administration of, any

22   institution.

23   (g) Within six months after the enactment of this

24   section, the Secretary, after consultation with the appro-

25   priate advisory council or councils, shall prescribe general

1 regulations covering the eligibility of institutions, and the

2 terms and conditions for approving applications.

3   (h) As used in this section the terms "construction"

4 and "cost of construction" include (A) the construction

5 of new buildings and the expansion, remodeling, and altera-

6 tion of existing buildings, including architects' fees and

7 the cost of acquisition of land, but not including the cost

8 of offsite improvements, and (B) equipping new buildings

9 and existing buildings, whether or not expanded, remodeled,

10 or altered.

11   (i) The Secretary shall administer the provisions of

12 this section by and through the Center.

91st CONGRESS
1st SESSION
H. R. 3295

IN THE HOUSE OF REPRESENTATIVES

JANUARY 14, 1969

Mr. SCHEUER (for himself, Mr. ADDABBO, Mr. BINGHAM, Mr. BURTON of California, Mrs. CHISHOLM, Mr. COHELAN, Mr. EDWARDS of California, Mr. FARBSTEIN, Mr. FRIEDEL, Mr. GILBERT, Mr. HALPERN, Mr. HATHAWAY, and Mr. HAWKINS) introduced the following bill; which was referred to the Committee on Education and Labor

---

A BILL

To provide for the establishment of a Commission on Afro-American History and Culture.

1   *Be it enacted by the Senate and House of Representa-*

2   *tives of the United States of America in Congress assembled,*

3   That (a) there is hereby established a Commission to be

4   known as the Commission on Afro-American History and

5   Culture (hereinafter referred to as the "Commission"). The

6   Commission shall be composed of eleven members, appointed

7   by the President from persons who are authorities on Afro-

8   American history and culture, American history, education,

9   journalism, communications, and other related fields.

I

1   (b) The President shall designate one of the members

2 of the Commission as Chairman, and one as Vice Chairman.

3 Six members of the Commission shall constitute a quorum.

4   (c) Members of the Commission shall each be entitled

5 to receive $100 per diem when engaged in the performance

6 of the duties vested in the Commission, including traveltime;

7 and while so engaged when away from their home or regular

8 place of business, they may be allowed travel expenses,

9 including per diem in lieu of subsistence, as authorized by

10 section 5703 (b) of title 5, United States Code, for persons in

11 Government service employed intermittently.

12   (d) The Commission shall meet at the call of the

13 Chairman or at the call of a majority of the members

14 thereof.

15   SEC. 2. (a) The Commission shall have the power to

16 appoint and fix the compensation of such personnel, as it

17 deems advisable, without regard to the provisions of title 5,

18 United States Code, governing appointments in the com-

19 petitive service, and the provisions of chapter 51 and sub-

20 chapter III of chapter 53 of such title, relating to classifica-

21 tion and General Schedule pay rates.

22   (b) The Commission may procure, in accordance with

23 the provisions of section 3109 of title 5, United States Code,

24 the temporary or intermittent services of experts or consult-

25 ants. Persons so employed shall receive compensation at a

1   rate to be fixed by the Commission, but not in excess of $75

2   per diem, including traveltime. While away from his home

3   or regular place of business in the performance of services

4   for the Commission, any such person may be allowed travel

5   expenses, including per diem in lieu of subsistence, as au-

6   thorized by section 5703 (b) of title 5, United States Code,

7   for persons in the Government service employed intermit-

8   tently.

9   SEC. 3. The Commission shall conduct a study of all

10 proposals to create a better understanding and knowledge of

11 the contributions of Afro-Americans and their heritage to

12 American history and culture.

13   SEC. 4. Within one year after the enactment of this Act,

14 the Commission shall submit to the President and the Con-

15 gress a comprehensive report on its study and investigation

16 which shall include its recommendations and such proposals

17 for legislation and administrative action as may be necessary

18 to carry out its recommendations. The Commission shall

19 cease to exist thirty days after such report is submitted.

20   SEC. 5. Total expenditures of the Commission shall not

21 exceed $500,000.

SECTION V

Statistics

This section contains brief statistical information in the areas of politics, education, labor, poverty, population, business and sports. The use of statistics for research purposes has been kept to a minimum in most of the interpretive articles in this book. Since the most up-to-date figures are not always available in all the areas mentioned above, those materials included here (with the exception of the sports information) have been chosen to illustrate trends. For further statistical information in these areas, students and interested readers may contact the sources cited below in each category. In the sports section, the coverage is completely up-to-date.

TABLE 1
Total Loans Approved vs. Minority Loans Approved
Monthly Comparison of FY 1960 to FY 1970

(Dollars in Millions)

FISCAL YEAR 1969

PROGRAM		JULY No.	JULY Amount	AUGUST No.	AUGUST Amount	SEPTEMBER No.	SEPTEMBER Amount	OCTOBER No.	OCTOBER Amount	NOVEMBER No.	NOVEMBER Amount	DECEMBER No.	DECEMBER Amount	JANUARY No.	JANUARY Amount	FEBRUARY No.	FEBRUARY Amount	MARCH No.	MARCH Amount	APRIL No.	APRIL Amount	MAY No.	MAY Amount	JUNE No.	JUNE Amount
Business (7a)	Total	669	$33.7	747	$35.6	906	$52.6	859	$48.3	755	$44.0	784	$44.2	778	$46.5	737	$43.2	723	$43.9	951	$54.5	817	$49.1	768	$48.2
	Minority	25	0.9	38	1.1	67	3.6	94	4.1	99	4.1	115	4.2	126	5.6	121	5.3	97	5.1	131	5.1	120	5.2	94	4.5
	Percent	4	3	5	3	7	7	11	8	13	9	15	9	16	12	16	12	13	12	14	9	15	11	12	9
EOL	Total	245	3.0	304	3.7	321	3.7	498	5.9	401	4.7	344	4.3	397	5.0	283	3.6	302	3.5	376	4.6	421	5.1	337	4.2
	Minority	120	1.6	155	1.7	189	2.3	329	4.1	280	3.3	276	3.4	288	3.8	217	2.7	233	2.9	278	3.6	319	4.0	234	3.2
	Percent	49	59	51	46	59	66	69	68	70	70	80	79	72	78	77	77	77	81	74	80	76	82	69	76
DBL	Total	13	1.1	19	1.6	19	1.6	26	2.6	19	3.5	28	3.5	25	3.1	25	2.7	22	2.2	17	2.4	30	3.3	38	5.0
	Minority	—	—	1	0.2	1	0.0	4	0.1	1	0.0	3	0.1	1	0.0	—	—	2	0.1	1	0.4	1	0.1	3	0.2
	Percent	—	—	6	12	5	—	15	4	5	—	10	3	4	—	—	—	9	5	6	17	3	3	8	4
DCL	Total	26	5.8	29	3.8	41	5.7	33	3.3	31	3.0	81	9.4	15	1.8	35	3.4	55	7.3	51	8.0	45	6.1	63	8.0
	Minority	—	—	2	0.3	—	—	1	0.4	4	0.3	22	1.7	—	—	1	0.3	5	0.7	13	1.6	5	0.2	3	0.4
	Percent	—	—	7	8	—	—	3	13	10	10	26	18	—	—	3	9	9	1	25	20	11	3	5	5
	Total Loans	953	$43.6	1099	$44.7	1287	$63.6	1416	$60.1	1206	$55.2	1243	$61.4	1215	$56.4	1080	$52.9	1102	$56.9	1395	$69.5	1313	$63.5	1206	$65.4
	Minority Loans	145	2.5	196	3.3	257	6.0	428	8.7	384	7.7	416	9.8	416	9.7	339	8.4	337	8.9	423	10.7	445	9.5	334	8.3
	Percent	15	6	18	7	20	9	30	14	32	14	33	15	35	17	31	16	31	15	30	15	34	15	28	13

FY 1969	No.	Amount
Total Loans	14,515	$693.0
Minority Loans	4,120	93.6
Percent	28	13

FISCAL YEAR 1970

PROGRAM		JULY No.	JULY Amount	AUGUST No.	AUGUST Amount	SEPTEMBER No.	SEPTEMBER Amount	OCTOBER No.	OCTOBER Amount	NOVEMBER No.	NOVEMBER Amount	DECEMBER No.	DECEMBER Amount	JANUARY No.	JANUARY Amount	FEBRUARY No.	FEBRUARY Amount	MARCH No.	MARCH Amount	APRIL No.	APRIL Amount	MAY No.	MAY Amount	JUNE No.	JUNE Amount
Business (7a)	Total	565	$30.3	700	$43.1																				
	Minority	99	4.8	113	5.2																				
	Percent	18	16	16	12																				
EOL	Total	328	4.1	311	3.9																				
	Minority	236	3.2	237	3.1																				
	Percent	72	78	76	79																				
DBL	Total	23	2.4	25	4.2																				
	Minority	2	0.1	1	0.2																				
	Percent	9	4	4	5																				
DCL	Total	26	4.0	68	7.4																				
	Minority	1	0.1	19	1.2																				
	Percent	8	3	28	16																				
	Total Loans	942	$40.8	1,104	$58.6																				
	Minority Loans	338	8.2	370	9.7																				
	Percent	36	20	34	17																				

EOL Econ Opportunity   FY Fiscal Year
DBL Displaced Business
DCL Devt Company

Note: Where "0.0" is used on this page, it indicates a sum less than $50,000. Where a "—" is used it indicates no dollars or numbers.

TABLE 2

Breakdown of Loans by Business

Business	Loan	Investment	Other Capital (Existing or Expected)	Employees Now*	Estimate In One Year
Janitorial	10,000	—	2,000	4	15
Soul Food Take Out	6,000	—	2,000	3	4
Service Station	6,500	—	—	5	6
Delivery	11,000	3,500	13,000(1)	7	12
Bus Transport	7,000	—	—	1(2)	3
Grocery	26,500	—	30,000	7	9
Furniture	5,000	—	5,000	3	6
Beauty Shop	7,500	—	—	3	6
Printing	10,000	2,000	85,1000	10	15
Cleaners	8,000	—	3,000	4	4
Grocery	30,000	—	15,000	8	7
Restaurant	15,000	—	23,000	6	8
	142,500	5,500	178,000	60	92
Auto Parts	7,000	—	32,000	3	5
Drive-in	14,500	—	15,000	6	7
Catering	10,000	—	20,000	4	8
Laundry	10,000	—	40,000	1	1
Men's Clothing	10,000	—	40,000	2	3
Computer Software	13,750	162,50	110,000	10	20
	65,250	16,250	257,000	26	44
	207,750	21,750	435,000	86	136

* Employees now or at time of opening including owner.
1) Loan application for $11,000—bank & SBA.
2) Several part time drivers excluded.
3) The statistics do not include five businesses financed by the bank, that are a direct result of XYZ's program.

TABLE 3

Occupied Housing Units, Classified by Condition and Plumbing Facilities: 1960 and 1966

[In thousands, except per cent]

ITEM	1960			1966 (prel.)		
	Total	White	Nonwhite	Total	White	Nonwhite
Total occupied units	53,024	47,880	5,144	57,856	52,030	5,826
Meeting specified criteria [1]	44,550	41,669	2,881	52,138	48,003	4,135
Not meeting specified criteria [2]	8,474	6,121	2,263	5,718	4,027	1,691
Per cent of total	16	13	44	10	8	29
In large cities [3]	(NA)	8	25	(NA)	5	16
In urban fringe	(NA)	7	43	(NA)	4	29
In smaller cities, towns, and rural	(NA)	23	77	(NA)	14	64

NA   Not available.

[1] Housing that is not dilapidated and has all basic plumbing facilities.   [2] Housing that is dilapidated or that lacks one or more of the following basic plumbing facilities: Hot running water in the structure, flush toilet for private use of members of the household, and bathtub or shower for private use of members of the household.

[3] Cities of 50,000 population or more in metropolitan areas.

Source: Dept. of Commerce, Bureau of the Census, and Dept. of Labor, Bureau of Labor Statistics; *Social and Economic Conditions of Negroes in the United States*, Series P-23, No. 24, and unpublished data.

TABLE 4

Housing Not Meeting Specified Criteria,* by Location, 1960 and 1966

	Nonwhite		White	
	1960	1966	1960	1966
United States	44	29	13	8
Large cities**	25	16	8	5
Suburbs	43	29	7	4
Smaller cities, towns, and rural	77	64	53	14

* Housing is classified as "not meeting specified criteria" if it either is dilapidated or lacks one or more of the following basic plumbing facilities: hot running water in the structure, flush toilet for private use of members of the household, and bathtub or shower for private use of members of the household.

Housing is reported as "dilapidated" if defects are so critical or so widespread that the structure would require extensive repairs, rebuilding, razing, or was of inadequate original construction. Information is collected also on housing condition rated as "deteriorating," that is, having one or more defects of an intermediate nature that require correction if the unit is to continue to provide safe and adequate shelter.

Based on these classifications, deteriorating and dilapidated housing for nonwhite households in the Nation as a whole was 45 percent in 1960 and 39 percent in 1966.

** Of 50,000 population or more in metropolitan areas.

Source: U.S. Department of Commerce, Bureau of the Census. Data for 1966 are preliminary.

TABLE 5

Homes With Selected Electrical Appliances: 1953 to 1969

[Wired homes in millions. As of January 1. Percentages based on total number of homes wired for electricity]

PRODUCT	1953		1960		1965		1968		1969	
	Number	Percent	Number	Percent	Number	Percent	Number	Percent	Number	Percent
Total number of wired homes	42.3	100.0	50.6	100.0	56.4	100.0	60.1	100.0	61.3	100.0
Air-conditioners, room	0.6	1.3	6.5	12.8	11.4	20.2	22.0	36.7	26.1	42.5
Bed coverings	3.6	8.6	10.8	21.3	18.3	32.4	25.4	42.3	28.0	45.6
Blenders	1.5	3.5	3.8	7.5	6.2	11.0	12.0	20.0	15.9	25.9
Can openers	(NA)	(NA)	(NA)	(NA)	11.1	19.7	20.7	34.5	24.2	39.4
Coffeemakers	21.6	50.0	27.0	53.4	38.6	68.5	47.8	79.6	50.8	82.9
Dishwashers	1.3	3.0	3.2	6.3	6.7	11.8	10.9	18.1	12.7	20.8
Disposers, food waste	1.4	3.3	4.8	9.5	7.6	13.5	10.8	18.0	12.6	20.5
Dryers, clothes [1]	1.5	3.6	9.0	17.8	13.7	24.2	20.8	34.6	23.8	38.8
Freezers, home	4.9	11.5	11.2	22.1	15.1	26.7	16.3	27.2	17.5	28.5
Frypans	(NA)	(NA)	20.6	40.7	27.6	49.0	31.1	51.8	32.7	53.4
Hotplates and buffet ranges	9.0	21.2	12.1	23.9	12.7	22.5	14.1	23.4	14.5	23.7
Irons, total	37.9	89.6	44.9	88.6	55.4	98.3	59.6	99.3	61.0	99.5
Steam and steam/spray	8.3	19.5	28.2	55.7	41.7	73.9	50.0	83.3	52.6	85.8
Mixers	12.6	29.7	27.0	53.4	39.7	70.4	47.1	78.5	49.3	80.5
Radios [2]	43.7	96.2	50.0	96.1	55.2	97.9	59.8	99.5	61.1	99.7
Ranges:										
Free-standing	10.2	24.1	15.3	30.3	18.0	31.9	20.5	34.1	22.2	36.2
Built-in			2.7	5.3	5.4	9.5	7.7	12.9	8.4	13.7
Refrigerators	37.8	89.2	49.6	98.0	56.0	99.3	59.9	99.7	61.1	99.8
Television:										
Black and white	19.8	46.7	45.5	89.9	53.1	94.1	58.9	98.1	60.3	98.5
Color	(X)	(X)	(NA)	(NA)	2.9	5.1	15.7	26.2	21.9	35.7
Toasters	30.0	70.9	35.6	70.4	45.8	81.1	52.6	87.6	54.7	89.3
Vacuum cleaners	25.1	59.4	36.7	72.5	45.8	81.2	55.3	92.9	57.1	93.1
Washers, clothes	32.2	76.2	42.0	83.1	49.0	86.9	56.6	94.3	58.1	94.8
Water heaters	5.8	13.8	9.4	18.6	13.1	23.2	15.7	26.1	17.0	27.8

NA Not available.   X Not applicable.   [1] Includes gas dryers.

[2] Prior to 1968, radio data based on total homes, as follows: 45,464,000 in 1953, 52,000,000 in 1960, and 56,860,000 in 1965.

Source: Billboard Publications, Inc., New York, N.Y.; *Merchandising Week*, annual statistical issues. (Copyright.)

TABLE 6

Housing Units—Tenure, Condition and Plumbing, Rooms, and Persons Per Room: 1960

[In thousands, except as indicated]

ITEM	Total units	UNITS OCCUPIED BY NONWHITE PERSONS		ITEM	Total units	UNITS OCCUPIED BY NONWHITE PERSONS	
		Total	Per-cent			Total	Per-cent
All housing units	58,324	5,153	8.8	ROOMS			
TENURE AND VACANCY STATUS				Units with—			
				1 to 3 rooms	11,704	1,661	14.2
				4 to 6 rooms	37,632	3,062	8.1
Owner-occupied units	32,796	1,974	6.0	7 or more rooms	8,987	430	4.8
Percent of all occupied	61.9	38.3	(X)				
Renter-occupied units	20,225	3,178	15.7	Median rooms per unit [1]	4.9	4.2	(X)
Vacant units	5,303	(X)	(X)	PERSONS			
CONDITION AND PLUMBING				Occupied units with—			
				1 person	7,405	811	11.0
Sound	46,915	2,797	6.0	2 persons	14,884	1,194	8.0
With all plumbing facilities	42,605	2,217	5.2	3 to 5 persons	24,713	2,026	8.2
Lacking only hot water	504			6 or more persons	6,019	1,122	18.6
Lacking private toilet or bath or running water	3,805	580	13.5	Median persons per unit [1]	2.9	3.2	(X)
Deteriorating	8,384	1,470	17.5	PERSONS PER ROOM			
With all plumbing facilities	4,766	627	13.2	Occupied units with—			
Lacking only hot water	353			1 person or less	46,891	3,696	7.9
Lacking private toilet or bath or running water	3,265	843	23.3	More than 1 person	6,130	1,457	23.8
Dilapidated	3,025	885	29.3				

X Not applicable.   [1] For definition of median, see preface.
Source: Dept. of Commerce, Bureau of the Census; *Congressional District Data Book, U.S. Census of Housing: 1960,* Vol. I, and unpublished data.

TABLE 7

Reported Enrollments, Fall 1968, in 11 State Universities and Land-Grant Colleges in 9 Eastern States

NAME OF INSTITUTION	FULL-TIME UNDERGRADUATE STUDENTS		ALL GRADUATE & PROFESSIONAL SCHOOL STUDENTS	
	TOTAL	NEGRO	TOTAL	NEGRO
University of Connecticut	9,821	167	1,975	19
University of Maine	8,237	12	705	1
Massachusetts Institute of Technology	3,907	28	3,274	20
University of Massachusetts	16,296	336	3,107	22
University of New Hampshire	6,000	45	1,200	5
Cornell University	10,019	233	4,009	28
State University of New York	68,742	1,439	8,509	134
Rutgers, State University of New Jersey	13,826	413	5,904	175
Pennsylvania State University	21,187	375	1,447	41
University of Rhode Island	6,339	51	2,005	10
University of Vermont	4,696	7	700	1
TOTALS	169,070	3,106 (1.84%)	32,835	456 (1.69%)

Source: Southern Education Reporting Service

TABLE 8
Reported Enrollments, Fall 1968, in 15 State Universities and Land-Grant Colleges in 7 Midwestern States

NAME OF INSTITUTION	FULL-TIME UNDERGRADUATE STUDENTS		ALL GRADUATE & PROFESSIONAL SCHOOL STUDENTS	
	TOTAL	NEGRO	TOTAL	NEGRO
University of Illinois	35,714	1,553	11,040	182
Southern Illinois University	27,132	1,688	4,754	321
Indiana University	27,364	750	11,000	300
Purdue University	22,971	390	6,980	168
Iowa State University	14,758	69	3,325	19
University of Iowa	13,183	84	6,323	44
Michigan State University	32,758	966	9,783	109
University of Michigan	20,148	546	15,089	251
Wayne State University	15,811	1,500	10,000	1,000
University of Minnesota	34,146	189	9,480	165
Kent State University	16,014	481	2,233	67
Miami University of Ohio	11,149	89	1,390	5
Ohio State University	29,516	767	5,542	139
Ohio University	15,480	619	1,479	11
University of Wisconsin	32,834	727	12,563	383
TOTALS	348,978	10,418 (2.98%)	110,981	3,164 (2.85%)

Source: Southern Education Reporting Service

TABLE 9
Reported Enrollments, Fall 1968, in 17 Originally All-Negro State Universities and Land-Grant Colleges in 16 Southern and Border States

NAME OF INSTITUTION (11 Southern States)	FULL-TIME UNDERGRADUATE STUDENTS		ALL GRADUATE & PROFESSIONAL SCHOOL STUDENTS	
	TOTAL	NON-NEGRO	TOTAL	NON-NEGRO
Alabama A&M College	1,930	6	146	30
Arkansas AM&N College	3,445	13	0	0
Florida A&M University	3,367	7	615	8
Fort Valley (Ga.) State College	1,963	1	139	0
Southern (La.) University	6,814	5	670	6
Alcorn (Miss.) A&M College	2,322	4	0	0
North Carolina A&T College	3,390	2	190	6
South Carolina State College	1,602	0	336	22
Tennessee A&I State University	4,372	6	164	0
Prairie View (Tex.) A&M College	3,576	30	482	29
Texas Southern University	3,330	12	470	30
Virginia State College	2,104	50	314	75
TOTALS	38,215	136 (0.3%)	3,526	206 (5.8%)

TABLE 9—(Continued)

NAME OF INSTITUTION	FULL-TIME UNDERGRADUATE STUDENTS		ALL GRADUATE & PROFESSIONAL SCHOOL STUDENTS	
(5 Border States)	TOTAL	NON-NEGRO	TOTAL	NON-NEGRO
Delaware State College	906	206	0	0
Kentucky State College	1,610	559	0	0
Maryland State College	717	83	0	0
Lincoln (Mo.) University	2,019	968	50	30
Langston (Okla.) University	1,336	41	0	0
TOTALS	6,588	1,857 (28.2%)	50	30 (60.%)
GRAND TOTALS, SOUTHERN AND BORDER STATES	44,803	1,993 (4.4%)	3,576	236 (6.6%)

Source: Southern Education Reporting Service

TABLE 10

Reported Enrollments, Fall 1968, in 26 State Universities and Land-Grant Colleges in 16 Western States

NAME OF INSTITUTION	FULL-TIME UNDERGRADUATE STUDENTS		ALL GRADUATE & PROFESSIONAL SCHOOL STUDENTS	
	TOTAL	NEGRO	TOTAL	NEGRO
University of Alaska	1,617	21	156	2
Arizona State University	14,818	141	5,499	20
University of Arizona	14,786	152	4,978	29
University of California	65,000	1,500	30,000	500
Colorado State University	12,789	91	2,572	10
University of Colorado	15,431	208	5,914	86
University of Idaho	5,724	12	749	2
Kansas State University	10,705	157	1,865	17
University of Kansas	13,671	315	3,858	74
Montana State University	6,679	7	677	0
University of Montana	6,645	21	840	3
University of Nebraska	19,944	419	4,910	57
University of Nevada	4,335	49	763	3
New Mexico State University	6,354	80	1,009	13
University of New Mexico	9,181	96	1,485	20
North Dakota State University	5,388	6	310	5
University of North Dakota	7,927	25	1,021	5
Oregon State University	12,531	61	1,960	10
University of Oregon	9,870	145	3,194	14
South Dakota State University	5,215	0	540	2
University of South Dakota	3,512	8	938	8
University of Utah	10,000	40	2,400	12
Utah State University	6,796	30	1,238	3
University of Washington	20,344	399	7,101	43
Washington State University	10,511	86	1,421	33
University of Wyoming	6,312	33	1,123	6
TOTALS	306,085	4,102 (1.34%)	86,521	977 (1.13%)

Source: Southern Education Reporting Service

TABLE 11

Per Cent Distribution by Years of School Completed for Persons 20 Years Old and Over, by Age and Race: 1969

	Less than 4 years high school	High school, 4 years	College, 1 year or more	Median years of school completed
WHITE				
20 and 21 years old	18.1	41.6	40.1	12.8
22 to 24 years old	19.6	44.8	35.7	12.7
25 to 29 years old	23.0	44.8	32.1	12.6
30 to 34 years old	27.3	44.9	27.6	12.5
35 to 44 years old	33.9	41.0	25.1	12.4
45 to 54 years old	40.7	39.3	20.0	12.2
55 to 64 years old	55.2	27.5	17.3	10.9
65 to 74 years old	67.6	18.9	13.4	8.9
75 years old and over	75.1	13.8	11.1	8.5
NEGRO				
20 and 21 years old	42.1	36.6	21.2	12.2
22 to 24 years old	43.9	37.1	19.1	12.2
25 to 29 years old	44.3	40.1	15.7	12.1
30 to 34 years old	49.8	36.7	13.5	12.0
35 to 44 years old	62.8	26.8	10.5	10.6
45 to 54 years old	70.8	18.9	10.3	9.1
55 to 64 years old	85.2	8.7	6.2	7.6
65 to 74 years old	89.7	5.5	4.9	6.1
75 years old and over	92.4	4.1	3.5	5.2

TABLE 12

Per Cent of Persons 25 to 29 Years Old Completing 4 years of High School or more, by Race and Sex: 1960 and 1966-1969

Year	Male		Female	
	White	Negro	White	Negro
1969	78	60	77	52
1968	76	58	75	54
1967	74	52	75	55
1966	73	49	74	47
1960	63	[1]36	65	[1]41

[1] 1960 data for Negroes and other races.

TABLE 13

Growth of Segregation in 40 School Systems in Southern, Border and Northern States, in Elementary Schools

State and city	Total elementary students	Total white students in elementary schools		Total Negro students in elementary schools		Negro students in schools 90 to 100 per cent Negro		Increase or decrease in Negro students in schools 90 to 100 per cent Negro; earliest year to latest year		Negro students in majority Negro schools		White students in schools 90 to 100 per cent white		Increase or decrease in white students in schools 90 to 100 per cent white; earliest year to latest year	
		Number	Per cent of total elementary students	Number	Per cent of total elementary students	Number	Per cent of total Negro elementary students	Number	Per cent increase or decrease	Number	Per cent of total Negro elementary students	Number	Per cent of total white elementary students	Number	Per cent increase or decrease
Southern															
Florida—Miami:															
1965–66	111,300	81,410	73.1	29,890	26.8	27,321	91.4	19,423	245.9	28,213	94.4	77,572	95.3	39,823	105.5
1960–61	93,440	72,348	77.4	21,092	22.6	21,066	99.9			21,066	99.9	72,348	100.0		
1950–51	45,647	37,749	82.7	7,898	17.3	7,898	100.0			7,898	100.0	37,749	100.0		
North Carolina—Charlotte:															
1965–66	43,300	30,205	69.8	13,095	30.2	12,533	95.7	5,346	74.4	12,533	95.7	28,622	94.7	10,411	57.2
1960–61	40,218	27,814	69.2	12,404	30.3	12,403	99.9			12,403	99.9	27,814	100.0		
1955–56	32,076	22,408	69.9	9,668	30.1	9,668	100.0			9,668	100.0	22,408	100.0		
1950–51	25,398	18,211	71.7	7,187	28.3	7,187	100.0			7,187	100.0	18,211	100.0		
Oklahoma—Oklahoma City:															
1965–66	44,924	35,389	78.8	9,535	21.2	8,628	90.5	6,175	251.7	9,231	96.8	34,010	96.1	10,308	43.5
1950–51	26,155	23,702	90.6	2,453	9.4	2,453	100.0			2,453	100.0	23,702	100.0		
Texas—Dallas:															
1965–66	95,935	69,504	72.4	26,431	27.5	21,840	82.6	12,558	135.3	23,883	90.3	62,633	90.1	21,818	53.5
1960–61	89,528	69,787	77.9	19,741	22.1	19,741	100.0			19,741	100.0	69,787	100.0		
1955–56	74,951	60,633	80.9	14,318	19.1	14,318	100.0			14,318	100.0	60,633	100.0		
1950–51	50,097	40,815	81.5	9,282	18.5	9,282	100.0			9,282	100.0	40,815	100.0		
Virginia—Richmond:															
1965–66	28,622	10,108	35.3	18,514	64.7	18,228	98.5	1,541	9.2	18,288	98.5	9,637	95.3	−1,435	−13.0
1960–61	27,759	11,072	39.9	16,687	60.1	16,687	100.0			16,687	100.0	11,072	100.0		
Border															
Delaware—Wilmington:															
1965–66	7,847	2,412	30.7	5,435	69.3	2,704	49.7	1,004	59.1	5,034	92.5	659	27.3	−3,600	−84.5
1960–61	6,959	3,114	44.7	3,845	55.2	1,487	38.6			3,449	89.7	1,545	49.6		
1957–58	6,866	3,993	58.2	2,873	41.8	1,563	54.4			1,766	61.5	1,581	39.6		
1950–51	5,959	4,259	71.5	1,700	28.5	1,700	100.0			1,700	100.0	4,259	100.0		
District of Columbia—Washington:															
1965–66	91,994	8,308	9.0	83,686	90.9	75,688	90.4	44,817	145.2	83,142	99.3	2,853	34.3	−25,674	−90.0
1960–61	80,279	13,498	16.8	66,781	83.2	55,806	83.6			66,001	98.8	6,902	51.2		
1955–56	67,384	22,415	33.3	44,969	66.7	33,055	73.5			42,972	95.6	14,804	66.0		
1950–51	59,398	28,527	48.0	30,871	52.0	30,871	100.0			30,871	100.0	28,527	100.0		

TABLE 13—(Continued)

State and city	Total elementary students	Total white students in elementary schools		Total Negro students in elementary schools		Negro students in schools 90 to 100 per cent Negro		Increase or decrease in Negro students in schools 90 to 100 per cent Negro; earliest year to latest year		Negro students in majority Negro schools		White students in schools 90 to 100 per cent white		Increase or decrease in white students in schools 90 to 100 per cent white; earliest year to latest year	
		Number	Per cent of total elementary students	Number	Per cent of total elementary students	Number	Per cent of total Negro elementary students	Number	Per cent increase or decrease	Number	Per cent of total Negro elementary students	Number	Per cent of total white elementary students	Number	Per cent increase or decrease
Border (Cont.)															
Kansas—															
Wichita:															
1965–66	41,938	36,381	86.7	5,557	13.3	3,531	63.5	575	19.5	4,955	89.1	34,509	94.8	6,218	22.0
1960–61	33,903	29,900	88.2	4,003	11.8	2,956	73.8	....	....	3,593	89.8	28,291	94.6	....	....
Maryland—															
Baltimore:															
1965–66	118,759	42,382	35.7	76,377	64.3	64,308	84.2	25,996	67.9	70,540	92.4	28,395	67.0	−24,123	−45.9
1960–61	105,989	45,684	43.1	60,305	56.9	50,673	84.0	....	....	56,416	93.6	34,025	74.5	....	....
1955–56	97,418	54,358	55.8	43,060	44.2	39,418	91.5	....	....	41,060	95.4	45,903	84.4	....	....
1954–55	94,627	54,914	58.0	39,713	42.0	38,312	96.5	....	....	38,672	97.4	52,518	95.6	....	....
Missouri—															
Kansas City:															
1965–66	47,991	27,647	57.6	20,344	42.4	14,068	69.1	7,670	119.9	17,426	85.7	18,027	65.2	−12,360	−40.7
1960–61	45,877	31,775	69.2	14,102	30.7	9,453	67.0	....	....	12,271	87.0	25,831	81.3	....	....
1955–56	42,401	33,525	79.1	8,876	20.9	6,500	73.2	....	....	7,666	86.3	29,414	87.7	....	....
1950–51	36,785	30,387	82.6	6,398	17.4	6,398	100.0	....	....	6,398	100.0	30,387	100.0	....	....
Northern															
California—															
Oakland:															
1965–66	35,639	15,033	42.2	18,570	52.1	9,043	48.7	9,043	....	15,455	83.2	7,547	50.2	−13,466	−64.1
1959–60*	37,214	21,548	57.9	14,453	38.8	1,110	7.7	....	....	10,274	71.1	12,190	56.5	....	....
1949–50*	30,466	25,628	84.1	4,305	14.1	....	....	....	....	2,632	61.1	21,013	82.0	....	....
Pasadena:															
1965–66	17,680	11,286	63.8	4,538	25.7	....	....	....	....	3,240	71.4	9,270	82.1	−314	−3.3
1963–64	17,114	11,682	68.3	3,746	21.9	....	....	....	....	2,785	74.3	9,966	85.3	....	....
1961–62	16,543	12,047	72.8	3,001	18.1	....	....	....	....	1,816	60.5	10,937	90.7	....	....
1955–56	13,793	11,536	83.6	1,374	10.0	....	....	....	....	706	51.4	10,457	90.6	....	....
1950–51	11,687	10,317	88.3	747	6.4	....	....	....	....	196	26.2	9,584	93.0	....	....
Sacramento:															
1965–66	28,743	19,387	67.4	3,869	13.5	....	....	−295	−100.0	1,689	43.6	15,920	82.1	181	1.2
1963–64	27,424	19,131	69.8	3,218	11.7	295	9.2	....	....	1,459	45.4	15,739	82.3	....	....
San Francisco:															
1965–66	49,813	21,331	42.8	14,337	28.8	3,031	21.1	1,452	92.0	10,369	72.3	13,879	65.1	−9,093	−39.6
1962–63	52,959	31,782	60.0	13,639	25.8	1,579	11.6	....	....	10,334	75.8	22,972	72.2	....	....
Connecticut—															
New Haven:															
1965–66	12,951	6,470	49.9	5,903	45.6	2,171	36.8	975	81.5	4,329	73.4	3,048	47.1	−367	−10.7
1964–65	12,851	6,786	52.8	5,515	42.9	2,023	36.7	....	....	3,812	69.1	2,624	38.7	....	....
1963–64	13,429	7,643	56.9	5,305	39.5	1,196	22.5	....	....	3,769	71.0	3,415	44.7	....	....

TABLE 13—(Continued)

State and city	Total elementary students	Total white students in elementary schools — Number	Total white — Per cent of total elementary students	Total Negro students in elementary schools — Number	Total Negro — Per cent of total elementary students	Negro students in schools 90 to 100 per cent Negro — Number	Negro 90 to 100 per cent Negro — Per cent of total Negro elementary students	Increase or decrease in Negro students in schools 90 to 100 per cent Negro; earliest year to latest year — Number	Increase or decrease Negro — Per cent increase or decrease	Negro students in majority Negro schools — Number	Negro in majority Negro schools — Per cent of total Negro elementary students	White students in schools 90 to 100 per cent white — Number	White 90 to 100 per cent white — Per cent of total white elementary students	Increase or decrease in white students in schools 90 to 100 per cent white; earliest year to latest year — Number	Increase or decrease white — Per cent increase or decrease
Northern (Cont.)															
Illinois—															
East St. Louis:															
1965–66	14,657	5,366	36.6	9,291	63.4	7,467	80.4	2,941	65.0	8,585	92.4	3,678	68.6	−673	−15.5
1962–63	13,242	6,026	45.5	7,216	54.5	6,434	89.2	.....	.....	6,899	95.6	5,184	86.0	.....	.....
1954–55	9,714	4,864	50.1	4,850	49.9	4,526	93.3	.....	.....	4,526	93.3	4,351	89.4	.....	.....
Peoria:															
1965–66	17,092	14,256	83.4	2,824	16.5	592	21.0	592	.....	2,454	86.9	12,779	89.6	4,604	56.4
1950–51	10,163	9,340	91.9	821	8.1	.....	.....	.....	.....	308	37.5	8,173	87.5	.....	.....
Indiana—															
Fort Wayne:															
1965–66	22,963	19,597	85.3	3,250	14.2	1,977	60.8	1,977	.....	2,694	82.9	17,183	87.7	1,138	7.1
1960–61	20,636	18,107	87.7	2,474	12.0	.....	.....	.....	.....	1,783	72.1	16,045	88.6	.....	.....
Indianapolis:															
1965–66	71,102	49,236	69.2	21,866	30.8	15,426	70.5	7,789	102.0	18,423	84.2	39,715	80.7	6,537	19.7
1960–61	59,547	42,699	71.7	16,848	28.3	11,945	70.9	.....	.....	13,356	79.2	34,461	80.7	.....	.....
1951–52	45,362	36,181	79.8	9,181	20.2	7,637	83.2	.....	.....	8,101	88.2	33,178	91.6	.....	.....
South Bend:															
1965–66	20,852	16,787	80.5	4,065	19.5	1,064	26.2	529	98.9	2,077	51.1	12,773	76.0	961	8.1
1963–64	21,032	17,206	81.8	3,826	18.2	588	15.4	.....	.....	2,627	68.7	14,090	81.9	.....	.....
1960–61	17,740	14,664	82.7	3,076	17.3	535	17.4	.....	.....	1,859	60.4	11,812	80.6	.....	.....
Massachusetts—															
Springfield:															
1965–66	19,061	14,830	77.8	3,689	19.4	567	15.4	567	.....	2,651	71.9	12,272	82.8	−489	−3.8
1963–64	19,417	15,588	80.3	3,386	17.4	.....	.....	.....	.....	1,989	58.8	12,761	81.8	.....	.....
Michigan—															
Ann Arbor:															
1965–66	9,748	9,046	92.8	702	7.2	.....	.....	.....	.....	.....	.....	7,477	82.7	290	4.0
1963–64	8,669	8,123	93.6	546	6.3	.....	.....	.....	.....	153	28.0	7,187	88.5	.....	.....
1965–66	194,338	85,226	43.9	107,461	55.3	77,654	72.3	.....	.....	98,274	91.5	55,395	65.0	.....	.....
1960–61	201,257	106,836	53.1	93,192	46.3	62,391	66.9	.....	.....	84,939	91.1	80,615	75.4	.....	.....
Detroit:															
1965–66	194,338	85,226	43.9	107,461	55.3	77,654	72.3	15,263	24.5					−25,220	−31.3
1960–61	201,257	106,836	53.1	93,192	46.3	62,391	66.9	.....	.....					.....	.....
Flint:															
1965–66	28,493	19,054	66.9	9,439	33.1	6,410	67.9	5,631	722.8	8,103	85.9	15,234	80.0	2,703	21.6
1959–60	24,751	18,261	73.8	6,490	26.2	2,711	41.8	.....	.....	6,156	94.9	16,309	89.3	.....	.....
1955–56	21,557	17,215	79.9	4,342	20.1	2,260	52.1	.....	.....	3,360	77.4	15,219	88.4	.....	.....
1950–51	15,398	13,456	87.4	1,942	12.6	779	40.1	.....	.....	1,681	86.5	12,531	93.1	.....	.....

TABLE 13—(Continued)

State and city	Total elementary students	Total white students in elementary schools — Number	Per cent of total elementary students	Total Negro students in elementary schools — Number	Per cent of total elementary students	Negro students in schools 90 to 100 per cent Negro — Number	Per cent of total Negro elementary students	Increase or decrease in Negro students in schools 90 to 100 per cent Negro; earliest year to latest year — Number	Per cent increase or decrease	Negro students in majority Negro schools — Number	Per cent of total Negro elementary students	White students in schools 90 to 100 per cent white — Number	Per cent of total white elementary students	Increase or decrease in white students in schools 90 to 100 per cent white; earliest year to latest year — Number	Per cent increase or decrease
Northern (Cont.)															
New Jersey—															
Newark:															
1965-66	53,266	12,404	23.3	36,805	69.1	18,881	51.3	6,528	52.8	33,238	90.3	4,604	37.1	−1,159	−20.1
1963-64	48,012	14,323	29.8	30,844	64.2	18,880	61.2	. . . .	. . . .	24,661	79.9	4,759	33.2	. . . .	. . . .
1961-62	43,460	16,057	36.9	25,353	58.3	12,353	48.7	. . . .	. . . .	21,503	84.8	5,763	35.9	. . . .	. . . .
New York—															
Albany:															
1965-66	8,744	6,217	71.1	2,527	28.9	. . . .	. . . .	. . . .	. . . .	1,869	74.0	4,134	66.5	−235	−5.4
1962-63	8,891	6,927	77.9	1,964	22.1	. . . .	. . . .	. . . .	. . . .	1,354	68.9	4,369	63.1	. . . .	. . . .
Buffalo:															
1965-66	49,219	31,007	63.0	17,016	34.6	13,106	77.0	3,907	42.5	15,097	88.7	25,131	81.1	5,930	30.9
1961-62	34,485	22,471	65.2	11,422	33.1	9,199	80.5	. . . .	. . . .	10,212	89.4	19,201	85.4	. . . .	. . . .
Syracuse:															
1965-66	17,611	14,263	81.0	3,348	19.0	. . . .	. . . .	. . . .	. . . .	1,679	50.2	9,937	69.7	−312	−3.0
1964-65	17,672	14,577	82.5	3,095	17.5	. . . .	. . . .	−667	−100.0	1,499	48.4	11,178	76.7	. . . .	. . . .
1962-63	14,974	12,785	85.4	2,189	14.6	667	30.5	. . . .	. . . .	1,258	57.5	10,249	80.2	. . . .	. . . .
Ohio—															
Akron:															
1963-64	33,797	25,570	75.6	8,174	24.2	3,347	40.9	1,954	140.3	5,568	68.1	6,801	26.6	−12,163	−64.1
1960-61	32,940	25,574	77.6	7,366	22.4	1,393	18.9	. . . .	. . . .	5,440	73.8	18,964	74.2	. . . .	. . . .
Cincinnati:															
1965-66	55,922	33,363	59.7	22,559	40.3	11,155	49.4	7,174	180.2	19,868	88.0	21,141	63.3	−1,422	−6.3
1960-61	51,030	33,597	65.8	17,433	34.2	10,935	62.7	. . . .	. . . .	13,605	78.0	24,520	73.0	. . . .	. . . .
1955-56	52,351	39,547	75.5	12,804	24.5	4,922	38.4	. . . .	. . . .	9,566	74.7	31,648	80.1	. . . .	. . . .
1950-51	40,038	30,973	77.3	9,110	22.7	3,981	43.7	. . . .	. . . .	6,442	70.7	22,563	72.8	. . . .	. . . .
Cleveland:															
1962-63	92,395	42,564	46.1	49,831	53.9	41,034	82.3	28,665	231.7	47,160	94.6	34,175	80.2	−5,501	−13.9
1952-53	70,614	49,075	69.5	21,539	30.5	12,369	57.4	. . . .	. . . .	18,174	84.4	39,676	80.9	. . . .	. . . .
Columbus:															
1965-66	66,215	48,913	73.9	17,302	26.1	5,933	34.3	4,267	256.1	13,986	80.8	37,651	77.0	18,032	91.9
1960-61	56,624	42,511	75.1	14,113	24.9	3,235	22.9	. . . .	. . . .	10,841	76.8	31,508	74.1	. . . .	. . . .
1955-56	39,341	32,189	81.8	7,152	18.2	2,677	37.4	. . . .	. . . .	4,720	65.9	26,369	82.0	. . . .	. . . .
1950-51	29,839	25,005	83.8	4,834	16.2	1,666	34.5	. . . .	. . . .	3,391	70.2	19,619	78.5	. . . .	. . . .
Oregon—															
Portland:															
1965-66	54,717	50,235	91.8	4,482	8.2	2,085	46.5	858	69.9	2,653	59.2	46,223	92.0	−688	−1.5
1964-65	55,246	51,012	92.3	4,234	7.7	1,548	36.6	. . . .	. . . .	2,635	62.3	46,701	93.3	. . . .	. . . .
1963-64	54,747	50,902	93.0	3,845	7.0	1,227	31.9	. . . .	. . . .	2,532	65.8	46,911	92.2	. . . .	. . . .

TABLE 13—(Continued)

State and city	Total elementary Students	Total white students in elementary schools		Total Negro students in elementary schools		Negro students in schools 90 to 100 per cent Negro		Increase or decrease in Negro students in schools 90 to 100 per cent Negro; earliest year to latest year		Negro students in majority Negro schools		White students in schools 90 to 100 per cent white		Increase or decrease in white students in schools 90 to 100 per cent white; earliest year to latest year	
		Number	Per cent of total elementary Students	Number	Per cent of total elementary students	Number	Per cent of total Negro elementary students	Number	Per cent increase or decrease	Number	Per cent of total Negro elementary students	Number	Per cent of total white elementary students	Number	Per cent increase or decrease
Northern (Cont.)															
Pennsylvania—															
Chester:															
1965-66	6,482	1,990	30.7	4,492	69.3	3,499	77.9	538	18.2	4,001	89.1	755	37.9	356	89.2
1963-64	6,311	2,148	34.0	4,163	66.0	2,961	77.1	......	......	3,573	85.8	399	18.6	......	......
Harrisburg:															
1965-66	8,208	4,456	54.3	3,752	45.7	2,025	54.0	−78	−3.7	3,048	81.3	2,505	56.2	−109	−4.2
1963-64	8,320	4,702	56.5	3,618	43.5	2,103	58.1	......	......	2,994	82.7	2,614	55.6	......	......
Philadelphia:															
1965-66	156,523	64,829	41.4	91,694	58.6	66,052	72.0	36,497	123.5	82,704	90.2	37,370	57.7	−34,356	−47.9
1960-61	148,464	71,246	48.0	77,218	52.0	60,636	78.6	......	......	53,820	75.5	70,619	91.5	......	......
1950-51	139,060	92,324	66.4	46,736	33.6	29,555	63.2	......	......	39,633	84.8	71,726	77.5	......	......
Pittsburgh:															
1965-66	47,363	28,717	60.6	18,646	39.4	9,226	49.5	6,000	186.0	15,428	82.8	17,883	62.3	−1,560	−8.0
1957-58	44,855	30,244	67.4	14,611	32.6	4,996	34.2	......	......	10,736	73.5	19,924	65.9	......	......
1955-56	43,699	30,693	70.2	13,006	29.8	4,204	32.3	......	......	9,338	72.1	19,387	63.1	......	......
1950-51	43,078	32,449	75.3	10,629	24.7	3,226	30.4	......	......	5,408	51.0	19,443	59.9	......	......
Utah—															
Salt Lake City:															
1965-66	22,066	19,893	90.2	361	1.6	......	......			.....	.....	19,212	96.6	−3,708	−16.2
1960-61	25,324	23,557	93.0	268	1.1	......	......			.....	.....	22,920	97.3	......	......
Washington—															
Seattle:															
1964-65	50,628	42,053	83.0	5,318	10.5	525	9.9	525	......	3,212	60.4	37,751	89.8	−10,295	−21.4
1962-63	54,455	46,407	85.2	4,960	9.1	576	11.6	......	......	3,207	64.6	43,128	92.9	......	......
1957-58	57,915	51,861	89.5	3,569	6.2	......	0.0	......	......	2,110	59.1	48,046	92.6	......	......
Wisconsin—															
Milwaukee:															
1965-66	75,033	55,230	73.6	19,803	26.4	14,344	72.4	13,028	990.0	17,204	86.8	47,648	86.3	9,752	25.7
1960-61*	66,423	53,716	80.9	12,707	19.1	8,559	67.4	......	......	10,990	86.5	49,743	92.6	......	......
1950-51*	43,487	40,916	94.1	2,571	5.9	1,316	51.2	......	......	1,716	66.8	37,896	92.6	......	......

* Estimated figures based on census and school enrollment data.

TABLE 14

Extent of Teacher Segregation in 75 School Systems in Southern, Border and Northern States, in Elementary Schools in 1965–66

State and city	Total elementary teachers	Total white teachers in elementary schools		Total Negro teachers in elementary schools		Negro teachers in schools 90-100% Negro		Negro teachers in majority-Negro schools		White teachers in schools 90-100% white	
		Number	Per cent of total elementary teachers	Number	Per cent of total elementary teachers	Number	Per cent of total Negro elementary teachers	Number	Per cent of total Negro elementary teachers	Number	Per cent of total white elementary teachers
Southern											
Alabama:											
Anniston	151	89	58.9	62	41.1	62	100.0	62	100.0	89	100.0
Tuscaloosa	248	133	53.6	115	46.4	115	100.0	115	100.0	133	100.0
Arkansas:											
Fayetteville	90	90	100.0	.....	.....	.....	.....	.....	.....	90	100.0
Forrest City	94	45	47.9	49	52.1	49	100.0	49	100.0	45	100.0
Helena	126	54	42.9	72	57.1	72	100.0	72	100.0	54	100.0
Hot Springs	111.5	92	82.5	19.5	17.5	19.5	100.0	19.5	100.0	92	100.0
Jonesboro	106	96	90.6	10	9.4	10	100.0	10	100.0	96	100.0
Little Rock	519	346	66.7	173	33.3	171	98.8	171	98.8	327	94.5
Pine Bluff	195	115.9	59.4	79.1	40.6	78.5	99.2	78.5	99.2	113	97.5
Florida:											
Miami	4,392	3,420	77.9	972	22.1	908	93.4	929	95.5	3,021	88.3
Tallahassee	366	191	52.2	175	47.8	175	100.0	175	100.0	191	100.0
Georgia: Atlanta	2,784	1,411	50.7	1,373	49.3	1,362	99.2	1,370	99.8	1,285	91.1
Mississippi:											
Hattiesburg	159	96	60.4	63	39.6	63	100.0	63	100.0	96	100.0
Vicksburg	118.6	55.6	46.9	63	53.1	63	100.0	63	100.0	55.6	100.0
North Carolina:											
Charlotte	1,688	1,208	71.6	480	28.4	469	97.7	469	97.7	1,102	91.2
Raleigh	413	287	69.5	126	30.5	126	100.0	126	100.0	287	100.0
Rocky-Mount	150.9	89.9	59.6	61	40.4	61	100.0	61	100.0	80.2	89.2
Winston-Salem	962	725	75.4	237	24.6	224	94.5	231	97.5	655	90.4
Oklahoma:											
Muskogee	169.1	132.1	78.1	37	21.9	37	100.0	37	100.0	120.4	91.1
Oklahoma City	1,396	1,138	81.5	258	18.5	246	95.3	252	97.6	1,040	91.4
South Carolina:											
Anderson	219	171	78.1	48	21.9	48	100.0	48	100.0	171	100.0
Columbia	612	355	58.0	257	42.0	257	100.0	257	100.0	355	100.0
Florence	267.7	152.7	57.0	115	43.0	115	100.0	115	100.0	152.7	100.0
Sumter	190.5	99	52.0	91.5	48.0	91.5	100.0	91.5	100.0	99	100.0
Tennessee:											
Knoxville	932.8	825.2	88.5	107.6	11.5	102.6	95.4	102.6	95.4	767.7	93.0
Nashville	1,934	1,497	77.4	438	22.6	433	98.9	434	99.1	1,279	85.5
Texas:											
Amarillo	724.5	675	93.2	49.5	6.8	49.5	100.0	49.5	100.0	658.25	97.5
Austin	1,022.7	849.2	83.0	174.5	17.0	164.5	94.3	164.5	94.3	766.7	90.3
Corpus Christi	887.5	861.5	97.1	26	2.9	16	61.5	19	73.0	758.5	88.0
Houston	4,994	3,441	68.9	1,553	31.1	1,548	99.7	1,551	99.9	3,255	94.5
Lubbock	762	702	92.1	60	7.9	53	88.3	55	91.6	625	89.1
Marshall	170	93	54.7	77	45.3	77	100.0	77	100.0	93	100.0
Texarkana	125	91	72.8	34	27.2	34	100.0	34	100.0	91	100.0
Wichita Falls	367	319	86.9	48	13.1	40	83.3	42	87.5	285	89.3
Virginia: Richmond ..	952	360	37.8	592	62.2	590	99.7	590	99.7	318	88.4
Border											
Delaware: Wilmington	357	182	51.0	175	49.0	99	56.6	166	94.9	28	15.4
District of Columbia:											
Washington	3,138	523	16.7	2,615	83.3	2,390	91.4	2,610	99.8	104	19.9
Kentucky:											
Lexington	209	141	67.5	68	32.5	38	55.9	52	76.5	58	41.1
Louisville	957	632	66.0	325	34.0	270	83.1	310	95.4	319	50.4
Maryland: Baltimore .	3,691	1,639	44.4	2,052	55.6	1,753	85.4	1,890	92.1	814	49.6
Missouri:											
Kansas City	1,617	1,142	70.6	475	29.4	392	82.5	433	91.1	609	53.3
St. Joseph	399	386	96.7	13	3.3	6	46.2	......	.....	336	87.1
St. Louis	2,633.9	1,147.5	43.6	1,486.4	56.4	1,413.9	95.1	1,439.9	96.8	613.5	53.4
New Mexico: Albuquerque*	1,567	1,531	97.7	23	1.5	.....	....	6	26.1	1.493	97.5

TABLE 14—(Continued)

State and city	Total elementary teachers	Total white teachers in elementary schools		Total Negro teachers in elementary schools		Negro teachers in schools 90-100% Negro		Negro teachers in majority-Negro schools		White teachers in schools 90-100% white	
		Number	Per cent of total elementary teachers	Number	Per cent of Total elementary teachers	Number	Per cent of total Negro elementary teachers	Number	Per cent of total Negro elementary teachers	Number	Per cent of total white elementary teachers
Northern											
California:											
Pittsburg*	449	401	89.3	22	4.9	2	9.1	2	9.1	52	13.0
San Diego	2,178	2,086	95.8	74	3.4	6	8.1	38	51.3	1,638	78.5
San Francisco**	1,676	1,353	80.7	114	6.8	20	17.5	57	50.0	736	54.4
Colorado: Denver	2,047	1,818	88.8	183	8.9	41	22.4	81	44.2	1,498	82.4
Connecticut:											
Hartford	1,158	1,003	86.6	150	13.0	15	10.0	99	66.0	390	38.9
New London	113	108	95.6	5	4.4	....	....	1	20.0	39	36.1
Illinois:											
Chicago	14,294	9,036	63.2	5,181	36.2	4,744	91.6	4,970	95.9	5,695	63.0
East St. Louis	461	204	44.3	257	55.7	222	86.4	238	92.6	122	59.8
Peoria	624	599	96.0	24	3.8	4	16.7	17	70.8	452	75.5
Indiana:											
Gary	996	349	35.2	623	62.4	501	80.4	523	83.9	232	66.4
Indianapolis	2,647	1,987	75.1	660	24.9	535	81.0	608	92.1	1,436	72.2
Massachusetts: Springfield	650	596	91.7	54	8.3	2	3.7	20	37.1	393	66.0
Michigan:											
Detroit	6,615	4,484	67.8	2,115	32.0	1,410	66.7	1,707	80.7	1,801	40.1
Flint	1,042	812	77.9	230	22.1	155	67.4	185	80.4	504	62.0
New Jersey: Camden	434	225	51.8	207	47.7	56	27.1	160	77.3	96	42.7
New York:											
Buffalo	1,922.8	1,720.1	89.5	202.7	10.5	162.6	80.2	171.7	84.7	963.4	56.0
Jamestown	195.5	193.5	99.0	2	1.0	......	....	....	....	152.5	78.8
Rochester	1,041	954	91.6	87	8.4	38	43.7	60	68.9	465	48.7
Schenectady	237	232	97.9	5	2.1	......	....	....	....	192	82.7
Syracuse	618	563.5	91.2	54.5	8.8	......	....	22	40.4	335.5	59.5
Ohio:											
Akron***	1,145.9	1,057	92.2	87.9	7.6	40.7	46.3	66.7	75.8	570	53.9
Cincinnati	1,778	1,327	74.6	451	25.4	223	49.4	361	80.0	615	46.4
Columbus	2,508	2,206	88.0	302	12.0	117	38.7	214	70.8	1,194	54.2
Oregon: Portland	2,548	2,411	98.1	47	1.9	13	27.7	17	36.2	2,039	84.6
Pennsylvania:											
Chester	227	115	50.7	112	49.3	101	90.2	105	93.8	26	22.6
Harrisburg	285	221	77.5	64	22.5	34	53.1	50	78.1	88	39.8
Philadelphia	4,357	2,529	58.0	1,828	42.0	1,437	78.6	1,679	91.8	767	30.3
Pittsburgh	1,556	1,373.3	88.2	182.7	11.8	109	59.7	160	87.6	553	40.3
Scranton	298	294	98.7	4	1.3	......	......	....	....	287	97.7
Washington: Seattle**	1,895	1,760	92.9	83	4.4	4	4.8	23	27.7	1,399	79.5
Wisconsin: Milwaukee	1,810	1,470	81.2	340	18.8	248	72.9	281	82.7	1,097	74.6

* Figures for 1966–67.
** Figures for 1964–65.
*** Figures for 1963–64.

TABLE 15

Pupil Desegregation in Eleven Southern States

	Desegregation Percentages					
	Fall 1967	Fall 1968			Fall 1967	Fall 1968
Alabama	5.4	7.4	South Carolina		6.4	14.9
Arkansas	16.8	23.3	Tennessee		18.4	24.3
Florida	18.0	24.1	Texas		26.1	38.9
Georgia	9.5	14.2	Virginia		20.4	25.7
Louisiana	6.7	8.8				
Mississippi	3.9	7.1	11-State Percentage		13.9	20.3
North Carolina	16.5	27.8				

Source: U.S. Department of Health, Education and Welfare

TABLE 16

Black Elected Officials In Southern States

	ALA.	ARK.	FLA.	GA.	LA.	MISS.	N.C.	S.C.	TENN.	TEXAS	VA.	TOTAL	
Legislators													
State Senate				2					2	1		5	31
State House			1	12	1	1	1		6	2	2	26	
City Officials													
Mayor	4	4	1		3	3	2	2				19	
City Council-Vice Mayor	37	9	28	15	19	30	43	22	8	10	18	239	259
Civil Service Board			1									1	
County Officials													
County Governing Board	6		1	5	10	4	1	4	6		2	39	
County Administration	2			1		1						4	58
Election Commission						15						15	
Law Enforcement Officials													
Judge, District Court							1		1			2	
Sheriff	1											1	
Coroner	1					2						3	
Town Marshal			1		4	1						6	89
Magistrate								4				4	
Constable	6		1		9	6			3			25	
Justice of the Peace	19	4			9	9			1		6	48	
School Board Officials													
School Board Members	7	37	1	7	9	6	10	2	3	9		91	91
TOTALS	83	54	35	42	64	78	58	34	30	22	28	528	528

Voter Education Project
Southern Regional Council
5 Forsyth Street, N. W.
Atlanta, Georgia 30303
November, 1969

TABLE 17

Voter Registration in the South
Summer-Fall 1969

STATE	WHITE VAP*	NEGRO VAP*	WHITE REGISTERED	% WHITE VAP REGISTERED	NEGRO REGISTERED	% NEGRO VAP REGISTERED	% NEGRO
ALABAMA	1,353,058	481,320	1,280,000	94.6	295,000	61.3	18.7
ARKANSAS	850,643	192,626	694,000	81.6	150,000	77.9	17.8
FLORIDA	2,617,438	470,261	2,465,000	94.2	315,000	67.0	11.3
GEORGIA	1,797,062	612,910	1,590,000	88.5	370,000	60.4	18.9
LOUISIANA	1,289,216	514,589	1,123,000	87.1	313,000	60.8	21.8
MISSISSIPPI	748,266	422,256	672,000	89.8	281,000	66.5	29.5
N. CAROLINA	2,005,955	550,929	1,572,000	78.4	296,000	53.7	15.8
S. CAROLINA	895,147	371,873	640,000	71.5	203,000	54.6	24.0
TENNESSEE	1,779,018	313,873	1,637,000	92.0	289,000	92.1	15.0
TEXAS	4,884,765	649,512	3,020,000	61.8	475,000	73.1	13.6
VIRGINIA	1,876,167	436,720	1,476,000	78.7	261,000	59.8	15.0
TOTALS	20,906,735	5,016,100	16,169,000	80.4	3,248,000	64.8	16.7

*VAP = Voting Age Population
Voter Education Project, Southern Regional Council, 5 Forsyth Street, N. W., Atlanta Georgia 30303
December, 1969

TABLE 18

High School Graduates and School Dropouts—Selected Characteristics: 1965 to 1968

[In thousands, except as indicated. As of October. Data for high school graduates relate to those not enrolled in college and include those who attended college prior to survey date; data for dropouts relate to persons not in regular school and not high school graduates. Based on samples and subject to sampling variability]

CHARACTERISTIC	GRADUATES				DROPOUTS			
	1965	1966	1967	1968	1965	1966	1967	1968
EMPLOYMENT STATUS								
Civilian noninstitutional population (16-21 yr. old)	4,898	5,058	5,176	5,417	2,986	2,878	2,827	2,734
Not in labor force	1,129	1,253	1,189	1,341	1,123	1,102	1,135	1,071
In labor force	3,769	3,805	3,987	4,076	1,863	1,776	1,692	1,663
Per cent of Population	76.9	75.2	77.0	75.2	62.4	61.7	59.9	60.8
Male	1,617	1,505	1,570	1,513	1,265	1,188	1,090	1,041
Female	2,152	2,300	2,417	2,563	598	588	602	622
White	3,375	3,391	3,530	3,598	1,469	1,380	1,341	1,315
Nonwhite	394	414	457	478	394	396	351	348
Employed	3,451	3,455	3,602	3,760	1,585	1,548	1,446	1,415
Per cent of labor force	91.6	90.8	90.3	92.2	85.1	87.2	85.5	85.1
Male	1,512	1,409	1,462	1,419	1,105	1,067	959	913
Female	1,939	2,046	2,140	2,341	480	481	487	502
White	3,116	3,116	3,231	3,344	1,266	1,230	1,173	1,153
Nonwhite	335	339	371	416	319	318	273	262
Unemployed	318	350	385	316	278	228	246	248
Per cent of labor force	8.4	9.2	9.7	7.8	14.9	12.8	14.5	14.9
Male	105	96	108	94	160	121	131	128
Female	213	254	277	222	118	107	115	120
White	259	275	299	254	203	150	168	162
Nonwhite	59	75	86	62	75	78	78	86
PER CENT DISTRIBUTION								
Occupation group of employed:								
Male	100.0	100.0	100.0	100.0	100.0	100.0	100.0	100.0
Professional, tech., and kindred wkrs	3.3	6.4	6.2	6.7	0.4	1.1	1.6	1.1
Clerical and kindred workers	13.1	12.1	11.6	10.7	3.5	4.1	4.5	4.5
Salesworkers	3.5	4.3	4.4	3.5	1.8	1.3	2.7	1.2
Craftsmen, foremen, and kindred wkrs	14.2	13.4	14.3	17.0	9.5	11.9	12.1	12.7
Operatives and kindred wkrs	37.1	36.2	35.3	33.6	39.3	40.8	39.4	39.8
Service wkrs., incl. private household	6.4	4.5	5.5	6.0	5.8	7.1	8.1	7.6
Farm laborers and foremen	4.6	3.8	3.5	3.5	12.2	10.8	9.4	10.7
Laborers, except farm and mine	13.6	15.5	14.7	13.6	25.2	20.3	19.4	21.5
Other	4.2	3.8	4.5	5.4	2.2	2.5	2.8	0.9
Female	100.0	100.0	100.0	100.0	100.0	100.0	100.0	100.0
Professional, tech., and kindred wkrs	4.6	6.6	6.5	6.6	–	–	1.2	1.4
Clerical and kindred wkrs	60.3	60.7	60.7	59.4	10.6	11.5	13.3	14.3
Salesworkers	4.8	4.5	5.1	5.3	6.0	3.5	6.9	5.7
Operatives and kindred wkrs	11.1	11.3	11.7	10.4	30.4	34.4	33.1	36.7
Service wkrs., incl. private household	17.5	14.8	13.3	16.2	40.3	44.5	38.5	35.1
Farm laborers and foremen	0.6	0.5	1.2	0.5	9.8	4.4	4.0	3.5
Other	1.1	1.6	1.5	1.6	2.9	1.7	3.0	3.3
Annual family income:[1]								
White	100.0	100.0	100.0	100.0	100.0	100.0	100.0	100.0
Less than $3,000	7.7	6.2	6.5	5.9	28.3	23.1	20.5	20.6
$3,000-$4,999	16.2	13.8	12.7	10.9	26.9	28.3	24.6	23.1
$5,000-$7,499	28.1	27.4	26.2	22.4	25.4	24.5	28.6	24.7
$7,500 and over	48.0	52.6	54.7	60.7	19.3	24.1	26.2	31.6
Nonwhite	100.0	100.0	100.0	100.0	100.0	100.0	100.0	100.0
Less than $3,000	28.3	37.9	27.9	22.4	50.8	45.9	39.3	41.0
$3,000-$4,999	32.7	22.9	31.2	23.5	28.4	29.7	42.3	33.5
$5,000-$7,499	26.6	23.5	21.3	26.9	16.8	17.1	13.4	17.6
$7,500 and over	12.5	15.7	19.5	27.2	4.0	7.3	5.0	7.9

– Represents zero.
[1] Includes only families of unmarried persons living with, and related to, head of household.
Source: Dept. of Labor, Bureau of Labor Statistics; Special Labor Force Report, Nos. 66, 85, 100, and forthcoming report.

TABLE 19

Voting Choices in Selected Cities in the
1968 Senatorial Elections

City	Democrat		Percentages		Republican		Percentages	
	City	Negro Areas	City	Negro Areas	City	Negro Areas	City	Negro Areas
Atlanta, Ga.	112,665	28,836	66%	71%	58,086	11,903	34%	29%
Charlotte, N.C.	42,418	7,359	63%	95%	24,817	359	37%	5%
Chicago, Ill.	881,848	271,955	64%	88%	491,104	36,202	36%	12%
Columbus, Ohio	74,007	13,751	45%	74%	89,436	4,776	55%	26%
Denver, Colo.	101,924	17,420	50%	75%	101,697	5,943	50%	25%
Kansas City, Mo.	86,549	28,339	59%	80%	60,303	7,098	41%	20%
Los Angeles, Calif.	593,795	85,990	60%	92%	393,433	7,887	40%	8%
Philadelphia, Pa.	499,800	149,557	62%	85%	305,597	2,563	35%	15%
Pittsburgh, Pa.	128,953	24,756	62%	86%	80,700	4,172	38%	14%
Raleigh, N.C.	36,226	3,371	62%	94%	21,887	215	38%	6%
St. Louis, Mo.	147,841	44,975	70%	93%	64,541	3,368	30%	7%

(Courtesy of J. Erroll Miller)

TABLE 20

Voting Choices in Selected Cities in the
1968 Congressional Elections

City	Congressional District	Democrat		Percentages		Republican		Percentages	
		City	Negro Areas	City	Negro Areas	City	Negro Areas	City	Negro Areas
Atlanta, Ga.	4th	17,543	7,082	58%	91%	12,741	672	42%	9%
Atlanta, Ga.	5th	63,183	34,293	44%	95%	79,258	1,775	56%	5%
Columbus, Ohio	12th	32,032	8,271	37%	70%	53,412	3,555	63%	30%
Columbus, Ohio	15th	20,986	3,579	33%	70%	42,836	1,520	67%	30%
Denver, Colo.	1st	91,199	14,855	52%	76%	82,677	4,651	48%	24%
Detroit, Mich.	13th	81,951	71,023	86%	87%	12,873	10,833	14%	13%
Detroit, Mich.	16th	30,987	12,161	88%	91%	4,340	1,211	12%	9%
Detroit, Mich.	17th	123,376	41,368	75%	86%	40,906	6,925	25%	14%
Kansas City, Mo.	4th	86,618	25,227	65%	86%	45,951	4,160	35%	14%
Kansas City, Mo.	5th	9,719	4,457	64%	74%	5,409	1,579	36%	26%
Los Angeles, Calif.	21st	63,875	63,875	91%	91%	6,143	6,143	9%	9%
Memphis, Tenn.	7th	13,132	10,924	87%	95%	1,910	598	13%	5%
Memphis, Tenn.	9th	43,797	18,689	39%	91%	67,142	1,822	61%	9%
Minneapolis, Minn.	5th	108,588	15,129	58%	65%	78,819	8,008	42%	35%
Pittsburgh, Pa.	14th	96,117	21,300	71%	73%	39,671	8,017	29%	27%
Raleigh, N.C.	4th	30,718	3,546	51%	97%	30,056	115	49%	3%
St. Louis, Mo.	1st	65,723	42,178	74%	89%	22,790	5,381	26%	11%

(Courtesy of J. Erroll Miller)

TABLE 21

Voting Participation in Selected Cities in the 1968 Presidential Election

City	Total Number of Persons Registered		Total Number of Persons Voting		Percentages	
	City	Negro Areas	City	Negro Areas	City	Negro Areas
Atlanta, Ga.	273,339	77,538	178,164	48,167	65%	62%
Charlotte, N.C.	104,434	14,363	74,139	8,833	71%	61%
Chicago, Ill.	1,722,618	416,683	1,471,355	330,628	85%	79%
Columbus, Ohio	200,009	31,048	177,513	24,999	89%	81%
Detroit, Mich.	774,288	350,447	610,687	270,118	79%	77%
East Chicago, Ind.	27,018	6,269	19,516	4,336	72%	69%
Gary, Ind.	103,516	47,756	72,193	33,546	70%	70%
Hammond, Ind.	61,040	1,741	43,798	1,164	72%	67%
Kansas City, Mo.	183,842	47,793	139,896	35,469	76%	74%
Los Angeles, Calif.	1,260,278	137,799	1,095,821	105,895	87%	77%
Memphis, Tenn.	252,815	81,493	184,102	53,703	73%	60%
Minneapolis, Minn.	258,087	34,185	193,192	24,108	75%	71%
Philadelphia, Pa.	1,004,091	231,833	843,427	179,426	84%	77%
Pittsburgh, Pa.	277,502	41,210	227,308	32,313	82%	78%
Raleigh, N.C.	88,902	7,620	67,157	5,281	76%	69%
St. Louis, Mo.	262,531	73,557	220,830	57,396	84%	78%

(Courtesy of J. Erroll Miller)

TABLE 22

Voting Choices in Selected Cities in the 1968 Presidential Election

City	Nixon				Humphrey				Wallace			
	City	Negro Areas	Percentages City	Percentages Negro Areas	City	Negro Areas	Percentages City	Percentages Negro Areas	City	Negro Areas	Percentages City	Percentages Negro Areas
Atlanta, Ga.	63,705	1,888	36%	4%	77,646	47,599	44%	94%	36,813	1,017	21%	2%
Charlotte, N.C.	38,081	270	51%	3%	24,323	8,459	33%	96%	11,735	104	16%	1%
Chicago, Ill.	452,914	32,935	31%	10%	874,113	281,615	59%	85%	.....	....	....	....
Columbus, Ohio	80,848	3,152	46%	13%	74,264	21,085	42%	84%	22,401	762	12%	3%
Denver, Colo.	92,013	4,864	44%	20%	106,081	19,088	51%	78%	11,404	608	6%	2%
Detroit, Mich.	119,829	29,401	18%	11%	427,396	223,252	70%	83%	50,369	9,916	8%	4%
East Chicago, Ind.	3,750	357	20%	8%	12,737	3,706	69%	88%	2,054	151	11%	4%
Gary, Ind.	17,475	2,081	25%	6%	44,043	29,488	63%	91%	8,917	904	13%	3%
Hammond, Ind.	3,944	60	42%	5%	3,657	1,030	39%	90%	1,697	52	18%	5%
Kansas City, Mo.	56,963	6,136	36%	17%	82,933	29,327	53%	77%	16,485	2,440	11%	6%
Los Angeles, Calif.	444,919	6,714	42%	7%	579,588	93,829	54%	92%	44,036	1,092	4%	1%
Memphis, Tenn.	56,127	2,077	30%	4%	71,290	47,873	39%	92%	56,885	2,297	31%	4%
Minneapolis, Minn.	70,016	6,862	36%	28%	114,721	16,091	59%	67%	8,455	1,155	4%	5%
Philadelphia, Pa.	254,153	22,044	30%	12%	525,768	153,990	62%	86%	63,506	3,452	8%	2%
Pittsburgh, Pa.	57,681	2,923	26%	9%	138,877	27,066	63%	87%	24,931	1,257	11%	4%
Raleigh, N.C.	28,928	130	43%	3%	20,979	4,731	31%	96%	17,250	38	26%	1%
St. Louis, Mo.	58,252	2,679	26%	5%	143,010	47,326	65%	94%	19,674	272	9%	1%

(Courtesy of J. Erroll Miller)

TABLE 23

Negro Participation on Local Draft Boards in Southern States in 1967 and 1968

	1967	1968		1967	1968
Alabama	0	3	Mississippi	0	0
Arkansas	0	35	Missouri	1	28
Florida	3	29	North Carolina	7	16
Georgia	2	17	South Carolina	1	12
Kansas	0	9	Tennessee	11	20
Kentucky	2	7	Texas	8	26
Louisiana	0	40	Virginia	12	27

As of August 1968, a total of 822 Negroes served on local boards across the country as compared to 278 at the start of 1967. In the calendar year 1967, 345 Negroes were added to local boards.

The 18-month study reflects nearly a 300 per cent increase in the number of Negroes serving on local boards and the number continues to grow.

TABLE 24

Negro Participation in the Armed Forces, 1968

Over 300,000 Negroes were on active duty with the armed forces as of September 30, 1968; they represent 8.8 per cent of the total active forces. Negro participation by service, by number and per cent, was as follows:

	Officer	Enlisted	Total
Army	5,646 (3.4)	153,516 (11.4)	159,162 (10.5)
Navy	352 (0.4)	31,809 (4.8)	32,161 (4.3)
Marine Corps	196 (0.8)	32,055 (11.3)	32,251 (10.5)
Air Force	2,461 (1.8)	78,422 (10.3)	80,883 (9.0)
Defense Dept. Total	8,655 (2.1)	295,802 (9.7)	304,457 (8.8)

TABLE 25

Labor Force by Age, Sex and Color

Age, sex and color	Total labor force				Civilian labor force			
	Thousands of persons		Participation rate		Thousands of persons		Participation rate	
	Dec. 1968	Dec. 1967	Dec. 1968	Dec. 1967	Dec. 1968	Dec. 1967	Dec. 1968	Dec. 1967
Total Male								
16 years and over	52,745	52,155	80.1	80.5	49,283	48,721	79.0	79.4
16 to 19 years	3,825	3,854	52.7	54.0	3,402	3,193	49.7	49.3
16 and 17 years	1,517	1,502	40.8	41.7	1,491	1,472	49.7	49.3
18 and 19 years	2,309	2,353	65.1	66.5	1,911	1,721	60.6	59.3
20 to 24 years	6,813	6,514	85.1	84.9	5,037	4,981	80.8	81.1
25 to 54 years	32,973	32,690	96.4	96.5	31,714	31,457	96.2	96.4
25 to 34 years	11,515	11,156	96.8	97.2	10,743	10,420	96.6	97.0
35 to 44 years	11,043	11,239	97.2	97.5	10,649	10,843	97.1	97.4
45 to 54 years	10,415	10,294	95.0	94.8	10,322	10,193	95.0	94.7
55 to 64 years	7,030	6,991	83.7	84.4	7,026	6,985	83.7	84.4
55 to 59 years	4,109	4,102	89.1	90.4	4,105	4,096	89.1	90.4
60 to 64 years	2,921	2,889	77.2	77.2	2,921	2,889	77.2	77.2
65 years and over	2,103	2,105	26.5	26.8	2,103	2,105	26.5	26.8
White Male								
16 years and over	47,465	46,945	80.4	80.7	44,358	43,818	79.4	79.6
16 to 19 years	3,370	3,394	53.4	54.6	2,984	2,782	50.4	49.6
16 and 17 years	1,353	1,321	42.0	42.2	1,329	1,293	41.5	41.7
18 and 19 years	2,017	2,073	65.4	67.1	1,655	1,489	60.8	59.4
20 to 24 years	6,016	5,752	85.0	84.7	4,408	4,352	80.6	80.7
25 to 54 years	29,694	29,467	96.8	97.0	28,583	28,356	96.6	96.8
25 to 34 years	10,279	9,966	97.1	97.5	9,603	9,310	96.9	97.4
35 to 44 years	9,940	10,127	97.6	98.0	9,590	9,768	97.5	97.9
45 to 54 years	9,476	9,373	95.5	95.3	9,390	9,278	95.5	95.3
55 to 64 years	6,451	6,389	84.4	84.8	6,447	6,384	84.4	84.8
55 to 59 years	3,767	3,754	89.9	91.0	3,764	3,749	89.9	91.0
60 to 64 years	2,684	2,635	77.8	77.3	2,684	2,635	77.8	77.3
65 years and over	1,934	1,942	26.6	26.9	1,934	1,942	26.6	26.9
Nonwhite Male								
16 years and over	5,280	5,210	77.3	78.0	4,926	4,903	76.1	76.9
16 to 19 years	455	460	47.8	49.8	418	411	45.7	46.9
16 and 17 years	164	181	33.5	37.9	162	178	33.3	37.5
18 and 19 years	291	279	63.0	62.5	256	232	59.9	58.1
20 to 24 years	798	762	85.4	86.7	629	629	82.2	84.3
25 to 54 years	3,279	3,223	93.0	92.7	3,130	3,100	92.7	92.4
25 to 34 years	1,237	1,190	94.7	94.3	1,140	1,110	94.3	94.0
35 to 44 years	1,103	1,112	93.7	93.8	1,059	1,075	93.5	93.6
45 to 54 years	939	921	90.2	89.4	932	915	90.2	89.4
55 to 64 years	579	601	76.7	80.3	579	601	76.7	80.3
55 to 59 years	342	348	81.0	84.2	342	348	81.0	84.2
60 to 64 years	237	254	71.3	75.6	237	254	71.3	75.6
65 years and over	169	163	25.5	25.1	169	163	25.5	25.1
Female								
16 years and over	29,873	29,372	42.2	42.2	29,835	29,337	42.2	42.2
16 to 19 years	2,821	2,851	39.8	40.9	2,811	2,840	39.7	40.8
16 and 17 years	1,121	1,068	31.0	30.4	1,121	1,068	31.0	30.4
18 and 19 years	1,700	1,782	49.0	51.5	1,691	1,772	48.9	51.4
20 to 24 years	4,414	4,240	55.6	55.7	4,397	4,226	55.5	55.6

TABLE 25—(Continued)

Age, sex and color	Total labor force				Civilian labor force			
	Thousands of persons		Participation rate		Thousands of persons		Participation rate	
	Dec. 1968	Dec. 1967	Dec. 1968	Dec. 1967	Dec. 1968	Dec. 1967	Dec. 1968	Dec. 1967
Female (Continued)—								
25 to 54 years	17,575	17,360	49.0	48.9	17,565	17,349	49.0	48.9
25 to 34 years	5,303	5,141	43.6	43.8	5,297	5,135	43.6	43.7
35 to 44 years	5,987	6,044	50.2	50.0	5,983	6,040	50.2	49.9
45 to 54 years	6,286	6,175	53.3	53.1	6,284	6,173	53.3	53.1
55 to 64 years	3,992	3,905	42.6	42.5	3,991	3,905	42.6	42.5
55 to 59 years	2,458	2,363	48.6	47.7	2,457	2,363	48.6	47.7
60 to 64 years	1,534	1,542	35.6	36.4	1,534	1,542	35.6	36.4
65 years and over	1,071	1,016	10.1	9.8	1,071	1,016	10.1	9.8
White Female								
16 years and over	26,070	25,554	41.4	41.2	26,036	25,522	41.3	41.2
16 to 19 years	2,522	2,514	41.3	41.7	2,513	2,505	41.2	41.7
16 and 17 years	1,016	958	32.6	31.7	1,016	958	32.6	31.7
18 and 19 years	1,505	1,556	50.3	51.9	1,497	1,547	50.1	51.7
20 to 24 years	3,830	3,710	55.1	55.4	3,816	3,697	55.0	55.4
25 to 54 years	15,165	14,901	47.8	47.4	15,155	14,891	47.8	47.4
25 to 34 years	4,482	4,268	42.1	41.5	4,476	4,263	42.0	41.4
35 to 44 years	5,114	5,168	48.7	48.4	5,111	5,165	48.7	48.4
45 to 54 years	5,569	5,465	52.6	52.3	5,568	5,464	52.6	52.3
55 to 64 years	3,576	3,509	42.0	42.0	3,576	3,509	42.0	42.0
55 to 59 years	2,188	2,108	47.8	47.0	2,188	2,108	47.8	47.0
60 to 64 years	1,388	1,401	35.3	36.3	1,388	1,401	35.3	36.3
65 years and over	976	920	10.0	9.7	976	920	10.0	9.7
Nonwhite Female								
16 years and over	3,803	3,818	49.0	50.4	3,799	3,815	49.0	50.4
16 to 19 years	299	336	30.6	35.5	298	335	30.6	35.4
16 and 17 years	105	110	20.9	22.6	105	110	20.9	22.6
18 and 19 years	195	226	40.8	49.1	194	225	40.7	49.0
20 to 24 years	584	530	59.3	57.2	582	529	59.2	57.2
25 to 54 years	2,410	2,459	58.5	60.5	2,409	2,458	58.5	60.5
25 to 34 years	821	873	55.0	60.0	821	873	55.0	60.0
35 to 44 years	872	876	61.3	61.5	872	876	61.3	61.4
45 to 54 years	716	710	59.4	59.9	716	710	59.4	59.9
55 to 64 years	415	396	48.6	47.5	415	396	48.6	47.5
55 to 59 years	270	255	56.2	55.0	270	255	56.2	55.0
60 to 64 years	145	141	38.8	38.0	145	141	38.8	38.0
65 years and over	95	96	11.5	12.1	95	96	11.5	12.1

TABLE 26

Employed Persons by Major Occupation Group, Color and Sex
(Per Cent Distribution)

Occupation group and color	Total		Male		Female	
	Dec. 1968	Dec. 1967	Dec. 1968	Dec. 1967	Dec. 1968	Dec. 1967
Total						
Total employed (thousands)	76,700	75,338	48,000	47,250	28,699	28,088
Per cent	100.0	100.0	100.0	100.0	100.0	100.0
White-collar workers	47.7	47.1	40.4	39.8	59.9	59.5
Professional and technical	14.0	13.7	13.8	13.4	14.4	14.2
Managers, officials and proprietors	10.2	10.0	13.6	13.4	4.4	4.3
Clerical workers	17.0	16.9	7.1	7.2	33.4	33.1
Sales workers	6.5	6.5	5.8	5.8	7.8	7.8
Blue-collar workers	36.2	36.1	47.6	47.4	17.1	16.9
Craftsmen and foremen	13.3	13.0	20.5	20.1	1.1	1.0
Operatives	18.4	18.6	20.2	20.5	15.5	15.5
Nonfarm laborers	4.5	4.4	6.8	6.8	.5	.4
Service workers	12.4	12.5	6.9	7.0	21.4	21.8
Private household workers	2.2	2.4	.1	.1	5.9	6.4
Other service workers	10.1	10.1	6.9	6.9	15.6	15.4
Farm workers	3.8	4.3	5.1	5.8	1.5	1.8
Farmers and farm managers	2.3	2.5	3.6	3.8	.2	.3
Farm laborers and foremen	1.5	1.8	1.6	1.9	1.3	1.5
White						
Total employed (thousands)	68,476	67,193	43,307	42,587	25,169	24,606
Per cent	100.0	100.0	100.0	100.0	100.0	100.0
White-collar workers	50.4	49.9	42.6	42.1	63.8	63.4
Professional and technical	14.8	14.4	14.6	14.2	15.1	14.9
Managers, officials and proprietors	11.1	11.0	14.7	14.6	4.8	4.7
Clerical workers	17.5	17.4	7.1	7.2	35.4	35.2
Sales workers	7.0	7.1	6.2	6.2	8.4	8.6
Blue-collar workers	35.3	35.4	46.2	46.2	16.6	16.7
Craftsmen and foremen	13.8	13.7	21.2	21.0	1.1	1.1
Operatives	17.8	18.1	19.4	19.6	15.0	15.3
Nonfarm laborers	3.7	3.7	5.6	5.6	.5	.4
Service workers	10.5	10.4	6.1	6.0	18.0	18.1
Private household workers	1.4	1.5	*	*	3.7	4.0
Other service workers	9.1	8.9	6.0	6.0	14.3	14.1
Farm workers	3.8	4.3	5.1	5.7	1.6	1.8
Farmers and farm managers	2.5	2.7	3.8	4.1	.3	.4
Farm laborers and foremen	1.3	1.5	1.3	1.6	1.3	1.4

TABLE 26—(Continued)

Occupation group and color	Total		Male		Female	
	Dec. 1968	Dec. 1967	Dec. 1968	Dec. 1967	Dec. 1968	Dec. 1967
Nonwhite						
Total employed (thousands)	8,223	8,145	4,693	4,663	3,530	3,482
Per cent	100.0	100.0	100.0	100.0	100.0	100.0
White-collar workers	25.4	24.2	19.8	18.6	32.9	31.7
Professional and technical	8.0	7.7	7.0	6.2	9.3	9.6
Managers, officials and proprietors	2.4	2.3	3.0	3.0	1.5	1.4
Clerical workers	12.8	12.2	7.9	7.8	19.3	18.2
Sales workers	2.3	2.0	1.9	1.6	2.9	2.5
Blue-collar workers	43.2	41.6	60.3	59.0	20.4	18.3
Craftsmen and foremen	8.4	7.4	14.0	12.4	.9	.7
Operatives	24.0	23.5	28.1	28.5	18.6	16.7
Nonfarm laborers	10.8	10.8	18.3	18.1	.9	.9
Service workers	28.0	29.7	14.8	16.1	45.6	47.7
Private household workers	9.3	9.9	.3	.4	21.2	22.6
Other service workers	18.7	19.8	14.5	15.8	24.4	25.1
Farm workers	3.4	4.5	5.1	6.2	1.1	2.4
Farmers and farm managers	.9	1.0	1.4	1.7	.1	.2
Farm laborers and foremen	2.5	3.5	3.7	4.5	1.0	2.2

* Less than 0.05 per cent.

TABLE 27
Employment by Month (Seasonally Adjusted) from December 1967 through December 1968
(In Thousands)

Characteristics	1968												1967
	Dec.	Nov.	Oct.	Sept.	Aug.	July	June	May	Apr.	Mar.	Feb.	Jan.	Dec.
White													
Total:													
Civilian labor force	70,769	70,457	70,000	70,123	69,871	69,995	70,105	69,609	69,560	69,892	69,959	69,355	69,686
Employed	68,695	68,369	67,789	67,848	67,630	67,655	67,761	67,415	67,437	67,654	67,655	67,154	67,391
Unemployed	2,074	2,088	2,211	2,275	2,241	2,340	2,344	2,194	2,123	2,238	2,304	2,201	2,295
Unemployment rate	2.9	3.0	3.2	3.2	3.2	3.3	3.3	3.2	3.1	3.2	3.3	3.2	3.3
Males, 20 years and over:													
Civilian labor force	41,652	41,345	41,261	41,322	41,385	41,369	41,350	41,042	41,137	41,268	41,419	41,260	41,295
Employed	40,984	40,575	40,434	40,497	40,566	40,517	40,454	40,238	40,364	40,441	40,548	40,425	40,448
Unemployed	668	770	827	825	819	852	896	804	773	827	871	835	847
Unemployment rate	1.6	1.9	2.0	2.0	2.0	2.1	2.2	2.0	1.9	2.0	2.1	2.0	2.1
Females, 20 years and over:													
Civilian labor force	23,299	23,313	22,979	22,976	22,691	22,831	22,785	22,672	22,531	22,652	22,616	22,467	22,812
Employed	22,565	22,591	22,205	22,151	21,887	22,046	22,026	21,943	21,797	21,908	21,821	21,669	21,997
Unemployed	734	722	774	825	804	785	759	729	734	744	795	798	815
Unemployment rate	3.2	3.1	3.4	3.6	3.5	3.4	3.3	3.2	3.3	3.3	3.5	3.6	3.6
Both sexes, 16 to 19 years:													
Civilian labor force	5,818	5,799	5,760	5,825	5,795	5,795	5,970	5,895	5,892	5,971	5,924	5,628	5,579
Employed	5,146	5,203	5,150	5,200	5,177	5,092	5,281	5,234	5,276	5,304	5,286	5,060	4,946
Unemployed	672	596	610	625	618	703	689	661	616	667	638	568	633
Unemployment rate	11.6	10.3	10.6	10.7	10.7	12.1	11.5	11.2	10.5	11.2	10.8	10.1	11.3
Nonwhite													
Total:													
Civilian labor force	8,894	8,674	8,601	8,509	8,728	8,859	8,802	8,837	8,815	8,919	8,819	8,639	8,892
Employed	8,361	8,110	7,963	7,937	8,190	8,245	8,164	8,272	8,227	8,301	8,187	8,085	8,281
Unemployed	533	564	638	572	538	614	638	565	588	618	632	554	611
Unemployment rate	6.0	6.5	7.4	6.7	6.2	6.9	7.2	6.4	6.7	6.9	7.2	6.4	6.9
Males, 20 years and over:													
Civilian labor force	4,562	4,500	4,458	4,485	4,523	4,532	4,554	4,567	4,569	4,591	4,565	4,504	4,547
Employed	4,409	4,332	4,249	4,302	4,355	4,373	4,384	4,399	4,386	4,400	4,369	4,312	4,391
Unemployed	153	168	209	183	168	159	170	168	183	191	196	192	156
Unemployment rate	3.4	3.7	4.7	4.1	3.7	3.5	3.7	3.7	4.0	4.2	4.3	4.3	3.4
Females, 20 years and over:													
Civilian labor force	3,547	3,443	3,417	3,346	3,397	3,479	3,460	3,484	3,427	3,478	3,486	3,386	3,527
Employed	3,336	3,242	3,203	3,141	3,200	3,230	3,229	3,281	3,212	3,261	3,251	3,167	3,273
Unemployed	211	201	214	205	197	249	231	203	215	217	235	219	254
Unemployment rate	5.9	5.8	6.3	6.1	5.8	7.2	6.7	5.8	6.3	6.2	6.7	6.5	7.2
Both sexes, 16 to 19 years:													
Civilian labor force	785	731	726	678	808	848	788	786	819	850	768	749	818
Employed	616	536	511	494	635	642	551	492	629	640	567	606	617
Unemployed	169	195	215	184	173	206	237	194	190	210	201	143	201
Unemployment rate	21.5	26.7	29.6	27.1	21.4	24.3	30.1	24.7	23.2	24.7	26.2	19.1	24.6

TABLE 28

Unemployed Persons by Duration of Unemployment, Sex, Age, Color and Marital Status for December 1968

Sex, age, color and marital status	Thousands of persons					Less than 5 weeks as a per cent of unemployed in group		15 weeks and over as a per cent of unemployed in group	
	Total	Less than 5 weeks	5 to 14 weeks	15 to 26 weeks	27 weeks and over	Dec. 1968	Dec. 1967	Dec. 1968	Dec. 1967
Total	2,419	1,303	814	165	137	53.9	50.3	12.5	15.3
16 to 21 years	932	564	282	55	31	60.5	52.6	9.2	12.5
16 to 19 years	728	429	236	44	20	58.9	54.0	8.7	12.8
20 to 24 years	435	277	123	21	14	63.7	53.1	8.1	11.6
25 to 44 years	678	326	240	59	51	48.1	48.9	16.2	14.9
45 years and over	579	272	215	40	53	46.9	46.0	16.1	21.0
Male	1,283	671	454	77	81	52.3	52.8	12.3	14.4
16 to 21 years	503	286	176	31	11	56.7	56.4	8.4	9.8
16 to 19 years	410	225	149	25	11	54.9	57.4	8.7	9.3
20 to 24 years	211	136	62	10	3	64.2	60.1	6.4	8.1
25 to 44 years	314	157	114	15	27	50.0	53.3	13.4	14.0
45 years and over	347	154	129	26	39	44.2	44.1	18.6	23.3
Female	1,136	632	360	88	56	55.6	47.3	12.7	16.2
16 to 21 years	428	278	107	24	20	65.0	48.2	10.2	15.7
16 to 19 years	317	203	87	18	9	64.1	49.7	8.6	17.1
20 to 24 years	223	141	60	11	11	63.2	45.4	9.7	15.3
25 to 44 years	363	170	127	44	23	46.8	45.5	18.5	15.2
45 years and over	232	118	86	15	14	50.8	49.2	12.2	17.3
White: Total	1,917	1,050	644	116	107	54.8	51.2	11.6	15.2
Male	1,051	556	374	56	64	52.9	53.2	11.5	15.0
Female	866	495	269	60	43	57.1	48.5	11.8	15.5
Nonwhite: Total	501	253	170	49	29	50.4	46.9	15.6	15.6
Male	232	116	80	21	16	49.8	51.1	15.8	11.7
Female	269	137	90	28	13	51.0	43.9	15.4	18.4
Male: Married, wife present..	562	272	211	34	45	48.5	51.3	14.0	17.3
Widowed, divorced or separated	105	55	34	7	10	52.2	45.8	15.8	18.6
Single (never married) .	616	344	210	36	26	55.9	55.6	10.1	10.7
Female: Married, husband present	559	308	185	39	27	55.1	49.8	11.9	12.8
Widowed, divorced or separated	194	105	67	15	6	54.1	43.4	11.1	19.0
Single (never married)	383	219	108	33	23	57.3	45.4	14.6	20.3

TABLE 29

Employment Status of Persons 16 Years and Over, in Urban Poverty and Other Urban Neighborhoods* by Color

(In thousands)

Employment status	Total		White		Nonwhite	
	2nd Quarter 1969	2nd Quarter 1968	2nd Quarter 1969	2nd Quarter 1968	2nd Quarter 1969	2nd Quarter 1968
TOTAL UNITED STATES						
Civilian labor force	80,513	78,919	71,624	70,066	8,889	8,852
Unemployment	2,747	2,803	2,160	2,218	587	585
Unemployment rate	3.4	3.6	3.0	3.2	6.6	6.6
URBAN POVERTY NEIGHBORHOODS						
Civilian labor force	6,395	6,511	3,739	3,808	2,656	2,703
Unemployment	363	373	151	177	212	196
Unemployment rate	5.7	5.7	4.0	4.6	8.0	7.3
OTHER URBAN NEIGHBORHOODS						
Civilian labor force	38,713	37,673	35,572	34,657	3,142	3,016
Unemployment	1,151	1,196	995	1,042	157	154
Unemployment rate	3.0	3.2	2.8	3.0	5.0	5.1

* Pertains only to standard metropolitan statistical areas (SMSA's) with populations of 250,000 or more.

TABLE 30

Employment Status of Persons 16 Years and Over, in Urban Poverty and Other Urban Neighborhoods,* by Color, Sex, and Age

(In thousands)

Employment status, sex, and age	Total		White		Nonwhite	
	2nd Quarter 1969	2nd Quarter 1968	2nd Quarter 1969	2nd Quarter 1968	2nd Quarter 1969	2nd Quarter 1968
MALES, 20 YEARS AND OVER						
Urban poverty neighborhoods						
Civilian labor force	3,564	3,634	2,195	2,219	1,369	1,414
Unemployment	120	146	71	89	59	58
Unemployment rate	3.4	4.0	3.2	4.0	4.3	4.1
Other urban neighborhoods						
Civilian labor force	22,558	22,137	20,899	20,544	1,659	1,593
Unemployment	384	388	331	348	52	40
Unemployment rate	1.7	1.8	1.6	1.7	3.1	2.5
FEMALES, 20 YEARS AND OVER						
Urban poverty neighborhoods						
Civilian labor force	2,342	2,350	1,265	1,286	1,077	1,065
Unemployment	133	116	52	43	81	73
Unemployment rate	5.7	4.9	4.1	3.3	7.5	6.9
Other urban neighborhoods						
Civilian labor force	13,023	12,484	11,759	11,294	1,263	1,191
Unemployment	384	396	334	339	50	58
Unemployment rate	2.9	3.2	2.8	3.0	4.0	4.9
TEENAGERS, 16-19 YEARS						
Urban poverty neighborhoods						
Civilian labor force	489	526	279	303	210	224
Unemployment	110	110	37	45	73	65
Unemployment rate	22.5	20.9	13.4	14.9	34.7	29.1
Other urban neighborhoods						
Civilian labor force	3,132	3,052	2,912	2,820	219	232
Unemployment	384	412	329	356	55	56
Unemployment rate	12.3	13.5	11.3	12.6	25.1	24.2

* Pertains only to SMSA's with populations of 250,000 or more.

TABLE 31

Department of Labor Negro Employment

	1961	1962	1963	1964	1965	1966	1967	1968*
Number of Negroes employed	1,222	1,524	1,780	1,740	1,772	1,938	2,182	2,276
Per cent of work force	18.01	18.20	19.25	19.57	19.76	20.89	23.32	24.11

Department of Labor Negro Employment by Grade Distribution

	GS–4 and below		GS–5 thru GS–11		GS–12 thru GS–18	
	Number	Per cent	Number	Per cent	Number	Per cent
1961	839	68.7	359	29.4	24	2.0
1962	968	63.5	509	33.4	47	3.1
1963	989	55.6	720	40.4	71	4.0
1964	840	48.2	812	46.7	88	5.1
1965	788	44.5	858	48.4	126	7.1
1966	829	42.8	950	49.0	159	8.2
1967	842	38.6	1,118	51.2	222	10.2
1968*	866	38.5	1,173	51.1	237	10.4

*Through June 30, 1968.
Source: U.S. Department of Labor.

TABLE 32

Employment Status and Reported Voter Participation of Persons of Voting Age, by Color: November 1966 and 1964

(Numbers in thousands.   Civilian noninstitutional population)

Employment status	Total		White		Nonwhite	
	1966	1964	1966	1964	1966	1964
Civilian labor force	69,204	66,926	61,455	59,283	7,749	7,643
Employed	67,331	64,423	59,984	57,342	7,347	7,081
Agriculture	3,446	3,929	3,008	3,267	438	662
Nonagricultural industries	63,885	60,494	56,976	54,075	6,909	6,419
Unemployed	1,873	2,503	1,471	1,941	402	562
Not in the labor force	43,596	43,677	39,750	40,069	3,846	3,608
VOTER PARTICIPATION RATE						
Civilian labor force	57.8	72.4	59.5	73.8	44.1	62.1
Employed	58.3	73.0	59.9	74.3	44.9	62.1
Agriculture	58.5	63.1	63.3	69.9	25.4	29.2
Nonagricultural industries	58.2	73.6	59.7	74.6	46.1	65.5
Unemployed	40.2	58.0	43.0	57.0	30.2	61.6
Not in the labor force	51.7	64.6	53.3	66.1	34.9	47.7

TABLE 33

Occupation and Reported Voter Participation of Employed Persons of Voting Age, by Color: November 1966 and 1964

(Numbers in thousands.   Civilian noninstitutional population)

Occupation	Total		White		Nonwhite	
	1966	1964	1966	1964	1966	1964
Total employed	67,331	64,424	59,984	57,343	7,347	7,081
White-collar workers	31,376	29,255	29,792	27,864	1,584	1,391
Manual workers	24,622	23,909	21,508	20,963	3,114	2,946
Service workers	8,117	7,579	5,869	5,468	2,248	2,111
Farm workers	3,216	3,681	2,815	3,048	401	633
VOTER PARTICIPATION RATE						
Total employed	58.3	73.0	59.9	74.3	44.9	62.1
White-collar workers	67.2	82.0	67.6	82.2	59.0	78.6
Manual workers	49.8	65.6	50.8	66.1	42.6	61.9
Service workers	49.0	65.8	52.0	67.5	41.4	61.6
Farm workers	59.4	63.7	64.0	71.0	26.4	28.9

TABLE 34

Family Income and Reported Voter Participation of Persons 21 Years Old and Over in Primary Families: November 1966 and 1964

(Numbers in thousands. Civilian noninstitutional population.   Income for preceding 12 months.)

Family income	Total		White		Nonwhite	
	1966	1964	1966	1964	1966	1964
Persons 21 years old and over	100,737	98,853	90,784	89,260	9,953	9,593
Under $3,000	14,042	16,812	10,747	13,112	3,295	3,700
$3,000 to $4,999	16,358	18,039	13,814	15,577	2,544	2,462
$5,000 to $7,499	24,991	25,319	22,998	23,717	1,993	1,602
$7,500 to $9,999	16,553	14,654	15,789	14,038	764	616
$10,000 and over	21,483	15,971	20,696	15,475	787	496
Income not reported	7,310	8,059	6,740	7,341	570	718
VOTER PARTICIPATION RATE						
Persons 21 years old and over	56.4	70.1	57.9	71.4	42.6	58.2
Under $3,000	43.2	53.3	46.6	56.0	32.1	43.4
$3,000 to $4,999	47.2	62.7	48.2	63.0	41.7	60.8
$5,000 to $7,499	55.0	72.4	55.3	72.4	51.3	73.0
$7,500 to $9,999	62.6	78.3	63.2	78.5	50.5	74.4
$10,000 and over	69.5	84.9	69.8	85.0	63.2	81.5
Income not reported	54.4	70.7	55.7	71.5	38.4	62.5

TABLE 35

Female Heads as a Per cent of All Family Heads in Central Cities, by Family Income
(1967 dollars)

	Total		White		Negro	
	1967	1959	1967	1959	1967	1959
All families	15	12	12	10	30	23
Under $2,000	44	38	36	31	61	51
$2,000 to $3,999	33	23	23	20	54	29
$4,000 to $5,999	22	11	20	11	27	14
$6,000 to $7,999	14	7	12	7	21	7
$8,000 to $9,999	8	7	8	7	12	6
$10,000 and over	5	5	5	5	6	9

The proportion of central city families headed by women has edged up in the past 8 years to 15 per cent in 1967. The proportion headed by women ranged from 44 per cent for families receiving income of under $2,000 in 1967 to only 5 per cent for those with incomes over $10,000.

In 1967, Negro families at the low income levels (under $4,000) were much more likely than white families to be headed by women, but the gap between the races narrowed significantly in the income brackets between $4,000 and $10,000 and virtually disappeared among families with incomes over $10,000.

TABLE 36

The Geographic Distribution of Hunger in the United States
(Similar data for subdivisions in Hawaii and Alaska was not available)

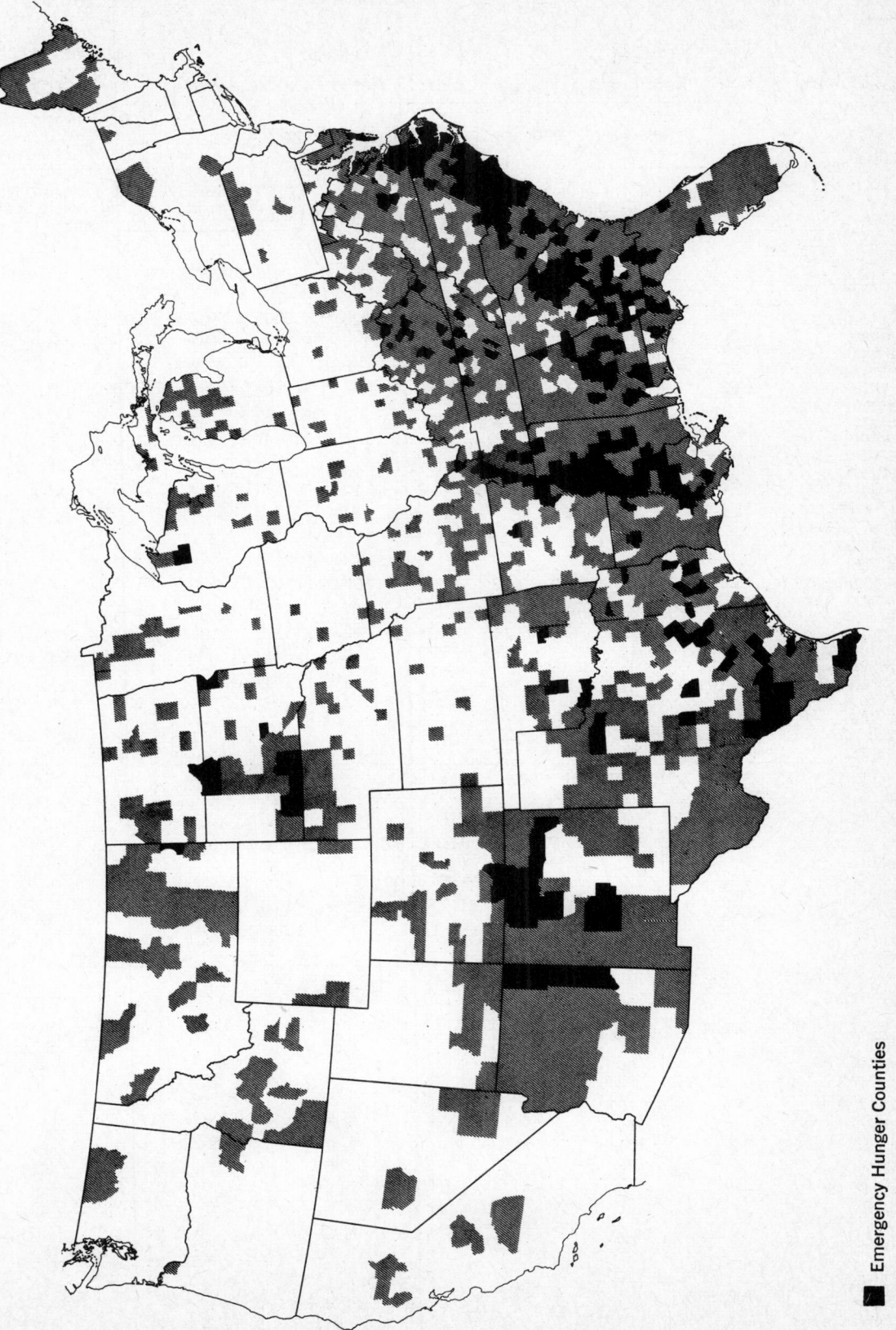

Source: New Community Press, Washington, D.C., Copyright © 1968

■ Emergency Hunger Counties

▨ Additional Counties with Serious Hunger Problem

TABLE 37

Families by Type and Color, by Region and Residence

Type of family	Region and residence (per cent by type of family)								Region and residence (per cent distribution by region and residence)			
	United States	North-east	North-central	South	West[1]	Urban	Rural non-farm	Rural farm	United States	North-east	North-central	South
TYPE OF FAMILY AND COLOR, 1960												
All families												
Nonwhite	100	100	100	100	100	100	100	100	100	14	16	64
White	100	100	100	100	100	100	100	100	100	28	32	27
Husband-wife												
Nonwhite	78	73	79	78	82	76	77	86	100	13	16	64
White	88	86	89	89	89	87	90	91	100	27	32	27
Other male head												
Nonwhite	5	5	5	5	5	5	5	5	100	15	15	63
White	4	4	4	3	3	3	3	5	100	34	32	23
Female head												
Nonwhite	18	22	17	18	13	20	18	9	100	17	15	64
White	9	10	8	8	8	10	7	4	100	32	29	26
TYPE OF FAMILY AND COLOR, 1960												
All families												
Nonwhite	100	100	100	100	100	100	100	100	100	16	18	55
White	100	100	100	100	100	100	100	100	100	26	30	27
Husband-wife												
Nonwhite	75	72	76	74	81	74	77	84	100	16	19	54
White	89	88	90	89	90	88	91	92	100	26	31	27
Other male head												
Nonwhite	4	4	4	4	4	4	5	5	100	17	17	55
White	3	3	3	2	2	3	2	4	100	33	30	23
Female head												
Nonwhite	21	23	20	22	15	22	19	11	100	18	18	56
White	8	9	7	8	8	9	7	4	100	30	27	28

[1] Includes Alaska and Hawaii in 1960. Note.—Because of rounding, sums of individual items may not equal totals.

TABLE 38

Type of Family

	Metropolitan areas, total		Central cities		Suburban rings	
TOTAL						
Number (millions)	32.2	28.6	14.6	14.7	17.6	13.9
Per cent	100	100	100	100	100	100
Husband-wife	86	88	82	84	90	91
Other male head	3	3	3	3	2	2
Female head	11	10	15	12	8	7
WHITE						
Number (millions)	28.6	25.8	11.8	12.4	16.8	13.3
Per cent	100	100	100	100	100	100
Husband-wife	88	89	85	86	90	92
Other male head	2	3	3	3	2	2
Female head	10	8	12	10	8	6
NEGRO						
Number (millions)	3.3	2.6	2.6	2.1	0.7	0.5
Per cent	100	100	100	100	100	100
Husband-wife	67	74	66	73	72	79
Other male head	4	4	4	4	6	3
Female head	29	22	30	23	22	18

Source: U.S. Bureau of the Census

TABLE 39

Per Cent Distribution by Characteristics of White and Negro Households and Famalies, for the United States and Regions: March 1966

Subject	United States		North and West		South	
	White	Negro	White	Negro	White	Negro
Size of Family						
All families	100.0	100.0	100.0	100.0	100.0	100.0
2 persons	34.2	28.7	34.2	28.5	34.2	28.9
3 persons	20.4	18.3	19.9	19.1	21.8	17.6
4 persons	19.7	15.5	19.6	16.7	20.1	14.5
5 persons	12.8	12.0	13.0	13.7	12.3	10.6
6 persons	6.9	8.2	7.1	7.9	6.6	8.4
7 persons	5.9	17.3	6.2	14.1	5.1	20.1
Average (mean) size	3.64	4.42	3.66	4.23	3.59	4.59
Related Children Under 18						
All families	100.0	100.0	100.0	100.0	100.0	100.0
No related children under 18	42.9	31.9	42.9	32.3	42.9	31.6
With related children under 18	57.1	68.1	57.1	67.7	57.1	68.4
1 related child under 18	18.0	18.2	17.5	17.3	19.3	19.0
2 related children under 18	17.7	14.4	17.3	16.2	18.6	13.0
3 related children under 18	11.0	12.4	11.3	14.0	10.3	11.1
4 or more under 18	10.4	23.0	11.0	20.3	8.9	25.4
Average (mean) per family	1.35	2.06	1.38	1.97	1.29	2.14
Average per family with child	2.37	3.02	2.41	2.90	2.26	3.13

Husband-wife families were much more prevalent among whites than among Negro families in both 1968 and 1960. In central cities, the proportion of husband-wife families among Negroes declined from 73 per cent to 66 per cent between 1960 and 1968.

About 8 out of every 10 families in the major cities in 1968 were headed by a man with his wife present. Within the suburban ring, 9 of every 10 families had both husband and wife present.

TABLE 40

Fertility Rates, by Color, United States, 1940-64 (per 1,000 women age 15-44)

Year	Nonwhite	White	Ratio, nonwhite to white	Year	Nonwhite	White	Ratio, nonwhite to white
	Births adjusted for under-registration				Births adjusted for under-registration—Continued		
1940	102.4	77.1	1.33	1956	160.9	116.0	1.39
1941	105.4	80.7	1.31	1957	163.0	117.7	1.38
1942	107.6	89.6	1.20	1958	160.5	114.9	1.40
1943	111.0	92.3	1.20	1959	162.2	114.6	1.42
1944	108.5	86.3	1.26				
1945	106.0	83.4	1.27				
1946	113.9	100.4	1.13		Registered births		
1947	125.9	111.8	1.13				
1948	131.6	104.3	1.26				
1949	135.1	103.6	1.30	1959	156.0	113.9	1.37
1950	137.3	102.3	1.34	1960	153.6	113.2	1.36
1951 [1]	142.1	107.7	1.32	1961	153.5	112.2	1.37
1952	143.3	110.1	1.30	1962 [2]	148.7	107.5	1.38
1953	147.3	111.0	1.33	1963 [2]	144.8	103.7	1.40
1954	153.2	113.6	1.35	1964	141.5	99.8	1.42
1955	155.3	113.8	1.36				

[1] Based on a 50-per cent sample of births, since 1951. Before 1951, based on total count.   [2] Excludes data for New Jersey.

Note.—Refers only to births occurring within the United States. Alaska included beginning 1959, and Hawaii, 1960. Rates for 1940, 1950, and 1960 are based on population enumerated as of April 1; for all other years, estimated as of July 1.

Source: *Vital Statistics of the United States, 1963,* Vol. I, *Natality,* table 1-2 for 1940-63; *Monthly Vital Statistics Report,* Col. 14, No. 8, table 1 for 1964. (U.S. Department of Health, Education, and Welfare.)

TABLE 41

Selected Characteristics of Families: 1967-1969

(Number in thousands)

	1969 White	1969 Negro	1968 White	1968 Negro	1967 White	1967 Negro
All families	45,437	4,646	44,814	4,589	44,110	4,560
Female head	4,053	1,327	4,008	1,272	4,032	1,138
Per cent of all families	8.9	28.6	8.9	27.7	9.1	25.0
Average number of own children under 18 per family:						
All families	1.27	1.80	1.29	1.78	1.30	1.76
Female head	1.03	1.95	1.01	1.98	0.98	1.93
Per cent of children of family heads living with both parents	91.9	67.2	92.2	67.3	92.4	71.0
Marital status of female head:						
Total	100.0	100.0	100.0	100.0	100.0	100.0
Married, husband absent	19.8	42.4	19.0	39.7	19.4	40.4
Separated	12.0	36.9	12.0	34.6	12.0	33.3
Other	7.7	5.6	7.0	5.1	7.4	7.3
Widowed	47.5	31.2	50.1	33.4	49.6	34.7
Divorced	22.8	12.8	21.9	13.1	21.9	13.3
Single	9.8	13.6	8.9	13.8	9.1	11.6

The proportion of nonwhite families headed by a female has increased since 1960, continuing the trend observed during the fifties. About 70 per cent of all nonwhite families are headed by a man with a wife present, compared to 90 per cent of white families.

TABLE 42

Fertility Rates, 1955-1966*

(Births per 1,000 women age 15-44)

	Nonwhite	White
1955	155	114
1956	161	116
1957	163	118
1958	161	115
1959	162	114
1960	154	113
1961	154	112
1962**	149	108
1963**	145	104
1964	142	100
1965	134	91
1966	126	86

* Births 1955-59 adjusted for underregistration.
** Excludes data for New Jersey.

Birth rates are higher among nonwhite than among white women. In recent years both nonwhite and white birth rates have dropped sharply.

Source: U.S. Department of Health, Education, and Welfare.

TABLE 43

Composition of Families, 1950, 1955, 1960, and 1966-1968

(Per cent)

	Husband-wife Nonwhite	White	Other male head Nonwhite	White	Female head* Nonwhite	White
1950	77.7	88.0	4.7	3.5	17.6	8.5
1955	75.3	87.9	4.0	3.0	20.7	9.0
1960	73.6	88.7	4.0	2.6	22.4	8.7
1966	72.7	88.8	3.7	2.3	23.7	8.9
1967	72.6	88.7	3.9	2.1	23.6	9.1
1968	69.1	88.9	4.5	2.2	26.4	8.9

* Female heads of families include widowed and single women, women whose husbands are in the armed services or otherwise away from home involuntarily, as well as those separated from their husbands through divorce or marital discord. In 1968, divorce and separation accounted for 47 per cent of the nonwhite female family heads and 34 per cent of the white.

Source: U.S. Department of Commerce, Bureau of the Census.

TABLE 44

Marital Status of Female Heads of Families

	Metropolitan areas, total		Central cities		Suburban rings	
	1968	1960	1968	1960	1968	1960
WHITE						
Number (millions)	2.7	2.1	1.5	1.3	1.3	0.8
Per cent	100	100	100	100	100	100
Single	10	12	12	14	7	9
Separated or divorced	37	31	37	31	38	32
Separated	13	11	13	11	13	10
Divorced	25	21	24	19	25	22
Married, husband absent	5	7	5	7	6	8
In Armed Forces	2	—	1	—	3	—
Other reasons	3	7	3	7	3	8
Widowed	48	49	47	48	49	51
NEGRO						
Number (millions)	0.9	0.6	0.8	0.5	0.1	0.1
Per cent	100	100	100	100	100	100
Single	15	13	15	13	11	9
Separated or divorced	54	45	55	46	49	38
Separated	38	32	39	34	33	25
Divorced	16	13	16	13	17	13
Married, husband absent	5	6	4	6	8	8
In Armed Forces	1	—	1	—	1	—
Other reasons	3	6	3	6	8	8
Widowed	26	36	25	35	31	45

— Rounds to zero

TABLE 45

Changes in the White and Negro Population, 1960 to 1968, and Per Cent White and Negro, by Age, 1968 and 1960

(Numbers in thousands. Total population including Armed Forces overseas)

Age	White				Negro				Per cent by race [1]		
	July 1, 1968	April 1, 1960	Change, 1960 to 1968		July 1, 1968	April 1, 1960	Change, 1960 to 1968				Negro
			Number	Per cent			Number	Per cent	White	Negro	Negro
All ages	176,663	159,467	+17,196	+10.8	22,354	18,916	+3,438	+18.2	87.8	11.1	88.6	10.5
Under 5 years	15,400	17,359	− 1,958	−11.3	2,859	2,731	+ 128	+ 4.7	83.2	15.4	85.4	13.4
5 to 13 years	31,703	28,341	+ 3,362	+11.9	5,066	4,049	+1,017	+25.1	85.1	13.6	86.6	12.4
14 to 17 years	12,982	9,785	+ 3,196	+32.7	1,908	1,273	+ 635	+49.9	86.2	12.7	87.7	11.4
18 to 24 years	19,983	14,032	+ 5,951	+42.4	2,633	1,785	+ 849	+47.5	87.5	11.5	87.8	11.2
25 to 34 years	21,124	20,317	+ 808	+ 4.0	2,565	2,435	+ 130	+ 5.3	88.1	10.7	88.3	10.6
35 to 44 years	20,984	21,657	− 673	− 3.1	2,375	2,322	+ 53	+ 2.3	88.7	10.0	89.6	9.6
45 to 64 years	36,865	32,673	+ 4,192	+12.8	3,572	3,146	+ 426	+13.5	90.4	8.8	90.6	8.7
64 years and over	17,622	15,304	+ 2,318	+15.1	1,376	1,176	+ 200	+17.0	92.1	7.2	92.4	7.1

[1] Base includes other nonwhite races, not shown in distribution.

TABLE 46

Summary of Social and Economic Characteristics of the White and Negro
Population, for the United States: March 1967 and April 1960

(Number in thousands. In general, the 1967 data in this report include members of the Armed Forces in the United States living off post or with their families on post, but exclude all other members of the Armed Forces. About 996,000 members of whom 906,000 were white and 63,000 were Negro, are included)

Subject	1967 (CPS)		1960 (Census)	
	White	Negro	White	Negro
Total population	172,198	21,631	158,838	18,849
SEX				
Male	83,771	10,358	78,348	9,098
Female	88,427	11,273	80,490	9,751
REGION [1]				
Per cent	100.0	100.0	100.0	100.0
Northeast	25.7	17.1	26.1	16.0
North Central	29.2	20.7	30.2	18.3
South	27.7	53.9	27.4	60.0
West	17.4	8.3	16.3	5.7
METROPOLITAN-NONMETROPOLITAN RESIDENCE				
Per cent	100.0	100.0	100.0	100.0
Metropolitan areas	64.2	67.9	62.8	64.7
In central cities	27.1	54.5	30.0	51.5
Outside central cities	37.1	13.4	32.8	13.2
Nonmetropolitan areas	35.8	32.1	37.2	35.4
YEARS OF SCHOOL COMPLETED				
Persons 14 years old and over	124,501	13,794	113,123	12,088
Median school years completed	12.0	9.7	11.0	8.6
Persons 14 to 24 years old	30,244	4,136	23,541	3,034
Per cent completed 4 years of high school	26.7	20.7	25.3	16.8
Median school years completed	11.4	10.4	11.0	9.9
Persons 25 to 34 years old	19,695	2,425	20,162	2,405
Per cent completed 4 years of high school	43.9	37.1	37.5	22.4
Per cent completed 4 years of college or more	15.0	5.6	11.7	4.3
Median school years completed	12.5	12.1	12.3	10.3
Persons 35 years old and over	74,562	7,233	69,420	6,649
Median school years completed	11.7	8.4	10.1	7.3
MARITAL STATUS				
Male, 14 years old and over	59,416	6,432	55,036	5,713
Per cent	100.0	100.0	100.0	100.0
Single	25.9	32.8	24.4	29.6
Married	68.9	59.7	70.3	63.3
Separated	0.9	5.4	1.0	5.7
Widowed	3.1	4.8	3.2	4.6
Divorced	2.1	2.8	2.1	2.4
Female, 14 years old and over	65,085	7,362	58,087	6,375
Per cent	100.0	100.0	100.0	100.0
Single	20.5	24.3	18.6	21.7
Married	63.9	57.8	66.7	60.3
Separated	1.5	9.0	1.3	8.9
Widowed	12.5	13.9	11.9	14.3
Divorced	3.1	4.1	2.8	3.7
CHARACTERISTICS OF FAMILIES				
Number of families	44,016	4,510	40,873	3,950
Per cent	100.0	100.0	100.0	100.0
Husband-wife	88.6	70.9	89.2	74.2
Other male head	2.3	4.1	2.7	4.2
Female head	9.1	25.0	8.1	21.7
Average size of family	3.62	4.38	3.58	(NA)

NA Not available.

[1] Represents 3-years average, 1965-67.

TABLE 47

Per cent Distribution of the Negro Population, by Region,*
1940, 1950, 1960, 1966, and 1968

	1940**	1950**	1960	1966	1968
United States	100	100	100	100	100
South	77	68	60	55	53
North	22	28	34	37	40
Northeast	11	13	16	17	18
North Central	11	15	18	20	22
West	1	4	6	8	8

* Except where noted, when data for regions are shown in this and succeeding tables, the standard Census definition for each region is used. In that definition, the South includes the States of the Old Confederacy as well as Delaware, the District of Columbia, Kentucky, Maryland, Oklahoma, and West Virginia.
** Data exclude Alaska and Hawaii.
NOTE.—In this report, numbers or percentages may not always add to totals because of rounding. More than half of all Negroes live in the South although the proportion is declining.
Source: U.S. Department of Commerce, Bureau of the Census.

TABLE 48

White and Negro Population—Per cent Distribution by Selected Characteristics: 1960 and 1968

1960 based on enumerated population as of April 1, and includes all members of the Armed Forces resident in the United States. 1968 based on Current Population Survey, as of March, and includes members of the Armed Forces living off post or with their families on post, but excludes all other members of the Armed Forces. See text, p. 1. For definition of median, see preface]

Characteristic		1960, TOTAL		1968					
		White	Negro	White			Negro		
				Total	Male	Female	Total	Male	Female
Total population	1,000	158,838	18,849	173,997	84,614	89,383	22,029	10,531	11,498
Nonfarm	1,000	146,962	17,367	164,747	79,808	84,939	20,935	9,971	10,964
Farm	1,000	11,876	1,482	9,251	4,806	4,445	1,094	560	534
AGE									
Per cent, all ages		100.0	100.0	100.0	100.0	100.0	100.0	100.0	100.0
Under 5 years		10.9	14.4	9.0	9.5	8.5	13.1	13.8	12.4
5-13 years		17.8	21.4	18.2	19.1	17.3	22.9	23.9	21.9
14-24 years		14.8	16.1	17.8	17.6	18.0	19.7	19.8	19.6
25-34 years		12.7	12.8	11.8	11.9	11.7	11.2	10.8	11.6
35-44 years		13.6	12.2	12.1	12.2	11.9	10.7	10.3	11.2
45-54 years		11.7	9.9 ⎫	21.1	20.8	21.3	16.2	15.7	16.6
55-64 years		9.0	6.9 ⎬						
65 years and over		9.4	6.2	10.1	8.9	11.2	6.3	5.8	6.7
Under 18 years		35.0	(NA)	34.6	36.3	33.0	44.5	46.6	42.6
18 years and over		65.0	(NA)	65.4	63.7	67.0	55.5	53.4	57.4
Median age	years	30.3	23.5	29.2	28.2	30.3	21.2	19.8	22.4
MARITAL STATUS									
Per cent, 14 years old and over		100.0	100.0	100.0	100.0	100.0	100.0	100.0	100.0
Single		21.4	25.5	23.6	26.4	21.1	30.6	34.9	26.8
Married		68.5	61.7	65.9	68.4	63.6	55.8	57.6	54.2
Spouse present		65.5	50.5	63.7	66.8	60.9	45.7	49.3	42.5
Spouse absent		2.9	11.2	2.1	1.6	2.6	10.1	8.2	11.7
Separated		1.1	7.4	1.2	0.9	1.4	7.9	6.3	9.4
Other		1.8	3.8	1.0	0.7	1.2	2.2	2.0	2.4
Widowed		7.7	9.7	7.8	3.0	12.3	10.0	4.8	14.5
Divorced		2.4	3.1	2.7	2.3	3.1	3.7	2.8	4.5
TYPE OF FAMILY									
Per cent, all heads of families		100.0	100.0	100.0	100.0	100.0	100.0	100.0	100.0
Husband-wife		89.2	74.2	88.9	97.6	(X)	68.0	94.0	(X)
Other male head		2.7	4.2	2.2	2.4	(X)	4.3	6.0	(X)
Female head		8.1	21.7	8.9	(X)	100.0	27.7	(X)	100.0

NA Not available.   X Not applicable.
Source: Dept. of Commerce, Bureau of the Census; U.S. Census of Population: 1960, Vol. I, PC(2)-1C, Nonwhite Population by Race, and Current Population Reports, Series P-20, forthcoming report.

TABLE 49

Population, by Race—States: 1940 to 1960

State	1940			1950			1960			
								Negro		
	White	Negro	Other races	White	Negro	Other races	White	Number	Per cent of all classes	Other races
U.S.	118,357,831	12,865,914	941,384	135,149,629	15,044,937	1,131,232	158,831,732	18,871,831	10.5	1,619,612
N.E.	8,329,146	101,509	6,635	9,161,156	142,941	10,356	10,242,389	243,363	2.3	23,615
Maine	844,543	1,304	1,379	910,846	1,221	1,707	963,291	3,318	0.3	2,656
N.H.	490,989	414	121	532,275	731	236	604,334	1,903	0.3	684
Vt.	358,806	384	41	377,188	443	116	389,092	519	0.1	270
Mass.	4,257,596	55,391	3,734	4,611,503	73,171	5,840	5,023,144	111,842	2.2	13,592
R.I.	701,805	11,024	517	777,015	13,903	978	838,712	18,332	2.1	2,444
Conn.	1,675,407	32,992	843	1,952,329	53,472	1,479	2,423,816	107,449	4.2	3,969
M.A.	26,237,622	1,268,366	33,499	28,237,528	1,875,241	50,764	31,280,078	2,785,136	8.2	103,238
N.Y.	12,879,546	571,221	28,375	13,872,095	918,191	39,906	15,287,071	1,417,511	8.4	77,722
N.J.	3,931,087	226,973	2,105	4,511,585	318,565	5,179	5,539,003	514,875	8.5	12,904
Pa.	9,426,989	470,172	3,019	9,853,848	638,485	5,679	10,454,004	852,750	7.5	12,612
E.N.C.	25,528,451	1,069,326	28,565	28,543,307	1,803,698	52,363	33,253,272	2,884,969	8.0	86,783
Ohio	6,566,531	339,461	1,620	7,428,222	513,072	5,333	8,909,698	786,097	8.1	10,602
Ind.	3,305,323	121,916	557	3,758,512	174,168	1,544	4,388,554	269,275	5.8	4,669
Ill.	7,504,202	387,446	5,593	8,046,058	645,980	20,138	9,010,252	1,037,470	10.3	33,436
Mich.	5,039,643	208,345	8,118	5,917,825	442,296	11,645	7,085,865	717,581	9.2	19,748
Wis.	3,112,752	12,158	12,677	3,392,690	28,182	13,703	3,858,903	74,546	1.9	18,328
W.N.C.	13,111,519	350,992	54,479	13,576,077	424,178	61,139	14,749,345	561,068	3.6	83,702
Minn.	2,768,982	9,928	13,390	2,953,697	14,022	14,764	3,371,603	22,263	0.7	19,998
Iowa	2,520,691	16,694	883	2,599,546	19,692	1,835	2,728,709	25,354	0.9	3,474
Mo.	3,539,187	244,386	1,091	3,655,593	297,088	1,972	3,922,967	390,853	9.0	5,993
N. Dak.	631,464	201	10,270	608,448	257	10,931	619,538	777	0.1	12,131
S. Dak.	619,075	474	23,412	628,504	727	23,509	653,098	1,114	0.2	26,302
Nebr.	1,297,624	14,171	4,039	1,301,328	19,234	4,948	1,374,764	29,262	2.1	7,304
Kans.	1,734,496	65,138	1,394	1,828,961	73,158	3,180	2,078,666	91,445	4.2	8,500
S.A.	13,095,227	4,698,863	29,061	16,041,709	5,094,744	45,882	20,047,496	5,844,565	22.5	79,671
Del.	230,528	35,876	101	273,878	43,598	609	384,327	60,688	13.6	1,277
Md.	1,518,481	301,931	832	1,954,975	385,972	2,054	2,573,919	518,410	16.7	8,360
D.C.	474,326	187,266	1,499	517,865	280,803	3,510	345,433	411,737	53.9	6,956
Va.	2,015,583	661,449	741	2,581,555	734,211	2,914	3,142,433	816,258	20.6	8,248
W. Va.	1,784,102	117,754	118	1,890,282	114,867	403	1,770,133	89,378	4.8	910
N.C.	2,567,635	981,298	22,690	2,983,121	1,047,353	31,455	3,399,285	1,116,021	24.5	40,849
S.C.	1,084,308	814,164	1,332	1,293,405	822,077	1,545	1,551,022	829,291	34.8	2,281
Ga.	2,038,278	1,084,927	518	2,380,577	1,062,762	1,239	2,817,223	1,122,596	28.5	3,297
Fla.	1,381,986	514,198	1,230	2,166,051	603,101	2,153	4,063,881	880,186	17.8	7,493
E.S.C.	7,993,755	2,780,635	3,835	8,770,570	2,698,635	7,976	9,338,991	2,698,839	22.4	12,296
Ky.	2,631,425	214,031	171	2,742,090	201,921	795	2,820,083	215,949	7.1	2,124
Tenn.	2,406,906	508,736	199	2,760,257	530,603	858	2,977,753	586,876	16.5	2,460
Ala.	1,849,097	983,290	574	2,079,591	979,617	2,535	2,283,609	980,271	30.0	2,860
Miss.	1,106,327	1,074,578	2,891	1,188,632	986,494	3,788	1,257,546	915,743	42.0	4,852
W.S.C.	10,569,596	2,425,121	69.808	12,037,250	2,432,028	68,294	14,090,149	2,768,203	16.3	92,903
Ark.	1,466,084	482,578	725	1,481,507	426,639	1,365	1,395,703	388,787	21.8	1,782
La.	1,511,739	849,303	2,838	1,796,683	882,428	4,405	2,211,715	1,039,207	31.9	6,100
Okla.	2,104,228	168,849	63,357	2,032,526	145,503	55,322	2,107,900	153,084	6.6	67,300
Tex.	5,487,545	924,391	2,888	6,762,534	977,458	7,202	8,374,831	1,187,125	12.4	17,721
Mt.	3,978,913	36,411	134,679	4,845,634	66,429	162,935	6,514,294	123,242	1.8	217,524
Mont.	540,468	1,120	17,868	572,038	1,232	17,754	650,738	1,467	0.2	22,562
Idaho	519,292	595	4,986	581,395	1,050	6,192	657,383	1,502	0.2	8,306
Wyo.	246,597	956	3,189	284,009	2,557	3,963	322,922	2,183	0.7	4,961
Colo.	1,106,502	12,176	4,618	1,296,653	20,177	8,259	1,700,700	39,992	2.3	13,255
N. Mex.	492,312	4,672	34,834	630,211	8,408	42,568	875,763	17,063	1.8	58,197
Ariz.	426,792	14,993	57,476	654,511	25,974	69,102	1,169,517	43,403	3.3	89,241
Utah	542,920	1,235	6,155	676,909	2,729	9,224	873,828	4,148	0.5	12,651
Nev.	104,030	664	5,553	149,908	4,302	5,873	263,443	13,484	4.7	8,351
Pac.	9,513,602	134,691	580,823	13,936,398	507,043	671,523	19,315,718	962,446	4.5	919,880
Wash.	1,698,147	7,424	30,620	2,316,496	30,691	31,776	2,751,675	48,738	1.7	52,801
Oreg.	1,075,731	2,565	11,388	1,497,128	11,529	12,684	1,732,037	18,133	1.0	18,517
Calif.	6,596,763	124,306	186,318	9,915,173	462,172	208,878	14,455,230	883,861	5.6	378,113
Alaska	39,170	141	33,218	32,808	(1)	35,835	174,546	6,771	3.0	44,850
Hawaii	103,791	255	319,284	114,793	2,651	382,350	202,230	4,943	0.8	425,599

[1] Not identified separately.

Source: Dept. of Commerce, Bureau of the Census; Sixteenth Census Reports, *Population*, Vol. II, *U.S. Census of Population; 1950*, Vol. II, Part I, and *U.S. Census of Population: 1960*, Vol I.

TABLE 50

Cities With 100,000 Inhabitants or More in 1960—Population, 1910 to 1960, and Area, 1960

[Increase from census to census includes that due to annexation of territory as well as to direct growth. "Cities" refers to political subdivisions which are incorporated as cities, boroughs, towns, or villages with the exception that towns are not recognized as incorporated places in New England States, New York, and Wisconsin. Land area figures, generally supplied by city engineers, have been revised to agree with those in the Bureau of the Census, *Area Measurement Reports*, Series GE-20]

CITY	1910	1930	1950	1960 Rank order	Total	Nonwhite Number	Per cent	Land area (sq. mi.)	Population per square mile
Akron, Ohio	69,067	255,040	274,605	45	290,351	37,894	13.1	53	5,448
Albany, N.Y.	100,253	127,412	134,995	93	129,726	10,972	8.5	19	6,757
Albuquerque, N. Mex.	11,020	26,570	96,815	59	201,189	5,925	2.9	58	3,457
Allentown, Pa.	51,913	92,563	106,756	116	108,347	847	0.8	18	5,921
Amarillo, Tex.	9,957	43,132	74,246	88	137,969	8,029	5.8	58	2,383
Anaheim, Calif.	2,628	10,995	14,556	123	104,184	712	0.7	25	4,118
Atlanta, Ga.	154,839	270,366	331,314	24	487,455	186,820	38.3	136	3,587
Austin, Tex.	29,860	53,120	132,459	67	186,545	24,739	13.3	45	4,109
Baltimore, Md.	558,485	804,874	949,708	6	939,024	328,416	35.0	78	11,993
Baton Rouge, La.	14,897	30,729	125,629	80	152,419	45,603	29.9	31	4,949
Beaumont, Tex.	20,640	57,732	94,014	102	119,175	35,004	29.4	69	1,720
Berkeley, Calif.	40,434	82,109	113,805	114	111,268	29,187	26.2	10	11,354
Birmingham, Ala.	132,685	259,678	326,037	36	340,887	135,267	39.7	63	5,420
Boston, Mass.	670,585	781,188	801,444	13	697,197	68,493	9.8	46	15,157
Bridgeport, Conn.	102,054	146,716	158,709	79	156,748	15,565	9.9	16	9,858
Buffalo, N. Y.	423,715	573,076	580,132	20	532,759	73,388	13.8	41	12,869
Cambridge, Mass.	104,839	113,643	120,740	119	107,716	6,787	6.3	6	17,374
Camden, N.J.	94,538	118,700	124,555	103	117,159	27,892	23.8	9	13,623
Canton, Ohio	50,217	104,906	116,912	109	113,631	11,147	9.8	14	7,946
Charlotte, N.C.	34,014	82,675	134,042	58	201,564	56,471	28.0	63	3,199
Chattanooga, Tenn.	44,604	119,798	131,041	92	130,009	43,226	33.2	37	3,552
Chicago, Ill.	2,185,283	3,376,438	3,620,962	2	3,550,404	837,656	23.6	222	16,014
Cincinnati, Ohio	363,591	451,160	503,998	21	502,550	109,682	21.8	77	6,569
Cleveland, Ohio	560,663	900,429	914,808	8	876,050	253,108	28.9	76	11,542
Columbus, Ga.	20,554	43,131	79,611	104	116,547	31,547	27.0	25	4,598
Columbus, Ohio	181,511	290,564	375,901	28	471,316	78,305	16.6	87	5,430
Corpus Christi, Tex.	8,222	27,741	108,287	74	167,690	9,327	5.6	37	4,520
Dallas, Tex.	92,104	260,475	434,462	14	679,684	131,211	19.3	254	2,676
Dayton, Ohio	116,577	200,982	243,872	49	262,332	57,547	21.9	34	7,693
Dearborn, Mich.	911	50,358	94,994	110	112,007	144	0.1	24	4,609
Denver, Colo.	213,381	287,861	415,786	23	493,887	35,261	7.1	68	7,295
Des Moines, Iowa	86,368	142,559	177,965	55	208,982	10,558	5.1	63	3,312
Detroit, Mich.	465,766	1,568,662	1,849,568	5	1,670,144	487,174	29.2	138	12,103
Duluth, Minn.	78,466	101,463	104,511	122	106,884	1,125	1.1	66	1,620
Elizabeth, N.J.	73,409	114,589	112,817	120	107,698	11,880	11.0	12	9,205
El Paso, Tex.	39,279	102,421	130,485	46	276,687	7,424	2.7	109	2,536
Erie, Pa.	66,525	115,967	130,803	87	138,440	6,745	4.9	19	7,403
Evansville, Ind.	69,647	102,249	128,636	86	141,543	9,389	6.6	34	4,127
Flint, Mich.	38,550	156,492	163,143	61	196,940	34,812	17.7	30	6,500
Fort Wayne, Ind.	63,933	114,946	133,607	78	161,776	11,989	7.4	36	4,544
Fort Worth, Tex.	73,312	163,447	278,778	34	356,268	56,922	16.0	138	2,578
Fresno, Calif.	24,892	52,513	91,669	90	133,929	13,123	9.8	27	4,960
Gary, Ind.	16,802	100,426	133,911	70	178,320	69,340	38.9	41	4,403
Glendale, Calif.	2,746	62,736	95,702	101	119,442	574	0.5	29	4,105
Grand Rapids, Mich.	112,571	168,592	176,515	71	177,313	14,778	8.3	27	6,567
Greensboro, N.C.	15,895	53,569	74,389	99	119,574	31,130	26.0	50	2,411
Hammond, Ind.	20,925	64,560	87,594	112	111,698	2,586	2.3	23	4,921
Hartford, Conn.	98,915	164,072	177,397	77	162,178	25,151	15.5	17	9,429
Honolulu, Hawaii	52,183	137,582	248,034	43	294,194	213,920	72.7	87	3,212
Houston, Tex.	78,800	292,352	596,163	7	938,219	217,672	23.2	321	2,923
Indianapolis, Ind.	233,650	364,161	427,173	26	476,258	98,684	20.7	70	6,794
Jackson, Miss.	21,262	48,282	98,271	84	144,422	51,629	35.7	47	3,106
Jacksonville, Fla.	57,699	129,549	204,517	60	201,030	82,744	41.2	30	6,723
Jersey City, N.J.	267,779	316,715	299,017	47	276,101	37,274	13.5	15	18,285
Kansas City, Kans.	82,331	121,857	129,553	98	121,901	28,327	23.2	20	6,005
Kansas City, Mo.	248,381	399,746	456,622	27	475,539	84,191	17.7	130	3,650
Knoxville, Tenn.	36,346	105,802	124,769	111	111,827	20,886	18.7	24	4,718
Lansing, Mich.	31,229	78,397	92,129	118	107,807	6,993	6.5	21	5,085
Lincoln, Nebr.	43,973	75,933	98,884	95	128,521	2,400	1.9	25	5,246
Little Rock, Ark.	45,941	81,679	102,213	117	107,813	25,352	23.5	25	4,313
Long Beach, Calif.	17,809	142,032	250,767	35	344,168	14,769	4.3	46	7,564
Los Angeles, Calif.	319,198	1,238,048	1,970,358	3	2,479,015	417,207	16.8	455	5,447
Louisville, Ky.	223,928	307,745	369,129	31	390,639	70,449	18.0	59	6,599
Lubbock, Tex.	1,938	20,520	71,747	94	128,691	10,427	8.1	75	1,709
Madison, Wis.	25,531	57,899	96,056	¹96	126,706	2,388	1.9	37	3,462
Memphis, Tenn.	131,105	253,143	396,000	22	497,524	184,725	37.1	129	3,851
Miami, Fla.	5,471	110,637	249,276	44	291,688	65,800	22.6	34	8,529
Milwaukee, Wis.	373,857	578,249	637,392	11	³741,324	65,752	8.9	90	8,255

TABLE 50—(Continued)

CITY	1910	1930	1950	1960 Population Rank order	1960 Population Total	1960 Population Nonwhite Number	1960 Population Nonwhite Per cent	Land area (sq. mi.)	Popu- lation per square mile
Minneapolis, Minn.	301,408	464,356	521,718	25	482,872	15,594	3.2	53	9,043
Mobile, Ala.	51,521	68,202	129,009	62	[2] 194,856	65,893	[3] 32.5	154	1,321
Montgomery, Ala.	38,136	66,079	106,525	89	134,393	47,432	35.3	30	4,421
Nashville, Tenn.	110,364	153,866	174,307	73	170,874	64,830	37.9	29	5,933
New Bedford, Mass.	96,652	112,597	109,189	125	102,477	3,333	3.3	20	5,255
New Haven, Conn.	133,605	162,655	164,443	81	152,048	22,665	14.9	18	8,264
New Orleans, La.	339,075	458,762	570,445	15	627,525	234,931	37.4	205	3,057
New York, N.Y. [4]	4,766,883	6,930,446	7,891,957	1	7,781,984	1,141,322	14.7	300	25,966
Bronx Borough	430,980	1,265,258	1,451,277	(X)	1,424,815	168,531	11.8	41	34,583
Brooklyn Borough	1,634,351	2,560,401	2,738,175	(X)	2,627,319	381,460	14.5	70	37,373
Manhattan Borough	2,331,542	1,867,312	1,960,101	(X)	1,698,281	426,459	25.1	23	74,814
Queens Borough	284,041	1,079,129	1,550,849	(X)	1,809,578	154,619	8.5	108	16,755
Richmond Borough	85,969	158,346	191,555	(X)	221,991	10,253	4.6	58	3,861
Newark, N.J.	347,469	442,337	438,776	30	405,220	139,331	34.4	24	16,814
Newport News, Va.	20,205	34,417	42,358	108	113,662	39,060	34.4	69	1,645
Niagara Falls, N.Y.	30,445	75,460	90,872	126	102,394	7,664	7.5	13	7,641
Norfolk, Va.	67,452	129,710	213,513	41	[2] 305,872	80,621	26.4	52	5,829
Oakland, Calif.	150,174	284,063	384,575	33	367,548	97,025	26.4	52	7,041
Oklahoma City, Okla.	64,205	185,389	243,504	37	324,253	42,282	13.0	299	1,086
Omaha, Nebr.	[5] 124,096	214,006	251,117	42	301,598	26,268	8.7	48	6,310
Pasadena, Calif.	30,291	76,086	104,577	105	116,407	17,967	15.4	22	5,220
Paterson, N.J.	125,600	138,513	139,336	85	143,663	21,353	14.9	9	16,705
Peoria, Ill.	66,950	104,969	111,856	124	103,162	9,776	9.5	15	7,066
Philadelphia, Pa.	1,549,008	1,950,961	2,071,605	4	2,002,512	535,033	26.7	129	15,584
Phoenix, Ariz.	11,134	48,118	106,818	29	439,170	25,651	5.8	187	2,344
Pittsburgh, Pa.	533,905	669,817	676,806	16	604,332	101,739	16.8	55	10,968
Portland, Oreg.	207,214	301,815	373,628	32	372,676	20,919	5.6	66	5,630
Portsmouth, Va.	33,190	45,704	80,039	106	114,773	39,681	34.6	18	6,521
Providence, R.I.	224,326	252,981	248,674	56	207,498	11,973	5.8	18	11,464
Richmond, Va.	127,628	182,929	230,310	52	219,958	92,331	42.0	38	5,834
Rochester, N.Y.	218,149	328,132	332,488	38	318,611	24,228	7.6	37	8,682
Rockford, Ill.	45,401	85,864	92,927	[1] 96	126,706	5,450	4.3	25	5,109
Sacramento, Calif.	44,696	93,750	137,572	63	191,667	24,296	12.7	45	4,278
St. Louis, Mo.	687,029	821,960	856,796	10	750,026	216,022	28.8	61	12,255
St. Paul, Minn.	214,744	271,606	311,349	40	313,411	9,317	3.0	52	6,016
St. Petersburg, Fla.	4,127	40,425	96,738	69	181,298	24,188	13.3	53	3,434
Salt Lake City, Utah	92,777	140,267	182,121	65	189,454	3,975	2.1	56	3,401
San Antonio, Tex.	96,614	231,542	408,442	17	587,718	43,221	7.4	148	3,966
San Diego, Calif.	39,578	147,995	334,387	18	573,224	44,712	7.8	195	2,944
San Francisco, Calif.	416,912	634,394	775,357	12	740,316	135,913	18.4	45	16,307
San Jose, Calif.	28,946	57,651	95,280	57	204,196	6,793	3.3	56	3,646
Santa Ana, Calif.	8,429	30,322	45,533	130	100,350	2,681	2.7	21	4,801
Savannah, Ga.	65,064	85,024	119,638	82	149,245	53,258	35.7	41	3,631
Scranton, Pa.	129,867	143,433	125,536	113	111,443	763	0.7	26	4,336
Seattle, Wash.	237,194	365,583	467,591	19	557,087	46,528	8.4	82	6,810
Shreveport, La.	28,015	76,655	127,206	76	164,372	56,719	34.5	36	4,630
South Bend, Ind.	53,684	104,193	115,911	91	132,445	13,169	9.9	24	5,542
Spokane, Wash.	104,402	115,514	161,721	68	181,608	4,508	2.5	42	4,293
Springfield, Mass.	88,926	149,900	162,399	72	174,463	13,361	7.7	32	5,504
Syracuse, N.Y.	137,249	209,326	220,583	53	216,038	12,281	5.7	25	8,539
Tacoma, Wash.	83,743	106,817	143,673	83	147,979	7,873	5.3	47	3,135
Tampa, Fla.	37,782	101,161	124,681	48	274,970	46,456	16.9	69	3,985
Toledo, Ohio	168,497	290,718	303,616	39	318,003	40,423	12.7	49	6,517
Topeka, Kans.	43,684	64,120	78,791	100	119,484	9,797	8.2	35	3,453
Torrance, Calif.	(6)	7,271	22,241	128	100,991	1,398	1.4	20	4,951
Trenton, N.J.	96,815	123,356	128,009	107	114,167	25,852	22.6	8	15,222
Tucson, Ariz.	13,193	32,506	45,454	54	212,892	9,278	4.4	71	3,003
Tulsa, Okla.	18,182	141,258	182,740	50	261,685	26,065	10.0	49	5,384
Utica, N.Y.	74,419	101,740	101,531	129	100,410	3,193	3.2	16	6,276
Washington, D.C.	331,069	486,869	802,178	9	763,956	418,693	54.8	61	12,442
Waterbury, Conn.	73,141	99,902	104,477	121	107,130	7,221	6.7	29	3,746
Wichita, Kans.	52,450	111,110	168,279	51	254,698	21,159	8.3	51	5,024
Wichita Falls, Tex.	8,200	43,690	68,042	127	101,724	8,551	8.4	38	2,677
Winston-Salem, N.C.	22,700	75,274	87,811	115	111,135	41,240	37.1	33	3,399
Worcester, Mass.	145,986	195,311	203,486	66	186,587	2,307	1.2	37	5,016
Yonkers, N.Y.	79,803	134,646	152,798	64	190,634	8,052	4.2	18	10,770
Youngstown, Ohio	79,066	170,002	168,330	75	166,689	31,905	19.1	34	4,961

X Not applicable.   [1] The cities of Madison, Wis., and Rockford, Ill., share the same rank of 96. In order to have the lowest rank equal to the number of cities presented, the number 97 is omitted.

[2] Revised population figure for Milwaukee, Wis., is 741,321; for Mobile, Ala., 202,779; for Norfolk, Va., 304,869.
[3] Based on revised total population figure, see footnote 2.
[4] Population shown is for New York City as now constituted.
[5] Omaha and South Omaha cities consolidated between 1910 and 1920. Combined population, 1910: 150,355.
[6] Not incorporated in 1910.

Source: Dept. of Commerce, Bureau of the Census; *U.S. Census of Population 1960*, Vol. I and *Area Measurement Reports*, Series GE-20.

TABLE 51

Population, Urban and Rural, by Color: 1950 and 1960

[In thousands, except per cent. An urbanized area comprises at least 1 city of 50,000 inhabitants (central city) plus contiguous, closely settled areas (urban fringe)]

YEAR AND AREA	Total	White	Nonwhite	PER CENT DISTRIBUTION		
				Total	White	Nonwhite
1950	151,326	135,150	16,176	100.0	100.0	100.0
Urban	96,847	86,864	9,983	64.0	64.3	61.7
Urbanized areas	69,249	61,925	7,324	45.8	45.8	45.3
Central cities	48,377	42,042	6,335	32.0	31.1	39.2
Urban fringe	20,872	19,883	989	13.8	14.7	6.1
Other urban	27,598	24,939	2,659	18.2	18.5	16.4
Rural	54,479	48,286	6,193	36.0	35.7	38.3
1960	179,323	158,832	20,491	100.0	100.0	100.0
Urban	125,269	110,428	14,840	69.9	69.5	72.4
Urbanized areas	95,848	83,770	12,079	53.5	52.7	58.9
Central cities	57,975	47,627	10,348	32.3	30.0	50.5
Urban fringe	37,873	36,143	1,731	21.1	22.8	8.4
Other urban	29,420	26,658	2,762	16.4	16.8	13.5
Rural	54,054	48,403	5,651	30.1	30.5	27.6

Source: Dept. of Commerce, Bureau of the Census; *U.S. Census of Population: 1960*, Vol. I.

TABLE 52

Cities Ranked by Negro Population

City	Negro Population 1960	National Rank, 1960 Negro	National Rank, 1960 Total	Per cent Negro 1960	Per cent Negro 1965*
New York	1,087,931	1	1	14%	18%
Chicago	812,637	2	2	23	28
Philadelphia	529,240	3	4	26	31
Detroit	482,223	4	5	29	34
Washington, D.C.	411,737	5	9	54	66
Los Angeles	334,916	6	3	14	17
Baltimore	325,589	7	6	35	38
Cleveland	250,818	8	8	29	34
New Orleans	233,514	9	15	37	41
Houston	215,037	10	7	23	23
St. Louis	214,377	11	10	29	36
Atlanta	186,464	12	24	38	44
Memphis	184,320	13	22	37	40
Newark	138,035	14	30	34	47
Birmingham	135,113	15	36	40	x
Dallas	129,242	16	14	19	21
Cincinnati	108,754	17	21	22	24
Pittsburgh	100,692	18	16	17	20
Indianapolis	98,049	19	26	21	23
Richmond	91,972	20	52	42	x
Oakland	83,618	21	33	23	x
Kansas City, Mo.	83,146	22	27	18	22
Jacksonville	82,525	23	61	41	x
Norfolk	78,806	24	41	26	x
Columbus	77,140	25	28	16	18
San Francisco	74,383	26	12	10	12
Buffalo	70,904	27	20	13	17
Louisville	70,075	28	31	18	x
Gary	69,123	29	70	39	x
Mobile	65,619	30	58	32	x
Miami	65,213	31	44	22	x
Nashville	64,570	32	73	38	x
Boston	63,165	33	13	9	13
Milwaukee	62,458	34	11	8	11

(X indicates no estimate was made for 1965)
* Census Bureau estimate
Source: U.S. Dept. of Commerce, Bureau of the Census.

TABLE 53

Net Migration, by Color—States: 1940 to 1950 and 1950 to 1960

[In thousands. Net migration comprises both net immigration from abroad and net interregional, interdivisional, and interstate migration according to the area shown. Includes movements of persons in the Armed Forces]

REGION, DIVISION, AND STATE	WHITE				NONWHITE			
	1940 to 1950		1950 to 1960		1940 to 1950		1950 to 1960	
	Number	Per cent	Number	Per cent	Number	Per cent	Number	Per cent
United States	[1] +1,522	[1] +1.3	+2,685	+2.0	[1] −160	[1] −1.2	−25	−0.2
Regions:								
Northeast	−173	−0.5	−206	−0.6	+483	+34.3	+541	+26.0
North Central	−948	−2.5	−679	−1.6	+632	+42.0	+558	+23.8
South	−538	−1.7	+52	+0.1	−1,597	−16.0	−1,457	−14.1
West	[1] +3,181	[1] +23.8	+3,518	+18.7	[1] +323	[1] +60.5	+332	+23.6
New England	+68	+0.8	−47	−0.5	+32	+29.9	+70	+45.6
Maine	−27	−3.2	−68	−7.5	(Z)	+1.8	+2	+67.7
New Hampshire	−1	−0.1	+11	+2.1	(Z)	+67.9	+1	+137.0
Vermont	−20	−5.4	−38	−10.1	(Z)	+30.8	(Z)	+20.0
Massachusetts	+8	+0.2	−119	−2.6	+14	+24.0	+25	+32.1
Rhode Island	+9	+1.3	−28	−3.6	+2	+16.0	+2	+13.7
Connecticut	+98	+5.8	+195	+10.0	+16	+46.5	+39	+71.1
Middle Atlantic	−242	−0.9	−159	−0.6	+451	+34.6	+472	+24.5
New York	−6	(Z)	−72	−0.5	+276	+46.0	+282	+29.5
New Jersey	−231	+5.9	+465	+10.3	+64	+27.8	+112	+34.6
Pennsylvania	−467	−4.9	−553	−5.6	+111	+23.5	+77	+12.0
East North Central	+75	+0.3	+178	+0.6	+594	+54.1	+521	+28.1
Ohio	+110	+1.7	+276	+3.7	+135	+39.7	+133	+25.6
Indiana	+57	+1.7	+19	+0.5	+40	+32.9	+45	+25.4
Illinois	−142	−1.9	−64	−0.8	+217	+55.2	+189	+28.3
Michigan	+146	+2.9	+30	+0.5	+189	+87.4	+127	+27.9
Wisconsin	−96	−3.1	−82	−2.4	+12	+47.5	+29	+68.4
West North Central	−1,023	−7.8	−857	−6.3	+38	+9.4	+37	+7.6
Minnesota	−175	−6.3	−101	−3.4	+2	+8.5	+4	+13.8
Iowa	−198	−7.9	−236	−9.1	+3	+14.3	+3	+12.3
Missouri	−222	−6.3	−158	−4.3	+32	+13.1	+28	+9.3
North Dakota	−119	−18.8	−103	−16.9	−2	−16.5	−2	−18.3
South Dakota	−74	−11.9	−90	−14.3	−5	−21.2	−5	−19.4
Nebraska	−139	−10.7	−121	−9.3	+4	+19.9	+4	+17.5
Kansas	−96	−5.5	−49	−2.7	+5	+7.1	+5	+6.5
South Atlantic	+604	+4.6	+1,189	+7.4	−531	−11.2	−542	−10.5
Delaware	+17	+7.2	+58	+21.0	+4	+12.1	+6	+14.6
Maryland	+231	+15.2	+284	+14.5	+39	+12.8	+36	+9.3
District of Columbia	−14	−3.0	−213	−41.1	+63	+33.6	+54	+19.2
Virginia	+194	+9.6	+84	+3.3	−26	−3.9	−70	−9.5
West Virginia	−219	−12.3	−406	−21.5	−16	−13.5	−40	−35.0
North Carolina	−95	−3.7	−121	−4.0	−162	−16.2	−207	−19.2
South Carolina	−24	−2.2	−4	−0.3	−207	−25.3	−218	−26.5
Georgia	−49	−2.4	−9	−0.4	−240	−22.2	−204	−19.2
Florida	+564	+40.8	+1,516	+70.0	+14	+2.7	+101	+16.6
East South Central	−694	−8.7	−845	−9.6	−591	−21.2	−620	−22.9
Kentucky	−349	−13.3	−374	−13.7	−17	−7.9	−15	−7.6
Tennessee	−97	−4.0	−216	−7.8	−47	−9.2	−57	−10.7
Alabama	−140	−7.6	−144	−6.9	−202	−20.5	−224	−22.8
Mississippi	−108	−9.7	−110	−9.3	−326	−30.2	−323	−32.7
West South Central	−448	−4.2	−292	−2.4	−475	−19.1	−295	−11.8
Arkansas	−259	−17.6	−283	−19.1	−157	−32.4	−150	−35.0
Louisiana	−2	−0.2	+42	+2.4	−145	−17.0	−92	−10.4
Oklahoma	−361	−17.1	−192	−9.5	−73	−31.5	−26	−13.0
Texas	+173	+3.2	+141	+2.1	−101	−10.9	−27	−2.7

TABLE 53—(Continued)

REGION, DIVISION, AND STATE	WHITE				NONWHITE			
	1940 to 1950		1950 to 1960		1940 to 1950		1950 to 1960	
	Number	Per cent	Number	Per cent	Number	Per cent	Number	Per cent
Mountain	+155	+3.9	+549	+11.3	+13	+7.7	+8	+3.6
Montana	−36	−6.7	−23	−4.0	−4	−22.4	−2	−11.4
Idaho	−28	−5.3	−41	−7.0	+1	+11.5	+1	+7.1
Wyoming	−2	−0.9	−19	−6.5	+1	+26.6	−1	−18.4
Colorado	+32	+2.9	+149	+11.5	+9	+52.2	+15	+52.9
New Mexico	+17	+3.4	+54	+8.5	−1	−1.5	−1	−2.9
Arizona	+135	+31.6	+340	+51.9	+2	+2.5	−10	−10.3
Utah	+6	+1.0	+9	+1.4	+3	+38.6	+1	+8.0
Nevada	+31	+29.8	+80	+53.2	+3	+45.6	+6	+63.0
Pacific	[1] +3,026	[1] +32.3	+2,970	+21.3	+310	[1] +85.4	+324	+27.4
Washington	+375	+22.1	+70	+3.0	+17	+44.5	+18	+28.6
Oregon	+278	+25.8	+10	+0.7	+8	+55.3	+6	+22.7
California	+2,373	+36.0	+2,791	+28.2	+285	+91.7	+354	+52.7
Alaska	(NA)	(NA)	+42	+45.5	(NA)	(NA)	−1	−3.0
Hawaii	(NA)	(NA)	+55	+48.0	(NA)	(NA)	−52	−13.6

NA Not available.   Z Less than 500 or 0.05 percent.   [1] Excludes Alaska and Hawaii.
Source: Dept. of Commerce, Bureau of the Census; Current Population Reports, Series P-25, No. 247

TABLE 54

Negroes as a Per Cent of Total Population by Location, Inside and Outside Metropolitan Areas, and by Size of Metropolitan Areas, 1950 1960, 1966, and 1968

	Per cent Negro			
	1950	1960	1966	1968
United States	10	11	11	11
Metropolitan areas	9	11	12	12
Central cities				
Central cities in metropolitan areas* of—	12	17	20	20
1,000,000 or more	13	19	26**	25
250,000 to 1,000,000	12	15	20**	18
Under 250,000	12	12	12**	12
Suburbs	5	5	4	5
Smaller cities, towns, and rural	11	10	10	10

* In metropolitan areas of population shown as of 1960.   ** Per cent nonwhite; data for Negroes are not available.
Source: U.S. Department of Commerce, Bureau of the Census.

TABLE 55

Mobility Status and Interregional Migration of the Negro Population 1 Year Old and Over, for the United States and Regions: March 1966 to March 1967

(Numbers in thousands)

Residence in 1966	Total		Region of residence in 1967			
	Number	Per cent	Northeast	North Central	South	West
INTERREGIONAL MIGRANTS						
Total persons	332	(X)	46	103	93	90
Northeast	76	(X)	(X)	8	54	14
North Central	77	(X)	10	(X)	29	38
South	149	(X)	35	76	(X)	38
West	30	(X)	1	19	10	(X)
Per cent	(X)	100.0	100.0	100.0	100.0	100.0
Northeast	(X)	22.9	(X)	7.8	58.1	15.6
North Central	(X)	23.2	21.7	(X)	31.2	42.2
South	(X)	44.9	76.1	73.8	(X)	42.2
West	(X)	9.0	2.2	18.4	10.8	(X)

X Not applicable.

TABLE 56

Mobility of the Population 1 Year Old and Over: 1968 to 1969

(Numbers in thousands)

	Total	White	Negro	Per cent distribution Total	White	Negro
Total	196,642	172,745	21,811	100.0	100.0	100.0
Same house	159,310	140,457	17,291	81.0	81.3	79.3
Different house	35,933	31,033	4,442	18.3	18.0	20.4
Same county	22,993	19,180	3,495	11.7	11.1	16.0
Different county	12,940	11,853	947	6.6	6.9	4.3
Abroad	1,399	1,255	78	0.7	0.7	0.4

Source: U.S. Department of Commerce, Bureau of the Census.

TABLE 57

Negro Population and Estimated Net Out-Migration of Nonwhites from the South,* 1940-1968

(In thousands)

	1940	1950	1960	1965	1968
Negro population in the South	9,905	10,222	11,312	11,233**	11,573**

	1940–50	1950–60	1960–65	1965–68
Nonwhite, average annual net out-migration from the South	159.7	145.7	94.6	80.3

* The South includes the States of the Old Confederacy as well as Delaware, the District of Columbia, Kentucky, Maryland, Oklahoma, and West Virginia.   ** Excludes Armed Forces living in barracks.
Source: U.S. Department of Commerce, Bureau of the Census.

TABLE 58

Change in Population by Type of Residence, 1960-1968

(Numbers in millions)

	Total 1968	1960	Per cent change	White 1968	1960	Per cent change	Negro 1968	1960	Per cent change
United States*	198.1	178.7	11	174.0	158.7	10	22.0	18.4	20
Metropolitan areas	128.0	112.4	14	111.3	99.4	12	15.2	11.9	27
Central cities	58.2	57.8	1	45.5	47.6	−5	11.9	9.5	25
Suburban rings	69.9	54.6	28	65.9	51.8	27	3.3	2.4	36
Metropolitan areas of 1,000,000 or more	70.0	61.2	14	59.8	53.9	11	9.3	6.8	36
Central cities	30.4	30.2	1	22.3	24.3	−8	7.5	5.6	34
Suburban rings	39.6	31.0	28	37.5	29.7	27	1.8	1.2	45
Metropolitan areas under 1,000,000	58.0	51.1	14	51.5	45.5	13	5.9	5.1	15
Central cities	27.8	27.6	1	23.2	23.4	−1	4.4	3.9	12
Suburban rings	30.2	23.5	28	28.3	22.1	28	1.5	1.2	26
Outside metropolitan areas	70.1	66.3	6	62.7	59.3	6	6.9	6.5	6
Central city population as a per cent of metropolitan area total:									
All metropolitan areas	45	51	(X)	41	48	(X)	78	80	(X)
Metropolitan areas of 1,000,000 or more	43	49	(X)	37	45	(X)	81	82	(X)
Metropolitan areas under 1,000,000	48	54	(X)	45	51	(X)	74	76	(X)

* All data presented in this report exclude Armed Forces living in barracks.   X Not applicable.
Source: U.S. Dept. of Commerce, Bureau of the Census.

TABLE 59

Selected Life Table Values: 1900 to 1967

[Prior to 1959, excludes Alaska, and 1960, Hawaii. Data prior to 1933 for death-registration States only; see text, p. 45. See also *Historical Statistics, Colonial Times to 1957*, series B 76-83 and B 92-100]

AGE AND SEX	WHITE					NONWHITE				
	1900-1902	1919-1921	1939-1941	1959-1961	1967	1900-1902 [1]	1919-1921 [1]	1939-1941	1959-1961	1967
ANNUAL RATE OF MORTALITY PER 1,000 LIVING AT SPECIFIED AGE										
At birth:										
Male	133.45	80.25	48.12	25.92	22.32	253.26	105.01	83.04	46.99	39.20
Female	110.61	63.92	37.89	19.64	16.82	214.75	87.49	66.82	38.28	32.39
Age 20:										
Male	5.94	4.27	2.12	1.59	1.77	11.89	10.85	(NA)	2.36	2.80
Female	5.54	4.33	1.45	0.56	0.61	11.39	11.59	(NA)	1.16	1.12
Age 40:										
Male	10.60	7.50	5.13	3.32	3.37	16.58	14.59	13.62	7.49	8.68
Female	9.31	6.76	3.68	1.90	1.93	15.56	15.37	11.81	5.61	5.19
Age 65:										
Male	41.66	34.99	36.85	33.89	33.61	54.18	38.93	(NA)	43.65	46.85
Female	36.41	31.68	26.43	17.42	16.17	54.07	43.36	(NA)	30.72	34.69
AVERAGE EXPECTATION OF LIFE IN YEARS										
At birth:										
Male	48.23	56.34	62.81	67.55	67.8	32.54	47.14	52.33	61.48	61.1
Female	51.08	58.53	67.29	74.19	75.1	35.04	46.92	55.51	66.47	68.2
Age 20:										
Male	42.19	45.60	47.76	50.25	50.2	35.11	38.36	39.74	45.78	44.8
Female	43.77	46.46	51.38	56.29	56.9	36.89	37.15	42.14	50.07	51.3
Age 40:										
Male:	27.74	29.86	30.03	31.73	31.8	23.12	26.53	25.23	28.72	28.3
Female	29.17	30.94	33.25	37.13	37.8	24.37	25.60	27.31	32.16	33.4
Age 65:										
Male	11.51	12.21	12.07	12.97	13.0	10.38	12.07	12.18	12.84	12.7
Female	12.23	12.75	13.56	15.88	16.5	11.38	12.41	13.95	15.12	15.8
NUMBER SURVIVING TO SPECIFIED AGE PER 100,000 BORN LIVE										
Age 20:										
Male	76,376	84,997	92,293	95,908	96,298	56,733	79,057	86,770	93,108	93,982
Female	78,978	87,281	93,984	97,135	97,486	59,053	80,154	88,505	94,660	95,485
Age 40:										
Male	64,954	75,733	86,880	92,427	92,583	42,989	61,353	72,830	85,744	85,013
Female	67,935	77,624	89,805	95,326	95,662	46,146	61,130	75,908	89,676	90,529
Age 65:										
Male	39,245	50,663	58,305	65,834	65,990	19,015	34,042	35,912	51,392	50,180
Female	43,806	54,299	68,701	80,739	81,486	21,995	31,044	40,718	60,825	64,255

NA not available.

[1] Negroes only. Negro population comprised 95 percent or more of corresponding nonwhite population.

Source: Dept. of Health, Education, and Welfare, Public Health Service: *U.S. Life Tables and Actuarial Tables, 1939-41*, *Vital Statistics—Special Reports*, Vol. 41 and Vol. 52, and annual report, *Vital Statistics of the United States*.

TABLE 60

Births and Birth Rates: 1950 to 1967

[In thousands, except as indicated. Prior to 1960, excludes Alaska and Hawaii. For 1950 and 1955, births adjusted for underregistration, except as noted; thereafter, registered births. See also Historical Statistics, Colonial Times to 1957, series B 6 and B 19-21]

ITEM	1950	1955	1960	1962	1963	1964	1965	1966	1967
Live births	3,632	4,104	4,258	4,167	4,098	4,027	3,760	3,606	3,521
Per cent urban [1]	60.6	61.0	62.3	62.6	62.9	54.0	54.5	54.6	54.6
White	3,108	3,488	3,601	[2] 3,394	[2] 3,326	3,369	3,124	2,993	2,923
Nonwhite	524	617	657	[2] 642	[2] 639	658	636	613	598
Male	1,863	2,103	2,180	2,132	2,102	2,060	1,927	1,846	1,803
Female	1,768	2,001	2,078	2,035	1,996	1,967	1,833	1,760	1,718
Males per 100 females	105.4	105.1	104.9	104.8	105.3	104.7	105.1	104.9	105.0
Birth rate per 1,000 population [3]	24.1	25.0	23.7	22.4	21.7	21.0	19.4	18.4	17.8
White	23.0	23.8	22.7	[2] 21.4	[2] 20.7	20.0	18.3	17.4	16.8
Nonwhite	33.3	34.7	32.1	[2] 30.5	[2] 29.7	29.1	27.6	26.1	25.0
Male	24.9	25.8	24.7	23.3	22.7	21.9	20.3	19.2	18.7
Female	23.3	23.9	22.8	21.5	20.8	20.2	18.6	17.6	17.0
Plural births per 1,000 live births	20.9	21.1	20.4	19.5	19.8	19.9	20.1	19.8	19.7

[1] Based on registered births. For definition of urban, see text, p. 2.

[2] Excludes data for residents of New Jersey since this State did not require reporting of color.

[3] For 1950 and 1960, based on population enumerated as of Apr. 1; for all other years, estimated as of July 1. Based on total population (in specific group) residing in area.

TABLE 61

Deaths and Death Rates: 1900 to 1967

[Prior to 1960, excludes Alaska and Hawaii. Excludes fetal deaths. Population enumerated as of April 1 for 1940, 1950, and 1960, and estimated as of July 1 for all other years. Data prior to 1933 for death-registration State only; see text, p. 45. See also Historical Statistics, Colonial Times to 1957, series B 129-136]

ITEM	1960	1965	1966	1967
DEATHS				
Total 1,000	1,712	1,828	1,863	1,851
Per cent urban [1]	65.9	56.4	56.5	56.4
White 1,000	1,505	1,605	1,634	1,627
Nonwhite 1,000	207	223	229	224
Male 1,000	976	1,035	1,053	1,046
Female 1,000	736	793	810	805
DEATH RATES [2]				
Total	9.5	9.4	9.5	9.4
White	9.5	9.4	9.5	9.4
Nonwhite	10.1	9.6	9.7	9.4
Male	11.0	10.9	11.0	10.8
Female	8.1	8.0	8.1	8.0
Age: [3]				
Under 1 year	27.0	24.1	23.3	22.3
1-4 years	1.1	0.9	0.9	0.9
5-14 years	0.5	0.4	0.4	0.4
15-24 years	1.1	1.1	1.2	1.2
25-34 years	1.5	1.5	1.5	1.5
35-44 years	3.0	3.1	3.1	3.1
45-54 years	7.6	7.4	7.4	7.3
55-64 years	17.4	16.9	17.0	16.7
65-74 years	38.2	37.9	38.4	37.5
75-84 years	87.5	81.9	81.7	79.0
85 years and over	198.6	202.0	200.5	194.2

NA Not Available.   [1] For definition of urban, see text, p. 2.
[2] Rate per 1,000 population (of specified groups) residing in area.
[3] Includes deaths for which age was not stated.
[4] Based on enumerated population adjusted for age bias in nonwhite population at ages 55-69 years.
Source: Dept. of Health, Education, and Welfare, Public Health Service; annual report, Vital Statistics of the United States, and unpublished data.

TABLE 62

Composition of Families, 1950, 1955, 1960, and 1966-1968

(Per cent)

	Husband-wife		Other male head		Female head*	
	Nonwhite	White	Nonwhite	White	Nonwhite	White
1950	77.7	88.0	4.7	3.5	17.6	8.5
1955	75.3	87.9	4.0	3.0	20.7	9.0
1960	73.6	88.7	4.0	2.6	22.4	8.7
1966	72.7	88.8	3.7	2.3	23.7	8.9
1967	72.6	88.7	3.9	2.1	23.6	9.1
1968	69.1	88.9	4.5	2.2	26.4	8.9

* Female heads of families include widowed and single women, women whose husbands are in the armed services or otherwise away from home involuntarily, as well as those separated from their husbands through divorce or marital discord. In 1968, divorce and separation accounted for 47 per cent of the nonwhite female family heads and 34 per cent of the white.

Source: U.S. Department of Commerce, Bureau of the Census.

TABLE 63

Families, by Characteristics: 1968

[Number in thousands.   As of March. Based on Current Population Survey; includes members of the Armed Forces living off post or with their families on post, but excludes all other members of the Armed Forces; see text, p. 1. For definition of families, see p. 9]

CHARACTERISTIC	ALL FAMILIES		NONWHITE FAMILIES	
	Number	Per cent	Number	Per cent
All families	49,832	100.0	5,020	100.0
COLOR				
White	44,814	89.9	(X)	(X)
Nonwhite	5,020	10.1	5,020	100.0
RESIDENCE				
Urban and rural nonfarm	47,151	94.6	4,800	95.6
Rural farm	2,683	5.4	219	4.4
SIZE OF FAMILY				
2 persons	16,889	33.9	1,341	26.7
3 persons	10,289	20.6	983	19.6
4 persons	9,467	19.0	848	16.9
5 persons	6,235	12.5	598	11.9
6 persons	3,549	7.1	448	8.9
7 or more	3,405	6.8	802	16.0
RELATED CHILDREN UNDER 18 YEARS OLD				
No related children under 18	20,728	41.6	1,516	30.2
1 related child under 18	9,176	18.4	969	19.3
2 related children under 18	8,801	17.7	854	17.0
3 related children under 18	5,469	11.0	565	11.3
4 or more	5,469	11.4	1,115	22.2
OWN CHILDREN UNDER 18 YEARS OLD	5,659	11.4	1,115	22.2
No own children under 18	22,024	44.2	1,943	38.7
1 own child under 18	8,741	17.5	854	17.0
2 own children under 18	8,484	17.0	787	15.7
3 own children under 18	5,246	10.5	499	9.9
4 or more	5,339	10.7	937	18.7
OWN CHILDREN UNDER 6 YEARS OLD				
No children under 6	36,114	72.5	3,400	67.7
1 child under 6	8,058	16.2	863	17.2
2 children under 6	4,296	8.6	505	10.1
3 or more	1,366	2.7	253	5.0
MARITAL STATUS OF HEAD				
Married, spouse present	43,291	86.9	3,471	69.1
Separated	1,023	2.1	(NA)	(NA)
Other married, spouse absent	405	0.8	(NA)	(NA)
Widowed	2,918	5.9	(NA)	(NA)
Divorced	1,230	2.5	(NA)	(NA)
Single	967	1.9	(NA)	(NA)
AGE OF HEAD				
Under 25	3,161	6.3	360	7.2
25-29	4,832	9.7	561	11.2
30-34	4,962	10.0	610	12.2
35-44	11,089	22.3	1,147	22.8
45-54	10,658	21.4	1,012	20.2
55-64	8,062	16.2	746	14.9
65-74	4,816	9.7	404	8.0
75 and over	2,254	4.5	180	3.6

NA Not available.   X Not applicable.
Source: Dept. of Commerce, Bureau of the Census; *Current Population Reports*, Series P-20.

TABLE 64

Major League Baseball, Selected Individual Leaders *

Batting

	American League			National League	
Rank	Name and Team		Rank	Name and Team	
3.	Reggie Smith, Bos.	.309	3.	Cleon Jones, N.Y.	.340
4.	Frank Robinson, Bal.	.308	5.	Willie McCovey, S.F.	.320
6.	Walter Williams, Chi.	.304	6.	Alex Johnson, Cin.	.315
11.	Don Buford, Bal.	.291	7.	Willie Davis, L.A.	.311
12.	Roy White, N.Y.	.290	12.	Hank Aaron, Atl.	.300

Runs Batted In

3.	Reggie Jackson, Oak.	118	1.	Willie McCovey, S.F.	126
8.	Frank Robinson, Bal.	100	4.	Lee May, Cin.	110
10t.	Reggie Smith, Bos.	93	5.	Ernie Banks, Chi.	106
13.	Willie Horton, Det.	91	7.	Hank Aaron, Atl.	97
20t.	Paul Blair, Bal.	76	8.	Billy Williams, Chi.	95

Hits

2.	Horace Clarke, N.Y.	183	3.	Lou Brock, St. L.	195
3.	Paul Blair, Bal.	178	4.	Bobby Tolan, Cin.	194
7t.	Reggie Smith, Bos.	168	5.	Billy Williams, Chi.	188
9t.	Frank Robinson, Bal.	166	11.	Curt Flood, St. L.	173
13.	Don Buford, Bal.	161	12.	Maury Wills, L.A.	171

Doubles

2.	Reggie Jackson, Oak.	36	3t.	Lou Brock, St. L.	33
4t.	Paul Blair, Bal.	32	3t.	Billy Williams, Chi.	33
6t.	Don Buford, Bal.	31	6.	Lee May, Cin.	32
8t.	Roy White, N.Y.	30	7t.	Curt Flood, St. L.	31
10.	Reggie Smith, Bos.	29	7t.	Willie Stargell, Pitt.	31

Triples

2t.	Horace Clarke, N.Y.	7	3t.	Lou Brock, St. L.	10
2t.	Reggie Smith, Bos.	7	3t.	Bobby Tolan, Cin.	10
7t.	Paul Blair, Bal.	5	3t.	Billy Williams, Chi	10
7t.	Frank Robinson, Bal.	5	6.	Nathan Colbert, S.D.	9
7t.	George Scott, Bos.	5	7t.	Willie Davis, L.A.	8
7t.	Roy White, N.Y.	5	7t.	Maury Wills, L.A.	8

Home Runs

	AMERICAN LEAGUE			NATIONAL LEAGUE	
Rank	Name and Team		Rank	Name and Team	
3.	Reggie Jackson, Oak.	47	1.	Willie McCovey, S.F.	45
7.	Frank Robinson, Bal.	32	2.	Hank Aaron, Atl.	44
10.	Willie Horton, Det.	28	3.	Lee May, Cin.	38
13t.	Paul Blair, Bal.	26	5.	Jim Wynn, Hou.	33
15t.	Reggie Smith, Bos.	25	6t.	Richie Allen, Phil.	32
			6t.	Bobby Bonds, S.F.	32

Runs Scored

1.	Reggie Jackson, Oak.	123	1.	Bobby Bonds, S.F.	120
2t.	Frank Robinson, Bal.	111	3.	Jim Wynn, Hou.	113
6.	Paul Blair, Bal.	102	6.	Bobby Tolan, Cin.	104
7t.	Don Buford, Bal.	99	7t.	Billy Williams, Chi.	103
15.	Reggie Smith, Bos.	87	8.	Willie McCovey, S.F.	101

Slugging

1.	Reggie Jackson, Oak.	.608	1.	Willie McCovey, S.F.	.656
6.	Frank Robinson, Bal.	.540	2.	Hank Allen, Atl.	.607
7.	Reggie Smith, Bos.	.527	3.	Richie Allen, Phil.	.573
12.	Paul Blair, Bal.	.477	4.	Willie Stargell, Pitt.	.556
14.	Willie Horton, Det.	.465	6.	Lee May, Cin.	.529

Stolen Bases

1.	Tommy Harper, Sea.	73	1.	Lou Brock, St. L.	53
4.	Joe Foy, K.C.	37	2.	Joe Morgan, Hou.	49
6.	Horace Clarke, N.Y.	33	3.	Bobby Bonds, S.F.	45
9t.	Paul Blair, Bal.	20	4.	Maury Wills, L.A.	40
11t.	Don Buford, Bal.	19	5.	Bobby Tolan, Cin.	26

Strikeouts

13t.	John Odom, Oak.	150	1.	Ferguson Jenkins, Chi.	273
13t.	Earl Wilson, Det.	150	2.	Bob Gibson, St. L.	269
			4.	Don Wilson, Hou.	235

Most Valuable Player
(First place votes in parentheses)

3.	Frank Robinson, Bal. (2)	162	1.	Willie McCovey, S.F. (11)	265
5.	Reggie Jackson, Oak.	110	3.	Hank Aaron, Atl. (2)	188
11.	Paul Blair, Bal.	28	6.	Tommy Agee, N.Y.	89

* To qualify, batters must have a minimum of 502 plate appearances and pitchers a minimum of 162 innings pitched.

t: Tied for that position in the standings

TABLE 65

Major League Baseball, Awards and Honors

Sporting News Rookie of the Year (AL): Carlos May, Chicago

Sporting News Comeback Player of the Year (NL): Tommy Agee, New York

Sporting News "Golden Glove" Awards (outstanding fielders): Curt Flood, St. Louis (NL); Bob Gibson, St. Louis (NL); Paul Blair, Baltimore (AL)

Chicagoan of the Year (by the Chicago Press Club): Ernie Banks, Chicago (NL)

Major League All-Star team as compiled by the wire services: Willie McCovey, San Francisco (NL); Hank Aaron, Atlanta (NL); Frank Robinson, Baltimore (AL); Reggie Jackson, Oakland (AL)

TABLE 66

Major League Baseball, Record Performance

Major League Records Set By National League Players

Most Home Runs, Right-Handed Batter (lifetime): 600, Willie Mays, San Francisco*

Most Years, 100-or-more Runs Scored: 14, Hank Aaron, Atlanta*

Most Years, Consecutive, 100-or-more Runs Scored: 14, Hank Aaron, Atlanta*

Most Years, Leading League in Total Bases: 8, Hank Aaron, Atlanta*

Most Years, 300-or-more Total Bases: 14, Hank Aaron, Atlanta*

Most Bases on Balls, Intentional (season): 45, Willie McCovey, San Francisco*

Major League Records Tied by National League Players

Most 2-Base Hits (game): 4, Billy Williams, Chicago, April 9

Making All of Club's Hits (game): 4, Billy Williams, Chicago, September 15

Most Home Runs, 3 Consecutive Games: 6, Lee May, Cincinnati, May 26-28

Most Strikeouts, 200-or-more Strikeouts: 7, Bob Gibson, St. Louis

Most Strikeouts, Inning, 9-Pitches: 3, Bob Gibson, St. Louis, May 12 (7th inning)

Most Assists by an Outfielder (inning): 2, Jim Hicks, St. Louis, May 6 (5th inning)

Major League Records Set by American League Players

Most Home Runs in the Month of April: 10, Frank Robinson, Baltimore

Most Putouts as a Catcher (lifetime): 9,162, John Roseboro, Minnesota

Most Chances Accepted as a Catcher (lifetime): 9,831, John Roseboro, Minnesota

Major League Records Tied by American League Players

Most Putouts by a Left Fielder (game): 11, Willie Horton, Detroit

Most Chances Accepted by a Left Fielder (game): 11, Willie Horton, Detroit

TABLE 66—(Continued)

National League Records Set

Most Games Played in League, Consecutive (lifetime): 982, Billy Williams, Chicago

Most Years, 100-or-more Extra Bases on Long Hits: 15, Hank Aaron, Atlanta*

Most Home Runs, League (lifetime): 600, Willie Mays, San Fancisco*

Most Home Runs, Outfielder (lifetime): 595, Willie Mays, San Francisco*

Most Strikeouts, Right-hander (season): 273, Ferguson Jenkins, Chicago

National League Records Tied

Most Years, 40-or-more Home Runs: 6, Hank Aaron, Atlanta

Most Years, Consecutive, 20-or-more Home Runs: 15, Hank Aaron, Atlanta

Most Bases on Balls (season): 148, Jim Wynn, Houston

Most Double Plays, Second Baseman (game): 5, Joe Morgan, Houston, May 4

American League Record Set

Most Home Runs for His Club (season): 47, Reggie Jackson, Oakland

Miscellaneous Records (1969) by National League Players

Most Total Bases: 332, Hank Aaron, Atlanta

Fewest Double Plays Grounded-into: 2: Lou Brock, St. Louis

Best Fielding Average, First Baseman: .997, Ernie Banks, Chicago

Best Fielding Average, Outfielder: .996, Vada Pinson, St. Louis

Longest Hitting Streak: 31 games, Willie Davis, Los Angeles. (During the streak, which ran from August 1st to September 3rd, he had 54 hits in 124 at bats for a .435 average)

Played in All of His Teams Games: Billy Williams, Chicago

Most Games Started: 42, Ferguson Jenkins, Chicago

Most Complete Games: 28, Bob Gibson, St. Louis

Miscellaneous Records (1969) by American League Players

Most Times Hit by Pitch: 13, Frank Robinson, Baltimore

Most Intentional Bases on Balls: 20, Reggie Jackson, Oakland

* Extended own Major League Record

(American League records courtesy the American League of Professional Baseball Clubs, Howe News Bureau, Statisticians; National League records courtesy the National League of Professional Baseball Clubs, Elias Sports Bureau, Statisticians)

TABLE 68

1968-69 National Basketball Association, Selected Individual Leaders

Scoring

Name and Team	Rank	Games	FG	FT	Pts.	Avg.
Elvin Hayes, S.D.	1	82	930*	467	2327*	28.4*
Earl Monroe, Balt.	2	80	809	447	2065	25.8
Bob Rule, Sea.	4	82	776	413	1965	24.0
Oscar Robertson, Cin.	5	79	656	643*	1955	24.7
Hal Greer, Phil.	7	82	732	432	1896	23.1

* League leader
Best performance (game): 66 points, Wilt Chamberlain, Los Angeles vs. Phoenix, 2/9/69

Field-Goal Percentage**

Name and Team	Rank	FG	Att.	Pct.
Wilt Chamberlain, L.A.	1	641	1099	.583*
Willis Reed, N.Y.	3	704	1351	.521
Walt Bellamy, Det.	5	563	1103	.510
Joe Caldwell, Atl.	6	561	1106	.507
Walt Frazier, N.Y.	7	531	1052	.505

* League leader
** Minimum 230 field goals made
Most field goals and attempts (season): 930 (2082 attempts), Elvin Hayes, San Diego
Most field goals (game): 29 (35 attempts), Wilt Chamberlain, Los Angeles vs. Phoenix, 2/9/69

Free-Throw Percentage**

Name and Team	Rank	FT	Att.	Pct.
Flynn Robinson, Mil.	4	412	491	.839
Oscar Robertson, Cin.	5	643*	767	.838
Bob Boozer, Chi.	9	394	489	.806
Chet Walker, Phil.	10	369	459	.804
Clem Haskins, Chi.	13	282	361	.781

* League leader
** Minimum 230 free throws made
Most attempts (season): 857, Wilt Chamberlain, Los Angeles
Most attempts (game): 24 (16 made), Wilt Chamberlain, Los Angeles vs. Cincinnati, 1/26/69
Most free throws (game): 21 (22 attempts), Flynn Robinson, Milwaukee vs. Atlanta, 2/17/69

TABLE 67

1968-69 Major-College Basketball, Selected Individual Leaders†

Scoring

Name and Team	Rank	Games	FG	FT	Pts.	Avg.
Calvin Murphy, Niagara	3	24	294	190	778	32.4
Spencer Haywood, Detroit	4	22	259	181	699	31.8
Marvin Roberts, Utah State	6	26	271	176	718	27.6
Bob Lanier, St. Bonaventure	8	24	270	114	654	27.3
Rich Travis, Oklahoma City	9	27	286	157	729	27.0

Best performance (game): 68, Calvin Murphy, Niagara vs. Syracuse, 12/7/68

Field-Goal Percentage**

Name and Team	Rank	FG	FGA	Pct.
Lew Alcindor, UCLA	1	303	477	.635*
Bob Lanier, St. Bonaventure	5	270	460	.587
Heyward Dotson, Columbia	11	148	262	.565
Greg Howard, New Mexico	15	155	277	.560
Spencer Haywood, Detroit	17	259	466	.556

* Led nation
** Minimum 140 field goals scored

Rebounds

Name and Team	Rank	Games	No.	Avg.
Spencer Haywood, Detroit	1	22	472	21.5*
Larry Lewis, St. Francis (Pa.)	2	24	495	20.6
Lamar Green, Morehead State	3	27	483	17.9
Booker Brown, Middle Tennessee	7	26	429	16.5
Joe Brunson, Furman	12	22	344	15.6

* Led nation
Best performance (game): 32, Spencer Haywood, Detroit vs. LaSalle, 2/21/69; 32, Willie Watson, Oklahoma City vs. Denver, 2/8/69

† One hundred ninety-three college basketball teams, which play most of their games against each other, are classified as "Major-College" or University Division teams. They represent the field of so-called "big-time" college basketball as judged by class of competition rather than seasonal strength. The basketball teams of all other four-year, accredited NCAA-member colleges comprise the College Division field.

TABLE 70

1968-69 National Basketball Association, Record Performances

Records Set

Most Points Scored (lifetime): 27,098, Wilt Chamberlain, Los Angeles (10 seasons)

Most Consecutive Games without Disqualification on Personals: 787, Wilt Chamberlain, Los Angeles

TABLE 71

1968-69 American Basketball Association, Selected Individual Leaders

Scoring

Name and Team	Rank	Games	2-Pt. FG	3-Pt. FG	FT	Avg.	Pts.
Connie Hawkins, Minn.	2	47	493	3	425	1420	30.21
Larry Jones, Den.	3	75	735	24	591	2133*	28.44
James Jones, N.O.	4	77	763	1	521	2050	26.62
Mel Daniels, Ind.	6	76	712	0	400	1824	24.00
Willie Somerset, N.Y.	7	74	583	36	484	1758	23.76

* League leader
Best performance (game): 57, Connie Hawkins, Minnesota vs. New York, 11/27/68

2-Point Field Goals

Name and Team	Rank	FG	Att.	Pct.
Bill McGill, Den.	1	411	745	.552*
Julian Hammond, Den.	2	329	601	.547
James Jones, N.O.	4	763*	1422	.537
Connie Hawkins, Minn.	5	493	949	.519
Tom Washington, Minn.	8	421	833	.505

* League leader
Most 2-point field goals attempted (game): 38, Mel Daniels, Indiana vs. New York, 3/18/69
Most 2-point field goals made (game): 25, Mel Daniels, Indiana vs. New York, 3/18/69
Best percentage of 2-point field goals made in a game (minimum of 10 attempts): 1,000, Roger Brown (14 of 14), Indiana vs. Denver, 1/25/69
Most 2-point field goals without a miss: 21, Roger Brown, Indiana, over a three-game span (last 3 of 15 vs. Miami, 1/22/69; 14 of 14 vs. Denver, 1/25/69; and first 4 of 12 vs. Denver, 1/29/69)
Most 2-point field goals attempted (season): 1531, Larry Jones, Denver

TABLE 68—(Continued)

Rebounds

Name and Team	Rank	Games	No.	Avg.
Wilt Chamberlain, L.A.	1	81	1712*	21.1*
Wesley Unseld, Balt.	2	82	1491	18.2
Bill Russell, Bos.	3	77	1484	19.3
Elvin Hayes, S.D.	4	82	1406	17.1
Nate Thurmond, S.F.	5	71	1402	19.7

* League leader
Best performance (game): 42, Wilt Chamberlain, Los Angeles vs. Boston, 3/7/69

Assists

Name and Team	Rank	Games	No.	Avg.
Oscar Robertson, Cin.	1	79	772*	9.8*
Lennie Wilkens, Sea.	2	82	674	8.2
Walt Frazier, N.Y.	3	80	635	7.9
Guy Rodgers, Mil.	4	81	561	6.9
Dave Bing, Det.	5	77	546	7.1

* League leader
Best performance (game): 22, Art Williams, San Diego vs. Phoenix, 1/28/68
(Copyright © 1969 by the National Basketball Association)

TABLE 69

1968-69 National Basketball Association, Awards and Honors

Official NBA All-Star Team

First Team	Second Team
Wesley Unseld, Baltimore (C)	Willis Reed, New York (C)
Oscar Robertson, Cincinnati (G)	Hal Greer, Philadelphia (G)
Earl Monroe, Baltimore (G)	
Elgin Baylor, Los Angeles (F)	

Most Valuable Player (Podoloff Cup): Wesley Unseld, Baltimore

Official NBA All-Rookie Team

Wesley Unseld, Baltimore
Elvin Hayes, San Diego
Bill Hewitt, Los Angeles
Art Harris, Seattle

Rookie of the Year: Wesley Unseld, Baltimore

TABLE 71—(Continued)

3-Point Field Goals

Name and Team	Rank	FG	Att.	Pct.
Stewart Johnson, Hou.	5	64	183	.380
Steve Jones, N.O.	7	52	151	.344
Charlie Williams, Minn.	8	66	212	.311
Charlie Vaughn, Minn.	12	145	523	.277
Willie Somerset, N.Y.	13	36	139	.259

Free Throws

Name and Team	Rank	FT	Att.	Pct.
Tony Jackson, Hou.	2	299	337	.887
Willie Somerset, N.Y.	5	484	583	.830
Fred Lewis, Ind.	8	419	510	.822
Ron Boone, Dal.	11	436	537	.812
James Jones, N.O.	15	521	647	.805

Most free throws attempted: 760, Larry Jones, Denver
Most free throws made: 591, Larry Jones, Denver

Rebounds

Name and Team	Rank	Games	Off.	Def.	Tot.	Avg.
Mel Daniels, Ind.	1	76	383	873*	1256*	16.52*
Tom Washington, Minn.	4	69	367	501	868	12.58
Connie Hawkins, Minn.	5	47	167	367	534	11.36
Jim Ligon, Ky.	7	75	328	491	819	10.92
Gene Moore, Ky.	8	76	318	499	817	10.75

* League leader
Most defensive rebounds (game): 23, Mel Daniels, Indiana vs. Kentucky, 10/26/68
Most defensive rebounds (game): 23 (ties record), Mel Daniels, Indiana vs. Kentucky, 10/26/68

Assists

Name and Team	Rank	Games	No.	Avg.
Don Freeman, Mia.	2	78	501	6.42
James Jones, Den.	4	77	437	5.68
Roger Brown, Ind.	5	75	345	4.60
Fred Lewis, Ind.	7	78	346	4.44
Willie Somerset, N.Y.	8	74	280	3.78

TABLE 72

1968-69 American Basketball Association, Awards and Honors

Official ABA All-Star Team

First Team	Second Team
Mel Daniels, Indiana (C)	Don Freeman, Miami (G)
James Jones, New Orleans (G)	
Larry Jones, Denver (G)	
Connie Hawkins, Minnesota (F)	

Most Valuable Player: Mel Daniels, Indiana

Official ABA All-Rookie Team

First Team	Second Team
Gene Moore, Kentucky (C)	Merv Jackson, Los Angeles (G)
Warren Armstrong, Oakland (G)	Don Sidle, Miami (F)
Ron Boone, Dallas (G)	George Stone, Miami (F)

Rookie of the Year: Warren Armstrong, Oakland

TABLE 73

1968-69 American Basketball Association, Record Performances

Records Set (season)

Most points scored (game): 57, Connie Hawkins, Minnesota vs. New York, 11/27/68

Most 2-point field goals attempted (game): 38, Mel Daniels, Indiana vs. New York, 3/18/69

Most 2-point field goals made (game): 25, Mel Daniels, Indiana vs. New York, 3/18/69

Most defensive rebounds (game): 23 (ties record), Mel Daniels, Indiana vs. Kentucky, 10/26/68

Best percentage of 2-point field goals made in a game (minimum 10 attempts): 1.000, Roger Brown, Indiana (14 of 14) vs. Denver, 1/25/69

Most 2-point field goals without a miss: 21, Roger Brown, Indiana over a three game span (last 3 of 15 vs. Miami, 1/22/69; 14 of 14 vs. Denver, 1/25/69; and first 4 of 12 vs. Denver, 1/29/69)

TABLE 75—(Continued)

Amateur

Amateur Athletic Union's 1969 All-America Boxing team (weight class in parentheses): Caleb Long, Washington, D.C. (12); Joe Bennett, Joliet, Ill. (125); Rudy Bolds, Pittsburgh, Pa. (139); Johnny Baldwin, Piney Point, Md. (156); Larry Ward, Milwaukee, Wisc. (165) and Dave Matthews, Cleveland, Ohio (175)

Coaches who served with the AAU's teams: "Pappy" Gault, Piney Point, Md., Head Olympic Coach; "Bubble" Klice, Kansas City, Mo., Assistant Coach vs. Russia in Moscow; Carlton Brooks, Fort Campbell, Ky., Assistant Coach vs. Mexico in Mexico City and Richard Pettigrew, Assistant Coach vs. South America in Venezuela

TABLE 76

Professional Boxing, Selected Championship Fights

Light Heavyweight

January 23—Bob Foster, Washington, D.C., knocked out Frank DePaula, Jersey City, N.J., in the 1st round to retain his title. The fight was held in New York and the referee was John LoBianco.

May 24—Bob Foster, Washington, D.C., knocked out Andy Kendall, Portland, Ore., 1:15 of the 4th round to retain his title. The fight was held in West Springfield, Mass., and the referee was Bill Connelly.

Welterweight

April 17—Jose Naples, Mexico, stopped Curtis Cokes, Dallas, Texas, in the 13th round to win the Title. The fight was held in Los Angeles and the referee was George Latka.

June 29—Jose Naples, Mexico, halted Curtis Cokes, Dallas, Texas, in ten rounds to retain his title. The fight was held in Mexico City and the referee was Ramon Berumen.

October 18—Jose Naples, Mexico, won a 15-round decision over Emile Griffith, New York, N.Y., to retain his title. The fight was held in Los Angeles and the referee was Dick Young.

Featherweight

January 23—Johnny Famachon, Australia, won a 15-round decision over Jose Legra, Spain, to win the vacant title. The fight was held in London and the referee was George Smith.

Bantamweight

March 7—Lionel Rose, Australia, won a 15-round split decision over Alan Rudkin, England, to retain his title. The fight was held in Melbourne, Australia, and the referee was Vic Patrick.

August 22—Ruben Olivares, Mexico, stopped Lionel Rose, Australia, 2:24 of the 5th round to win the title. The fight was held in Los Angeles and the referee was Larry Rozadilla.

(Courtesy of *Ring* magazine)

TABLE 74

Professional Boxing, Ring Magazine World Ratings

(As of December 31, 1969)

Heavyweights (over 175 pounds)
Champion: Cassius Clay, Houston, Tex.

Group I
1. Joe Frazier, Philadelphia, Pa.

Group II
1. Leotis Martin, Philadelphia, Pa.
2. Jimmy Ellis, Louisville, Ky.
3. Mac Foster, Fresno, Cal.
5. Sonny Liston, Las Vegas, Nev.
8. Al Jones, Miami Beach, Fla.

Light Heavyweights (not over 175 pounds)
Champion: Bob Foster, Washington, D.C.

Group I
1. Dick Tiger, Biafra
2. Jimmy Dupree, Jersey City, N.J.

Group II
1. Ray Anderson, Akron, Ohio
2. Hal Carroll, Syracuse, N.Y.
8. Gomeo Brennan, Bahamas

Middleweights (not over 160 pounds)
Group I
1. Freddie Little, Las Vegas, Nev.

Group II
2. Emile Griffith, New York, N.Y.

Welterweights (not over 147 pounds)
Group I
3. Percy Pugh, New Orleans, La.

Group II
1. Hedgemon Lewis, Detroit, Mich.
4. Curtis Cokes, Dallas, Tex.

Junior Welterweights (not over 140 pounds)
Group I
2. Adolph Pruitt, St. Louis, Mo.

Group II
4. Jimmy Robertson, San Francisco, Cal.
6. Larry Harding, Los Angeles, Cal.
9. Eddie Perkins, Chicago, Ill.

Lightweights (not over 135 pounds)
Group I
2. Ismael Laguna, Panama

Group II
8. Lloyd Marshall, Newark, N.J.

Junior Lightweight (not over 130 pounds)
Group I
1. Ruben Navarro, Los Angeles, Cal.
4. Alton Colter, Phoenix, Ariz.

Featherweights (not over 126 pounds)
Group II
4. Jose Legra, Spain
7. Dwight Hawkins, Los Angeles, Cal.
8. Lionel Rose, Australia

Bantamweight (not over 118 pounds)
None

Flyweights (not over 112 pounds)
Group II
12. Raton Mojica, Nicaragua
(Courtesy of *Ring* magazine)

TABLE 75

Boxing: Awards, Honors and Records

Professional

Edward J. Neil Trophy: Joe Frazier
Ring's "Fight of the Year": June 23, Joe Frazier vs. Jerry Quarry
Ring's Progress Award: Mac Foster
Elected to Boxing's Hall of Fame: Jersey Joe Wolcott
Al Buck Memorial Award (Manager of the Year): Yancy Yank Durham

TABLE 77

Major-College Football, Selected Individual Leaders†

Rushing*

Name and Team	Rank	Games	Plays	Yards	TDs
Joe Moore, Missouri	3	10	260	1312	5
Clarence Davis, So. Cal.	5	10	282	1275	9
Ron Poe James, New Mexico St.	7	10	258	1181	8
Duane Thomas, W. Texas St.	9	10	199	1072	10
Lee Bouggess, Louisville	10	10	267	1064	6
Bob Gresham, West Va.	11	10	190	1057	8

* Those with over 1,000 yards gained

Passing

Name and Team	Rank	Games	Att.	Comp.	Int.	Pct.	Yards	TDs
Jimmy Jones, So. Cal.	69	10	193	78	10	.404	1102	12
Cleve Bryant, Ohio U.	90	10	127	60	7	.472	733	7
Stahle Vincent, Rice	100	10	100	51	7	.510	556	3
Bill Triplett, Mich. St.	126	10	117	37	12	.316	735	6

Pass Receiving*

Name and Team	Rank	Games	Cght	Yards	TDs
Elmo Wright, Houston	7	10	63	1275	14
Fred Mathews, Bowl. Green	10t	10	57	528	6
Ron Shanklin, No. Texas St.	12t	10	56	874	10
Bob Moore, Oregon	15t	11	54	786	10
Larry Carter, Marshall	15t	10	54	663	3
Mack Herron, Kansas St.	19t	10	52	652	1
Ernie Jennigs, Air Force	21t	10	52	652	

* Those with over 50 receptions
t: Tied for that position in the standings

TABLE 77—(Continued)

Scoring

Name and Team	Rank	Games	TDs	XPT	FG	Pts
Mack Herron, Kansas St.	2	10	21	0	0	126
Stan Brown, Purdue	6t	10	18	0	0	108
Jim Braxton, West. Va.	8	10	12	24	3	105
Bob Moore, Oregon	10	10	15	2	0	92
Elmo Wright, Houston	11t	11	14	6	0	90
Dave Buchanan, Arizona St.	11t	10	15	0	0	90

t: Tied for that position in the standings

Total Offense

Name and Team	Rank	Games	Plays	Yards	TDR*
Joe Moore, Missouri	57	10	260	1312	5
Clarence Davis, So. Cal.	60	10	282	1275	9
Ron Poe James, New Mexico St.	70	10	259	1181	8
Jimmy Jones, So. Cal.	72	10	278	1168	15
Duane Thomas, W. Texas St.	85	10	201	1072	10

* Touchdowns-responsible-for are player's TDs rushed and passed for
† One hundred eighteen college football teams, which play most of their games against each other, are classified as "Major-College" or University Division teams. They represent the field of so-called "big-time" college football as judged by class competition rather than seasonal strength. The football teams of all other four-year, accredited NCAA-member colleges comprise the College Division field.
(Copyright © 1969 by National Collegiate Sports Services)

TABLE 78

Major-College Football, Awards and Honors

The consensus All-America team as compiled from the first and second All-American teams of the American Football Coaches Association, the Football Writers Association of America, the Associated Press, United Press International, Look Magazine, the Sporting News and the Newspaper Enterprise Association: Charlie Pittman (HB), Penn State; Ken Burroughs (SE), Texas Southern; Mike Ballou (LB), UCLA; Jack Tatum (LB), Ohio State; Don Parish (LB), Stanford; Curtis Johnson (DHB), Toledo; Jim Gunn (DE), Southern California and Al Cowlings (DT), Southern California.

TABLE 79

American Football League, Selected Individual Leaders

Rushing

Name and Team	Rank	Att.	Yards	Avg.	Long	TDs
Jim Nance, Bos.	2	193*	750	3.9	43	6*
Mike Garrett, K.C.	4	168	732	4.4	34	6*
Floyd Little, Den.	5	146	729	5.0*	48	6*
O. J. Simpson, Buff.	6	181	697	3.9	32	2*
Matt Snell, N.Y.	7	191	695	3.6	34	4

* League leader
Best performance: 166 yards in 29 attempts, Floyd Little, Denver vs. Cincinnati, 10/10
Longest gain: 83 yards, Jesse Phillips, Cincinnati vs. Oakland, 11/2

Pass Receiving

Name and Team	Rank	No.	Yards	Avg.	Long	TDs
Al Denson, Den.	3	53	809	15.3	62	10
Alvin Reed, Hou.	4	51	664	13.0	43	2
Warren Wells, Oak.	5	47	1260*	26.8*	80	14*
Mike Garrett, K.C.	8	43	432	10.0	41	2
Jerry Levias, Hou.	9t	42	696	16.6	86*	5

* League leader
t: Tied for that position in the standings

Scoring

Name and Team	Rank	TD-R	TD-P	Tot.	Points
Warren Wells, Oak.	5	0	14*	14*	84
Mike Garrett, K.C.	16	6*	2	8	48
Eric Crabtree, Cin.	18t	0	7	7	42
Charles Frazier, Bos.	18t	0	7	7	42
Carl Garrett, Bos.	18t	0	5	2	42

* League leader
t: Tied for that position in the standings
Best performance: 18 points, Brad Hubbert, San Diego; Otis Taylor, Kansas City; Warren Wells, Oakland

Punt Returns

Name and Team	Rank	No.	Yards	Avg.	Long	TDs
Jim Thompson, Den.	1	25	288	11.5*	40	0
Speedy Duncan, S.D.	2	27	280	10.4	38	0
Jerry Levias, Hou.	3	35*	292*	8.3	46	0
Max Anderson, Buff.	4	19	142	7.5	30	0
Eugene Morris, Mia.	5t	25	172	6.9	38	0

* League leader
t: Tied for that position in the standings
Longest return: 64 years, Noland Smith, Kansas City vs. Boston, 9/21

Kickoff Returns

Name and Team	Rank	No.	Yards	Avg.	Long	TDs
Jim Thompson, Den.	1	18	513	28.5*	63	0
Carl Garrett, Bos.	2	28	792	28.3	63	0
Speedy Duncan, S.D.	3	21	587	28.0	52	0
Eugene Morris, Mia.	4	43*	1136*	26.4	105*	1
O. J. Simpson, Buff.	5	21	529	25.2	73	0

* League leader

Interceptions

Name and Team	Rank	No.	Yards	Avg.	Long	TDs
Emmitt Thomas, K.C.	1	9*	146		45	1
Dave Crayson, Oak.	2t	8	132		76*	1
George Byrd, Buff.	4t	7	95		32	1
Jim Hill, S.D.	4t	7	92		42	0
Speedy Duncan, S.D.	6t	6	118		72	1
Bobby Howard, S.D.	6t	6	50		19	0
Miller Farr, Hou.	6t	6	48		35	0

* League leader
(Copyright © 1969 by the American Football League and Elias Sports Bureau)

TABLE 80

National Football League, Selected Individual Leaders

Rushing

Name and Team	Rank	Att.	Yards	Avg.	Long	TDs
Gale Sayers, Chi.	1	236*	1032*	4.4	28	8
Calvin Hill, Dall.	2	204	942	4.6	55	8
Larry Brown, Wash.	44	202	888	4.4	57	4
Leroy Kelly, Cleve.	7	196	817	4.2	31	9
Andy Livingston, N.O.	8	181	761	4.2	18	5

* League leader
Best performance: 151 yards, in 22 attempts, Leroy Kelly, Cleveland vs. Green Bay, 12/7
Longest gain: 80 yards, Clint Jones, Minnesota vs. Chicago (TD), 11/2

Pass Receiving

Name and Team	Rank	No.	Yards	Avg.	Long	TDs
Charlie Taylor, Wash.	2	71	883	12.4	88	8
Harold Jackson, Phil.	3	67	1079	16.1	63	9
Roy Jefferson, Pitt.	4	65	1116*	17.2	65	9
Charles Harraway, Wash.	6	55	489	8.9	64	3
John Gilliam, St. L.	9	52	997	19.2	84	9

* League leader
Best performance: 10 receptions, John Gilliam, St. Louis, Mel Farr, Detroit; Charley Taylor, Washington; Dick Gordon, Chicago; Bob Wallace, Chicago

Scoring

Name and Team	Rank	TD-R	TD-P	Ex. P	FG	Points
Gene Mingo, Pitt.	17	0	0	26	12	62
John Gilliam, St. L.	18t	1	9	0	0	60
Leroy Kelly, Cleve.	18t	9	1	0	0	60
Paul Warfield, Cleve.	18t	0	10	0	0	60
Charlie Harraway, Wash.	21t	6	3	0	0	54
Harold Jackson, Phil.	21t	0	9	0	0	54
Ray Jefferson, Pitt.	21t	0	9	0	0	54
Gene Washington, Minn.	21t	0	9	0	0	54
Travis Williams, G.B.	21t	6	3	0	0	54

Best performance: 24 points (4 TDs), Ben Hawkins, Philadelphia vs. Pittsburgh, 9/28

Punt Returns

Name and Team	Rank	No.	Yards	Avg.	Long	TDs
Alvin Haymond, L.A.	1	33	435	13.2*	52	0
Rickie Harris, Wash.	2	14	158	11.3	86*	1*
Bob Hayes, Dall.	3	18	179	9.9	50	0
Charlies West, Minn.	6	39*	245	6.3	55	0
Mel Renfro, Dall.	7	15	80	5.3	34	0

* League leader

Kickoff Returns

Name and Team	Rank	No.	Yards	Avg.	Long	TDs
Bobby Willis, Det.	1	17	563	33.1*	96	1
Jim Duncan, Bal.	2	19	560	29.5	92	1
Bo Scott, Cleve.	3	25	722*	28.9	65	0
Les Shy, N.O.	4	16	447	27.9	57	0
Dave Hampton, G.B.	5	22	582	26.5	78	1

* League leader
Longest return: 101 yards (TD), Don McCall, Pittsburgh vs. Minnesota, 11/23

Interceptions

Name and Team	Rank	No.	Yards	Long	TDs
Mel Renfro, Dall.	1	10*	118	41	0
Lem Barney, Det.	2t	8	126	32	0
Earsall Mackbee, Minni.	4t	6	100	38	0
Mike Howell, Cleve.	4t	6	21	11	0
Herb Adderley, G.B.	7t	5	169*	80	1
Rudy Redmond, Atl.	7t	5	50	32	0
Kermit Alexander, S.F.	7t	5	39	22	0
Jim Johnson, S.F.	7t	5	18	18	0

* League leader
(Copyright © 1969 by the National Football League and Elias Sports Bureau)

TABLE 81

Professional Football, Awards and Honors

Consensus All-Star Teams*

Offense

Pos.	National Football League — Name and Team	American Football League — Name and Team
SE	Roy Jefferson, Pittsburgh; Charley Taylor, Washington; Paul Warfield, Cleveland; Gene Washington, Minnesota	Alvin Reed, Houston
TE	Charlie Sanders, Detroit	
OT	Bob Brown, Los Angeles; Charlie Cowan, Los Angeles	Winston Hill, New York
OG		Gene Upshaw, Oakland
OB	Calvin Hill, Dallas; Leroy Kelly, Cleveland; Gale Sayers, Chicago	Mike Garrett, Kansas City; Floyd Little, Denver; Jim Nance, Boston

Defense

Pos.	National Football League — Name and Team	American Football League — Name and Team
DE	Carl Eller, Minnesota; Deacon Jones, Los Angeles; Jim Marshall, Minnesota	Rich Jackson, Denver
DT	Alan Page, Minnesota	Buck Buchanan, Kansas City
MLB		Willie Lanier, Kansas City
OLB	Dave Robinson, Green Bay	
CB	Herb Adderley, Green Bay; Lem Barney, Detroit; Cornell Green, Dallas; Jim Johnson, San Francisco	Bobby Bell, Kansas City; George Webster, Houston; Willie Brown, Oakland; Emmitt Thomas, Kansas City
S	Mel Renfro, Dallas; Mike Howell, Cleveland	Dave Grayson, Oakland

Awards

Associated Press NFL Offensive Rookie of the Year: Calvin Hill, Dallas Halfback

United Press International NFL Rookie of the Year: Calvin Hill, Dallas Halfback

NFL Defensive Rookie of the Year: Joe Greene, Pittsburgh Tackle

NFL Offensive Rookie of the Year: Calvin Hill, Dallas Halfback

AFL Rookie of the Year: Carl Garrett, Boston Halfback

United Press International AFL Comeback Award: Jim Nance, Boston Fullback

* Based on the first and second all-star teams selected by Associated Press, United Press International, Pro Football Hall of Fame and other minor polls.

Picture Credits

The editor is grateful to the many libraries and special collections whose personnel have aided in the search for unusual and interesting photographs for this special section.

Index